MAGILL'S
LITERARY ANNUAL

1987

MAGILL'S LITERARY ANNUAL

1987

*Essay-Reviews of 200 Outstanding Books
Published in the United States during 1986*

With an Annotated Categories Index

Volume One
A-Mari

Edited by
FRANK N. MAGILL

SALEM PRESS
Pasadena, California   **Englewood Cliffs, New Jersey**

LIBRARY OF CONGRESS CATALOG CARD No. 77-99209
ISBN 0-89356-287-4

FIRST PRINTING

PRINTED IN THE UNITED STATES OF AMERICA

PUBLISHER'S NOTE

Magill's Literary Annual, 1987, is the thirty-second publication in a series that began in 1954. The philosophy behind the annual has been to evaluate critically each year a given number of major examples of serious literature published during the previous year. Our continuous effort is to provide coverage for works that are likely to be of more than passing general interest and that will stand up to the test of time. Individual critical articles for the first twenty-two years were collected and published in *Survey of Contemporary Literature* in 1977.

For the reader new to the Magill reference format, the following brief explanation should serve to facilitate the research process. The two hundred works represented in this year's annual are drawn from the following categories: fiction; poetry; literary criticism and literary history; essays; biography; autobiography, memoirs, diaries, and letters; history; current affairs and social science; science; and miscellaneous. The articles are arranged alphabetically by book title in the two-volume set; a complete list of the titles included can be found at the beginning of volume 1. Following a list of titles are the titles arranged by category in an annotated listing. This list provides the reader with the title, author, page number, and a brief one-sentence description of the particular work. All contributing reviewers for the literary annual are listed alphabetically in the front of the book as well as at the end of their reviews. At the end of volume 2, there are two indexes: an index of Biographical Works by Subject and the Cumulative Author Index. The index of biographical works covers the years 1977 to 1987, and it is arranged by subject rather than by author or title. Thus, readers will be able to locate easily a review of any biographical work published in the Magill annuals since 1977 (including memoirs, diaries, and letters—as well as biographies and autobiographies) by looking up the name of the person. Following the index of Biographical Works by Subject is the Cumulative Author Index. Beneath each author's name appear the titles of all of his or her works reviewed in the Magill annuals since 1977. Next to each title, in parentheses, is the year of the annual in which the review appeared, followed by the page number.

Each article begins with a block of top matter that indicates the title, author, publisher, and price of the work. When possible, the year of the author's birth is also provided. The top matter also includes the number of pages of the book, the type of work, and, when appropriate, the time period and locale represented in the text. Next, there is the same capsulized description of the work that appears in the annotated list of titles. When pertinent, a list of principal characters or of personages introduces the review.

The articles themselves are approximately two thousand words in length. They are original essay-reviews that analyze and present the focus, intent, and relative success of the author, as well as the makeup and point of view of the work under discussion. To assist the reader further, the articles are supplemented by a list of additional reviews for further study in a bibliographic format.

As mentioned above, history-oriented books are once again included in *Magill's Literary Annual*, as they were prior to 1983. Readers who are especially interested in biography, history, and current affairs are invited to consult the twelve-volume *Great Events from History* and the *Great Lives from History*, which covers significant historical figures.

LIST OF TITLES

LIST OF TITLES

TITLES BY CATEGORY

ANNOTATED

TITLES BY CATEGORY

TITLES BY CATEGORY

page

page

page

Wild Birds: Six Stories of the Port William
Membership, The—*Wendell Berry*............................989
Six stories which center on Wheeler Catlett, his family, and friends during a thirty-year period and which focus on tradition, family, communal values, and the sanctity of the land

POETRY

All of Us Here—*Irving Feldman*................................ 29
The eighth collection by a poet of great gifts and increasing wisdom, this book presents Irving Feldman at his best so far

Collected Poems—*Geoffrey Hill*..................................146
A collection made up of five earlier volumes published between 1959 and 1984, together with a short sequence appearing for the first time

Collected Poems—*Charles Tomlinson*............................151
A long-awaited volume that gathers the work of one of the foremost contemporary British poets

Collected Poems of William Carlos Williams, Vol. I:
1909-1939, The—*William Carlos Williams*......................155
Williams' early work offers an ideal opportunity for reassessment of an intensely American writer whose influential later poetry sometimes leads to a simplified view of his overall achievement

Dream Work—*Mary Oliver*..219
An analysis of the ties between nature and the poet

Edwin Denby: The Complete Poems—*Edwin Denby*................223
A lyric description of the interrelation of place and its human inhabitants

Hurricane Lamp—*Turner Cassity*................................415
A description of the paradoxes that define human life and behavior

Land of Superior Mirages: New and Selected Poems—
Adrien Stoutenberg..461
A complex, vivid, and personalized drama of nature, history, and time is Adrien Stoutenberg's poetic legacy

Last Poems—*Paul Celan* 466
The most celebrated figure in contemporary German poetry reflects on the Nazi Holocaust and his own approaching death in this bilingual collection of surreal, minimalist poems

TITLES BY CATEGORY

page

page

**But Do Blondes Prefer Gentlemen? Homage to Qwert
Yuiop and Other Writings**—*Anthony Burgess* 94
In this collection, a professional man of letters considers primarily works and issues of literary scholarship, but also language, music, and contemporary culture in the widest sense

Complete Prose of Marianne Moore, The—*Marianne Moore* 165
A chronological collection of Moore's published prose works

**End Papers: Essays, Letters, Articles of Faith, Workbook
Notes**—*Breyten Breytenbach* 242
A collection of Breytenbach's political writings from both in and out of prison, plus comments on contemporary culture and literary theory

Going to the Territory—*Ralph Ellison* 331
A collection of sixteen thought-provoking essays on the black experience in America, on the concept of American democracy, on the poetics of the novel, and on various other aspects of American culture

Less Than One: Selected Essays—*Joseph Brodsky* 471
Literary, political, and autobiographical essays by one of the most talented living Russian poets

Letters from Prison and Other Essays—*Adam Michnik* 477
Incisive essays by a historian who was a founder of the important organization known as KOR (Workers' Defense Committee) and of Solidarity, the independent workers' union

**Man Who Mistook His Wife for a Hat: And Other
Clinical Tales, The**—*Oliver Sacks* 516
A collection of twenty-four unusual case histories from the neurological practice of Dr. Oliver Sacks

Marriage and Morals Among the Victorians—
Gertrude Himmelfarb 525
A survey of the accomplishments and influence of a number of important historical figures from the late eighteenth to the mid-twentieth centuries

Sense of Sight, The—*John Berger* 754
A collection of John Berger's nonfiction writing, including essays, travel pieces, and poems, reflecting the author's preoccupation with the meaning of art in the twentieth century

Taking the World in for Repairs—*Richard Selzer* 836
A lyrical quest for love and art, through memoir and short story

page

TITLES BY CATEGORY

page

BIOGRAPHY

page

page

page

page

Roots of Conflict: British Armed Forces and Colonial
  Americans, 1677-1763—*Douglas Edward Leach* 732
  A history of the relations between British armed forces and Colonial Americans in
  the century of Anglo-French colonial wars

Siege: The Saga of Israel and Zionism, The—
  Conor Cruise O'Brien 776
  A clearly and comprehensively written history of Zionism from its pre-Herzl days,
  of mandatory Palestine, and of the State of Israel from its founding to 1985

Soviet Paradox: External Expansion, Internal
  Decline, The—*Seweryn Bialer* 807
  A penetrating study of the Soviet Union, revealing its internal weaknesses and im-
  perial ambitions

Thinking in Time: The Uses of History for Decision-
  Makers—*Richard E. Neustadt and Ernest R. May* 853
  A guide to principles of using historical precedent in the formulation of public-
  policy decisions

Tombee: Portrait of a Cotton Planter—
  Theodore Rosengarten, Editor 875
  A diary kept by a young cotton planter of the South Carolina Sea Islands before
  and after the Civil War, with a helpful, lengthy editor's introduction

Underground Empire: Where Crime and Governments
  Embrace, The—*James Mills* 896
  An in-depth look at the international narcotics trade and at the not entirely success-
  ful efforts of American law enforcement agents to combat this trade

Vanished Imam: Musa al Sadr and the Shia of
  Lebanon, The—*Fouad Ajami* 901
  Dilemmas in the religious and ideological orientation of Lebanon's Shiite minority
  were reflected in the teachings and organizational work of its most remarkable mod-
  ern leader, Musa al-Sadr

Voyagers to the West: A Passage in the Peopling of America
  on the Eve of the Revolution—*Bernard Bailyn* 917
  A comprehensive analysis of emigration from Great Britain in the New World on
  the eve of the American Revolution

War Without Mercy: Race and Power in the Pacific War—
  John W. Dower 947
  A study of the diverse attitudes of the Japanese about the United States, and Ameri-
  can attitudes about the Japanese, during World War II

page

page

MISCELLANEOUS

page

CONTRIBUTING REVIEWERS FOR 1987 ANNUAL

Michael Adams

J. Stewart Alverson

Terry L. Andrews

Stanley Archer

Edwin T. Arnold

Jean W. Ashton

Bryan Aubrey

David Axeen

Dean Baldwin

Dan Barnett

Carolyn Wilkerson Bell

Richard P. Benton

Mary G. Berg

Meredith Berg

Gordon N. Bergquist

Dale B. Billingsley

David Warren Bowen

Albert Hall Bowman

Harold Branam

Gerhard Brand

Peter A. Brier

Jeanie R. Brink

J. R. Broadus

Keith H. Brower

Rosemary M. Canfield-Reisman

Karen Carmean

John Carpenter

John Christie

John J. Conlon

Robert J. Forman

Margot K. Frank

Leslie E. Gerber

Dana Gerhardt

Richard Glatzer

Manfred Grote

Daniel L. Guillory

Terry Heller

Greig E. Henderson

Erwin Hester

Jane Bowers Hill

Elvin Holt

Ronald Howard

Linda T. Humphrey

Theodore C. Humphrey

Philip K. Jason

Ronald L. Johnson

Judith L. Johnston

Carola M. Kaplan

Cynthia Lee Katona

Steven G. Kellman

Barbara E. Kemp

Paul B. Kern

Henderson Kincheloe

Wm. Laird Kleine-Ahlbrandt

James B. Lane

Saul Lerner

Leon Lewis

Elizabeth Johnston Lipscomb

Janet E. Lorenz

Judith N. McArthur

Steven A. McCarver

Mark McCloskey

Margaret McFadden

Ric S. Machuga

Paul D. Mageli

Charles E. May

Laurence W. Mazzeno

Sally Mitchell

Robert H. Morace

Gordon R. Mork

Katharine M. Morsberger

Robert E. Morsberger

Edwin Moses

John M. Muste

Stella Nesanovich

Peter West Nutting

James W. Oberly

George O'Brien

Patrick O'Donnell

Robert M. Otten

Thomas R. Peake

David Peck

Robert C. Petersen

Robert L. Peterson

Jennifer L. Randisi

Thomas Rankin

John D. Raymer

Martin Ridge

Bruce Robbins

Michael C. Robinson

Mary Rohrberger

Joseph Rosenblum

Robert Ross

Marc Rothenberg

Victor Anthony Rudowski

David Sadkin

Scott Sawyer

Joachim J. Scholz

Patricia Sharpe

T. A. Shippey

R. Baird Shuman

Anne W. Sienkewicz

Thomas J. Sienkewicz

Harold L. Smith

Ira Smolensky

Madison U. Sowell

Michael Sprinker

Leon Stein

Gerard H. Strauss

James Sullivan

Daniel Taylor

Henry Taylor

Shelly Usen

Ronald G. Walker

Craig Werner

Bruce Wiebe

John Wilson

Michael Witkoski

Harry Zohn

MAGILL'S
LITERARY ANNUAL

1987

AN ACADEMIC QUESTION

Author: Barbara Pym (1913-1980)
Publisher: E. P. Dutton (New York). 182 pp. $15.95
Type of work: Novel
Time: Approximately 1970
Locale: A provincial university town in England

A comedy of manners which centers on the professional and private lives of a small group of people connected with a provincial English university

Principal characters:
ALAN GRIMSTONE, a young anthropology lecturer at a provincial English university
CAROLINE GRIMSTONE, the narrator, his wife
CRISPIN MAYNARD, an eminent scholar and head of the anthropology department
COCO JEFFREYS, a research fellow
KITTY JEFFREYS, his mother
DOLLY ARBORFIELD, Kitty's elder sister
IRIS HORNIBLOW, a young sociologist at the university

Loyal readers of Barbara Pym's novels will be pleased with the posthumous publication of *An Academic Question*, following so soon after the appearance of *Crampton Hodnet* in 1985. The novel has been made available through the editorial efforts of Hazel Holt, Pym's literary executor. Working from the notes and drafts which Pym accumulated during the late 1960's and early 1970's, she has made available a delightful novel which will be a valuable addition to the eleven others in the Pym canon. Pym herself did not expect the novel to be published, although she commented that "perhaps my immediate circle of friends will like to read it." Her discouragement was understandable following her failure, throughout the 1960's and well into the 1970's, to find a publisher for any of her manuscripts. This was a distressing period for her in which she became convinced that her career as a novelist was over. It is not difficult to see, in retrospect, why her efforts met with such little success in the 1960's. The poet Philip Larkin succinctly expressed it in a letter to a friend at Faber and Faber, one of the publishers who had turned down Pym's *An Unsuitable Attachment*: "I feel it is a great shame if ordinary sane novels about ordinary sane people doing ordinary sane things can't find a publisher these days. This is the tradition of Austen and Trollope, and I refuse to believe that no one wants its successors today. Why should I have to choose between spy rubbish, science fiction rubbish . . . or dope-taking nervous-break-down rubbish?"

Fortunately, Pym is now back in favor, and *An Academic Question* is likely to consolidate further her still growing reputation. It is set in a provincial English university town, and like most of Pym's novels, the plot is slight. It centers on the academic rivalry between two members of the sociology and anthropology department. A young scholar, Alan Grimstone, publishes an article which challenges the theories of the professor of the department, Crispin Maynard. Grimstone has dishonestly obtained important material from the papers of a dying missionary in the local old people's home, but after a few twists and turns of the plot, he escapes detection. The second element of the plot is Grimstone's extramarital affair with the assistant editor of the journal that is publishing his article.

Yet Pym, as is her custom, avoids treating these events in highly dramatic fashion. The chief interest of the novel is not in what happens, but in Pym's characteristically understated wit, her wry observations, through the medium of the narrator, Grimstone's wife, Caroline, about the rituals of academic life. It is in Pym's acute awareness of all the nuances of social intercourse, her observation of the small details of behavior which reveal large things about people that her success lies. Chief of these rituals is communal eating and social drinking. Much of the novel takes place at dinner or luncheon parties. Even the hardworking Alan Grimstone is more interested in the progress of the Yorkshire pudding than in the book review he is writing, and the editor of an academic journal fondly looks back on a "memorable asparagus mousse" as if it were a great work of art. Small pleasures count for much in Pym's novels.

Caroline, known as Caro, is not a typical Pym heroine, in that she is a young married woman rather than a middle-aged spinster. She has married slightly below herself (or so her mother believes) and sees herself as a frustrated graduate wife. She is not ambitious and finds herself taking a part-time job at the university library, along with other graduate wives "striving to fulfill [them]selves with useful work." She often reflects on her sense of inadequacy and ignorance, but this stems more from her intelligence and self-awareness than any lack of it. She can see through and beyond the closed world of others.

Through Caro, Pym gently satirizes the solemn rat race of academe, where the most important thing in life is what one publishes and where one publishes it (making sure certainly that one send offprints to all the right people). Caro has learned to keep up appearances and refrains from making jokes about the odd titles of articles in learned anthropological journals. She is quite ready to enjoy the annual Dabbs Memorial Lecture (to be given by the "able" young Iris Horniblow) until she finds that the dead hand of the sociologist's jargon has ruined it, and she regards the "ongoing" professional rivalry with detached amusement, not having more than a dutiful interest in her husband's attempts to climb the academic ladder.

Anthropologists appear in many of Pym's novels, and Pym often commented on the similarity between the work of the anthropologist and the novelist. Each is concerned with the detached, objective observation of human behavior. Much of the amusement to be gained from *An Academic Question* is in seeing the tables turned, the anthropologists themselves becoming the objects of study. This is cleverly brought out in the title of the Dabbs Memorial Lecture: patterns of neighborhood behavior in various suburban communities, since it is these very patterns of behavior which are the subject of the novel. As Caro's colleague Heather Armitage comments, unconscious of the significance of her remark: "It does make one feel that there are opportunities for fieldwork on one's own doorstep."

Indeed, Caro makes a good researcher. Like Mildred Lathbury in Pym's novel *Excellent Women* (1952), she has the ability to step outside herself and observe with an objective eye the odd behavior of others. In the midst of a party, for example, Caro comments: "Carefully, cautiously, with a cool eye and as much detachment as I could muster, I peeped at myself and Alan, as it were lifting the corner of a curtain or peering through a chink in a lighted window." At one point she studies the people in a railway carriage, as if she were indeed a sociologist or "even a novelist storing useful material." She has an engaging habit of reflecting from the individual to the general, passing on to the reader her thoughts about life.

These reflections, appropriately enough for a Pym novel, are never dogmatic. Caro's thoughts tend to turn back on themselves, self-questioning, doubting the affirmative statement of a moment before. There is no convenient simplification of the complexity of life. This is brought out by the second element in the plot, Caro's marriage to Alan. They are a restrained, "civilized" couple (Caro's sister thinks that it would be better if they shouted and threw things at each other, but that is not their way). Nevertheless, she is bored with him. She has no opportunity to share in his work and thinks that he looks on her as "a meddling, ignorant servant who might use a valuable manuscript for lighting the fire." All she ever seems to do, she comments regretfully, is represent him at funerals and memorial services for recently demised anthropologists. Yet in spite of this, she does not regard the marriage as having irretrievably broken down. She remains, in a way, in love with him and does not think them incompatible.

The situation comes to a head when she discovers her husband's infidelity—but then everything that happens serves to undercut and minimize this moment of potential drama. Readers of Pym's novels will be familiar with such a pattern. No one reacts much to Caro's situation; none of her friends can respond in the way that she needs. Her friend Dolly Arborfield, an elderly spinster who is more interested in animal life than human, is brooding over the loss of her favorite hedgehog and regards Caro's news as unimportant. It should not affect her marriage, she says (a thought which Alan also expresses). Caro's friend Coco, the effeminate, clothes-conscious research fellow, is sympathetic, but at the moment she most needs closeness and comfort, he is concerned only with brushing an insect off her dress. He can give her nothing. Her sister Susan, working as a social worker in a "difficult" area of London, expects such infidelity as a matter of course and wonders why it did not happen sooner. When Caro meets the offending woman, a friendly, hopelessly disorganized girl called Cressida, there is no direct, emotional confrontation, and she realizes that she has been taking the incident far too seriously. After a brief stay with her mother, she returns to her husband and the affair is never mentioned again. The business of daily living goes on much as before.

As happens so often in Pym's novels, the lives of the main characters do not change very much. Alan continues to work far into the night, and Caro hears the tap of the typewriter while she lies awake in bed, just as she had done before she learned of his affair. Time will heal, or will not heal; the final outcome is left open. One of the last exchanges between Caro and Alan ends with a question from him to her which "hung in the air, unanswered." Caro herself observes on the last page of the novel how "ongoing" life is. She is referring to the probability that the academic dispute will continue in future issues of the journal, but the sociological jargon conveys an additional meaning: Life is organic process, nothing is ever neatly resolved or "finished"—the irresolvable ambiguities and complexities of life must be quietly accepted and lived through. Dreams must be tailored to suit circumstances and realistic prospects.

An Academic Question is certainly a realistic novel; romantic, idealized love plays little part in it. Caro learns, for example, that even her mother settled for second best in marriage, having been in love with someone else at the time. This is a fact which Caro had never suspected, and it suggests that even the best of relationships may hide disappointed dreams.

The down-to-earth realism is also noticeable in the setting. The new university buildings look as if they had been made from a child's box of bricks; a dead pigeon lies in the little moat around the library building; an ugly piece of modern sculpture is covered in graffiti. It is not the sort of place where dreams come true, a fact which is emphasized once more when Caro, out walking, sees what she had thought from a distance were attractive flowers turn out to be no more than discarded candy wrappers. "How narrow our lives become" she laments at one point, and indeed this seems to be one perspective that the novel suggests. When she visits a nursing home, she observes that the old peoples' lives are narrowed down so much that they seem to be entirely contained in the boxes of personal possessions which they bring in with them. Finally, death, whether of the old missionary Stillingfleet or of one of Dolly's hedgehogs, casts a faint but continual shadow over the novel. Kitty Jeffreys, whose life consists of nostalgia for the good old days she spent in the West Indies, and her son Coco, full of self-love and pride in his appearance, cannot bear even to hear death discussed.

Yet Caro is not unhappy. Life lived within narrow confines need not be depressing. After all, Dolly's life revolves around trivia, and with her sentimental reverence for animal life she is one of the more open and likable characters in the book. At one point Caro sees her arranging hedgehog droppings into a neat pile and queries the usefulness of such an endeavor. Dolly replies, "Oh, what does it matter what *use* they are! It's enough to see such tangible evidence of another kind of life!" The book concludes with Dolly's platitudes about hibernating hedgehogs that will be seen again in the spring (they are "ongoing" too). The trivial, the seemingly insignificant, has the last word. It is to Barbara Pym's credit that she could not only observe human behavior with an acute and unjudging eye but also had the artist's ability to give to the dull daily round of living the dignity and validity it surely possesses.

Bryan Aubrey

Sources for Further Study

Booklist. LXXXII, August, 1986, p. 1663.
Chicago Tribune. August 26, 1986, V, p. 3.
Kirkus Reviews. LIV, July 1, 1986, p. 968.
Library Journal. CXI, August, 1986, p. 172.
The London Review of Books. VIII, September 4, 1986, p. 20.
Los Angeles Times Book Review. September 14, 1986, p. 6.
New Statesman. CXII, August 15, 1986, p. 31.
The New York Times Book Review. XCI, September 7, 1986, p. 25.
Publishers Weekly. CCXXX, July 11, 1986, p. 53.
The Wall Street Journal. CCVIII, September 9, 1986, p. 26.

ACROSS

Author: Peter Handke (1942-   )
Translated from the German by Ralph Manheim
Publisher: Farrar, Straus and Giroux (New York). 138 pp. $14.95
Type of work: Novel
Time: The 1980's
Locale: Salzburg, Austria

A middle-aged man is torn from his life as an intense observer of reality by an act of violence whose repercussions force him across the threshold of previous self-conceptions and into a complex search for a renewed identity

> *Principal character:*
> ANDREAS LOSER, a teacher of classical languages and an amateur archaeologist

Since several of Peter Handke's scandalously deconstructionist plays were published in English in 1969, his work has appeared regularly in the United States, with translations now numbering more than a dozen. Considering the widespread reluctance of American publishers to venture into the marketing of avant-garde literature from Europe, Handke's track record is clearly remarkable, especially as it has been achieved by an author whose sparse reconstruction of reality is as daunting to established tastes as was once his dissection of hollow linguistic conventions. That his work has been able to enlist for almost fifteen years the devoted services of the immensely gifted translator Ralph Manheim has undoubtedly helped to strengthen Handke's reputation in this country as the best-known postmodern writer of the German-speaking world.

Across (published in Germany in 1983 as *Der Chinese des Schmerzes*), appearing in English only one year after Handke's *Slow Homecoming*, must be read as a further attempt by the author to advance his heroes beyond their tainted existence as historical beings to a higher world of timeless harmony. "Child Story," the last of the three interrelated prose narratives that constitute *Slow Homecoming*, concludes with the narrator and his adolescent daughter painting over the swastikas which some benighted perpetrator of history had painted onto the birdhouses of a nearby forest. Yet these malignant symbols of Germany's unique historical guilt cannot simply be erased by the strokes of a brush. *Across* takes the logical, though troublesome, next step by involving its protagonist in a kind of preventive murder against the murderous movers of time.

"The Viewer Is Diverted," the first of three dialectically arranged stages in the development of the hero, provides a slow, deliberate, and at times laboriously minute exposition. Andreas Loser—the first-person narrator, who insists that his family name does not refer to the English meaning of the word but must be traced back to an Austrian dialect term meaning "to listen"—belongs to Handke's growing portrait gallery of meticulous and passionate observers. Wife and children Loser has left some time ago. He now lives like a hermit in a drab apartment in an inconspicuous suburb of Salzburg. As a devoted amateur archaeologist, he has learned that finding something is actually less important and less rewarding than to look "for what was missing, for what had vanished irretrievably—whether carried or merely rotted away—but was still present as a vacuum, as empty space or empty form." Playfully he calls himself a thresholdologist, one who during an archaeological excavation concentrates on finding the thresholds from which the whole layout of a site can frequently be deduced. All through the story, the threshold serves Loser as the symbol for the one spot in the vacuum of the times from which the reconstruction of reality must proceed. His continuing preoccupation with the topography of Salzburg and its vicinity is intended to provide him with a more than accidental, merely historical entry to his life and world. Yet the threshold from which the surroundings could be viewed as a transhistorical configuration has so far eluded his intense scrutiny. The objects, though clearly outlined, remain curiously disassociated from one another: "In one corner of my room a ball of dust lit by the floor lamp moved about, and in the sky a vapor trail drawn by a blinking metallic pencil flashed in the sun. At the bottom of the canal, clumps of moss drifted about. Out in the bog, a herd of deer jumped across a drainage ditch."

The results of his archaeological digs into past and present Loser writes up at his desk, in front of four carefully selected objects. Three of them are to remind him of the indestructible peace of primordial forms, of existence as "calm, radiant sea." The fourth object, on the other hand, is a troublesome presence and a much more telling indicator of Loser's true state of mind. An egg-shaped lump of clay that Loser retrieved from a thornbush on an island in the Mediterranean turns out to be the puzzling home of an insect in black armor. Only once has the furtive creature sortied forth to allow the startled archaeologist a glimpse of his most unsettling companion.

Loser, too, has recently been lured from the safe haven of his hermit's existence. Jostled by a pedestrian in one of the crowded streets of the inner city, he responds, to his own surprise, instinctively and with unexpected force by pushing back so violently that the other falls to the ground. Though completely unrepentant about his outburst of aggression, Loser realizes that a number of contradictory feelings have left him "in suspense, or in a state of 'in-decision.'" He takes a leave of absence from his school in order to have the time to confront himself, as he seems poised on the threshold of new things to come.

One evening, on the way home from an extended walk, just at the moment when the peace of night has melted the boundaries which usually separate objects and subjects so painfully from one another, the calm of Loser's soul is cruelly disturbed by a row of election posters that clutter the

harmony of the landscape with their strident impostor faces. Mechanically
he kicks the first of the wooden signboards, only to find it, quite literally,
unanchored in reality. Quickly and effortlessly he disposes of the whole row
of intruders by throwing them into an adjacent canal, where they sink instantly. Walking on without remorse, Loser, nevertheless, cannot avoid asking himself: "Was this a case of wanting to commit murder?" For the moment, he still shies away from acknowledging such momentous implications.
Only too soon, however, another event will bring to an end all further
evasions.

The title of the next segment, "The Viewer Takes Action," sets the tone
for the inevitable climax. A few days later, Loser walks to his monthly card
game at a friend's house. The soothing timelessness of the game's orderly
pursuits has become for him the longed-for ideal of all communal interactions and almost the only social activity in which he still participates voluntarily, even eagerly. On his way, Loser strays into one of the few enclaves
of nature in the city and loses himself in the prehistorical starkness of its
nightly life. Once again, he is rudely awakened from his contemplation, this
time by the noxious sight of a freshly painted swastika on a beech tree.
Sensing the defacer's presence nearby, Loser picks up a stone to pursue this
satanic propagator of a symbol which for Loser represents "the cause of all
my melancholy—of all melancholy, ill humor, and false laughter in this
country." He quickly hunts down the spoiler of natural peace and, propelled
by "an unaccustomed impersonal strength," slays him with one well-aimed
throw. Unconcerned about the legality or even the morality of his act, Loser
quickly disposes of the disgustingly anonymous man and immediately re-
gains his composure, smacking his lips aloud as he "experienced a sense of
triumph at having killed."

His return to the charmed circle of the card players strikes Loser initially
as quite unproblematic. Still, a surprising fatigue hints at the turmoil within
him. When after the game the friends part ways, Loser cannot return home.
He descends into the bleak underworld of the nightly city. Even when finally
back in the safe precincts of his apartment, he no longer finds the solid
presence of his beloved objects truly therapeutic. Loser, having trapped
himself in a historical act, suddenly feels excluded from the pacifying sway
of nature's unchanging objectivity. For historical man, and Loser has invol-
untarily reentered that creature's precarious realm, any victory over time
can only be guaranteed by the tenuous human power of memory. To extend
memory beyond the narrow bounds of human life, to build memory as a
threshold to permanence, Loser's historical act must strive not to be forgotten. Loser, consequently, sets out to find an appropriate witness to his deed.

"The Viewer Seeks a Witness" contains some of the most baffling turns in
the hero's erratic course toward personal renewal. At first, Loser is completely paralyzed by a sensory confusion which distorts the sounds and forms

of his daily life. Even his body feels strangely out of reach. To emphasize the significance of Loser's predicament, Handke makes sure that the reader is aware of the time during which these events take place. The murder was committed on the Wednesday of Holy Week. Loser's subsequent travails reach their greatest intensity on the following Friday and Saturday. By integrating the fate of his hero into the mythical sequence of death and resurrection—Loser is not a Christian and therefore does not view the Easter events in their historical uniqueness—Handke points the way toward a resolution of the conflict between the necessary course of nature and the accidental course of history by appealing to the predictable recurrences of archetypal myths.

Rejuvenated, Loser embarks on a series of excursions that take him in quick succession to the airport of Salzburg, the old age home of his senile mother, Vergil's birthplace in northern Italy, and to a former vacationing spot on the island of Sardinia. What these erratic journeys apparently have in common is Loser's desire to see and measure himself in the eyes of others. Yet none of the forced encounters can solve the enigma of his identity until, back in Salzburg, he recognizes his face in the tilted mirror of a supermarket as resembling that of his son. Convinced that his son represents his own future in history, Loser returns to his family to make the adolescent boy the witness of his burdensome act. An epilogue shows Loser on a small bridge near his apartment as he watches in solemn joy the people who pass him on their way home from work. The threshold has apparently been located. "Peace, mischief, quietness, gravity, slowness, and patience" flow from it. The story of Loser's future can begin.

From the moment Handke stepped into the literary limelight with his spectacularly successful play *Publikumsbeschimpfung* (1966; *Offending the Audience*, 1969), his career as a writer has often been summarized with the help of this programmatic title as representing one continuous assault on public sensibilities. The shrill antics of the *enfant terrible* have long since given way to a no less consciously chosen posture of magisterial aloofness, yet a cold and annihilating fury can still be sensed behind the mask of calm composure. Nevertheless, when allowed to lower his guard, Handke, as always, is eager to transpose objects and events of everyday life into a realm of serene enchantment. Where the reader is invited to touch with Loser the petal of a hibiscus, to join the peaceful circle of his card-playing friends, or to stand with him ankle-deep in the muck of Sardinia's Lago di Barratz, nothing else seems to matter, and the perception of reality becomes its own reward.

Yet there remains the central, the unassimilable fact of the remorseless murder. Even if one does not judge the deed by the common standards of law and morality, the question of why and to what end Handke insists on the sinister occurrence still needs to be answered. Does Handke really suggest that it is a necessary step in Loser's ascent to ever new heights of perceptual maturity? If so, should the price not be considered inhumanly high? Loser's search for a witness at least indicates that such a deed must have ramifications that lead beyond the good conscience of any individual. The epilogue, nevertheless, shows the hero as splendidly isolated as before. The renewed composure appears to be the achievement not of remembrance but of forgetfulness. That Handke views the events as prologue to a story, rather than the story itself, leaves him with many tantalizing options. For the moment, however, the reader takes leave of Loser more disturbed than captivated by his regained peace of mind.

Joachim J. Scholz

Sources for Further Study

Best Sellers. XLVI, October, 1986, p. 248.
Booklist. LXXXII, June 15, 1986, p. 1498.
Kirkus Reviews. LIV, April 15, 1986, p. 566.
Los Angeles Times. June 25, 1986, V, p. 6.
The New York Review of Books. XXXIII, August 14, 1986, p. 37.
The New York Times Book Review. XCI, July 27, 1986, p. 13.
Publishers Weekly. CCXXIX, April 25, 1986, p. 67.

ACTUAL MINDS, POSSIBLE WORLDS

Author: Jerome Bruner (1915-   )
Publisher: Harvard University Press (Cambridge, Massachusetts). 201 pp. $15.00
Type of work: Essays

A unified collection of essays which argues for the constructive nature of the human mind and the importance of the narrative imagination

In the early 1960's, Jerome Bruner, then a professor of psychology at Harvard University, published a collection of what he called "fugitive essays" entitled *On Knowing: Essays for the Left Hand* (1962), in which he argued that to understand the nature of human cognition one needed an approach which went beyond that provided by the conceptual tools of the psychologist, an approach whose primary medium of exchange was the "metaphor paid out by the left hand." Such is the way of the poet, Bruner said then, for poets' hunches and intuitions create a grammar of their own. Bruner has done a considerable amount of important work in the fields of knowledge acquisition, education, and cognitive psychology since that collection. Now he returns to the topic of the poetic way of knowing in this sequel of sorts to his "left hand" essays, for which a group of essays written for various occasions between 1980 and 1984 have been revised and reorganized.

The result is a unified argument, developed in three stages. Part 1 contrasts two modes of thought: the paradigmatic, or the logical and scientific mode, and the narrative mode. Part 2, which constitutes the central section of the book, deals with the basic worldview of constructivism, a view Bruner shares with such thinkers as Nelson Goodman and Lev Vygotsky, which claims that there is no given world "out there," at least no meaningful world, but rather that reality is constructed by the human mind. Part 3 suggests some of the implications of these ideas for education and for culture in general.

Bruner's return to his earlier interest in poetic modes of thought has been stimulated by his sympathetic reading of literary theory and criticism of the 1970's and 1980's, beginning with the revival of the Russian Formalists, continuing with the works of Claude Lévi-Strauss, Roman Jakobson, and Roland Barthes, and culminating with the deconstructionist theories of Jacques Derrida and the reader-response and speech-act theories of Wolfgang Iser. It seems that much recent literary theory reaffirms Bruner's earlier conviction that there is something about the nature of human knowledge to be learned from the poet's way of creating meaning.

Bruner begins by tackling what he considers to be a basic problem: Can a psychology of literature be developed that will explain why some stories succeed and others fail to engage the reader? He is, however, also concerned with why and how stories can trigger multiple readings. Bruner's central thesis, which does not stray far from his earlier thoughts of twenty-five years ago, is that there are two modes of thought, each providing distinctive ways of constructing reality: the logico-scientific mode, or the paradigmatic, and the "other" mode, what he calls the narrative mode. His primary concern is with the latter, the less understood of the two.

Bruner tries to synthesize the work of such thinkers as Tzvetan Todorov, Victor Turner, and Hayden White, who suggest that there are underlying "deep structures" of narrative. He then attempts to integrate their ideas with the phenomenological and speech-act theories of Wolfgang Iser and others; thus are introduced the notions of intention, presupposition, and what Bruner calls "subjunctive reality" (the story's allowance for the reader to give play to his imagination to "rewrite" the story), all of which focus on the role of the reader rather than on the underlying nature of the text.

In applying Todorov's structuralist theories of transformations, Bruner administered empirical testing, where his subjects were asked to read and "tell back" pieces of good narrative or exposition; these tests were designed not only to determine differences between the two modes but also to shed light on how the creation of "virtual" texts (variants of the given text) depends on the reader. Critics have been trying to gauge reader response at least since 1935, when I. A. Richards published his pioneering and controversial *Practical Criticism, a Study of Literary Judgment.* Such efforts have always produced unsatisfactory results in their simplicity and reductiveness. Indeed, when one goes to Bruner's appendix and reads his subject's retelling of James Joyce's short story "Clay" alongside the original, one finds the sort of unexamined plot summary that would not be tolerated in a freshman English class. Bruner's reader responds as if the story of Maria in "Clay" were a real event, not a narrated story. To use the terms Bruner borrows from the Russian Formalists via Jakobson and Todorov, Bruner's reader responds only to the *fabula,* that is, the event as event, not to the *sjuzet,* the event as it is structured by the writer and therefore must be processed by the reader.

In the second part of the book, Bruner develops what he describes as his central ontological conviction—that there is no primary reality against which one can compare a possible world. Bruner's view, not an uncommon one in contemporary literary theory, but a view that goes against the grain of pragmatic American philosophy (with the exception of those adherents of William James's early notion of multiple realities), suggests a more complex relationship between literature and reality than the conventional mimetic notion that literature imitates life. In the essay entitled "The Transactional Self," Bruner argues that insofar as one often accounts for one's actions and events in terms of drama, narrative, and story, it might better be said that life imitates art.

Bruner's primary ally for this view is Harvard philosopher Nelson Goodman. In such books as *Ways of Worldmaking* (1978) and *Of Mind and Other Matters* (1984), Goodman asserts that, despite one's commonsense notion, there is no "real world" which comes before or exists independently of human symbolic activity. Placing such crucial and central emphasis on man as *animal symbolicum*, as such thinkers as George Berkeley, Immanuel Kant, and Ernst Cassirer have done previously, Goodman's constructivism eliminates the distinction between science and art, which argues that the logico-scientific method is the only means by which reality can truly be known. For Goodman, and also for Bruner, both science and art grow out of common constructional activities.

The constructivist point of view has important implications for the humanities, making the study of art and literature as important as scientific study. For if reality is a creation of the human imagination, then reality is indeed a continuous story constantly being told and retold by those who both observe and participate in its events. Thus, each person's life is a story constructed from the same kinds of conventions that make literary stories possible. Reality is created by the same kinds of tropes, metaphors, and genres that are used in literature. Consequently, if one wishes to understand human reality, one would do well to understand literature first.

Such a point of view would explain the current popularity of reflexive fictions and films, that is, works which, rather than simply being about some preexistent "real" world outside themselves, are about their own fictional or filmic processes. Rather than being examples of self-indulgent art or industry in-jokes, as they are sometimes perceived, such novels as John Fowles's *The French Lieutenant's Woman* (1969) and such films as *The Stuntman* (1980) suggest that if reality is indeed a fictional process, then the only way for art to reflect reality is to embody self-consciously those very processes.

In the last three essays in *Actual Minds, Possible Worlds*, Bruner applies his constructivist point of view to the relationship between thought and emotion, to the language of education, and to the relationship between theories of human development and culture. The primary implication of the constructivist view regarding education, writes Bruner, is that a culture constantly re-creates itself as it is reinterpreted by its members. Thus, a culture is a forum for negotiating and renegotiating meaning, and it follows that the constant re-creating of meaning should be a part of the educational process. Although Bruner recognizes that this idea runs counter to the more traditional view of education as being a transmission of knowledge, he insists on the importance of this extension of his earlier notions of "discovery learning," or what Jean Piaget has called "learning by inventing."

In the classroom, the practical implications of this point of view would be a shift to a stance in which the teacher expresses the hypothetical nature of knowledge, in which the teacher, rather than transfer information to the student, invites him to extend his own world of wonder and possibility to encompass the teacher's own. Much of the process of education, writes Bruner, consists of the ability to distance oneself from what one knows to reflect on one's knowledge. The language of education, insists Bruner, cannot be the language of so-called uncontaminated fact and objectivity but, rather, must express a stance and invite counterstance. If a student fails to develop any sense of reflective intervention, he will always be operating from the outside in, absorbing information without reflecting upon it. The language of education should be the language of a culture being created, not of knowledge being consumed.

In the afterword to *Actual Minds, Possible Worlds*, Bruner summarizes and responds to two articles, one by George Steiner, the other by Todorov, which appeared in the *Times Literary Supplement* in 1985. Both Steiner and Todorov disagree with the nihilistic deconstructionist view that a text can mean nothing (if nothing exists but discourse, then discourse can only refer to discourse) and with the pragmatic deconstructionist view that a text can mean everything (only a reader can give a text meaning, and thus the most "interesting" interpretation is the best interpretation). Bruner is less anxiously concerned than Steiner and Todorov with a philosophical point of view that he calls a "harebrained perspectivalism that is now living out its sunset in Paris and New Haven and in the intellectual suburbs." He regards both the view that the text means nothing and the view that the text means everything as excesses reflecting the revolution of thought in the twentieth century in science, philosophy, politics, and art—that is, excesses resulting from the idea that one's concern should not be with what one knows but rather with how one knows.

For Bruner, interpretations of a literary work can be judged according to their rightness, but their rightness cannot be determined by a correspondence to a primary "real" world "out there." The function of art, he concludes, is not to reflect external reality, whatever that is, but to open one up to dilemmas and to the hypothetical, to make the world less banal and fixed, to make what seems obvious less so. As such, art is an instrument of imagination and freedom and, thus, one's only hope against what Bruner calls "the long gray night."

Charles E. May

Sources for Further Study

Booklist. LXXXII, March 15, 1986, p. 1045.
Kirkus Reviews. LIV, February 1, 1986, p. 177.
The New York Times Book Review. XCI, March 23, 1986, p. 43.
Publishers Weekly. CCIX, February 14, 1986, p. 64.

THE AFFAIR
The Case of Alfred Dreyfus

Author: Jean-Denis Bredin (1929-   )
Translated from the French by Jeffrey Mehlman
Publisher: George Braziller (New York). Illustrated. 628 pp. $24.95
Type of work: Political, cultural, and social history
Time: Primarily 1894-1907
Locale: France

An account of the Dreyfus Affair, by far the most complete, the most balanced, and the most interesting single volume work on the subject

> *Principal personages:*
> ALFRED DREYFUS, a captain in the French Army; accused of treason
> LUCIE DREYFUS, his wife
> MATHIEU DREYFUS, his brother and constant supporter
> MARIE CHARLES ESTERHAZY, a major in the French Army; the real traitor
> HUBERT JOSEPH HENRY, a lieutenant colonel in the French Army; part of the conspiracy against Dreyfus and a forger of documents
> AUGUSTE MERCIER, a general in the French Army and Minister of War (1893-1895); a principal conspirator
> GEORGES PICQUART, a lieutenant colonel (later general) in the French Army; defender of Dreyfus
> MERCIER DU PATY DE CLAM, a major in the French Army and a principal conspirator against Dreyfus
> ÉMILE ZOLA, a novelist and the most noted defender of Dreyfus

On October 15, 1894, Alfred Dreyfus, an obscure captain of infantry in the French Army, was arrested for high treason, specifically for providing military information to Germany. The effects of this seemingly unimportant action were to convulse France for the next twelve years and are still to be found in various guises in the France of the late twentieth century. The Dreyfus Affair, as it came to be called, was and is probably the most famous (or notorious) *cause célèbre* in the history of Western civilization.

The Affair has produced thousands of books, pamphlets, and articles. This latest recounting of and commentary on The Affair by Jean-Denis Bredin, originally published in France in 1983 as *L'Affaire* and ably translated by Jeffrey Mehlman, will certainly not be the last book on the subject, but it is one of the best. Because of its wealth of detail, its treatment of background, and its balanced and judicious view of all the issues, it is the one basic book that should be read by anyone interested in The Affair, its origins, and its effects. The author, a highly respected lawyer and professor of law at the University of Paris, is also a modern historian and a frequent contributor to French periodicals. He has brought to this comprehensive study all the best qualities of the legal mind and temperament; it could only be wished that all the lawyers involved in The Affair had displayed the same qualities.

After his arrest in October, 1893, Dreyfus was tried by court martial and, on the basis of forged evidence, suppressed documents, perjured testimony, against a background of press-fueled anti-Semitism, was found guilty and sentenced to military degradation and perpetual deportation. In January, 1895, Dreyfus was degraded before the army and sent to Devil's Island, where he arrived in March to spend the next four years and three months. As Bredin makes clear in several memorable chapters, counterpointed against the continuing events in Paris, Devil's Island was Hell. Dreyfus was subjected to special supervision, severe restraints, and petty, demeaning regulations. Clearly, he was expected to die there, as most transportees did, but he stubbornly refused to acquiesce.

At home, meanwhile, his wife, Lucie, his brother Mathieu, and Colonel Georges Picquart sought every avenue of appeal and searched for new evidence. Picquart discovered that the real spy was almost certainly a Major Marie Charles Esterhazy of the French Army. As the result of a public letter by Lucie Dreyfus, the press again began to choose sides and ask questions. The result was a redoubled effort by the military to cover up (more forgeries) and to blacken the reputation of Picquart. Esterhazy was brought before a court martial in January, 1898, and acquitted. Two days after the acquittal, The Affair was forever transformed from a search for justice for one man into a social, religious, and political upheaval and debate about the very nature of the French state and French life. The turning point was the publication of "J'accuse" by the famous novelist Émile Zola. In his pamphlet, Zola made it perfectly clear that the struggle was now to be that of the traditional republican virtues, especially truth and justice, against the religious passion, the military spirit, and the devotion to hierarchies characteristic of what may be termed the French Establishment. Dreyfus had become a symbol; henceforth, one's political and social values would be measured by where one stood on the Dreyfus Affair. Among the Dreyfusards tended to be found Socialists, intellectuals, republicans and those with a passion for individual liberty. Ranged against them tended to be monarchists, the military, many Catholics, and those with a passion for order, tradition, and obedience. Many enrolled on one side or the other to further their own personal agendas. For many, Dreyfus was guilty because he was a Jew. For many, the army could do no wrong simply because it was the army.

The Dreyfusard cause suffered two setbacks in early 1898 when Zola was found guilty of slander of the Minister of War and Colonel Picquart was dismissed from the service because of his activities on behalf of Dreyfus. Though the anti-Dreyfusards kept winning battles, the war was going against them. As the result of various trials and legal proceedings, more and more evidence appeared in public, and the anti-Dreyfusards found themselves fighting more rearguard actions.

At the end of August, 1898, Commandant Hubert Joseph Henry, the principal forger, admitted his guilt and committed suicide. By the end of 1898, Dreyfus' innocence had been clearly demonstrated, and he was returned from Devil's Island and accorded a new court martial in September, 1899. Against all the evidence, the army once again found him guilty.

Within days of the verdict, however, Dreyfus accepted a pardon. Some of his supporters and lawyers opposed the pardon and wished to carry on the struggle for complete reversal of the original verdict, because the clear implication was that one could not be pardoned for something one has not done in the first place. Nevertheless, on September 19, 1899, Dreyfus became a free man once again. Complete rehabilitation would, however, have to wait another seven years. Finally, as a result of hearings and proceedings before a multitude of courts, in July, 1906, the High Court of Appeal found Dreyfus completely innocent of any charges against him. He was restored to the army (as was Picquart) and awarded the Cross of the Legion of Honor.

The ins and outs of this whole long series of events is fascinating to follow; the narrative presents a wealth of melodrama, as one outrageous event follows upon another. Bredin, who has mastered a great mass of detail and set it out with clarity without skimping on the evidence, has the novelist's ability to let a scene speak for itself. Though he is clearly on Dreyfus' side, he does not sermonize nor does he indulge in heated or outraged rhetoric—though certainly he is presented with numerous opportunities. The tone throughout remains cool and judicious. As might be expected from a professor of law, Bredin is especially good on the trials, the court martials, and the sessions of the legislature. The author manages to bring out all the drama inherent in the court proceedings; he captures vividly moments and personalities.

Ultimately, the book, like The Affair itself, is more than the story of one man. Bredin has firmly set The Affair in its time and place, mastered the background, and supplied a context: Dreyfus and The Affair are not seen in isolation but as a part of the flow of French life that they were. In particular does Bredin set the anti-Semitism of the time in its place. Dreyfus was not initially arrested because he was a Jew, but the fact that he was a Jew had much to do with the conduct of the case and with public attitudes. Bredin carefully traces the growth of anti-Semitism in France from about 1880 and in several chapters estimates carefully the contribution of The Affair to anti-Semitism and the contribution of anti-Semitism to The Affair.

Bredin ably examines a number of currents of French thinking and brings these to bear upon the narration of the events of The Affair: the spirit and reputation of the army; the national desire for revenge and restoration after the embarrassing defeats of the war of 1870; the growth of what may be

called the intelligentsia; the place and power of the Press. Thus, the reader
is offered a rounded picture rather than an isolated series of events. The Affair took place in a real place and time, and Bredin provides that place and
time in such a way as to make the events, however outrageous, at least
understandable and believable. Bredin not only masters events but also
ideas. He reveals the divisions in French society and how The Affair influenced political careers and events.

The final chapters of the work are noteworthy. After accounting for all
the persons of The Affair, Bredin surveys its consequences. He distinguishes
those things that were of that time and place only and those things that are
still to be found in present-day France. It is here that he is at his most judicious and where he applies the full play of mind to the events of history.
He is suggestive rather than dogmatic and never goes beyond his evidence.
He does not try to claim too much for The Affair, but he is clear that the
divisions and conflict raised by it are not all of the past. Moreover, in his final chapter, Bredin extends the "meaning" of The Affair beyond France to
the whole world and into the heart of individuals.

In the course of the book several themes are educed which have become
all too common. For example, national security was frequently invoked by
the anti-Dreyfusards as a means to protect individuals or reputations; the
argument was advanced that to find the army guilty of any sort of under-
handed dealings would cause a crisis of confidence in the army and thus
weaken the government. As another example, the narrative includes the sor-
did details of a cover-up that extended to the highest levels of government
and the military, with perjured testimony and much stonewalling. Again,
there is here a built-in warning about political generals and a politicized
military. Perhaps most notably, the reader is presented with ample evidence
of the power of the press, both for good and for ill. Without it, The Affair
would never have come to the public eye.

It would be satisfying to report that, once Dreyfus' innocence was established, everyone lived happily ever after. Regrettably, Dreyfus' lawyers fell
out among themselves and with Dreyfus; some members of the Dreyfusards
never spoke to one another again. The villains of the piece—except for
Henry, who committed suicide—did not come to the end that poetic justice
would seem to demand. Mercier remained a senator and died in 1921; du
Paty de Clam fought bravely and was wounded in World War I; Esterhazy
fled to England, where he died rich in 1923.

Of Dreyfus himself, one learns that broken in health from his stay on
Devil's Island, he retired from the army in 1907. He was recalled to duty at
the outbreak of war in 1914, served throughout the war, participating in several of its bloodiest battles, and retired again in 1919 as a colonel. He died
in July, 1935. He seems not to have been, at least outside his family, a particularly warm or outgoing person. He continued, all through his ordeal, to

protest his innocence. Bredin judges that his heroism consisted in surviving and refusing to give in to death. It is ironic, or perhaps fitting, that Dreyfus, all through The Affair, not only proclaimed his innocence but also trusted that he would be vindicated. His love of his country emphasized the ideals of justice and truth; he could never believe that his France, which he saw as founded on those ideals, would not right his wrongs. Though the course was long and twisting and entailed much suffering, he was proved right.

Gordon N. Bergquist

Sources for Further Study

The Atlantic. CCLVII, February, 1986, p. 83.
Choice. XXIII, May, 1986, p. 1442.
Commentary. LXXXI, May, 1986, p. 68.
Library Journal. CXI, January, 1986, p. 82.
The New York Review of Books. XXXIII, February 27, 1986, p. 3.
The New York Times Book Review. XCI, January 26, 1986, p. 11.
The New Yorker. LXII, March 17, 1986, p. 110.
Publishers Weekly. CCXXVIII, December 6, 1985, p. 67.
Time. CXXVII, March 24, 1986, p. 86.
Washington Post Book World. XVI, January 26, 1986, p. 1.

ALEXANDER POPE
A Life

Author: Maynard Mack (1909-   )
Publisher: W. W. Norton and Company (New York), in association with Yale University Press (New Haven, Connecticut). Illustrated. 975 pp. $22.50
Type of work: Literary biography
Time: 1688-1744
Locale: England

A scholarly biography of the eighteenth century English poet Alexander Pope, which relates the poet to his own times and analyzes his literary achievement

> *Principal personages:*
> ALEXANDER POPE, an English neoclassic poet
> MARY WORTLEY MONTAGU, Pope's friend, a learned English lady
> MARTHA BLOUNT, a spinster, neighbor, and friend of Pope
> TERESA BLOUNT, her younger sister
> HENRY ST. JOHN, Viscount Bolingbroke, an English Tory politician and philosopher
> JONATHAN SWIFT, an English author and satirist
> COLLEY CIBBER, poet laureate, actor, and dramatist
> ROBERT WALPOLE, Whig prime minister during most of Pope's productive period

Fame and reputation have not dealt evenly with Alexander Pope, the leading English poet of the early eighteenth century. Following his death, he was generally ranked among the greatest of English poets, but his reputation declined during the Romantic period, when neoclassicism fell into disfavor. In the twentieth century, Pope has found enthusiastic readers, although their numbers are small. His place in literary history remains secure, yet he is studied as a poet of a remote era and remote sensibility rather than as a living influence upon contemporary literature. In his lengthy biography of the poet, Maynard Mack has attempted to depict Pope's life, to clarify his literary principles and values, and to interpret his achievements.

As Mack points out, Pope's remoteness from the present results, in part, from his view of the purpose of poetry and literature. Pope believed that poetry had an important function in society at large as an influence on manners, morals, and taste—it should appeal not merely to aesthetic sensibilities but to reason as well, and the poet indeed had a legitimate role as an adviser to rulers and political leaders. Even Pope's age was hostile to this exalted view of poetry, for the rulers of England, the first Hanoverian kings, who neither read nor spoke English, cared little about English literature. Moreover, the great prime minister of Pope's era, Sir Robert Walpole, was contemptuous of poetry and poets. Readers of a later age, even those who agree with Pope's exalted view of literature, encounter an additional burden, for those poets who address the issues of their own day, particularly if they address them in satire as Pope did, produce works containing topical allusions and contemporary references that inevitably become obscure.

Pope did not allow himself to become discouraged by official indifference or disapproval, for he did not rely on the patronage of the great. Instead, he achieved independence through his ability to bargain with booksellers, becoming the first truly professional man of letters in English literature. Those who received official patronage, notably the poets laureate—such as Nahum Tate, Laurence Eusden, and Colley Cibber—are all but forgotten. For modern readers, Pope's contribution remains in the epigrammatic wit of his couplets and countless expressions that have passed into English idiom and have become familiar maxims—"A little learning is a dangerous thing," "To err is human, to forgive divine," "Be not the first by whom the new are tried"—a decidedly lesser immortality than he would have desired.

In addition to the disadvantages stemming from Pope's view of literature, another obvious one must be noted. It lies in the same epigrammatic wit that made Pope's brief passages memorable—for he wrote primarily in heroic couplets, the rhymed iambic pentameter lines that reveal numerous rhetorical and poetic conventions, chiefly intricate and varied patterns of repetition. Pope brought the couplet to its perfection in English poetry, largely through making the verse form of John Dryden more regularly balanced and end-stopped. Yet in modern times the verse form can be appreciated by few readers. A scattered few couplets are easily recalled; hundreds following successively in a single composition cause most readers to lose the poem's thought and structure. They seem restrictive and artificial rather than artful. The decline of the couplet form inevitably had an adverse effect on Pope's fame as a poet.

In the poetry of a neoclassic writer such as Pope, little about the poet's life is revealed. John Dryden, the greatest literary figure in England during the final part of the seventeenth century, once remarked that however little a man said about himself, it was too much. As with many other legacies from his predecessor, Pope seems to have taken this one to heart. It implies much about the mental outlook of the neoclassic artist: respect for traditional forms and values over the subjective experience of the present, awareness that the individual's life is brief and fleeting, and recognition that in the long run only deeds and works matter. There can be little doubt that an author's distrust of the subjective makes the biographer's task more difficult, and Pope compounds the difficulty by appearing often under a mask or an assumed persona. Nevertheless, through a meticulous and admirable scholarly approach, Maynard Mack provides the reader with a thorough account of Pope's life and works set within the history of his own times. Mack succeeds in creating a fuller portrait of the subject than has been achieved heretofore.

Mack divides his account into four parts, derived primarily from the stages of Pope's literary career: "Beginnings, 1688-1708"; "The Road to

Fame, 1709-1720"; "Works and Days, 1720-1733"; and "'My Countrys Poet,' 1733-1744." In the first section, Mack sketches Pope's family background, education, and other early influences. The remaining three sections trace the development of Pope's life, times, and literary career, beginning with idyllic, pastoral poetry, moving to verse essays and translations, and finally to mature epistles and satires. This threefold pattern for the poet's career, as Pope knew, resembled the patterns of the lives of Vergil, Edmund Spenser, and John Milton. The poet's ultimate achievement was the epic, written toward the end of his life. Pope himself planned an epic on British mythical history, but he did not live to complete this ambitious project.

The great central and most admirable truth about Pope's life is that he rose to fame and fortune despite numerous disadvantages. With no assistance from the English government, he became the chief poet of the nation. Apart from historical and literary liabilities, biographers must deal with two major personal disadvantages to Pope during his lifetime—his religion and his health. Carefully probing the history of Pope's time and his life records, Mack goes further than any previous biographer toward explaining the disadvantages of Pope's Catholic faith. Reared in a Catholic family, the only son of an affluent merchant, Pope faced difficulties throughout his life. Barred from public schools and universities, he was educated by tutors and briefly at Catholic schools. His family lived at Binfield near Windsor, probably in part because laws forbade Catholics from living in London. Among a host of anti-Catholic laws were those subjecting Catholics to double taxation and forbidding them to own horses. At times during Pope's early life, owing to Jacobite plots and uprisings, anti-Catholic hysteria reached such heights that Catholics feared for their safety. Pope's name offered an invitation to his enemies to arouse animosity against him by referring to "Popery." He had no chance for official appointments or rewards, and throughout his life the threat of persecution hung over him because of his faith. Though he was urged by friends to convert to the Church of England and though he himself showed little zeal for the old faith, he remained true to the church of his fathers. Drawing upon modern psychology, Mack points out that Pope's identification with a persecuted minority left psychological scars.

Pope's life was disturbed even further by his early contracting of Pott's disease, a form of tuberculosis of the bone that attacked and gradually disfigured his spine. It is thought that he contracted the disease from his wet nurse, though its effects did not become apparent until his early adolescence, about age twelve, when he began to exhibit a decided stoop. Always frail in health and on strict regimens, he suffered constant inconvenience in early life. Only very late in life did he experience severe pain, when, in order to walk, he was forced to wear an iron brace enclosing his torso. Because of his spinal disfigurement, he stood only about four and a half feet tall. He himself referred to his life as one long disease, yet he overcame this disadvantage too. His numerous enemies satirized his physical defects as well as his Catholicism in their indiscriminate attacks.

His affliction had other untoward effects as well, rendering all but impossible any normal sexual relationship. Mack suggests that during his lifetime Pope was probably in love with at least three women: Lady Mary Wortley Montagu and Teresa and Martha Blount, two Catholic spinsters who lived near Pope's villa at Twickenham. The affection toward Lady Mary led to mutual acrimony and distaste, that with Teresa Blount ended with Pope's establishing an annuity for her, and with Martha, an enduring friendship that lasted until the poet's death. Mack demonstrates that Pope's expressions of love were guarded, as if he feared rejection; one indication is his inclination to write with increasing ardor as the actual distance from his correspondent increased, as seen in his letters to Lady Mary. Mack concludes plausibly that in no instance was Pope's love requited.

Socially and intellectually, Pope's life centered on his numerous friends— poets, artists, noblemen, philosophers. The young Pope, whose parents were in their mid-forties when he was born, was inclined to seek friends much older than himself, men who had made their mark and whose careers were already in decline. Moreover, they were selected from those who were interested in art, men such as the poet William Walsh, the dramatist William Wycherley, and the actor Thomas Betterton. It was Walsh who had told Pope that England had produced great poets and correct poets, but no great poet was correct. Pope accepted this challenge as a goal for his own career. His seeking friendships with older successful artists suggests an attempt to get on with his literary career, the serious business of his life.

Among Pope's numerous friends were the writer Jonathan Swift, John Gay, John Arbuthnot, and other wits of the age. Pope accepted invitations to the houses of many wealthy noblemen, particularly after he achieved fame and wealth. His lifelong friend, the philosopher-politician Henry St. John, influenced Pope's literary career through his ideas. Most of Pope's friendships were fortunate for him, partial compensations for his disappointments and disadvantages.

In addition to a thorough chronological account of Pope's life, Mack provides a good critical survey of Pope's poetry and literary achievement through analyses of the works, giving the general reader a sound introduction to the works. One comes away with an understanding of Pope's contribution to English literature. Mack takes standard critical and scholarly approaches, eschewing esoteric literary theory, though his approach varies depending on the nature of the work under analysis and its place in Pope's productive career. For example, in the early poems "Windsor Forest" and "To an Unfortunate Lady," Mack prefer to stress the biographical hints and suggestions found in the poems' contents, allusions, and references, particularly to places. When he comes to the translations of Homer, which established Pope's fortune, Mack points out Pope's merits as translator by drawing comparative passages from other translations, the dominant critical method being comparative analysis of texts. When he turns to *Essay on Man* (1733-1734), Mack clarifies the poem's intellectual contexts and elucidates the poem's major ideas. His emphasis is both varied and judicious.

Upon the approaching tricentennial of his birth, Pope has begun to gain the attention of scholars and has been less neglected than in previous years. Mack's book, which is destined to be the standard biography for decades to come, pays tribute to a professional poet whose influence upon the English-speaking world has rarely been exceeded. In doing so, Mack has made Pope's literary art more accessible to modern readers.

Stanley Archer

Sources for Further Study

The Atlantic. CCLVI, December, 1985, p. 112.
Christian Science Monitor. LXXVIII, February 12, 1986, p. 21.
Contemporary Review. CCXLVII, November, 1985, p. 277.
Encounter. LXVI, January, 1986, p. 38.
History Today. XXXV, October, 1985, p. 60.
Kirkus Reviews. LIII, September 1, 1985, p. 938.
Library Journal. CX, September 1, 1985, p. 102.
Los Angeles Times Book Review. November 24, 1985, p.11.
The Nation. CCXLII, March 1, 1986, p. 245.
The New Republic. CXCIV, March 3, 1986, p. 33.
New Statesman. CX, August 23, 1985, p. 24.
The New York Review of Books. XXXIII, March 13, 1986, p. 29.
The New York Times Book Review. XCI, March 2, 1986, p. 11.
Times Literary Supplement. September 13, 1985, p. 997.
Washington Post Book World. XVI, February 9, 1986, p. 10.

ALL GOD'S CHILDREN NEED TRAVELING SHOES

Author: Maya Angelou (1928-   )
Publisher: Random House (New York). 210 pp. $15.95
Type of work: Autobiography
Time: The early 1960's
Locale: Accra, Ghana

The fifth volume of Maya Angelou's serial autobiography narrates the author's sojourn in Ghana in the early 1960's and explores the black American's search for roots and home

Principal personages:
MAYA ANGELOU, the narrator
GUY, her son, a college student at the University of Ghana
JULIAN MAYFIELD, an expatriate black American novelist and journalist
ALICE WINDOM and
VICKI GARVIN, other black American expatriates, her housemates
SHEIKHALI, her French-speaking lover from Mali
MEMBERS OF THE REVOLUTIONIST RETURNEES, a group of expatriate black Americans

Maya Angelou is writing perhaps the longest series of autobiographical volumes in contemporary American letters. The serial autobiography has a distinguished history, and other black Americans have written their life histories in several parts. Frederick Douglass, Langston Hughes, and Richard Wright are names that come immediately to mind. What is unique about Angelou, however, is the number of autobiographical works she has produced, bringing her into the company of women who have published multivolume memoirs or diaries—women such as Anne Morrow Lindbergh or Anaïs Nin.

The form that Angelou is creating is indeed akin to memoir, but it still has the crafted, worked quality of the true autobiography. She writes with a doubleness of point of view (the narrator's perspective at the time of the event as well as at the time of telling) and uses the telling incident to underline overall theme, as the wise teller makes sense of her life. Journals or diaries cannot do this, being written to the moment, and a memoir cannot either, since it is chronological only, usually with little attention to theme or structure and much emphasis on famous persons. What Angelou is doing is more like fiction, with her own life as raw material.

In her first volume, *I Know Why the Caged Bird Sings* (1969), the metaphor of the cage unifies the work, beginning with the young girl who believes that she is in reality white with long blonde hair, caged in a dark skin and kinky hair, and continuing as she learns pride in being black and female from her strong grandmother and mother, both caged in a racist society. By the end, the cage is metamorphosed into Angelou's protective arm over her newborn son; she is sixteen and unmarried.

In *Gather Together in My Name* (1974), the horror of drug use by loved ones is brought home in her worsening relationship with her brother and her own adventures as a single mother in the racist California of the early 1950's. Subsequent volumes, *Singin' and Swingin' and Gettin' Merry like Christmas* (1976) and *The Heart of a Woman* (1981), treat more peregrinations of the intrepid traveler Angelou—a world tour with the cast of *Porgy and Bess* and her short-lived marriage to an exiled South African freedom fighter, residing in New York and then in Cairo. Always, however, she deals with the problem of being an outsider in her own society, and always she deals with the double jeopardy facing one who is black and female.

In *All God's Children Need Traveling Shoes*, Angelou describes her sojourn in Ghana, at a time when many black Americans were hungrily exploring their heritage, searching for "home" and the meaning of home. Visiting Accra to enroll her son Guy at the University of Ghana, she is forced to remain and must give up a new job in Liberia when he is seriously hurt in a car accident. Her adventures with the black American expatriate community, in the newly independent Ghana of Kwame Nkrumah, make stimulating reading. There are unforgettable portraits of such notables as W. E. B. Du Bois' wife, Shirley, Malcolm X, writer Julian Mayfield, and various West African chiefs; there are even better vignettes of Angelou's encounters with her hairdresser (who tells her fortune), her houseboy (whom she educates), and the media and journalism establishment of Ghana (which despite her wide experience wants to exploit her).

The expatriate black community in Accra is fascinating. Like such communities everywhere, it is united by its common national origin. These people would probably not be good friends if they were in the United States. Yet black Americans feel their foreignness in Africa, and they come together to talk about home and occasionally to indulge in soul food. A package of sausage to which were added greens and biscuits could bring tears. Conversation and jokes in a supportive setting, the quick wit and repartee of the black American community—this was as much a part of the home that Angelou longed for as soul food.

The present volume continues the exploration of being black and female, adding also the dimension of roots and home. Tellingly, the strength which Angelou gains in Africa comes primarily from the female side of her heritage, from *Mother* Africa: Her hairdresser Comfort, the women whom she meets at the university where she is employed, Efua Sutherland (the playwright and dancer), a Ewe market woman, the women who mistake her for a Bambara woman, the women with whom she shares a house—these are elements of the matriarchal tradition that sustains her. The men are famous and exciting—Malcolm X, Julian Mayfield, Nkrumah, Du Bois, Sheikhali (her French-speaking lover from Mali)—but in the end they offer little. It is from other women that she learns about herself, about Africa, and about her own need for home. The women support her when she is depressed; understand her difficulties with her son; are sympathetic when she breaks up with Sheikhali; accept her as kin and guest in the rural bush country by feeding her, taking her to the communal bath, and giving her a place to sleep.

Three incidents in the book stand out, all of them furthering the theme of home, home for black Americans. The first is the visit of Malcolm X. Malcolm X visited Ghana in the early 1960's, right after his trip to Mecca, in the last period of his life, when he was shifting away from the separatist teachings of Elijah Muhammad and deciding that blacks and whites must work together for peace and justice. This account is a fascinating look at Malcolm's mind in this transition period as well as the political intrigue that prevailed as the American black community in Accra tried to arrange an audience with Nkrumah. Angelou is in the center of it all, being persuaded, finally, that her place and home is not Africa; she should be back in America, carrying on the real struggle. In this case, the pivot in the situation is a woman, Shirley Du Bois.

The second incident is Angelou's trip to Berlin to play in a production of Jean Genet's *The Blacks*, with the all-black Broadway cast. The incident shows her unflinching willingness to confront the harsh ambiguities of the postwar German mentality. While there she is invited to the home of a German family, and she takes with her an Israeli actor whom she has met in the hotel. During the meal, the conversation turns to ethnic jokes, with Angelou baiting the Germans to reveal their Nazi background. Again she learns something about her own psyche and her own longing for home. She tells a Br'er Rabbit story, but a scatological and racist joke told by one of the family members makes her physically ill. At the end of the visit, his true motive is apparent; he wants Angelou to smuggle traditional artwork out of West Africa. In this incident she clearly acts as an American: No African would have been as brazen as she in hunting out the racism of her host.

The third incident provides the climax of the book. On a trip to eastern Ghana, several incidents reveal her clairvoyance and suggest a kind of racial memory. She irrationally "remembers" a bridge over a river that was notoriously unsafe in past generations; she is "recognized" by an Ewe market woman because of her facial features and six-foot height. Angelou discovers her roots, as descendant of a tribe that had been wiped out by slavery, except for a few orphan children who hid in the forest when the slavers came. It seems that Angelou has come home; she is showered with vegetables and tears from the market women. Again, it is the women who recognize her features from generations back—women who have preserved the history of that lost group through their telling and retelling, women who try to make restitution for the sins of their fathers by readopting Angelou into their midst. Finally, however, this is not home; she does not know even a single word in the local language.

As a result of this incident, Angelou understands more clearly than ever where she belongs. Yes, she is African, but she is American too, and home is in the United States. She decides to return to America to take part in the struggle for equality, to become a part of Malcolm's organization. She understands, finally, that the role of an expatriate, even a black American expatriate, is not for her. As she says, "Many of us had only begun to realize in Africa that the Stars and Stripes was our flag and our only flag, and that knowledge was almost too painful to bear."

The book is interestingly structured, with no chapter divisions, only section breaks for each vignette. This technique makes the text flow more easily, suggesting the art of a *griot*, or traditional West African storyteller. The metaphors used in the descriptions, however, often seem forced and not as organic as in earlier Angelou works. Similes such as "arguments as pointed as broken bones" and "like a rain forest on a moonless night" jump out at the reader and add little to the text. Perhaps this writing was done quickly, with little revision.

In any case the reader's mind is stimulated by Angelou's depiction of the West African scene and by her honest analysis of the thorny problem of identity for black Americans. Home, learns Angelou, is not in Africa, although it takes Africa to teach her about home.

Margaret McFadden

Sources for Further Study

Booklist. LXXXII, February 1, 1986, p. 778.
Kirkus Reviews. LIV, January 15, 1986, p. 98.
Library Journal. CXI, March 15, 1986, p. 64.
Los Angeles Times Book Review. April 13, 1986, p. 4.
The New York Times Book Review. XCI, May 11, 1986, p. 14.
The New Yorker. LXII, April 14, 1986, p. 110.
Publishers Weekly. CCXXIX, February 21, 1986, p. 159.
School Library Journal. XXXII, August, 1986, p. 113.
Time. CXXVII, March 31, 1986, p. 72.
Washington Post Book World. XVI, May 11, 1986, p. 11.
The Women's Review of Books. IV, October, 1986, p. 17.

ALL OF US HERE

Author: Irving Feldman (1928-   )
Publisher: Viking Penguin/Elisabeth Sifton Books (New York). 81 pp. $17.95; paper-
   back $8.95
Type of work: Poetry

*The eighth collection by a poet of great gifts and increasing wisdom, this book
presents Irving Feldman at his best so far*

When Irving Feldman's prodigal verbal gifts are under control, which is
most of the time, his poems provide some of the richest pleasures available
in contemporary literature. In an earlier book, *Leaping Clear* (1976), Feldman occasionally overindulged his affection for playful sound effects; in this
collection, though the sound effects are frequently dazzling, there are no
more than three words which seem likely to set some teeth on edge. Along
with this greatly increased tact, one finds here a profound wisdom, an ability to speak clearly and compassionately of the nearly unspeakable. This wisdom is not at all new in Feldman's work; he has been a keen observer of the
urban scene for a long time, and his sense of the tragicomic, as well as of
the purely tragic, is among the gifts that have sustained him the longest.

Feldman writes often of the city, and sometimes of the academic world,
with its shifting notions of what ethics and good sense might be. These
worlds are not everyone's, and there are things one needs to know in order
to enter Feldman's poems. This is especially true in the case of this book's
title sequence, a group of twenty poems arising from an exhibition of sculptures by George Segal. Fortunately for Feldman and his readers, this necessity has been brilliantly dealt with in the design of the book, whose cover
photograph is of *The Brick Wall*, a 1970 Segal sculpture in which his characteristic plaster casts of actual if anonymous people are shown walking along
in raincoats. Whatever this phase of Segal's art amounts to as time passes, it
seems a fair bet that Feldman's poems will contribute heavily to our ways of
responding to it.

Yet it is not as art criticism that the poems themselves have their being.
Like the best of that class of poems whose points of departure are works of
art, they are no more dependent on Segal's sculptures than other poems are
dependent on one's knowledge of the Trojan War, for example, or the death
of Abraham Lincoln, or the normal behavior of cows and dogs. Furthermore, the jacket illustration turns out to be useful primarily to those who
are not helped by the sequence's opening poem, "—*OH, IT'S ALL SO*,"
which consists of snippets of gallery conversation at the exhibit, such as the
following:

> —*These statues are plaster casts of real people?*
> . . . .
> —*To me it's like a wax museum.*

—Of victims? That's a new one.
....
—What's this guy got that I don't have?
I'll tell you what. Connections, man, connections.

—God, sometimes I feel just the way they look.

—I think he sympathizes with people.
He must be a nice man.

—I don't know what it is about these statues . . .

The remaining poems in the sequence constitute a meditation on the help-lessness with which people try to puzzle out the meanings of their little lives. At first, the viewer compares his state to that of the sculptures, and feels alive, more with it (since the sculptures are in backgrounds suggestive of a decade past). As the sequence progresses, however, the thinking dark-ens; the sculptures remind him of a stockroom where great marble classics lie pell-mell or of the last vestiges of some holocaust. The threat of human extinction next occurs to him when he sees the sculptures as "our fleet fore-runners in prospective elegy,/ champions, pioneers of the missing future."

Nearer the end, the sculptures suggest again the frozen last moments of people who could say what they were doing when the world ended, but then the human heart must occasionally contrive some comfort:

> We should envy them, no? Immortality
> experienced from within must seem just such
> imperturbable ordinariness as theirs,
> repose deep in the simple heart of averageness,
> which death, raiding along the frontier, must take
> forever to reach.
>   The eternal verity of
> their middle way nourishes with safety and seemliness.

The final poem in the sequence, "They Say to Us," is one of the few po-ems in it which could be completely detached from the sculptures as a takeoff point; it portrays the ordinary ritual of looking at someone's family photographs, listening to the brief, identifying phrases—*"Of course, you never met him"*—and making polite responses.

> It is all very important.
> This ritual is profound,
> solemn, religious—we feel it,
> become weighty ourselves,
> judicious, like gods:
> even and merciful in judgment,
> simple, courteous and worthy.
> Now we hand the photos back.

> There they are—"little William,"
> "her brother," "the neighbor's girl"—
> all of them pressed close
> in a single pack in dark
> and radiant density.
> All of us here
> are deeply satisfied.

In such ordinary ways, the sequence seems to suggest, people put one another away for good, until their sensitivities—battered and calloused as they are from the speed at which their lives rush by—grow too dull to prevent their extinction. The most pessimistic reading might even be that people's sensitivities become so bruised that they wish for extinction, but, suffused as it is with a tragic view and tone, the sequence contains many passages whose dignity and beauty are enough to counteract a thoroughly pessimistic attitude. Even in view of the atomic imagery in the passage above—"pressed close/ in a single pack in dark/ and radiant density"—and the frightening ambivalence of the last two lines, the brilliance and, let it be said, majesty of some of the lines in this sequence are finally exhilarating. The threat of annihilation is the most urgent theme of the twentieth century, so it has often been dealt with hysterically. To confront it in language that sometimes stands comparison with Wallace Stevens' "Sunday Morning" requires not only poetic skill of a very high order but rare courage as well.

The six poems in the second section of *All of Us Here* embrace a wide range of subjects, but their deft placement and arrangement, and the weight of the title sequence, reveal unifying tones and attitudes. "Our Father" is a moving evocation of a childhood in which the father's mysteriousness arose from his living in two worlds—that of work and the home. Like millions of other men, he moved from one to the other, to the bafflement of children, yet was a child himself:

> How then can we renew his acquaintance, that boy
> lost in the man, this man missing in the world,
> walking among all that must be inexplicable?
> And how are we to thank him properly?
> who salted our cheerful, selfish tongues with farewell,
> and gave us his name to ponder, to pass on, to keep.

"River" and "An Atlantiad" make a complex pairing; the first is a short and exquisitely phrased characterization of the water in a river, dependent on anthropomorphism; the second begins as a description of the Atlantic, seen from Rockaway Beach, fraught with attributes that must also be described in human terms, even when what is described is recognized as nonhuman. At the end, though, the speaker is engulfed by the ocean, and as he is sucked outward and downward, clings hilariously and sadly to "our humble/· perspective, our merely personal view," pitifully threatening law-suits. These two lessons in the dangers of solipsism are followed by "The Judgment of Diana," in which Feldman's finest qualities combine with apparent flawlessness; aside from the much more ambitious title sequence, this is the best poem in the book.

"The Judgment of Diana" is a six-page combination of narrative and meditation which takes rise from a trivial moment. Six middle-aged poet-professors are gathered in a living room, blundering toward decisions about the coming year's schedule of visiting poets; a female student of remarkable androgyny and prole-chic garb is present, but she is being ignored or, worse, being treated with benign neglect. She stalks out, finally, leaving the speaker to imagine her as one of Diana's spear-carriers, roving through sky or stony landscape, in pursuit of greater game than these six satisfied professors could ever be. The poem's fourth and final section takes the story line a few years along and finds the woman still at work on her thesis, still posting in hallways notices of feminist gatherings, perilously on her way to becoming a middle-aged poet-professor herself, while the speaker muses over the possibility that only he, of the men gathered that evening, saw the power inherent in her departure from the meeting.

So much for story line, which will have some careless readers yawning la-zily about academic poetry and the irrelevance of Greek myth. Yet Feld-man's concerns take the poem far beyond the confines of an academic gath-ering; in language at once colloquial, witty, and grand, he makes a stately meditation that moves from gender and generation gaps through the terrors of the accomplished and tenuously comfortable, to a moving contemplation of the works of time, and the human willingness to surrender to the forces of convention. At the end of the first section, for example, having estab-lished the scene and the situation, he offers this sad, amusing look at the room:

> Wherever pigeonholes are, pigeons must be,
> and spats and bespatterings of the dovecote
> —a roocooing featherweight hierarchy—
> where, hoisted on the shoulders of the years
> to our modest perches, we loafed alright
> in a living room, each of us floating out
> upon the perilous divan of his dossier,
> or *vita*'s leaky pneumatic pouf, out along
> the whirling margin of a great unknown.

Two more poems complete the first section of the book. The first is "Summer's Sublet," in which a man finds himself absorbing the life of an old friend in whose apartment he is living through the summer, while she is up north. It begins to seem that she has reached a willingness to let life go, and he is watching it go, as things in the apartment seem to come to life or disappear. "The Call" is a brief but effective poem about people's willingness to tell others what they want to hear, especially if they might be to blame for what might otherwise be said.

Section 3 consists entirely of a single poem, "The Flight from the City," a poem of some fourteen pages which contains the three words mentioned in the opening paragraph of this review. The narrative and dramatic situation of this poem is hard to pin down with precision; it is a dialogue, in which an interrogator of threatening anonymity elicits from one Kleinwort his account of a nightmare vision of disaster in the City. The suggestion of the final holocaust is hard to resist, but there are passages in the poem which indicate that this could be a vision of the present rather than of the near future; the dehumanizing pressures of city life can fairly be portrayed in images of hideous destruction and suffering. At the beginning of the poem, Kleinworth gives his name and then amends it to Hummingblood; later, a strongarm associate of the police inspector is identified as Hurtingbrute, and near the end of the poem, the inspector says that his name is Harmingbad, "formerly your baby brother." These three names seem heavy-handed, even as they make their valid points: This is the human body, these three characters are versions of one another, people must love one another or die. Yet despite the ambivalence of the situation, and the perhaps excessive preachiness of these names, the power of Hummingblood's descriptions of chaos hurtles the reader forward; as a vision of what man may already have become, this poem is more terrifying than it would be if it were taken purely as a vision of what might happen.

The book ends on a note of curious lightness; the final section consists entirely of the poem "Art of the Haiku," in which an extra syllable in the first line sets up provocative ripples:

> "His finger then, now yours
> here, where master stopped, went back,
> counted syllables.

This is a witty, if comparatively slight, conclusion to a collection throughout which one marvels at masterful craftsmanship and compassionate humanity.

Henry Taylor

Sources for Further Study

Booklist. LXXXIII, October 1, 1986, p. 184.
Choice. XXIV, October, 1986, p. 306.
The Economist. CCC, September 20, 1986, p. 102.
Library Journal. CXI, July 16, 1986, p. 88.

The New Republic. CXCV, July 14, 1986, p. 28.
The New York Times. CXXXV, July 15, 1986, p. C13.
Publishers Weekly. CCXXIX, May 16, 1986, p. 65.

ARAB AND JEW
Wounded Spirits in a Promised Land

Author: David K. Shipler (1942-   )
Publisher: Times Books (New York). 596 pp. $22.50
Type of work: Current history
Time: 1979-1984
Locale: Israel

A fascinating, often tragic account of the many ways in which Jews and Arabs of present-day Israel perceive one another

> *Principal personages:*
> DAVID HARTMAN, an Israeli rabbi and Jewish Orthodox philosopher
> CORDELIA EDVARDSON, a Swedish-Jewish Holocaust survivor and journalist
> SALAH TAAMRI, a Palestinian Arab and the leader of a prisoner's committee
> RIFAT TURK, an Israeli-Arab soccer star
> BRUCE COHEN, an American rabbi and the founder of "Interns for Peace"

David Shipler, who is neither an Arab nor a Jew, served as the Jerusalem bureau chief for *The New York Times* from 1979 to 1984; in 1982, he covered the war in Lebanon. This fascinating and powerful book is the result of five years of intensive study of the mutual images and stereotypes that have developed between Arabs and Jews in present-day Israel. The areas he studied include the West Bank, the Gaza Strip, the annexed portions of Jerusalem, and the Golan Heights. His often contradictory conclusions are the result of wide-ranging interviews and an intensive study of the history, literature, films, school textbooks, and newspapers of the region. This is a portrait of two peoples living alongside one another whose history has been shaped by the conflicts of war, terrorism, religion, and nationalism. They occupy a tiny, but vital piece of land that is a cradle of civilization and of vital concern to the peace of mankind. His subjects include Jews, Muslims, and Christians, moderates and extremists on both sides, religious and secular people, and those who wish to further understanding.

As the subtitle indicates, the book is a study of hurt feelings and bodies and of the reasons for these wounds. Some of the mutual perceptions are the result of hard realities, others of misunderstanding and ignorance, still others of a failure of communication. Shipler explores these mutual perceptions and misperceptions in three dimensions. First he surveys those forces that have contributed to aversion and tension. Then he describes the multifaceted range of images and stereotypes that Arabs and Jews have of one another and the range of their interactions, from open hostility to grudging respect. The book ends with a brief, but moving account of attempts at reconciliation.

Shipler examines the problem from an impressive number of vantage points that include the effects of war and terrorism, class divisions and personal contacts, relations between Judaism and Islam, sexual fears and intermarriage, popular aspirations, and the effects of the Holocaust on the conflict between Jews and Arabs. The result is not only a richly informative study but also a refreshing and a deeply caring book.

The time frame of *Arab and Jew: Wounded Spirits in a Promised Land* is limited mainly to the generation of Jews and Arabs that has grown up since June of 1967; that is, a generation that has known mainly war and conflict. It is in this period that Israel has become a storm center of world events. Every chapter of this work reflects the drama and significance of this area.

The author sets the tone of his book by remarking on the passionate frankness and amazing diversity of the troubled democracy that is Israel. This country that is the size of the state of New Jersey is a land of conflicting opposites—Jews and Muslims, desert and farm, sea and hills. Had the Arabs accepted the partition of Palestine in 1947, says Shipler, Israel would be far tinier than it is today. Instead, a series of wars led to the conquest of the West Bank, the Golan Heights, part of Jerusalem, and the Gaza Strip.

In the streets and alleys of Jerusalem, Jews and Arabs walk past one another quickly, pretending not to acknowledge one another's presence. "Zionist" is a fearsome word in the Arab vocabulary, while "Palestinian" conjures up similar emotions in the Jews, for each word attacks the other's aspirations and legitimacy. Though Shipler maintains that Jerusalem is safer than New York City (one of many comparisons with America), Palestinian terrorist attacks and Jewish retaliation feed on each other and erode human decency. They make otherwise stable people irrational while expanding and hardening political extremes. Even those Israelis who advocate toleration for the Arabs fear and mistrust the Arabs because of terrorist incidents.

The power of ideology is an important theme of this book. In the Middle East, nationalism and religion have reinforced each other, and the result is an explosive mix. Islamic and Jewish fundamentalism are on the increase. The right-wing Jewish movement of Meir Kahane that seeks to expel Arabs from Israel and the "born again" Jewish settlers on the West Bank are gaining in appeal. On the other side are the Muslim brotherhoods that see Israel as a cancer in the Arab world, an intolerable affront to Arab unity and pride that can be removed only by a holy war. Yet, both Arabs and Jews venerate Abraham as their common ancestor and both pray at his tomb in Hebron, while Hebron seethes with conflict. Unfortunately, some educated Arabs have in recent decades appropriated the teachings of Nazi anti-Semitism that depict the Jews as irredeemably satanic. This fuels the fires of hatred and suspicion all the more.

Shipler's portrait of reciprocal myths and stereotypes between Jews and Arabs is most revealing and often tragicomic. These images have emerged as a result of decades of proximity and hostility. Many Jews look upon Arabs as violent, lazy, dirty, craven, primitive, exotic, and irrational. In return, many Arabs view Jews as violent, immoral, materialistic, alien, arrogant, and imperialistic. Some portrayals of Jews in Syrian children's textbooks are shockingly crude and inhuman. Israelis are reluctant to be treated at Arab hospitals and vice versa, but they will consent to do so in life-and-death situations. Despite their proximity, Arabs and Jews are often ignorant of one another's language, culture, and customs. There are more Israeli Arabs who learn Hebrew than there are Israeli Jews who bother to learn Arabic, probably because some Arabs need Hebrew to function and advance in Israeli society.

Class divisions often accentuate the hostilities between Jews and Arabs. Many Arabs do the menial jobs and the heavy labor. This can lead to resentment. In addition, there are sexual fears on both sides, particularly Jewish fears of Arab violence. Both Arabs and Jews bitterly oppose intermarriage; couples who intermarry are usually ostracized by their family and friends.

These negative images that Arabs and Jews have of one another are ironic, says Shipler, for their languages and religions have some points of similarity. Moreover, Jews often view Arabs in much the same way in which Arabs see Jews—as shrewd, greedy moneylenders and as physically threatening.

The contrasting ways in which Arabs and Jews interpret the Holocaust are both revealing and tragic. Indeed, Israeli Jews and Arabs alike use the Holocaust as a moral reference point, a vehicle of outrage against one another. The Jews use the Holocaust to justify the existence of the State of Israel and to illustrate the vulnerability of Israel in a hostile world. Many Arabs maintain that they also paid the price for the Holocaust because Israel was created at their expense and that the Jews are practicing aggressive behavior against them.

In one of the most moving episodes in the book, Shipler recounts his visit to the Israeli-built Ansar prison camp in Southern Lebanon. He was accompanied by Cordelia Edvardson, a Swedish reporter and survivor of Auschwitz. During their visit, Salah Taamri, a Palestinian Arab and spokesman for the prisoners, led the prisoners in chanting "Ansar is Auschwitz." Shipler was outraged at the comparison, which trivializes the Holocaust by comparing the extermination of a people with the overcrowded conditions of a prison in time of war. He hoped that Edvardson would rebuke the prisoners, but her reply was understated: "Auschwitz was an extermination camp. Children and elderly people did not come out alive." Why did she not tell Taamri that she herself had been in Auschwitz? "'It would have been unfair,' she said. 'He was behind bars, and I was free.'"

Shipler provides a fascinating portrait of the Israeli Arabs; that is, those who live in the unoccupied areas of Israel. Israeli Arabs are moderate in their outlook toward the Jews. Many respect the achievements of the State of Israel, but they are torn between their desire to succeed in Israel and their loyalty to their Arab identity. The Bedouin tribes of the desert, on the other hand, keep to themselves and maintain their ancient traditions. The Druze tribesmen are a case unto themselves, distinct from both Muslims and Christians. They are very loyal to Israel yet maintain their identity. Some Israeli Arabs have risen to fame. Rifat Turk is an Arab soccer star who plays on an Israeli team. He is idolized by many for his athletic brilliance and his sportsmanship, but he is mistrusted by other Arabs and Jews, who view him as an opportunist. Such are but a few of the complexities in the relationships of Arabs and Jews.

Despite the tensions and reciprocal negative stereotypes, Shipler sees some hopeful signs of reconciliation in Israel. Interfaith communities have recently been established to provide communication and cooperation between young Arabs and Jews. Rabbi Bruce Cohen has founded an organization called "Interns for Peace" in Arab and Jewish communities. A faint, but hopeful dialogue has started. It is surprising that Shipler fails to discuss the small, but important peace movement among Israeli students and intellectuals—this is the major omission of his book.

Despite the police methods of search and detention that are sometimes used against Arabs, Israel remains a democracy that is surrounded by authoritarian states and cultures. A huge rally of four hundred thousand Israelis, one-tenth of the population, was held in Tel Aviv to demand an inquiry into the massacres of Palestinian refugees in the Sabra-Shatila camps in Lebanon. These massacres were committed by Arabs, albeit under Israeli occupation. The book ends with a touching story of an Israeli soldier's mother who was a Holocaust survivor. She questioned her son when he came home from his military service in Lebanon. Had he known about the massacres? She would not let him into the house until he had cleared himself of involvement in the Sabra and Shatila massacre.

Arab and Jew ends on a note of uncertainty. Shipler maintains that Arabs and Jews will not escape from one another. They will find peace only by looking into one another's eyes. This is good advice that can promote mutual understanding, but it is the sort of optimistic romanticism that can only exist on the level of individuals and small groups. The politicians on both sides remain closed to such advice. The gap between Arabs and Jews in Israel remains so great that one cannot even see the eyes of the other. Yet Shipler is certainly right about one thing: Only if the wounded spirits begin to be healed can there be any hope for a promised land.

Leon Stein

Sources for Further Study

Booklist. LXXXIII, September 1, 1986, p. 4.
Chicago Tribune. September 7, 1986, XIV, p. 33.
Christian Science Monitor. LXXVIII, October 2, 1986, p. 25.
Kirkus Reviews. LIV, August 15, 1986, p. 1279.
Library Journal. CXI, November 15, 1986, p. 101.
Los Angeles Times Book Review. October 26, 1986, p. 2.
The New Republic. CXCV, November 10, 1986, p. 38.
The New York Times Book Review. XCI, September 28, 1986, p. 1.
Publishers Weekly. CCXXX, August 1, 1986, p. 63.
Washington Post Book World. XVI, October 26, 1986, p. 4.

ARCTIC DREAMS
Imagination and Desire in a Northern Landscape

Author: Barry Lopez (1945-   )
Publisher: Charles Scribner's Sons (New York). Illustrated. 464 pp. $22.95
Type of work: Scientific adventure
Time: 1986, with historical flashbacks
Locale: The Arctic

*A detailed recounting of scientific expeditions to the Arctic, with considerable atten-
tion to the stark beauty of the landscape and to the dreams that have motivated people
to seek out this harsh land through the centuries*

As terrestrial frontiers go, the circumpolar regions have long been man's
most formidable and mysterious. In *Arctic Dreams: Imagination and Desire
in a Northern Landscape*, Barry Lopez, whose earlier writings about nature,
in such books as *Desert Notes: Reflections in the Eye of a Raven* (1976), *Of
Wolves and Men* (1978), *River Notes: The Dance of Herons* (1979), and *Winter Count* (1981), have won for him enthusiastic plaudits, focuses on the
northern circumpolar regions, particularly the area between the Bering
Strait and the Davis Strait.

Lopez, who has made several trips to the Arctic, has observed his sources
closely and recorded the fruits of his observations meticulously. He has also
done extensive research on the Arctic at the Arctic Institute of North
America in Calgary, Alberta, and the results of his research are, in particular, detailed in the last chapters of the book. These chapters focus on the
various expeditions that have through the centuries explored this frozen
landscape.

Lopez handles his materials with the meticulous care of a scientist, with
the visual sensitivity of a painter, with the cadences and insights of a poet,
and with the ingenuous awe of a man to whom the Arctic has revealed wonders that border on the religious. His first-person narrative is deceptively
casual, disarmingly nonchalant; its flow and its careful use of language remind one of the best of E. B. White's writing.

Even though many sections of the book are highly specialized, they are
nevertheless easily accessible to nonspecialists. Reading that is simultaneously this hard and this easy points to writing that is carefully calculated,
penetratingly observed, and effectively revised. Lopez knows his material
well and reacts to it enthusiastically. He also knows his audience and understands precisely how to share with them the enchantment that he has found
in the extreme North.

Part of the scientific allure of the Arctic is that its ecosystem is only ten
thousand years old, dating to the retreat of the Wisconsin ice. This makes it
the youngest ecosystem and, to many, the most interesting on the planet. By
comparison, the history of man, from Cro-Magnon to the late twentieth
century is four times older.

Lopez demonstrates some of the intense drawing power the Arctic has on humans, who sometimes are drawn so much into the majesty of the nature that surrounds them in the far North that they lose judgment and put themselves at great risk. Lopez himself was at times in imminent peril, but at such moments, he felt detached, somehow removed from the danger. On one occasion, his clothing became wet and froze on his person.

> I began to recognize in the enduring steadiness another kind of calmness, or relief. The distance between my body and my thoughts slowly became elongated, and muffled like a dark, carpeted corridor. . . . I knew I had to get to dry clothes, to get them on. But desire could not move my legs or arms. They were too far away. I was staring at someone, then moving; the soaked clothes were coming off. I could not make a word in my mouth.

In passages such as this one, ever replete with rich similes and vivid metaphors, Lopez captures the detached quality that overtakes one in the Arctic. He depicts with precision the difference in how one views the demarcations of time and space that exist in this frozen world about which he is writing.

Lopez writes accurately and passionately about the legendary explorers who have left their mark on the northern Arctic regions and about the Eskimos who inhabit them. He depicts individual Eskimos bent on testing outsiders who come to explore or exploit the area. In some cases they rob the intruders, in others they help them.

The Eskimos are fighting a losing battle against the white man and against an industrialized civilization that threatens the fragile Arctic environment. Lopez cites historical evidence to suggest that as much as 90 percent of the indigenous population of the Arctic has died off from such diseases as pneumonia, tuberculosis, smallpox, diphtheria, and poliomyelitis as the white man has made incursions into the area in ever-increasing numbers during the nineteenth and twentieth centuries.

Lopez is at his best when he writes about the animals of the region. He pictures a society of animals, most of them predatory, that have adapted not only to the extremes of cold that characterizes the Arctic but also to the twenty-four hours of darkness that constitute their diurnal cycles in winter and to the twenty-four hours of sunlight that constitute their diurnal cycles in summer.

The denning animals, notably the polar bear, hibernate, although not in the ways that many people imagine. The pregnant female polar bear is the one most likely to construct a den and retreat into it for half the year, living on her fat and awaiting the birth of her cubs. Male polar bears and females that are not pregnant are not nearly so consistent in their patterns of hibernation as the pregnant female is, although all polar bears live essentially off their fat during the winter, to such an extent that they may lose half their body weight in the months between October and April.

A pregnant female will construct a den only large enough for her to move around in, building a tunnel to it that will accommodate her body, a passageway about two feet in diameter. As the arrival of her cubs nears, she will construct space for them because they will be in the den with her for up to two months after birth, during which time they grow from about one pound to twenty-five pounds in weight. They live on their mother's milk, which is among the richest of known milks, surpassing even that of seal milk in nutrient value.

Lopez traces a swift evolution from the brown bear to the polar bear which, in some cases, stands twelve feet high and, in summer, may in some cases weight more than a ton. He notes that adaptation in the Arctic is greatly accelerated in most species. Certainly failure to adapt through evolution would result in extinction.

The polar bear, whose hair is hollow and stands erect so that it does not mat, can dry itself by shaking and by rolling around in the snow. The layers of fat that insulate it from the extremes of the cold water in which it must hunt seals, provide it simultaneously with nourishment during the long winter. An underlayer of wool protects it from the cold winds. The polar bear produces so much heat that heat retention would be a greater problem to it than the cold were it not for the fact that its footpads and other less insulated body areas conduct heat away from it.

Lopez writes with feeling and with a remarkable depth of knowledge and understanding about the Arctic creatures, such as lemmings, ringed seals, horned narwhals, musk oxen, beluga and bowhead whales, caribou, the crustaceans and fish of the Bering Strait, booming walruses, and varied bird life. He writes in a celebratory way about these wonders of nature, existing as they do in a remarkably hostile and predatory environment which, through the millennia, has been balanced, however, precariously, in such a way that it has endured.

Lopez depicts nonliving things, such as the huge icebergs that he encounters as he sails toward the Strait of Belle Island, with the same sort of zeal that characterizes his writing about Arctic animals:

> The first icebergs we had seen . . . listing and guttered by the ocean, seemed immensely sad, exhausted by some unknown calamity. We sailed past them. Farther north they began to seem like stragglers fallen behind an army, drifting, self-absorbed, in the water, bleak and immense. It was as if they had been borne down from a world of myth, some Götterdämmerung of noise and catastrophe.

He then compares them to fallen pieces of the moon. It is this sort of writing and this level of analogical observation—images of caribou moving across the land like wood smoke in a snowstorm or of whales whose skin is the color of a bruise—which distinguish this book and make it comparable to the best of Loren Eisley's scientific writing for general readers.

The manner in which Lopez discusses the types of ice in *Arctic Dreams* brings to mind the Whorf-Sapir Hypothesis, formulated by Benjamin Lee Whorf and Edward Sapir, according to which the language of various social groups indicates the relative values these groups places on various items. For example, shepherds have many words to describe grass, because the types of grass on which their flocks feed is of considerable importance. Similarly, the types of ice that exist in the Arctic are so numerous that each type demands a special word to indicate its unique qualities. It is a matter of life and death to know precisely what kind of ice one is about to encounter, and Lopez recounts in detail the kinds of ice that one finds in the far northern reaches. He also goes into the dynamics of ice, telling how it forms and how some types move with such inexorable and crushing force that anything in their path will be annihilated.

Lopez also devotes considerable attention to a discussion of light in the northern reaches. He compares the colors of the snow-covered earth to those of a desert, to ochres and siennas, to gray greens.

> Arresting color in the Arctic is found more often in the sky, with its vivid twilights and aurora borealis. . . . Arctic skies retain the colors of dawn and dusk for hours in winter. On days when the southern sky is barely lit for a while around noon, layers of deep violet, of bruised purples and dense blues, may stretch across 80° of the horizon, above a familiar lavender and the thinnest line of yellow gold.

Lopez notes the effect of Arctic light upon the nineteenth century school of luminist painters, about whom he writes knowledgeably. Indeed, his many apt allusions to painting and to architecture reveal a considerable breadth of learning in the fine arts, and these comparisons enhance the book substantially.

Although *Arctic Dreams*, winner of the 1986 American Book Award in the category of nonfiction, is not strident, it certainly makes a fervent ecological statement. Perhaps Lopez's tendency to understate permits this book to make its ecological point more effectively and permanently than a polemical statement could have. His environmental concerns are both apparent and informed.

R. Baird Shuman

Sources for Further Study

Booklist. LXXXII, January 1, 1986, p. 643.
Business Week. April 14, 1986, p. 20.
Choice. XXIII, May, 1986, p. 1390.
Christian Science Monitor. LXXVIII, March 7, 1986, p. 22.

Kirkus Reviews. LIV, February 1, 1986, p. 188.
Library Journal. CXI, March 1, 1986, p. 102.
The New York Times Book Review. XCI, February 16, 1986, p. 1.
The New Yorker. LXII, March 17, 1986, p. 110.
Publishers Weekly. CCXXIX, January 24, 1986, p. 65.
Time. CXXVII, March 10, 1986, p. 74.

AROUND THE DAY IN EIGHTY WORLDS

Author: Julio Cortázar (1914-1984)
Translated from the Spanish by Thomas Christensen
Publisher: North Point Press (San Francisco, California). Illustrated. 288 pp. $22.50
Type of work: Essays, criticism, and memoirs

A collection of occasional pieces from a master of contemporary South American fiction displaying the range of his interests, from jazz to surrealist art, from fantasy to scenes of poverty in Calcutta, from the erotic to the grotesque

Julio Cortázar, best known for his constructivist fictions including *Hopscotch* (1963), *62: A Model Kit* (1968), and *We Love Glenda So Much and Other Tales* (1981), was, along with Gabriel García Márquez, Jorge Luis Borges, and Carlos Fuentes, one of the most bountiful sources of the modern renaissance in Central and South American fiction. His death in 1984 marked a watershed of sorts: The first generation, to whom Borges served as godfather, was passing away, and the effects of its remarkable outpouring, moving north (though this is only one of the directions in which it moved), was being felt by a new generation of "fabulists" in Great Britain, Canada, and the United States. *Around the Day in Eighty Worlds* could serve either as an introduction to or as a retrospective of Cortázar's work: Though most of the pieces included were collected between 1967 and 1969, and published originally in two books, *La vuelta al día en ochenta mundos* (1967) and *Ultimo round* (1969), the variety of styles and interests they exhibit gives the reader an indication of the range of Cortázar's work over his long career. Here, one can find a formal, critical tribute to the Cuban novelist José Lezama Lima alongside a compelling recollection of a Louis Armstrong jazz concert in Paris. A horrific remembrance of a visit to the Howrah Railroad Station in Calcutta appears in the same volume as descriptions of the antics of Cortázar's anarchists of the imagination, the Cronopios. In essence, *Around the Day in Eighty Worlds*, as the inversion of the Jules Verne title suggests, is a chaotic voyage through the "worlds" of Cortázar's capacious vision. The collection, abundantly illustrated with photographs, surrealist graphics, and line drawings, might be seen as a collage or an almanac of Cortázar's imagination which can be read sporadically, at will, in a disorderly fashion. As the reader is invited to do in his fiction, in this assemblage of autobiographical fragments, critical essays, travelogues, satires, and flights of fancy, he can travel digressively through Cortázar's "eighty worlds" constructing his own view of the author's mind and memory.

While *Around the Day in Eighty Worlds* is a "miscellany" in the truest sense of the word, it does reflect a series of concerns which have been central to Cortázar's writing throughout his career. Certainly one of these is his interest in "reflexivity," or speculation upon the act of making fiction within fiction itself. For example, in "The Broken Doll," an essay illustrated with what appears to be twenty-four negative prints of a child's doll gradually undergoing disassembly beneath the covers of a doll-size bed, Cortázar discusses the "intentions" and "uncertainties" of *Hopscotch* and *62: A Model Kit*. Of his writing, Cortázar says,

> We know that attention acts as a lightning rod. Merely by concentrating on something one causes endless analogies to collect around it, even to penetrate the boundaries of the subject itself: an experience that we call coincidence, serendipity—the terminology is extensive. My experience has been that in these circular travels what is really significant surrounds a central absence, an absence that, paradoxically, is the text being written or to be written. In the years I was working on *Hopscotch*, this saturation reached the point that the only legitimate response was to accept without comment the meteor shower that came through the windows of streets, books, conversations, and everyday circumstances and to convert them into the passages, fragments, and required or optional chapters of the *other* that formed around an ill-defined story of searches and missed encounters; that, in large part, accounts for the method and presentation of the story.

This elaborate analogy describes the method of Cortázar's writing in general, as it does the way in which *Around the Day in Eighty Worlds* is assembled. Rather than controlling external reality through his art or creating a masterful illusion, Cortázar suggests that he, as artist, is merely a conduit for the "meteor shower" of information that comes to him through books, films, and the noise of everyday life. He argues that story is an "absence," a kind of vortex around which the fragments of a discursive reality whirl or, perhaps, the black background upon which the artist arranges his verbal collage. In quoting a famous passage from Vladimir Nabokov's *Pale Fire* (1962), Cortázar notes that the essence of his fiction is "not text but texture"; that is, not a transparent representation of the real or the illusory but an interweaving of plots, information, and discourses into a "web" of narrative. Reinforcing these points visually is the photo-essay of "the broken doll," which shows the piece-by-piece destruction of the doll: The disassembly of the doll both parallels and acts as counterpoint to Cortázar's remarks upon the assemblage of his fiction from fragments. The photos are disturbing in that, in some frames, the doll looks like a real little girl; a frame where the doll's pose is frankly erotic is followed by one where a limb has been broken. The commentary provided by the photographs reflects the nature and intent of much of Cortázar's fiction: to blur the difference between the real and the artificial; to show the attractions and distractions of eroticism and violence, while suggesting that the dividing line between them is not as clear as one might wish.

Cortázar is equally interested in that primary quality of fiction—time. Several items in *Around the Day in Eighty Worlds* raise the issue of time in fiction, especially those, such as "Journey to a Land of Cronopios" or "Julios in Action," which involve a strange creature, the Cronopio. While Famas are overbearing, and while Esperanzas are ambitious, Cronopios are sensitive, paradoxical, artistic types who care little for logic, order, and time schedules. A typical Cronopio, getting ready for a journey, is described thus:

> On Thursday the Cronopio gets his bags ready early, which is to say he throws two toothbrushes and a kaleidoscope into them and then sits back to watch his wife fill them with the necessary things; but as she is as much Cronopio as he, she forgets the most essential things, . . . and at that moment the telephone rings and the embassy informs them that there has been a mistake and that he was supposed to take last Sunday's plane, which precipitates a dialogue full of pointed remarks between the Cronopio and the embassy, and they hear the snap of the luggage opening, and fuzzy teddy bears and dried starfish escape, and the end of it all is that the plane will leave next Sunday, and please bring five full-face photos.

Louis Armstrong appears as a Cronopio in "Louis, Super-Cronopio," thus typifying the supreme traits of the Cronopio as aleatory, anarchistic, and childlike.

Cronopios refuse to conform to traditional notions of time and place; these traits are to be found on a more serious level in one of many of Cortázar's portraits of the artist, "Marcel Duchamp; Or, Further Encounters Outside of Time." Cortázar writes that his "relationship" with Duchamp (standing for all the relationships between Cronopios, or artists) is a game:

> The games of time (which Alejo Carpentier calls the wars of time—wars of the flowers, games of Russian roulette) are games of billiards where caroms on a single surface reduce before and after to mere historical conveniences. This afternoon I had a game with Marcel Duchamp, another game among many.

Cortázar goes on to describe a chance literary encounter beginning with Duchamp's visit to Buenos Aires in 1914, some memories of which are recorded in an interview which comes into Cortázar's hands nearly fifty years later. In the interview, Duchamp recalls a sculpture he created in his Buenos Aires hotel room. The sculpture is made of "little bits of rubber bathing caps. . . . At the bottom of each piece there was a thin rope and these were tied to the four corners of the room, so that when you entered the room you couldn't move around because these ropes blocked your way." Cortázar then describes an essay he wrote in 1958 or 1959 (the impreciseness of the time is significant; the essay, entitled "Of Another Bachelor Machine," appears in this volume)—years before he read the interview—in which he describes a room so filled with rope that no one can move through it. Whether Cortázar has made up this remarkable coincidence of time and artistry is unimportant: A Cronopio himself, he believes that simultaneity takes precedence over normal chronology, that chance, rather than priority and logic, rules in the literary universe. As is the case for so many other modern writers such as Nabokov, Borges, and Samuel Beckett, time for Cortázar is a relative quality, and one is likely to find in his world that the notation or passing of time takes place through repetition and synchronization, and always through the warping of clock time.

Cortázar has been observed to be one of the most important experimental writers in contemporary literature. Appropriately, *Around the Day in Eighty Worlds* is filled with various examples of Cortázar's experimentalism, from the absurdist parodies of "Regarding the Eradication of Crocodiles from Auvergne" and "With Justifiable Pride" to the perspectival enigmas of "Stairs Again" and "Of Another Bachelor Machine." Cortázar's interest in altering one's accepted notions of time and fictionality is matched by his concern to show that, as the title of this book indicates, what one normally refers to as "reality" is a heterogeneous collection of worlds that are multiple, contradictory, and paradoxical in their constitution. Thus, in "I Could Dance This Chair, Said Isadora," Cortázar discusses the possibility of a "prelogical" attitude toward reality:

> I am referring to the intuition of archaic, magical origin that there are phenomena, even physical objects, that are what they are and the way they are because, in some sense they also are or could be other phenomena and other things; that the reciprocal action of a conjunction of elements that the intelligence perceives as heterogeneous can release analogous interactions in other conjunctions apparently separate from the first—as is understood in sympathetic magic by at least four fat and cranky women who still stick pins into wax figures; and that there exists a profound identity between one conjunction and the other, outrageous as that may seem.

Many of the essays, stories, and reflections in *Around the Day in Eighty Worlds* portray this view of reality or, more accurately, depict a piece of it while undermining any notion of that reality becoming singular or monolithic. Disjunction, conjunction, parallelism, and analogy may be seen as the primary items in Cortázar's narrative toolkit. For example, the piece entitled "It Is Regrettable That" is composed of a series of sentence fragments following from the title ("Our living room is fairly large, but to think that in it Robert"; "We don't have too much furniture, which leaves a lot of room to receive parents and friends when they come to"; "Me in the chair by the lamp and my wife almost always on the stool where she can"). The collection of fragments does not add up to a story in the usual sense, but the fragments' elliptical nature allows the reader to imagine a series of possible stories, all related to an ambiguous and regrettable minor domestic tragedy. By negation, Cortázar reinforces the conception of a multiple and fragmentary reality in "Short Feature." Here, in a paragraph, the reader is given the "whole" story of a tourist's encounter with a treacherous hitchhiker, complete with an O. Henryesque surprise ending. All the details needed to comprehend the nature of the tourist's tragic mistake and the meticulousness of the hitchhiker's perfect crime are provided, yet something—the "story" itself, is missing. How, for example, might the tourist's demise be a fitting (or undeserved) end to his life? Will the hitchhiker's crime be punished, or is this a world in which the shrewdness of the criminal is held up against certain unmentioned moral values? In this way, Cortázar parodies the notion that single stories reflect single worlds, or that in reading a story, one can never know all that there is to know. Equally, if Cortázar's worlds are multiple and fragmentary, they are also labyrinthine funhouses where a shift in perspective generates a different reality. In "Nights in Europe's Ministries" (based, perhaps, on his own experience in the field of diplomacy), Cortázar writes of a ministry in Helsinki where

> one night I . . . discovered a secret garden, the garden of the minister or of a judge, a small garden enclosed by high walls. I descended an iron staircase from the balcony and everything was on a miniature scale, as if the minister were a dwarf. I felt again the incongruity of my being in this garden inside this palace inside this city inside this country thousands of miles from the place I had lived all my life, and I thought of the white unicorn imprisoned in a small enclosure imprisoned in the blue tapestry imprisoned in the Cloisters prison in New York.

The Chinese-box effect of this vision is countered by the sense of incongruity and miniaturization where perspective, itself, becomes a way of knowing and organizing a world through, in this case, the confining vehicle of analogy. Given this view, the reader is compelled to accept the jarring incongruities of a collection where a defense of fantasy occurs in the same volume as a wrenching, graphic view of a child eating offal in India.

While the quality of the individual pieces in *Around the Day in Eighty Worlds* is occasionally uneven, one could hardly wish for a better introduction to Cortázar's work. True, its eclecticism may irritate some readers, but this can also be perceived as one of the collection's strongest qualities. Indeed, the book, as it stands, is arguably a kind of cultural encyclopedia, a "voyage" through Cortázar's version of modernism and postmodernism, where the reader will encounter such personages as Charlie Parker, Jules Verne, Raymond Roussel, René Magritte, Pablo Neruda, and Thelonious Monk. This rich and fitting tribute to Cortázar is meant, then, to be read in bits and pieces, text and illustrations intermingling, never from front to back but—in the manner of a true Cronopio—anarchistically, at random, with a sense of irony, humor, and outrage at the incongruities of imposed and imagined realities.

Patrick O'Donnell

Sources for Further Study

Booklist. LXXXII, February 15, 1986, p. 845.
The Kenyon Review. LIV, March 15, 1986, p. 407.
Kirkus Reviews. LIV, March 15, 1986, p. 407.

The New York Times Book Review. XCI, May 4, 1986, p. 9.
Publishers Weekly. CCXXIX, February 21, 1986, p. 155.
Saturday Review. XII, May, 1986, p. 74.
Washington Post Book World. XVI, March 30, 1986, p. 1.

BEACHMASTERS

Author: Thea Astley (1926-   )
Publisher: The Viking Press (New York). 185 pp. $14.95
Type of work: Novel
Time: The 1980's
Locale: Kristi, a South Pacific island

Beachmasters *records a doomed native rebellion on a South Pacific island, vividly revealing its effect on the islanders, both natives and colonials*

> *Principal characters:*
> TOMMY NAROTA, the leader of the rebellion, whose presence is felt throughout, even though he appears seldom
> GAVI SALWAY, a boy for whom the rebellion becomes a passage to manhood
> DISTRICT AGENT CORDINGLEY, a representative of British Imperialism at its worst
> CHLOE OF THE DANCING BEARS, a fading prostitute, the epitome of the decadent white islander
> BONSER, a crude, rough opportunist, ready to use the rebellion for his own gain
> PÈRE LEYROUD, a tired and doubting missionary priest

Australian novelist Thea Astley said in an interview that the idea for *Beachmasters* came to her on seeing a television account which showed the arrest of a native leader who had attempted to bring a tiny South Pacific island into independence. As might be expected, the larger powers of France and Great Britain squelched the short-lived rebellion and arrested its leader. Astley went on to explain that the desolate picture of this ancient and gentle islander being led to jail touched that sympathy she had always felt for the misfit: the person who dares to reject the accepted pattern, whether it be to defy the mores of small-town Australia, often the subject of her previous work, or to take on world powers the way the rebel leader had.

As a fictional rendering of an insignificant rebellion on an obscure island, *Beachmasters* succeeds, providing a detailed account of the events leading to the rebellion, its actuality, and its aftermath. The events, as Astley says, are "so quick to tell. So long in the happening." Through the work's taut narrative structure, the substance of revolution does emerge. Opportunists smuggle weapons to the natives, a mercenary advises, a radio announcer with a BBC accent broadcasts the victory of the ill-prepared troops and the establishment of a provisional government, the soldiers carry out senseless destruction and practice indiscriminate cruelty, the involvement of Western business interests reveals itself, and the short-lived euphoria that accompanies such ill-fated events arises, then vanishes. Astley handles these matters with characteristic irony but at the same time shows compassion for the pawns of colonialism, a condition she deplores, much like the character in the novel who asks:

How could he speak honestly of the criminality of colonialism, the banditry of planters and trading empires, of the fools of men who strutted on the red carpets of tradition sustained by a bit of coloured rag, centuries of acute class distinction and a belief in their own godhead?

Yet the novel turns into more than a record of a rebellion or a diatribe against colonialism, no matter how effectively it handles both. Instead, *Beachmasters* is essentially a religious novel, and the political events serve as a vehicle for the larger matters that concern Astley in all of her work: evil and guilt and redemption.

The cliché of a tropical paradise appears when Island Kristi, often called Eden, comes to life in a number of poetic passages, where lines such as "the mango trees blue in the butterscotch morning" capture its undeniable beauty. More often, however, the lost Eden dominates, when the island is said to have "a stinking climate where there was no weather, only hot and hotter with rampaging wets in the monsoon months, quick sunsets and sudden daylights as the world cracked open like an egg and everywhere this spinach green, this straining blue." So the Eden has evolved into a hell for the white Europeans who have no right to be there. Outcasts from their own world—whether they be government officials representing the controlling powers, missionaries, teachers, prostitutes, mercenaries, opportunists— the outsiders have sought to find an Eden but have polluted it, then are expelled from it. Likewise, there seems little hope for the natives, corrupted by the influences of Western colonialism, including Christianity, which they have been told moves closer to the truth than do their own religions. Island Kristi, once the rebellion subsides, becomes a part of a larger group of islands to which the colonial powers soon grant independence, only to institute a more subtle form of colonial rule—or bondage.

In Thea Astley's world, then, evil and guilt prevail, and redemption eludes those who seek it. "The stench, the flies and the incredible beauty of the first days of Eden" combine to form an undeniable force against which no human has power; like Gavi Salway, for whom the revolution turns into a test of his impending manhood, the searcher can only weep once confronted with the contradictions of beauty and stench, good and evil, redemption and damnation. The revolution, the Eden-Hell, and the tainted natives comprise a background for the narrative's concentration on the tortured lives of the Europeans. Again, with the economy which Astley practices, she brings to life a wide assortment of seekers and losers, revealing just enough about their past to establish their present. Among the more memorable are District Agent Cordingley, whose failure, pomposity, and cowardliness the strains of the rebellion only magnify; Chloe of the Dancing Bears, who stayed on during World War II to entertain the American soldiers, then, immersed in decadence, never left the island; Bonser, describing himself as "a rough-as-guts bugger," who attempts to use the revolution for his own gain;

and Père Leyroud, the priest to whom "on desperate evenings...God refused answers from the dusty tabernacle of the chapel." A dozen or so more of what one character calls "we abandoned ones" weave in and out of the story, trying to grasp the evil that paralyzes them and searching for the not-to-be-found redemption that will free them. Young Gavi may well be the only one to attain some sort of peace when he trembles with recognition in the presence of the island's single pure man, Tommy Narota, the leader of the revolution.

Whereas Astley takes a dim view of the human condition, she does appear to believe in language, as though somehow through the strength of words she might discover the answers she seeks in all of her work. Lorimer, an innocent among "the abandoned ones" on the island, writes in his diary: "Trying to carve out a good sentence. There's little else to do. I might as well give myself up to that." Astley, like Lorimer, tries always "to carve out a good sentence," a practice for which critics have long taken her to task. Her intricately wrought language should not, however, be considered mere verbal gymnastics. The style which Astley employs, to the delight of some readers and to the consternation of others, will only be appreciated when apprehended as a means to understanding the presence of evil and the absence of redemption, much as a religious litany serves for the worshiper in the building of a bridge to the divine presence. When Astley's stylistic brilliance is thus approached, its close wedding to her thematic concerns becomes evident.

Appropriately, much of her imagery is drawn from the forms and rituals of Roman Catholicism, but most often she distorts those familiar metaphors. Here, for example, Astley ridicules commercialism on the island through an irreverent comparison to the climactic moment of the Mass:

> "Salvaging something from the basilicas of Dixie Chicken. That's the killer. The High Mass of Colonel Sanders, offered at a pizzeria in downtown Lena. For this is my body, the Colonel says, with twenty-nine secret ingredients. Take this and eat in commemoration of me."
> Even Bonnard had to laugh. "You've forgotten to consecrate the Pepsi."

Throughout the novel, the most ordinary events are compared to the Mass, common things to stigmata or to the mark of Ash Wednesday, unlikely people to disciples, to mendicants, or to priests. In an interview, Astley called herself a "lapsed Catholic," but she added that the rituals of Roman Catholicism "stimulate the metaphor glands and heighten the sense of guilt."

In her Australian novels, Astley captures the rhythms and the speech of her countrymen; similarly, in *Beachmasters*, she integrates into the novel "Seaspeak," the island mixture of native tongues, French, and English. Seaspeak, while lending authenticity to the work, also acts in the narrative as a social and racial determiner, once more stressing the central place of language in all parts of the human experience.

Although *Beachmasters* covers fewer than two hundred pages, its complexity demands much of the reader. When approached with the kind of attention it solicits, the novel yields not only a painstaking record of rebellion against colonialism but also a penetrating examination of the eternal questions concerning evil and redemption, whose answers are embedded in a litanylike narrative, so "well carved" that it is both lucid and impenetrable, never quite giving up its meaning. For there exist no easy answers to the questions *Beachmasters* poses.

Robert Ross

Sources for Further Study

Australian Book Review. LXXII, July, 1985, p. 17.
Best Sellers. XLVI, July, 1986, p. 123.
Kirkus Reviews. LIV, March 1, 1986, p. 314.
Library Journal. CXI, April 1, 1986, p. 160.
The New York Times Book Review. XCI, June 22, 1986, p. 12.
Publishers Weekly. CCXXIX, March 21, 1986, p. 75.
Quill & Quire. LII, April, 1986, p. 41.
South Central Review. III, Summer, 1986, p. 90.
Times Literary Supplement. November 15, 1985, p. 1295.
Washington Post Book World. XVI, June 8, 1986, p. 10.

BEARING THE CROSS
Martin Luther King, Jr., and the
Southern Christian Leadership Conference

Author: David J. Garrow (1953-   )
Publisher: William Morrow and Company (New York). 800 pp. $19.95
Type of work: Biography and historical survey
Time: 1929-1968

The life story and public career of Dr. Martin Luther King, Jr., with principal focus on his leadership of the Southern nonviolent black movement and his personal burdens and achievements in that role

> *Principal personages:*
> MARTIN LUTHER KING, JR., president of the Southern Christian Leadership Conference (SCLC) and major spokesman for the Southern nonviolent movement from 1955 to 1968
> RALPH DAVID ABERNATHY, his closest personal companion and organizational aide who succeeded him as president of SCLC in 1968
> CORETTA SCOTT KING, his wife
> STANLEY LEVISON, a controversial white supporter of King who provided financial backing and who aggravated the Federal Bureau of Investigation's suspicions of King and of his organization
> FRED SHUTTLESWORTH, a major leader of the Birmingham Civil Rights efforts who was deeply involved in the 1963 campaign and many others
> WYATT TEE WALKER, executive director of SCLC from 1960 to 1964 and a strategic realist who prepared much of SCLC's planning for the Birmingham campaign
> ANDREW J. YOUNG, a leader of SCLC's Citizenship Education Program and later close aide of King, executive director of SCLC after Walker

The South in which Martin Luther King, Jr., was born in 1929 had changed little in regard to race relations since Reconstruction. King grew up in comparatively privileged and protected conditions close to the Ebenezer Baptist Church on Auburn Avenue in Atlanta, Georgia, which his father pastored. Precocious and self-conscious, young King did not at first intend to follow his father and maternal grandfather in the Baptist ministry, but he learned early the power of the spoken word and longed to be important and influential. Although more isolated than poorer blacks from the direct impact of racism, he did not escape it entirely and frequently witnessed his family's spirited opposition to it.

King excelled as a student and was graduated from high school early. During World War II he studied at Morehouse College in Atlanta. There, and later at Crozer Seminary in Pennsylvania and Boston University, he became adept at analyzing philosophy and social theory and prepared for a church ministry. By 1954 he was ready to assume the pastorate of the Dexter Avenue Baptist Church in Montgomery, Alabama, as he was completing his doctoral dissertation at Boston University. In Montgomery, King was drawn into the new wave of black resistance to segregation and racism that was emerging in several Southern cities. Albeit reluctantly, King became the leader of the Montgomery Improvement Association that spearheaded a 381-day boycott of Montgomery's segregated transit system triggered in December, 1955, by the refusal of a local black seamstress, Rosa Parks, to comply with demands that she yield her seat to a white man on a crowded bus.

The familiar story of King's rise to prominence in Montgomery is told in elaborate detail by David J. Garrow. A particular emphasis of Garrow's account, however, is less typical: On January 27, 1956, at a particularly trying juncture in the boycott, King had a profound spiritual experience that Garrow identifies as seminal in King's public career. Alone, discouraged, and virtually ready to quit the effort, King wrestled within himself with the implications of Christian experience and his own calling as a leader. From pain and frustration King moved to confidence and resignation to God's will. "I didn't have to worry about anything. I have a marvelous mother and father," he recalled. They were far away in Atlanta, however, and unable to come to his rescue this time. With that realization, King placed his faith in God's presence in his own life.

> And it seemed at that moment that I could hear an inner voice saying to me, "Martin Luther, stand up for righteousness. Stand up for justice. Stand up for truth. And lo I will be with you, even until the end of the world." . . . I heard the voice of Jesus saying still to fight on. He promised never to leave me, never to leave me alone. No never alone. No never alone. He promised never to leave me, never to leave me alone.

Over the years King returned to this experience when resistance was particularly intense or when he was uncertain about his own capacities or role. Indeed, there were many such occasions. Just a year after the experience of January, 1956, and only weeks after the successful completion of the Montgomery boycott which resulted in the Supreme Court decision that ruled in favor of the blacks, King helped to organize the Southern Christian Leadership Conference (SCLC). Garrow provides extensive details of SCLC's early development and institutional structure without losing his primary focus on King the man. In a series of conferences in Atlanta, New Orleans, and Montgomery in 1957, SCLC took shape under the influence of King, his close friend and aide Ralph David Abernathy, pacifist Bayard Rustin, white Socialist attorney Stanley Levison, and a host of others, particularly Southern black ministers from Tallahassee, Birmingham, Mobile, and other sites across the South.

King was chosen president of SCLC and held that post until his death in 1968. At first, the organization had limited resources and a hazy focus that militated against a repetition of the Montgomery success. Ella J. Baker, who was never particularly fond of King or willing to accept the male chauvinism she saw among the black ministerial leadership of SCLC, was its first executive director. Baker and King moved quickly to draw into the nonviolent camp the unexpected energy of the sit-in movement that flourished in 1960 and 1961. The young people of the movement had already been influenced by Indian leader Mohandas K. Gandhi's commitment to nonviolent resistance, and the transition was relatively smooth. The Student Nonviolent Coordinating Committee (SNCC) that was formed at Shaw University in Raleigh, North Carolina, in April, 1960, however, had a mind of its own and was never fully led by King or any other mainstream black spokesperson. Nevertheless, the King mystique carried over into the work of SNCC, despite differences between King and SCLC in the 1962 Albany campaign and other activist efforts of the early and middle 1960's.

In 1963, in the historic Birmingham campaign, King and SCLC reached a new pinnacle of influence but not without difficulty. There were tensions with local black leaders who feared destructive disruption of the economy and with Birmingham's principal black activist, the Reverend Fred Shuttlesworth, who feared that King and SCLC might make an easy compromise, thus leaving Birmingham's blacks in an unimproved condition after the campaign. Garrow frankly explores these problems and the role of the Kennedy Administration in trying to avoid a bloodbath in Birmingham.

The Birmingham compromise was hardly finished when King helped to lead a massive march on Washington, D.C., in August, 1963. A cooperative endeavor of many civil and human rights organizations, the march drew more than two hundred thousand people and many prominent speakers. For King, it was the high tide of his public career. His "I Have a Dream" speech at the Lincoln Memorial became the epitome of his public message. Yet, at the time, trouble still loomed in Birmingham, and the proposed Civil Rights bill placed before Congress by President John F. Kennedy was far from assured passage. Just days after the speech, furthermore, four young black girls were killed by a dynamite blast in their Sunday school classroom at the Sixteenth Street Baptist Church in Birmingham. In November, President Kennedy himself was killed, a fact that stunned King and moved him to point out the systemic hatred and violence that seemed to mar American society.

King's career after Birmingham was a complex mixture of successes and personal anguish. More honors lay ahead. He was named *Time* magazine's "Man of the Year," and he received the 1964 Nobel Prize for Peace. Increasingly, however, King was a troubled man. The nonviolent movement symbolized by King seemed to reach an impasse following passage of the 1964 Civil Rights Act and, after the violent Selma campaign, the enactment of the Voting Rights Act of 1965. The hard-fought Chicago campaign of 1966 resulted in some fundamental improvements in housing and jobs, but in the North King met serious resistance from both whites and blacks. A tide of militancy was obvious among many blacks who questioned the efficacy of the Southern nonviolent tactics. King was moved by the spectacle of urban ghetto riots both before and after the Chicago effort and sought to redirect their destructive tendencies. Solution to this problem, however, eluded him.

Nor was his effort to revise the Johnson Administration's policy in the Vietnam War successful. King lost support not only in the administration but also among many moderate blacks by his crusade against that war. Increasingly he was, Garrow implies, isolated and troubled. A number of SCLC endeavors were beset by difficulties in this period, including the projected Poor People's Campaign of 1968. King apparently hoped to move the nation with a new movement mentality, focusing on the plight of the poor and shifting national priorities from the Vietnam struggle to eliminating poverty.

This period found King increasingly caught up in his personal needs, especially what Garrow calls his "sexual athleticism." Repeatedly, it is reported, King turned to women for short-term, and in a few cases, longer romantic relationships. Away from home for weeks at a time, and in a strained relationship with his wife, Coretta Scott King, the SCLC president engaged in numerous love affairs. Most of them, says Garrow, were temporary but important to King's quest for acceptance and satisfaction. Further, the Federal Bureau of Investigation (FBI) kept King's private life under constant surveillance, bugging hotel rooms and other points along King's many journeys. In an effort to discourage King and to discredit him as a national leader, the FBI continually spied on him and his associates. While other biographers have touched on this thorny subject, Garrow presents the fullest coverage to date and takes it all quite seriously.

In Garrow's account, King appears as a man driven to martyrdom by the pressures of the FBI, by his alienation from a growing segment of the American mainstream, and by his personal pain. According to Garrow, King began to shift from his original relatively moderate stance on social issues. With his primary emphasis after Selma upon socioeconomic reform, King became increasingly absorbed in matters related to poverty, housing, social acceptance, and economic justice.

King's friends noticed his preoccupation with his own death and his apparent weariness. Garrow quotes extensively the observations of several men and women who witnessed his strained state in 1967 and 1968. His sermons and speeches, including his last formal address in Memphis just before his death on April 4, 1968, were replete will allusions to death and bearing the cross. In meticulous detail, Garrow traces King's final steps in Memphis and his assassination on the balcony of a motel as he departed for yet another rally.

There is so much coverage here of King's public life and the SCLC that it is inappropriate to focus only on the frank exposé of his private life. Garrow's long treatise works through all the major Civil Rights campaigns and several lesser ones, and it contains valuable biographical information on a host of personalities. Garrow's emphasis on King's sexual encounters and on his preoccupation with bearing the cross, however, are central to his interpretation of King's life.

Many people who knew King personally will likely doubt some of the material Garrow has presented, nor is it certain that his image of King as a man, especially in the period after Selma, is accurate. That King was a "waning light" has been affirmed by writers since before his death, yet many who carried on his work recall another King: still dynamic and hopeful, still charismatic and trusting, and hardly bent on self-destruction. What Garrow has done calls for further analysis. Yet it will be some time before the details will be enlarged or the scope of coverage exceeded.

Garrow's greatest strength is the depth of his research. Each footnote has many citations, and he has gone through thousands of pages of FBI material as well as more typical Civil Rights research sources. That he has done a thorough and sophisticated job of reporting is obvious. It remains true, however, that Martin Luther King, Jr., and the movement he led were complex and have a continuing life. If Garrow has correctly noted the seminal role of the January, 1956, inner experience, he has not probed the depths of King's spiritual life in regard to his temptations and shortcomings. Nor is the image of a martyr totally convincing. Why was King looking to the Poor People's Campaign with such intensity? What were his actual political aspirations after Chicago? Does Garrow, or anyone, know the real story of King's private life and struggles? These are pressing questions that have not been answered but have only been suggested by Garrow's account.

Despite his real and imagined flaws, Martin Luther King, Jr., was a deeply religious man. His inner moral struggles elicited Pauline-like wrestlings of the spirit. He continued to preach against sexual license and moral laxity. In Garrow's account, a deeper dimension of the human King, as opposed to the idealized version, comes through. *Bearing the Cross: Martin Luther King, Jr., and the Southern Christian Leadership Conference* will be one of the starting points of future scholarship. There is still, however, much room for exploration of both the details and the interpretation of King's life and career. Garrow has earned a significant place, by this and other studies of King, in contemporary scholarship, but his tendency to hold back from fuller analysis should also be noted.

Thomas R. Peake

Sources for Further Study

Best Sellers. XLVI, February, 1987, p. 433.
Booklist. LXXXIII, January 1, 1987, p. 670.
Kirkus Reviews. LIV, October 15, 1986, p. 1553.
Library Journal. CXI, November 15, 1986, p. 90.
Los Angeles Daily Journal. C, January 16, 1987, p. B18.
The New Republic. CXCVI, January 5, 1987, p. 34.
The New York Review of Books. XXXIII, January 15, 1987, p. 3.
The New York Times Book Review. XCI, November 30, 1986, p. 1.
Publishers Weekly. CCXXX, October 31, 1986, p. 51.
Time. CXXIX, January 19, 1987, p. 24.

THE BEET QUEEN

Author: Louise Erdrich (1954-   )
Publisher: Henry Holt and Company (New York). 338 pp. $16.95
Type of work: Novel
Time: 1932-1972
Locale: Argus, North Dakota

A tough yet empathetic novel exposes the loneliness and craving that keep people separate even when their lives intersect

> *Principal characters:*
> MARY ADARE, a difficult, unlovable, independent businesswoman, who as a girl of eleven was deserted by her mother
> KARL ADARE, her brother, three years older, perpetually rootless and wandering
> SITA KOZKA, their beautiful cousin
> CELESTINE JAMES, a half Chippewa, once Sita's best friend
> WALLACE PFEF, the chief booster of the town of Argus and a perpetual bachelor
> DOT ADARE, Celestine's daughter

Louise Erdrich's second novel is set in the same part of North Dakota as her award-winning *Love Medicine* (1984) and covers much the same stretch of time. A few characters reappear—Eli Kashpaw, Officer Lovchik, Dot Adare. Both books are made up of semi-independent chapters in various narrative viewpoints, some of which have been published as short stories. Yet in texture, effect, and theme, the novels are very different. *The Beet Queen*, for all its occasional zaniness, is a bleak book; its people do not connect with one another or with the land. They are so repressed that their hunger for love and family breaks out in sudden, inarticulate excess that makes people flee for fear of being devoured. The technical facility and the careful thematic control reveal new facets of Erdrich's skill.

Although *The Beet Queen*, like *Love Medicine*, is made up of interwoven stories, it has a more linear structure. *Love Medicine* was a tapestry, a weaving and touching and crossing that created constantly surprising new patterns; *The Beet Queen* is constructed to a plan, revealing how pieces which interlock can still retain borders and boundaries that keep them from blending. Possibly the structure of the two books reveals one difference between the German and the Chippewa elements of Erdrich's heritage—at any rate, her subject here is townspeople, and the central figures are un-rooted and non-Indian.

The story begins and ends with scenes of flight—literal flight, in airplanes. Like many other pieces of the plot, these two scenes are improbable enough to verge on the surreal, yet their matter-of-fact narration makes them seem almost ordinary, while their metaphoric or expressive content fuels the meaning of the tale. As the book opens, in 1932, Mary and Karl Adare's mother, Adelaide, hops aboard a fairgrounds airplane with a seedy barnstormer billed as "The Great Omar, Aeronaught Extraordinaire," and disappears from their lives. Mary and Karl are illegitimate; Adelaide's married lover died in a freak accident which may have been suicide. The kids hop a freight headed for Argus, where their Aunt Fritzie and her husband, Pete, own a butcher shop. Karl, in a moment of panic, jumps back on the train; Mary is taken in by Aunt Fritzie (to the intense jealousy of Fritzie's own daughter, Sita) and soon also steals Sita's best friend, Celestine James. The remainder of the novel traces the intersection of their lives at scattered intervals over the next forty years.

Yet though the characters are connected, their stories are marked by disruption and disconnection. Parents desert or die; children are fostered by sisters or aunts (or craved by pseudoparents). Wallace Pfef—Chamber of Commerce president, Jaycee activist, the man who brings sugar-beet prosperity to Argus—provides an excuse for remaining single by displaying the picture of a "dead fiancée" he bought at a farm auction, but even so he fails to recognize his homosexuality until, well into adulthood, he encounters Karl in a hotel room. Because they have never seen their emotions reflected or mirrored by others, the book's central figures are so needy that their fierce hungers and bizarre attempts to satisfy their cravings are immediately self-defeating.

At eleven, Mary regrets Karl's loss primarily because she feels weak if she has no one to protect and look out for. In Aunt Fritzie's house, she spies out ways to be useful: "I planned to be essential to them all, so depended upon that they could never send me off. I did this on purpose, because I soon found out that I had nothing else to offer." Mary is an unattractive and unlovable character—yet Erdrich writes with such empathy that one cannot help caring about her. Mary's grasping and conniving and her fierce selfishness are her only defense against a world which has given her nothing voluntarily.

Karl also remains fixed for life in a rather adolescent emotional pattern created by his early experience. Riding the rails at age fourteen and overwhelmed by yearnings that he does not analyze, Karl seeks closeness with another man, initiates a homosexual encounter, and declares his love. When it is rejected, Karl's life is set; forty years later he is still a rover, a traveling salesman for one gimcrack after another, never again willing to expose his feelings.

Another motif in *The Beet Queen* has to do with women's social roles. None is shown to be satisfactory. Adelaide abandons motherhood, leaving behind a nursing infant (as well as Karl and Mary) when she flies away. The beauty-queen ideal of prettiness and popularity is effectively destroyed by the title alone, without even waiting for the tragicomic irony of the sugar-beet festival that ends the book. Yet Mary's life as an independent businesswoman also lacks something. As she says:

I did not choose solitude. Who would? It came on me like a kind of vocation, demanding an effort that married women can't picture. Sometimes, even now, I look on the married girls the way a wild dog might look through the window at tame ones, envying the regularity of their lives but also despising the low pleasure they get from the master's touch.

Mary had once been tempted, by Celestine's half brother Russell Kashpaw; she invited him to dinner, dressed carefully, even drew on eyebrows in a futile attempt to coax him. Nevertheless, as she says flatly, "I don't know coaxing from a box lunch." Yet if the detached characters are unfulfilled, so is Sita, who more closely conforms to expected behavior. An attractive, self-centered adolescent who is quite reasonably jealous when Mary takes part of her room, her hand-me-down clothes, her best friend, and her parents' interest, Sita has conventional adolescent dreams—to model in a department store, to marry a perfect man. Her first marriage is a compromise, but her second is to a man with money, education, manners. In it she has episodes of insanity; most appropriately, she loses her voice.

The "Beet Queen" of the title is Dot Adare. She is Celestine's daughter and Mary's niece; Karl's child by biology and Wallace Pfef's because he delivered her when Celestine went into labor during a blizzard. Bullying, spoiled, fierce, and erratic, Dot becomes the focus of everyone's frustrated love and yearning. Mary so craves Celestine's child that the two of them compete to be important to Dot, and in the process they leave her undisciplined and unhappy. Essentially, the characters have had no way to learn love; they try to matter to others but never achieve connections that can sustain warmth and comfort. Celestine discovers and enjoys her sexuality but does not like having a man living in her house. Mary and Celestine force themselves on Sita when she is dying. Necessity makes all of them independent and, as a consequence, uncomfortable with evidence of others' care. Karl speaks of the brief period when he stayed with Wally Pfef:

> As his only experience, I was some sort of God he worshipped by acting like he was my personal maid. He ironed everything I wore, washed my shirts fresh, brought coffee, squeezed oranges because I said I liked real juice, and cooked up big dinners every night. An ash wouldn't drop from my cigarette but that he'd catch it in his bare palm and brush it into a wastebasket. Sleeping with him was no different from that. He'd do anything to please me, but didn't have the nerve to please himself. . . . He drove me out of my mind with attention, and even though I did feel sorry for him there was no question, ever, of staying.

The novel is tidily structured with repetitions, reversals, and a series of "Night" chapters—one for each central character—that provide moments of personal confrontation and epiphany. The book begins with Adelaide running away from her children and ends with Dot's escape from her parents and parent figures—who include those same children. The nuance of each individual's voice is clear. One pair of them, furthermore, lose the ability to speak: Sita in marriage, and Russell Kashpaw after a stroke. There are other interesting parallels between the two (as well as their similar situation in the book's final scene). Russell, coming back from World War II as the town's most decorated hero, is offered a job in the bank even though he is an Indian—yet a second war ruins Russell, as a second marriage ruins Sita, and both become voiceless and powerless.

Like Edgar Lee Masters in *Spoon River Anthology* (1915) or Sherwood Anderson in *Winesburg, Ohio* (1919), Erdrich peels back the surface of an American small town and discovers not simply a worm in the Eden but a complex life that is touching, comic, and bizarre. The first-person monologues are a particularly appropriate narrative technique because the characters remain so fiercely, protectively, helplessly isolated—despite the interconnections of their lives. It is a measure of her great skill that Erdrich has centered the novel on a group of people who are all difficult and unlovable, yet she has avoided satire—while still writing comic scenes—and has treated her characters with attention and empathy.

The novel's physical background is also significant. The non-Indian residents of the piece of North Dakota that is almost off the map are not so connected to the land as the Chippewa of *Love Medicine*; the setting seems grimmer and less permanent. In 1932, when the book opens, "the topsoil was so newly tilled that it hadn't all blown off yet, the way it had in Kansas." The residents of Argus are still exhausted by their struggle with an inhospitable land. In addition, they are townspeople rather than farmers or hunters, living in a place made a town by virtue of its railway and grain elevator and, later, its highway and beet-sugar refinery. The buildings cling precariously to an earth they are not at home with: The butcher shop is concrete and stucco, Sita's restaurant is a ship beached thousands of miles from the nearest ocean, Wally Pfef's modern split-level house perches above open blizzard-swept acres. The simple struggle against blistering heat, drought, snow, and the need to think about the state of the tires before visiting someone at night silently mark the character of the people who live in such a place.

Although it lacks the wild joy of some passages in *Love Medicine*, *The Beet Queen* has a multitude of rich scenes and memorable lesser characters, including Fleur Pillager, pulling her peddler's cart on grooved wheels along the railroad track, and the schoolyard miracle that makes Mary Adare temporarily a marked child. There are also quiet moments that sink in later, especially in the continuing relationship between Celestine and Mary, two women aging together.

Among other things, *The Beet Queen* works backward to create a heritage and past for the Dot Adare who appeared, pregnant with Garry Nanapush's child, in one chapter of *Love Medicine*. Now in progress is a book that will look at the years before *Love Medicine* began, and a fourth is projected to examine the future of the Albertine/Lipsha generation and pick up characters such as *The Beet Queen*'s Father Jude. As Louise Erdrich peoples her world, it grows wonderfully more full and deep.

Sally Mitchell

Sources for Further Study

Belles Lettres. II, November/December, 1986, p. 9.
Booklist. LXXXII, July, 1986, p. 1562.
Chicago Tribune. August 31, 1986, XIV, p. 29.
Commonweal. CXIII, October 24, 1986, p. 565.
Kirkus Reviews. LIV, July 15, 1986, p. 1042.
Library Journal. CXI, August, 1986, p. 168.
The Nation. CCXLIII, November 1, 1986, p. 460.
The New Republic. CXCV, October 6, 1986, p. 46.
The New York Times Book Review. XCI, August 31, 1986, p. 2.
Publishers Weekly. CCXXX, July 4, 1986, p. 60.
The Wall Street Journal. CCVIII, September 2, 1986, p. 24.

BIRD OF LIFE, BIRD OF DEATH
A Naturalist's Journey Through a Land of Political Turmoil

Author: Jonathan Evan Maslow (1948-   )
Publisher: Simon and Schuster (New York). 249 pp. $17.95
Type of work: Travelogue
Time: The 1980's
Locale: Guatemala

An essay, with political and social insights, of a trip into the highlands of Guatemala to see and study the rare quetzal and to investigate its chances of survival

Principal personages:
JONATHAN EVAN MASLOW, a free-lance writer and "fanatical birder"
MICHAEL KIENITZ, a photographer

The quetzal was one of those birds one first encountered collecting stamps many years ago. Its picture came along in a special packet prepared by the stamp companies to tantalize the young and entice them to spend their allowance. In addition to birds, one could also buy an assortment of fish, horses, dogs, and tropical fruits. One had to sort them out, track down the countries from which they came, and ever so carefully paste them in an album, using the translucent stamp hinges that one would fold before licking but that would usually stick to one's fingers. In each bird packet there would usually be one or more quetzals because Guatemala featured it on many of its stamps of low value. This small picture, however, gave little idea of the bird's majesty, as it was printed on very cheap paper, in no more than two colors, and drawn by rather untalented artists. Once mounted in the album, the quetzal did not seem out of place with the drab pictures of dictators and architectural monstrosities that routinely appeared on the other stamps of that country.

Stamp collecting, one was told, would increase one's awareness of the world, be one's guide to faraway places and of times past. The editors of the stamp album would try to push one along by providing short, helpful descriptions of the countries whose canceled postage one was saving. One learned that Guatemala was "discovered" in the early sixteenth century by Spanish explorers, who found there an incredible Mayan civilization, and that the country in time grew to be one of the most populous in Central America—90 percent of its people were Indians or mestizos, while the small percentage of Spanish descendants made up the ruling class. The natives sold their handicrafts to the tourists; they raised coffee and bananas and worked in the forests, which yielded chicle for chewing gum. There was also a growing oil industry, and the national emblem was the quetzal.

Trouble is, most people's knowledge of Guatemala never seemed to go beyond that found in the "Around the World" stamp album. Nothing in that book with those tiny pieces of paper glued neatly in rows told anything of the repressive conditions under which most of the country's people have lived since the sixteenth century. Jonathan Maslow says that his trip to Guatemala to go bird-watching was motivated by an obsessive curiosity about nature, but he ultimately found more than he bargained for. "Dust, grit, smoke, weeds, garbage, slops, marl, excrement, packing crates, naked kids with bloated bellies, drunks lying in the gutters, and looming over everything an enormous billboard showing... some girl in designer jeans." His description of the slums of Guatemala City is not to be found on any of the country's stamps. "How do poor people take it?" he asks. "Why don't they burn the whole thing down and start over again? What have they got to lose?" Before his journey is over, he will begin to provide some answers.

In 1524, Pedro de Alvarado, one of Hernán Cortés' unruly lieutenants, arrived from Mexico at the head of a column of 120 horsemen and three hundred foot soldiers to conquer the land for the Spanish crown, enslave the inhabitants, rob them of their wealth and, in many cases, their lives. These foreign plunderers were thoroughly convinced that what they were doing had the blessing of the king and God. Alvarado, a homicidal maniac, was given the greatest opportunity of his life to satisfy his lust for blood. His war against the civilian population initiated what Maslow describes as "the tradition of genocide that has bedeviled Guatemala as it greatest shame down to the present day."

Though future dictators never quite seemed to measure up to the murderous panache of Alvarado, this was often not through want of trying. That the ruling classes would run roughshod over the natives was taken for granted. In the state of siege which currently exists, the campesino villages are habitually destroyed, the men massacred, the women raped, the children left destitute or even killed along with their mothers. The bloodshed is mostly confined to the remote areas of the country and is often not publicized. Journalists do not usually write about things that they are not allowed to see, which accounts for the standpoint of the rest of the world: out of sight, out of mind. Amnesty International has branded Guatemala one of the world's worst violators of human rights. When Maslow was writing his book, the chief hangman was born-again Christian President-General Efraín Ríos Montt, who gave the army the power to arrest "subversives" and sentence them to death without the right of appeal or pardon.

Maslow writes of visiting an adobe church sanctuary perched on a long steep hill behind the provincial capital of Salamá. The atmosphere inside the church is one of tranquillity and peace, with polished black-and-white floor tiles leading to votive tables covered with lace-embroidered cloths gleaming white beneath the weight of candles; the altar is bedecked with long-stemmed lilies, gladioli, and baby's breath, all of which is flanked by brightly colored Mayan-style paintings decorating the sidewalls. Mute evidence of the routine horror under which most of the rural Guatemalan people live is pinned and taped to the rear wall, where there are hundreds of snapshots of persons who have vanished. The photos are mainly of teenage Indian boys and girls with rotting teeth and scared looks; near the pictures, relatives have "scrawled messages on scraps of paper—a name, the date and place of their relative's disappearance, or a prayer to the Virgin for their safe return."

"By fear and sword I might bring these people to the service of His Majesty," Alvarado wrote in a dispatch to Cortés, describing how he had recently obliterated the Mayan capital of Utalán and burned its leaders at the stake. It used to be thought that the natives were glad to serve their Ladino masters, but revolts and uprisings and incessant guerrilla warfare have put that myth to rest. In fact, almost every generation since the conquistadores arrived has been touched by serious civil unrest. To escape the terror, as of 1986, Guatemalan Indians have been crowding into Mexico at the rate of about two hundred thousand a year—this out of a total Guatemalan population of seven million. Guatemalan soldiers, not content to let them go in peace, at one time pursued them across the border, sometimes killing them in refugee camps, until the Mexicans reinforced their southern frontier.

Maslow's account of his attempts to observe the resplendent quetzal never frees itself from a sense of foreboding and doom. Thus it contrasts markedly with the mood set in his previous book, *The Owl Papers* (1983), a cheerful presentation of owl watching in history and mythology, complete with a boat trip off Martha's Vineyard. Although Maslow tries to restrain his sense of moral indignation, he is not always successful. On the other hand, sometimes it seems that he has unnecessarily pulled his punches; for example, he does not mention one of Guatemala's most extravagant ecological and human disasters: the large-scale development project in the Northern Transversal region, which ravished the topography and tossed campesino families off their land like refuse. Nor does he refer to the escapades of the United Fruit Company. How can one talk about Guatemala without mentioning the United Fruit Company? This multinational, together with the United States Central Intelligence Agency and State Department (then headed by John Foster Dulles), arranged a military coup to bring about the collapse of the reformist government of Jacobo Arbenz.

The military has been in power ever since, still fighting its self-righteous war against any opposition, which it automatically brands as a Communist insurgency. The Moscow connection to Guatemalan military officers began three centuries before the birth of Vladimir Ilyich Lenin. Maslow bitterly observes that in the United States, "the gringo gods speak the private language of Cold War abstractions. If only Central America were really so simple." Some things are. "How do poor people take it? Why don't they burn the whole thing down and start over again?" These are questions born of frustration with the inaction of others. Yet how does one prevail against a government which remains indifferent to the social and economic needs of its citizens and whose response to their demands comes from the mouths of Uzis? Burn the whole thing down? The masses would be doing the general a favor.

The shy and gentle quetzal, the bird of freedom, is hardly an appropriate national emblem for Guatemala. More fitting would be the black vulture, the zopilote, a bird that is much more hardy and tenacious and aggressive. Whereas to Maslow the brilliantly plumed quetzal was elusively difficult to find, its numbers dwindling, its nesting grounds increasingly constricted as they are being systematically ravaged, the vultures were everywhere. Death was everywhere and often a public affair. Getting close to study the creatures at firsthand, even coming to within a few feet, was no problem. When the vultures were feeding, nothing else mattered. "They had no true pecking order, but lunged at each other willy-nilly, snapping their beaks and flapping their wings like fighting cocks. They barked, woofed, snuffled, snorted, wheezed, and hissed at each other in a constant struggle for a place at the dinner table." Yet, these odious, hardworking scavengers were performing a valuable service, especially in a country whose leaders do not put a high priority on public sanitation.

In Central America, Maslow says, a fundamental hostility has existed between the Ladino and the natural environment. The Ladino sees it as something to conquer in order to destroy, not, as believed in North America, in order to improve. For the Ladino, therefore, the destruction of the wilderness is almost good in itself; conservation is always an affront to progress. Faced with this justification for rapacity and greed, the quetzal, its number forever growing smaller, is understandably facing extinction. Maslow undertook his journey in July, when the likelihood of encountering the bird was not as great as it would have been during the mating season in the spring. Still, his quest was not in vain: He saw six of the birds, two of which were the coveted, prodigiously colored and plumed adult males. The sightings left him transfixed. "I was practically unaware of time, frozen in ecstasy: I had never seen a more deliciously feathered creature."

Maslow denies that he has written a true travelogue, and in a sense he is right, especially as the term is currently used to describe those short sections that one skims in the Sunday supplement. Maslow's book fits in with those more expansive accounts of erudite travelers of the nineteenth century, who believed that their obligation went beyond a mere description of places and things, often blending in sociology, politics, and philosophy. In their accounts, the addition of ornithology would hardly have created a stir. "In writing about the Quetzal," Maslow argues, "I have attempted a kind of essay in political ornithology—a field that does not quite exist, at least yet."

In a quest story, is the object of the quest important? Maslow presents a fairly free-ranging text with observations of waitresses, street vendors, tourist guides, and hotel clerks, a description of one of his dreams, an analysis of cultural despoilation, a sober description of man-made environmental calamity, and a vivid description of vultures methodically tearing apart the carcass of a dog. The book hops easily from early modern history to contemporary society; it provides admirable descriptions of nature, descriptions that are as brightly colored as the Mayan pattern blankets which Maslow bought in the market at Antigua: "Granite heights that looked clawed by blind and angry titans pitched into patches of lowland rainforest, blooming in erotic dishevelment: a restless topography that would be all things at once, display all seasons, demonstrate all climates, contain the living evidence of all ages, conjure all the varied forces of nature." Thus, Maslow invites the reader to participate in his love of nature and share his sense of shock at its cruel destruction. He is a worthy guide.

Wm. Laird Kleine-Ahlbrandt

Sources for Further Study

Booklist. LXXXII, May 1, 1986, p. 1280.
Kirkus Reviews. LIII, December 15, 1985, p. 1382.
Library Journal. CXI, March 1, 1986, p. 87.
The New York Times Book Review. XCI, March 9, 1986, p. 13.
Publishers Weekly. CCXXIX, January 10, 1986, p. 78.
Smithsonian. XVII, May, 1986, p. 164.
Texas Monthly. XIV, June, 1986, p. 157.

BLESSINGS IN DISGUISE

Author: Alec Guinness (1914-   )
Publisher: Alfred A. Knopf (New York). Illustrated. 238 pp. $17.95
Type of work: Memoirs
Time: 1914 to 1986
Locale: England, the Mediterranean, the United States, Mexico, and Cuba

The great actor Alec Guinness recalls his boyhood, war experiences, highlights of his career, and artists he has known

> *Principal personages:*
> ALEC GUINNESS, an actor
> MERULA GUINNESS, his wife
> MARTITA HUNT, an actress
> SYBIL THORNDIKE, an actress
> JOHN GIELGUD, an actor
> EDITH SITWELL, a poet
> EDITH EVANS, an actress
> ERNEST MILTON, an actor
> RALPH RICHARDSON, an actor
> PETER BULL, an actor
> TYRONE GUTHRIE, a director and producer

Herbert Pocket, Fagin, Marley's Ghost, Disraeli, eight members of the D'Ascoigne family, the man in the white suit, Father Brown, Cardinal Mindzenty, Colonel Nicholson, Gully Jimson, Prince Faisal, Marcus Aurelius, Julius Caesar, Yevgraf Zhivago, Charles I, Pope Innocent III, Adolf Hitler, Sigmund Freud, Obi-Wan Kenobi, George Smiley, Professor Godbole, Hamlet, Richard III—behind these and a host of other characters Alec Guinness has concealed himself. A consummate actor since the 1930's on stage, screen, and television, Guinness has been a self-effacing person who has shunned publicity and whose scandal-free private life has provided no grist for the tabloids. In his autobiographical *Blessings in Disguise*, Guinness finally removes the makeup and appears in his own person.

The fact that he turns out to be as good a writer as he is an actor should be no surprise, for he won an Oscar nomination for his screenplay for *The Horse's Mouth* (1958). Indeed, Guinness' writing ability was in a way responsible for the beginning of his screen career, for in 1939 he adapted Charles Dickens' *Great Expectations* for the stage and played the role of Herbert Pocket, with Martita Hunt as Miss Havisham. David Lean, not yet a film director, saw the show and told Guinness that he planned to film it as soon as the war was over. Lean kept his word and made the film in 1946, with Guinness and Hunt repeating their roles. *Great Expectations* is arguably the greatest Dickens film ever made, and in it, Guinness made an auspicious screen debut. It led in turn to Lean selecting him to costar as Fagin in *Oliver Twist* (1948). Guinness' versatility got him the part of the D'Ascoigne family (six of them murdered) in *Kind Hearts and Coronets*

(1949), and from there he was on his way to two Oscars (one for best actor, the second a special award for his entire career) and a knighthood.

Yet his path was not easy, and his beginnings were difficult. Born in 1914, Guinness never knew for certain who his father was, and part of the book is a lifelong search for a father. Guinness recalls being "born to confusion and totally immersed in it for several years, owning three different names until the age of fourteen and living in about thirty different hotels, lodgings and flats." If he was "pursued by his infantile demons," however, he also had many good angels to guide him on his way. Much of the book is a tribute to them.

Blessings in Disguise is not so much an autobiographical narrative as it is a series of sketches, loosely chronological, focusing on those good angels, with Guinness casting himself in a supporting role. To begin with, there was an ancient Dickensian woman who seemed to haunt the ground-floor front of a large gloomy house where five-year-old Guinness would be left alone for hours. A former actress, now "an impoverished Miss Havisham" without a wedding cake but with a partially eaten rice pudding under her bed, she became his secret friend and taught him to use his imagination to conjure up theatrical images. She was succeeded by Nellie Wallace, a vaudeville star, and then by Sybil Thorndike and Lewis Casson, who befriended the stage-struck sixteen-year-old Guinness and remained lifelong friends. If Guinness were in part responsible for getting Martita Hunt her best-known role as Miss Havisham, he was repaying a favor, for when he was a gangling, unknown twenty-year-old, she took him under her wing and coached him. Another good angel, John Gielgud, whom Guinness had dared approach for coaching, directed him to Miss Hunt; when the penniless young man was auditioning, Gielgud staked him to twenty pounds, expressed faith in him, and later got him his start at the Old Vic playing Osric in William Shakespeare's *Hamlet*. Tyrone Guthrie also encouraged the young actor, sent him to Elsinore to play Osric again with Laurence Olivier, Vivien Leigh, and Michael Redgrave, and years later brought him to star as Richard III in the opening season at Stratford, Ontario.

An entire chapter, with full-dress portrait, is devoted to each of these people as well as to Sydney Cockerell, Edith Sitwell, Edith Evans, Shakespearean actor Ernest Milton (who, Guinness claims, played the greatest Hamlet he ever saw), and Ralph Richardson. Others who appear prominently but do not receive as full a treatment are Grace Kelly (she and Guinness for years kept up a private joke in which each arranged for a tomahawk to be slipped into the other's bed), Noël Coward, Laurence Olivier, Vivien Leigh, Sophia Loren, Ernie Kovacs, Fidel Castro, George Bernard Shaw, Graham Greene, Dylan Thomas, Evelyn Waugh, Anthony Quayle, Peter Bull, Ernest Hemingway, and Pope Pius XII, not to mention other theatrical friends and associates.

Guinness seems to have total recall; he re-creates dialogue and describes, like a stage setting, the details of his friends' rooms and dress from fifty years ago. He has a novelist's ability to create scene and character with vivid, memorable vignettes. By contrast to the usual celebrity biographies and memoirs, which tend to be superficial hackwork, Guinness' is the work of a literary artist. Indeed, Guinness reveals himself to be a lifelong lover of literature, immersing himself over the years in Thucydides, Shakespeare, John Milton, Dickens, Greene, and T. S. Eliot, among others, and he always has a small library with him on his travels.

The book's longest chapter is an account of Guinness' adventures (or rather misadventures) in the British navy during World War II. Though Guinness showed plenty of courage in the Mediterranean and the invasion of Italy, he was no swashbuckler; his recollections sound like a Guinness film comedy, such as *All at Sea* perhaps, with numerous nautical mishaps, including putting a swinging bridge out of commission. At the same time, however, he stood up to incompetent officers.

Guinness displays an immense tolerance for eccentricity, injury, and insult from his friends. "Who can one hit, if not one's friends?" asked Ralph Richardson one evening when Guinness came to dinner, and, for no reason, punched Guinness in the jaw. When Guinness dared defend Ludwig van Beethoven, whom Edith Sitwell pronounced a bore, she did not let him forget the incident for two years, declaring, "Alec Guinness is *not* a Plantagenet." Martita Hunt had a bizarre way of greeting him—partly deafening him by clapping her hands over his ears. When he began playing leading roles, John Gielgud asked him, "Why don't you stick to the little people you do so well?" Guinness portrays his friends warts and all, not hiding their theatrical vanities and temperaments, but he defends them fiercely, remains devoted to them, and is generous with his tributes. Modest about himself, his only boast is, "I am unaware of ever having lost a friend."

A Catholic convert, Guinness devotes a chapter to his religious pilgrimage from schoolboy experiences with Anglicanism, youthful atheism, dabblings into Quakerism, Buddhism, Anglo-Catholicism, Tarot (to which he became addicted until the cards gave him the horrors and he threw them into the fire), and finally, after overcoming initial reluctance and testing himself by a stay in a Trappist monastery, to Roman Catholicism. Always ready to acknowledge his human failings, Guinness nevertheless communicates throughout the book an appealing serenity.

Guinness also possesses an appealing modesty, applying to himself Samuel Johnson's admonition, "Almost all absurdity of conduct arises from the imitation of those we cannot resemble." He has no melodramatic sins and scandals to confess, and he is free from self-abasement, but he can be critical of his performances. He never mentions his Oscars and makes little of his knighthood, making it appear a reward for his subduing hostility toward

Great Britain at a Mexican film festival. His greatest blessing seems to be his marriage of almost fifty years, and he pays an eloquent tribute to his wife, Merula: "I cannot imagine life without her or what it would have been like had I never known her or had not had the courage to suggest marriage."

Guinness writes considerably more about his beginnings as an actor than about his later stage and screen career, and while the book is valuable as theatrical history, one wishes for more. There is practically nothing about his understudying Olivier in *Hamlet*, nothing about his playing the Fool to Olivier's Lear, nothing about starring in *The Cocktail Party*, nothing about filming *The Bridge on the River Kwai* in Ceylon and *Lawrence of Arabia* in Jordan, very little about his classic Ealing comedies, nothing about the later films (including *Star Wars*), little about productions and his interpretation of his roles. There is enough left out to make two or three more books, and *Blessings in Disguise* is so good that one hopes that Guinness, like David Niven, will write another volume or two of memoirs.

Robert E. Morsberger

Sources for Further Study

The Atlantic. CCLVII, April, 1986, p. 131.
Christian Science Monitor. LXXVIII, March 18, 1986, p. 28.
Library Journal. CXI, March 15, 1986, p. 76.
The London Review of Books. VII, December 5, 1985, p. 21.
Los Angeles Times Book Review. March 23, 1986, p. 10.
The New York Review of Books. XXXIII, March 27, 1986, p. 21.
The New York Times Book Review. XCI, April 6, 1986, p. 14.
Punch. CCLXXXIX, October 16, 1985, p. 58.
Time. CXXVII, March 17, 1986, p. 89.
Washington Post Book World. XVI, March 2, 1986, p. 3.

THE BLOOD OF KINGS
Dynasty and Ritual in Maya Art

Authors: Linda Schele (1942-   ) and Mary Ellen Miller (1952-   )
Foreword by Emily J. Sano
Preface by Michael D. Coe
Publisher: George Braziller (New York). Illustrated. 335 pp. $45.00
Type of work: Art history

Based on historically documented ideals of kingship and religious ritual, The Blood of Kings *entirely revises modern thinking about Maya civilization*

In 1816, the English poet John Kcats expressed his enthusiastic discovery of Homer in George Chapman's Elizabethan translation by likening his experience to the discovery of a new planet or to the Spanish discovery of the Pacific Ocean. That wild delight which Keats described is precisely the condition contemporary readers experience on first looking into *The Blood of Kings: Dynasty and Ritual in Maya Art* in which Linda Schele and Mary Ellen Miller present to the modern world an astonishingly new version of the Maya in a generally accessible form. Produced in connection with the 1986 exhibition *The Blood of Kings: A New Interpretation of Maya Art* shown at the Kimball Art Museum in Fort Worth, Texas, and the Cleveland Museum of Art, this richly illustrated and elegantly written work focuses in its eight chapters on the eight principal elements of the exhibit. It also contains a ground-breaking introduction in four parts as well as informative sections on the Maya calendar and on the recently decoded hieroglyphic writing system, the solution to the mystery of the Maya. The study is, thus, far more than a conventional exhibit catalog.

Michael D. Coe, in his preface to the work, places the book in its proper historical context as a culmination and definitive statement of the revolution in Maya studies since the mid-1960's. He agrees with the authors that blood was the mortar of ancient Maya ritual life, and, in addition, he traces the short but meteoric history of the breaking of the hieroglyphic code. The slow acceptance of the Russian Yuri Knorosov's revival in 1952 of Bishop Diego de Landa's long-discredited sixteenth century recording of a Maya alphabet led to the epoch-making discovery in 1960 by Harvard University's Tatiana Proskouriakoff that the Maya inscriptions had historical context. The twenty-five years of Maya studies that followed have been a golden age of collaboration among linguists, epigraphers, art historians, archaeologists, and ethnologists, one fruit of which is the present volume.

The speculative theories about the Maya most broadly adopted in the 1950's and still quite evident in works published in the 1980's are discredited here by the evidence of the Maya themselves in their recorded history on the stelae, temples, palaces, tombs, and artworks of Mesoamerica. *The Blood of Kings* replaces a highly romanticized conjectural image of the Classic Lowland Maya civilization (fl. A.D. 250-900) as a peaceful, primitively agrarian theocracy attended by anonymous calendar priests who were learned in astronomy and lived in ceremonial centers to which the general populace was invited to witness spectacle and ritual with irrefutable evidence that the Maya lived in cities, had a highly advanced agricultural system, engaged in constant warfare among their city-states, and were ruled by dynastic kings who commissioned major artworks to memorialize themselves and ensure their place in history and who shed their own blood and that of their captives in bloodletting rituals that had dynastic, religious, and cosmic significance. Drawing upon varied sources in other fields in addition to those in their disciplines of art and art history, the authors provide a comprehensive guide to the Maya that is informative to neophytes, satisfying to amateur Maya enthusiasts and useful to students, teachers, and scholars in the field, and that leads to a realistic vision of a culture and civilization built upon the blood of its divine kings. This vision is never clearer than in the treatment of the edifices and artifacts beautifully and carefully photographed by Justin Kerr and reproduced in 122 color plates, the three hundred original drawings by Linda Schele, and the fifty other black-and-white illustrations.

In their introduction, the authors provide not only a clear sense of the divisions of Maya history and salient points about geography and agriculture but also an overview of the modern invention of the ancient Maya, the basics about the Maya calendar, a primer on the characteristics of Maya art, and a discussion of Maya gods and icons that all proceed from new readings of the Maya glyphs and iconography. The wealth of knowledge amassed since 1960 is amply evidenced and expertly used to explain the phenomenon that the Maya are only now emerging from a misty prehistory to become a people with a written history dating from 50 B.C., a history principally celebratory of such kings as Pacal of Palenque, Bird Jaguar of Yaxchilán, and Yax-Pac of Copán. The notion of kingship here espoused and explained is not that of a single Maya emperor but of kings who ruled concurrently in different parts of Mesoamerica.

The emphasis on blood is an important new element in the general understanding of the Maya: Their kings let blood on every important occasion in the life of the individual and community, a fact powerfully illustrated by the comparison of a sanitized nineteenth century drawing and a modern one of a detail from Yaxchilán Lintel 17. The former, by Annie Hunter, shows only the stylized head of a woman; the latter gives a fuller and more faithful rendering, complete with the rope which Lady Balam-Ix draws through a hole in her tongue in a blood sacrifice. In the lintel she is accompanied by her husband, King Bird Jaguar, he of the twenty captives, blood lord of Yaxchilán, who is about to let his own blood by piercing his male member on February 18, A.D. 752, on the occasion of the birth of his son and heir, Shield Jaguar II. Lady Balam-Ix does not undergo the additional pain her predecessor, Lady Xoc, had in lintel 24 (a work attributed to the affection-ately named Cookie Cutter Master), where the rope is pierced with thorns in a ritual bloodletting dated October 28, A.D. 709, in the reign of Shield Jaguar, Lady Xoc's husband. These are but two of scores of examples of what is now known of the gory written history of the Maya kings.

In Chapter 1, "The Royal Person," the authors argue that the surface ho-mogeneity of much Maya art spanning a thousand years can be attributed to the fiercely conservative traditions of the Maya and the consequently highly stylized elements of their very formal art. Moreover, the rituals in which the king was always a principal actor were important chiefly for what occurred and not for who the king was. In these rituals, spiritual beings (gods, ances-tors) came into bodily existence in the vessel of the king: The participants became the gods they portrayed, while the gods became flesh in the partici-pants. The costumes and regalia of the kings in these rituals, including ritual wars, were therefore also constant and became the conduits and instruments through which and in which sacred power was accrued.

The discussion of Maya kingship and the rites of accession persuasively underscores the notion that since public art and architecture sought to define the nature of political power and its role as a causal force in the cos-mos, the king (or sometimes queen) directed artistic production for the same purpose that he directed religious activity—to reinforce a cosmic worldview in which the king's divine right and spiritual and temporal legiti-macy were most emphatically shown to exist on the stelae of the highlands and the public buildings of the lowlands. One principal way of documenting the social and cosmic order was to demonstrate how, in seven formal stages, a human of royal blood was transformed into a king, sometimes over a lengthy period of time. Among those stages were rituals in which the king wore traditional regalia, manifested himself to the public, let blood, took captives in war, displayed the captives on scaffolding, sacrificed them by heart excision, and finally ascended the scaffolding to the throne. In this transformation into a complete king, the ruler nourished and sustained the gods through sacrifice and became the vehicle through which the sacred and the profane interacted.

The courtly life of the royal temples and cities, with royal families includ-ing about one hundred people, placed a major emphasis on literacy, as evidenced in the tales of the Monkey Scribes from the *Popol Vuh*, a frag-ment of the greater Maya *Book of the Dead*. These scribes, present at the creation, were instrumental in giving form to humans fashioned out of maize. It is thus a fitting return that one focus of courtly activity was ritual bloodletting to fertilize and regenerate nature itself, including the regenera-tion of life-sustaining vegetation, and that this ritual was both publicly done and publicly enshrined in the Maya "billboards" of the lowlands and stelae of the highlands by new generations of scribes.

Another element of royal life, the mystical Vision Quest, was achieved by massive blood loss (and the consequent release of endorphins); its aim was to call forth the gods, incarnate them in the visionary king, and thereby draw the power of the supernatural into the daily lives of the Maya. In one powerful representation from Yaxchilán Lintel 25, Lady Xoc ritually induces a hallucinatory vision of a giant-rearing serpent on the day of Shield Jaguar's accession, October 23, A.D. 681. Issuing from the mouth of the vision serpent is the warrior Jaguar, possibly an ancestor or possibly a variant of a Jaguar god.

Blood similarly played a major role in the ritual warfare and captive sacrifices in that the king's function was to capture enemies, while himself avoiding capture, and to sacrifice them (often after prolonged torture) to satisfy the gods' demands for the blood of others as well as the blood of royal persons. Frequently this ritual sacrifice of captives took place in the blood sport of the ball game.

Some of the more fascinating elements of Maya and all Mesoamerican architecture and culture are the ball court and the ball game. Referring to the *Popol Vuh*, the authors point out that the game had a crucial role in the mythology of death and sacrifice. They persuasively and successfully illustrate that the sacrificial death of the loser by decapitation depicted at Chichén-Itzá, for example, had the threefold purpose of publicly celebrating the capture of enemies, of offering blood to the gods to ensure continuing fertility of the natural world, and of extinguishing enemies of the kingdom. The Classic Maya used not only the ball courts but also the steep stairs of their pyramids for the ball game; evidence strongly suggests that the sacrificial captives, some already dead, some not, were trussed into ball shapes for the final play on the stairs, as at Yaxchilán and Tikal. So much for the national pastime of peace-loving farmers.

A pervasive sense of death is ubiquitous in Maya art, much of which is funerary and concerns the underwater hell of Maya mythology, Xibalba, a place of trial where one could outwit the lords of death, as did the Hero Twins of the *Popol Vuh*, and thus achieve an apotheosis, resurrection, or rebirth, or, if losing the contest of wit, face extinction. Much, in fact, of the mythology, funerary art, and provisions placed in tombs suggests that death was a journey the challenges of which were known. The death of a king held many meanings for the Maya: As a replacement of the gods among men he would rejoin the gods; as an ancestor he would continue to influence his own replacements; as an absent lord he would leave his people in great danger until the accession of a new king.

Kingship, as the authors suggest, was not only local and terrestrial but also cosmic in its origins, actions, and effects in the living cosmos of the Maya where the king was a transformer and sacred conduit of the gods. This cosmos, encoded in and now finally communicated through Maya art, consists of mystery as well as ancient logic and science and is a sacred world filled with awesome power and beauty that produced a civilization in which blood and sacrifice held society together, gave individual lives meaning beyond themselves, and in which the bases of the social order were royal genealogy and descent. Schele and Miller more than succeed in opening out that cosmos, its kings, and other rituals to the contemporary world in a unified, coherent exegesis of the symbolic art of the Maya. Their volume adds immensely to the public knowledge of a very public art, and it does so cogently and beautifully.

The one overwhelming question that haunts anthropologists, archaeologists, and historians still remains unanswered: What caused the Maya civilization to collapse and disappear as a major, organized civilization about the year 900 A.D.? The authors touch upon the several theories of volcanic cataclysm, wholesale captivity and slaughter, devastating plagues, and a combination of like events. This final mystery of the Maya, however, is one which even their artists and scribes did not survive to record. Nevertheless, the first written history of the Americas, a record spanning one thousand years, is at last becoming available in all of its fullness and is presently available in part in this extraordinary book.

John J. Conlon

Sources for Further Study

Ceramics Monthly. XXXIV, October, 1986, p. 77.
Choice. XXIV, November, 1986, p. 466.
Library Journal. CXI, October 1, 1986, p. 88.
The New York Review of Books. XXXIV, February 26, 1987, p. 3.
The New York Times. August 6, 1986, p. 19.
Publishers Weekly. CCXXX, July 4, 1986, p. 54.
Times Literary Supplement. September 26, 1986, p. 1075.

BLOOMERS ON THE LIFFEY
Eisegetical Readings of Joyce's *Ulysses*

Author: Paul van Caspel (1912-   )
Publisher: The Johns Hopkins University Press (Baltimore, Maryland). 281 pp.
    $27.50
Type of work: Literary criticism

Paul van Caspel, an experienced translator as well as a Joycean of long standing, examines the best-known translations and critical studies of James Joyce's Ulysses, *correcting many misapprehensions and misinterpretations while providing an engaging overview of Joyce's masterpiece*

James Joyce's epic novel *Ulysses* (1922) is clearly one of the most analyzed, annotated, criticized, translated, interpreted, and misinterpreted novels ever written. Paul van Caspel's selected references list implicitly attests this through its eight-and-a-half single-spaced pages. Paradoxically, this plethora of criticism has discouraged many general readers from even attempting their own reading of Joyce's masterpiece. Too often, the criticism has become mired in obscurities, biographical trivia, sociological underpinnings, and psychological subtexts. Fifty years worth of academic criticism has, in effect, shelved *Ulysses* for many who are attracted to Joyce's works but who never get much further than the lyricism of *Dubliners* (1914) or, if fortunate, *A Portrait of the Artist as a Young Man* (1916).

Van Caspel's *Bloomers on the Liffey: Eisegetical Readings of Joyce's "Ulysses"* is, accordingly, a work of critical housecleaning. Though he could be accused either of hubris or of being a literary reactionary by his bold intention to challenge even "untouchable" critics such as Richard M. Kain, William Y. Tindall, or Hugh Kenner, not to mention the sacrosanct reminiscences of Frank Budgen, van Caspel is actually quite sure of his position whenever he presents a new interpretation or argues for an emended version in one or another of the many translations of *Ulysses* which he considers here. His long experience and thorough grounding in English, French, German, Italian, Spanish, and Swedish (not to mention his native Dutch) allow him to move freely through the labyrinths many translators have made of Joyce's already often obscure but daedal prose.

The full title of van Caspel's book implicitly reveals its dual purpose, for this is a handbook for the general reader as well as a sourcebook for the experienced Joycean. The "Bloomers" of the title are not only the legion of critics who have sprung up in the wake of *Ulysses*'s publication but also the thousands of readers who have accompanied Joyce's protagonist Leopold Bloom on his day-long odyssey through Dublin. Significantly, while most criticism is exegetical, drawing from a work in order to analyze, van Caspel's is "eisegetical," guiding readers into Joyce's novel whether for the first or the fiftieth time. The distinction is not merely one of semantics. In a sense, van Caspel would like his readers to lay aside, temporarily at least, both preconceptions concerning Joyce's text and prejudices about its interpretation. He holds the obvious but often-forgotten view that Joyce wrote *Ulysses* primarily to create a work of art. Other levels of meaning, whether sociological, biographical, or structural, are, accordingly, secondary to this major purpose.

Primarily because the book is eisegetical in its intent, its organization is logical and taut. Van Caspel presents his analysis in eighteen episodes corresponding to those of Joyce's novel. Asking only that readers be familiar with *Ulysses*'s major scenes, he dutifully traces the critical tradition throughout and provides page references not only to the Random House edition (1961) but also to the recent synoptic text of Hans Walter Gabler (1984).

Van Caspel makes several varieties of observations. The first, of greatest interest to readers fascinated by Bloom, Stephen Dedalus, and the colorful personalities among whom they circulate, involves character delineation. A typical van Caspel synthesis draws upon Dedalus' interview with his superior Mr. Deasy in the "Nestor" episode. Van Caspel contrasts Dedalus' need for self-respect and discipline with the actual state of affairs presented in *Ulysses*, in episodes 1 and 2. Dedalus is ashamed of his teaching position, seems largely ineffective as a teacher, and never is seen teaching, merely hearing lessons or coaching Sargent in algebra. He accepts his small salary of £2.19 with embarrassment at Deasy's fussiness. (Significantly, Deasy's name is pronounced daisy.) He also receives Deasy's wrongheaded views on politics and history and promises to show Deasy's letter on foot-and-mouth disease to editor friends at the *Evening Telegraph* and the *Irish Homestead* for possible publication.

Van Caspel's examination of this sequence notes Dedalus' willingness to compromise with principle to maintain his relationship with Deasy, whom he does not respect, yet his unwillingness to kneel in prayer to a god in whom he does not believe in order to please his dying mother. Though Dedalus vows to resign his teaching position, he determines to do so by telegram rather than in person, and he still seeks out his editor friends, Crawford and Russell. Implicit in this sequence is the theme of compromise, not only personal but artistic as well.

Bloom is also willing to tolerate moral compromise. He too holds a letter for most of the day, received under the pseudonym Henry Flower from his mistress, Martha. Though Bloom destroys its envelope, he preserves the letter itself and uses it during the day to buoy and influence his mood. Van Caspel's careful eisegesis here serves to emphasize the opposing forces of spirituality and sensuality in Bloom's personality. Bloom suddenly finds himself in All Hallows; the church seems to him an ideal place for a lovers' rendezvous, but his worried self-question "Who is My Neighbour?" recalls the lawyer's question to Christ in Luke 10:29. Christ's answer is the parable of the Good Samaritan. Bloom feels hatred for overly devout "crawthumpers," even as he recalls Martha's proposal of a meeting "one Sunday after the rosary."

A second class of observations, combined with van Caspel's episode-by-episode analysis, concerns Joyce's use of personal, arcane, or obscure references. Van Caspel notes prevailing critical views as well as more obvious interpretations before providing the *lectio difficilior*, his own inevitably more obscure reading of the text. He does not allow himself to become mired in these obscurities, however, and usually presents quite solid arguments for the interpretations he prefers. For example, Bloom's recollection of Athos, the old dog Bloom's father had entrusted to his son in his suicide note, recalls Odysseus' dog Argos at the most obvious level. After this, one thinks of the mountain monastery in eastern Greece, also appropriate considering Bloom's prevailing mood, which is one of isolation from his family as well as his family line. Van Caspel suggests associations with the Alexandre Dumas, *père*, novels *Les Trois Mousquetaires* (1844; *The Three Musketeers*, 1846) and *Le Comte de Monte-Cristo* (1844-1845; *The Count of Monte-Cristo*, 1846). Their dates of publication made them likely reading for Bloom's father, and the second chapter of *A Portrait of the Artist as a Young Man* records that Dedalus had read them in the evenings in "ragged translation." Athos thus acquires a third, as well as an unobtrusive and noncontradictory, level of meaning: The first of Dumas' musketeers had lent his name to old Bloom's dog, and Dumas' works were in Joyce's thoughts as he wrote both *A Portrait of the Artist as a Young Man* and *Ulysses*.

The third and final variety of van Caspel's observations concerns the manifold problems inherent in translations of *Ulysses*. This is obviously the most original feature of van Caspel's study as well as the area of greatest interest to him, given his background as linguist and translator. Van Caspel runs some risk here of interrupting his readable and coherent commentary with discussions of interest primarily to scholars; nevertheless, language experimentation is an important part of *Ulysses*, and van Caspel aims at a grand synthesis in his own book: not only to clear away the contradictory and miscellaneous criticism which has fastened itself to Joyce's novel but also to write one critical text of interest to scholars and nonscholars alike. The remarks on translation, then, serve to bring van Caspel's book above the level of the *Ulysses* handbooks, far too many of which are filled with pedestrian and uninspired notes.

Some of van Caspel's remarks on language involve obvious but long-retained errors of mistranslation. For example, in the fourth episode Bloom glances at the letter he has received from his daughter, Milly. He recalls the silly "moustachecup, sham crown Derby" she had given him and remembers the amberoid necklace he had given her as well as "putting pieces of folded brown paper in the letterbox for her." From what follows, Bloom had clearly written and sent some amusing poems to his daughter when she was a young girl. It amuses him still to recall the incident. Van Caspel notes the mistaken use of the reflexive in both the French ("Elle s'envoyait des bouts de papier") and the older German translations ("steckte für sich Stücke gefalteten"). Both translations imply that Milly had sent herself the poems, obviously wrong given the context. Even in the midst of such corrections, however, van Caspel provides an insightful addendum. Much later, Molly recalls in her soliloquy that she had amused herself as a girl in Gibraltar by sending letters to herself "with bits of paper in them." Van Caspel surmises that Molly might have suggested sending the poems to Milly, who would have been about four years old at the time.

Passages such as those cited above reveal the reason van Caspel's book is so successful at the synthesis he intends. He never forgets that *Ulysses* is like a tapestry in which questions of language support and illuminate details of plot. Just as important, van Caspel does not belabor his arguments. His arrangement by Homeric episodes allows easy parallel reading of Joyce's text, while his bibliography provides enough critical material to satisfy all but the most insatiable Joyce scholar.

Robert J. Forman

Sources for Further Study

Choice. XXIV, November, 1986, p. 481.
Library Journal. CXI, July 16, 1986, p. 87.

BOSTON BOY

Author: Nat Hentoff (1925-   )
Publisher: Alfred A. Knopf (New York). 176 pp. $15.95
Type of work: Autobiography
Time: The 1930's and 1940's
Locale: Boston

A digressive, anecdotally rich memoir about Nat Hentoff's first twenty-eight years, the pre-New York City part of his life when he was initiated into the world of jazz and left-wing Democratic Party politics

> *Principal personages:*
> NAT HENTOFF, the author
> CY HENTOFF, his father
> LENA KATZENBERG HENTOFF, his mother
> FRANCES SWEENEY, a reforming newspaper publisher
> JAMES MICHAEL CURLEY, onetime Boston mayor

In person, Nat Hentoff is an unprepossessing man. Slight of build, a little disheveled, mildly absent-minded, a trifle out of focus, lacking rhetorical fire, he seems for all the world like a retirement-age Jewish academic. This indeed he might well have become, save for the jazz, the politics, and the contentiousness he absorbed in his youth in Boston. The Hentoff of this memoir is startlingly different from the personage one encounters on the current college-lecture circuit—wearily reasserting left-liberal strategies to combat Reaganism. For *Boston Boy* is a thoroughly lively, completely absorbing exploration of Hentoff's first twenty-eight years. Those who have followed his curiously meandering career since his arrival at *Down Beat* magazine will find this book an invaluable source of insights about Hentoff's well-known passions: First Amendment liberties, civil rights, the possibilities of the public schools, and music. Also, the book is certain to become a basic text for those interested in the rise of the "New York intellectuals" of the 1950's and 1960's, of which Hentoff was a dissident specimen. Thus, *Boston Boy* deserves comparison with such works as Irving Howe's *A Margin of Hope* (1982), an intellectual autobiography—covering roughly the same period—of *Dissent*'s famous editor. (William Phillips' *A Partisan View: Five Decades of the Literary Life*, 1984, is another title of relevance here, as is Alfred Kazin's *New York Jews*, 1978.) Best of all, however, *Boston Boy* is simply a good read—vivid, narratively interesting, lumpy with stories and portraits and provocations.

While *Boston Boy* indulges in the digressive, anecdotal, block-and-gap formlessness permitted the "memoir," it is possible to see the writing as an exploration of three themes. These include the forbidding allurements of Orthodox Judaism; the liberating power of jazz and jazz culture; and the greatness of inclusive, ethnically rich Democratic Party politics.

In his writings and public debates, Hentoff frequently proclaims his atheism. It is therefore a bit surprising to discover in *Boston Boy* a thorough-going preoccupation with Judaism. The book opens with this sentence: "I would not have known I had been excommunicated had it not been for the news reports." Hentoff proceeds to explain how, in 1982, a group of rabbis expelled him from the faith for his signature on a *New York Times* advertisement protesting Israel's invasion of Lebanon. Hentoff's tone is whimsical. He only wishes, he says, that he might have been present to state his case: "And I would have told them about my life as a heretic, a tradition I keep precisely because I am a Jew, and a tradition I was strengthened in because I came to know certain jazz musicians at so early an age that they, not unwittingly, were my chief rabbis for many years." Yet the reader also senses that Hentoff is relieved that the court had no real authority, for, as the reader learns, he wants very much to remain within the house of Judaism—if perhaps only in that special room reserved for God's protesting sons.

That Hentoff had something to rebel against is clear enough from the first third of the book. His childhood and adolescence were heavily patterned by exacting regimes: school; heder; shul; music lessons; paying jobs. His father was Orthodox but not fanatically so. Born in Russia, he emigrated to America to escape service in the army of the czar, only to find himself fighting in an American uniform in France. Painter, union organizer, haberdasher, Cy Hentoff lost his shop in the Great Depression and became a traveling salesman. Nat was expected to work—his first job was with a Yiddish-speaking fruit peddler—and achieve the highest marks in school.

While the boy accepted the demands of school and work, he grew increasingly resentful of religious disciplines. Upon reaching the seventh grade, he was admitted to Boston Latin School (BLS), the famous public institution that has produced such luminaries as Cotton Mather, Benjamin Franklin, Ralph Waldo Emerson, and Leonard Bernstein. The secular perspectives absorbed at BLS began to compete with those inculcated in Hebrew school. Hentoff disputed his Jewish teachers, was expelled, and barely made it through his bar mitzvah. It is telling that one of *Boston Boy*'s major symbols is Hentoff's memory of eating a huge salami sandwich in a busy public place on Yom Kippur, the Day of Atonement, the day of fasting. "This despicable twelve-year-old atheist is waiting to be stoned. Hoping to be stoned. But not hit," writes Hentoff sardonically. He returns over and over to this memory. It reminds him of his vocation as an oppositional figure, a dissenter.

Hentoff's posture, however, is decidedly that of loyal opposition. He writes whimsically, movingly, of a Sabbath morning in 1974 when, after thirty-six years, he returned again to a synogogue for religious services. The occasion was the bar mitzvah of his elder son. While Hentoff had not encouraged the boy to take this step, he was surprised by the awareness of significance it aroused. It was a moment when "I felt the ghosts of all whose name, in one spelling or another, I bear, whispering with satisfaction that they had not been abandoned." So Hentoff, while dissenting theologically from the orthodoxy of his Jewish neighborhood in Roxbury, has remained a cultural Jew. "I have not abandoned our people," he writes, "whatever *they* might think."

The "conversion" of Jewish youths to Afro-American jazz is hardly a new story. One thinks of George Gershwin, Benny Goodman, Gene Goldkette, Ben Pollack, and critic Leonard Feather. Indeed, the creative interaction of Jewish and African musical traditions is a fascinating chapter in American cultural history. Hentoff's memoir sheds interesting light on this process. He recalls a summer morning in his tenth year when he walked past a music store on Washington Street. A speaker above the door broadcast loudly the newest hits of the big bands of the day.

> I was suddenly stopped by a fierce wailing of brass and reeds, a surging, pulsing cry of yearning that made me cry out too. I'd never before yelled in public; it was not something a Boston boy, especially a Boston Jewish boy wandering outside the ghetto, could ever satisfactorily explain to one of *them*. But I didn't care. All I cared about were those sounds.

The passion grew. He collected records, went to Sunday jam sessions at the Ken Club, began speaking to the jazzmen, and took them on as "foster fathers." Hentoff admired them and emulated them "because they had so much life in them by contrast with practically all the other adults I knew." The only thing he really cherished in Jewish liturgical practice was the sad, fierce melismatic singing of the hazan, the cantor, who, as he once explained to Charles Mingus, is the man whose soul carries in it the "Jewish blues," thousands of years old. In jazz, Hentoff found a parallel blues tradition elaborated and magnified.

Hentoff's musical preoccupations did not challenge his school career at first, but they did awaken in him a taste for the bohemian and avant-garde that would soon have major consequences for his life path. Meanwhile, a fateful decision about college was taken. At Boston Latin, Hentoff had conceived the notion that Greek should be his academic avenue. He therefore applied only to Boston College, home of a model program in classical studies. It did not occur to Hentoff that the Jesuits might have a Jewish quota. They did, and he did not gain admission. He thus was forced to opt for the nonprestigious, non-Jewish, working-class environment of another Boston school, Northeastern University, which proved to be a vital experience in forming Hentoff's well-known populism.

Also, near the Northeastern campus was the Savoy Café, a jazz club on the edge of a black ghetto, where intellectualism, "race-mixing," and legendary music held sway. Nat Hentoff became a fixture of the Savoy, and one of the best parts of *Boston Boy* is his account of musical, racial, and marital adventures in and around the Savoy. Hentoff met Miriam Fonda Sargent, his first wife, at the Savoy. More important (the marriage only lasted eight months), he became thoroughly immersed in the jazz world, befriending such figures as Sidney Bechet, Bunk Johnson, Jo Jones, Rex Stewart, Duke Ellington, and Lester Young.

At the same time, Hentoff was gaining notice at Northeastern because of his editorship of the *Northeastern News*. He worked to transform the paper from a university news sheet to a muckraking, investigative, irreverent witness. Hentoff brought a mature talent to the task, for at the age of fifteen, he had gone to work as a reporter for the *Boston City Reporter*, a crusading paper owned and edited by Frances Sweeney. A Roman Catholic in the Dorothy Day reform tradition, Sweeney tried to expose corruption in municipal and state government as well as call the Catholic Church to a higher standard of conduct. She was particularly upset by the failure of William Cardinal O'Connell to censure anti-Semitism among the faithful, especially the brand of anti-Jewish rhetoric purveyed by the infamous Father Charles Coughlin. Hentoff was devastated by the sudden death of Sweeney in 1944; *Boston Boy* is dedicated to her.

Sweeney's reformist politics tell the reader much about Hentoff's subsequent stances. Like Sweeney, he was captivated with Franklin Delano Roosevelt ("In our ward, he took ninety-six percent or more of the vote every time"). He hewed a left-center course, buoyed by the promise of coalition building among like-minded progressives. His early distrust of Jewish religious sectarianism created a distaste for vanguard, elitist structures of all sorts. When he was seventeen, he read Arthur Koestler's *Darkness at Noon*, which confirmed his anti-Stalinism and awakened his interest in the rights of dissenters. Over the years, he has displayed a surprising admiration for the perspectives of social Catholicism. Indeed, Hentoff's most recent pronouncements have been influenced by and supportive of the statements of American Catholic bishops on the nation's economy. Further, he has angered innumerable feminists and leftists by defending in the pages of *The Village Voice* the prolife antiabortion perspectives of Joseph Cardinal Bernardin.

There will surely be further installments in Hentoff's autobiography, and one trusts that they will be as stimulating as *Boston Boy*. No doubt they will prove controversial. Many of the New York intellectuals who traveled with Hentoff in the late 1950's and early 1960's have become quite conservative in recent years. Hentoff's stay-the-course posture will certainly infuriate writers in the *Commentary* orbit. To be sure, there are many things about Hentoff that show why it is that liberalism could have fallen on such bad times.

Perhaps the most conspicuous thing about Hentoff's intellectual posture is that it presupposes strong conserving cultural structures against which the dissenter can react. What has occurred in the postwar period, however, is the radical weakening of all such structures. Neither mainline churches nor mainline Jewish organizations hold and form individuals as they once did. As Robert Bellah has brilliantly shown in *Habits of the Heart* (1985), Americans are deeply tentative about commitments to groups and are increasingly drawn into "life-style enclaves" where many collective norms can be held at arm's length.

In this cultural context, Hentoff's affectionate rejection of Judaism seems an inappropriate response to the tradition that nourished him. If he finally affirms that tradition, then he is obliged to work for its revitalization. The crisis of the hour forbids any noncommittal standing on the sidelines. Hentoff simply needs to face the historic truth about liberalism; namely, that it came into existence at a time when authoritative communities were strong, and it is locked in a historic dance with these communities. When these communities begin to wane, the liberal's *raison d'être* disappears. Some readers will properly admire the rabbis who were willing to excommunicate Hentoff: At least they were expressing concern for the communities that gave Hentoff so much against which to protest. In their secret hearts, these rabbis might fancy having the luxury of existing in a dissident, critical, oppositional zone outside the synagogue and yeshiva. What perhaps prevents them from making this move is the wisdom that, for all their viciousness, communities are the proper setting for the rearing of fully moral human beings. So they labor on in the dreary work of community building.

In the end, one comes to admire the choice of Nick Hentoff, Nat's son, who—to his father's amazement—returns to organized Judaism after seeing *Fiddler on the Roof*. The fact that Nat did not try to hinder or resist his son certainly proves that his liberalism has ceased to mean as much to him as he pretends. "Why not then go the full way?" one might want to ask. If mere embarrassment and the desire to maintain image are what prevents Hentoff from actively serving the cause of historic Judaism, then one must wonder if Hentoff's liberalism has not degenerated into quailing and preciosity.

Leslie E. Gerber

Sources for Further Study

Booklist. LXXXII, April 15, 1986, p. 1175.
Boston Magazine. LXXVII, December, 1985, p. 22.
Christian Science Monitor. LXXVIII, May 2, 1986, p. B1.
Kirkus Reviews. LIV, March 1, 1986, p. 368.
Library Journal. CXI, March 15, 1986, p. 64.
New Leader. LXIX, June 16, 1986, p. 17.

The New Republic. CXCIV, June 16, 1986, p. 41.
The New York Times Book Review. XCI, April 27, 1986, p. 34.
Publishers Weekly. CCXXIX, February 21, 1986, p. 160.
Washington Post Book World. XVI, April 20, 1986, p. 9.

THE BUILDING

Author: Thomas Glynn (1935-   )
Publisher: Alfred A. Knopf (New York). 371 pp. $18.95
Type of work: Novel
Time: The 1980's
Locale: Brooklyn, New York

A surrealistic novel consisting of a series of episodes that together form a montage of all that is depraved and corrupt in the modern world

> *Principal characters:*
> LOWELL, the protagonist, whose desire it is to fix broken buildings
> SANCHEZ, an official at Housing, Preservation, and Development (H.P.D.), who hires Lowell
> HECTOR, an employee at H.P.D., who is confined to a wheelchair, possibly as a result of the Vietnam War

In the preface to his novel *The Building*, Thomas Glynn quotes a Navajo "House Blessing":

> May it be delightful my house,
> From my head may it be delightful,
> To my feet may it be delightful,
> Where I lie may it be delightful,
> All above me may it be delightful,
> All around me may it be delightful.

Everything in the novel that follows this poem, however, is in utter contradiction to it. The Building itself, constructed as a multiple dwelling place, is a surreal mix of the once magnificent and the immediately grotesque, built at a time in history when floors were parqueted and doors were made of real oak, when spacious lobbies had marble floors and gold-leaf ceilings and when individual apartments contained room enough for families to grow, for children to be born and mature, for parents to work and retire in a sufficient allotment not only of space but also of hope and fulfillment of the American Dream. The dream, however, has become a nightmare. The courtyard of the Building now contains garbage to the height of the first floor. The lobby, dark and dank, is brown from blood from muggings and cluttered with marble that has been broken by sledgehammers. Elevators do not work. On the doors that still stand are rivets of dozens of locks that inhabitants have used to try to protect themselves at night. Rivers, following the line of pipes, run through the apartments. Electrical storms cause instant fires. Walls ooze blood or are smeared with excrement; apartments are filled with roaches, rats, moths, vermin of all description; the roof has holes and the chimney is crumbling.

The Building is filled with people, described in such abundant detail that they become figures larger than life, like characters in myth. There is

Steckler, who is supercharging a Chevy Nova in his apartment; Cuzz, a part-time mugger and drug addict; Mother Ozmoz, whose gestation period is eight months and who produces children back to back, three children every two years. There is an African dictator who lives in the Building with ten wives, his exalted pillow bearer, and a man who intones the hour every hour. There is the artist Stern, who paints only Madonnas using naked models, who are usually numbed by cold and hunger. There are two muggers named Visa and MasterCharge; the Wilson sisters, former acrobatic dancers who can still tie themselves into a knot; a man who worships roaches and a superintendent who worships wood; and a grossly overweight female paraplegic who mistakes rape for love.

These characters are only a few of the many who are introduced early in the novel. The chapters in this first section are primarily self-contained character sketches; consequently, no sustained narrative line emerges. Rather, recurring image patterns, like that of fire and various kinds of religious worship, provide necessary unifying elements and build toward the apocalyptic conclusion. Dwarf and Lunatic, for example, at various places in the novel, imagine fire and flames engulfing the Building as walls collapse and people shout and cry as they attempt to escape. A veritable microcosm of the city of New York—which, in turn, is a microcosm of the world—the Building is peopled with humans of every race and kind, who worship spirits, both holy and demonic, in as many diverse ways as there are religions being practiced.

The first half of the novel concludes with an epiphany that provides a kind of conclusion. The owner of the Building has become convinced by one of the tenants that millions of tiny insects are gnawing at the Building, chewing through pipes and eating insulation, and that larger animals are eating windowsills and short-circuiting wires, leaving excrement in empty apartments, and bringing down plaster from ceilings. The owner hires an exterminator, who goes from apartment to apartment in a kind of magic incantation shouting out his presence, ringing bells, and warning of danger. As he goes, he spreads a brown liquid, driving most of the apartment dwellers from the Building. Rather than destroy the pests, however, the exterminator himself is destroyed. Hosts of fireflies descend upon him, surrounding him with pure light, and they carry him off in a ball of white.

In chapter 22, Glynn introduces a protagonist of sorts—an idealist named Lowell—and narrative continuity begins, since Lowell functions, in some way, in almost every episode subsequent to his first appearance. This continuity of plot line is surprising; it is almost as if the novel begins again with a line of action that will take it to a different conclusion—which, indeed, it does.

Lowell, who has always thought of himself as a social worker, has a degree in English and philosophy, and is a weight lifter on the scale of an Olympic athlete. Coming out of an interlude of madness, Lowell decides with the zeal of a monomaniac that he will fix broken buildings and that he will hire himself out to a city agency that fixes such buildings. He goes to the department of Housing, Preservation, and Development (H.P.D.), which turns out to be itself a microcosm of Brooklyn. Hector, an employee there, explains to Lowell: "We got wops, spades, spics, kikes, chinks, all on quota, everything on quota. . . . We got welfare, hopheads, junkies, boozers, perverts, ex-cons. We got it all, and it's all on quota because they say we gotta hire minorities and so we do, but this whole . . . city is one big minority. They're ain't no . . . majority anymore." Hector continues to liken H.P.D. to Brooklyn, declaring that Brooklyn is a fantasy, a subterfuge, and that Brooklyn "collects those who are about to be flushed down the toilet— loonies, weirdos, dingbats, crazies, psychopaths."

Though Glynn's style clearly places him in a postmodernist mode with such writers as Günter Grass, William S. Burroughs, Thomas Pynchon, Gabriel García Márquez, and such earlier writers as Jorge Luis Borges and Franz Kafka, to the extent that Glynn's absurd black humor is a mirror of his sense of moral outrage, he is most like Joseph Conrad. Indeed, toward the end of the novel, Glynn introduces a man named Kurtz, who sports a dark, precise beard and a navy P-jacket and who resembles his namesake in Joseph Conrad's *Heart of Darkness*, a story that reverberates with horror. Kurtz places African statues on platforms nailed to the wall of his apartment. He spends most of his time in the cellar digging or moving objects around. MasterCharge tells Lowell that Kurtz is crazy, that in the cellar he is rolling in the dirt and dancing with natives.

Following Kurtz's appearance, Lowell thinks that someone or something must set bounds to the carnage, the violence, and the horror. He thinks that limits must be set on the kinds of sacrilege that can be committed. He believes that if there is no God in Heaven, then one will have to be invented to punish those who find new varieties of sacrilege to commit.

The last chapter of the novel documents the destruction by fire of the Building. The fire is started by arsonists hired to torch it for the owner, who believes that he can thus redeem the Building for back taxes. As the fire gathers strength and burns, making its way into all parts of the Building, people stream out through the exits or jump from windows or off the roof. Some are caught inside and burn to death. Others reach the safety of the street. Finally, as the entire Building fills with smoke and fire, "all fears, all dreams, all hopes, burn, melt, explode, and the Building, as if in a dance, turns slowly, almost pirouettes, and falls."

One of the inhabitants of the building is a writer. When the fire reaches his apartment, he crumples up the pages of his manuscript and then throws them one by one at the flames hoping to extinguish the fire or "at the very least . . . cause a parting in the fire, like that in the Red Sea, so the writer can make his/her escape." The extent of the horror becomes clear as Glynn extends his metaphor to include not only Brooklyn but also all of New York and then the entire world. Nothing, Glynn seems to be saying, not even art, can help. Man is absurdly whirling his way toward his ultimate destruction.

Mary Rohrberger

Sources for Further Study

Booklist. LXXXII, November 15, 1985, p. 450.
Kirkus Reviews. LIII, November 15, 1985, p. 1207.
Library Journal. CXI, January, 1986, p. 101.
The New York Times Book Review. XCI, January 26, 1986, p. 12.
Publishers Weekly. CCXXVIII, November 1, 1985, p. 56.
Time. CXXVI, December 30, 1985, p. 76.

BUT DO BLONDES PREFER GENTLEMEN?
Homage to Qwert Yuiop and Other Writings

Author: Anthony Burgess (1917-   )
Publisher: McGraw-Hill Book Company (New York). 589 pp. $24.95
Type of work: Essays and reviews

In this collection, a professional man of letters considers primarily works and issues of literary scholarship, but also language, music, and contemporary culture in the widest sense

This volume by Anthony Burgess consists of very nearly two hundred short essays, or short reviews of other writers' books, published in several journals (notably the *Times Literary Supplement*, *The New York Times*, and the *Observer*) over a period of some seven years. Naturally, the main impression they make is of variety. Subjects often repeated include the problems of biography, attitudes toward religion, the utility of dictionaries, and the relation between literature and popular fiction, but a reader dipping into the volume at random may find himself faced with thoughts on Canada, on syphilis, on dialectology, or any one of literally scores of apparently unrelated topics. What, one must ask, is the point of producing such a volume? What also is the point of reading it—for in doing so, one is reading collectively works meant to be read singly and thus going against the author's prime intention at the moment of composition.

To the first question Burgess himself gives a kind of answer, which is self-justification, or as he puts it, "writer's guilt." Writers are supposed to be lazy, he points out. People think that *he* is lazy. This book proves that even between novels he has been doing something. Beneath this reason, one feels, there lies a less cynical one, which is (as Burgess also points out) that writing a short essay to a set length on a topic set by someone else, such as a literary editor, is a form of discipline. It makes the writer subordinate his personality to a clear task, and it tells him virtually immediately whether he has succeeded or failed. Discipline is a quality by which Burgess sets great store, and this collection can be seen, in a way, as a sort of "sonnet-cycle"— a sequence of works each of them within clear and unalterable formal bounds. As with a sonnet-cycle, too, the reader has the option of reading singly or collectively. To read one or two sonnets or essays is normal and legitimate; to read many together creates a different experience, predominantly that of recognizing emotional or thematic unity beneath apparent diversity. This latter point is perhaps the strongest reason for considering Burgess' pieces together.

As the volume's title suggests, one of Burgess' continuing preoccupations is male-female relations and the developing theory of feminism. His attitude is, to say the least, a thoroughly old-fashioned one. Few modern thinkers, male or female, would, for example, agree with his declaration that for him to offer his seat to a woman on a bus or the tube train is a reaction "wholly biological in origin," which he should not apologize for because it is "built into my glands." His reaction, as many would point out to him, cannot be biological because, if it were, most other men would share it, which they very clearly do not. Burgess' is in fact a cultural reaction, which may indeed be unalterable but nevertheless was learned. It is clear that Burgess means no harm by his courtesy. Still, courtesy clearly if benevolently implies that a woman is not a man's equal but needs to be cared for. Burgess titles his opening article "Grunts from a Sexist Pig"; he means it ironically, but there can be little doubt that "sexist" is what he indeed is.

What, however, does "sexist" mean? This is exactly the kind of question that fascinates Burgess, and one on which he has strong views. The latest definition of sexist, given by the *Oxford English Dictionary Supplement*, volume 4 (1986), is "one who advocates sexism," while sexism itself is defined as "the assumption that one sex is superior to the other" and, further, "conformity with the traditional stereotyping of social roles on the basis of sex"—as, for example, deciding who should stand or sit. The dictionary seems to have defined a broad attitude both precisely and fairly. Against that, Burgess believes that in many mouths sexist has become a meaningless insult directed against a nonmember of one's own faction, as with so many political terms, one being the term "fascist." He may, then, be a sexist in the dictionary sense of the term, but not in the factionalist sense. The underlying question is whether the meaning of a word is conferred by authority or by usage or, to put it another way—since even the authority of the *Oxford English Dictionary* rests entirely on the codification of past usage—whether words are allowed to change their meaning. Here Burgess betrays interesting ambivalence.

To begin with, Burgess is well aware that the meaning of a word always changes, as does its form and pronunciation. In one of his most interesting pieces, "Firetalk," which deals with the problems Burgess encountered creating an imaginary prehistoric language for the film *Quest for Fire*, he sets out across the page a sequence of grammatical paradigms in five dead languages from Gothic to Sanskrit, making the point that though they appear different all derive from one common ancestral form. If word usage has undergone change from pre-Sanskrit periods, though, why stop now? Yet Burgess opposes change of word meaning in modern English, associating one idiom after another with laziness, aggression, vagueness, or intellectual vice. He cites a number of examples. "Virago" is a rather foolish name for a women's publisher, he says, because "virago," as every dictionary states, means a scold, a shrew. Sentences such as "Hopefully I'll hear from you on Monday" fill him with horror, he asserts (even though he is guilty of such misuse himself) because "hopefully" implied, not very long ago, an emotional state and could never be used as a stand-in for "I hope that." This latter idiom is a borrowing from the German *hoffentlich* and should be resisted. "Gay" should mean cheerful, never homosexual; "chauvinistic" should apply only to people who are excessively patriotic; "pejorative" should not be pronounced with stress on the second syllable, peJORative, but with it on the first, PEjorative. Burgess, in a phrase, is linguistically as well as culturally intensely conservative.

This, though, is a matter of choice and even of reason, and not (as too many readers may prejudicially assume) of mere ingrained lack of courage or of imagination. To return to the subject of feminism, Burgess' recurrent point is not that relations between men and women should remain as they were when he grew up (which would be the viewpoint of a merely thoughtless conservative), but that in the attempts to change such relations feminists too often abandon fact in favor of dogma—and this, he believes, is in the long run invariably disastrous. Students of English dialect, he notes, have found that men are more reliable informants than women because women tend to give the answers they regard as "correct." Their intentions are good, but they prevent scholars from finding out what people actually say, and this is information which is disappearing all the time. By contrast, he praises Kingsley Amis' misogynist novel *Stanley and the Women* (1984), not for its misogyny but for the total accuracy of its dialogue; this quality, he thinks, is closely related to the author's immunity to ambition, fashion, and dogma of any kind.

Clearly, Burgess worships fact in proportion as he distrusts theory. What did they actually *say*? is a repeated question. Did Christ on the Cross say "*Eli, Eli, lama sabacthani*" (Lord, Lord, why hast thou forsaken me") or "*Elie, elie*" ("O Sun, O Sun, why. . .)? Could Christ have been a sun worshiper? Burgess seems to think this question almost less important than the one from which it springs, which is whether Christ might have used the Greek word *helios* in the vocative case and "in its demotic unaspirated form," that is, without the initial "h." Similarly, did Christ say (again in Greek) that it was as easy for a rich man to enter the kingdom of Heaven as for a camel (*kamelon*) to pass through the eye of a needle? Or did he say as for a rope (*kamilon*)? It could even have been an early mishearing. Nevertheless, Burgess says, when he tried to work these questions into a television film on Christ, the fact, the linguistic datum, was not considered "cinematic" enough. The modern world, Burgess implies, rejects facts, and words, and is, accordingly, at the mercy of both. It is a striking and novel point of view.

Yet as a direct result of his theory-rejecting stance, Burgess proves very hard to categorize. He is ambivalent over language change, at once conservative and up-to-date. His general approach, as described above, could be said to be characteristically English in its pragmatism, yet Burgess observes that his books sell better in France than in Great Britain or the United

States, shows a rare familiarity with French and Italian language and literature, and at one point claims for himself the highly unpragmatic title of structuralist. In the same way, many of his remarks sound almost irritatingly academic—demotic vocatives, for example, or "thetatismus"—but Burgess shows frequent and open contempt for the academic system, with its students who seek only simple solutions and its professors who aim only for tenure. Burgess is anti-Soviet but also anti-American, a Catholic but also a freethinker, a writer famous for his Dystopian work who nevertheless proclaims that science fiction is dull—the list of (apparent) contradictions stretches out almost perversely. One of the most interesting of these, perhaps, is Burgess' uncertainty as to what kind of writer he himself is. Are his works "literary" or not?

Actually, Burgess thinks that this question should not be asked. Living writers, he argues, should not be studied. His stance on the whole, however, is deeply critical of the nonliterature which he believes is taking over the Western world, dismissing for example, John le Carré's spy stories as "best-selling deadweights," and being even ruder about better-known authors. Nevertheless, he admits with apparently inconsistent honesty, this kind of writing is not the cynical trick it seems. A uniqueness of *some* kind is needed, and no one knows exactly what it is: sheer information? raw narrative strength? a yang of adventure to go with a yin of philosophy? Furthermore, Burgess muses, he himself does not know why his one major best-seller, *A Clockwork Orange* (1962), reached that status. His agent was reluctant even to send it in.

But Do Blondes Prefer Gentlemen? Homage to Qwert Yuiop and Other Writings is continually fascinating, quirky, unpredictable. It is at its best, perhaps, when dealing with close analysis of style—the account of F. Scott Fitzgerald's written-to-order magazine fiction is excellent on what remained individual even within the format of *The Saturday Evening Post*—or with subtle elucidation of cultural stereotypes, as over the image of the blonde in American society. Sometimes his analysis is open to academic question. Burgess may be right in thinking that the English language is, or was once, "a kind of creole," but he is surely wrong in believing that its mixed formations resulted from contact between Normans and Anglo-Saxons. Burgess, however, has a second shot at the same topic in another review and succeeds in coming closer to the mark with the suggestion that the cause was contact between Scandinavians and Anglo-Saxons (with Normans only as an added confusion). This kind of self-correcting accuracy is typical Burgess and grows naturally from his devotion to fact. *But Do Blondes Prefer Gentlemen?* is full of facts, and everyone can learn something from it. It appears also as the work of an immensely subtle, and still unwearied, defender of an intellectual tradition felt to be increasingly under threat.

T. A. Shippey

Sources for Further Study

American Spectator. XIX, March, 1986, p. 43.
Booklist. LXXXII, March 1, 1986, p. 940.
The Guardian Weekly. CXXXIV, May 4, 1986, p. 18.
Kirkus Reviews. LIV, February 1, 1986, p. 178.
Library Journal. CXI, March 15, 1986, p. 69.
National Review. XXXVIII, July 18, 1986, p. 61.
The New York Times Book Review. XCI, March 30, 1986, p. 19.
Publishers Weekly. CCXXIX, January 24, 1986, p. 66.
Washington Post Book World. XVI, March 9, 1986, p. 1.

CAPTAIN KIDD AND THE WAR AGAINST THE PIRATES

Author: Robert C. Ritchie (1938-   )
Publisher: Harvard University Press (Cambridge, Massachusetts). Illustrated.
  306 pp. $20.00
Type of work: Biography and history
Time: The end of the seventeenth century
Locale: The Caribbean, New York, England, and the Indian Ocean

An absorbing account of the brief and violent career of England's most famous pirate, with a background picture of the economic, social, and political forces which contributed to the rise and the decline of seventeenth century piracy

> *Principal personages:*
> WILLIAM KIDD, a pirate captain
> BENJAMIN FLETCHER, a corrupt English governor of New York
> RICHARD COOTE, EARL OF BELLOMONT,
> SIR EDWARD HARRISON, DUKE OF SHREWSBURY, and
> JOHN, LORD SOMERS, sponsors of Kidd
> ROBERT CULLIFORD, a pirate captain

Robert C. Ritchie's account of the brief and violent career of Captain William Kidd, the most famous (or notorious) pirate of the seventeenth century, separates him largely from the aura of romantic legend which attached to Kidd's name after his death. There are gaps in the story because Kidd and most of the men who sailed and fought for or against him—and survived—were men of action and limited education who had either no interest in or ability at keeping orderly records of their actions and their lives. After Kidd's capture he wrote about himself and what he had done, but he was trying then to save his neck and thus his writing is suspect. In his desperation, he found it easy to lie or to claim that others had lied about or double-crossed him.

Piracy had been practiced for centuries before Kidd took it up. Greek and Roman historians reported it. Viking piracy flourished in the North Atlantic during the Middle Ages. At the end of the seventeenth century, William Kidd was only one among many whose depredations endangered or snuffed out the lives of sailors, ship passengers, and slaves; who stole cargoes; and who burned or sank ships belonging to merchant companies in Europe, the Americas, Asia, and Africa.

Piracy falls into three categories. These include officially sanctioned piracy, commercial piracy, and marauding.

Sir Francis Drake's famed round-the-world voyage from 1577 to 1579, which included attacks on Spanish ships, was actually a pirate voyage, but he shared his rich plunder with Queen Elizabeth, and she honored him as an English patriot. Still, to the Spanish emperor he was a pirate. Robert Cecil, Earl of Salisbury and secretary to both Elizabeth and James I, financed Richard Gifford's piracy and received part of the spoils.

Piracy played a part in the early development of the empires of Great

Britain, France, and the Netherlands as they followed in the wake of the earlier colonizers, Spain and Portugal. Since Spain could not guard all of its scattered territory in the New World, the English, French, and Dutch grabbed what they could get in the West Indies. Pirates roamed the Caribbean, usually avoiding the well-armed navy ships but attacking merchant ships, which lacked the firepower to protect themselves. The defeated ships were sometimes seized as prizes but were often destroyed after having been plundered.

The officially sanctioned pirates were dignified by the name privateers, and supposedly they were patriotically aiding their countries by privately supporting the hard-pressed navies during periods of war. Attacking merchant ships and removing their cargoes of varied goods and treasures could weaken an enemy country's economy and hasten the end of a war. After peace had been achieved, though, many of the pirates were unwilling to give up actions which had produced excitement, adventure, and sometimes rich rewards. They had grown skillful, bloodthirsty, and greedy, and they turned to wholesale marauding.

The marauders first appeared in the Mediterranean about 1570. Later they cruised the Caribbean, around the southern tip of Africa, and into the Indian Ocean. Ritchie remarks that they "wandered the seas, dividing and coalescing like amoebas."

Almost nothing is known of the life of William Kidd before he began his career of piracy, which lasted a little more than a decade and ended with his hanging in London in 1701. According to tradition, he was born in Greenock, Scotland, about 1645, into the family of a Presbyterian minister. When he first appeared in records he was a buccaneer in the Caribbean. A short time later, he was captain of the *Blessed William* (for the British king William of Orange), a twenty-gun ship renamed after having been stolen from the French members of a French-English crew by the English sailors, and serving as a privateer under orders from Captain Thomas Hewetson of the Royal Navy ship *Lion*.

Captain Kidd's shift from privateering to marauding occurred during a time of political turmoil and the early economic and geographic development of England from a small island nation into a far-ranging and rich empire. England and France were at war, and the ships of the two nations often engaged in battles as they sailed to and from the New and the Old World. Some attacks were made on ships anchored in harbors while part of their crews were ashore, leaving the ships nearly defenseless either to fight or to flee. Both England and France were establishing colonies on Caribbean islands and on mainland America. The rapidly developing English navy needed increasing numbers of ships and men for the sea wars. Private ships frequently supplemented those of the regular navy in the warfare. Often sailors from either merchant or pirate ships were impressed into naval service after losses from battle, accidents, or disease.

Kidd fought successfully against several French ships in the Caribbean, but his men stole the *Blessed William* while he was ashore at Nevis. Then, given a new ship, the *Antigua*, by Christopher Codrington, governor of Antigua, Kidd sailed for New York and in 1690 aided the new governor there, Colonel Henry Sloughter, in capturing the city following an insurrection.

In 1691, in New York, Kidd married a rich widow, and for a time he settled down as a peaceful burgher, fathering two daughters. The lure of adventure and profit was too strong to resist, though, and in 1695 he set sail in the *Antigua* for London to seek a royal commission as a privateer.

Backed by several wealthy English partners and armed with a commission both to prey on enemy merchantmen and to hunt pirates, Kidd in 1696 sailed in a new ship, the *Adventure Galley*, in search of possible rich rewards. First, however, he returned to New York to add men to a scanty crew and to visit his family. Then he headed for the Indian Ocean, where pirates had been preying on merchants.

Though Kidd's mission was to hunt pirates, he himself turned to piracy after rounding the horn of Africa. Short on supplies, plagued by an unhappy crew (some because they had volunteered for privateering, not piracy), and increasingly worried about his "leaky and rotten" ship, Kidd stopped a small merchantman, seized food and money, and abducted its captain to guide him and a Portuguese sailor to serve as a "linguistor," or translator.

Desperately needing water, Kidd sailed into the Indian port of Carnor where, unfortunately for him, his piracy was suspected by two inquiring and observant East India Company visitors to his ship. Also, some of Kidd's men deserted and betrayed him by informing on him. Loyalty to a leader did not rank high among pirates.

After a voyage of many months and thousands of miles, Kidd's men had grown restive. Though they had volunteered to serve on a "no-prey, no-pay" basis, they were tired of waiting for the riches of which they had dreamed. A battle with a Portuguese ship had ended with the wounding of several of Kidd's men and with his flight when a large rescue ship hove in sight. His men urged an attack on a ship belonging to the East India Company, but he persuaded them against it. Frustration, misery, and anger built up until the ship's gunner, William Moore, challenged Kidd's authority, and Kidd killed him by smashing his head with a wooden bucket. Kidd had made a fatal mistake, but it would be some time before he would pay for it.

At last piracy began to succeed for Kidd when he captured or robbed several ships and sold their cargoes or distributed some of their goods among his men as their shares of the booty. When he reached Saint Marie, a pirate settlement on an island near Madagascar, his deteriorating *Adventure Galley* was accompanied by two of his prizes. On Saint Marie, Kidd could buy supplies and plan future actions, and his men could entertain themselves with drinking, slave women, gambling, fighting, and even killing.

Temporarily harboring also on Saint Marie was Robert Culliford, a former shipmate of Kidd who was now a pirate captain. When he left the island he took with him most of Kidd's disgruntled crew. Kidd was left with only a few men, boys, and slaves. It was time, he decided now, to give up pirating and concoct a plausible story to tell when he reached an American port and later England. He would omit his intended and his actual piracy, and he would blame his men for having turned against and deserted him. He and the few men who remained with him might avoid hanging if they could convince their hearers.

There was one serious flaw in his plan. The rotting *Adventure Galley* had been burned. Kidd would have to use one of his captured ships, originally the *Quedah Merchant* but now named the *Adventure Prize*. The cumbersome ship had an easily recognizable Indian structure, and it might be very difficult to explain convincingly why he was sailing it.

Kidd had set out for the Indian Ocean in 1696; now two years later he was beginning his return voyage. He did not know that he was coming back from the East at a time when such freebooting as he had indulged in was much less likely to be forgiven than formerly. The moral climate had altered. He had stirred the anger of the East India Company by his lawlessness. With the geographical, political, and mercantile development of what would soon become (in 1707) the British Empire, there had come an increased respect for law, order, and discipline. Piracy was a symbol of disorder; it must be stopped. Kidd was now not only the most notorious pirate, but he had also come, as Ritchie says, "to symbolize all pirates." The search was on for him. A cat-and-mouse game would be played, with Kidd dodging or hiding wherever he could to escape capture or destruction.

How Kidd managed the long, difficult, and dangerous voyage from the East to the West Indies is not known. At the first of several stops in the Caribbean, he learned the frightening news that the English government, at the urging of the East India Company, had declared him a pirate and had ordered "an all-out manhunt."

On the Spanish island of Hispaniola, Kidd bought a sloop, the *Saint Antonio*, from a trader who took over (and later burned) the unwieldy *Quedah Merchant*. As Kidd moved north along the Atlantic coast, rumors spread about the immense wealth he was supposedly carrying.

During Kidd's long absence, one of his backers, the Earl of Bellomont, had been appointed governor of New York, Massachusetts Bay, and New Hampshire. After removing his corrupt predecessor, Governor Benjamin Fletcher, and sending him back to England, Bellomont set about the moral improvement of rowdy New York, long a pirate haven. On a trip to Massachusetts, Bellomont arrested two pirates from a stolen treasure ship. The governor of New Jersey arrested six pirates and seized their treasure-filled chests. Kidd arrived (probably on Long Island) at the height of the excitement.

Following a reunion with his family, Kidd sent a friend to Massachusetts to feed Bellomont a tale of his having been forced into piracy by threats of death from his crewmen. He added the lie that the *Quedah Merchant* was in the West Indies with a rich cargo. Bellomont sought proof of the statements. Finally Kidd met Bellomont in Boston and pleaded his case before a council there. The council did not swallow his farfetched story. On Kidd's third appearance before the council he was arrested.

Through patronage, the unknown buccaneer had risen to power and wealth as a pirate captain. Now his patrons would control his fall. The Whig junto which had teamed with Kidd were being denounced by Tories in Parliament as members of a government "that sent its own thieves to graze among upright traders." Kidd was a handy Jonah to be tossed overboard if the Whigs were to weather the political storm.

The *Advice* was sent to Boston to fetch Kidd and thirty-one other prisoners and return them to England. When the ship arrived after a cold, stormy voyage, Kidd was ill. He tried to escape his almost certain doom by writing to two of his patrons and repeating the lies he had told in Boston. In a fit of despondency he asked to be shot, not ignominiously hanged. He even asked for a knife to kill himself. Finally tried on May 8 and 9, 1701, he was convicted first of the murder of William Moore, his rebellious gunner, and then of multiple piracies. His desperate offer to Robert Hardy, Tory speaker of the House of Commons, to recover £100,000 hidden in the West Indies was ignored. The treasure did not exist anyway.

In a drunken speech before his hanging, Kidd assailed the "false" testimony of his turncoat friends. The hanging itself was marked by black comedy. The rope tore, and the dazed Kidd had to be taken up the ladder by the hangman for a second try. This finished him, or did it? The real Kidd was gone now, his corpse to be left for a while as a "terror to all that saw it," and then buried. The Captain Kidd of legend, though, would live on in countless tales of buried treasure. Ritchie regards these as only pleasant fables. Actual pirates gambled, lavishly spent their money, or took it home; they did not bury it. Very few invested it and settled down.

Ritchie's absorbing story of Captain Kidd makes clear why such careers as his and those of other pirates were possible. Politicians and merchants in America and England condoned and even encouraged piracy because they profited or expected to profit from it. As the Colonial merchants in such ports as New York, Philadelphia, and Boston became firmly established, however, they chose to carry on an orderly commerce and to rid themselves of the pirates and their excesses.

In England, the Tory opposition to such deals as that which linked Whig politicians and a pirate captain brought a temporary end to the Whig ascendancy in Parliament and an improvement in mercantile morality. Piracy had not been ended, but with the hanging of Kidd and a number of other pirates it would no longer flourish as it had for a century.

Henderson Kincheloe

Sources for Further Study

Best Sellers. XLVI, December, 1986, p. 353.
Booklist. LXXXIII, October 15, 1986, p. 311.
Kirkus Reviews. LIV, September 1, 1986, p. 1357.
Library Journal. CXI, November 1, 1986, p. 94.
The New York Times Book Review. XCI, October 19, 1986, p. 31.
Smithsonian. XVII, October, 1986, p. 175.

CHEKHOV

Author: Henri Troyat (1911-   )
Translated from the French by Michael Henry Heim
Publisher: E. P. Dutton (New York). Illustrated. 364 pp. $22.50
Type of work: Literary biography
Time: 1860-1904
Locale: Russia; notably Taganrog, the Ukraine, Moscow, Saint Petersburg, Sakhalin
    Island, and the Crimea; and other parts of Asia and Europe, including Italy,
    France, and Germany

The life and times of the great playwright and short-story writer are recaptured in a well-rounded and sympathetic study of the personal events that shaped his literary accomplishments

Principal personages:

ANTON PAVLOVICH CHEKHOV, a major literary figure who was the author of important short stories and plays

PAVEL EGOROVICH CHEKHOV, his father, for many years a grocer and shopkeeper

ALEKSEI SERGEEVICH SUVORIN, a major publisher of journals and books in Saint Petersburg

LEO NIKOLAYEVICH TOLSTOY, a major Russian novelist and literary writer

MAXIM GORKY, an important literary writer with a bent for social criticism

LIDIIA ALEKSEEVNA AVILOVA, a celebrated actress and one of Chekhov's romantic interests

OLGA LEONARDOVNA KNIPPER, an actress who became Chekhov's wife during the last three years of his life

KONSTANTIN SERGEEVICH STANISLAVSKY, a renowned actor and director who performed in some of Chekhov's plays

During his lifetime Anton Pavlovich Chekhov won renown as Russia's most accomplished playwright; his short stories were widely read and discussed for their evocation of the human tragedies and social problems of his time. Chekhov insisted that his literary calling was artistic: He worked to convey certain qualities of human nature that were exemplified in the settings and dramatic situations he created. In contrast to other Russian masters of his period, his works betrayed little didactic intent; social criticism was leavened by wry humor and a bemused tolerance for the various human failings of his characters. Above all his productions were distinguished by a technique where atmosphere and description transcended the limitations of plot and action. Readers and audiences debated whether Chekhov was an optimist or a pessimist as they responded to a literature that bore its own particular hallmarks of modernism.

Literary histories and surveys of the genres where Chekhov was active are wont to depict the author as reticent and reserved; his life had few of the momentous and extraordinary occurrences that figure in the biographies of other great Russian writers. To be sure, there has been enough to arouse the interest of researchers. Chekhov was the grandson of a serf; his father was a merchant who ultimately fled imprisonment for debt. The author's years as a student, his training as a physician, and the difficult early years of his medical practice have been recounted in studies of his life. The prolific efforts of his early literary career, the difficult road to acceptance as a major prose writer and dramatist, and his travels and mingling in literary circles took place during a relatively brief life span. Chekhov, who lived in the Ukraine, Moscow, and the Crimea, also left a description of his visit to the eastern penal outpost on Sakhalin Island; during his later years he also spent some time in Italy, France, and Germany. His collected letters, which in one recent edition were published in twelve volumes, attest his concerns with the business of authorship and wavering loyalties between medicine and literature; they also bear testimony to the tragically parlous state of his health during much of his adult life. Nevertheless, he has often been considered an elusive figure, rather guarded in mentions of his personal life, who at times seems imperceptibly to blend with the settings and situations he created.

In his own right Henri Troyat is a literary figure of consequence; prior to his work on Chekhov he published about forty novels as well as short stories and other works of fiction. Of Russian birth, he has lived in France since the age of nine; in some of his works he has undertaken to render the history and culture of his original homeland comprehensible to the French reading public. Some of his fictional works deal with themes taken from Russian history, such as episodes from the reigns of Peter the Great and Catherine the Great. Other novels have historical settings, such as Napoléon's invasion of Russia in 1812 or the Russian Revolution and civil war. Troyat's use of Russian publications for original source materials has been turned to advantage in works of nonfiction, mainly biographical studies. Before undertaking the present work, he produced five major studies of classical Russian writers, of which his biography of Leo Tolstoy (first published in 1965; an English translation appeared in 1967) in particular was widely acclaimed. Other efforts include four biographies of Russian rulers, from Ivan the Terrible to Alexander I; he is also the author of a broader historical survey of Russian politics and society under the last czar. His study of Chekhov marks his return to concerns with literary men, after a hiatus since the French publication of his biography of Nikolai Gogol in 1971.

Troyat does not claim to have uncovered new or unusual information about his subject; nor does he engage in prolonged analysis or interpretation of Chekhov's works. His biographical schema is straightforward and sequential. At the same time, by a judicious selection from the author's published statements and the works of his contemporaries, Troyat on the whole succeeds in calling back Chekhov's circumstances and surroundings. Born in 1860 in Taganrog, a Ukrainian city on the Sea of Azov, the boy underwent a difficult childhood. His father, Pavel Egorovich Chekhov, administered disciplinary beatings on a regular basis; young Anton also derived little from an education that was heavily dependent upon the rote learning of classical languages. Neither the grimy routines of his father's business, as a merchant of liquor and foodstuffs, nor the pious incantations dispensed by local religious functionaries had positive effects on him.

A major transition took place in 1876; the family business failed, and Chekhov's father, who had seemed so formidable on the domestic front, ignominiously and furtively sought relief from his creditors by moving to Moscow. Chekhov's first literary productions, short stories, and humorous sketches were composed shortly thereafter, and subsequently he began to write frequently as a means of support for his studies at the University of Moscow. Only a tepid response was elicited when his work was first reviewed for publication, and indeed some of his early writing has not survived at all. Encouraged by a doctor friend of the family, Chekhov became a medical student; all the while he continued to produce a stream of short efforts for satirical journals in Moscow. Although he had his share of tribulations with unresponsive editors, or those who paid him only after a struggle, by the early 1880's a literary career of sorts was under way; during a period of four years he produced some three hundred prose pieces under various pseudonyms. It remained for Chekhov to refine his technique while drawing ever more upon his experiences and his powers of observation.

Chekhov's medical practice never quite assumed comparable importance, though for some time he considered it his primary calling. He did treat patients in Moscow, in Saint Petersburg during a typhus epidemic, and while he lived in the Ukraine. He was conscientious and indeed may have limited his opportunities for financial gain by taking a number of cases where he knew that there was no real chance for payment. His work as a physician brought before him an odd assortment of individuals from high and low stations in society and, thus, also furnished material for his writing. All the while his literary production continued. Of major importance was his relationship with Aleksei Sergeevich Suvorin, one of Russia's leading publishers, whom Chekhov met during a visit to Saint Petersburg in 1885. Many of his thoughts about life and literature were revealed in the numerous letters he sent this literary sponsor. Chekhov won critical plaudits with his novella-length story "The Steppe," and in 1888 a collection of his short fiction, *V sumerkakh* (in the twilight), was awarded the prestigious Pushkin Prize from the Russian Academy of Sciences.

Certain characteristic traits derived from his formative years also affected Chekhov's later life, and Troyat depicts these features most ably without going beyond the actual evidence at hand. After the collapse of his father's business, major responsibilities devolved upon the young author; he had moreover to look after other family members. His two older brothers were not only dissolute but sometimes also drunken and disruptive; Chekhov tolerated them while avoiding extremes of moralism or indulgence. His life in major cities and in the provinces brought him directly in contact with the unsentimental realities of Russian life; in his writing he did not flinch at acknowledging unfortunate truths. Some of his experiences were separated by long periods of time from their reappearance in fictional guises. The habit, ingrained early in his career, of writing in quantity may also have strengthened the stoicism that is exhibited in the peculiarly ironic standpoint of his works. Chekhov's recorded comments reveal a gentle, self-effacing soul who was unwilling to take his own efforts too seriously, and, as Troyat demonstrates, his patient, unassuming character is amply attested in the letters and memoirs of many of his contemporaries. One may indeed be struck by the contrast between his quiet, dignified bearing and the turbulent, troubled existences of other literary men, including those who associated with Chekhov.

Some of Chekhov's writing presented his personal experiences and observations directly, rather than in oblique, reworked forms. In certain respects this was the case with his study of the criminal detention system. In 1890, he traveled through Siberia and performed an inspection tour of Sakhalin Island, on the Pacific Ocean, which then was used as a penal colony. In a narrative account he recorded his impressions and stated his deeply felt revulsion against the brutal excesses of corporal punishment. He held decidedly mixed feelings about the convict population, where widespread moral degradation held sway. (In another context, such impressions formed the basis for his story "Ward No. 6.") Traveling onward, he sailed on a ship that circled the continent of Asia. A tour of Europe took him to Vienna, Venice, Rome, Naples, and Paris, but he found little real inspiration in Western cities. He bought a small estate well removed from Moscow and attended to medical concerns in his district; at one time he took part in combating a cholera epidemic. Although his literary output may have slackened from the frenetic pace of his student days, stories such as "The Grasshopper" won notice for their evocation of troubled domestic relations, in this instance an unwise love affair. Chekhov's studies of peasant life aroused interest because of their displacement of heroic stereotypes with the somber truths the author had gathered from those around him.

As Troyat makes clear, Chekhov was wary of political or ideological commitments; yet he had the knack of forming and stating his own positions forthrightly and unequivocally without putting off those around him. When Suvorin was denounced in some quarters for his support of the government, Chekhov remained on friendly terms with the celebrated publisher. At other times, Chekhov took issue with Suvorin over such controversies as the use of force against rioting students and the Dreyfus Affair in France; nevertheless, he also defended the other man's freedom to reach his own judgments.

Relations with other literary men were similarly respectful; indeed, during the last years of his life Chekhov frequently conferred with others of his calling. He first met Tolstoy, Russia's single most famous author, in 1895. He showed the well-known novelist great deference but in time parted company with Tolstoy over religious and social issues. Many of Tolstoy's preachments on the moral imperative in literature were received with noncommittal response on the part of Chekhov, and on his side Chekhov took issue with Tolstoy's idealized conception of the peasantry. Also prominent in the literary circle that sometimes gathered around Chekhov was Maxim Gorky, the most forward and outspoken social critic among leading Russian writers of that period. Although Gorky accepted Chekhov's advice on literary style, he promoted fiction with a more openly activist intent. When Gorky was expelled from the Russian Academy of Sciences in 1902, Chekhov resigned his own membership in that institution as a gesture on behalf of the free exchange of ideas. Lacking the pronounced political convictions of many other intellectuals, Chekhov was essentially liberal-minded, able to tolerate many forms of opinion and arriving at his own positions as issues of the day arose. He had a clear sense of civic duty and a basic patriotic identification with his native country. In 1897 he assisted in the gathering of official census data for his district. Somewhat implausibly, in view of his failing health, he offered to perform military service in a medical capacity, both in 1896, during an Anglo-Russian crisis over the Middle East, and when the Russo-Japanese war broke out in 1904.

In many ways the opposite of a womanizer, Chekhov in some letters dismissed amorous inclinations in gentle but reproving tones. Here it is noteworthy that Troyat, while stating what is fairly known about his subject's intimate life, does not surmise or speculate where the evidence is inconclusive. It would seem that Chekhov did not entirely approve of romantic passion, though he did carry on the occasional pursuit of various women, notably actresses, whom he knew from professional connections. He continued to see one of them, Lidiia Alekseevna Avilova, for about ten years. In her memoirs she claims, somewhat extravagantly, that he was utterly devoted to her; his letters, however, show a measure of reluctance and uncertainty that must have restrained his ardor. It is suggestive of his state of mind as well that, in various guises, themes of unfulfilled or hopeless love made their appearance in his writing. Troyat suggests that this was the case with "The Lady with the Dog," where tragedy ensues when a hitherto unfeeling middle-aged man is swept up suddenly in romantic abandon. When Chekhov was nearly forty he formed a lasting attachment; he came to know the actress Olga Leonardovna Knipper, a bright, vivacious woman who was nearly ten years younger than he. Her impulsive, energetic temperament contrasted pleasantly with his shy, taciturn demeanor. They were together both in theatrical rehearsals and on vacation travels in various southern portions of the Russian empire.

He joyfully returned her affection, and, even with pessimistic prognostications about his health, she agreed to marry him in 1901. Ironically enough, while he was pleased with her performances in major roles from his plays, their years together were marred by her extended absences for theatrical productions in which she continued to take part.

Chekhov's career as a playwright was rather slow in getting under way. Troyat traces the author's development in this area, for it became a major concern in his literary activity. His earliest dramatic work, a tragedy in four acts that would have required more than seven hours to perform, was rejected by producers in Moscow; it was only published posthumously, under the title *Platonov* in 1923. Chekhov turned to farces and one-act plays, and then he expanded upon incidents in his own life, including, for example, the shooting of a wild bird on his estate to create *The Seagull*. On its opening night in Saint Petersburg in 1896, the audience was restive and openly abusive. Chekhov was mortified and remained suspicious even when the critical reception subsequently became favorable. When writing for the theater, Chekhov confronted demands different from those of prose composition; he worried greatly as he revised and emended his plays. During rehearsals he consulted anxiously sometimes with Konstantin Stanislavsky, Russia's most celebrated actor and director. In spite of occasional sharp differences of opinion, both men were immensely gratified when Chekhov's plays gained popular acceptance. In Moscow, *Uncle Vanya* won favorable reviews when it opened in 1899; among others, Gorky praised it highly. Further success attended the premiere of *Three Sisters* in 1901. Chekhov's last play, *The Cherry Orchard*, with a provincial setting similar to that which the author had known, added yet another note of triumph to his career as a playwright. By the time it was staged, however, in 1904, he was not long for the world.

Ill health stalked Chekhov most of his adult life. He contracted tuberculosis rather early, and at the age of twenty-four he began coughing blood. Bronchitis, phlebitis in one leg, and hemorrhoids also troubled him. He accepted illness gracefully—indeed he apologized to visitors when he was sometimes discomfited by his chronic lung complaints—but at times he also voiced a certain weariness and fatalism that probably were derived from his weakened state. Partly to alleviate his condition he traveled to France and Germany; in 1898 he had a house built in the Crimea where he composed his last works. The disease in his lungs seemed inexorably to haunt him, and at times he grimly estimated the number of years left to him. There were occasions when he was too ill to attend the theater or, indeed, to leave his home. When he was in a condition to travel, he eventually determined to consult a leading specialist in Germany. His tubercular condition was treated at Badenweiler, a spa on the outskirts of the Black Forest; he seemed briefly to improve before he succumbed altogether in July, 1904.

With this delicate, bittersweet account of Chekhov's life, Troyat provides a clear and distinct portrait of his subject that brings into clear focus the salient issues that affected the great writer's work. Without insinuating or obtruding, and without trespassing beyond the written record, Troyat has performed his task as a biographer incisively and with great empathy. It may be indeed that this work benefits from Troyat's own literary background and experience, as the joys and sorrows of creative composition are called to mind in Chekhov's case. It is unlikely that this biography will supersede existing scholarly works, which already are fairly numerous, but it should rekindle interest in Chekhov among general readers. It may be as well that this type of work, which draws upon both research in the Russian sources and the efforts of sustained literary insight, is particularly suited to Troyat's approach.

J. R. Broadus

Sources for Further Study

Booklist. LXXXIII, September 15, 1986, p. 97.
Kirkus Reviews. LIV, September 1, 1986, p. 1364.
Library Journal. CXI, November 1, 1986, p. 91.
Los Angeles Times Book Review. November 16, 1986, p. 4.
The New York Review of Books. XXXIII, December 4, 1986, p. 21.
The New York Times Book Review. XCI, December 28, 1986, p. 12.
Publishers Weekly. CCXXX, August 29, 1986, p. 383.
Time. CXXVIII, November 10, 1986, p. 103.
Vogue. CLXXVI, October, 1986, p. 268.
The Wall Street Journal. CCVIII, November 18, 1986, p. 30.

CHILDREN OF LIGHT

Author: Robert Stone (1937-   )
Publisher: Alfred A. Knopf (New York). 258 pp. $17.95
Type of work: Novel
Time: The mid-1980's
Locale: Hollywood and Bahía Honda, a film location on the Baja peninsula in Mexico

Gordon Walker is quickly coming unglued, and he flees to Mexico to find his old love, Lu Anne, but their rekindled romance only brings disaster to them both

Principal characters:
GORDON WALKER, a Hollywood screenwriter and occasional actor
LU ANNE BOURGEOIS (LEE VERGER), an actress suffering from schizophrenia
AL KEOCHAKIAN, Walker's agent
SHELLEY PEARCE, Keochakian's associate and Walker's occasional lover
WALTER DROGUE, JR., the director on the Mexican film location
DONGAN LOWNDES, a New York journalist in Mexico doing an article on the filming

Children of Light is a contemporary fictional nightmare in which drugs and alcohol and mental illness are both the causes for the aimlessness and destructiveness of the characters and symbols for the human condition.

Gordon Walker is a successful screenwriter and actor whose life is rapidly coming unraveled. He has just returned to Hollywood after a summer playing King Lear in Seattle, and things are not going well. He thought he knew "how to endure, and what it was that got you through. There was work. There were the people you loved and the people who loved you." These things, however, no longer work for Walker: His wife (Connie) has left him, he is estranged from his two teenage sons (Tom and Stuart), he cannot write, and he has become increasingly dependent on drugs and alcohol to get him through his daily crises—to say nothing of the larger anxieties (such as fear of death) that constantly assail him. Like Lear, Walker "hath ever but slenderly known himself," and the prospects for further self-knowledge seem remote. Bitter, desolate, his life poisoned by the cocaine and vodka he ingests, he has "a vision of his life as trash." He needs to "reinvent" himself but knows that this time it will not "be easy to get straight."

Walker is looking for a new dream but escapes instead into an old one, Lu Anne Bourgeois, an actress and his former lover who is on the Baja coast filming Walker's ten-year-old adaptation of Kate Chopin's turn-of-the-century novel about emerging feminist consciousness, *The Awakening*. No one wants Walker in Mexico—both his agent and his agent's secretary try to dissuade him—but Walker drives down to Bahía Honda anyway, to escape his demons and find salvation in Lu Anne. When he arrives, he realizes that "on a whim, he had come to a place where he was without friends to see a woman whom he had no business to see."

For Lu Anne has demons of her own—what she calls the "Long Friends" of her schizophrenia—and the two people only feed each other's fears and fantasies. Like Walker, Lu Anne has recently been deserted by mate and children, and she is barely holding herself together now. She completes a crucial scene from the end of *The Awakening*, in which Edna Pontellier walks into the ocean, and she tells Walter Drogue, Jr., the director of the film, using one of Edna's lines, "If I must choose between nothingness and grief, I will choose grief." She also chooses to share mescal and cocaine with Walker and quickly comes unraveled herself. Certainly, the Bahía Honda location is not a particularly healthy one, for even the strongest character, as all the film people here seem bent on self-destruction or the destruction of one another, and there is the added ingredient of Dongan Lowndes, a New York journalist who has come to Mexico to witness and record the disintegration of film and stars.

After one especially ugly party scene, where all the film people attack one another mercilessly, Lu Anne and Gordon flee by car and then by plane and end up in a deserted Baja valley where they had once been on location years before and where Lu Anne thinks that they will find a religious shrine. Instead they find a pigsty, and here they enact their final mad, drunken scene, saved only by the Mexican police, who have been called by suspicious locals. On the way back to Bahía Honda, Lu Anne convinces Gordon to stop for a swim in the ocean, and she successfully completes her role as Edna Pontellier and drowns herself. In the brief epilogue to the novel, a sober but suffering Walker is not even able to attend the Hollywood memorial service for Lu Anne Bourgeois.

Children of Light explores the horrific world of drugs, alcohol, and mental illness, and it is Robert Stone's intention to elevate these maladies into metaphors for the human condition, but his novel never quite succeeds. Clearly, this is a novel about spiritual and psychological disintegration, about people mired in the pigsty of their own lives, but the book itself gets mired in the same place. It is hard to identify with, let alone like, characters bent on such massive self-destruction.

It is interesting, from a literary point of view, how often Hollywood resists easy fictionalization. Many writers have seen the film world as a perfect symbol for what is wrong with American culture (the unabashed materialism, the glittering superficiality), but few have been able to capture it (F. Scott Fitzgerald and Nathanael West are two exceptions).

Children of Light is best on the scene and scenery of Hollywood in the opening of the novel and, later on, the mechanics of filmmaking in Mexico. Walker has a liquid lunch with his agent, Al Keochakian, at Musso and Frank's in Los Angeles and drinks with his occasional lover, Shelley Pearce, later that night in Laguna Beach, and both scenes smack of the shallowness and artificiality of the film life. On the whole, Stone's exposition and description are stronger than his dialogue, which often reads like the low-budget films his characters are trying to avoid, and several scenes stand out as symbolic film ideas. In one, Walker watches the filming from a cliff in Baja and falls in love with Lu Anne anew; later he realizes that it was her stand-in doing the scene. "There's your poetry, he thought. Your movies."

What also works in the novel is the literary symbolism. This is a very literary novel, with constant references throughout to William Shakespeare and to Kate Chopin. Walker has played every character in *King Lear*, and late in the novel he says, "I could spend the rest of my time on earth playing Lear." In many senses he is still playing the role, for the novel is clearly about the tragedy of a man bringing his own house down around him. It is, in dramatic terms, Shakespeare done in modern dress.

Lu Anne completes the tragedy. The final scene, played out on a deserted hilltop in a tropical downpour, is similar to the crucial scene in *King Lear*, where Lear rants at the storm-tossed night. In the novel, it is Walker who is playing the Fool and Lu Anne who goes mad. This symbolism dovetails neatly with *The Awakening*. Walker had written the screenplay's Edna Pontellier with Lu Anne in mind; choosing "grief" earlier, she chooses "nothingness" at the close of the novel and completes the tragedy as Edna Pontellier. *Children of Light* thus operates on several levels, and the literary symbolism reinforces its feminist and psychological themes.

The religious symbolism in the novel is similarly rich. Lu Anne enters a church in search of some stability (in a scene that may remind the reader of Lady Brett Ashley in Ernest Hemingway's *The Sun Also Rises*), but when she looks up at the cross, "she saw that the hanged Christ nailed to the beams had become a cat." In her final mad scene—which she believes is a version of "baptism, renewal and rebirth" acted out on "holy grounds"— she smears Walker with pig manure. " 'Now you get the blessing.' She reached out and rubbed the stuff on his forehead in the form of a cross." It is not religion that is being desecrated here; rather, the religious symbolism is pointing up the emptiness and meaninglessness of contemporary human life and the inability of these characters to achieve any kind of salvation. Lu Anne's final solace is in the sea.

Stone's language and imagery are particularly impressive. The novel is filled with sentences that reverberate ("Delirium was a disease of darkness"), and his use of imagery is often poetic. The "light" of the title, for example, is seen through a prism in the novel and shines in a number of directions. Light is what is necessary for filming; it is also essential for sight. It is the glow off the silver screen, and at the same time it is also vision. Finally, it is what the characters—the children of light—lack, what fails to illuminate their lives or their dreams.

Stone is a very talented writer, the author of several widely acclaimed novels. *Dog Soldiers*, which won the National Book Award in 1975, dealt with drugs in America after the Vietnam War. More recently, *A Flag for Sunrise* (1981) captured the political and moral confusion of Central America. *Children of Light*, however, like so many novels before it, seems to have broken up against the tinsel walls of Hollywood. Perhaps Hollywood looks so easy to capture; perhaps the corruptive power of the film capital is so strong that it weakens even the talents who are trying to capture it. In either case, *Children of Light* is one of those cases in which the writing is better than what it all adds up to. The novel is held together, not by character and story (which hold most successful books together), but by imagery and symbolism, and they are barely enough. Like Bruce Jay Friedman's *About Harry Towns* (1974), a collection of short stories on the same subject, *Children of Light* mixes drugs and alcohol and ends up a confused story of substance abuse and spiritual deterioration in the film capital.

David Peck

Sources for Further Study

Booklist. LXXXII, January 1, 1986, p. 642.
Christian Science Monitor. LXXVIII, March 17, 1986, p. 26.
Commonweal. CXIII, May 23, 1986, p. 305.
Library Journal. CXI, March 1, 1986, p. 110.
Los Angeles Times Book Review. March 23, 1986, p. 3.
The New York Review of Books. XXXIII, April 10, 1986, p. 23.
The New York Times Book Review. XCI, March 16, 1986, p. 1.
The New Yorker. LXII, June 2, 1986, p. 105.
Publishers Weekly. CCXXIX, January 24, 1986, p. 62.
Time. CXXVII, March 10, 1986, p. 72.

THE CHIMPANZEES OF GOMBE
Patterns of Behavior

Author: Jane Goodall (1934-   )
Publisher: The Belknap Press of Harvard University Press (Cambridge, Massachusetts). Illustrated. 674 pp. $30.00
Type of work: Ethological study
Time: 1960-1985
Locale: Gombe, Tanzania, on the eastern shore of Lake Tanganyika

A comprehensive study of all aspects of chimpanzee behavior in the wild, based on twenty-five years of fieldwork by the author both individually and as director of a team

> *Principal personages:*
> FIGAN, an alpha male chimpanzee for three periods in a decade
> FLO, a high-ranking matriarch who has often been a mother and grandmother
> GOBLIN, a follower of Figan, eventually his supplanter
> MIKE, a low-ranking male who used kerosene cans to bluff his way to alpha status
> PASSION, an infant-killer and cannibal

The Chimpanzees of Gombe: Patterns of Behavior is the record of an ethological study that has already lasted more than twenty-five years. It was in 1960 that Jane Goodall first went to Gombe National Park, on the eastern shore of Lake Tanganyika in Tanzania, and began the process of watching chimpanzees, at first at a distance and through binoculars, but later—as the chimpanzees became habituated to human presence—at increasingly close quarters and with the help of teams of students and locally recruited field assistants. The Gombe project has had to survive several crises, including the kidnaping of four team members by Zairian rebels in 1975, but it has nevertheless maintained both continuity and methodological rigor.

The length, and the naturalness, of the Gombe observations have important effects not only on the quantity but also on the quality of the data recorded. As Goodall indicates, if her study had closed after a mere decade, the myth of "the gentle, peace-loving ape" would have remained and gained new credit by being placed on an apparently reliable scientific basis. After 1970, however, two sequences of events took place to shatter this myth, one being the division of the chimpanzee community near the research center into two groups, which led to an outbreak of what one can almost call warfare, and the other being the cannibalistic attacks of one chimpanzee female on the infants of all the other females, behavior apparently individual and unmotivated but nevertheless involving and capable of being transmitted to a new generation in the person of the female's one daughter. Chimpanzee behavior varies, then, and limited observations place one in danger of drawing general conclusions from biased data. A further point in favor of the

Gombe project, though, is that as a result of long familiarity, Goodall and her colleagues can quite simply recognize individual chimpanzees, say with absolute certainty how they are all related at least maternally, and even—despite the normal promiscuity of chimpanzee life—make good guesses at fatherhood. The importance of this for any study of behavior cannot be overestimated. At the simplest level it makes it possible to identify recurrent patterns, such as persistent challenging and struggles for dominance among the males; it allows conclusions to be drawn even about such seemingly unapproachable matters as whether chimpanzees have an incest taboo; and it enables the observers to see not "chimpanzees" as a whole, but as individuals, with their own peculiarities and deviations from average or expected behavior. It is not too much to say that the mere raw data on which *The Chimpanzees of Gombe* is based are of a different kind from those of almost any other animal study, being at times closer to anthropology than to ethology.

This, however, adds a further dimension of interest to Goodall's book. Recent work on DNA and on immunological differences has only confirmed the original strong feeling that chimpanzees (and gorillas) are very close to human beings indeed. It is even possible that all three are "sibling species," physically and genetically closer to one another, for example, than dogs and foxes, or horses and zebras. In all that Goodall writes, accordingly, there is a strong and overt element of comparison. In what ways are chimpanzees like people? What are the major remaining differences? Does observing them provide clues to the behavior of early man, as Goodall had hoped it would at the beginning of the study? What is the significance of the very obvious correspondence of chimpanzee behavior with the behavior of present-day man?

Goodall considers all these points in many different ways. The question of language has long been a vexed one. Early attempts to bring captive chimpanzee infants up as humans and teach them to speak were unsuccessful; much more successful, though still debated, were the attempts to teach chimpanzees sign language. What do they do, however, when left to themselves? Typical of this study is the very close and careful analysis of the Gombe chimpanzees' "vocal repertoire," from the "pant-grunt," always directed up the social hierarchy and never down, to the "waa-bark," associated with fights (but often emitted by bystanders, seemingly out of sympathy), to the food-grunt, the nest-grunt, the "huu" of puzzlement or anxiety, and no less than four distinguishable types of screams. Such distinctions could be made only on the basis of long experience; linking noises to contexts must take even longer. In the end, though, Goodall is confident that contexts can provide enough clues to lead one reliably to the motivations behind the sounds—calls showing, for example, the change from fear to defiance as a victimized chimpanzee detects the approach of an ally. Such questions are not likely to arise in captivity; the range of contexts is too narrow. In the closely observed wild, however, it is even possible to approach such issues as whether chimpanzee communities have different "dialects" (probably yes) and whether individuals can "tell each other" anything. Here the answer is more probably no. Yet, Goodall notes, the fear and dislike felt by chimpanzee mothers for the cannibal and infant-killer Passion was clearly communicated in some way even to males, though one cannot imagine that the males knew exactly what had happened.

When it comes to emotions, Goodall is particularly definite. It may seem "anthropomorphic" to say that chimpanzees feel such complex emotions as distress or annoyance, but the belief that they do is based on very much the same kind of information as that which leads us to infer their existence in fellow human beings. Small chimpanzees poking and molesting their elders are clearly "teasing" (and provoking much the same response as in human society). The very small chimpanzee who watched a large male stamping and drumming on a tree, only to go over later, deliver a few stamps, and then gently and cautiously tap the same tree twice with his knuckles, was clearly practicing (and as clearly learning). Goodall remarks that Goblin was seen rehearsing displays on his own before making his bid to become "alpha male"—the dominant male in the community. She is even prepared to say—and once again the subjective remark is based on strong objective data as to normal chimpanzee behavior—that Humphrey, the alpha male from 1970 to 1972, sensed the potential threat from his eventual supplanter Figan before the rivalry had been openly declared.

At points such as these, one is getting close to the "mind" of the chimpanzee, and many readers of Goodall's study will be convinced of the similarity of that mind to the human. The meticulously recorded struggles for dominance of the Gombe males make compelling reading because of the familiarity of the strategies and the personality types: Jomeo, for example, the large, powerful male with almost no dominance drive; Goblin, who rises to alpha status by the sheer determination of his aggression, if at the cost of marked sexual difficulties; or Evered, the defeated alpha male who consoles himself in defeat by long periods of withdrawal and by siring more infants than any of his rivals. Yet how far can one go with these comparisons? Can one say, for example, that chimpanzees feel love, practice war, and show aversion to incest?

The last question is the easiest, being answerable at least statistically. Copulation between mothers and sons is rare, even when the mother is in estrus and mating with all available males; the same is true of relations between brother and sister. On occasions when "incest" of this kind does take place—as with the clearly abnormal Goblin—it may be over the very active disapproval and evasion of the female concerned. There seems to be, then, a chimpanzee feeling of some kind against certain types of incest, though whether it is instinctive or on what it is based cannot be told.

As for warfare, Goodall is in no doubt that the intercommunity conflicts which led to the extermination of the Kahama community were different from the normal dominance fighting of chimpanzee life. The chimpanzees as a whole are unexpectedly efficient predators, hunting and killing large numbers of colobus monkeys, baboons, bushpigs, and even, although rarely, human infants. When they kill other animals, though, they do it by flailing, biting to the brain, or tearing off limbs, all quite abnormal in dominance contests, but much more like their behavior when fighting other chimpanzees to kill. Why they should want to kill one another is not clear. This, however, raises an issue of particular interest throughout Goodall's book; namely, the correspondence of chimpanzee life to theories of natural selection.

It is a Darwinian tenet that natural selection operates through the individual, not the group. It may make sense for the group for one individual to sacrifice his own interests to it, but that individual will lose by doing so, and insofar as he loses time or energy (or life), he becomes less competitive against others in terms of reproduction and is more likely to be "bred out." Altruism, and waste, ought both to be selected against in a Darwinian world. Yet chimpanzees show the latter both in the time they spend on dominance struggles, although being an alpha male seems to confer very little reproductive advantage, as the case of Evered shows, and in the risks they take in intercommunity warfare, a proceeding that once again seems to confer no clear benefit in either the capture of females or even the elimination of other males' potentially competing offspring. Altruism is just as evident in chimpanzee society and just as difficult to defend in Darwinian terms. Goodall is at times attracted by the concept of 'the selfish gene," as explained by the Oxford biologist Richard Dawkins. When the juvenile male Prof seizes his tantrum-throwing baby brother Pax's hand and leads him away from the dangerous Goblin, it is a risk for Prof and an unselfish action toward a potential competitor; it does, however, save Pax's genes, which are largely the same as Prof's. A foolish action considered individually could then be a wise action considered genetically. Alternatively, one could say that Prof is showing love, and of this there are many clearer and more touching examples within the highly supportive, if violent, society that Goodall describes.

Not only human, but also humane, behavior is identifiable among the Gombe chimpanzees. Such behavior presents a challenge to crudely Darwinian explanations; it also erodes one's sense of the line between human and animal, just as Goodall's methodology refuses to acknowledge a distinction between scientific rigor (expressed in statistics) and patient receptivity (expressed in anecdotes). Goodall remains certain that there are differences of kind, and not only of degree, between human and chimpanzee, and she points in the end to three elements: language, conscious unselfishness, and comprehension of suffering. The main effect of her book, however, is to make many formerly perceived differences untenable. Humans are not the only creatures that laugh, avoid incest, possess a conscience, or make war on their kind. A subject surrounded by myth and prejudice has been greatly clarified here by the elementary, if demanding, techniques of waiting, watching, and recording.

T. A. Shippey

Sources for Further Study

Chicago Tribune. November 9, 1986, XIV, p. 6.
Choice. XXIV, December, 1986, p. 649.
Christian Science Monitor. LXXVIII, August 27, 1986, p. 20.
Economist. October 18, 1986, p. 95.
Kirkus Reviews. LIV, September 1, 1986, p. 1344.
Library Journal. CXI, August, 1986, p. 160.
Los Angeles Times Book Review. December 28, 1986, p. 8.
Ms. XV, December, 1986, p. 14.
Nature. CCCXXIII, October 30-November 5, 1986, p. 765.
New Society. October 31, 1986, p. 31.
The New York Times Book Review. XCI, August 24, 1986, p. 1.
Smithsonian. XVII, November, 1986, p. 212.

CITIES ON A HILL
A Journey Through Contemporary American Cultures

Author: Frances FitzGerald (1943-   )
Publisher: Simon and Schuster (New York). 414 pp. $19.95
Type of work: Cultural history
Time: The 1960's to the mid-1980's
Locale: The United States

*A description of four contemporary American communities—the homosexual com-
munity of San Francisco, the religious community of Jerry Falwell, the retirement
community of Sun City, Florida, and the community of Bhagwan Rajneesh in Oregon*

> *Principal personages:*
> HARVEY MILK, leader of the gay community of San Francisco who
> was murdered in 1978
> JERRY FALWELL, pastor of Thomas Road Baptist Church in Lynch-
> burg, Virginia, and titular head of the Moral Majority
> DEL WEBB, developer of Sun City, Florida
> BHAGWAN SHREE RAJNEESH, guru and spiritual leader of Rajneesh-
> puram in Oregon
> MA ANAND SHEELA, Rajneesh's secretary and the administrative
> head of Rajneeshpuram

Cities on a Hill: A Journey Through Contemporary American Cultures is
basically a description of four different types of communities in contemporary America and an attempt by the author to link them conceptually. Frances FitzGerald focuses on the Castro, the gay community of San Francisco;
the congregation of Jerry Falwell and the Thomas Road Baptist Church of
Lynchburg, Virginia; the retirement community of Sun City, near Tampa,
Florida; and the community of Bhagwan Shree Rajneesh in Oregon. Although FitzGerald's descriptions of the activities of the communities are often in minute detail, they often lack adequate analysis. Nevertheless, Fitz-
Gerald has selected four interesting communities, and her account provides
valuable information on their inner workings.

The primary question that FitzGerald addresses is what these four communities say about American society in the 1980's. To answer this question,
she leads her readers through a thoughtful reflection on the nature of early
nineteenth century American society and reform communities. Her analysis,
which summarizes much of the scholarship on the topic, is the best part of
her book and well worth its price. Early nineteenth century American society is FitzGerald's paradigm for comprehending and explaining the nature
and characteristics of contemporary society.

The major change sweeping American society in the early nineteenth century was the gradual development of industrialism. While the growth of
technology and the factory system was slow, industrialism was well under
way in New England and upstate New York by the 1830's and 1840's. The
factories brought to Rochester, New York, and other communities large

numbers of young, frequently unmarried laborers. These transients, usually living alone, lacked discipline and spent their leisure hours drinking, fighting, and intimidating the people of the community. They also lacked good work habits. Most of all, these young people, alone and without families, lacked manners, social standards, and moral values. In the face of their rowdyism and hooliganism, the citizens of Rochester seemed helpless—until they called upon Charles Grandison Finney to save their community (as he would similarly save others in upstate New York, New England, and Ohio).

Finney was the foremost revivalist of the time. During his six-month stay in Rochester, he led daily revival meetings, terrified the sinners and brought them to God, trained a cadre of evangelists who would continue his tactics, and rescued Rochester from the clutches of Satan. Finney's frenzied young people turned upstate New York into "the Burned-Over District" and ended rowdiness. For Paul E. Johnson, in *A Shopkeeper's Millennium* (1978), Finney represented the successful effort on the part of "Gentlemen of Property and Standing" to control urban laborers. The change wrought by Finney, however, was much broader than the establishment of social controls, as may be seen in the works of such writers as Mary P. Ryan (*Cradle of the Middle Class*, 1981).

Finney unleashed a revivalistic storm that spread to all segments of society and contributed to the disintegration of that society. A new nuclear family structure emerged from Finney's brand of revivalism. Given the dog-eat-dog nature of the developing industrial world, the family became a "Haven in a Heartless World," a sanctuary. In the haven of the home, middle-class values of gentility developed primarily through the efforts of women. The role of nurturing such values became gender-linked. The males of the family would be expected to develop initiative, self-reliance, toughness, ruthlessness, industry, thrift, and competitive resourcefulness to cope with the working world, while at home they and their families would be bound together by affection, kindness, and gentility. Women played an especially important role in bringing religion to the family and to society. Thus two different value systems developed together in nineteenth century America, and Finney played an important part in their emergence.

This extraordinary change in nineteenth century American society was the result of what anthropologist A. F. C. Wallace spoke of as a "revitalization movement." The intense religious emotionalism of Finney's revival eventuated in the destruction of the reigning image of society and of the individual throughout "the burned-over district" and the establishment of a new vision. This new vision, in fact, became the basis of many different views of the good society and the responsibilities of the individual. Finney was a so-called perfectionist who believed that the individual could be perfected, that society could be redeemed through individual efforts and that Christ would return to such a redeemed society. The revitalization that he inspired contributed to the rise of many reform and utopian movements, both religious and secular. Mormonism, the Oneida Community, Seventh Day Adventists, Fourieristic Phalanxes, the feminist movement, Swedenborgianism, abolitionism, temperance, Sabbatarianism, and other movements all shared in this revitalization of the vision of society and belief in human perfectibility.

In the twentieth century, the central vision of American society has also been disintegrating, according to FitzGerald. While the major change that spawned nineteenth century revivalism was the coming of industrialism, the major change transforming twentieth century America is the coming of postindustrial society. Not only is the nature of work and industry being radically transformed, but also traditional American society is being transformed. As FitzGerald states, American society is "changing its costumes, its sexual mores, its family arrangements, and its religious patterns." This process of change has brought in its wake a "revitalization movement." FitzGerald argues that the gay community, Falwell's fundamentalist community, the Sun Citians, and Rajneeshpuram are all examples of revitalization in twentieth century America.

While much divides the four communities described by FitzGerald, the author maintains that they have much in common as well. All the communities are "transformative"; they each have sought the transformation of American society. Each has sought transformation in the image of that society and its membership, and as a result, each has disavowed and rejected the past and attempted to shape a new present and a unique future. In FitzGerald's view, all are anti-intellectual and historical manifestations of pragmatic experimentalism. In theory, membership reflects equalitarian commitment in a society that "had no past but only a present and a future." Focusing on the future and rejecting the past, all participate in millennial or apocalyptic anticipation and longing. Finally, all these groups are part of "the tradition of radical dissent, separation, and heroic struggle to build a new world on hostile ground."

FitzGerald thus outlines a bold and thought-provoking thesis, using historical analysis of nineteenth century American reform to discover the mechanisms by which a society transforms itself from one value system and social configuration to another. Her effort to use the early nineteenth century as a model for twentieth century social change is insightful; the problem is that she has trivialized her hypothesis by the selection of her examples. The gay community of the Castro, the religious followers of Jerry Falwell, the Sun Citians, and the followers of Bhagwan Rajneesh do not provide the strongest evidence of her theory. In fact, she seems less inclined to demonstrate the validity of an interesting theory than to provide exciting gossip for her readers—the lengthiest part of the book (on Rajneeshpuram) supplies the most titillation and is the section that is least supportive of her thesis.

Moreover, she is unable, based on her examples, clearly to define the changed society and value system of which she claims her examples are illustrative. Thus, one must question the seriousness of FitzGerald's effort to provide an analysis and explanation of contemporary society; curiously she even ignores standard works, such as Christopher Lasch's *The Culture of Narcissism* (1979).

The first community that FitzGerald describes is the gay community of the Castro in San Francisco. The year 1978 was a good year for homosexuals throughout the United States. They flocked to San Francisco because of a growing national awareness of San Francisco's favorable treatment of homosexuals. In 1978, the gay population of the city doubled and the growth continued. Throughout this period, Harvey Milk, a city supervisor, served effectively as spokesman for the interests of the gay community. While the gay community was well represented in San Francisco politics and government, it evolved its own unique social institutions, such as separate churches, business establishments, and entertainment centers. FitzGerald speaks of the inhabitants of the Castro participating in a "sexual free-for-all." Curiously, homosexual men are especially active sexually while lesbian women are more discreet. The liberated atmosphere spurred an increase in "experimentation with new techniques" and a significant growth in the number of cases of sexually transmitted diseases. In a highly self-indulgent atmosphere, the gay community of the Castro ignored the possibility that the sexual joyride could be physically dangerous, emotionally troubling, and morally reprehensible and that sexuality alone might not be a suitable foundation for a community and its value system.

In the years following 1978, the Castro has been beset by major problems. On November 27, 1978, Harvey Milk was shot dead. The story of the subsequent trial and conviction of his murderer, Dan White, was scarcely important in comparison with the demise of the Castro's most effective and dedicated leader. No one would fully replace Milk, and the Castro would gradually decline in political clout and the esteem of city government. Far more important was the fact that by the early 1980's, Acquired Immune Deficiency Syndrome (AIDS) had struck the Castro. FitzGerald documents the community's efforts to cope with AIDS by attempting to reduce sexual activity among its members, but there was, initially, great reluctance to end the sexual free-for-all. Enormous pressure was required, for example, to close the gay public baths, major centers of sexual activity. The gay community's attitude eventually changed, however, because it had to cope with the rapidly growing AIDS epidemic. FitzGerald regards the change as an example of growing maturity.

FitzGerald's account of the Castro is mostly anecdotal. There is little discussion of the community as a community and almost no analysis of the value system. Are sexual indulgence and outlandish dress the foundations of community or society? FitzGerald has supplied little in her description of the Castro that supports her general thesis of the transformation of twentieth century American social values.

FitzGerald's treatment of Jerry Falwell's community and activities is based on two occurrences—one that took place in 1981 and the other in 1985. During these years, Falwell's major efforts lay in stimulating a fundamentalist religious revival and in creating a voting bloc of religious fundamentalists. Falwell was effective in using the media to enhance and support his revival. He also broadened the base of his voting bloc—the Moral Majority—to include Catholics, Mormons, and Orthodox Jews. Centering his work on his congregation in Lynchburg, Virginia, Falwell successfully attracted a rising middle class to the Thomas Road Baptist Church, a congregation willing to attribute its growing financial success to Divine intervention. Falwell perceives his role, as Finney did, as perfecting and redeeming the United States, so that a regenerate society will bring the day of the Second Coming. Putting together a fundamentalist voting bloc will hasten the coming of the Kingdom of God. Anyone who disagrees with Falwell's political view or does not adhere to his fundamentalism is working against the Second Coming.

While Falwell often takes an aggressive stance against his enemies, his followers see him as representing love. In Falwell, authority and love are combined, so that his followers accept his aggressiveness and refuse to criticize, often for fear of "God's vengeance." Seeing the world in black-and-white terms, Falwell and his followers cannot empathize with a differing point of view, virtually declaring a holy war against the political and spiritual opposition. Such militancy changed somewhat in the years from 1981 to 1985. Falwell became increasingly interested in the entire world and its salvation: He sailed "far away from the rock of doctrinal purity" by investing much time, effort, and money in his own university, Liberty University. While he has often despaired of the future of the United States and the world, classes go on at Liberty University, and the school looks to the future with hope. It is clear that FitzGerald intends her description of Falwell and his community as an important and relevant contribution to her general thesis of the transforming of American society, yet it is difficult to find much that is new in Falwell and his followers or to discern something that cannot already be seen in the revivalism of Finney, Lyman Beecher, Dwight Moody, Billy Sunday, or other historic American revivalists and the fundamentalist congregations to which they ministered.

FitzGerald has truly identified something new and unique in America in her brief section on Sun City, Florida, developed by Del Webb. Having cast off their past and close ties with family, having no jobs but an adequate income, and facing a future of growing disability and eventual death, the Sun Citians constitute a truly equalitarian society. They are constantly busy with daily activities and volunteer wørk, and, in the absence of nearby family, they have substituted neighbors and friends for their extended family. What is lacking, however, in FitzGerald's account is a detailed analysis of the value system of the Sun Citians.

The final section of FitzGerald's book describes Rajneeshpuram, the community that Bhagwan Rajneesh established in Oregon in 1981, run by Ma Anand Sheela, the guru's secretary and second-in-command. FitzGerald has written an overly long description of the day-to-day operation of the community, from Bhagwan Rajneesh's earliest work as a guru in India, through the establishment of the Oregon community and the disputes with local residents, to the final demise of the community and the paranoia of Sheela. There is far more detail here than most readers will require to recall the children's story about the Emperor and his new clothes. Rather than constituting a community based on shared values, Rajneeshpuram's deluded citizens desperately wanted to believe. What they did share, aside from their desire, was participation in the "Human Potential Movement." Their involvement in the movement led them to see life in Rajneeshpuram as its extension. It might well have been wise for FitzGerald to have focused on the human potential movement as an example of changing American values rather than on the short-lived community of Rajneeshpuram.

Cities on a Hill will undoubtedly attract considerable attention because it is the work of the Pulitzer Prize-winning author of two important studies—*Fire in the Lake* (1972) and *America Revised* (1979)—and because it deals with at least three very controversial topics—homosexuals, Jerry Falwell, and Bhagwan Rajneesh. FitzGerald's thesis regarding the disintegration of twentieth century American society and the emergence of a postindustrial value system, however, is inadequately sustained; FitzGerald proves to be a far better reporter than analyst, social critic, and historian of contemporary American culture.

Saul Lerner

Sources for Further Study

Booklist. LXXXIII, September 1, 1986, p. 4.
California Magazine. XI, November, 1986, p. 54.
Kirkus Reviews. LIV, September 15, 1986, p. 1416.
Los Angeles Times Book Review. October 26, 1986, p. 1.
The New Republic. CXCV, October 20, 1986, p. 38.
The New York Times Book Review. XCI, October 12, 1986, p. 11.
Newsweek. CVIII, November 3, 1986, p. 75.
Psychology Today. XX, December, 1986, p. 70.
Publishers Weekly. CCXXX, August 15, 1986, p. 62.
Washington Post Book World. XVI, September 28, 1986, p. 1.

COLLABORATORS

Author: Janet Kauffman (1945-   )
Publisher: Alfred A. Knopf (New York). 134 pp. $13.95
Type of work: Novel
Time: The 1960's
Locale: Mennonite tobacco-farming country in Pennsylvania

An intense, poetic novel celebrates the strength and pain of the bond between mother and daughter

> *Principal characters:*
> ANDREA DORIA (Dovie), the narrator, a child and adolescent who studies her mother in search of herself
> MOTHER, a Mennonite farmer and woman of strength
> RUTH, an old friend of the mother who has become a scholar
> MARLENE BEECHER, a non-Mennonite who teaches grade school and does farm work
> JONAS, Andrea Doria's younger brother

Janet Kauffman's first novel is, on the surface, an intensely personal story set in a curious backwater of American society. Because Kauffman writes with a poet's economy and evocative skill, however, *Collaborators* also serves, in the manner of a myth or fairy tale, to encode a fantasy with much broader resonance. The subconscious material here given conscious expression involves union, incomplete separation, and reabsorption: the process through which mothers are re-created in and by their daughters.

The book's first half conjures up a close, earthbound relationship between the child Andrea Doria—always called Dovie—and her mother (who, like most children's mothers, has no name except Mother). The child's view of her mother is a compound of awe, admiration, mystery, and desire; if she is at times almost overwhelmed by her mother's omnipotence, that omnipotence is wholly necessary to her security. Because the story is transmitted through the child's visual and sensual memory, Andrea Doria's father and brother scarcely seem to exist—as in the narcissistic world of childhood only the self is important. She is enmeshed with her mother, her shadow, her apprentice, ultimately her collaborator.

The chapters are short, like the fragments of memory that remain from childhood—intensely vivid but with little sense of context or connection. The narrative voice, though clearly that of Andrea Doria as an adult, does not provide linkages or interpretation. Thus for the reader, also, there are puzzles and mysteries: A child can never know all of a parent's secrets. It is this blurring of "reality" that gives the specific events of Dovie's childhood their universal resonance. Does one understand the truth by knowing what really happened and how it can be explained, or is there indeed a truer reality in the residue of feeling that remains unexamined and therefore ingrained? The subjective nature of the scenes makes them serve not only as scenes from Dovie's story—a narration about someone else—but also as metaphors that reveal the workings of the unconscious, just as a dream can tell truth by presenting the impossible.

The fragmentary scenes that conjure up childhood's mother are laden with the specific sensory details that burn into the mind at moments of intense emotion, especially when the emotion is too contradictory or too threatening to face. In one early scene expanded from a story in Kauffman's collection *Places in the World a Woman Could Walk* (1983), Andrea Doria lies on the beach in her mother's shadow. She feels fragile and boneless, compared to her mother's sturdy frame; there is a sense of homelessness, as of an exile cast forth from her native land and fearful of further change. The images of separation anxiety are almost overwhelming; the child is only intermittently aware of her own body and feels safe only when sure of her mother's attention:

> I'm small enough to lie beside her and use her shade. There, I am invisible; I am in hiding, in the only darkness she offers me. But if I raise my head and look over my chin into the daylight, I can see the blond unshaven hair on her calves, glitters of sand among the hairs, and, beyond her legs, clear strips of navy-blue ocean and white sky. The things I see have, as frame, one of my mother's limbs; that's how she places herself, convenient, dismembered, for such compositions. She doesn't realize that her body is breakable, but for me each glimpse of her, whole, is a resurrection. I believe it is she, not I, who attaches her body this closely at the edge of everything. When I look up, there is an arm, a leg....

When her mother gazes at the ocean or speaks of Ruth, her own girlhood friend, Dovie aches with the withdrawal of attention; knowing that her mother will soon go for another swim, she uses the time to prepare herself, "so I will not hold my breath the whole time."

In addition, the setting and characterization are full of fascination. Dovie's mother is no plastic suburban "mom" but a woman of strength and complexity, a strong-boned Mennonite farmer with individualistic and sometimes subversive personal convictions. The tobacco land was originally hers; marriage simply added a neighboring farm. Mother and daughter do hard physical labor in the fields and stripping sheds, talking as they work. Their communication is abbreviated, truncated, allusive; the mother writes words in the tobacco dust and then wipes them away, as if a whole range of experience and meaning can be communicated by a sparse word. She tells Dovie about her lovers about the love of a man's body, and also about good and evil:

> Goodness has nothing to do with convention, my mother said. It has nothing to do with sentiment.
> She made distinctions.

Goodness was passion—an ongoing, cumulative passion, a hoard of energies and decencies stockpiled against the day evil, that armored slug, turned up in the garden. And evil, of course, was not sin. Sin was what human beings *did*, when they acted most freely according to nature.

Evil was something else; it violated nature. It was loathsome, pestilential, chaotic. It showed itself always as violence—an explosive.

The sights and sounds and smells of the setting are vivid and sensuous but not idyllic; the state prison that sits "not quite out of sight" at the edge of the farm is both reality and metaphor. On the day Dovie first menstruates, her mother tells her about a sexual assault she had once experienced, but the details are so contradictory that even the listening child suspects that her mother's tale screens something she will not or cannot let herself remember.

The narrative voice recognizes that truth may be hidden when events are retold and invites readers to make their own unconscious and metaphoric connections. For all that Dovie describes herself as her mother's "apprentice," for all the dependence and awe and admiration that make her seem in danger of being overwhelmed, the book's opening passage warns of the ambiguities and the need to look beneath the narrative:

My mother lied to me about everything. She told me she believed in Hell. She told me she was a pacifist, a good Mennonite, and could never kill, not even in self-defense. She crooned and ranted and cooked up powerful storms of lies that held like uncalled-for weather over my childhood.... On the sly she told me, and more than once, that the world had nothing to do with God.

At mid book, just after Dovie has passed through puberty, her mother has a sudden stroke, and Dovie becomes her mother's second self—her collaborator in living—in a series of scenes that are, once again, both poignantly detailed in themselves and also invitations to metaphorical elaboration. At the moment that Dovie becomes physically a woman, she also turns into the mother of her memory, the woman who had defined both "woman" and self for her. Exercising the helpless limbs, she becomes her mother's muscle. She takes up her mother's friendship with Ruth—the woman who, after high school, cut her hair, took off her Mennonite covering, moved to the city, and became a scholar. Dovie had been jealous of Ruth as a child because she perceived that her mother's love for Ruth was a love between adults and of a different quality from a mother's love for a child who is part of herself. After her mother's stroke, Dovie also begins to see (and see to) her father and brother. When she has achieved—or been thrust into—an ego of her own, she grows aware of other people.

Once one has passed into adulthood, the mother that existed in childhood is forever lost. In the specifics of *Collaborators*, illness makes Andrea Doria's mother an outsider and exempt from Mennonite rules: She is allowed a television, a zippered robe, a glass of brandy at night. Although everyone says, officially, that she is recovered, she is quicker, lighter, less solid; Andrea Doria is the large one in the house now. As Dovie was boneless early, her mother now seems to lack substance. In series of dreams, Andrea Doria—who bears a name made famous by a sinking ship—sees her mother plunge into watery depths and then herself looks out at an undersea world through the drowning woman's eyes.

Kauffman's writing is evocative, intense, and selective. She uses the narrator's eye to compose scenes as a painter as well as a poet:

> Through the summer, Jonas's hair bleached out blond, almost as light as my mother's, and from where I sat in the living room that night, his hair and the top of his ear rose up above my mother's head. If I glanced at my mother, what I saw was a woman with half-curled, half-straight hair, a woman with one ear on the side of her head, one coming out the top. She might have had one or two extra legs, if I'd wanted to look.

The style thus encourages readers to look beneath the surface of the composition. It is not always easy to explain precisely what happens in a particular scene or to piece together a distinct narration of events. Yet the technique reflects the operation of memory: It is storytellers who create links and achieve coherence by filling in "what must have happened" or "what it means" when re-creating scenes from the past. Nor is it easy to separate the reality and the fantasy. The fantasy, however, provides clues about what is repressed and therefore cannot be remembered and may thus be more true and more universal than the particular reality.

Kauffman's technique is so vivid that one can hardly avoid experiencing the scenes. What one does with them probably depends on the ways they impinge on one's own fantasies and memories. *Collaborators* provides both an unforgettable depiction of a woman worth remembering and a mythic rendering of the mother-daughter bond, the transition from girlhood to womanhood, and the reproduction of mothering. As Dovie passes into adolescence she begins to spin words in her head in the same way that her mother wrote words in tobacco dust and left them for her daughter to erase. The final collaboration is Dovie's telling of her speechless mother's story— her re-creation for her own daughter of a memory that communicates a sense of womanhood with all of its vigor, its contradictions, its drive to independent self-creation, and its sense that self is necessarily entangled with other human selves.

Sally Mitchell

Sources for Further Study

Chicago Tribune. March 9, 1986, XIV, p. 39.
Kirkus Reviews. LIV, February 1, 1986, p. 156.

Library Journal. CXI, May 15, 1986, p. 78.
Los Angeles Times Book Review. May 11, 1986, p. 1.
Ms. XIV, April, 1986, p. 83.
The New Republic. CXCIV, April 21, 1986, p. 34.
The New York Times Book Review. XCI, April 20, 1986, p. 17.
Publishers Weekly. CCXXIX, January 17, 1986, p. 61.
The Village Voice. XXXI, April 29, 1986, p. 50.

THE COLLECTED LETTERS OF DYLAN THOMAS

Author: Dylan Thomas (1914-1953)
Edited, with an introduction, by Paul Ferris
Publisher: Macmillan Publishing Company (New York). 982 pp. $45.00
Type of work: Letters
Time: 1931-1953
Locale: Primarily Wales, England, and New York

More than a thousand letters provide a running commentary on the boisterous, undisciplined, and ultimately tragic life of the Welsh poet

Principal personages:
JOHN MALCOM BRINNIN, an American poet and lecturer
PRINCESS MARGUERITE CAETANI, an editor and patron of the arts, Thomas' patron from 1949
JOHN DAVENPORT, a critic and literary figure, coauthor with Thomas of *The King's Canary*
DESMOND HAWKINS, a novelist, critic, and broadcaster
CAITLIN THOMAS, Dylan Thomas' wife
VERNON WATKINS, a Welsh poet
OSCAR WILLIAMS, an American poet, anthologist, and Thomas' unofficial literary agent

Following his definitive biography of Dylan Thomas in 1977, Paul Ferris has completed a further labor in the same field, a collection of more than a thousand of Thomas' letters, covering more than nine hundred pages of text. This collection (originally published in England in 1985) chronicles a period of more than twenty years, ranging from the wordy exuberance of the adolescent poet in the 1930's to the increasingly sad and desperate letters written in the years immediately preceding his tragic death in 1953 in New York as a famous, and notorious, figure. Seven hundred of these letters have not been published before, and although they will not lead to any radical reassessment of Thomas' life or character—the Thomas story is too well-known and documented for that—the collection as a whole does give continuous insight into one of the brightest and wildest literary figures of the twentieth century.

The bulk of the early letters are to Pamela Hansford Johnson, an aspiring poet, later to succeed as a novelist, who had written to Thomas following the publication of one of his early poems. An enthusiastic and lengthy correspondence followed, in which they exchanged and criticized each other's work. The young Thomas, writing from his boyhood home in Swansea, Wales, gives many clues to the spirit that motivated his early, obscure, self-absorbed poetry, which caused such a stir in literary circles when his first collection, *18 Poems*, was published in 1934.

Not yet fully confident of his own powers (hardly surprising in a young man of nineteen), Thomas acknowledges to Johnson that he may be only a "freak user of words." Although he is "in the path of Blake," he is "so far behind him that only the wings on his heels are in sight." When Thomas digs into some of the conceptions and assumptions underlying his work, however, many of his comments are illuminating. When Johnson complains of the "ugliness" of much of his poetry, by which she probably meant his excessive use of anatomical imagery, he declares, "Every idea, intuitive or intellectual, can be imaged and translated in terms of the body, its flesh, skin, blood, sinews, veins, glands, organs, cells, or senses. Through my small, bonebound island I have learnt all I know, experienced all, and sensed all." In another early letter, this time to Trevor Hughes, a friend from Swansea living at the time in London, he writes that "it is my aim as an artist... to prove beyond doubt to myself that the flesh that covers me is the flesh that covers the sun, that the blood in my lungs is the blood that goes up and down in a tree," a concept brilliantly realized in many of his youthful poems, most notably perhaps in the complex, unified and unifying imagery in the famous "The Force That Through the Green Fuse Drives the Flower." To another early literary acquaintance, Glyn Jones, Thomas describes this as "the cosmic significance of the human anatomy." In his own curious and self-occupied way, he was intuitively grasping an ancient idea: the correspondence between microcosm and macrocosm—that man is a world in little and the universe is a man writ large.

Thomas freely admits to the obscurity that riddled his early poetry. In a previously unpublished letter to Desmond Hawkins, who was at that time literary editor of the magazine *Purpose*, he writes, "I agree that much of the poetry is impossibly difficult; I've asked, or rather told, words to do too much." Sometimes he is severe in his self-judgments, as, for example, regarding *18 Poems*: "a poor lot, on the whole, with many thin lines, many oafish sentiments... & much highfalutin nonsense." He confesses to Glyn Jones that his sonnet sequence "Altarwise by Owl-Light," in which he seems to reach new heights of opacity, reads almost like a "mad parody" of his own style. (His explanation of the first two lines of the first of these sonnets is particularly illuminating, since it is hard to see how anyone could have divined it without Thomas' help.)

Thomas disliked theoretical discussions of his own, or anyone else's, poetry. He writes to an inquiring friend, "You asked me to tell you about my theory of poetry. Really I haven't got one," and to Hawkins he says that "it isn't theories that choke some of the wilder and worser lines, but sheer greed." To his early critics and correspondents, he denies any connection with surrealism ("I have very little idea what surrealism is") or any suggestion that his poetry is the product of automatic writing. On one of the few occasions that he gave any detailed explanation of his method or technique, he explained to Henry Treece, a young poet who, as early as 1937, was preparing a book-length study of Thomas' poetry: "Each image holds within it the seed of its own destruction, and my dialectical method...is a constant building up and breaking down of the images that come out of the central seed, which is itself destructive and constructive at the same time." Out of this conflict of images, he attempts "to make that momentary peace which is a poem.... All warring images within it should be reconciled for that small stop of time." Thomas returns more than once to this Blakean idea of the conflict of opposites, most notably in the newly available letter to Hawkins. In an explanation of his poem "I Make This in a Warring Absence When," he comments that "I made as many contraries as possible fight together, in an attempt to bring out a *positive* quality," and in a note at the foot of the page Thomas adds, "negate each other, if they could; keep their individualities & lose them in each other." The debt to Blake is clear.

By the mid-1930's, with the publication of his second book, *Twenty-five Poems*, Thomas was building a reputation for himself as an exciting and promising new poet. He now spent much of his time in London, and the friendship with Pamela Johnson had turned into a brief love affair that did not long survive Thomas' wild behavior. It was during this period that he began to cultivate carefully another kind of reputation—as the Bohemian poet, always likely to flout convention and behave outrageously, especially when drunk (which Thomas frequently was).

These years set the pattern for the future. Thomas refused to earn money from anything but the sale of his poems and short stories, claiming that he could not find, and was not fit for, any other kind of work. Consequently, he was usually poor, and this led him into an increasingly disorganized and chaotic life-style. He was frequently on the move, from one temporary (usually free) lodging to another, and he was notoriously unreliable. Eventually his irresponsibility proved to be as much of a burden to himself as to others. His apologies, for broken appointments and unanswered letters, for rude or thoughtless behavior, run like a leitmotif through his correspondence. They are sometimes candid and revealing and foreshadow the despair of later years: "My selfish carelessness and unpunctuality I do not try to excuse as poet's properties. They are a bugbear & a humbug. The selfish trouble is that I myself have had to put up with these seriously annoying faults for so long that I've almost come to think other people can bear them."

Thomas' friends, however, usually forgave him his faults, even when pushed to the limit (such as when he failed to turn up for the wedding of his close friend, the poet Vernon Watkins, at which Thomas was to have been best man). The secret of the loyalty which he undoubtedly inspired in his friends lay not only in the fact that he was quite obviously a poet of superior gifts but that he was also uproariously funny company, a wonderful storyteller with a gift for improvisation and exaggeration—the perfect drinking companion. Also, he was so obviously unconcerned, through a curious blend of innocence and cunning, with the practical business of earning a living that others felt compelled to support him. Thomas certainly knew how to exploit the patience and generosity of his friends; many letters contain desperate appeals for money. At one point, when mulling over a proposed scheme to solicit regular donations from a circle of literary acquaintances, he writes to John Davenport, "I think I should concentrate...on getting my living-money from *people* and not from poems." Yet whenever Thomas had money, he seemed incapable of handling it wisely. Throughout his life, he avoided responsibility and seemed bent on reckless, self-destructive behavior.

Many times in his letters, Thomas obliquely suggests his lack of confidence, his helplessness in the face of the world, in spite of the image of the *bon viveur* he had created for himself. He is full of self-deprecating remarks, especially about his appearance (he describes his own face as a "red, blubbery circle mounted on ballooning body"); he refers often to his "littleness" (a word used perhaps subconsciously to elicit sympathy); and he dwells often on his ill health, whether real or imaginary. A previously unpublished letter to Vernon Watkins, discovered by Watkins' wife after her husband's death, and dated 1945, reveals a deeply troubled personality: "The ordinary moments of walking up village streets, opening doors or letters, speaking good-days to friends or strangers, looking out of windows, making telephone calls, are so inexplicably (to me) dangerous that I am trembling all over before I get out of bed in the mornings to meet them." Behind the social mask, Dylan Thomas struggled to cope with a disabling melancholy and introspection.

Yet there is no doubt that, whatever his faults and inadequacies, Thomas was ruthlessly dedicated to his craft. To a journalist who was preparing an article about him, he commented that he often covered a hundred sheets of paper to produce a single verse. "I work extremely slowly, painfully, in seclusion." Sometimes, he seems to have exerted his technical skill almost for the sake of it, as in the unusual rhyme scheme of the author's prologue to the *Collected Poems 1934-1952* (1952), where the first line of a 102-line poem rhymes with the last, and so on, until the two central lines rhyme with each other. (He writes to E. F. Bozman, his editor at Dent, "Why I acrosticked myself like this, don't ask me.") This concern with technique even extended to the shape of the poem on the printed page, as can be seen not only from the elaborate and unusual structure of "Vision and Prayer," but also in "Into Her Lying Down Head," the typographical exactitude of which is not apparent to the casual reader, but Thomas (as one of his letters to Vernon Watkins shows) labored hard to get it right.

Some of the most interesting letters in the collection are those more than thirty previously unpublished letters to Thomas' wife, Caitlin. Thomas had met Caitlin Macnamara, a high-spirited and tempestuous Irish girl from County Clare, and a year his senior, in 1936; they were married the following year. It was a turbulent marriage, but Thomas remained genuinely in love with her to the end. Many of the surviving letters were written from London during World War II. Thomas had managed to avoid military service and had found employment writing scripts for propaganda films. Others are from Thomas' first trip to America, where he spent three months on a highly successful nationwide reading and lecturing tour in 1950, and from Iran, where he was temporarily employed by the Anglo-Iranian oil company as scriptwriter for a documentary film. These letters are full of childlike declarations of love ("I love you, more and more and more the longer I am without you. I cannot go on without you, for you are forever too wonderful and I can only say Cat my darling you are my sweetheart..."); of his loneliness ("I am as lonely as the grave"); and of his utter helplessness without her. He desperately clung to Caitlin as his one source of love and security. Caitlin, on the other hand, had grown increasingly dissatisfied, unhappy with Thomas' inability to provide an adequate income for her and their three children, and upset by his affair with an American woman. A letter, reproduced in this collection, which she wrote in early 1953 to their American friends Oscar Williams and his wife, Gene Derwood, conveys bitterness and disillusionment. Thomas, she says, has virtually given up writing "for the actor's ranting boom, and lisping mimicry," and as a consequence "anything he sells is either a rehashed bubble and squeak of adolescence, or a never to be fulfilled promise in the future."

Toward the end of his life, Thomas' letters become even more desperate. To his patron Margaret Taylor (the wife of historian A. J. P. Taylor) he writes, "I have gout in my toe, phlegm on my lungs, misery in my head, debts in the town, no money in my pocket, and a poem simmering on the hob." The playful tone of earlier letters has gone; Thomas is now an unhappy, depressed man, unable to cope with his responsibilities and seeing no way of escape. His creative output had declined and caused him endless frustration and worry: "My room is littered with beginnings, each staring me accusingly in the eyes." Only six complete poems were written in the last four-and-a-half years of his life, when he and his family moved back to the village of Laugherne, in South Wales, to live in a cottage provided by Taylor at minimal rent. He seems to have spent as much time carefully drafting and redrafting letters as he did poems, and his excuses for missed appointments and unfinished work became more elaborate and more full of self-pity and self-disgust. His unreliability in delivering promised manuscripts eventually made employers such as the BBC wary of him. Although to the outside world he appeared to be a successful poet and broadcaster, and his income was steadily rising, he never managed to set his affairs in order. His early and tragic death in New York in 1953, at the age of thirty-nine (as a result of complications arising from a long drinking bout), was, with hindsight, predictable. It was almost as if he had himself scripted his own demise, as a final way of escape.

At their best, the letters of Dylan Thomas are highly entertaining. Full of irreverent, often vulgar, humor, the words tumble out fast—spun, spilled, and savored by a man for whom language had almost magical power. Others, particularly those from his last years, make painful reading. Yet few would dispute that out of the boisterous chaos of his life Thomas managed to write some of the finest lyrics of the twentieth century. Indeed, many of the poems which have proved most popular, as well as the radio play *Under Milk Wood* (1954), were written in his final, tormented years. His incomparable reading voice, so full of rich intensity, survives on gramophone records. Had he been able to enjoy his full measure of years, he would perhaps have found a new lease of creative life in television, a medium which would have suited him so well, but which at the time of his death was only in its infancy.

A final word should record that Thomas has been well served by his editor, Paul Ferris. As well as making a much larger number of Thomas' letters available, Ferris has considerably improved the texts of letters which were included in Constantine Fitzgibbon's selection, published in 1966. Ferris' footnotes are invaluable. Concise and unobtrusive, they rarely leave the reader in the dark concerning names, events, and allusions mentioned in the text. An informative and fair-minded introduction, and a comprehensive index, complete a valuable edition.

Bryan Aubrey

Sources for Further Study

Booklist. LXXXII, May 1, 1986, p. 1277.
Contemporary Review. CCXLVII, November, 1985, p. 278.
Kirkus Reviews. LIV, April 1, 1986, p. 519.
Los Angeles Times Book Review. May 25, 1986, p. 1.
The New Republic. CXCV, August 11, 1986, p. 33.
The New York Review of Books. XXXIII, April 24, 1986, p. 15.
Publishers Weekly. CCXXIX, March 14, 1986, p. 91.
Time. CXXVII, April 21, 1986, p. 73.
Times Literary Supplement. May 2, 1986, p. 475.
Washington Post Book World. XVI, May 4, 1986, p. 1.

THE COLLECTED LETTERS OF JOSEPH CONRAD
Volume II: 1898-1902

Author: Joseph Conrad (1857-1924)
Edited, with an introduction, by Frederick R. Karl and Laurence Davies
Publisher: Cambridge University Press (New York). Illustrated. 483 pp. $44.50
Type of work: Letters
Time: 1898-1902
Locale: Kent, England

    The second of eight projected volumes of the collected letters of a major British novelist

> *Principal personages:*
> JOSEPH CONRAD, a Polish-born seaman-turned-novelist in his adopted tongue, English
> JESSIE CONRAD, his wife
> BORYS CONRAD, their newborn son
> H. G. WELLS, a novelist and friend of Conrad
> JOHN GALSWORTHY, a novelist, friend, and benefactor of Conrad
> FORD MADOX FORD, a novelist with whom Conrad collaborated on *The Inheritors* and *Romance*
> JAMES BRAND PINKER, Conrad's literary agent
> EDWARD GARNETT, a publisher's reader and critic, who early in Conrad's career encouraged him in his work
> ROBERT BONTINE CUNNINGHAME GRAHAM, a Socialist writer and a close, enduring friend of Conrad
> STEPHEN CRANE, a famous American poet, novelist, and journalist, and a friend of Conrad
> CORA CRANE, a former brothel keeper and the first woman war correspondent, who traveled as Crane's wife

If the greatest potential pleasure in reading the letters of a great writer during a particularly fertile period in his life is to gain insight into the creative process, then this second volume of Joseph Conrad's letters is a disappointment. Although in this four-year period Conrad wrote much of his finest fiction, including "Youth," "Typhoon," "The End of the Tether," *Lord Jim* (1900), and *Heart of Darkness* (1902), he says little in his letters about these works except to disparage them, while making clear that he considers them minor in comparison to the novel *The Rescue* (1920), which he was having great difficulty finishing (and which he did not in fact complete until 1919). Indeed, these letters and the period of life they reflect are clear illustrations of one of Conrad's favorite literary themes, that reality often belies appearances.

On the surface, this was a good period in Conrad's life. He and his wife, Jessie, moved to a spacious house in the country, and their son, Borys, was born. In addition, Conrad acquired a new literary agent, J. B. Pinker, who treated him generously, gave him encouragement, and almost always tolerated his delays. Conrad, moreover, developed a number of close friendships with other literary men, including Stephen Crane, John Galsworthy, H. G.

Wells, Robert Cunninghame Graham, and Ford Madox Ford. His friendship with Ford led to a successful collaboration on two novels, *The Inheritors* (1901), and *Romance* (1903). His work of this period received consistently favorable reviews, and his growing recognition was capped by Pinker's publication of a collection of his stories, entitled *Tales of Unrest* (1898).

Despite these apparent successes, Conrad frequently expressed disappointment in his work, remained ambivalent about his son, suffered bouts of depression and illness, and worried incessantly about money problems, expending much of his energy in concocting wild schemes for making additional income. These miseries were further exacerbated by guilt at his apparent desertion of his native land and Polish language for England and English and by despondency following the early death from tuberculosis of his beloved friend Stephen Crane.

The most curious aspect of Conrad revealed in these letters is his peculiarly dismissive attitude toward some of his finest work of this period. He refers to "Youth" as merely "a bit of life," which "could have been made better if it had fallen into better hands." He calls *Lord Jim* "the sort of rot I am writing now," deeming it "not worth troubling about" and pronouncing the second installment "too wretched for words." Similarly, he calls "Typhoon" "too silly for words." Even *Heart of Darkness*, which he values for its topicality and sustained idea, "is terribly bad in places and falls short of my intention as a whole."

Nor do these statements reveal a false modesty or a disingenuous courting of praise. Rather, Conrad suffered from chronic self-doubt: "The doubt of form—the doubt of tendency—a mistrust of my own conceptions—and scruples of the moral order." Accordingly, he sees his work as suffering from "want of power" and concludes, "The *Outcast* is a heap of sand, the *Nigger* a splash of water and *Jim* a lump of clay." This self-mistrust leads him to fret, "I am afraid there's something wrong with my thinking apparatus." Because of these self-doubts, he worked agonizingly slowly and consistently failed to meet deadlines. He also consistently underestimated the length of his finished stories and therefore frequently produced stories twice their projected length. Most painful of all, he censored his own ideas so severely that, as one letter reveals, he would sit at the typewriter all day, creating entire chapters in his head, without recording a single word of them.

To a certain extent, these difficulties stemmed from his lingering misgivings about his belated choice of vocation and about his expatriation. In letters to Polish friends and relatives, he too vigorously attempts to defend his allegiance to English life and letters. "It does not seem to me that I have been unfaithful to my country by having proved to the English that a gentleman from the Ukraine can be as good a sailor as they, and has something to tell them in their own language." Yet he says of writing as a profession, "It is a fool's business to write fiction for a living. . . . The unreality of it seems to enter one's real life, penetrate into the bones, make the very heart beats pulsate illusions through the arteries."

In actuality, these gloomy reflections on his vocation merely reflected his pervasively gloomy outlook on life. This outlook not only pervades his works but also often made the entire enterprise of art seem futile to him and prevented him from writing. He moreover saw human nature as ineradicably flawed, his audience as hopelessly unredeemable, and writing itself as mere illusion: "All is illusion—the words written, the mind at which they are aimed, the truth they are intended to express, the hands that will hold the paper, the eyes that will glance at the lines." In a previously published letter to Cunninghame Graham, he states:

> Man is a vicious animal. His viciousness must be organised. Crime is a necessary condition of organised existence. Society is fundamentally criminal—or it would not exist. Selfishness preserves everything—absolutely everything—everything we hate and everything we love. . . . That is why I respect the extreme anarchists. . . . One compromises with words. There's no end to it.

Despite this bleak view of human nature, Conrad was able to enjoy warm, confiding relationships with a diverse group of friends, including the utopian Socialist H. G. Wells, the traditional novelist of family saga, John Galsworthy, and the bon vivant man of letters, Ford Madox Ford. To all of them, as well as to literary acquaintances, such as Arnold Bennett, Conrad wrote responses at their request to their current works, criticizing their writing with insight and incisiveness, yet with delicacy and tact.

In general, the letters show him to be a most generous appreciator and defender of the talents of others. Most notable is his defense of Henry James, in which he argues against the assertion that James does not write from the heart. With great acuity, Conrad observes, "His heart shows itself in the delicacy of his handling. . . . He feels deeply and vividly every delicate shade. We can not ask for more." Perhaps this insight into James helps to explain Conrad's own intense concern to explore minutely—even exhaustively—the motivation of his characters and the implications of their actions.

In general, it is Conrad's comments upon the words of others rather than upon his own writings that offer the greatest insight into his own work. Thus, the reader may understand his letter urging Galsworthy to more skepticism in his work, maintaining that skepticism is "the tonic of minds, the tonic of life, the agent of truth—the way of art and salvation." As Conrad maintains, the writer must not side too much with his characters but "must preserve an attitude of perfect indifference." Again, the reader thinks of Conrad, not Bennett, when Conrad tells his fellow novelist, "Now realism in art will never approach reality. And your art, your gift should be put to the service of a larger and freer faith." Likewise, Conrad is describing his own style when he states to Elsie Hueffer, "Sometimes a sentence is too precisely finished. . . . Indubitably a less precise expression makes for a greater precision of effect in nine cases out of ten."

Whatever his misgivings and awareness of his shortcomings, Conrad never doubted his methods. Disclaiming kinship with past authors, he proclaimed his work "modern." Repeatedly advising writers to get at the truth in indirect or oblique ways and to get at reality by departing from realism, Conrad in his letters to other writers gives the reader insight into his own artistic aims and techniques.

On the whole, this collection of Conrad's letters is an interesting and eminently readable volume, largely because of the excellence of the editing. The editors provide many useful features, including a fine introduction, a number of illustrations, and a map of the south of England, where Conrad lived. Other helpful supplementary features include a chronology of the important events of Conrad's life and an alphabetical list and description of all of Conrad's correspondents. One of the most commonsensical features of the edition is that it assumes that most readers will not read the volume cover to cover or in sequence; thus, the editors provide information in footnotes more than once. Throughout, the letters are fully and conveniently annotated.

On the whole, this collection of letters will be valuable to Conrad scholars for its clear, accurate, and complete presentation of Conrad's correspondence at various crucial stages in his life. It will also be of great interest to general readers for its illuminating portrait of a writer who managed to create enduring works of art despite self-doubt, pressing deadlines, ill health, and penury.

Carola M. Kaplan

Sources for Further Study

The Guardian Weekly. CXXXV, August 31, 1986, p. 22.
Listener. CXVI, August 21, 1986, p. 23.
The London Review of Books. VIII, October 9, 1986, p. 22.
The New York Times Book Review. XCII, January 25, 1987, p. 16.
The Observer. August 17, 1986, p. 22.
Spectator. CCLVII, August 16, 1986, p. 18.
Times Literary Supplement. August 29, 1986, p. 931.

THE COLLECTED LETTERS OF W. B. YEATS
Volume I: 1865-1895

Author: W(illiam) B(utler) Yeats (1865-1939)
Edited, with an introduction, by John Kelly and Eric Domville
Publisher: Oxford University Press (New York). Illustrated. 548 pp. $29.95
Type of work: Letters
Time: 1865-1895

The collected letters of W. B. Yeats up to the age of thirty reveal primarily his work to encourage Irish literature and culture, and his developing ideas about poetry

This is the first of a many-volumed collection of the letters of William Butler Yeats, perhaps the most unreservedly acclaimed modern poet in the English language. Almost half the letters in this superbly edited volume have not been previously published. Although there are some letters from his boyhood, the great bulk of them span the years 1887 to 1895 when Yeats was in his twenties and working passionately for the cause of Irish literature and his own career as a poet and man of letters.

These early letters are filled with business—the business of recovering and encouraging Irish literature and, at the same time, forwarding his own career. As such, they are not deeply reflective or self-conscious but filled with the ambition and enthusiasm of a young poet with great plans. Many of the letters are perfunctory in the sense that they merely seek or communicate information.

Interspersed throughout the letters, however, are references to the great concerns of Yeats's youth and entire life. Chief among those is his concern to engender in the Irish people an appreciation for their cultural past and an enthusiasm for a new Irish literature in the present. These letters are full of what came to be known broadly as the Irish Literary Revival, a diverse movement whose aims are fairly summarized in a letter Yeats wrote to a Dublin newspaper in 1895:

> Our "movement" . . . has denounced rhetoric with . . . passionate vehemence. . . . It has exposed sentimentality and flaccid technique . . . but, at the same time, it has persuaded Irish men and women to read what is excellent in past and present Irish literature, and it has added to that literature books of folk-lore, books of history, books of fiction, and books of verse. . . . Nor is it a self-conscious endeavour to make a literature, but the spontaneous expression of an impulse which has been gathering power for decades.

The Irish Literary Revival was the cultural counterpart of a growing Irish political nationalism. Yeats repeatedly calls in these letters for an Irish literature that is not slavishly imitative of English forms, but that grows out of and celebrates the "wild Celtic blood, the most un-English of all things under heaven."

Yeats's letters attest the difficulty of the task he set for himself. He describes Ireland as a land which loves language yet does not read. It had little of the literary infrastructure—libraries, publishers, books (especially genuinely Irish ones), literary organizations—necessary to preserve, much less continue to create, a national culture. Standing squarely in the way of solving these problems was the ever-present political squabbling of Ireland and what many saw as a pervasive spiritual and intellectual lethargy.

Nevertheless, Yeats threw himself into the fray with energy and optimism. Included in this collection are letters to other Irish writers, such as the poet Katharine Tynan, encouraging them to explore their Irishness in producing the literature their country needs. Yeats frequently sought help in his own efforts to collect and publish Irish folklore and legends. There are repeated letters to newspapers and publishers pushing specific projects and the Irish Literary Revival as a whole, and Yeats does not avoid public and private battle with those whom he thinks stand in the way.

One can sense Yeats growing weary and somewhat less optimistic in this crusade in his later twenties. He more or less gave up on his initial hope that the peasant masses would embrace the movement and began to concentrate instead on persuading the intellectual and artistic elite to become the backbone of the effort. He admits that the standard of Irish life has forced many with talent to seek fame and fortune abroad, but he takes heart in the example of Walt Whitman that writers who are initially ignored or reviled at home may one day be recognized as the voice of their people.

As a young man Yeats clearly saw his work for the Irish Literary Revival as his most valuable contribution to his country and the one most likely to win for him a place in Irish literary history. His letter of 1895 to Tynan reveals the mixture of pride, determination, and frustration that characterizes much of his early correspondence:

> Whether the coming generations in England accept me or reject me, the coming genera-
> tions in Ireland cannot but value what I have done. I am writing at the end of the day &
> when I am tired, this endless war with Irish stupidity gets upon my nerves. Either you or
> I could have more prosperous lives probably if we left Ireland alone, & went our own
> way on the high seas—certainly we could have more peacable lives. However if the sun
> shine in the morning I shall be full of delight of battle & ready to draw my bow against
> the dragon.

While fighting the good fight for Irish culture, Yeats was simultaneously launching his own career as a poet and man of letters. Among the delights of reading these letters is coming across the casual inclusion of a later famous poem such as "The Lake Isle of Innisfree" and watching his views of poetry develop.

In these years, beauty and spirituality in poetry were clearly paramount for Yeats. At twenty-one, Yeats wrote a letter to a high school friend which reveals the aesthetic that underlies much of his early poetry. While criticizing the novels of George Eliot, he declaims with youthful assurance: "In literature nothing that is not beautiful has any right to exist." Anticipating his later notion of the "spiritus mundi" (and Carl Jung's "collective unconscious"), he declares that Eliot "knows nothing of the dim unconscious nature[,] the world of instinct which . . . is the accumulated wisdom of all living things." He completes his revealing dismissal of Eliot by the claim that she had not "imagination or spirit enough," adding,

> She is too reasonable. I hate reasonable people[;] the activity of their brains sucks up all the blood out of their hearts. I was once afraid of turning out reasonable myself. The only business of the head in the world is to bow a ceaseless obeisance to the heart.

Yeats's earliest poetry shows exactly this Romantic preference for the heart over the head, for the world of spirit and beauty over that of intellect and practicality. This aesthetic fit nicely with his attempt to incorporate Irish myth and folklore into his work and to write a musical, symbolistic poetry that appealed to intuition and the human heart.

At the same time, Yeats wanted to write a new poetry that incorporated the past without being bound by it. He wanted to be modern and yet avoid the spiritual deadness of the modern world. He saw as early as 1888 that his poetry was "almost all a flight into fairy land" and "not the poetry of insight and knowledge but of longing and complaint—the cry of the heart against necessity." He expressed the hope to write one day a different kind of poetry, a hope that was triumphantly fulfilled in his later life.

The general direction of that fulfillment is adumbrated in a comment Yeats made a year later about a play on which he was working: "The plot will be the best I have yet worked on—being both fantastic and human—human enough to rouse peoples [sic] sympathies, fantastic enough to wake them from their conventional standards." Here in miniature is the great goal of Yeats's life and art: to wed this world and the transcendent one, the real and the ideal, the material and the spiritual, the world of Irish politics and Irish fairies.

This quest for ultimate unity was the driving force in all that Yeats did, and evidence of it is scattered throughout these letters: He is anxious about a world that is increasingly scientific, materialistic, and rationalistic; he fears that such forces, symbolized for him by the England of the late Industrial Revolution, are squeezing out the imagination and the spirit, and that mystical Ireland has much to offer, if only it will recognize its great resources.

This yearning for spirituality and transcendence primarily accounts for Yeats's well-known attraction to the occult. In a letter written in 1892 to John O'Leary, the Irish revolutionary so influential on the young Yeats, Yeats connects his study of the occult with his writing of poetry, claiming that magic is "next to my poetry the most important pursuit of my life." Without it, he claims, he could not have written much of what he had.

For Yeats, the occult was not an investigation into evil, but an attempt to reach spirituality, and thereby consistent with all that he did. In this same letter to O'Leary, Yeats writes,

> The mystical life is the centre of all that I do & all that I think & all that I write. . . . I have all-ways considered my self a voice of what I beleive [sic] to be a greater renaisance [sic]—the revolt of the soul against the intellect—now beginning in the world.

Yeats talks easily of meeting fairies in the fields outside Sligo. He offers interpretations of his friends' visions. He joined occult societies, the most famous led by Madame Helena Blavatsky, accepting some of their activities as genuine while passing off others as charlatanism. In all of this, Yeats displayed his hunger for transcendence and his willingness to pursue it wherever it might lead.

There are many other items of interest in these letters. Here is recorded the beginning of his relationships with women who would shape his life— Olivia Shakespear and Maud Gonne. Here also is his testimony to the importance of his boyhood days in Sligo, to his dislike of London, and to his opinion of writers such as George Bernard Shaw (shallow), Leo Tolstoy (joyless), and William Blake (wonderful). All of this is supported with abundant and unusually helpful editorial material, making this first volume of Yeats's collected letters the beginning of a definitive and indispensable tool in Yeats studies.

Daniel Taylor

Sources for Further Study

Booklist. LXXXII, June 1, 1986, p. 1429.
Choice. XXIII, July, 1986, p. 1680.
Library Journal. CXI, July, 1986, p. 78.
Listener. CXV, March 20, 1986, p. 24.
The London Review of Books. VIII, April 3, 1986, p. 9.
Macleans. XCIX, June 9, 1986, p. 58.
The New Republic. CXCIV, May 12, 1986, p. 33.
The New York Review of Books. XXXIII, August 14, 1986, p. 14.
The New York Times Book Review. XCI, June 29, 1986, p. 14.
Times Literary Supplement. March 7, 1986, p. 235.

COLLECTED POEMS

Author: Geoffrey Hill (1932-   )
Publisher: Oxford University Press (New York). 207 pp. $18.95
Type of work: Poetry

A collection made up of five earlier volumes published between 1959 and 1984, together with a short sequence appearing for the first time

In the introduction to an earlier collection of Geoffrey Hill's poems, *Somewhere Is Such a Kingdom* (1975), the critic Harold Bloom described Hill as "the strongest British poet now alive." This is a considerable accolade. One may, however, wonder slightly about the adjective "British." Hill is in many respects a cosmopolitan poet, writing with increasing frequency about France, drawing on Spanish and German poetry, and clearly influenced by several American poets as well. For all that, he seems very much less "British" (a term which includes Scotland and Wales as well as Northern Island) than "English." Many of Hill's qualities are those central to the English tradition. His writing seems often to be "under glass," produced by an intelligence of extreme detachment and self-consciousness. Social embarrassment is a common theme, as is self-distrust. Hill has a trick of building up to a major assertion, a gesture of passion, but then catching himself in the act, withdrawing. Yet he is at the same time a "strong" poet, as Bloom observes, capable of assuming an authoritative or, even, quasi-prophetic voice, and of writing with a mythic intensity. Other recurrent themes of his include the major public events of the twentieth century and of previous centuries, among them war and genocide. His poetry is often one of strong and direct sensuality; he is a great evocator of the natural world.

If there is an overriding feeling within Hill's poems, however—it is too evasive to be called a theme—it must be the feeling of loss. In his 1978 collection *Tenebrae* (reprinted in this volume, along with all the other poems to be mentioned), he heads one poem with the German epigraph *Es ist ein Land Verloren*, translatable literally as "There is a lost land." That is not how Hill translates it, but the notion of a lost country, or, more precisely, of an unattainable country within the mind, colors much of his poetry. Very often this country is that of his own memories of childhood: *Mercian Hymns* (1971) is set in "Mercia," at once the old Latin term for the Anglo-Saxon kingdom of King Offa in the eighth century and Hill's private term for the rural Worcestershire of his own boyhood. The most obvious feature of that collection is its anachronism. Hill brings together an archaic language of the far past, of rune stones, wergilds, and fire dragons, with a studied colloquialism sometimes ironically vulgar, sometimes childish. The result is characteristically ambiguous. In one way, Hill appears to be pointing to ways in which England has declined, dwindled—the great victories of the Anglo-

Saxon conquerors now remembered only as names for small, suburban houses. In another way, he indicates direct continuity and achievement. The coins of King Offa still preserve his face and power; his name is still familiar (from "Offa's Dyke," the long earthwork that divides much of England from Wales); there is a sense of pride lurking in Hill's memories of a boyhood in wartime as fierce as anything from the remotest past. Nevertheless, both the recent past of childhood and the far past of Mercia have receded, gone back to the same country, the land indeed "called Lost."

What besides the inevitable passing of time motivates Hill's feelings of loss? To this there must be many answers. One is a loss of political innocence. *Mercian Hymns* is prefaced by an epigraph on "the conduct of government," which laments the way in which public morality has become a thing apart from private morality. More nostalgically, the sequence of thirteen sonnets in *Tenebrae* titled "An Apology for the Revival of Christian Architecture in England" contains three sonnets described as "A Short History of British India." They are once more "spectator-poems," in which Hill looks on at a historical process as if at a pageant or spectacle, yet their overall point is that a certain simplicity, a certain directness of rule, has gone from the world, never to be revived but perhaps to be regretted. This loss of innocence is, however, not only, and, not even primarily, a British concern. Like so many of the writers of the twentieth century, Hill shows also that he has been deeply marked by the horrors of World War II, events which (one should remember) would very probably have seemed unthinkable in any civilized European state even in the year when Hill was born. History, however, falsified the European confidence in progress. Accordingly, Hill's earliest collection, *For the Unfallen* (1959), contains "Two Formal Elegies: For the Jews in Europe"; *King Log* (1968) begins with the poem "Ovid in the Third Reich"; *Mercian Hymns* draws, as has been said, on wartime memories; and even *Tenebrae* includes a poem centered on Dietrich Bonhoeffer, the pacifist German theologian eventually executed for his part in a plot to kill Adolf Hitler. The point which Hill draws in all these meditations is an obvious one: that the horrors of the Holocaust cannot be safely distanced but point to an evil potential in all humanity. Hill, however, does not forget that this knowledge is a new knowledge or, at least, a revived one. The nineteenth century was different from the twentieth.

Feeling for historical change is nevertheless subordinate in Hill to a feeling for the human condition regardless of time, though this too is dominated by a sense of lost innocence. There is a puzzle in the title of Hill's first collection, *For the Unfallen*. In Christian theology, all mankind, with the exception of Christ, is "fallen" as a result of original sin. Divine grace can repair the effects of the Fall but does not annul the fact of it. "The unfallen," then, do not exist. Is Hill referring to another Fall, not that of Adam and Eve? Does he mean the adjective in some other sense, not "primally innocent," perhaps, but much more simply "alive" or "untempted"? Answering this question takes one further into the realm of Hill's developing private mythology.

Aptly enough, the first poem in Hill's first collection is titled "Genesis," and it follows the biblical six days of Creation. Yet the "I" of the poem cannot be God, must be in some sense the poet, and the poet's "Genesis" shows a strange oscillation between renunciation of the flesh (and with it the entire natural order of breeding and predation) and eager acceptance of it. "By blood we live," Hill declares, near the end. It may be "Christ's blood." Yet even that seeming return to a traditional religious statement is muted by two parallel conditional clauses at the very end of the poem, whose effect is to suggest that there are doubts, facts which if scrutinized make the tame-seeming Christian order untenable.

In the broadest possible terms, one could say that Hill (like many other writers of the twentieth century) perceives a crisis of faith, caused by a new awareness of human and of natural cruelty. If this is the way of the world, how can that world be reconciled with divine love? In this dilemma, Hill writes one poem after another on traditional themes but with untraditional answers—for example, "Genesis," "Canticle for Good Friday," "Annunciations," "The Pentecost Castle," "Hymns to Our Lady of Chartres." *Tenebrae* means "shadows," but it is also the name given to the services at the end of Easter Week, held by tradition with all tapers in the church extinguished in mourning for Christ's death and in expectation of his Resurrection. It is significant that "Canticle for Good Friday" centers on "Doubting Thomas" (see John, 20:24-29), the apostle who refused to believe in the Resurrection until he had seen and handled the very wounds of Christ. Hill appears himself, very often, as a skeptic who would like to believe. In the seven sonnets of "Lachrimae," in *Tenebrae*, Hill repeatedly addresses his "Crucified Lord," asking in effect why Christ should bother with a heart that will not harbor him—the heart of a Thomas or, indeed (he suggests), a Judas—especially as the "judas-kiss" he writes of is itself the act of devotion, possibly even the act of poetry, turned to treachery for all of its good intentions by an insidious lack of real conviction. Hill, in poems such as these, is close to the traditional sin of theological despair, in a downward spiral of doubt and distrust only accelerated by the failure of each attempt to break out. Once more Hill adds an element of historical irony by taking the words of Saint Robert Southwell—a Jesuit priest executed in hideous fashion in 1595 in the reign of Queen Elizabeth—and reversing them within his poetry. As with the poems on "British India," he seems to be looking back wistfully to an earlier and simpler age when even intelligent and self-conscious men could be immune to doubt and act without fatal introspection.

Hill's admiration for Southwell (and King Offa) is, however, paralleled by admiration for characters more nearly contemporary to himself and thus much more likely to be caught in the mire of doubt. Yet some appear to have escaped it—for example, Bonhoeffer—and Hill is quick to celebrate any modern gallant achievement. His most recent major work, *The Mystery of the Charity of Charles Péguy* (1983), celebrates a little-known French writer, born in 1873, whose life appears as a mixture of violent paradoxes and even futilities, until, in a gesture of unpredictable patriotism, he went to battle as an infantry lieutenant of the reserve, only to be killed in action on the first day of the Battle of the Marne in September, 1914. Throughout the long poem in his memory, Hill broods on the symbolic contradictions of Péguy's life—the gallant ambition, the life marked by defeats, the obscure death in a beetroot field—that ends, however, on the first day of a victory which was to save Paris and to save France. How could Péguy preserve his faith, in God, in France, Hill seems to ask (still a bystander, still a skeptic)? It is, to him, a "mystery" in both senses, something baffling and a religious rite from which noncelebrants such as himself are rigorously shut out.

Hill's emotional stance is one of painful passivity. He is quick to reject solutions. Easy faith is impossible for him, he has no trust in mere ritual observance, he refuses to fall back on the common academic position of genteel humanism. Often, indeed, he writes quasi-satirically about the world of dinner parties and conversations from which he feels excluded. Any show of acceptance, of merely "muddling through" life as best one can, is likely to anger him. A final question must be: What is there that is *positive* in Hill's poetry? To this several suggestive answers at least can be made. It is worth noting that Hill is attracted to simple poetic forms, sonnets, quatrains, even (in "The Pentecost Castle" in *Tenebrae*) nursery rhyme. His language, often obscure, can be very plain. At its best, this gives him a gnomic and prophetic quality, in which he appears as an Isaiah, or a Jeremiah, come to scourge the modern world out of its complacency. Horror is rarely far from his writing, whether it be natural, political, or historical (as in his sequence on the English "Wars of the Roses," centering on the bloody Battle of Towton, 1461, fought close to Hill's former home). At the same time, Hill's admirations are strong and his affections deep. His poetry is full of love for the English countryside, though it is an "Amor Carnalis" for a "terre charnelle."

T. A. Shippey

Sources for Further Study

British Book News. December, 1985, p. 750.
Christian Science Monitor. LXXVIII, September 5, 1986, p. B2.
Punch. CCXC, June 18, 1986, p. 100.

Spectator. CCLV, November 30, 1985, p. 28.
Times Literary Supplement. April 4, 1986, p. 363.
World Literature Today. LX, Summer, 1986, p. 472.

COLLECTED POEMS

Author: Charles Tomlinson (1927-   )
Publisher: Oxford University Press (New York). 351 pp. $29.95
Type of work: Poetry

A long-awaited volume that gathers the work of one of the foremost contemporary British poets

Charles Tomlinson's *Collected Poems* reprints, in the sequence in which they appeared, all of his collections from *The Necklace* (1955) through *The Flood* (1981). Not included is the later collection *Notes from New York* (1984); Tomlinson's first book of poems, the pamphlet *Relations and Contraries* (1951), is represented here by a single poem—one which, as he notes in the preface, "stands in the present volume as a kind of prelude to what follows." The book itself is lovely, compact (more British than American in size), with one of Tomlinson's graphics decorating the front jacket. Why there is no index is a mystery.

This volume should provoke a wider critical appreciation of Tomlinson's achievement. His work has always had its champions—most notably Hugh Kenner, who was instrumental in the publication of Tomlinson's first full-length collection, *Seeing Is Believing* (1958), in the United States after its rejection by numerous English publishers. (A belated and slightly expanded British edition was published in 1960, and it is that version which is reprinted here.) In his superb book *Eight Contemporary Poets* (1974), Calvin Bedient began his chapter on Tomlinson with an unequivocal assertion— "Charles Tomlinson is the most considerable British poet to have made his way since the Second World War"—and went on, in what remains the best single reading of Tomlinson, to substantiate that judgment. Still, if Tomlinson's advocates have been of the first rank, his work has not been brought to the attention of American readers as has that of, for example, Ted Hughes or Philip Larkin. There are, it seems, two closely related reasons for this relative neglect, an understanding of which will bring Tomlinson's distinctive qualities into focus.

First, there is the matter of the strong American affiliations in Tomlinson's work—repeatedly noted by critics and fully acknowledged by the poet himself in *Some Americans: A Personal Record* (1981), which, in addition to offering memorable portraits of Ezra Pound, Marianne Moore, William Carlos Williams, George Oppen, Louis Zukofsky, and Georgia O'Keeffe, traces Tomlinson's own development, the shaping of his mind and style. At the same time, Tomlinson has been open to other traditions outside those of his native England; himself active as a translator, he has edited *The Oxford Book of Verse in English Translation* (1980).

Assimilating these influences, Tomlinson has fashioned a poetic language that is neither aggressively local (in the manner of much British poetry of the 1970's and 1980's) nor remotely "American" English. In Kenner's formulation, Tomlinson is "the first poet to have learned a way of being distinctly English by mastering an idiom markedly international. Consequently he can write English, in England, as though it were a foreign tongue of amazing resources, at his thorough if somewhat wary command." That is a brilliant description of Tomlinson's style, for what is striking about his scrupulous English is precisely its detachment from any locatable community of speakers.

This, then, is the first reason for Tomlinson's lack of visibility: He is British, but not in the way that Americans expect British to be. Tomlinson's linguistic detachment, however, his deliberate giving up of the resources of local idiom, cannot really be separated from his way of seeing the world. To some readers, he seems cold. This is the second barrier to appreciation of his work. The excitement of the *Collected Poems* lies in Tomlinson's triumph over these potential liabilities, which are transformed into the hallmarks of his highly original style.

One senses that originality immediately in the first poems in this volume, despite the obvious debts to Ezra Pound and Wallace Stevens. *The Necklace*, comprising only fifteen short poems, takes its title from Stevens: "The necklace is a carving not a kiss." Here, the opposition between "a carving" and "a kiss" adumbrates what Tomlinson has described as his "basic theme—that one does not need to go beyond sense experience to some mystic union, that the 'I' can only be responsible in relationship and not by dissolving itself away into ecstasy or the Oversoul." Tomlinson's preference for the carved, his distrust of undisciplined emotion, could (and occasionally does) produce poetry that is excessively abstract. What saves him, for the most part, from this fate is his deep responsiveness to the natural world. There is a remarkable lack of self-absorption in these poems of a young man, and a gift for unforced delight in perception, as in these lines from "Nine Variations in a Chinese Winter Setting":

> Pine-scent
> In snow-clearness
> Is not more exactly counterpointed
> Than the creak of trodden snow
> Against a flute.

From the beginning, however, Tomlinson has resisted the reductionism of commonsense realism: His rock-solid sense of things and textures, finding a congeniality between the temper of British empiricism and the fiercely American vision of William Carlos Williams, is balanced by a keen interest in the process of perception and the shaping power of the imagination. The claims of the latter are astringently argued in "The Art of Poetry":

> At first, the mind feels bruised.
> The light makes white holes through the black foliage

Or mist hides everything that is not itself.
But how shall one say so?—
The fact being, that when the truth is not good enough
We exaggerate. Proportions

Matter. It is difficult to get them right.
There must be nothing
Superfluous, nothing which is not elegant
And nothing which is if it is merely that.

Tomlinson is justifiably celebrated as a poet of observation; for that reason it is important to say that he is also a poet of imagination. "Mushrooms," from a much later collection, *The Shaft* (1978), explicitly and brilliantly treats the relation between observation and imagination. "Eyeing the grass for mushrooms," the poet begins, "you will find/ A stone or stain, a dandelion puff/ Deceive your eyes—their colour is enough/ To plump the image out to mushroom size. . . ." Such illusions have their own value, the poet suggests, instructing the seeker to "waste/ None of the sleights of seeing . . ."; in the poem's concluding lines, he celebrates the life-giving power of the imagination in harmony with the observing eye:

For realer than a myth of clarities
Are the meanings that you read and are not there:
Soon, in the twilight coolness, you will come
To the circle that you seek and, one by one,
Stooping into their fragrance, break and gather,
Your way a winding where the rest lead on
Like stepping stones across a grass of water.

"Mushrooms," with its rhymes and glancing rhymes, is a reminder of Tomlinson's range. There is indeed abundant formal variety in this volume. In the later collections, though there are still few poems that scan according to traditional metrics, rhyme is much more frequent; one also finds a handful of prose pieces. Many of the poems collected in *A Peopled Landscape* (1963) follow Williams' "three-ply measure"; this form, which also reflects the influence of Marianne Moore, is well suited to Tomlinson's discursive style, and it is a pity that he has rarely returned to it since that time.

A particularly fine example from *A Peopled Landscape* is "The Impalpabilities," which begins with an acknowledgment of all that eludes clear definition:

It is the sense
     of things that we must include
          because we do not understand them
the impalpabilities
     in the marine dark
          the chords
that will not resolve themselves
     but hang

in an orchestral undertow
dissolving
(celeste above shifting strings)
yet where the dissolution
gathers the echoes
from an unheard voice. . . .

A different kind of poet might stop there (as many contemporary poets would, content to say that much cannot be said). It is characteristic of Tomlinson that, even as he evokes "the impalpabilities," he describes a natural scene with extraordinary fidelity and with an intellectual clarity that recalls the similes of Dante:

and so the wood
advances before the evening takes it—
branches
tense in a light like water,
as if (on extended fingers)
supporting the cool immensity
while we meditate the strength
in the arms we no longer see.

Those closing lines sound a religious note, one that recurs throughout Tomlinson's work, almost always in this form, implicit and guarded. In a poem from *The Flood*, entitled "Instead of an Essay," there is, however, a rare explicitness concerning the religious sense that informs this volume, and the poem, not one of Tomlinson's best, is worth noting for that reason. It is addressed to the poet and critic Donald Davie; writing to his friend, Tomlinson names himself "Brother in a mystery you trace/ To God, I to an awareness of delight/ I cannot name. . . ." The illustration by Tomlinson that graces the jacket of the *Collected Poems* is dated, titled, and signed in a fine hand, the letters tiny but legible: *Ode to Joy*. It is a fitting icon for this book, which asks its readers to share in the poet's awareness of delight.

John Wilson

Sources for Further Study

British Book News. November, 1985, p. 690.
Christian Science Monitor. LXXVIII, December 17, 1986, p. 23.
The London Review of Books. VIII, February 20, 1986, p. 20.
The Observer. January 12, 1986, p. 47.
Times Literary Supplement. March 21, 1986, p. 308.

THE COLLECTED POEMS OF WILLIAM CARLOS WILLIAMS
Volume I: 1909-1939

Author: William Carlos Williams (1883-1963)
Edited, with notes, by A. Walton Litz and Christopher MacGowan
Publisher: New Directions (New York). 579 pp. $35.00
Type of work: Poetry

Williams' early work offers an ideal opportunity for reassessment of an intensely American writer whose influential later poetry sometimes leads to a simplified view of his overall achievement

Sharing the long-standing American obsession with "unmediated" experience, William Carlos Williams struggled throughout his career with and against the idea of a modernist poetic tradition. Williams most certainly wrote in a modernist matrix; the problems he considers and his interest in technical experimentation connect him on a general level with T. S. Eliot, Ezra Pound, H. D., and Langston Hughes. His third published collection, *Spring and All* (1923), for example, opens with a standard modernist complaint concerning the aesthetic insensitivity of the mass audience. Setting himself apart from Eliot and Pound, both of whom had achieved a higher degree of early success, Williams indirectly repudiates their densely allusive style, which frequently juxtaposed American experiences with "Old World" or "classical" materials. Williams first denounces the "constant barrier between the reader and his consciousness of immediate contact with the world" and then proceeds with a blistering attack on "THE TRADITIONALISTS OF PLAGIARISM" who "led yesterday and wish to hold their sway a while longer. It is not difficult to understand their mood. They have their great weapons to hand: 'science,' 'philosophy,' and most dangerous of all 'art.'" From the beginning, then, Williams presented himself as a kind of populist "antimodernist": a radical, pragmatic, skeptical, intensely American individual.

This was an elaborate persona: as complex, sincere, and deceptive as the personae of Walt Whitman, Williams' most obvious ancestor; Hughes, the contemporary who (without acknowledgment on either side) did the most to realize Williams' theoretical project; or Allen Ginsberg, the most visible of his problematic descendants. The first volume of *The Collected Poems of William Carlos Williams* provides an excellent opportunity for reconsidering the early stages of Williams' career, which are frequently overshadowed by his more influential later work, particularly *Paterson* (1946-1958). With the exception of a few juvenile poems explicitly repudiated by the poet, this exquisitely produced and expertly edited volume contains all the poetry Williams published prior to 1940. Editors A. Walton Litz and Christopher MacGowan have done an exemplary job in creating a text which is at once academically sound and highly readable. Their notes, placed unobtrusively at the back of the volume, provide full textual histories and incorporate many of Williams' previously unavailable comments on individual poems.

Examining the circumstances of Williams' emergence helps clarify his attitude toward and position in the American modernist tradition he so deeply distrusted. Like most young American poets during the first two decades of the century, Williams felt a deep dissatisfaction with available models. In *The Tempers* (1913) and *Al Que Quiere!* (1917), Williams explores various styles, most notably those of Robert Browning and the Elizabethan lyricists, without notable success. Williams was already practicing medicine in Rutherford, New Jersey (a profession he would pursue throughout his life), and his early struggles to find an authentic voice coincided with the emergence of Eliot and Pound as major voices associated with "Imagism" and "Vorticism," the latter an early attempt to codify the approach to tradition which would characterize the most influential strain of Anglo-American modernism. By the time Eliot published *The Waste Land* in 1922, Williams had already declared his aesthetic independence. Throughout the 1920's, he would develop an alternative American modernism incorporating a desire for unmediated perception, an awareness of the impact of observer on event, an embrace of the American vernacular experience, and a style which was at once sparse and multigeneric.

Williams' poem "Portrait of a Lady," a satiric revision of Pound's "Portrait d'une femme," specifically rejects the reliance on allusion which had assumed a central aesthetic significance for modernism as early as 1917 when Pound began to publish the first *Cantos*. Williams treats allusion as a form of mediation, part of the problem rather than a possible solution to the aesthetic difficulties of the modern poet. "Portrait of a Lady" opens by self-consciously avoiding the use of simile, which for Williams implied the distancing of experience: "Your thighs *are* appletrees/ whose blossoms touch the sky" (emphasis added). The remainder of the poem amounts to an aggressive engagement with, and repudiation of, the Pound-Eliot strain of allusive modernism. Williams presents a sequence of questions—"Which sky?" "what sort of man was Fragonard?" "Which shore?" "Which shore?" "Which shore?" "Which shore?"—each distracting attention from the immediate perception. The closing reiteration of the initial image—"I said petals from an appletree"—seems to endorse a Whitmanesque immersion in experience. Yet the poem is not as transparent as it would seem. Its subject matter is not a real woman but a painting, Fragonard's *The Swing*. Even while he repudiates allusion as a mediating distraction, Williams alludes to a representation, an already mediated version of an infinitely regressing "pure experience."

Such ironic complexities both establish Williams as a modernist and caution against any simplistic apprehension of him as an anti-Eliot, a posture he occasionally relished and reinforced. Poems of the early 1920's such as "The Desolate Field," "Queen-Anne's-Lace," "The Widow's Lament in Springtime," and "The Great Figure" demonstrate Williams' increasing awareness that no experience is entirely unmediated. "Queen-Anne's-Lace," for example, differs from "Portrait of a Lady" in that it foregrounds the impact of the observing sensibility. Its opening images present subject—and by extension the process of the poet who describes that subject—in terms of negation: "Her body is not so white as/ anemone petals nor so smooth— nor/ so remote a thing." Implicitly questioning the "objective" stance frequently attributed to his early work, Williams acknowledges that the observer inevitably alters the experience: "Wherever/ his hand has lain there is/ a tiny purple blemish." By the end of the poem, the mind of the poet— like the hand of the rapist-florist-lover—has destroyed the object it has set out to preserve, leaving only "a pious wish to whiteness gone over—/ or nothing." This relativistic awareness—not entirely dissimilar from that articulated in more abstract terms by Wallace Stevens—informs the remainder of Williams' career.

Despite Williams' claims to the contrary, he shares many of these concerns with mainstream modernism. As many of his aesthetic heirs recognize, the uniqueness of Williams' poetry stems much more directly from his insistence on the aesthetic significance and potential of American vernacular experience. Section 18 of *Spring and All*, for example, sounds the nativist tone which will receive its strongest expression in *Paterson*: "The pure products of America/ go crazy." In pursuing the etiology of the madness, Williams' prose-poetry experiments of the 1920's immerse poet and reader in the American environment. The October 28 entry in *The Descent of Winter* (1928) announces the birth of a New Jersey "hero," Dolores Marie Pischak. Williams catalogs the details—people, streets, bars—of her hometown. The brilliance of the approach rests on the tension between Williams' ever-shaping mind—which implies the possibility of order, if not quite sanity— and the intractable forces mediating the baby's experience from birth. Throughout his early poetry, Williams writes most powerfully when he encounters these forces directly. He thrives on the presence of machines, of urban landscapes, of people only half-conscious of the forces shaping their lives. By contrast, many of Williams' "nature" poems—particularly after the period of discovery in the early 1920's—frequently seem pale versions of Stevens' or Eliot's psychological meditations.

These, then, are the thematic concerns clearly established in Williams' poetry by 1939: the celebration of unmediated experience; the awareness of the mediating mind; the concern with American vernacular culture. It is, however, Williams' technical experimentation that ultimately defines the reception and influence of his sensibility. Williams himself viewed most of the work included in this volume of the collected poems as part of an extended apprenticeship during which he found his voice, developing the techniques he would employ more successfully in *Paterson*, *The Desert Music* (1954), and *Pictures from Brueghel* (1962). Williams' technical experiments take two basic forms, both related to his desire for a pure American voice. On the one hand, long poems such as *Spring and All* and *The Descent of Winter*, like prose works such as *Kora in Hell* (1920) and *In the American Grain* (1925), reflect Williams' abiding interest in multigeneric collage forms. Culminating in *Paterson* (but realized more effectively by Hughes in "Montage of a Dream Deferred"), this aspect of Williams' voice amounts to a modernist extension of the Whitman catalog, a method of incorporating vernacular voices—newspaper clippings, overheard conversation, and so on—into a single poetic structure, which ideally calls into question its own mediating presence. The second major direction of Williams' technical experimentation focuses more on specific details than global structures. By 1940, Williams had abandoned traditional prosody—regular meter, rhyme, line breaks, and so forth—almost entirely. His alternative prosody, which would later coalesce in the concept of the "American meter," emphasizes oral rhythm, sparse language, and line breaks, reflecting the poet's perceiving process. "Man and Nature" typifies the lyrical aspect of Williams' mature voice. An early one-stanza version of the poem (reprinted in the notes of this volume) begins with the tumult of a passing ambulance. It concludes:

> . . . Gone. Leaving
> only the cat that with
> green eyes and dragging
> tail slinks hesitant
> across the endless
> chasms of the streets

In the final version, Williams places the ambulance in the first stanza, before concluding:

> The cat remains,
> green eyes and dragging
> tail under
> the frozen street light.

The changes emphasize Williams' commitment to compression and precision. Eliminating small words ("the," "with," "that") and abstract description ("hesitant," "endless," "chasms"), he reduces the word count by 50 percent. Each line focuses on a single unit of perception. After realizing that he sees the cat, the persona isolates the detail that attracted his attention (the green eyes). Responding to a motion, he then identifies it as the cat's tail. Finally, his perception expands to include the context. All judgment, all comment, is left to the reader who in experiencing the poem participates in a process similar to that of the poet experiencing the original scene.

In addition to providing the opportunity to reexamine Williams' poetic development, this volume suggests several paradoxes relating to his substantial influence on younger poets. Rebelling against what they perceived as the New Critical attempt to divorce poetry from experience, many younger poets of the 1950's, particularly those associated with the Black Mountain School and/or the Beat Generation, championed Williams in his anti-Eliot persona. Distrustful of the academic influence and political conservatism of the Eliot-Pound strain of modernism, poets such as Ginsberg sought alternate poetic ancestors, transitional figures connecting them back with Whitman's radical vernacular aesthetics. Williams was in many ways made to order; he had chosen America over exile, the vernacular over erudition, direct perception over academic research, the living city over classical ruins. While Ginsberg's celebration of Williams (complemented by Williams' prefaces to Ginsberg's widely read and discussed *Howl and Other Poems*, 1956) certainly served to introduce the poet's work to a much larger audience, it also mediated the reception of the work, emphasizing its expansive social elements. The primary effect of the mediation was to diminish the significance of nuance, both psychological and aesthetic, in Williams' work. Although poets such as Robert Creeley and Denise Levertov appreciated both aspects of Williams' work, the 1960's in effect replaced the introspective ironic stylist of the early lyrics with the urban chronicler of *Paterson*. The mediation seems doubly ironic in the light of the emergence of Wallace Stevens as a major poetic influence on numerous poets who began writing during the 1970's. Much of what younger poets derived from Stevens—the emphasis on the rhythm of the perceiving mind and the elaborate reflexive ironies, though not the intricate music of Stevens' poetry is present in Williams' pre-*Paterson* work. Perhaps the great virtue of the first volume of *The Collected Poems of William Carlos Williams* is that it encourages the rediscovery of an early Williams whose presence has been obscured by his own substantial shadow.

Craig Werner

Sources for Further Study

Booklist. LXXXIII, January 15, 1987, p. 746.
Library Journal. CXI, October 1, 1986, p. 100.
The New York Times Book Review. XCI, January 4, 1987, p. 3.

COLLECTED STORIES
1948-1986

Author: Wright Morris (1910-   )
Publisher: Harper & Row, Publishers (New York). 274 pp. $17.95
Type of work: Short stories

A collection of twenty-six previously published short stories spanning the career of one of America's most respected novelists

Although Wright Morris is better known as a novelist than as a short-story writer, having received both the American Book Award and the National Book Award in the past for his efforts in that genre, these stories, which were previously published in such magazines as *The New Yorker*, *Harper's Bazaar*, *American Mercury*, and *Esquire*, and which span almost forty years of his distinguished career, indicate his abiding interest in the short-story form.

Since its inception in American literature with the works of Edgar Allan Poe, the short story has depended on certain unique conventions: It has tended to be more symbolic than realistic; it usually focuses on an event that breaks the routine of everyday life; and it frequently places heavy emphasis on its ending. Morris obviously knows and has control of these unique conventions, for many of these twenty-six stories can be read as textbook cases of the twentieth century short story, even if they do not always exhibit the special illumination or genius of such short-story specialists as Bernard Malamud, Eudora Welty, or, more recently, Raymond Carver.

Morris' stories share a number of themes and techniques which reappear so frequently that they might be called personal or artistic obsessions. For example, Morris is quite fond of using domestic animals as central figures in his stories. In "The Cat in the Picture," a retired army officer rents a studio with his wife and begins painting. When a stray cat comes through the skylight and begins sleeping with the couple, the retired captain finds it an intrusion and begins to harass it by throwing his paint tubes at it. In the background of the story is a continuing unarticulated friction between the captain and his wife that ends with his separating from her. When he opens the suitcase his wife has packed for him, he finds, sandwiched between his clothes, the body of the dead cat with red paint, looking like blood, on its mouth. The cat serves primarily as a metaphoric catalyst for the unspoken conflict between the captain and his wife, for when he discovers the body of the dead animal, he realizes that it is the living part of the picture that his wife had always urged him to paint but which he had never seemed capable of producing.

Other stories which make use of animals as central metaphoric embodiments of human conflicts are "Drrdla," "The Cat's Meow," "Victrola," and "Fellow Creatures." The first of these, "Drrdla," named for the sound made

by a cat which has strayed into the basement, deals once again with a growing estrangement between a husband and wife for which the cat serves as an
emblem. In this case the cat suggests the sexual arousal of the wife, who
heretofore has been a reserved, scholarly type. With the arrival of the cat,
however, she becomes a "female creature" awakened to life and in need of
being satisfied both by her husband and by another man who lives with the
couple.

The central metaphor, indeed the central character, in "The Cat's Meow"
is a cat named Bloom, which has laryngitis and is therefore presented as an
enigmatic voiceless creature, whereas the central figure in "Victrola" is a
dog, so named because he reminded his former owner of the dog in the
RCA advertisement listening to "his master's voice." A dog is also a catalyst
in the story "Things That Matter," whereas a leghorn pullet figures centrally
in "Fellow Creatures."

Another obsessive characteristic appearing frequently in Morris' stories is
the theme of alienation, for many of the stories focus on a stranger in a
strange land, a character experiencing a sense of being lost in an alien world
and unfamiliar with its customs. In "Since When Do They Charge Admission," a Kansas couple travel to San Francisco during the hippie heyday of
the 1960's to visit their married daughter and are taken to a nude beach for
a picnic. The father, however, is more fascinated with a crow he sees on the
beach, so domesticated that, doglike, it buries a bone he gives it. At the
conclusion of this inconclusive story, his wife says that it is typical of him to
drive all that way to look at a crow.

In a similar story about a man thrown out of his element and unsure how
to respond to it, "Glimpse into Another Country," the protagonist, a shel-
tered academic type, flies to New York City to consult a doctor. The story is
told from such a distanced omniscient point of view that the protagonist
seems detached from his surroundings in a dreamlike way. Under the influence of this dreamlike state, he buys his wife an expensive string of pearls,
gets caught up in a bomb scare in a department store, and then is accosted
by a group of young boys to whom he willingly, but needlessly, gives the
pearls. This is another inconclusive Morris piece that seems less a formally
tight story than an experience of the innocent caught in a world he neither
understands nor desires to understand.

The central Morris story illustrating this theme (which takes both its title
and its setting from a story by Ernest Hemingway) is "In Another Country."
The protagonist is an American male who has come to Spain to see Ronda,
a place he stumbled onto in Hemingway's book about bullfighting, *Death in
the Afternoon*. At the climactic point of the story, the protagonist shares the
romantic experience of looking at a beautiful landscape with a native. When
he leaves, he shakes the man's outstretched hand and gives him a chocolate.
Later he realizes that the man wanted money and must be telling others the

story about the silly tourist who thought that he was sharing a moment of religious communion with him.

More terrifying examples of this theme of a stranger in a strange land are "The Customs of the Country," in which a European peasant who works as a custodian at a private school watches a young boy drown a child in a creek, and "Here Is Einbaum," a story about a Jewish refugee from the Nazi death camps. In the final story in the collection, "The Origin of Sadness," Morris traces the life of a paleontologist, who, since his childhood on the plains of Kansas, has been drawn toward nature's silent but symbolic messages in fossilized life forms. His love of fossils suggests also a passion for survival, a refusal to accept extinction. Having returned home because of his mother's illness, he walks through an arroyo he often visited as a child. Slipping on the steep slopes, he injures his hip and cannot move. As the snow falls on him, he is pleased to reflect that the ice will get to him before the searchers do, transforming him into one of the fossils he has spent his life seeking.

"In Another Country" repeats as well another theme often found in Morris' stories: a self-conscious literary theme about a character who is seduced by a piece of fiction or by an author into entering a purely literary and therefore idealistic world, only to discover that reality is unlike that depicted in the fictional world. Two other stories which focus on this theme are "Going into Exile," which deals with a character who attempts to enter into the fictional world of William Faulkner, and "The Character of the Lover," in which a young man fancies himself F. Scott Fitzgerald's idealistic hero in *The Great Gatsby*. In the first of these two stories, a character goes to Jefferson, Mississippi, hoping to meet Faulkner. When he, along with his companion, is taken into the home of a Southern lawyer, what he confronts is a parody of the Southern life he has come to know in the works of Faulkner. In the second of these stories, a young man who works at a drugstore reads *The Great Gatsby* and decides that Gatsby is the character of a lover with which he most identifies. As a result, he slaps a customer for making an anti-Semitic remark and loses his job.

The fictional characters in which Morris seems most interested are primarily middle-aged or elderly men who seem strangely detached from their environment and the people around them. They go through life so narrowly focused or so lost within their own idealistic obsessions that they seem incapable of dealing with the world at large. Consequently, Morris' primary theme in these stories is the character's confrontation with a threat to his isolated detachment.

One of the most significant technical implications of this theme is the creation of a detached point of view or persona to tell the story. Most often the voice is that of a disengaged and distanced observer. For example, in an early story, "The Sound Tape," a nameless and faceless man tells the story of a neighbor who has devoted his life to training his child to think and talk like himself. It is the man's wife who uses the term "the sound tape" to refer to the daughter who seems to do little else but parrot her father. The story makes sense as a case in which a man needs to create a mirror reflection of himself, especially since he cannot find any sympathy or identification with his wife. The conclusion of the piece, however, when the father and daughter commit suicide in a closed car because of the reelection of Harry Truman, seems to reduce the complexity of its theme to absurdity.

The same flat and disinterested voice tells the story of "The Safe Place," about a colonel who is hurt in a chemical explosion and put in a hospital ward where he meets Hyman Kopfman, a hopeless case who has lost an arm and a leg because of a blood disease. As Hyman becomes progressively worse, the colonel becomes progressively better, until finally Hyman dies "quite decently" during the night, just before the release of the colonel. A similarly grotesque story, told once again in the same flat monotone voice of the indifferent observer, is "Fiona," which deals with a young woman whose life has been conditioned by a childhood experience in which she found what she thought was a doll frozen in the ice, only to discover later that it was an infant. When her husband is found dead face-up in the food freezer, she will not allow the authorities to thaw him out, believing that if he remains frozen he will stay alive. Like the colonel in "The Safe Place," she somehow benefits by the death of the other, for she looks younger now that her husband's future is taken care of.

The short stories of Wright Morris, from the earliest story in this collection, "The Ram in the Thicket," to the most recent, "Things That Matter," reflect an author who has mastered the conventions of the traditional, well-made short story. The genius of the short stories of Morris and other twentieth century practitioners of this form, such as John Cheever, Philip Roth, and Joyce Carol Oates, is the ability to create a realistic sense of ordinary people who are mysteriously caught up in the dreamlike world of symbolic disruptions. Furthermore, the successful short-story writer must walk a fine line between the creation of characters who are believable and deserving of sympathetic identification and the creation of a highly formal, sometimes almost ritualistic, situation that is less real than it is aesthetically controlled.

Morris is well aware of these contrasting characteristics of the short-story form, as, for the most part, these stories reveal. Although Morris' writing career began in the early 1940's, roughly half the stories collected here were written in the 1980's—a sign perhaps that Morris has turned away from the novel to devote more of his creative energies to the stringent demands of the short story. His success in this medium is attested by the fact that two of his stories from the 1980's, "Victrola" and "Glimpse into Another Country," have been included in both the annual *Prize Stories: The O. Henry Awards* and the *Best American Short Stories* collections. Although Wright Morris will perhaps always be best remembered as a master of the novel, his work in the short-story medium deserves attention by anyone interested in modern American fiction.

Charles E. May

Sources for Further Study

Kirkus Reviews. LIV, September 1, 1986, p. 1319.
Los Angeles Times Book Review. December 7, 1986, p. 1.
The New York Times Book Review. XCI, December 14, 1986, p. 7.
Publishers Weekly. CCXXX, September 5, 1986, p. 91.
Time. CXXVIII, December 1, 1986, p. 71.

THE COMPLETE PROSE OF MARIANNE MOORE

Author: Marianne Moore (1887-1972)
Edited, with an introduction, by Patricia C. Willis
Publisher: The Viking Press/Elisabeth Sifton Books (New York). 733 pp. $24.95
Type of work: Essays, reviews, and miscellaneous prose

A chronological collection of Moore's published prose works

The Complete Prose of Marianne Moore, which was published in anticipation of Marianne Moore's centenary in 1987, presents all of her published prose except for letters, interviews, and quotations in the writings of others. The body of the text consists primarily of reviews and essays in chronological order of publication; the works published when Moore was editor of *The Dial* (1921-1929) are subdivided by kind into reviews, "Comment" (the name of a regular feature in *The Dial*), and "Briefer Mention," containing one-paragraph notices of books published. The appendix comprises separate sections for "letters to the editor," dust-jacket blurbs for the works of others, miscellaneous short pieces, book lists, and questionnaire responses. The editor, Patricia C. Willis, curator of the Marianne Moore Collection at the Rosenbach Museum and Library, Philadelphia, supplies a four-page introductory appreciation and notes of the original place and date of publication at the end of each piece.

Although Moore's reputation will continue to be based primarily upon her poetry, this collection affords readers the opportunity to trace over the course of some sixty years her influence as a critical reader and her refinement as a prose stylist. Her acutely perceptive sensibility and delicately resilient control are displayed everywhere in the text, and by making available virtually the whole corpus of her work, this volume reinforces Moore's important position in twentieth century American letters.

Even the earliest works, eight stories and a review published between 1907 and 1909 in the literary magazine of Bryn Mawr College, Moore's alma mater, show the characteristically precise diction that later typified all of her writing, even though the felicity of language in these pieces is obscured by mannered, derivative settings and slight plots. In spite of these defects, however, the undergraduate pieces are interesting because they show that Moore's turn to nonfiction prose and criticism was deliberately chosen, not coerced through lack of other talents: In her later career, she abandoned fiction in favor of poetry, and prose became the medium through which she surveyed the literary world. These stories do not hint at the acute critical intellect that, within fifteen years of their publication, would establish itself as a potent voice in American literary culture.

To be a literary critic requires first of all that one be a reader. The "Briefer Mention" section shows more succinctly than any other how broad and deep Moore's reading ran. These capsule reviews are marvels of economy and productivity: Few of the 125 she published in *The Dial* ran to more than 250 words, and to some of the monthly numbers she contributed as many as four short notices. Books of poetry, criticism, and literary history predominate, but the number also includes works on history, politics, art, music, philosophy, and the popular culture of various historical periods. This breadth of reading, astonishing in itself, is matched by the terse and pungent (although seldom pugnacious) judgment of the work's quality and worth. In poetry and other literary works, Moore swiftly picks out the best and most original elements in each book, pointing out, where necessary, infelicities or "disaffecting" characteristics that mar its quality. In other works, Moore states the principal subject or argument, summarizes its development, and finally judges its success and stature in the range of work on similar subjects. In each case, regardless of the work's kind or quality, Moore demonstrates a sympathetic understanding both of the author and of the reader: On the one hand, she points out excellences that might escape a hasty reader; on the other, she warns against the superficial or defective reasoning of an inexpert writer. Considered as a part of Moore's own work overall, the "Briefer Mention" section accurately outlines her intellectual wealth and range for the larger portrait that the rest of the volume completes at greater length and with finer detail.

Important in this larger portrait are the numerous longer reviews that Moore wrote throughout her career. Her manner in the capsule reviews is characteristic also of the full-scale reviews that appeared not only in *The Dial* but also in *The Nation*, *The New Republic*, *The New York Review of Books*, and *The New York Times Book Review*. As a whole, the longer reviews provide ample insight into and definition of the sometimes vague phrase "a woman of letters." Whatever her other concerns and interests, from these reviews it is apparent that Moore was in touch with the key movements not only in American letters but also with parallel forms and movements in England and Europe.

The list of poets whose work she reviewed includes most of the major names in modern literature in English as well as many less familiar. From these reviews can also be traced a genealogy of modern poetry with its complex affiliations of developing styles and personalities. Frequent references to William Butler Yeats, to whom Moore evidently looked as the precursor of modernism, appear throughout the reviews. She writes more specific and detailed analyses of her contemporaries, pointing out their individual glories and weaknesses with impartial generosity: W. H. Auden. T. S. Eliot, E. E. Cummings, H. D., Gertrude Stein, Wallace Stevens, William Carlos Williams—to mention only the most prominent—are all treated in specific reviews of their various published works and in more general assessments of their work. It is Ezra Pound, however, who occupies the central place in Moore's assessment of the period as a whole. Moore carefully notes each addition to Pound's *Cantos*, commenting not only upon the detailed complexity of many individual poems but also upon the development and unity of the whole series; in her treatment of other figures, she often uses Pound's work as an explicit or implied standard of value for comparison.

Each review conveys the sense of Moore's complete grasp and appreciation of the poet's work. This evident familiarity with the poet's work, coupled with a general and synthetic view of the literary tradition, is the greatest strength of Moore's critical approach, manifested repeatedly in her ability to assemble telling groups of brief quotations that reveal the genius of the poet whose work she discusses, and then to elucidate the patterns and themes those quotations outline in relationship to the broader movements of the literary tradition. The cumulative effect of these longer reviews is to impress the reader again with the evidence of Moore's lively knowledge and experience of literature, put to forceful, dramatic use in the interpretation and criticism of the best that modern poetry could offer.

This is not to say that Moore's criticism is uniformly laudatory or that her catholicity of taste recognizes no defects or inferiorities. On the whole, both the interest of her readers and the discrimination of her judgment seem to have led her to the best and most important poetry, but the occasional negative review gives point and force to the quality of her other, more positive assessments. Especially in the negative reviews, Moore's stylistic control becomes in itself a satisfaction that somehow justifies the defective work she examines. When she says of one poet, for example that he "is hampered to the point of self-destruction by his imperviousness to the need for aesthetic self-discipline," the deadly precision of the judgment causes the reader to look again at (that is, to re-view) the work under discussion for confirmation. It is in this return to the poem by which the reader tests and validates both the poet and the critic: In this regard and despite her mastery of form and language, Moore is repeatedly the most self-effacing of critics.

In a 1921 *Dial* review of Eliot's *The Sacred Wood*, Moore observes: "The connection between criticism and creation is close; criticism naturally deals with creation but it is equally true that criticism inspires creation. A genuine achievement in criticism is an achievement in creation." The relationship between Moore's critical reviews and her independent essays proves the accuracy of this observation as applied to her own work. Many of her essays turn finally on her meditations about some critical insight to another writer's work, whether poet, novelist, or nonfiction prose writer. At times, the source work may be a literary monument—Geoffrey Chaucer, William Shakespeare, and John Milton; Dante, Michel Eyquem de Montaigne, and Johann Wolfgang von Goethe; Plato, Aristotle, and Confucius all appear frequently in this regard—but at other times, the stimulus may be the history of *The Dial* under her editorship, Abraham Lincoln's rhetoric, the Brooklyn Bridge, or baseball, to which she was fanatically devoted. Whatever the subject, her essays move, as do her critical reviews, from the elucidation of telling detail to the perception of a fresh and comprehensive insight. The forty-three essays in the "Comment" section, owing to their publication in *The Dial*, tend to be the most regularly literary in the collection, but even here Moore often moves from some specific incident of observed experience to its cognates or reflection in poetry or fiction, pointing out again and again how intimate is the connection between the two worlds. In the many essays written after the *Dial* period, when Moore's literary reputation was enormous, the range of subjects is far broader; all the essays, however, participate in that fruitful connection between criticism and creation that Moore remarked in Eliot's work.

The chronological arrangement of the volume means that, for the most part, reviews, essays, and miscellaneous pieces follow one another unpredictably, and neither the table of contents nor the index provides much help to the reader interested in tracing Moore's ideas about modern poetry or any other subject. While this lack of categorical order may complicate such studies, the order of the book gives a clear perspective on the development of Moore's prose style, which is one of the most captivating stories in the volume and the only one that runs through each piece. In a 1922 *Dial* review, Moore observed that "any writer of strong personality is a stylist, the style varying from the stereotyped in rhetoric and sentiment as the personality varies"; as before, the accuracy of her perception is proved by its appositeness to her own work. Although the earlier works clearly anticipate the style of the later pieces, her sixty years of experience as a writer refined and perfected her style until she achieved an almost absolute control of word choice, sentence variety, and tone. As a late anecdote reveals in both its substance and form, this stylistic capability occasionally leaves less gifted persons confused: "Always, in whatever I wrote—prose or verse—I have had a burning desire to be explicit; beset always, however carefully I had written, by the charge of obscurity. Having entered Bryn Mawr with intensive zeal to write, I examined, for comment, the margin of a paper with which I had taken a great deal of trouble and found, 'I presume you had an idea if one could find out what it is.'"

Over the details of style, Moore demonstrates her mastery on almost every page. Many of her sentences give the impression of almost chiseled sharpness and texture, without any stuffiness or lapidary self-consciousness. Like so much else in this volume, Moore's style can also be explained partly as the effect of her zealous and lifelong habit of reading. Most frequently cited are English writers: Sir Francis Bacon, Sir Thomas Browne, John Milton, John Bunyan, Samuel Johnson, and Thomas Babington Macaulay—all renowned for their stylistic achievements—but also William Blake, Lewis Carroll, and Anthony Trollope, just as noteworthy, although usually for other reasons. Perhaps more important than the English writers are the nineteenth century American classics, some of whom were associated with the original *Dial*: Washington Irving, Henry David Thoreau, Nathaniel Hawthorne, as well as Lincoln, Edgar Allan Poe, and Henry James. These writers, together with those whom Moore knew through a broad familiarity with European literature, affected her style especially in its range of sentence structure and variety: Moore's capacity to vary sentence length is almost unrivaled by prose stylists in the modern period. Finally, the overall impression of her writing throughout the volume—of geniality, worth, intelligence, and wit—marks Marianne Moore as one of the most original and gifted prose writers of the twentieth century. This volume is a fitting memorial of her contribution to American letters.

Dale B. Billingsley

Sources for Further Study

Booklist. LXXXIII, September 1, 1986, p. 20.
Christian Science Monitor. LXXVIII, December 17, 1986, p. 23.
Kirkus Reviews. LIV, September 1, 1986, p. 1351.
Library Journal. CXI, September 15, 1986, p. 89.
The Nation. CCXLIII, December 27, 1986, p. 742.
The New Republic. CXCV, December 29, 1986, p. 30.
The New York Review of Books. XXXIII, December 4, 1986, p. 40.
The New York Times Book Review. XCI, November 30, 1986, p. 13.
Publishers Weekly. CCXXX, October 17, 1986, p. 48.

CRABGRASS FRONTIER
The Suburbanization of the United States

Author: Kenneth T. Jackson (1939-   )
Publisher: Oxford University Press (New York). Illustrated. 396 pp. $21.95
Type of work: Social and economic history
Time: The beginning of the nineteenth century to the 1980's
Locale: The American city and suburb, with occasional excursions to European and
Japanese urban settings

*A history of American suburbs and cities, their inhabitants, their planners, and their
troubled relationships with one another*

> *Principal personages:*
> ANDREW JACKSON DOWNING, a mid-nineteenth century architec-
> tural critic and the first national popularizer of the romantic
> suburban ideal
> HENRY FORD, an engineer, entrepreneur, and visionary of produc-
> tion and automobility
> WILLIAM J. LEVITT, the creator of the post-World War II automo-
> bile suburb for white veterans and their booming families

Kenneth T. Jackson's careful survey of the American suburb, *Crabgrass
Frontier: The Suburbanization of the United States* (winner of both the
Parkman and Bancroft prizes), is also a history of the suburb's ambivalent
relationship to its opposite number, the American city. The city gives birth
to the suburb by making its existence possible and desirable. The suburb,
born in rebellion against the city and its inhabitants, treats its ancestor with
contempt and conspires with its favorite uncle, Sam, to deny the city the
care and respect it has earned. Although the suburb has had some come-
uppance since the 1973 oil embargo, it remains unrepentant. Jackson's thorough and enlightening synthesis of the evidence in his analysis of the stages
of this generational conflict leaves little doubt of his sympathies. The suburbanization of the United States is understandable, given the many incen-
tives manufactured to encourage white flight from the central city. Yet, the
process was emphatically not inevitable, as Jackson's comparison to the European experience suggests, and cannot be recommended to others in the
future.

In one sense, the recurring urge to move to new havens on grassy plots
outside official urban boundaries is in fact nothing more than the conventional American pattern of "leaving home"—striking out on one's own to
put down new roots. Within metropolitan constraints, suburban pioneers
reenact the drama of Daniel Boone moving west when the pressure of population made him feel confined. From another perspective, however, the suburb is the leading product of the American growth machine. Here the frontier is less a psychological safety valve and more the scene of speculative
profits being turned by making it easy to escape the problems represented

by the city and its inhabitants. In this sense, the creators of the suburb are the real-estate developers, aided by transportation innovations and assisted at every step by government officials.

The role of local and state officials in this process of growth and movement is easy to imagine and generally well-known. Jackson's most important contribution to our knowledge of this urban-suburban interplay is, however, his research into the federal government's assistance to suburban sprawl and, particularly, to the way federal policies insured that the American suburb would be a major focus of a drive to protect and extend racial segregation. The dream of living in a detached house with other "people like us" at a reasonable commuting distance from commercial and industrial necessities is embedded in the nation's culture and psychology. Abundant cheap land and relatively high per-capita wealth helped make that dream possible, but the suburban dynamic was much more than an exercise in popular consumer sovereignty. Jackson concludes that "suburbanization was not an historical inevitability created by geography, technology, and culture, but rather the product of government policies. In effect, the social costs of low-density living have been paid by the general taxpayer rather than only by suburban residents."

As he reviews United States history, Jackson reminds the reader that the suburb had a history before the automobile and the *Father Knows Best* sitcom of the 1950's. Consistent with the term's etymology, the first American suburbs in the eighteenth and nineteenth centuries were slums, squalid and inferior working-class areas where housing was cheap because it was so far from employment and from the more fashionable city centers. These original cities were organized for a population which moved on foot or by horse and saw no reason to live at some remove from their productive endeavors. Ironically, the first Americans to flee the city for racial reasons were antebellum urban slaves allowed to "live out." They put as much distance as they dared between themselves and their masters; the outlying New Orleans black districts were called "suburb sheds."

The reversal of this initial relation between urban core and suburban periphery began before the Civil War. Jackson presents Brooklyn Heights, with Walt Whitman of the Brooklyn *Eagle* looking on, as the first example of what would be the modern suburb. Whitman found it "highly edifying" to contemplate the early morning "phrenzy exhibited by certain portions of younger gentlemen" rushing for places on the ferry which would take them to work in New York City. There were two key elements in the transformation of Brooklyn. The ferry, an efficient transportation link which brought commuters within range of employment, made former farmland available to be redivided for reconveyance as suburban real estate. Before that, however, the new vision of Brooklyn's future had taken shape in the mind of an entrepreneur named Hezekiah Beers Pierrepont, who had lost his importing business to pirates in 1797, married the daughter of New York State's largest landowner, and settled down in Brooklyn. He began buying farmland and harbor frontage, entered politics as a village trustee with a special interest in street planning and road improvement projects, and befriended Robert Fulton, in whose steamboat projects he invested. After Fulton began steamferry service to Manhattan in 1814, Pierrepont was able to begin reaping the profits from the small lots he had surveyed and held off the market.

The modern suburb was, in other words, a product of the American version of the industrial revolution and the burst of entrepreneurial activity the new age of steam initiated. The technology of urban transportation developed rapidly. After the steam ferry came the horse-drawn omnibus operating under city-granted franchise. Then came the various rail-borne vehicles: horsecars, commuter railroads, cable cars, electric streetcars, and subways. Through this long history of transportation innovation, capped in the twentieth century with that most revolutionary of vehicles, the automobile, the combination of land speculation with political influence never varied much from the original pattern suggested by Pierrepont. The long-run result was the development of metropolitan conurbations where population growth was usually greatest on the periphery. In a pattern which Jackson tracks for more than a century, central urban districts lose both population and socioeconomic status to the periphery, and the relative differences in density between downtown and suburb decrease.

More important for individual experience may have been the steady increase in the length of time the head of the household spent traveling to work. Jackson's appendix offers extensive data on the willingness of attorneys in various East Coast cities to accept longer and longer "commutes" in the past century. As the physical distance between home and middle- or upper-class employment grew, so too did the psychological separation of private and public spheres. The household, now compartmentalized as a feminine sphere, lost its productive role as men employed by commercial and industrial capital increasingly left home to work. In the new intensity and uncertainty of modern life, the home took on new significance as a refuge and also took on a new shape in the suburbs. The detached single-family house in a quiet green landscape was urged as the ideal of modern aspiration, a soothing therapeutic antidote to urban commercial-industrial stress. As in so many other facets of this modernization, Walt Whitman was available to read the cultural lesson in this development: "A man is not a whole and complete man," he announced, "unless he owns a house and the ground it stands on."

By giving the suburb a history before Henry Ford, Jackson reminds the reader of its romantic origins, how suburban design was part of the grand tradition of urban park design, represented in the United States by Frederick Law Olmstead, and how the single-family house cooperated in the softening of the effects of industrialization. The latter comes through most clearly in fascinating statistics, which show how quickly the foreign-born recruits to industrializing American embraced the suburban frontier, how specifically American the mystique of the detached house was. At the turn of the twentieth century, immigrants were more likely to own their own houses than native-born white Americans. When soon thereafter the question was posed "Why is there no socialism in the United States?" one powerful answer was at the end of major urban streetcar lines. Small wonder that Friedrich Engels saw home ownership as the most effective block to class consciousness or that the premier post-World War II speculative builder, William Levitt, could chortle, "No man who owns his house and lot can be a Communist. He has too much to do."

The comparison to European experience suggested here is another very useful perspective which Jackson adds to his survey, but that juxtaposition also emphasizes the racial facet of America's culture and institutions. However much Stockholm differs from Chicago in physical organization or appearance, the long sorry history of racial segregation in American cities gives America's urban history a complexity which more homogeneous societies have missed. It is also in this light that the differences in government urban policies between the United States and the rest of the Western world may most profitably be viewed. In general, it has been the white American experience to move from farm to city to suburb; black Americans have only made the first step—escaping Southern agriculture for urban life, for they have been largely prevented from making the move to suburbia.

In this most original contribution to our knowledge of cities, Jackson goes beyond the story of how the federal government encouraged suburbs in the 1950's by building interstate highways, bulldozing "blighted" urban areas to renew them, and gearing federal and state tax policies to the interests of homeowners. In his reading of the history of the Home Owners Loan Corporation (HOLC), Jackson pays due respect to the fact that this 1933 New Deal initiative saved a million mortgage holders from foreclosure in its first two years of operation and, in so doing, established the "long-term, self-amortizing mortgage with uniform payments spread over the whole life of the debt" as a viable, indeed desirable, financial instrument. More important, he points out, was the way the HOLC established nationwide appraising standards.

Whatever the benefits for uniformity, this system also made "red-lining" a national policy. It may be objected that categorizing neighborhoods for appraising purposes according to their age, density, ethnic makeup, and proximity to neighborhoods higher or lower on these scales was only to register reigning public views. Jackson is certainly not interested in identifying any culprit other than the free-floating racism prevalent then and later. Nevertheless, the federal ratification of local prejudices created a repetitive series of self-fulfilling prophecies. "Residential Security Maps" were secretly established in local HOLC offices, with neighborhoods which were coded A, B, C, and D and marked in green, blue, yellow, and red boundary lines respectively. The Federal Housing Administration and Veterans Administration housing bureaucrats later took over these maps and the policies they implied. Bankers structured loan policies in accord with these official ratings, lawyers wrote racial and ethnic restrictions into deeds, and real-estate agents carried the word to uninitiated buyers and sellers. Thus the suburban demography described on these secret maps shaped America's future suburban inheritance.

In a footnote, Jackson chides another study of urban-suburban process for displaying too much passion and too little research. Until his final chapter, Jackson's book risks the opposite judgment. He is himself in the middle of an explosion of interest in urban history, no small part of it sparked by his own work and that of his students, but he occasionally seems determined to get it all in one volume. Any serious student of urban history will want this book for its footnotes alone. One can only hope that urban policymakers might be drawn to the book for its relentless demonstration of the choices which have made the United States the world's first and most suburban nation and for Jackson's conclusions that those were choices which no other nation can afford to imitate.

David Axeen

Sources for Further Study

American Historical Review. XCI, June, 1986, p. 755.
Best Sellers. XLV, January, 1986, p. 394.
Choice. XXIII, January, 1986, p. 779.
Journal of American History. LXXIII, June, 1986, p. 227.
Library Journal. CX, September 1, 1986, p. 196.
The New Republic. CXCIV, March 10, 1986, p. 34.
The New York Times Book Review. XCI, April 27, 1986, p. 14.
Psychology Today. XX, July, 1986, p. 74.
Wilson Quarterly. C, No. 1, 1986, p. 151.

CRUSOE'S DAUGHTER

Author: Jane Gardam (1928-   )
Publisher: Atheneum Publishers (New York). 224 pp. $12.95
Type of work: Psychological novel
Time: 1904-1986
Locale: Northeast England

The story of Polly Flint's life, from her arrival at the home of her aunts, the yellow house on the marsh, to her final stand against the destruction of that house and her isolated way of life eighty-two years later

> Principal characters:
> POLLY FLINT, the narrator and protagonist
> MARY YOUNGHUSBAND, her serious aunt
> FRANCES YOUNGHUSBAND, her gentle aunt
> AGNES WOODS, a widow who lives with the Younghusbands
> PAUL TREECE, a young poet who loves Polly
> THEO ZEIT, a Jewish neighbor whom Polly loves
> REBECCA ZEIT, Theo's sister
> ARTHUR THWAITE, a friend of the Younghusbands, owner of Thwaite House

Because Jane Gardam's fiction generally focuses on a young protagonist's gradual discovery of the world, her first three novels were published in the category of children's (or young adult) fiction. It soon became clear, however, that Gardam's work eluded this generic label, and subsequent books—published simply as fiction—have received critical acclaim, including several literary awards.

Many of Gardam's young protagonists see themselves as fictional characters and therefore must come to terms with reality by discarding not only the illusions of childhood but also the certainties of fiction. Such is Polly Flint's problem in *Crusoe's Daughter*.

Robinson Crusoe's island was his refuge from shipwreck, his home alone and then with his man Friday until rescue and return to England, where supposedly he wrote his story. The situation of Polly Flint, Crusoe's admirer and spiritual daughter, is quite different. At the age of six, Polly is deposited with her dead mother's sisters on her "island," a yellow house on a marsh, Oversands, to which visitors come regularly and from which the people who are Polly's companions as frequently go. Left on her island, Polly spends her life looking for footprints in the sand, discovering people to whom she might be important, and, when they desert her, turning to Crusoe as a model of courage and self-discipline.

Certainly the house to which her ship-captain father brings Polly is an improvement over foster care in Wales, where a drunken, sluttish woman had abused Polly for seemingly watching and judging her. Her father departs from Oversands to be lost at sea, and Polly is cared for by her aunts, Mary and Frances Younghusband, grumpy Mrs. Agnes Woods, and an outspoken maid. Like Crusoe, she has the physical necessities but feels as isolated as if her island were a geographical fact. Prodded to be good, she obliges, even, as she realizes later, living lies in order to be praised—though being praised for conformity is not the same as feeling loved. Polly does not feel important to anyone.

As Polly's life proceeds, those who seem to care for her continue to disappear. Her father deposits her at Oversands and dies. Aunt Frances marries the vicar and sails for India, where she, too, dies, and it is not until much later that Polly learns that her gentle aunt had sent letters to her, letters that were cruelly intercepted by Mrs. Woods. Aunt Mary abandons Polly in order to go to her beloved convent. Because she has trained her niece to be good, Mary can leave her in the care of Mrs. Woods. Thus Polly is called from some days of happiness with Arthur Thwaite, who is actually her grandfather, at his Yorkshire home.

In one significant scene, young Polly is reading *Robinson Crusoe* on the beach, comparing her isolation to Crusoe's. As she glances across the sands, she sees a speck, and the speck gradually becomes a pony trap carrying Rebecca and Theo Zeit. Perhaps it is at this moment that Polly begins to love Theo, begins to hope that she will be important to him. Theo, however, is merely another occasional visitor to her island, casually affectionate but easily distracted by his manipulative mother. There is one blissful period with the Zeits at New House when Polly feels pretty and accepted, even loved by Theo, who has held her in his arms and promised to come to her room at night. Instead of Theo, his mother appears, and Polly is sent packing like a poor relation, expelled with her new party dress before the guests for whom she has helped to prepare can arrive. Later, Theo reappears, stirs her passions, and responds to her letters of unveiled desire. His letters, however, suddenly stop, and Polly learns that he is marrying another girl. At this point, Polly abandons attempts to escape her emotional island and retreats into apathy and alcohol.

If Polly Flint is a castaway, the fault does not lie with her or even with those who quite humanly find other interests and desert her. A very young child may well be placed among people who are kind but indifferent, but a male child, Polly realizes, would have been sent out into the world, where he could have found meaningful work, friends, interests, perhaps finally lovers. If she had been a boy, Polly writes to Aunt Frances, who herself escaped into marriage, the money would have been found for school. "But because I am a girl, Aunt Frances," Polly writes, "I was to be stood in a vacuum. I was to be left in the bell-jar of Oversands. Nothing in the world is ever to happen to me."

As Polly observes the lives of other women, she comes to realize that passivity is expected of them. The rescuer must come to them; perhaps a subdued beacon is permissible. In her own family, there was a grandmother yoked to a sexless husband. Her affair with Arthur Thwaite produced Polly's own mother, though it broke the heart of Thwaite's fiancée, the grim Aunt Mary, who had no option left but her religious mania. For years, Aunt Frances had been "close to" the vicar; only when she learned that he was bound for India did she "beard him" (shockingly) and persuade him to marry her. Again, the result was less than happy. He died on the ship and she in India. Nevertheless, the costume picture which found its way to Polly suggested that there may have been enough excitement on the ship to make Frances' venture worthwhile.

Even the Younghusbands' first maid was thwarted by society's expectations of women. She was not permitted to bring her illegitimate child to Oversands. Because he needed a man and a proper family, because the yellow house demanded respectability, he was taken from her. After his death from influenza, the maid left the household, with bitter words for those who had forced her into passive acceptance of social rules.

Neither religion nor marriage, society's two sanctioned options for marooned women, strikes Polly as a particularly satisfactory escape route. Both, she observes, soon deteriorate into habits, and even though a well-regulated life may keep one sane during a period of isolation, it should not extinguish the desire to escape. Unschooled, unmarried, unemployable, Polly finds herself looking for a purpose. For a time, like countless other unhappy women, she gives herself to the yellow house. For a time, she makes translations of *Robinson Crusoe*, which are unneeded and which will never be published. At last penniless, she permits her maid to set the yellow house up as a lodging house. Finally, she is saved from her isolation and her drunkenness by the maid's marriage to a headmaster and her own consequent involvement in the school. Her final salvation has significantly come through no act of her own but, rather, through the maid's managing to capture a husband.

Because she has not been asked in marriage, either by Paul Treece, a poet, who was killed in World War I, or by Theo Zeit, who married another girl, Polly Flint is denied the female consolation of children, as she has been denied the expression of her passion. Her traumatic first menstruation and the subsequent nuisances of the female biological system seem to have been a meaningless punishment. Yet unexpectedly, Polly does have children, first those at the school, later the two daughters of Theo Zeit, who take refuge with her in flight from Germany in 1939. After the war, Theo himself comes to her briefly before his death, but the lovers do not marry because, as his younger daughter says, "It was not important."

In the end, Polly has her final interview with Crusoe. Holed up at Oversands, now to be torn down for a nuclear waste site, Polly is besieged as well as marooned. Crusoe sums up her life: reading, being good, having children love her. "A quiet life. But Godly—and some of that because of me. As a life, not bad. Marooned of course. But there's something to be said for islands." Ironically, Polly has outlived the adventurers—Frances, Paul Treece, Theo, Theo's wife—at least in terms of years.

While Jane Gardam's novel seems to be a simple first-person narrative, covering eighty-two years of Polly Flint's life, it is actually a complex book which demands more than a single reading. The parallels between the island life of Crusoe and the entire life of Polly are skillfully drawn as Polly rereads and reinterprets *Robinson Crusoe*, which is in a sense her bible. Although his isolation and hers have different causes, Polly emulates Crusoe's practical courage. Sometimes, too, she better understands her own despair by remembering his despair; when Theo abandons her, Polly feels as Crusoe did when his own escape attempt had been thwarted.

Although Polly tells her own story in the past tense, she does not reveal family secrets until the point at which they are revealed to her, nor does she voice mature wisdom at a place in the book where she is merely six or sixteen. The result of this gradual development is an immediacy for the reader at every step of Polly's life. Why Gardam concludes her novel with two dialogues, one between a journalist and Theo's daughter, and one between Polly and Crusoe, is a bit difficult to understand. If an objective statement were necessary at the conclusion, young Beccy Zeit Boagey and Robinson Crusoe himself would certainly be perceptive enough to make it; Polly, however, should have been able to speak for herself, as she has done throughout the book. Nevertheless, if this is a flaw, it is one only because the author has handled point of view so well up to this point that no change seems called for. In the clear but subtle jumps in time, in the genuine ring of the dialogue, in the restrained but effective evocation of the landscape, in the richness of fabric resulting from the allusions to Daniel Defoe, Jane Gardam is a master of technique. In creating Polly Flint, a unique daughter of Crusoe, Gardam has shown herself to be a first-class contemporary novelist.

Rosemary M. Canfield-Reisman

Sources for Further Study

Kirkus Reviews. LIV, January 15, 1986, p. 74.
Library Journal. CXI, February 15, 1986, p. 193.
London Review of Books. VII, June 20, 1985, p. 20.
The New York Times Book Review. XCI, April 27, 1986, p. 39.
Publishers Weekly. CCXXIX, January 31, 1986, p. 365.
Spectator. CCLV, November 30, 1985, p. 29.
Times Literary Supplement. May 31, 1985, p. 599.
Washington Post Book World. XVI, April 21, 1986, p. 3.

CURRANNE TRUEHEART

Author: Donald Newlove (1928-   )
Publisher: Doubleday & Company (Garden City, New York). 394 pp. $17.95
Type of work: Novel
Time: 1958
Locale: King James, New York

In a novel, when madness is made metaphor and the condition is shown to be endemic, no reader can expect a happy ending; nor is there one, for in spite of Jack Trueheart's true heart, Curranne is not cured

> *Principal characters:*
> JACK TRUEHEART, the protagonist, a recovered alcoholic and writer
> CURRANNE, his wife, who has a history of mental problems
> STELLA, Jack's mother
> CAROL GARRITY, Curranne's mother
> LEOPOLDA, a former alcoholic who facilitates a local group-therapy session for Curranne, Jack, and some out-patients from a local mental institution

In his fictions, Donald Newlove attempts to delineate two dimensions of reality/illusion: insanity and alcoholism. In his first novel, *The Painter Gabriel* (1970), Newlove explored madness; in *Leo and Theodore* (1972), alcoholism. In *Curranne Trueheart*, Newlove brings the two states together, emphasizing their symbolic relationship in an initial paragraph whose implications reverberate throughout the novel: "What could be more hopeless than a madwoman marrying a drunk? But cities have always been full of crazy people and alcoholics who marry. That lasting love can grow from such a union—such a fearful matching of cracks—is a miracle."

The madwoman is Curranne, born Garrity, whose name changes five times and whose habitats at least as many. The one constant in her life seems to be intermittent commitments to mental hospitals and lengthy psychoanalyses by psychiatrists who are clearly never as intelligent as she. Though Curranne desires sanity with every spiritual fiber of her being, a moral fiber interferes. She is constitutionally unable to make distinctions between two ontological positions: She is unable to accept lies or to accommodate herself to half-truths or to confuse the banal with the fresh, the prosaic and trite with the authentic, the misguided with the categorically true. Nor can she make clear distinctions between "fact" and "fiction," "truth" and "illusion," the "literal" and the "metaphoric," and "inner" and "outer" reality."

Curranne's inability to confuse the sententious with the discriminatory works positively for her husband, Jack, making it possible for her to guide him to a better understanding of the world around him, and with her help, he is able to make the necessary adjustments to living that life apparently calls for. Because of Curranne, Jack, a recovered alcoholic, becomes a writer capable of accepting love and of expressing incontrovertible joy and grief. In Jack's memories, Curranne miraculously continues to live. Nevertheless, for Curranne, her inability to distinguish between her hallucinatory and waking worlds, between the symbolic and the prosaic, between the metaphoric and the literal is a negative, the cause of her schizophrenia, her extreme pain, and her eventual suicide.

When Jack first meets Curranne in the library, he is thirty years old; he has spent eleven years in the marines and four in the air force. His marriage of less than two years, which produced one child, has ended in annulment because of his failure to provide. Desiring to be a writer, he returns to his home in King James, moves back into his mother's house, and gets a job on a local newspaper. He knows that his writing problems and his inability to make lasting relationships with people are the result of his own powers of perception. After he meets Curranne, he is serious in thinking that he can help her, but "it takes titanic labor for me to get skin-deep even in my writing—my power of character analysis is more Stan Laurel than D. H. Lawrence. I can't take it in, much less make it up. People pass right through me." When Curranne first reads a sample of Jack's writing, she zips through three pages in thirty seconds and is direct, even brutal, in her comments to him. His writing, she tells him, is not authentic; it is "strawberry-flavored baloney. . . . No attack, all marshmallow." In the same way, she attacks him for his drinking, telling him that alcohol will kill him; for her, a clear head is paradise.

When Curranne first meets Jack, it has been fifteen years since she was first institutionalized. All the men in her life she characterizes satirically as geniuses: her father, who was a drunk and abandoned his wife and children; her nineteen-year-old bridegroom, who, questioning his maleness, joined the marines in World War II with the noble purpose of becoming a man; her second husband and the father of her two sons, who was a painter; and a third husband, who produced television programs. Unlike Jack, who spent two years in a community college and then quit to become a writer, Curranne went to a university, majored in English, and was graduated Phi Beta Kappa with a New York State teaching certificate, which she uses during times of relative sanity for substitute teaching in the public schools.

The quality of Curranne's intelligence is clear in the opening section of the novel (parts 1 through 4); her reactions to Jack's ridiculous "literary" parties, her informative discussions, her acute analyses both of his problems and writings, and her choices and limitations show her acute awareness not only of cultural history but also of the immediate world around her. Only at secondhand does the reader hear of her "bizarre" behavior, as, for example, when her mother tells Jack about Curranne's tirades about banking, about what Curranne believes to be Chase Manhattan's manipulation of the world and Nelson Rockefeller's demoniac schemes and frauds. Curranne's mother says that when her daughter was in school, her ambition was to be White House surgeon-in-residence so that she could sterilize the Oval Office daily. According to her mother, Curranne is also an activist who was arrested twice in the Chase Manhattan bank for disturbing the peace. Once Curranne rented a safe-deposit box at the Bank of America, loaded it with rotting meat, and never went back.

Part 5 of the novel abruptly changes point of view. Parts 1 through 4 are related by Jack in the first person; parts 5 through 9 are told from Curranne's viewpoint. This second part of the novel, however, is not as effective as the first. Whereas the often brilliant epigrammatic style used in the opening sections is well suited to Jack's character and ambitions, no clearly different style emerges here to characterize Curranne. The effect is that of Newlove attempting to enter the mind of Curranne in order to provide another dimension to her character but failing because he either has not or cannot fully understand her inner experiences. Despite these problems, this center section plots Curranne's inexorable movement to complete paranoia, which, in turn, makes totally credible her suicide as a painfully felt and authenticated need to escape. Though the style seems inappropriate, the reader learns in a firsthand way of Curranne's struggles, her hallucinations, her imagined abuse by her father and her psychiatrist, and by Nelson Rockefeller, who has assumed for Curranne the role of incubus, sexually using her by means of brain waves. In addition, the long group-therapy sessions depicted in this section often seem not only to fill up time and space, providing a sense of duration for the reader who knows what the eventual outcome must be, but also, unfortunately, to provide an additional handy vehicle for some pithy wisecracks and empty dialogue.

When Newlove moves in parts 10 and 11 to a third-person viewpoint, the major focus is on Curranne, though one might wonder what is achieved by another shift in point of view. Perhaps the author's purpose is to prepare the reader for the epilogue, which is a brilliant piece of writing, reminiscent in tone and theme to the endings of some of Vladimir Nabokov's astonishingly brilliant novels, where the dead are reborn into the art form, there to experience one kind of everlasting life that the writer and/or persona, too, may share.

In the epilogue, Jack returns as narrator, chastened, wiser, a provider for his daughter, no longer alcoholic, no longer needing the veneer of the witty or the support of an epigram for an epigraph, but able to write with the kind of simple lucidity that helps one to define the sane. Perhaps, after all, the shifts in point of view are a necessary prerequisite to the novel's conclusion. Perhaps, however, if the shifts had been handled more skillfully, a reader would understand more clearly the need to get through the cacophonies to the silence of a perfectly realized word. Whatever the case, the epilogue makes it clear that Jack's conflict is, for Newlove, the controlling one throughout the book, that Jack, not Curranne, is the novel's protagonist, and that Curranne has effected a cure, if not for herself, for him and their child: "Life heals the hardest death. The power that rekindled you on that winter bench still enspirits our wildflower daughter. When I see her wise gray-green eyes, and watch your tender Chaplin-grin—my God, I want you back. How much more I could give you now! But only your smiling strength remains."

Mary Rohrberger

Sources for Further Study

Best Sellers. XLVI, April, 1986, p. 7.
Kirkus Reviews. LIII, December 1, 1985, p. 1285.
The New York Times Book Review. XCI, February 23, 1986, p. 18.
Publishers Weekly. CCXXVIII, November 29, 1985, p. 37.

THE CYCLES OF AMERICAN HISTORY

Author: Arthur M. Schlesinger, Jr. (1917-   )
Publisher: Houghton Mifflin Company (Boston). 473 pp. $22.95
Type of work: Political history
Time: 1607-1986
Locale: The United States

A collection of analytical essays on themes in American political history, emphasizing recurrent cycles in domestic and foreign policy

An interpretive and synthesizing journey through American history and politics is an ambitious enterprise that only a distinguished senior historian could undertake with confidence, and perhaps only Arthur Schlesinger could manage it with such energy and style. Most of the fourteen essays in *The Cycles of American History* are adapted and reworked pieces from the voluminous body of articles that Schlesinger has published since the 1950's. They represent an informed but hardly dispassionate attempt to isolate and explain patterns and trends in domestic and foreign policy. Schlesinger's liberal biases are readily apparent and as readily admitted: He admires presidents of broad vision, such as the Roosevelts and John F. Kennedy, while conservatives such as Jimmy Carter (whom he likens to Grover Cleveland) and Ronald Reagan stand very low in his estimation. His purpose in this collection is to explain how and why such variations in leadership recur in American history.

The essays are grouped into two main categories, foreign policy and domestic affairs, each discussing half a dozen topics. Two long thematic pieces set forth the themes that inform the rest of the book. In "The Theory of America: Experiment or Destiny?" Schlesinger identifies two central traditions on which the self-image of the early American republic was grounded. One viewed the young nation as a bold but risky experiment in democratic government, undertaken in the face of historical evidence that republics tended to be short-lived and self-destructive. The Founding Fathers considered their enterprise an uncertain one for which a successful outcome could by no means be predicted. A coexisting countertradition, rooted in the Calvinist ethos and growing stronger over time, proclaimed America as a country with a special destiny, or, in John Winthrop's words, a "redeemer nation" that would serve as an example and guide for the old, unsanctified world.

The centerpiece essay of the book, "The Cycles of American Politics," follows up on this dialectic between pragmatics and ideology, experiment and destiny, by dividing United States history into alternating cycles, roughly thirty years long, dominated either by private interest or public purpose. A private-interest phase is inward-looking and dominated by capitalist values: making money, expanding markets, and keeping government under a tight rein lest it become a burdensome interference. A public-interest phase, by contrast, is outward-looking and idealistic, characterized by a preoccupation with debating issues, solving problems, redressing injustices. In public-interest eras, the function of government changes from static to dynamic; it becomes an agent and instrument of change. Both phases are naturally self-limiting. After a prolonged period of public-interest activism, idealism wears thin and crusading impulses spend themselves; people are worn out with causes and turn with relief to the quieter, self-interested pastimes of getting and spending until the cycle swings back again. Applying the model to the twentieth century, for example, Schlesinger identifies the first two decades, the era of Progressive reform at home and war for democracy abroad, as a public-interest phase. Disenchanted and tired, the nation then gladly returned to "normalcy" and private interest until Franklin D. Roosevelt's New Deal, World War II, and Harry S Truman's Fair Deal ushered in another period of intense public activism. The Eisenhower years brought another period of respite before the plunge into Kennedy's New Frontier and Lyndon B. Johnson's Great Society. The trauma of the late 1960's and early 1970's then swung the cycle back toward private interest. Thus Schlesinger sees the "Reagan revolution" as merely the culmination of a predictable phase that should at some point in the decade of the 1990's give way to another period of public activism.

In Schlesinger's words, "the public-private equation and the experiment-destiny equation overlap rather than coincide." Thus, "experimentalists" such as Theodore and Franklin Roosevelt and "predestinarians" such as Woodrow Wilson devoted themselves equally to the public purpose, while a pragmatic Dwight D. Eisenhower and an ideological Reagan have shared a common devotion to the private interest. The public-private cycle corresponds to liberal and conservative political philosophies but is not circumscribed by party labels; Republican or Democratic dominance does not guarantee the emergence of one or the other. A Republican can be an activist—Theodore Roosevelt is a prime example—and a Democrat such as Cleveland can preside over a private-interest period. The cyclical pattern is entirely self-generating and independent of external events such as the business cycle. The New Deal was inspired by the Depression, but Progressivism sprang up during a period of prosperity, and the two serious depressions of the last thirty years of the nineteenth century had no effect on the conservative temper of the period.

Using the experiment-destiny and the public-private interest dichotomies as explanatory models, Schlesinger then turns his attention to foreign affairs. He finds no correlation between the public-private cycle and Frank L. Klingberg's foreign-policy cycle, which proposes a periodic alternation between "extroversion," or the willingness to exert diplomatic, military, or economic pressure in pursuit of American interests abroad, and "introversion," a concentration on domestic needs. He does, however, see a relationship between Klingberg's foreign cycle and his own domestic one in the sense that each phase of the domestic cycle defines the national interest in accordance with its own values, which it then incorporates into foreign policy. Public-purpose eras support democratic center-to-left-leaning regimes abroad, while private-interest periods tend to interpose market values into international affairs and thus to prefer authoritarian and right-wing governments that can guarantee the security of American corporations and investment capital.

Schlesinger's interpretation of foreign policy links these "cyclical fluctuations of withdrawal and return" to his experiment-destiny model of American history. The tension between pragmatism and ideology, he believes, is responsible for the tendency to alternate between realism and idealism in the conduct of foreign affairs. The realistic or pragmatic school assumes that the United States shares the weaknesses and self-serving impulses common to all societies. The moralists, for whom Wilson has been the most eloquent and Reagan the most recent spokesman, claim superior virtue and wisdom for the United States and attempt to endow it with a messianic character and a mission to make the world over in its own image. Schlesinger finds the moralistic school of foreign policy both distasteful and dangerous, "profoundly alien to the Constitution" and to the ideas of the intensely practical Founding Fathers, who regarded the international balance of power as a necessity. "Ideology," Schlesinger argues, "is the curse of public affairs because it converts politics into a branch of theology and sacrifices human beings on the altar of dogma." It "insists on the escalation of local troubles into global crises," and in an age of nuclear escalation it can put the very future of the human race at risk. He pleads for the conduct of foreign policy in terms of national interests rather than ideological abstractions and moral absolutes: "Humanity has no choice but to find ways to crawl back from the edge of the abyss."

Historiographical debate is the primary focus of the two longest essays in the foreign-policy section. In "America and Empire," Schlesinger takes on William Appleman Williams and his disciples in the Open Door school of American foreign-policy studies, who claim that the search for markets has always been the predominant motive behind the country's foreign policy. Citing numerous instances of "historical malpractice" in the published works of the Open Door historians, Schlesinger contends that American economic growth has always been based on the domestic rather than the foreign market; he cites the country's historically protectionist attitude, as expressed in its consistently high tariff policies, as evidence against a global search for markets. He faults the Open Door historians for simplistically equating imperialism with the pursuit of economic advantage and points out that noncapitalist nations, notably the Soviet Union, are empire seekers too. Schlesinger argues instead for a geopolitical interpretation of imperialism and contends that a desire for strength in order to protect political self-interest—what William L. Langer has termed "preclusive imperialism"—underlies American (and Russian) imperialism. He follows up on this theme in "Why the Cold War?" where he rejects the revisionist attempt of the Open Door historians to lay the blame on American empire-seeking and focuses instead on each country's perceived geopolitical needs and the realities of the balance of power. He joins the postrevisionist school of Cold War analysts in concluding that the escalation of tensions and misunderstanding was inevitable given the conflicting ideological imperatives that colored the two countries' views of the postwar world.

The essays on domestic policy are among the most thoughtful in the book. In discussing the government's role in the economy, Schlesinger returns to the theme of public-purpose and private-interest political cycles and links them to the argument, as old as the nation itself, concerning the degree of activism that should be permitted the national government. He contends that laissez-faire economic theory is not one of the articles of faith on which the republic was founded (the legacy of the Founding Fathers was a "mixed" economy of public and private interests) and that the alternation between affirmative economic management (Franklin Roosevelt, Truman, Kennedy, Johnson) and noninterventionist negativism (Ulysses Grant, Cleveland, Calvin Coolidge, Reagan) corresponds to the alternation between the public-interest and private-interest phases of the political cycle. Ironically, the players have switched sides since the early republic, when it was the Hamiltonian private-interest faction that sought affirmative government and the Jeffersonian public-purpose group that denounced it.

Schlesinger also reflects on the state of the Imperial Presidency, a phrase that he himself contributed to the political lexicon, and finds presidential accountability still unchecked in the post-Watergate era. The executive's appropriated war-making powers and the "secrecy system" (security classification of documents and the withholding of information from Congress and the public) are as characteristic of the Reagan White House as they were of the Nixon Administration, and the size of the staff that insulates the chief executive from the outside world has increased with every successive administration. "The vital difference between the early republic and the Imperial Presidency resides not in what Presidents did but in what Presidents believed they had the inherent right to do," Schlesinger emphasizes. Early presidents circumvented the Constitution with caution, taking care to have legislative majorities and broad congressional delegations of authority to back up their actions. By contrast, "in the late twentieth century Presidents made sweeping claims of inherent power, neglected the collection of consent, withheld information *ad libitum* and went to war against sovereign states." He lays the blame for the Imperial Presidency on the failure of Congress to exercise its constitutional authority and its willingness to surrender legislative prerogatives to the executive.

In a long discursive piece entitled "The Future of the Vice Presidency," Schlesinger traces the growth in the second half of the twentieth century of an "institutional Vice Presidency" to complement the Imperial Presidency. Although the office still has scant function, the decline of party influence and the rise of the electronic media have given it increasing visibility.

By virtue of his only constitutionally prescribed duty, presiding over the Senate, the vice president was traditionally regarded as a legislative officer; gradually in the twentieth century he has become an adjunct of the executive and an obedient echo for the Imperial President. (The shift of the vice presidential quarters reflects this changed emphasis: His office moved from the Capitol to the Executive Office Building under Kennedy and into the West Wing of the White House under Carter.) Schlesinger argues that the vice presidency has long outlived its original purpose, that of fostering a sense of nationhood for the young republic by forcing presidential electors to cast two ballots, one of which would presumably be for an individual outside the elector's own state. It is demonstrably not a training ground for the presidency, since most chief executives (including those who have risen from the number-two spot themselves) exclude the vice president from the inner sanctum of power. Nor is it required to ensure succession in the event of the president's death; nearly every other democratic nation in the world functions without a vice president by investing power in a chief legislative officer and calling a special election to choose a new president. Moreover, since the passage of the Twenty-fifth Amendment, which permits the president to appoint a vice president (with congressional approval) if the office becomes vacant, the vice presidency has become a potentially antidemocratic route to the presidency. The Gerald R. Ford-Nelson A. Rockefeller Administration illustrated the unanticipated consequences of the Twenty-fifth Amendment, which was "carelessly conceived in the High Noon of the Imperial Presidency." Schlesinger would repeal it and abolish the vice presidency, substituting a called election in the event of a president's death in office.

Conservatives will take issue with a number of Schlesinger's views, but he defends them skillfully, with illuminating forays into the language of the Constitution and the writings of the Founding Fathers. Schlesinger's admirers will relish *The Cycles of American History*, and even the unpersuaded should find it engaging.

Judith N. McArthur

Sources for Further Study

American History Illustrated. XXI, January, 1987, p. 48.
Booklist. LXXXIII, October 1, 1986, p. 186.

Los Angeles Times Book Review. October 26, 1986, p. 1.
National Review. XXXVIII, November 7, 1986, p. 48.
The New Republic. CXCV, December 1, 1986, p. 28.
The New York Review of Books. XXXIII, November 6, 1986, p. 3.
The New York Times Book Review. XCI, November 16, 1986, p. 13.
Newsweek. CVIII, October 27, 1986, p. 98.
Publishers Weekly. CCXXX, September 5, 1986, p. 96.
Time. CXXVIII, December 1, 1986, p. 72.
USA Today. V, October 31, 1986, p. 40.
The Wall Street Journal. CCVIII, November 21, 1986, p. 26.

CZESLAW MILOSZ AND THE INSUFFICIENCY OF LYRIC

Author: Donald Davie (1922-   )
Publisher: University of Tennessee Press (Knoxville). 92 pp. $8.50
Type of work: Literary criticism

An extended essay which seeks to demonstrate that Czesław Miłosz repudiated the lyric mode of poetic expression in favor of more heterogeneous forms that are better suited to reflect the complexity of twentieth century experience

Donald Davie, a noted British poet and critic, currently holds the position of Andrew W. Mellon Professor of Humanities at Vanderbilt University, and the text of *Czeslaw Milosz and the Insufficiency of Lyric* is an augmented version of the John C. Hodges Lectures which Davie delivered at the University of Tennessee in February, 1984, under the title "Poetics of the Unfree World: Czeslaw Milosz." As he himself states, his involvement with Miłosz's work started in the early 1950's, "having during that period indulged an amateurish and intermittent interest in Polish poetry generally." His primary interest in the poetry of Poland was formerly focused on the work of Adam Mickiewicz, especially the epic poem *Pan Tadeusz: Or, The Last Foray in Lithuania* (1834). In 1956, Davie published an essay called *"Pan Tadeusz* in English Verse" as part of a symposium edited by Wacław Lednicki and issued under the title *Adam Mickiewicz in World Literature.* Featured within Davie's essay are a number of his own poetic adaptations of selected passages from a prose translation of this renowned epic by George Rapall Noyes that came out in 1917. His efforts to extract the latent poetry from Noyes's prose version of *Pan Tadeusz* came to full fruition in 1959 with the publication of a short series of poems entitled *The Forests of Lithuania.* Oddly enough, both Mickiewicz and Miłosz were born in the region that was formerly designated as the Grand Duchy of Lithuania prior to the partitions of Poland during the latter part of the eighteenth century.

On the occasion of the Swedish Academy's announcement that Miłosz had been selected as the 1980 recipient of the Nobel Prize for Literature, those unfamiliar with the history of Eastern Europe had difficulty comprehending how a Polish poet could have been born and reared in a region that is now a constituent part of the Soviet Republic of Lithuania. Despite his own longstanding interest in the poetry of Poland, Davie confesses that he himself finds the Polish-Lithuanian roots of Miłosz to be "a tangle that no outsider and perhaps few Poles can understand." This statement appears in the author's preface to *Czeslaw Milosz and the Insufficiency of Lyric.* Here, Davie uses the occasion to express his disappointment with Miłosz's novel *The Issa Valley* (1955), at least with the English translation published in 1981. He maintains that this novel, the plot of which focuses on a young boy's coming of age in rural Lithuania during World War I, does little to clarify any questions pertaining to the author's roots. It would have been helpful if Davie had taken the trouble to inform the reader that Miłosz was but three years of age at the outbreak of World War I and that his family spent the war years in Russia owing to the fact that his father, a civil engineer by profession, had been drafted into the czar's army. After the Bolsheviks seized power in Russia, the Miłosz family returned to the newly independent Baltic states for a few years but finally decided to settle down in the city of Wilno. This city, although once the capital of ancient Lithuania, had long been a predominantly Polish-speaking cultural center and was a part of a fully restored Poland between 1922 and 1939. Hence, *The Issa Valley* can scarcely qualify as autobiography.

Since Davie provides scant biographical data about Miłosz, most readers will want additional background material on this score. To begin with, Miłosz was born in an area of Europe where Polish, Lithuanian, and German blood intermingled over the centuries, and his own ancestry is a mixed one. It can, however, be established through legal documents that his father's forebears had been speakers of Polish since the sixteenth century. Nevertheless, Miłosz takes great pride in his Lithuanian origins and even derives a perverse pleasure from the fact that Lithuania was the last country in Europe to adopt Christianity. The city of Wilno, where his family eventually settled, had a population of two hundred thousand. Approximately 60 percent of the people who lived there used Polish as their mother tongue, and more than a quarter of the inhabitants were Yiddish-speaking Jews. Most of the others spoke either Lithuanian or Russian. The city was called Vilnius by the Lithuanians, Wilno by the Poles, and Vilna by the Jews and the Russians. Miłosz apparently alluded to this disparity in nomenclature when he published a collection of poems in 1969 under the title *Miasto bez imienia* (city without a name). Vilnius is today the capital of Soviet Lithuania.

After being graduated from the King Stefan Batory University with a Master of Law degree, Miłosz received a fellowship in literature from the Polish government enabling him to study in Paris during the years 1934-1935. Upon his return to Poland, he obtained employment with the Polish Radio Corporation in Wilno and later in Warsaw. His career as an administrator came to an abrupt end when the Germans attacked Poland on September 1, 1939. By this time Miłosz had already published two collections of poetry. Under the German occupation he became active as a writer for the resistance movement and even managed to publish a volume of his own poetry clandestinely. After the Red Army liberated Poland from more than five years of Nazi rule, Miłosz joined the diplomatic corps and was posted as a cultural attaché in Washington, D.C., from 1946 to 1950. He then was transferred to Paris, where he served as first secretary for Cultural Affairs. In 1951, shortly after the practice of "Socialist Realism" became mandatory for all Polish writers, he decided to break with the home government in Warsaw and to start life anew by working as a free-lance writer in

France. After a decade of extraordinary literary productivity, Miłosz was invited to lecture on Polish literature at the University of California in Berkeley during the academic year 1960-1961. In 1961, he decided to settle in Berkeley after he was made an offer of tenure as a professor of Slavic languages and literature. He became a naturalized American citizen in 1970 and eventually retired from active teaching in 1978 with the honorary rank of Professor Emeritus. He married in 1944 and is the father of two sons.

Davie begins his critique of Miłosz's poetry with a discussion of several poems that are now part of an English-language collection entitled *Bells in Winter* (1978). It was Davie's exposure to the contents of this volume that initially led him to rethink his views on the nature of poetic discourse. In Davie's view, Miłosz's concept of poetry entails a rejection of John Keats's principle of "negative capability." According to this Keatsian dictum, such a state occurs "when a man is capable of being in uncertainties, mysteries, doubts, without any irritable reaching after fact and reason.... With a great poet the sense of Beauty overcomes every other consideration, or rather obliterates all consideration." Miłosz, in contrast, has argued that the true mission of a poet should be defined as "a passionate pursuit of the real," and his own poetry constitutes an explicit repudiation of Keats's equation of truth with beauty. He believes that the lyric mode is an insufficient vehicle for registering the complexity of twentieth century experience. It is Davie's contention that, in order to attain these complex aesthetic objectives, Miłosz has abandoned the fixed standpoint of the traditional lyricist in favor of flitting, changeable standpoints on the part of the speaker. He goes on to assert that "Milosz characteristically seeks poetic forms more comprehensive and heterogeneous than any lyric, even the most sustained and elaborate." This generalization concerning Miłosz's poetry forms the central thesis of Davie's book.

Davie maintains that Miłosz began writing poetry as a lyricist and that he did not begin to break with this tradition until midway through his career. As a consequence, Miłosz's use of the personal pronoun "I" can be a source of misunderstanding on the part of the reader. For Davie, therefore, it is crucial to take note of the fact that the first-person singular may be employed in two distinct ways. As a case in point, he cites the example of Walt Whitman, insisting that the use of "I" in *Leaves of Grass*, especially in the section entitled "Song of Myself," is meant to include everyone. Davie identifies this nonlyrical quality as the "dithyrambic voice," after the Greek choric hymns that were originally recited in honor of the god Dionysus. Here, Davie seeks to bolster his argument by invoking the distinction that Friedrich Nietzsche draws between the Apollonian and Dionysian modes of aesthetic expression. It is Nietzsche's position that the dramatic dialogues within a Greek tragedy represent an affirmation of individuality, whereas the choral passages constitute a suppression of individuality. On this basis,

Davie feels justified in drawing a distinction of his own between the lyrical "I" of a poet such as William Wordsworth and the dithyrambic "I" of a poet such as Miłosz. Another genre which Davie identifies as having influenced Miłosz is that of the idyll. In an appendix devoted to Miłosz's wartime poetry, he underscores the idyllic aspects of a work entitled "The World: A Naive Poem" that was written in 1943.

Conditions in Warsaw during the German occupation were the opposite of idyllic, yet Davie does not believe that the ordeal of those war years played any decisive role in shaping Miłosz's views on the nature of poetry. He points out that Miłosz, while still a student at the University of Wilno, became affiliated with a coterie of local poets who soon came to be labeled "catastrophists" because of the apocalyptic premonitions expressed in their poetry. Davie, furthermore, links Miłosz to the vatic tradition that prevailed among Polish poets of the Romantic era whose mission it was to keep the cause of national independence alive. Foremost among these prophetic poets is Mickiewicz, and Davie refers to him repeatedly throughout his exegesis of Miłosz's poetry. Also mentioned by Davie in passing is Juliusz Słowacki, a man approximately ten years younger than Mickiewicz and his chief rival for the title of *wieszcz* (national bard). It is useful to recall that when a two-volume collection of Słowacki's earliest poetic endeavors appeared in print, Mickiewicz dismissed it as "a church without a God inside," since the content was completely devoid of any political or religious ideology. Mickiewicz's sentiments on this occasion are echoed by Miłosz himself in the poem called "Dedication," where he poses the rhetorical question: "What is poetry which does not save/ Nations or people?" This poem serves Davie as a point of departure for some concluding remarks pertaining to the distinction between the lyrical "I" and the dithyrambic "I."

While Davie frequently discusses poems which Miłosz wrote in response to the inhumanity of Nazi oppression, there is little mention of those pertaining to Soviet tyranny. One of the most memorable protests against the Communist regime imposed on Poland in the aftermath of World War II is enshrined in the lines which Polish workers belonging to the Solidarity movement selected to serve as an inscription on the monument erected outside the shipyards in Gdańsk for the purpose of commemorating the strikers who died during demonstrations against the government in 1970. These lines are taken from a work that originally appeared in 1953 as part of a collection of poems published in exile under the title *Światło dzienne* (daylight) and run as follows:

> You who have harmed the upright man
> Bursting out in laughter at his troubles,
> Be not secure. The poet remembers.
> You may kill him—another will be born.
> Deeds and dialogues will be recorded.

Thus, verse that previously circulated clandestinely in *samizdat* form could now be read on a public square in broad daylight. Davie, for his part, has paid the poet a similar honor by writing *Czeslaw Milosz and the Insufficiency of Lyric.*

Victor Anthony Rudowski

Sources for Further Study

Library Journal. CXI, July 16, 1986, p. 84.
The London Review of Books. VIII, December 4, 1986, p. 12.

DARKNESS

Author: Bharati Mukherjee (1940-   )
Publisher: Penguin Books (New York). 199 pp. $5.95
Type of work: Short stories
Time: The 1980's
Locale: The United States and Canada

These twelve stories treat in varied ways, often metaphorically, the conflicts East Indians face as they adjust to life in Canada and the United States

In an autobiographical account from *Days and Nights in Calcutta* (1977), Bharati Mukherjee describes herself as a " 'Third World Woman Writer' living in North America." She had been born into a middle-class Brahman family in Calcutta, educated at Catholic schools there, then in Europe, finally at a university in the United States where she married a Canadian. At the time, she was teaching at a Canadian university, and she had defined her place as an artist in such a limited manner; then, after living in Canada for fourteen years, she moved in 1980 to the United States. This change affected her attitude so sharply that in the introduction to *Darkness* she is able to say: "I see myself as an American writer in the tradition of other American writers whose parents or grandparents had passed through Ellis Island." Explaining how she shed her role as an expatriate to take on the more gratifying one of immigrant, Mukherjee notes that she now possesses "a set of fluid identities to be celebrated" rather than the "mordant and self-protective irony" she had practiced previously.

Although the stories collected here are not autobiographical, they do reflect the disparity Mukherjee sees between the expatriate and the immigrant. The expatriate narratives set in Canada vibrate with bitterness, rejection, and defeat, whereas the immigrant stories taking place in the United States seem about to explode with awareness. Yet "about to explode" carries significance always, for the troubled immigrants find no easy solution for their disassociation. In fact, their struggle with "Indianness" becomes a metaphor to depict the gratuitous cruelty, the broken identities, and the conflict between sexes that dominate much contemporary writing. Thus the stories—the immigrant ones more so than the expatriate—transcend their inherent "Indianness" to embrace the metaphorical immigrants who seek stability in a world of shifting patterns. As Mukherjee points out in the introduction to *Darkness*: "Indianness is now a metaphor, a particular way of partially comprehending the world."

The best of the expatriate stories, "The World According to Hsü," follows the misadventures of a Canadian couple who stumble into a military coup when they are on an idyllic holiday on an island off the African coast. Yet the wife, an Indian by birth, feels safer surrounded by revolutionaries than amid Canadians whose violence against Asians she recounts to her disbelieving North American husband. Later, sitting alone in the barricaded hotel among a "collection of Indians and Europeans," the expatriate from Canada decides that "no matter where she lived, she would never feel so at home again." Such assurance fails to come to the characters in the other two Canadian stories, "Isolated Incidents" and "Tamurlane," where both the Canadians and the expatriates suffer from violence and disillusionment. Only the woman in "Isolated Incidents," who had escaped Canada and succeeded as a singer in the United States, finds happiness. The narrative rests on a meeting between the star and her childhood friend Ann, who stayed behind and with a now-shattered idealism had gone to work for a human-rights agency handling the discrimination complaints of Asians, Africans, Jamaicans, and others from warm climates who "found reasons for staying where Ann herself, on bad days, found few." The despair she faces each day eventually seeps into her consciousness, and in a crowded restaurant she shouts at one of her clients: " Nothing is fair! . . . There isn't any justice." Her outburst describes aptly the events in "Tamurlane," a brutal account of a Toronto police raid on an Indian restaurant whose crippled cook sinks a cleaver into a Mountie's arm, then holds his passport in front of his face, only to be struck by a bullet.

These two stories point up Mukherjee's belief that Canada has failed as a multiracial nation. Unlike "The World According to Hsü," neither story attains the grace of personal discovery that bonds shattered identity. In the introduction to *Darkness*, Mukherjee admits that "the purely 'Canadian' stories . . . were difficult to write." They are also difficult to read, for the thinly veiled polemicism and near literalness make them less universal than the other narratives.

Three of the immigrant stories, "A Father," "Nostalgia," and "Hindus," depict outwardly Westernized Indians who at unguarded moments are possessed by a blurred vision of their past; when they try to put that vision into focus, they find their newly acquired present blurred. Mr. Bhowmick, in "The Father," lives in a high-rise in Detroit with his employed wife and daughter, works as an engineer, and enjoys all mechanical conveniences, even dreams of a Club Med vacation. Still, he keeps an image of the goddess Kali-Mata in his bedroom and prays to her at length each morning before eating his French toast and commuting to work. Yet when he discovers how his unmarried daughter became pregnant, he cannot reconcile the disparity between his traditional Indian beliefs and his borrowed Western sophistication. Thus an act of violence ensues, but it is an act altogether personal, not national as in "Tamurlane."

The single stroke which ends "Nostalgia" turns symbolic rather than literal, for through its performance a wealthy Indian doctor cleanses himself and by means of this purgation begins to restore the delicate balance that he maintains between the world he inhabits and the world that at times inhabits him. One evening, he discovers in an Indian shop a woman so lovely that he imagines her the epitome of Indian womanhood. After dinner in an ethnic restaurant, followed by lovemaking in a room above it, he realizes the falseness of his nostalgia: The woman is a prostitute in the employ of a blackmailer. To erase the memory of such an encounter so that he might return to his Western life demands the dramatic and symbolic gesture that he makes.

"Hindus" draws its meaning from another sole incident, which in a way amplifies all the stories in *Darkness*. When an Indian woman working for a New York publisher speaks in Hindi to a client, an associate unwittingly says to her: "I had no idea you spoke Hindu." Instead of pointing out the error, the Indian editor concludes that "there's a whole world of us now, speaking Hindu," an unfolding of thought that brings her closer to grasping her own identity.

Female identity, or the lack of it, dominates "Angela," "The Lady of Lucknow," and "Visitors." The first story gains its strength through the way it plays the horror of Angela's early life in Bangladesh against the security of the midwestern home into which she was adopted as a refugee child. Her body scarred and her memory filled with the suffering she had seen and experienced, Angela wonders if her suitor, an Indian doctor, can free her through marriage, as "he tempts with domesticity. Phantom duplexes, babies tucked tight into cribs, dogs running playfully off with barbecued steak." At the same moment, shreds of childhood memories haunt her: "Legless kids try to squirm out of ditches. Packs of pariah dogs who have learned to gorge on dying infant flesh. . . ." Will she, Angela seems to be asking, trade her freedom for a new kind of bondage if she succumbs to the role of the traditional Indian wife and the stifling attention of the Indian doctor?

Two far more fortunate women emerge in the other stories. Both wives of successful Indians well situated in American business, they come from the protected environment of upper-class Indian homes. Yet, in spite of the Western luxury which they now enjoy, they both thirst for romance in the self-satisfied society that they have entered. One tries to overcome her disaffection through an affair, the other through duty. Their inner lives unhaunted by memories of destruction but plagued instead by a longing for the exotic qualities they imagine having left behind, the two women suffer the same indefinable anguish that Angela does. "Visitors" asks the question which might well be the first step toward completeness for all three:

> Why then is she moved by an irresistible force to steal out of his bed in the haven of his expensive condominium, and run off into the alien American night where only shame and disaster can await her?

Though darkness prevails among the immigrants, its lifting might come about once they dare to step beyond the confining boundaries that they have created for themselves, once they dare to chance the trials and perils of assimilation.

"Courtly Vision" serves as an epilogue to the collection. Inspired by a Moghul miniature painting, the story evokes the actual sixteenth century Indian city of Fatehpur-Sikri built by Emperor Akbar, who for unknown reasons left with his people after only fourteen years of occupancy. The city stands today, still deserted, as an archaeological oddity. More important, the story details Mukherjee's fictional style, which in itself resembles a Moghul miniature: the sparsity but exactness of detail; the cleanness; the humor; the rich texture; the sweeping vistas in microscopic plainness. As the emperor in the story leaves his doomed city, he commands the court painter:

> *Give me total vision. . . . Hide nothing from me. . . . Tell me who to fear and who to kill but tell it to me in a way that makes me smile. Transport me through dense fort walls and stone grilles and into the hearts of men.*

Mukherjee must have heeded, too, the emperor's command. Her vision is like that of one her characters, Shawn Patel in "Saints." The son of an American mother and an Indian father, he captures the essence of Mukherjee's art in the revelation of his own secret: "How wondrous to be a visionary. If I were to touch someone now, I'd be touching god." Mukherjee proves herself a visionary, one who looks into the hearts of men and women, sends them—along with her readers—into the darkness, then almost into the light.

Robert Ross

Sources for Further Study

Booklist. LXXXII, January 1, 1986, p. 658.
Books in Canada. XIV, August, 1985, p. 21.
Macleans. XCVIII, August 19, 1985, p. 51.
The New Republic. CXCIV, April 14, 1986, p. 36.
The New York Times Book Review. XCI, January 12, 1986, p. 14.
Quill & Quire. LI, August, 1985, p. 43.
Times Educational Supplement. December 20, 1985, p. 17.

DEATH VALLEY AND THE AMARGOSA
A Land of Illusion

Author: Richard E. Lingenfelter (1934-   )
Publisher: University of California Press (Berkeley). Illustrated. 664 pp. $39.95
Type of work: History
Time: 1850-1930
Locale: Death Valley, California

An exhaustive account of Death Valley during the invasion and reign of white miners, con men, newspapermen, and dreamers during the late nineteenth and early twentieth centuries

> *Principal personages:*
> DEATH VALLEY SCOTTY, a quintessential flimflam artist
> ALBERT M. JOHNSON, his financial backer
> THE MONTGOMERY BROTHERS, the initiators of the Bullfrog gold rush
> "BELLERIN TECK" (ANDREW LASWELL), one of the valley's first pioneers and settlers
> FRANK "SHORTY" HARRIS, a single-mule prospector

Richard E. Lingenfelter's unstated thesis in his comprehensive history of Death Valley is that the restless American pioneer spirit and fantasy thrived in a vacuum. There are 470 pages of text, 110 pages of footnotes, and fifty-four pages of bibliography that make up the author's very tangible story of illusion. Lingenfelter tells of credulity and fantasy at work in the latter half of the nineteenth century and the early decades of the twentieth. The void this faith inhabited is the lowest geographical elevation in the United States—282 feet below sea level by latest survey—where summer heat scalds and the air holds no moisture. Sitting in shade, if one finds shade in Death Valley, the basking visitor can lose more than two gallons of water to dehydration in eight hours. Climatic extremes to the side, Lingenfelter's subject is what happened when this innocently empty world was invaded by white men in the nineteenth century.

Ancient campsites argue that humans have lived in Death Valley for at least ten thousand years. A variety of Indian tribes, including Shoshones, Paiute, and Kawaiisu, subsisted on pinenuts, mesquite beans, jackrabbits, chuckwallas, and an occasional bighorn sheep. If pinenuts were scarce the Indians suffered; if not, they thrived. Summers were hot, but the rest of the year was pleasant, and the Panamint Mountains towering to eleven thousand feet on the valley's west side provided an escape from dreadful summer days. Living in the valley for centuries without the white man's terminology for hell and damnation, the Indian failed to develop a mythology commensurate with the place's malevolent genii. Their lives seem typified by gratitude for available sustenance. Their home came to be known as Death Valley when white immigrants arrived or attempted to travel through the valley in wagons. The disasters they suffered, Lingenfelter demonstrates, were never as horrible as the disasters reported. Lingenfelter argues that the strangers were expert fictioneers, skilled at sending horrors onto the sand and canyons by their imagination's projectors. Their tendency to pile rumor upon rumor, imagined death upon imagined death, created the monstrous illusion they obscurely seemed to need—Death Valley. Death by thirst seen once, or heard about once, was sufficient to fuel visions of hundreds of such calamities. The valley floor, with the arrival of the "forty-niners," gold seekers, cattle rustlers, and the surreal panorama of civic life—newspapers, banks, whorehouses, stock exchanges—became less an environment than a stage where dreams masquerading as men acted scenes as brief as they were similar in plot. The performances were viewed from the nation's financial centers with imperfect clarity but absolute interest. At one time during the gold boom in Death Valley, the two biggest stocks on the New York Exchange were from Death Valley mines.

Lingenfelter, a research physicist at the University of California, San Diego, devoted the spare time of five years to researching Death Valley history. His research methodology and published record are in their methodical thoroughness the antithesis of the histrionic impulsiveness which created the subject upon which he focused. A glance through the footnotes section reveals a forest of citations from extinct and still existing newspapers, surveyors' reports on the first explorations of the valley, mining journals, New York stock-market periodicals, city registers, company prospectuses, and personal letters. The bibliography contains what appears to be every manuscript, thesis, court case, government publication, and book on Death Valley and its obscurest happening. All but a few paragraphs in Lingenfelter's book terminate with a footnote, which explains the extensive data base collected at the end of the book.

Lingenfelter's desire is clearly to secure, compile, and organize a mass of information. He is less interested in interpreting the story he has amassed than in getting all of it down. This at-times plodding accounting makes for a book the historian will read from beginning to end, while the general reader will sample. Whoever the reader, he will be fascinated by the subject for the same reason that Lingenfelter seems to be—that so much life and energy could exist as it did in such a place. Any account of the white man's greed, restlessness, dreams, and repeated losses when faced with the American frontier is hard to resist, containing as it does the familiar insensitive, unreligious white man arrogantly staking claim to a world previously untouched by a "claiming" psyche. Lingenfelter's book is doubly interesting in this light, because very little existed in Death Valley to be claimed, yet the distinctive white need for finds and treasure flourished anyway.

After the brief chapter on the various Indians who lived in the valley, Lingenfelter presents this "white history" of Death Valley—a spectacle of

crime, gold fevers, borax prospectors, swindles, con artistry, minimal profits, and large deficits. The first whites to enter were horse traders moving
stock between California and New Mexico. The horse traders attracted vermin, raiders known as Los Chaguanosos, who rustled horses in California
for buyers in the Mississippi Valley. Next came the gold seekers of 1849,
otherwise known as "argonauts," as in the company Jason kept when pursuing the fleece. The story of the forty-niners Lingenfelter titles "More Lost
Than Found." He disentangles several distinct stories from what is in his
words "the most repeated, though frequently, garbled, tale in the history of
Death Valley." To condense again what he unravels, the story of the argonauts in Death Valley is that of wagon trains lost, fantastic gold discoveries,
deaths from thirst, impossible rescues, and unminable claims. Though the
invaders fared poorly in the mass, there were among them individuals who
saw a profitable vein:

> For those who tried to work its minerals, the remoteness of Death Valley was a much
> greater problem than were occasional Indian raids. But to those who chose to work the
> stockholder instead, Death Valley's remoteness was a vital ingredient for success.

Lieutenant Robert Bailey was the first successful miner of speculators'
pockets, and he set a precedent followed by many others. The method he
used was primitive, but its effectiveness indicates how blind rich men can be
when they "see" a chance to grow even richer. Bailey showed silver-studded
rock to San Francisco investors after arriving from Death Valley. An assay
showed the ore to be worth $16,342 per ton. Bailey assured his listeners that
the lode from which the rock came was endless. Its endlessness was
stretched to suddenly remembered extensions as more suckers appeared.
Speculators paid Bailey twelve thousand dollars cash for half interest in one
wing of the lode and established the Bailey Silver Mining Company. The
Comet Silver Mining Company followed on its heels to work another arm of
the ore, which a suspicious geologist proved to be a rock concocted in a fur-
nace in Bailey's backyard. By then, however, Bailey had disappeared and
staged an identification of his mutilated remains in the wilds of the San
Joaquin Valley. The real Bailey was still living thirty years later in San
Diego, working as a bartender and fondly recounting the swindle to his
customers.

While Bailey was the first to capitalize on the illusory Death Valley
strike, the master of the technique was Walter Edward Scott, better known
as Death Valley Scotty. By the time he went to work on investors, the San
Francisco lode was much less gullible, so he traveled to New York with his
amazing samples and stories. The ethos of the Wild West accompanied
Scotty, and he knew well the tricks of the showman from working as a rider
in Buffalo Bill Cody's shows. Scotty's first catch was the third vice president
of the Knickerbocker Trust Company, Julian M. Gerard. Scotty described

an imaginary claim, and Gerard surrendered the cash to begin mining it. Scotty's imaginary mines kept newspapers in headlines across the United States. His true craving was publicity, and the gold myth fueled his seemingly transparent joyride. A play was written and performed to dramatize his life while he was still fabricating it. Everything he did was offstage, as reported by the media. A second backer of Scotty, Albert Johnson, came to California to see the mine for himself. Scotty staged an ambush to scare off the determined Johnson, but it backfired when Scotty's brother stopped a bullet. When news of the ambush, which Scotty called off by yelling out to the attackers to stop shooting, reached the San Bernardino sheriff, Scotty's con seemed to be finished. Yet while newspapers proclaimed the truth about the mystery man, Johnson continued feeding him money, stubbornly believing that real discoveries had been made and that Scotty was hiding them by his elaborate antics. Twenty years after the ambush, Johnson and Scotty were still together, and while Scotty never provided Johnson with his gold mine, Johnson became a permanent zookeeper for Scotty, finally building a castle for him in the wasteland which is today the valley's main tourist attraction. The final joke was played on Johnson when, nearing the completion of the lavish project, he learned that he was building it on land he did not own; his own property was a mile away from the castle. Johnson and Scotty had to surrender the castle to the government. Scotty had not adapted to castle life anyway, as he slept in the kitchen on a cot and ate pickles and crackers. His meat was illusions, not actual wealth.

Lingenfelter's chapters on the fast talkers, Scotty, Bailey, and their ilk, are exhaustive. Thorough as well are those on the actual miners of gold, silver, borax, and copper. With the exception of borax, which made a fortune for Francis Marion Smith, mining in Death Valley was mainly sound and fury culminating in worthless stock certificates. This story repeated itself again and again. Mines were either superficially promising or too expensive to run. Tremendous effort went into developing technology for retrieving and processing, but with few exceptions the mines were lost causes. The interesting part of Lingenfelter's account of the mining boom is his depiction of the rise and fall of the towns. News of a strike created a small town overnight in the middle of nowhere. Rhyolite, at its peak, claimed four thousand citizens, daily newspapers, running water, a stock exchange, and three-story buildings. A participant in numerous strikes. Frank "Shorty" Harris, recalled the Bullfrog strike, which saw towns mushroom from the flats simultaneous with the disappearance of others:

> Men were leaving town in a steady stream with buckboards, buggies, wagons and burros. It looked like the whole population of Goldfield was trying to move at once. . . . They all got the fever and milled around, wildeyed, trying to find a way to get out to the new "strike". . . . I saw one man who was about ready to cry because he couldn't buy a

jackass for $500.00. . . . Men who didn't have anything else started out on that seventy-
five mile hike with wheelbarrows; and a lot of 'em made it alright.

Lingenfelter spares no detail depicting the life of these cities, from the
Fourth of July baseball games with neighboring towns to the occasional
gunfights. Lingenfelter relishes the fatuousness inherent in these rootless
places and people. He finds one story illustrative as an image of the point-
less energy that drove people. Joe Simpson, a drunk, killed a man while on
a bender and was hanged without trial by the citizenry. The town doctor
was curious to discover evidence in Joe's brain of damage which would
explain the senseless murder, so he decapitated the corpse and after exploring the brain put the skull in a bag suspended from the floor joists of his,
the doctor's, house. Some women concerned with providing Joe a proper
burial went by night with their buggy to transport the body, but they lost
interest after traveling a ways and left the body on the sands when it fell off
the buggy.

There were shrewd men in the vicinity as well. The Montgomery brothers, George and Bob, found the gold in the last decade of the nineteenth
century which led to the largest boom in Death Valley mining. Their find
coincided with the arrival of the automobile and diesel engines, thus sim-
plifying and speeding up the mining process. Yet it is the theme of delusion
that Lingenfelter sees controlling the valley's history. The valley generated
from its arid hollows a resonance in the early visitor's brain, propagating tall
tales and wild visions. One rumor told of fountains shooting forth scalding
blood. Preachers heard the wails of the damned coming through the valley
floor and called it the roof of Hell. Another speculated that Death Valley
was the blasted remains of the original Eden. Entire wagon trains of people
perished in the mass; poison gas filled the visitor's lungs. Lingenfelter produces the litany of disasters and terror with an affectionate, dry scientist's
searchingness. He seems to say without stating it that the generic white
transient needed the generic wilderness to appease the emptiness within. If
he, the transient, were tired of fantasizing terrors, he could fantasize gold,
entire mountains of it.

Lingenfelter consistently downplays the valley's intimidation and emphasizes the visitor's dramatic contributions. He tells of Erich von Stroheim
shooting a film in the valley one summer in the 1920's. The film, titled
Greed, ran, when finished, twenty-four hours. The studio heads demanded
cutting and ruined the masterpiece, in the director's view. Without elaborat-
ing on it, Lingenfelter demonstrates the parallel between Death Valley and
Hollywood—places where men could "make it big." This reader would have
liked more interpretive asides from Lingenfelter, but it is probable that,
after five years' research on men chasing illusions, he decided to let the facts
speak for themselves.

Bruce Wiebe

Sources for Further Study

Booklist. LXXXIII, September 1, 1986, p. 26.
California Magazine. XI, July, 1986, p. 32.
Choice. XXIV, November, 1986, p. 370.
Kirkus Reviews. LIV, May 1, 1986, p. 701.
The New York Times Book Review. XCI, August 24, 1986, p. 15.

DELIRIUM ECLIPSE AND OTHER STORIES

Author: James Lasdun (1958-   )
Publisher: Harper & Row, Publishers (New York). 200 pp. $15.95
Type of work: Short stories
Time: The mid-1980's
Locale: England

A collection of nine stories dramatizing contemporary consciousness throughout English society

The stories in *Delirium Eclipse and Other Stories* are richly lacquered things. James Lasdun's determination to get colors, scents, shadings of light and shadow down (in what often reads like a prose gone lush) gives his work an art for art's sake quality. His way of writing recalls the sensuous models of Walter Pater's prose of the late nineteenth century; "to burn with a gem-like flame" seems at times to become an end in itself. Indeed, so intense is Lasdun's descriptive prose that the reader may get the impression he is reading a poet in disguise, or perhaps a prose-poet more interested in atmosphere than plot. At times he names too many flowers, traces a shading of color or light a bit too closely. John Keats was like that in his earlier poetry, and there is quite a bit of Romantic naturalism in stories such as "Delirium Eclipse," where the protagonist drowns in the vertigo of India's smells, sights, and sounds, or "Heart's Desire," in which the hero is a voyeur who spares neither himself nor the reader the graininess of virtually every sensuous detail—from the feel of an artichoke leaf to the glimpse of a girl's naked back.

Nevertheless, it would be grossly superficial to dismiss these brilliant stories, a first collection by a twenty-seven year-old Englishman, as precious or self-consciously pursuing a latter-day literary aestheticism. Many pack a powerful blow, a trenchant psychological or social comment, that at once shakes the reader free of the hypnotic effect of Lasdun's own language and imagery and proves that the style is part of the effect; that what seems ornate and decorative is actually sly, ironic—in all cases, pertinent. Lasdun reminds one that the greatest modern British short stories are those of D. H. Lawrence and that the genius of short-story telling requires more of rendering than telling, more of symbolic suggestion than plotting.

In "Dead Labor," Lasdun juxtaposes with cruel irony the luxurious temptations of the self-indulgent life and the moral demands of principle and social responsibility. This story almost gives away the whole show of Lasdun's art, because here the sinuous and sensual details are openly seductive and corrupting. In addition, the story is about writing, and the hero makes a choice; he forsakes morally aware writing—the shaping of his radical mentor's fragments, the leavings of a dying idealist—for the banal and commercialized sensuousness of slick magazine commentary on gourmet dining. This hack work also gets him the sexual favors of a young journalist who uses her body to woo him away from his obligations to the dying radical. The story ends with the hero humiliated by a magician in a tawdry nightclub setting. The inference for Lasdun's fictive intentions is clear: Writing that is not virtuous, that substitutes virtuosity for virtue, is parasitic and self-destructive. The story takes its title from the heading the dying radical Samuelson appended to the top of his notes. The quotation from Karl Marx follows: "Capital is dead labor which, vampire-like, lives only by sucking living labor, and lives the more, the more labor it sucks."

No "dead labor" Lasdun's stories—their descriptive magic seems to feed on life, but the end result is always the exposing of that intention as a protagonist's substitution for true perception. His heroes seem to be feeling intensely, and they often do, but they also often—and the reader always—learn that their intensity is a lie, that openness to experience can be as much a falsification as the denial of experience. For example, in the collection's title story, "Delirium Eclipse," a shallow young agronomist combines the seduction of a beautiful English girl with field work in developing India's agriculture. He takes risks with food and sanitation that make him very ill and cause him to wallow in a delirium of fever and jealousy. In the collection's last story, "Heart's Desire," the protagonist-hero permits himself the voyeur's pleasure of total immersion in the experience of others. He enjoys also the satisfaction of a kind of disinterested heroics by saving an upper-class girl from being raped by her social peers. Yet he does this without revealing his presence; he merely throws rocks into a pool to frighten the rapists away. By staying in the dark and not revealing his identity to the rescued damsel, he is indulging a withering detachment as well as feelings of class inferiority. In both these stories, what the main characters see, hear, smell, and feel is what they experience—and it is not enough.

Lasdun can play this theme—the experience of sensuousness and the sensuousness of experience—with interesting variations. In "Escapes," an African college professor has a night out in Paris with a "Nordic" girl. Throughout the entire evening he thinks that he is impressing her, and Lasdun brilliantly conveys the way one's senses can betray one into thinking that one is secure. When she leaves him at her doorstep to go home alone, he is left with the problem of catching the last metro. Failing to find an exit at his station, he thrashes about in endless corridors of white tile before finally breaking out of what has become a terrifying trap. This is clearly a symbolization of white terror no less powerful than Joseph Conrad's heart of darkness was a symbolization of the European's fear of barbarism. Racism, like beauty, is in the eyes of the beholder.

An astonishing story is "The Siege." A young girl from a nameless totalitarian country somewhere in Eastern Europe does domestic service for a London bachelor, a Mr. Kinsky. He is a musician and has surrounded himself with precious objets d'art. He declares his love for the girl. When pressed by Mr. Kinsky to tell him if there is "anything" he could do to make her love him, she finally blurts out, "Get my husband out of jail!" Her husband is a political prisoner in her homeland. There now ensues an incredible and suspenseful plot. Piece by piece, Mr. Kinsky sells his beautiful possessions. He does this so gradually that it only becomes obvious to the girl after a time. They do not communicate, but he plays hypnotic pieces on a great piano. The music slowly possesses the girl. He sends her notes that promise her husband's eventual release from prison. Finally, he sells the piano itself. He is divesting himself of his own world of luxurious possessions, the only world he has, to release a man from jail married to a woman he loves. He is doing this because she has said she would love him if he could succeed in freeing her husband. Mr. Kinsky's heroic desire—his strength in giving up one sensuousness for the fleeting possibility of another—is too much for the girl. She becomes his lover the very morning her husband's taxi arrives.

Peter A. Brier

Sources for Further Study

Booklist. LXXXII, May 1, 1986, p. 1282.
Chicago Tribune. September 5, 1986, V, p. 3.
Kirkus Reviews. LIV, May 1, 1986, p. 661.
Library Journal. CXI, June 15, 1986, p. 78.
The New York Times Book Review. XCI, August 3, 1986, p. 12.
Publishers Weekly. CCXXIX, June 6, 1986, p. 56.
Washington Post Book World. XVI, August 24, 1986, p. 3.

DESSA ROSE

Author: Sherley Anne Williams (1944-   )
Publisher: William Morrow and Company (New York). 236 pp. $15.95
Type of work: Historical novel
Time: 1847
Locale: Alabama and Iowa

Dessa Rose is a young slave woman who fights for her freedom; the novel thereby challenges the traditional, largely sexist historical perspective on the role of slave women in the resistance movement

Principal characters:
DESSA ROSE, a young slave woman who fights for her freedom
KAINE, the father of Dessa's baby
RUTH "RUFEL" SUTTON, a white woman who harbors runaway slaves
ADAM NEHEMIAH, a journalist conducting research for a book on slave revolts
NATHAN, a slave who helps rescue Dessa
HARKER, a slave who plans and directs the slave-selling scheme and leads his fellow slaves to freedom

Dessa Rose, a novel in three parts, recounts the story of a young slave woman's courageous struggle to secure her freedom. As the novel begins, Dessa Rose, the pregnant protagonist, is being held in the local sheriff's root cellar, pending the birth of her baby, after which she is sentenced to hang for her role in a violent slave revolt. During the lonely hours of her confinement, Dessa dreams of her last days on the plantation of her former owner, Mr. Terrell Vaugham. She remembers her work in the fields and her love for Kaine, the plantation's gardener and father of her unborn child. Much of the first section of the book explores Dessa's preoccupation with her life on the plantation, especially the chain of events that leads to her incarceration in the root cellar.

Adam Nehemiah, a white journalist gathering information for a book on methods of preventing slave revolts, obtains permission from the sheriff to question Dessa about her role in the revolt. Dessa, however, artfully evades the journalist's questions, choosing instead to talk about her life with Kaine on the Vaugham Plantation. By reconstructing her final days on the plantation, Dessa hopes to impose some measure of order on her past, to make sense of it. The central conflict in this section of the novel arises from Dessa's refusal to comply with the journalist's persistent requests for specific details about the revolt. The section ends with Dessa being rescued from the root cellar by two slaves, Harker and Nathan—an event which leaves the unsuspecting journalist and self-styled expert on slaves feeling humiliated and angry. He vows to find her and bring her back to be hanged.

In part 2, the scene shifts to an isolated farm in northern Alabama where Dessa's rescuers take her and her newborn baby. Ruth Sutton, the owner of the farm, permits runaway slaves to live on the farm in exchange for their help with the crops. The hostility that erupts between Ruth and Dessa becomes the central focus of this section. In the pivotal scene, Dessa is outraged by Ruth's claim that her recently deceased mammy loved her. Given Dessa's experiences in slavery, she cannot conceive of any conditions under which a slave could love his or her master. Dessa forces Ruth to acknowledge the selfish, superficial relationship she had with her mammy of eleven years. When Ruth cannot recall Mammy's given name, the truth of Dessa's charge becomes painfully evident, casting doubt over her previously unshakable faith in Mammy's love. The tension between the two women threatens to disrupt Ruth's arrangement with the other runaway slaves.

In the final section of the novel, Harker and Nathan persuade Dessa and Rush to lay aside their personal enmity and participate in a scheme to raise money to finance the slaves' escape to freedom. Ruth, who is desperately in need of money, is promised half the profit. According to the plan, Ruth, posing as owner of the runaway slaves, will sell them to various buyers. The slaves will then escape and meet Ruth at an agreed-upon location and be resold in the next town. Traveling together from town to town, Dessa and Ruth come to know and respect each other.

Dessa Rose is a skillfully drawn, multidimensional character. As a young slave on the Vaugham Plantation, Dessa dreams of escaping to the north with Kaine, where she hopes that they can rear their children free from the constant threat of beatings and separations that haunt slave families. Tragedy strikes, however, before she can realize her dream of freedom. Kaine unexpectedly attacks Vaugham with a hoe, prompting him to kill Kaine. As Kaine lies dying, he tries to explain the meaning of his act to Dessa. Dessa comes to view Kaine's attack on their master as a bold act of self-liberation, an assertion of his manhood. Inspired by Kaine's example, the normally quiet, nonaggressive Dessa Rose surprises the plantation community when she attacks her master and mistress. For this offense, she is whipped, branded, and sold to a slave trader. Although she is barely fifteen years old and nearly eight months pregnant, Dessa Rose plays a decisive role in the revolt of the slaves traveling with her en route to the slave market. Survivors of the uprising credit Dessa with killing several guards single-handedly. Thus, Dessa reaches within herself and finds tremendous resources of courage and strength.

Like Dessa Rose, Ruth Sutton is a dynamic, sensitive, and courageous woman. A native of Charleston, South Carolina, Ruth grew up in a family of slave owners. Because of her background, Ruth viewed all slaves, including her beloved mammy, as somewhat less than human. When she is abandoned by her husband, estranged from her family, and ostracized by her white neighbors, Ruth comes to depend on the fugitive slaves for companionship as well as for their labor on her farm. After Dessa's arrival and their subsequent confrontations, Ruth's attitude toward slaves begins to change. For example, she acts as wet nurse for Dessa's baby, reversing the usual situation in which the slave woman nurses white babies. Moreover, Ruth becomes romantically involved with Nathan, a runaway slave living on the Sutton farm.

While Ruth's dramatic change of heart toward the slaves may appear contrived or improbable at first, a close reading of the text suggests two explanations for her shift in attitude. First, Ruth's change of mind occurs while she is totally isolated from the influence of white people who would insist that she maintain the traditional posture toward slaves. Furthermore, Ruth's new behavior is fully consistent with her innate sense of honesty and compassion which the fugitive slaves manage to awaken. Consequently, Ruth becomes an enlightened opponent of slavery.

Another interesting character is Adam Nehemiah, the son of a mechanic, who yearns for acceptance by the elite class of planters. He hopes to gain access to that exclusive group by establishing a reputation as an expert on slave management. Having achieved some success with his first book on this topic, Nehemiah sets out to write another book in which he plans to analyze the causes of slave revolts and propose ways to prevent them from occurring—information sure to attract the attention of wealthy slave owners whose life-style he finds infinitely appealing. Therefore, Nehemiah sees Dessa Rose as an invaluable source of data for his research. He is portrayed as an arrogant, insecure man whose obsession with social status undermines his moral integrity. Although Nehemiah's main function is to provide a context for the narrative of Dessa's past, rather than to influence the plot, he is, nevertheless, an intriguing character.

Dessa Rose features several notable minor characters. Harker is a strong, intelligent slave who plans and coordinates the slave-selling scheme. He falls in love with Dessa Rose and helps her to regain her lost sense of order and stability. Nathan, the slave who assists Harker in rescuing Dessa from the root cellar, forces Dessa to confront her own racism by showing, through his sincere romantic relationship with Ruth, that race need not be a factor in the growth of love between two people. Two other minor characters, Jemina and Linda, are slaves who perform significant acts of courage that further illustrate the slave woman's role in the resistance against slavery.

The central theme of *Dessa Rose* challenges the myth of the passive, cowardly slave women, who, with only a few exceptions, lacked the courage and the will to play an active role with male slaves in the resistance against oppression. A related theme explores the painful struggle of a slave woman and a white woman to transcend their individual histories, to bridge the gap between their cultures in order to build a friendship.

The main theme of the novel is embodied in Dessa's interpretation of her master's wanton destruction of Kaine's precious banjo and of Kaine's violent act of retribution. The omniscient narrator reports Dessa's perception of these tragic events: "Master had smashed the banjo because that was what . . . he felt like doing. And a nigger could, too. This was what Kaine's act said to her. He had done; he was." Dessa's acts of resistance following Kaine's death shatter the image of the complacent, nonviolent slave woman that most slave owners accepted as realistic. Indeed, after reviewing accounts of Dessa's participation in the coffle revolt, Adam Nehemiah concludes: "Truly, the female of this species is as deadly as the male." Clearly, Dessa Rose is symbolic of the countless slave women whose acts of heroism in the resistance movement are lost to history or ignored by sexist historians.

Courage of a different kind is highlighted in the secondary theme. Dessa Rose, a runaway slave and Ruth Sutton, a white woman whose husband owns slaves, must summon the courage to develop the mutual trust and respect that genuine friendship demands. Dessa's experiences in slavery leave her cynical and hostile toward whites. She sees white people as "wicked and treacherous" and insists that "white woman was everything I feared and hated." Ruth must learn to relate to slaves as human beings. As Dessa and Ruth work together in the slave-selling scheme, they get to know each other, and their preconceived stereotypical notions of each other begin to diminish and the barriers fall.

The crucial event in the development of the secondary theme occurs when Dessa Rose helps Ruth defend herself against a white man's attempt to rape her. Pondering the experience, Dessa concludes, "I hadn't knowed white mens could use a white woman like that, just take her by force same as they could with us." This startling revelation moves Dessa Rose closer to an acceptance of Ruth as a friend. Dessa finally triumphs over her deep-seated hatred of white people when Ruth risks her own safety to rescue her from the clutches of Adam Nehemiah, who tracks Dessa down and has her arrested on suspicion of being a fugitive slave. Summing up her new perception of Ruth, Dessa declares: "She was good."

This theme exploring the liberation of Ruth and Dessa from their racial prejudices is reflected in Ruth's acknowledgment of a profound change in her attitude toward slavery. She tells Dessa: "I don't want to live round slavery no more; I don't think I could without speaking up." Not only do Ruth and Dessa Rose share the actual journey associated with the slave-selling scheme, but they also complete a remarkable metaphorical journey that lifts them above and beyond the misconceptions and racial antagonisms that separated them earlier in their relationship.

Dessa Rose is based on a short story by Sherley Anne Williams titled "Meditations on History." First published in Mary Helen Washington's *Midnight Birds: Stories by Contemporary Black Women Writers* (1980), "Meditations on History" focuses on a young slave girl named Odessa who is condemned to hang for her role in a violent slave uprising, but she, like Dessa Rose, is rescued before the sentence is carried out. Williams skillfully reshapes the story and integrates it into the fabric of her novel, retaining the story's main characters, basic structure, and plot. By deleting superfluous descriptive passages that often impede the narrative flow in the short story, Williams manages to incorporate a substantially improved version of the original story into *Dessa Rose*.

Like most contemporary black women writers, Sherley Anne Williams is engaged in the struggle for control of the images of black women in American literature. In *Dessa Rose*, Williams portrays slave women as equal partners with slave men in the resistance movement, forcing readers to see slave women in a new light.

Elvin Holt

Sources for Further Study

Essence Magazine. XVII, August, 1986, p. 38.
Kirkus Reviews. LIV, May 15, 1986, p. 748.
Library Journal. CXI, June 15, 1986, p. 80.
Los Angeles Times. August 8, 1986, V, p. 1.
Ms. XV, September, 1986, p. 20.
The New York Times Book Review. XCI, August 3, 1986, p. 7.
The New Yorker. LXII, September 8, 1986, p. 136.
Publishers Weekly. CCXXIX, May 30, 1986, p. 53.
Washington Post Book World. XVI, August 3, 1986, p. 11.

DOSTOEVSKY
The Stir of Liberation, 1860-1865

Author: Joseph Frank (1919-   )
Publisher: Princeton University Press (Princeton, New Jersey). Illustrated. 395 pp.
    $29.50
Type of work: Literary biography
Time: 1860-1865
Locale: Primarily Saint Petersburg, Russia

The third volume of a projected five-volume study of a literary genius who became one of the masters of modernity

> *Principal personages:*
> FEODOR MIKHAILOVICH DOSTOEVSKY, a great Russian novelist and
>   literary figure
> MIKHAIL DOSTOEVSKY, his devoted older brother
> MARYA DIMITRIEVNA DOSTOEVSKY, his unstable first wife
> APOLLINARIA SUSLOVA, his sadistic mistress for two years
> IVAN TURGENEV, a distinguished Russian novelist and literary
>   figure
> NIKOLAY CHERNYSHEVSKY, a radical critic and novelist whose ideas
>   Dostoevsky vehemently opposed
> NIKOLAY STRAKHOV, Dostoevsky's journalistic ally who became his
>   enemy and unreliable first biographer
> APOLLON GRIGORYEV, Dostoevsky's friend who contributed to his
>   periodical *Time*
> ALEXANDER HERZEN, an influential social critic and editor

Joseph Frank, professor emeritus of comparative literature at Princeton University and now a professor of Slavic languages and literature at Stanford University, is engaged in one of the most ambitious and illuminating literary projects of the late twentieth century: a five-volume study of the tumultuous life and career of Feodor Dostoevsky, who identified and summoned to compelling imaginative life large lands of psychological, political, and aesthetic modernity.

Frank's first volume, subtitled *The Seeds of Revolt, 1821-1849* (1976), highlighted the rapturous reception of Dostoevsky's initial novel, *Bednye lyudi* (1846; *Poor Folk*, 1887), but also described the relative failure of his second book, *Dvoynik* (1846; *The Double*, 1956)—a judgment that has been reversed by modern critics. Frank's second volume, subtitled *The Years of Ordeal, 1850-1859* (1983), dealt with Dostoevsky's life in the 1850's, when he wrote no significant works but experienced monumental changes in his life, spending four of those years as a convict in Siberia and another four as a soldier in one of the Siberian regiments of the Russian army. This third volume, *The Stir of Liberation, 1860-1865*, focuses on a complex five-year period prior to the quartet of great novels that began with *Prestupleniye i nakazaniye* (1866; *Crime and Punishment*, 1886). During this time Dostoevsky wrote voluminously, producing both fiction and journalism; engaged in acrimonious controversies with sociopolitical opponents; witnessed the liberation of the serfs in 1861 and the consequent social upheavals that convulsed Russian society; made two trips to Europe; became the editor of two important periodicals; experienced a tormented affair with the writer Apollinaria Suslova; suffered debilitating epileptic attacks; and saw his consumptive first wife and beloved brother die in 1864, within three months of each other.

Since Frank specializes in intellectual history, his study subordinates the melodramatic personal struggles, stirring anecdotes, and narrative sweep that have fascinated such previous biographers as David Magarshack, Marc Slonim, and Henri Troyat. Instead, he stresses the sociocultural context in which his subject lived and wrote, taking particular care to analyze the great contemporaneous issues in which Dostoevsky participated heart and soul. The result is especially revealing in Frank's learned analysis of Dostoevsky's energetic journalistic career in the early 1860's—a phase that most critics have neglected in their eagerness to discuss the major novels.

The Dostoevsky who returned to Saint Petersburg in mid-December, 1859, after some ten years in Siberia, had matured enormously as a result of having confronted mortality and having discovered the starkly egoistic drives dominating his fellow convicts. He had undergone a conversion crisis that caused him to emphasize the inner life over the exterior environment and to affirm the Christian virtues of love and self-sacrifice, compassion and forgiveness. Frank emphasizes that Dostoevsky's attacks of epilepsy, which began during his prison-camp servitude, filled him with an intensely blissful—albeit brief—sense of rapturous plenitude and cosmic harmony. He was tremendously moved by Ivan Turgenev's meditative essay, *Gamlet i Don Kikhot* (1860; *Hamlet and Don Quixote*, 1930), identifying himself with the courageous, fideistic Don, whom he regarded as morally superior to the skeptical, disillusioned Hamlet. Eight years later, the quixotic type was to serve as the major model for Prince Myshkin, the generous and compassionate, all-too-saintly protagonist of *Idiot* (1868; *The Idiot*, 1887).

With his brother Mikhail, Dostoevsky founded a monthly magazine, *Vremya* (*Time*), whose initial issue appeared in January, 1861. Among its leading contributors were two close associates of Dostoevsky, Nikolay Strakhov and Apollon Grigoryev. The former—later to become the first Dostoevsky biographer—had a well-trained, coolly philosophic mind against which Dostoevsky whetted his own in frequent, long conversations. Dostoevsky, however, was more attracted to the tempestuous, alcoholic Grigoryev, an authority on Aleksandr Pushkin, when he was not debauching his energy in the company of Gypsies. Grigoryev worked out a cultural typology of post-Pushkin Russian literature as a battle between "predatory" and "meek" literary types. Much of Dostoevsky's later work dramatizes this division, with the predatory characters Westerners, the meek characters authentically Russian Slavophiles.

Both men advocated moderately Slavophile sociopolitical programs that influenced Dostoevsky. They called their beliefs "a return to the soil"— *pochvennichestvo*—and named themselves *pochvenniki*. They foresaw a new Russian cultural synthesis that would fuse the common people and their intellectual superiors, insisting that such a change should occur through gradual evolution rather than drastic revolution. At this stage, Dostoevsky was not yet ready to embrace all the Slavophilic concepts, which centered on a total rejection of the European Enlightenment in general and Czar Peter the Great's Westernizing reforms in particular. Dostoevsky did, however, express frequent admiration for the *raskolniki*—the Old Believers who dissented from the Greek-inspired reforms of the Russian liturgy and therefore caused a *raskol* (schism) within the seventeenth century Russian Church.

During the 1840's, Dostoevsky had been with those Westerners, headed by the great critic and reformer Vissarion Belinsky, who had campaigned against Slavophile ideas; in turn, Slavophiles had severely criticized his first two novels. Frank reminds the reader, however, that Dostoevsky was always a Russian nationalist—even during his most liberal phase—and by the early 1860's he had come to share the Slavophile insistence—also strongly proclaimed by the otherwise left-leaning Alexander Herzen—that the *mir*, the Russian commune, constituted "a moral-social principle superior to Western individualism and egoism," with Russian peasant life achieving an admirably egalitarian moral harmony. It was not until after his second, wretchedly unhappy trip to Europe in 1863 that Dostoevsky was ready to join the Slavophiles in pressing the differences—indeed, opposition—between Russia and Europe in fundamentally religious terms. He now endorsed the bitter anti-Catholicism of Slavophile theology, tracing mankind's evils "back to the Roman Catholic pope's assumption of the temporal power once possessed by the Roman emperors."

The first issue of *Time* carried the eighty-seven-page first installment of Dostoevsky's novel *Unizhennye i oskorblyonnye* (1861; *The Insulted and Injured*, 1887). It derived clumsily from the Gothic tradition of the *roman-feuilleton*, the melodramatic thriller, with a plot that featured venality, betrayal, intrigues galore, and incredible coincidences. The book is generally regarded as Dostoevsky's worst work of fiction: tritely plotted, diffusely narrated, and at times embarrassingly bathetic. Its villain, the cruel Prince Valkovsky, asserts a doctrine of absolute egoism; he is the first of several Dostoevskian characters who parody the gospel of "rational egoism" advanced by Dostoevsky's leading radical foe, Nikolay Chernyshevsky, in such treatises as *Esteticheskie otnosheniya iskusstva k deistvitel'nosti* (1855; *Aesthetic Relation of Art to Reality*, 1953) and *Antropolo gicheskii printsip v filosofii* (1860). Dostoevsky refused to accept Chernyshevsky's logic that reason and self-interest would ultimately unite, with egoism becoming beneficence through rational calculation. Valkovsky belongs to the tradition of the unprincipled seducer prominent in the libertine fiction of the Marquis de Sade and Pierre Choderlos de Laclos, with Valkovsky's name a slavification of Valmont, the rake in Laclos' *Les Liaisons dangereuses* (1782; *Dangerous Connections*, 1784; also as *Dangerous Liaisons*, 1962). In looking ahead, he prefigures such problematic characters as Svidrigailov in *Crime and Punishment* and Stavrogin in *Besy* (1871-1872; *The Possessed*, 1913).

In the spring of 1862, the leaflet *Young Russia*, written by a twenty-year-old radical, climaxed a series of waves pounding sociopolitical agitation against the shore of established institutions and creating an atmosphere of panic and hysteria among many Russians. The pamphlet insisted on "a bloody and pitiless revolution . . . utterly overthrowing all the foundations of present society." Simultaneously with *Young Russia*'s circulation, a series of fires raged in Saint Petersburg for two weeks, leaving thousands of people homeless. That same spring, Turgenev published *Ottsy i deti* (1862; *Fathers and Children*, 1867), whose brusquely militant protagonist, Bazarov, frightened conservative readers into showering Turgenev with a hail of abuse. To his honor, Dostoevsky, having read the novel immediately on its periodical circulation in March, wrote Turgenev a long letter conveying his admiration. Unfortunately, this letter has been lost. Turgenev's grateful reply, however, has not been:

> You have so fully and sensitively grasped what I wished to express in Bazarov that I can only raise my hands in astonishment—and satisfaction. It is as if you had slipped into my soul and intuited even what I did not think necessary to utter. I hope to God that what you have said is not only the sharp penetration of a master but also the direct understanding of a reader—that is, I hope to God everyone sees even a part of what you have seen!

Frank notes that *Time* was the only important Russian periodical that treated *Fathers and Children* with informed understanding in the 1860's.

In 1862, the bond between Dostoevsky and Strakhov began to loosen; eventually they were to become enemies, with Strakhov denouncing Dostoevsky bitterly and scurrilously in a letter he wrote to Leo Tolstoy in 1880. Their differences were more temperamental than ideological. While both strongly opposed the left-wing radicalism of Chernyshevsky, Nikolay Dobrolyubov, Mikhail Bakunin, and others, Strakhov insisted on a severely Augustinian reading of human nature: It is "rotten to the core," and none of the radicals should escape the direst punishment. Dostoevsky, to the contrary, maintained that remorse and repentance were always possible, and the hope of redemption should never be renounced.

Time was to be suppressed by the czarist regime in May, 1863, but during its last nine months it carried not only a large number of Dostoevsky's articles but also two of his books, *Zapiski iz myortvogo doma* (1861-1862; *Notes*

from the House of the Dead, 1915) and *Zimnie zametki o letnikh vpechat-
leniyakh* (1863; *Winter Notes on Summer Impressions*, 1955). The cause for
Time's demise was the government's misunderstanding of a subtle article by
Strakhov on the Polish character: It was deemed insufficiently anti-Polish
during a period when Russian opinion was bitterly hostile to Polish aspirations for independence.

As for *Notes from the House of the Dead*, it is a memoir, thinly disguised
as a novel, of Dostoevsky's Siberian prison experiences, which strongly
stamped the rest of his life. Frank remarks that Turgenev and Tolstoy parallel Dostoevsky's work with personal accounts of their own: Turgenev's
Zapiski okhotnika (1852; *A Sportsman's Sketches*, 1932) and Tolstoy's *Sevas-
topolskiye rasskazy* (1855-1856; *Sevastopol Stories*, 1887). The three great
contemporaries share the same unifying theme: the initiation of a member
of the educated upper class into the customs of the proletariat. For Turgenev, the Russian peasant's rich life of imaginative beauty makes his serf status all the more cruel; Tolstoy, anticipating *Voyna i mir* (1865-1869; *War and
Peace*, 1886), contrasts the unassuming heroism of the peasantry to the van-
ity and artifice of the aristocracy; Dostoevsky is the most scathing of the
three in denouncing serfdom as an abhorrent evil, showing the ordinary
Russians in revolt against its enslavement and sympathizing with their readi-
ness to use force against their oppressors. It is no wonder that radicals
admired Dostoevsky's depiction of the peasantry—at the same time that he
disapproved of the radicals' advocated remedies for solving Russia's excru-
ciating dilemmas.

Winter Notes on Summer Impressions is a book-length travel journal in
which Dostoevsky excoriates Europe as a dying culture: morally stultified,
horrifyingly materialistic, in unashamed pursuit of worldly gains. Dostoevsky had visited London's nineteen-acre Crystal Palace, dedicated to the
exhibition of science's and technology's latest achievements, and taken it as
a malign symbol of the "unholy spirit of modernity," the monstrous beast of
the apocalypse. In *Winter Notes on Summer Impressions*, he regards European society, no matter how economically prosperous, as an "ant-heap" of
warring egoisms—every individual against every other individual. In contrast, Russia is capable of the "instinctive mutual relation between the individual and the community in which each desires only the welfare of the
other." Genuine brotherhood, Dostoevsky concludes, requires "a voluntary,
totally conscious sacrifice of oneself in the interests of all, made under no
sort of compulsion." Despite the French Revolution's slogan *liberté, égalité,
fraternité*, neither France nor Europe in general, according to Dostoevsky,
is able to attain such a spiritually exalted peak; the Russian folk psyche,
however, is. Growing increasingly eschatological, Dostoevsky declares that
Russia is a chosen nation, with its soul rooted in a Christian ethic of self-
sacrifice rather than in a European-instigated, utilitarian concept of self-

interest. Hence, to propagate the second doctrine, as the socialists do, is to destroy the first.

Winter Notes on Summer Impressions clearly anticipates many of the major symbols and motifs of *Zapiski iz podpolya* (1864; *Notes from Underground*, 1954), but before Frank analyzes that work he devotes several chapters to narrating Dostoevsky's painful private life in 1863 and 1864. He was morosely unhappy in his marriage with Marya, whose tuberculosis continued to worsen, as did her crises of hysterical rage—thus becoming a model for the embittered Katerina Ivanovna in *Crime and Punishment*. He felt drained by demanding editorial and literary obligations. He had to suffer the depressing effects of epileptic attacks that assailed him at increasingly shorter intervals. He fell victim to a gambling impulse-neurosis whenever he visited Europe. Worst of all, however, was his passion for Apollinaria Suslova.

Polina, as he called her, was twenty-three to his forty-three when they met during the winter of 1862. She was an assertive Russian feminist who wrote periodical articles and scorned conventional public opinion. By the time she and Dostoevsky reunited in Paris in the spring of 1863, however, for what he hoped would be a honeymoon trip of sorts through France and Italy, their relationship had already begun to sour: She had been seduced and quickly abandoned by a Spanish lothario, Salvador, with whom she had humiliated herself. Polina took such vengeance as she could in her turn by tantalizing Dostoevsky sexually, provoking his desire, only to frustrate it. The most amusing situation of their association occurred on a boat in Italy when Dostoevsky chanced to meet the twenty-four-year-old Alexander Herzen, Jr., the critic's oldest son. Dostoevsky introduced Polina as a distant relative to avoid gossip reaching his wife's ears back in Russia. Young Herzen then engaged Polina in an ardent courtship throughout the voyage. To maintain appearances, Dostoevsky even encouraged Polina to give Herzen her card and to write to him later.

Circumstances continued to punish Dostoevsky. Marya finally died on April 15, 1864, after an emotionally draining last winter and spring. His brother Mikhail received permission to publish another periodical, *Epokha* (*Epoch*), but could not raise enough subscriptions to keep it solvent. On July 10, Mikhail died, overtaxed by financial worries as well as a liver ailment. *Epoch* had to be sold to creditors.

Meanwhile Dostoevsky's banked literary-ideological fires were stirred by the 1863 publication and subsequent great popularity of Chernyshevsky's didactic novel, *Chto delat?* (1863; *What Is to Be Done?*, 1883). Believing that Turgenev's protagonist, Bazarov, in *Fathers and Children* had been drawn to caricature the radical Dobrolyubov, Chernyshevsky retaliated with an icily logical superman, Rakhmetov, who is incredibly self-disciplined and steel-nerved in his fictive career as an invincible revolutionist and rationalist.

As in his previous texts, Chernyshevsky affirmed rational egoism as the panacea for all human problems, having his characters earnestly work toward an earthly paradise. Perhaps as a direct taunt to Dostoevsky, Chernyshevsky chose as an icon for his rational utopia the very Crystal Palace that Dostoevsky had derided as the acme of modern materialism. Dostoevsky rose to the challenge, writing *Notes from Underground* primarily as a satirical parody of Chernyshevsky's views. This extraordinary work, which laid the fictional foundation for Dostoevsky's mature novels, has become so celebrated that it need not be discussed here.

Dostoevsky, Frank has demonstrated in his masterfully learned and lucidly written study, has finished his literary apprenticeship and adolescence and was ready for the first of the four great texts which were to establish him as arguably the greatest psychological novelist in the annals of literature. Frank's account of the fertile years that produced these masterpieces will be eagerly awaited.

Gerhard Brand

Sources for Further Study

Booklist. LXXXIII, December 1, 1986, p. 543.
Christian Science Monitor. LXXVIII, September 5, 1986, p. B1.
Chronicle of Higher Education. XXXIII, September 10, 1986, p. 8.
National Review. XXXVIII, November 21, 1986, p. 61.
The New York Review of Books. XXXIII, September 25, 1986, p. 11.
The New York Times Book Review. XCI, August 31, 1986, p. 8.

DREAM WORK

Author: Mary Oliver (1935-   )
Publisher: The Atlantic Monthly Press (Boston). 90 pp. $8.95
Type of work: Poetry

An analysis of the ties between nature and the poet

Mary Oliver seems to mean by the title of her collection of poetry *Dream Work* an intuitive as well as deliberate movement toward a nature-oriented perception of oneself. Dreams are an important vehicle for this movement, and nature is both in them and the goal toward which they move, the goal being life in its truest sense. If this sounds like Romanticism, it is, but with a twist. Instead of viewing man as a dimly divine creature discovering godhead in nature, Oliver's Romanticism leaves out the divine aspect and the human egotism; she regards nature simply as the best place for a person to see where he or she belongs.

For Oliver, nature is hard to avoid. It is an overwhelming presence, and the way one pays attention to it is not mainly through reason but through the subconscious and through intuition. In order to find out what nature is all about, one must be feelingly open to it. At first, at least, nature is frightening. In "Banyan," she shows how the organisms in nature are inexorable, beginning as seeds and ending as insatiable growth. Not only is nature hungry, predatory, as in "Bowing to the Empress," but also impersonal. The destructive forces in nature see no link with their human victims because they cannot. There is no love or hate in them as there is in people, which makes them hard for people to accept. Yet accept them people must, for nature is as much man's home as it is the home of anything else in it, and people acknowledge these forces—some of them, at least—by living with nature's dangers, as in "The Waves," and by personifying its dark power, as in "The Chance to Love Everything."

One may talk about nature, but one cannot talk to it, for it has no mind. Except for man, the creatures of nature simply act. They do not think about what they do ("The Turtle"), they do not talk about what happens to them ("The Shark"). What goes on, however, inside these creatures, inside organisms, parallels what goes on inside man on the level of instinct. It is on this level that man's unique ability to think about himself finds its best use—in showing him, through dreams and imagination, that his isolation in pride or despair is foolish, that his meaning is embedded in the features of nature itself.

Aside from her liking for nature, how does Oliver find this out? She does so through dreams. What are dreams to her? They are the opposite of that mental activity which seeks to hide or control. They force one to face oneself, to admit one's guilt and fear, to go beyond the boundaries one imposes on one's perception. In "Rage," Oliver sees her father dreaming about her.

His guilt forces him to see how badly he hurt her psyche by hiding his love for her. She presents her own dream about him in "A Visitor," in which she does not cringe from him as she used to but faces him as the cruel and hollowed-out person he was, and, realizing the longing in him for expiation, she accepts him into herself, thus finally freeing herself from the paralysis of which he was the source. Indeed, one of the main lessons of dreams for Oliver is that the feelings which stunt and free people are most accessible to them in their sleep.

If dreams teach Oliver to trust her feelings, nature teaches her feelings— often through the analogues and personifications she brings to bear on them—what life is really all about. In "Whispers," she learns that the paralysis of self-absorption has little to do with the healthy life that nature leads in its humdrum fashion. She finds that when she is in nature and patient with herself, she gradually opens to the life it shares with her. In "Sunrise," the sun, its warmth, teaches her happiness. In going back to its source, the river in "The River" shows her what progress toward a sense of home means. She sees that nature is not merely a clash of forces resulting in exhaustion but that, for example, the male wind helps to impregnate the female earth. In "Clamming," her vision of her place in the food chain in nature reveals to her how healthy such a system is. In "Trilliums," she exults in the energy she detects in nature, even as she acknowledges the hardship of expending such energy, and she is fascinated by the way nature's creatures act without thinking ("The Moths"). A dream tells her—or nature tells her through a dream—that she is one with nature's movements, that she is the fire in wood and the growth in a flower.

In all such episodes with nature, Oliver believes that it is her imagination that is being appealed to, not her rational mind. Her imagination comes alive when she lets the animal deep inside her work on it from the bottom up, as it were. In this way, nature is a kind of muse, sometimes leading her to give voice to the destruction it causes ("Storm in Massachusetts, September 1982") and the destruction its destroying creatures undergo ("The Shark").

Oliver is not a passive student of nature. She believes that she must act on its lessons. First she must face the pain of which she is afraid in her personal life, then, through acceptance of her weakness and through an intuitive openness with herself and her nonhuman surroundings, work to attain the kind of health that nature displays. In "The Fire," watching the progress of a natural ruin, she is forced to return to her past, to the things in it that hurt her deeply, to the basic structure of her own organic life. Only then can she escape the past and break the paralysis that has kept her from doing anything useful. Thus, she can analyze her dreams properly ("Members of the Tribe") and take joy in building a place for herself in the world ("The House").

Besides being attentive to the lessons of dreams and nature, and trying to apply them to the way she perceives and conducts her life, Oliver sometimes focuses on art. She connects it with madness in "Robert Schumann" (where the composer is in an asylum) and in "Members of the Tribe" (where she is). Schumann's art seems to have kept him afloat in his madness, countering its depression with enthusiasm occasioned by spring and Clara, the woman who became his wife. Art, in this case, is in tune with good feelings and with nature in the season of rebirth. Regarding herself, Oliver says that her breakdown preceded her art. Before she could create, she had to understand what was wrong with her, and this included analyzing her bad dreams. Having done this, she looks to other poets to find out how to think about herself as an artist. She decides that they are poor role models, not because there is so much unhappiness in their work but because they focus their creative energy on death. They are egomaniacs in their own bleakness; they do not seem to believe in the kind of health she wants to have in her life and reflect in her poetry. This requires, she thinks, humility, which, in "Members of the Tribe," Michelangelo's helper had, awed by the work his master produced. Because of his healthy attitude and his humble position, this man lived to an advanced old age. Death for him was more of an afterthought than something around which to organize his life.

This is the kind of humility and earthiness that Oliver admires in Stanley Kunitz. The poet in "Stanley Kunitz" is patient, doing the hard and simple work of his craft as though he were gardening. This view of poetry brings it in line with the processes of nature, which are not magical so much as drawn out and grubby. The true gardener or poet understands this; the true successes of writing, like gardening, come after a long time of tending, weeding, and pruning.

Mary Oliver is among the more philosophical pastoral poets currently writing in the United States. She is not content merely to express her psychological difficulties in pastoral settings; she treats nature, in giving her life, as a source of ontological truth, and she tries to give it more than personal meaning. In this sense, as noted above, she is a Romantic, and as such, she adopts a childlike stance as she faces nature. She wants to appear open, cleansed, simple, and in so doing, she often seems somewhat silly and cute. She has no sense of humor, it seems, and thus her poetry lacks a certain common sense. Carefully elegant as her style is, her personifications of nature, for example, amount to pathetic fallacies. If she were a real child, for whom everything is new, including language, her perceptions might be somewhat fresher than they indeed are.

Mark McCloskey

Sources for Further Study

Booklist. LXXXIII, September 1, 1986, p. 22.
Choice. XXIV, November, 1986, p. 480.
Library Journal. CXI, June 1, 1986, p. 126.
The Nation. CCXLIII, August 30, 1986, p. 148.
Prairie Schooner. LIX, Fall, 1985, p. 108.

EDWIN DENBY
The Complete Poems

Author: Edwin Denby (1903-1983)
Edited, with an introduction, by Ron Padgett
Publisher: Random House (New York). 194 pp. $16.95; paperback $7.95
Type of work: Poetry

A lyric description of the interrelation of place and its human inhabitants

Edwin Denby: The Complete Poems shows the poet's lifelong concern with how environments—especially cities—define, and are defined by, those who live in them. Through the lens of setting, people are shown to be joined sometimes by their isolation from one another and sometimes by their common desires. Edwin Denby often uses himself as an example of such isolation and of the ways in which it is overcome. The importance of place in his perception of human loneliness and endeavor derives from his travels on the one hand and his long stay in New York City and his summer sojourns in Maine on the other.

The city is often a collection of people who do not belong to one another. They want love so badly for themselves that they do not see that everyone else wants the same thing. As in one of the songs in *The Sonntag Gang*, when people do find love, they may keep it a secret. The longer one goes without the fulfillment of love, the more the mind suggests that it is impossible, thus helping to isolate one even further from other people. At times this yearning is no more than lust, which warm weather fuels, and it leads less to a true joining than to a selfish moment that cannot last. Even the parts of the body may seem not to belong to the person who has them but to function as parasites on his life. When it comes to the fruits of love, a man's restlessness may make him run away from the woman who loves him, and a child may end up on his own, like the derelict boy in "Legend (After Victory)" who is full of hate, rage, and impotence.

Denby uses himself to itemize the details of not belonging to anyone. At best, two people may love each other and make no secret of it, but in the end they are mysteries to each other. Part of his own mystery is the monstrous alter ego he conceives for himself in "A Sonnet Sequence: Dishonor." There is shame and guilt in this self-image, and they make him feel unlovable, confirming him in his isolation. He may be the only one who sees this, but what he thinks others see of him in "Snoring in New York—An Elegy" does not really bridge the gap between him and them. His true public image is complex enough: his age, his intensity, his femininity. He also looks, he thinks, "like a priest, a detective, a con," mainly because people do not care or have time to look further, and if they do not, how can he belong to them or they to him? Even his loft apartment can be an alien place, giving him cabin fever and driving him out. A place he knew in his youth can also make him feel that he does not belong there in his maturity; this happens in "Brindisi," where nostalgia is powerless to sweeten the sour experience of alienation. "In Rome," too, he shows how isolated he feels; this time it is the natives who spur these feelings, regarding him superficially as a tourist.

When it comes to the places where people live, however, it is the integration between the two that Denby often notices. The life of cities depends on the human diversity that characterizes it. In "Syracuse," visitors and natives alike make for a rich mixture, and in "To peer at the common man as a hero," the city acts as a magnet to the downtrodden, stressing their unity rather than their individual discontinuity. The city, in fact, orders the chaos of disconnection, though the name of this common order may be nothing more than money. The city belongs to its inhabitants the way clothes belong to their wearer, Denby says in "Northern Boulevard," and in "A New York Face," he sees bridges as the faces that cross them, blank as those faces may be. In the end, any place that humans live for a long time is saturated with their feelings. People may not belong to one another, but they do belong to the places in which they live.

This is true of landscapes as well as cities. Sky and light characteristics of a place provide images of integration between such a place and the people in it. The ruins of civilization in a landscape join the human past with the human present, as in "Sant'Angelo d'Ischia" and "Forza d'Agro," and a landscape can cause feeling as well as be full of the memory and threat of passion, in both cases becoming an extension of the human. Weather works this way, too, bringing (in the guise of summer or spring, for example) a tone to place that inclines its dwellers to idleness and desire.

Denby details how he himself is made to feel less lonely and cut off in the world. He is fond of cats, and they appear in many poems as his companions. Along with roaches, he presents them as his roommates in "Awakening, look into sweet," and they are his bedmates in "New Year's near, glass autumn long gone." Grief ties him to a favorite cat that died in "Born in my loft, dancer untame," and he sees himself joined to the cat, in that death will relieve him, as it has the cat, of his anger. Death is also the source of his seeing, in "A Domestic Cat," that life itself is what joins him and his cat together.

Sometimes Denby's surroundings make him forget his loneliness. His loft, where he has lived for many years, gives him a sense of belonging. When it warms up in winter, it links him through nostalgia with his dead cat and with a lover who has disappointed him, just as the pictures in it link him to his friends who have made them. The simple landscape of his summer home, and his pleasant habits there, also make him feel at home.

In his isolation, Denby prizes human contact. He is aware that common speech ties him to other people. His friends lighten his gloomy inwardness in "Mycenae," and because he is with them in "Via Appia," he feels at one with his foreign surroundings. He likes having his friend the photographer Rudy Burckhardt's family around him, going to parties and to dinner at the house of friends who have named their baby after him. When his friend the painter Franz Kline dies, he sees, as he was close to the man and his work, that art itself draws people together because it reveals the beauty in their miserable environments.

Denby's art is very much like primitive painting. It is unself-conscious and meticulous, not slick in the ways that fashion dictates and not overawed by tradition or put off by it. Most of his poems are sonnets, but he uses straight talk, idiom, and his own quirky phrasing and rhymes to fill up the form. He has, in fact, made it new, as Ezra Pound would have said. He molds the meter of his traditional forms to his own ends, too. Denby, a dancer in his youth, and a dance critic in his later years, brought a kind of choreography to his poems that sets them apart from the smoother and less lively efforts of those who still practice meter. Even when there is a strong reflective aspect to his poems, as when he considers the ruins of civilization and the complex nature of his own spirit, he is open and blunt, and he always has an eye for small, endearing details. Finally, as with primitive painters, his art was more important to him than what people might think about it. Most of his work was published through the efforts of others, not his, and he never liked talking about it in public. In this sense, let alone because of the work itself, he stands as a corrective to much contemporary poetry and the way it is presented.

Mark McCloskey

Sources for Further Study

Booklist. LXXXII, August, 1986, p. 1655.
The New York Times Book Review. XCI, November 2, 1986, p. 28.
Publishers Weekly. CCXXIX, February 28, 1986, p. 120.

EISENHOWER, AT WAR
1943-1945

Author: David Eisenhower (1947-   )
Publisher: Random House (New York). 997 pp. $29.95
Type of work: Military history
Time: 1943-1945
Locale: Europe

A close examination of the Western Alliance during the last eighteen months of World War II

Principal personages:
> OMAR N. BRADLEY, Commander, United States First Army in France; Commander, Twelfth Army Group
> ALAN BROOKES, Chief of Imperial General Staff, 1941-1945
> DWIGHT D. EISENHOWER, Supreme Commander of Allied Expeditionary Forces, 1944-1945
> HARRY C. BUTCHER, aide-de-camp (naval) to Eisenhower during the war
> WINSTON CHURCHILL, Prime Minister of Great Britain, 1940-1945
> GEORGE C. MARSHALL, United States Chief of Staff, 1939-1945
> BERNARD L. MONTGOMERY, Commander in Chief, British Twenty-first Army Group, Europe
> GEORGE S. PATTON, JR., Commander, United States Third Army, Europe
> FRANKLIN D. ROOSEVELT, Thirty-second President of the United States, 1933-1945

In *Eisenhower, at War: 1943-1945*, David Eisenhower (hereafter referred to as Eisenhower) attempts to achieve two basic objectives: a thorough discussion of the Western Alliance during the last year and a half of World War II and a balanced analysis of his grandfather's contribution to Allied victory. The result is a detailed, usually thoughtful, and sometimes ponderous volume of almost one thousand pages. With the exception of occasional flashbacks, the book is organized chronologically. Although the author attempts no final appraisal of his subjects, he does pause from time to time in the narrative to offer evaluations of particular personalities and events. The fact that the book tends to quit rather than conclude is perhaps largely a consequence of its position as the first volume of a projected trilogy on the public life of Dwight D. Eisenhower (hereafter referred to as Ike).

For better or worse, the outstanding quality of *Eisenhower, at War* is its wealth of detail. The descriptions are in many cases literally day-by-day. Thus when events are inherently dramatic the narrative moves along in good order. The Normandy invasion offers a particularly good example. After months of meticulous preparation, Operation Overlord (the code name of the invasion) was finally ordered to proceed on the basis of predictions that indicated a short period of favorable weather. Once initiated, the operation took on a life of its own. Soldiers became actors in a vast pageant. Each participant had carefully rehearsed his own part and knew that the success of the operation was largely dependent upon the sum of individual faithfulness to assigned roles. The action itself is so compelling that virtually any detail serves to heighten reader interest. The resulting description is crisp and exciting.

A second advantage of Eisenhower's close description of events is that the reader tends to view the war as a participant rather than an observer who, knowing the outcome, imposes hindsight on the narrative. Again, to use the example of Operation Overlord, the generally informed reader knows well enough that, following moments of savage fighting on the beaches, the Allies ultimately prevailed. All too frequently the reader leaps to the conclusion that the final result was more or less inevitable. The slow but steady movement toward the German border seems inexorable. Although it is certainly fair to conclude, as did most non-Germans at the time, that the weight of superior Allied manpower and resources would eventually crush the German will to continue in the war, the result of particular battles prior to the penetration of the Rhine in early 1945 was very much in doubt. The Normandy beachhead, for example, was tenuously established and precariously maintained during the first seventy-two hours of its existence. The adversary was well trained and well equipped. Had Adolf Hitler resolved to destroy the Allied offensive at its birth, as General Erwin Rommel and Karl Rundstedt urged, rather than during its infancy, the result might have been very different. The failure of Operation Overlord in turn would have severely tested the Western Alliance and undermined Anglo-American claims to equal credit with the Soviet Union for defeating the Fascist partners, Germany and Italy.

A rigorously chronological approach further serves to impress upon the reader the intensely political nature of the Anglo-American relationship. One of the distinctive contributions of this book is the case that it makes for the political significance of Operation Anvil. This operation was conceived as an adjunct to Operation Overlord. As originally planned, a Franco-American force would land in Marseilles to coincide with the Normandy invasion. This army would then proceed up the Rhone River and eventually occupy the right flank of the Allied offensive. The Anvil offensive promised multiple military advantages. Most obviously, it would tie down German units in the south of France and thus insure that they would not be diverted to Normandy. In addition, the liberation of Marseilles would open a much-needed port facility. Finally, the operation would provide a means whereby French troops training in North Africa could be brought into the war in significant numbers.

Inasmuch as Operation Anvil was ultimately delayed until August, it was overshadowed by the already-established front in northern France. Hence it has received little attention from military historians. Eisenhower, however, has discovered Operation Anvil's importance as a political issue. Throughout the fighting in North Africa, Sicily, and Italy, Great Britain had been the senior partner in the Anglo-American alliance. Whereas the United States was committed to the earliest possible opening of a second front somewhere in Holland, Belgium, or the northwest coast of France, the British favored a more peripheral strategy that centered in the Mediterranean. Although Winston Churchill hotly denied that he opposed the eventual opening of a second front, the priority that he assigned to such an operation was sufficiently low as to cause many Americans to question the distinction between indefinite postponement and outright opposition. At the Teheran Conference in November-December, 1943, Franklin D. Roosevelt won grudging British approval for the long-awaited opening of the second front the following spring. Historians are virtually unanimous in regarding this agreement as marking the point at which essential control of the alliance shifted. The United States now became the senior partner. Its will would largely determine Anglo-American strategy for the remainder of the war.

Nevertheless, as Eisenhower repeatedly shows, decision making was never as clean as outward appearances suggested. The British persistently argued for flexible responses to the war effort. Thus they reserved the right to change their minds at a later date if circumstances warranted. Churchill exercised this option after the Teheran Conference, contending until the end of the year that Operation Overlord should be deferred beyond the following spring. His pleas fell on deaf ears. Preparations to convert southern England into a gigantic staging area for Operation Overlord were already under way, preparations that increasingly constituted an imperative for the operation itself.

If the British had become reconciled to the inevitability of Operation Overlord in the spring of 1944, however, they were by no means ready to accept demotion to junior partner in the alliance. Operation Anvil, not Operation Overlord, became the crucial test of that latter and, from the British viewpoint, a far more important issue. Whereas Operation Overlord required the diversion of manpower and materials that might have been used to reinforce the Allied position in Italy, Operation Anvil proposed to recruit its American contingent from units already active in the Italian theater. In short, the practical effect of Operation Overlord was mainly to place the British-controlled Italian campaign on hold; the practical effect of Operation Anvil was to enlarge the American-controlled French theater at the direct expense of the Italian theater. Operation Anvil, more than any other single episode in the war, represented the erosion of British status and power, and British leaders reacted in predictable ways. Churchill especially would not be reconciled. Time and time again he resurrected the issue. He argued, pleaded, wept, and even threatened to resign unless Operation

Anvil were canceled or incorporated more directly into the Normandy theater, but to no avail. Even though the British would valiantly try to recover lost ground by subsequently arguing that the final Western assault on Germany should take the form of a single left-flank thrust under the command of General Bernard Montgomery, that effort was destined to failure. Discounting the military wisdom of a concerted thrust as opposed to a broad-front strategy, no matter who was in charge, the brutal political reality was that the United States, which increasingly dominated the military effort on the Western front, would be the arbiter of military policy as well.

A chronological approach might well serve to intensify the drama of inherently dramatic events, discourage the unfair use of hindsight, and impress the reader of the contentious nature of political issues, but in other respects it is not so useful. Not only has Eisenhower chosen to discuss events chronologically, but he has also done so in huge blocks. The chapters average more than eighty pages. As a result, the narrative lacks clear focus. More than likely, a given chapter will include treatment of at least two of the three principal fronts as well as policy discussions involving heads of state, the three groups of chiefs of staff, and field commanders. Added to this mélange are frequent references to Ike's personal life, many of which take the form of rather intrusive flashbacks. Thus the narrative wanders snakelike through the vast quantities of disparate materials the author feels constrained to include. The point here is not that the use of a chronological approach is necessarily ineffective or that the narrative is too inclusive but, rather, that the author has compounded the discursive quality inherent in such an approach by neglecting to take adequate charge of his material.

The same might well be said of the author's coverage of policy decision making. As much time as Eisenhower devotes to discussions involving policy at all levels, it is curious that he fails to prepare the reader to understand how policy was created. In theory, military policy was to be determined by the Combined Chiefs of Staff (CCS) which was permanently headquartered in Washington, D.C. When it was impossible for the British joint chiefs to meet with their American counterparts, the British position was represented by a joint staff mission which, for most of the war, was headed by the very able field marshal Sir John Dill. The CCS was subject to direction by Churchill and Roosevelt but in practice functioned more as an independent authority than as a conduit in its relationship to theater commanders. In the individual theaters, the command structure was thoroughly integrated. If the theater commander was American (as in the case of Western Europe), the deputy would be British. The field commanders were a mix of both nationalities. Regardless of nationality, however, in matters concerning military operations, field commanders were subject to the authority of the theater commander.

This thoroughgoing commitment to Anglo-American cooperation did not always work as planned. Although military operations were subject to CCS control, personnel and supplies were not. Thus Ike could replace American field commanders serving under him, but not British field commanders. In addition, as the war progressed, the United States increasingly dominated the production of war materiel. Since the CCS had no jurisdiction over the disposition of supplies, British field commanders were directly dependent upon Ike for resources above and beyond those available from British sources. To complicate matters further, as the conflict wore on, Churchill especially bypassed the CCS in favor of dealing with Ike directly. All these factors tended to diminish the authority of the CCS and, with it, the spirit of Anglo-American cooperation.

The absence of a specific description of the command structure leaves the reader to figure out for himself the relationships among the various levels of authority. Knowledge of these relationships helps to explain, for example, why General Montgomery, a field commander, could behave as independently as he did in his relationship with Ike, who functioned as his immediate superior. Although Montgomery was obliged by the rules to obey Ike's direct orders, he reserved the right to interpret those instructions or even ignore them pending reconsideration. There is no question that Montgomery acted as boldly as he did partly because he knew that Ike did not have the authority to fire him. Knowledge of the command structure also helps to explain why Ike acted with evident greater assurance as the war moved into its final phases. Whereas Eisenhower sees this change as the result of a "growth in office," which is no doubt partly true, it also seems true that Ike's heightened sense of assurance was affected by his control of American supplies. Even though the CCS pressured Ike into shifting a larger portion of his strength to the left flank, thereby enhancing Montgomery's prestige, Ike was determined to maintain a broad-front offensive into Germany. His control of supplies was an important factor in determining his success in implementing his own strategy. When systematic German resistance along the Western front broke down in March, 1945, it was the American Twelfth Army Group under General Omar Bradley that led the drive into the German heartland. General Montgomery's Twenty-first Army Group in contrast was assigned to mop up in northern Germany and Denmark.

Despite his failure to provide a clear context for understanding the complex and often colorful relationships among those in command, Eisenhower is most judicious in evaluating the strengths and weaknesses of the individuals themselves. The centerpiece of these discussions is Ike himself. The supreme commander was often criticized, by Americans as well as British, as being too conservative and indecisive, a charge Eisenhower admits has some merit. His conservative nature, according to these critics, is best displayed in his choice of a broad-front strategy. Ike consistently rejected British advice to attempt to end the war quickly by concentrating Allied forces on the left flank, thereby reducing the center and right flank to holding actions. Montgomery and British Chief of Staff Sir Alan Brooke, who were the most persistent advocates of such a strategy, argued that a "left hook" under Montgomery's command offered great promise of reaching Berlin quickly, thus ending the war. Since the debate over the wisdom of the left-hook strategy is unresolvable, there seems little point in summarizing the arguments in this essay. It is sufficient to point out that Ike's position, rather than his nationality or native conservatism, dictated his rejection of the left hook in favor of a broad-front strategy. As supreme commander, Ike's primary concern (perhaps his only legitimate concern) was to adopt strategies that guaranteed victory. By the beginning of 1945 at the latest, the evident fact of the war was that the superior resources of Great Britain, the United States, and the Soviet Union ensured an Allied victory in the foreseeable future. To crush the German will and capacity to continue a hopeless struggle seemed the most prudent method of securing unconditional surrender. The use of a broad-front strategy was best suited to this objective.

Political considerations reinforced Ike's commitment to a broad-front strategy. Whatever its merit as a military strategy, a left-hook drive on Berlin was a virtual political impossibility. It is hard to imagine that the United States, or even France for that matter, would have acquiesced in a plan designed to allow a British-led force to administer the coup de grace to Germany while the remaining American and French forces provided secondary support. A broad-front strategy offered the only mechanism by which American, British, and French forces could work productively in harness. Ike's willingness on occasion to "loan" the United States Ninth Army and elements of the First Army to Montgomery was a concession to these political realities rather than a display of indecisiveness.

Eisenhower, at War fails to live up to the claims made for it by its publisher. It does not "profoundly recast our perception of World War II and its consequences." On the other hand, it is much more than a memorial to a larger-than-life public figure by an awestruck grandson. In the final analysis, *Eisenhower, at War* is a serious and very comprehensive study of the last eighteen months of World War II from the perspective of the supreme commander. As such, it is not, or could it be expected to be, free of controversy or error. Nevertheless, the book's shortcomings must be balanced against its strengths, and on balance *Eisenhower, at War* is a valuable addition to the growing literature on World War II.

Meredith Berg

Sources for Further Study

The Atlantic. CCLVIII, August, 1986, p. 85.
Kirkus Reviews. LIV, July 15, 1986, p. 1088.

Library Journal. CXI, September 15, 1986, p. 80.
Los Angeles Times Book Review. September 21, 1986, p. 1.
The New York Review of Books. XXXIII, September 25, 1986, p. 30.
The New York Times Book Review. XCI, September 14, 1986, p. 1.
Newsweek. CVIII, September 1, 1986, p. 83.
Publishers Weekly. CCXXX, July 25, 1986, p. 176.
Time. CXXVIII, September 15, 1986, p. 95.
The Wall Street Journal. CCVIII, September 12, 1986, p. 30.

EMILY DICKINSON

Author: Cynthia Griffin Wolff (1936-   )
Publisher: Alfred A. Knopf (New York). Illustrated. 608 pp. $25.00
Type of work: Literary biography
Time: 1830-1886
Locale: Amherst, Massachusetts

An insightful and skillfully written biography which stresses the interior life of the poet, especially her struggle with Trinitarian Christianity and nineteenth century notions of womanhood

> *Principal personages:*
> EMILY ELIZABETH DICKINSON, an American poet
> EMILY NORCROSS DICKINSON, her mother
> EDWARD DICKINSON, her father
> SAMUEL FOWLER DICKINSON, her grandfather
> THOMAS WENTWORTH HIGGINSON, her literary adviser
> OTIS PHILLIPS LORD, her lover

Writing a biography of Emily Dickinson is necessarily a perilous and ambitious undertaking, partly because a whole cluster of myths and misunderstandings still clings to this enigmatic New England writer and partly because her internal life is colorless in the extreme. Emily Dickinson did not marry; she rarely left her home in Amherst, Massachusetts (except for a year or so at Mount Holyoke Female Seminary and very brief visits to Philadelphia and Boston, the latter for much-needed medical attention to her eyes). There is, in fact, nothing remarkable about this brilliant, auburn-haired woman except for the fact that she wrote some 1,775 poems during her lifetime and by general account is one of the finest poets to have lived and written in America. Her voice and her verse forms are unique: Emily Dickinson must be considered an American original. It is fitting, then, that Cynthia Griffin Wolff takes great pains to show the American roots of this creative genius while at the same time debunking many of the wrongheaded notions that have persisted in the popular imagination.

Without trying to create an image of Emily Dickinson as the girl-next-door, Wolff demonstrates that the poet was an outgoing and gregarious adolescent who formed deep friendships with many girls—and boys—of her acquaintance. She was not socially awkward, nor was she insulated from diverse and stimulating company, since Amherst was an intellectual center and the Dickinson home served as a meeting place for many of the bright young men in her father's and older brother's social circles. Although certain strains and distances always typified her relations with her parents, Emily was clearly a devoted daughter who admired her father and nursed her mother through years of declining health (one of the primary obstacles to Emily's marital plans). It is true that the poet kept mainly to herself during her declining years, but she chose this path voluntarily. At no time was she a recluse, hermit, or misanthrope: She had a genuine and ready sense of wit, a playful sense of humor, and a genuine affection for children. The poet played with her niece Mattie by lowering gingerbread and cookies in a basket from her second-story bedroom window.

Emily Dickinson's readers over the decades have found even sweeter and more substantial nourishment in her posthumously published work, especially the monumental variorum edition edited by Thomas Johnson and published in 1955. To understand the mind that created those extraordinary poems, it is necessary to appreciate the dominance of the Dickinson clan on the Amherst scene. Emily's grandfather, Samuel Fowler Dickinson, the founding father of Amherst College, poured his life's fortune into the bank account of the fledgling institution. He was also instrumental in creating the decidedly theological slant of the early curriculum; in fact, Samuel Fowler Dickinson helped to begin the period of great religious revivals which shook the town of Amherst to its very foundations. His granddaughter Emily grew up, then, with the constant pressure for religious conversion, and the thesis of Wolff's biography is that Emily Dickinson rejected this pressure (and other social pressures) in order to carve out a unique cultural niche suitable for her survival as a poet.

Emily's father, Edward Dickinson, lacked his father's fiery Puritanical vision (even though he read the Bible aloud on a daily basis), but he possessed an uncanny business sense that helped him manage the finances of Amherst College brilliantly. He married Emily Norcross, a woman who communicated in a strange manner of indirection and evasion. One always had to guess what Emily Norcross intended, and this odd behavior manifested itself even during their courtship when Edward could not extract a simple yes or no to his proposal of marriage. Her elliptical style seems to have been passed on directly to her daughter, and Wolff makes a very convincing case that Emily Dickinson's elaborate poetic riddles are, like Emily Norcross' evasive responses, a sophisticated strategy for not being discovered. As poignant and unsettling as her best poems are, they always conceal as much as they reveal.

In order to place Emily Dickinson and her family in a more understandable context, Wolff devotes roughly the first quarter of the biography to the general social conditions prevailing in New England during the fourth and fifth decades of the nineteenth century while Emily was growing up. Death was the constant companion of everyone alive at this time. Only a fraction of the population lived beyond childhood. Infant mortality rates were high throughout this period, and death by tuberculosis (or consumption, as it was called) was commonplace. Many member of Emily Norcross' family died from this lingering and painful ailment, and Emily could view the frequent burials of Amherst citizens from the vantage point of her second-story window, which provided an excellent view of the Amherst cemetery. The whole process of burial and mourning was elaborately institutionalized. Tombstones were decorated with emblems from a well-known vocabulary of death: angels, skulls, skeletons, hourglasses, bats, and serpents biting their tails. The text of *Emily Dickinson* is beautifully illustrated with photographs of the Dickinson family, homes, and friends—and with reproductions of tombstones and pages from emblem books, such as Edward Hitchcock's *Religious Lectures on Peculiar Phenomena* (1850). Surrounded by the ubiquitous presence of death, Emily Dickinson responded with the full force of her artistic power, writing almost obsessively on the subject. Some of her finest poems (such as "Because I could not stop for Death," 712) reenact the poet's frequent psychological sparring with this powerful and implacable enemy:

> Because I could not stop for Death—
> He kindly stopped for me—
> The Carriage held but just Ourselves—
> And Immortality.

The business of tending the sick and the dying fell inevitably to women because mid-nineteenth century American culture was still sharply divided along gender lines. Women could not vote, many of them died in childbirth, and their only sphere of permissible activity was the home. Obstetrical practices of the day were primitive and cruel by modern standards; many mothers and their fetuses died because of the brutal and senseless application of forceps. Emily Dickinson's mother was forced to spend most of her life in isolation at home while her increasingly famous husband became a politician and went off to Springfield and Boston for extended periods of time. Mrs. Dickinson fell victim to fits of loneliness and depression, conditions which only exacerbated her other ailments. Her daughter the poet faithfully attended her during these years of suffering, staying on duty many nights in a process called "watching." Even Edward Dickinson and his journalist friend Samuel Bowles published antifeminist tracts during Emily Dickinson's lifetime—and they were enlightened, highly educated professionals. Edward Dickinson strongly rejected any attempt to grant women suffrage, and Bowles (liberal in all other matters) believed that a woman's place was emphatically in the home. Wolff might very easily have given a strictly feminist rendering of these events, and, although her interpretation of women and their plight is highly sympathetic, it never becomes ideological or overstated. Wolff lets the facts speak eloquently for themselves, suggesting, for example, that the poet's failure to publish significantly during her lifetime—only six poems were published while she was alive—was the result of a closed literary culture which accepted women's writing only if it conformed to expected subject matter and tone. The world was ready for saccharine and sentimental verses but not for the original and ironic utterances of Emily Dickinson. The poet's attempts to break into publishing all ended fruitlessly—even her celebrated effort to gain the attention of Thomas Wentworth Higginson, who simply did not understand the remarkable verse being sent to him by the young woman from Amherst.

More controversial, perhaps, is Wolff's discussion of Christianity and Dickinson's complex reaction to it. Clearly, Dickinson stood like a rock as wave after wave of Trinitarian revivalism swept over the tiny community of Amherst. She refused to be converted, and finally she quit attending church altogether. These acts of defiance did not mean that the poet had ceased to be a Christian or even a believer, but they do signify her originality of purpose and natural suspicion of conformity. Surely the poet must have questioned the all-too-emotional faith of the Amherst Congregationalists and their stultifyingly narrow prescriptions for salvation, but Wolff goes on to suggest that Dickinson needed to reject traditional Christianity to make a psychological space for her writing. In this reading, Dickinson becomes another Jacob (Wolff's favorite image) struggling with God for her identity. Perhaps this account is accurate, but some readers will recall that other poets (John Milton and John Donne come readily to mind) made great poetry precisely because of their accommodation to traditional Christianity. Essentially, Wolff argues that Dickinson could liberate herself only by rejecting traditional patterns of behavior wherever she encountered them. Obviously, Dickinson rejected the traditional role of woman in her day; it is not at all clear, however, that she rejected Christianity, and, if she did, that she was obliged to do so by her poetic vocation.

Nevertheless, Wolff offers insightful ideas about Dickinson's stylistic development, noting, by frequently quoted letters, that the poet needed visual reassurance to validate every event. She had to see in order to believe; her letters are filled with instances of her literally demanding to see someone or something. This visual preoccupation translated into the rich visual imagery that controls and enhances her best poems. Also convincing is Wolff's close analysis of stylistic trademarks (dashes and key phrases) which appear first in the letters, then in the poems. In fact, the letters often contain poems as integral parts of their structures, not merely as afterthoughts or addenda. As Wolff dramatically proves, the poetry was a logical extension of the letters—and Emily Dickinson wrote hundreds upon hundreds of letters.

Also useful is Wolff's discussion of the many different "voices" which the poet adopted to suit her various aesthetic purposes—a tactic she used in the letters as well. Dickinson might adopt the voice of student, housewife, lover, bride, or child. Artistically, this use of voices allowed the poet to introduce appropriate and complex lines of imagery for each particular voice and to pun on various terms used by both the adopted voice and the real voice. Of all her strategies of indirection, the use of these voices is probably the most effective, and Wolff is especially sensitive to the nuances and possibilities inherent in them all.

Although Emily Dickinson corresponded with—and occasionally met—three men (Samuel Bowles, Thomas Higginson, and the Reverend Charles Wadsworth), her intentions seem to have been purely literary. Such was not the case with Judge Otis Phillips Lord, a widower who enjoyed a frankly passionate and physical (though unconsummated) relationship with Dickinson. About 1878, she wrote to him: "I will not let you cross—but it is all your's [sic], and when it is right I will lift the Bars, and lay you in the Moss—You showed me the word." For whatever reason—her devotion to her mother or her perverse desire to be separated from the one she obviously loved passionately—Dickinson did not accede to Lord's wishes that they be married, and he died shortly thereafter, in 1884. Two years later she would join him in the kingdom of death she had so often described in her poems.

Cynthia Griffin Wolff once served as a guide and interpreter at the Dickinson House in Amherst. In *Emily Dickinson* she is that wisest of guides: outspoken when necessary, informative, knowledgeable, and above all sensitive to the silences and dark places that will always be part of the Emily Dickinson story.

Daniel L. Guillory

Sources for Further Study

Booklist. LXXXIII, October 1, 1986, p. 183.
Christian Science Monitor. LXXVIII, November 13, 1986, p. 29.
Kirkus Reviews. LIV, October 1, 1986, p. 1502.
Library Journal. CXI, October 15, 1986, p. 97.
Los Angeles Times. December 12, 1986, V, p. 38.
The Nation. CCXLIV, January 31, 1987, p. 117.
The New Republic. CXCVI, March 2, 1987, p. 40.
The New York Times Book Review. XCI, November 23, 1986, p. 7.
Publishers Weekly. CCXXX, October 3, 1986, p. 102.
Washington Post Book World. XVI, November 23, 1986, p. 1.

ENCHANTMENT

Author: Daphne Merkin (1954-   )
Publisher: Harcourt Brace Jovanovich (San Diego, California). 288 pp. $16.95
Type of work: Psychological novel
Time: The late 1950's to the late 1970's or early 1980's
Locale: New York City

A penetrating novel in which a young woman explores her past, particularly her relationship with her mother

> *Principal characters:*
> HANNAH LEHMANN, the protagonist, twenty-six years old
> WALTER LEHMANN, her father, a stockbroker
> MARGOT LEHMANN, her mother
> LILY LEHMANN, her censorious oldest sister
> RACHEL LEHMANN, the second daughter in the family
> BENJAMIN LEHMANN, her oldest brother
> ERIC LEHMANN, the middle son
> ARTHUR LEHMANN, the youngest child

The title of this novel refers to the spell that Margot Lehmann has unintentionally placed upon her youngest daughter, Hannah Lehmann, the protagonist, who at twenty-six is so obsessed with her mother that she cannot live her own life. In order to come to terms with her past, Hannah, who tells her story in the first person, recalls incidents in what seems to be a random pattern, but which actually is a carefully structured narrative, in which each of the eighteen chapters of the book deals with a particular theme or setting or aspect of Hannah's life.

The Lehmanns are a wealthy Jewish family who live luxuriously on Manhattan's Upper East Side, with a full staff of servants, and summer in their own second home. Neither Hannah's mother nor her friends can understand the child's desire to belong to some other family. After all, as Margot points out, she has everything. Nor do the other children have what Margot calls Hannah's "Orphan Annie" complex. From babyhood, however, Hannah has longed for more than her mother could give, longed for a mother who would bake cookies, hug her to a motherly bosom, and, above all, think that she was perfect.

Margot is a practical, realistic person, who declares that she wishes her epitaph to read: "She never made mountains out of molehills." As the novel progresses, Margot springs into life as a vigorous, independent woman who can enchant the reader almost as much as she has enchanted Hannah. Margot cannot be summed up as easily as Hannah's cookie-baking, ideal Jewish mother can be, simply because she is complex and, indeed, fascinating. She is frugal, practical, and insensitive to an adolescent girl's faddy needs, yet she buys expensive shoes for herself. While capable of fury, at other times she placidly assures the histrionic Hannah that everything will be all right. Her detachment drives Hannah to despair, yet there is something admirable in Margot's refusal to accept the responsibility for her daughter's neuroses. Indicted for past actions, she points out that that was the past, then cuts off discussion as if she is bored with it. Hannah's tantrums result only in Margot's ironic admission that she is a bad mother, but, as she points out, Hannah has not lacked for food, clothing, or shelter. When Hannah cuts herself with manicure scissors, attempting to get her mother's attention, Margot bandages her, tells her that her feelings are foolish, and goes out. None of Hannah's strategies produces the desired results. Margot's detachment always triumphs.

Although the struggle between Hannah and Margot permeates the entire novel, some chapters focus on incidents involved in other relationships. For example, the ninth and the thirteenth chapters deal with Hannah's father, Walter Lehmann. Walter is a man who, as Hannah realizes, belongs to his wife; he is not susceptible to the charms of little girls. In Hannah's words, he is "not seducible." Busy with his work, his religious and civic activities, his social life, and his marriage, he does not give his daughters the special attention which all of them would like and which Hannah craves. Although Walter seems to be aware of Hannah's desperation and does his best to help, making her his coat-check child when she is little, taking her to a dinner when she is older, the closeness of his relationship to his wife precludes the kind of closeness which alone would satisfy Hannah, and indeed, she is so besotted with her mother, so unable to appreciate her father as a sexual being, that it is unlikely any effort on his part would be helpful.

A number of the chapters explore Hannah's perceptions about her brothers and sisters. One would think that if the parents seemed distant, brothers and sisters so near in age would have formed alliances and intimacies with one another. Hannah does not believe this to be true. When a dinner guest comments on the closeness of the children, Hannah thinks:

> But hasn't she noticed that we are all miles apart even as we sit together at the Shabbos table? That Eric holds his tie up close and studies its pattern of polka dots as though someone has asked him for an exact count? That Arthur says nothing when he is here and that he disappeared from the table a while ago? . . . What Mr. and Mrs. Hans, securely enclosed in their guestdom, don't know is everything of importance.

Earlier during the dinner, while members of the family respond to one another's statements, generally with disagreement, Hannah voices her real grievance: "No one listens to anyone in this family. We never have."

If *Enchantment* were merely the heroine's—perhaps the author's—statement of grievances, however, it would not be the kind of work which holds the reader's attention to the very last page, as indeed this narrative does. Daphne Merkin has the gift of bringing her characters to life, particularly Margot, Walter, and Hannah, through accurate observation and sometimes hilarious dialogue. After a lengthy fight between Hannah and her sister Lily, which Margot has vainly attempted to stop, she "has enough." Without regard for later reports to psychiatrists, she backs off from both the squabblers: "You're both bitches. You deserve each other. Don't play with each other if you can't keep peace!" As an adolescent, pining for a coat as spectacular as Sharon Levi's rabbit skirt, Hannah appeals to her mother, "I'm just trying . . . to give you a sense of the competition at school. It's ruthless." Pulling out a conservative gray coat, Margot answers flatly, "Ignore it." There is a missing pencil episode that is delightful, too. Walter, who is always praised by his wife for his rationality, has a favorite lead pencil. No other pencil will do. The subsequent search, which permits the various children to voice their various grievances, leads to five-year-old Arthur, who keeps repeating, "My pencil," without any realization of the fact that his father is as obsessed by the pencil as he. This subtle leveling of the adults, which reveals the children who still exist within them, is one of the interesting patterns in Merkin's novel.

In other ways, too, Merkin transcends the mere childish statement of grievances. By the end of the novel, Hannah has begun to realize that her family is composed of human beings and that her mother, in particular, is enchanting partially because she is complex. Although as a child, playing "Orphan Annie," Hannah believed that every other mother was preferable to her own, as the process of recollection proceeds, she has to admit that her mother should not be castigated simply because she could not be as loving all the time as she was some of the time—when she took Hannah for a treat after shopping; when she let the young girl help her with her makeup; or when she telephoned the mother of the bully Naomi Litt. Whatever Hannah's psychiatrist says about Margot's deficiencies, Margot is ready to admit to them, but she must make the obvious point: "I did the best I knew how." At this point Hannah seems to understand that the emotions her mother stirs in her must finally be her own problem. "What do we expect from our mothers but absolute fealty?" she asks herself, and the answer is clear: The child's expectation is impossible.

When her psychiatrist suggests that Hannah look for love, she realizes that her own feelings for her mother have predisposed her to romantic disaster, that she is always drawn to men who display indifference toward her. She will never find anyone, Hannah muses, who will love her as much as her little nephew Max. Understanding herself, forgiving her mother, however, perhaps she will now be as free to search for love as she is in the dream that concludes the novel. If she meets rebuffs, perhaps her mother's consistent answer will at least make sense to her: Stay calm; things will work out. In a final poignant and hilarious interchange, Hannah asks her mother dramatically whether she thinks that she will ever get married. "I suppose so," she says, "You can always get divorced." Then comes the usual reassurance, which, after all, is as much as most mothers can say: "Don't worry.

Everything will turn out fine." Hannah can finally admit that for all the "disowned longings" for which her mother may have been responsible, "there are also the things she didn't overlook." Finally accepting of the past, Hannah can move into the future.

It is obvious that, whatever the autobiographical content of *Enchantment*, Merkin keeps a distance between her protagonist and herself. Throughout the novel, those who are accused of denying Hannah a normal development are never presented to be as bad as Hannah thinks they are. Through scene and dialogue, the first-person narrator reveals more than she knows that she is revealing. By the end of the novel, the reader is merely waiting for her to attain the same conclusions that he has already reached. Merkin's artistry as well as her perception are to be commended.

Although Daphne Merkin has published some short fiction in various periodicals as well as some critical articles, *Enchantment* is her first novel. The subject—that of mother-daughter relationships—has become a popular one, and the situation—the daughter who continues to seek her mother's approval—is frequently treated in modern fiction. What is unusual is the complex handling of point of view, the brilliant rendering of dialogue, and the prevailing good humor in Merkin's version of the mother-daughter story.

Rosemary M. Canfield-Reisman

Sources for Further Study

Chicago Tribune. September 14, 1986, XIV, p. 5.
Christian Science Monitor. LXXVIII, September 29, 1986, p. 22.
Kirkus Reviews. LIV, July 1, 1986, p. 964.
Library Journal. CXI, August, 1986, p. 171.
Los Angeles Times Book Review. September 14, 1986, p. 2.
The New York Times Book Review. XCI, October 5, 1986, p. 7.
Publishers Weekly. CCXXX, July 18, 1986, p. 79.
Washington Post. August 27, 1986, p. D2.

END PAPERS
Essays, Letters, Articles of Faith, Workbook Notes

Author: Breyten Breytenbach (1938-   )
Publisher: Farrar, Straus and Giroux (New York). 270 pp. $16.95
Type of work: Political and cultural memoir
Time: 1967-1986
Locale: Europe and South Africa

> *A collection of Breytenbach's political writings from both in and out of prison, plus comments on contemporary culture and literary theory*

It is a sad comment on the times to note how many of the most memorable titles of the latter half of the twentieth century have belonged to books which describe an individual's struggle against the tyranny and terror of vicious political systems. The Argentinian Jacobo Timerman's *Prisoner Without a Name, Cell Without a Number* (1980), the Italian Primo Levi's *The Periodic Table* (1975), the Cuban Armando Valladares' *Against All Hope* (1985), and the Russian Alexander Solzhenitsyn's *The First Circle* (1968) and *The Gulag Archipelago* (1973-1975) are all the work of men who have been incarcerated because of their refusal to comply with the demands of a social system which they considered an illegal infringement upon the universally acknowledged rights of man. In each case, their imprisonment has also been a consequence of their determination to speak directly against a tyrannical government. Levi and Timerman have returned from prison to see the emergence of genuine democratic reforms in their countries, and although Solzhenitsyn and Valladares have had to accept exile in the refuge of the United States, their work stands as a continuing testament to the endurance and resilience of the human spirit, offering some kind of encouragement to all of their countrymen continuing the struggle and some kind of consolation to the citizens of the world who might just as easily give in to despair upon consideration of the percentage of the human race that lives now—and has always lived—under some form of tyranny.

The South African writer and painter Breyten Breytenbach—Afrikaner by birth, exile in Paris for ten years by choice, self-described in mid-life as a "Whitish Afrikaans-speaking South African African"—felt compelled to return from Europe in 1975 to help organize resistance among members of the "white tribe" to the diabolical system of Apartheid (Breytenbach always capitalizes the term). Entering his country under an alias, he was arrested and convicted for treason, and he spent seven years in jail, two in solitary confinement. His account of those days, *The True Confessions of an Albino Terrorist* (1985), has been described as both "defiantly unesthetic" and "modest and refreshing," an indication of the singularity of his voice and stance. It brought Breytenbach almost immediate celebrity among writers in the Western world, a somewhat ironic occurrence since his work as a poet was previously invisible beyond his home country and visible there only to members of a closed audience of a culture he was attacking. Partly as a result of this fame, Breytenbach has accepted the opportunity to publish *End Papers*, a series of occasional, personal, casual, and polemical essays, political addresses, poems, and fragments that defy characterization. Aside from his understandable eagerness to reach a wider audience concerning his convictions about Apartheid and the political situation in South Africa, Breytenbach candidly confesses that he is pleased to publish an accumulation of varied material so that he can "get it over and done with" and move on to new territory in his work.

It is this combination of artistic ambition with a sense of the developing self as an aesthetic construct and a total commitment to work toward the political evolution of his homeland that makes Breytenbach, at his best, such an intriguing writer. The connections between his political activity and creative endeavors stem from his conviction that it is not possible to write truthfully in the service of or in collusion with a system that denies freedom to its subjects. His central contention is that by enslaving the black majority of its people, the minority white tribe which rules South Africa (his "people," the Afrikaans) has enslaved itself as well. Both the jailer and prisoner are enchained by the moral corruption that is the primary product of Apartheid.

End Papers, because of the diverse nature of its contents, its political and its artistic focus, has been organized by two directing precepts in order to give it more than a random structure. The first one is chronological, leading Breytenbach to arrange his thoughts and remarks in roughly the order in which they were written, but they are preceded by a section called "Pretext," which is an introduction designed to prepare the reader for what is to follow: to establish a context for perception. Following the chronologically arranged material, there is a final section called "End Notes," which gives the author another opportunity to comment on and extend the insights and arguments of the twenty years between the mid-1960's and the mid-1980's from the perspective of the sensibility that has been formed by the experience of those decades. The second precept is an important aspect of Breytenbach's aesthetic credo. Because it is important for the author to reinforce and expand his sense of himself as an author of imaginative literature (he has been called the "leading poet" of the Afrikaner language and has translated some of his own work for *End Papers*), Breytenbach is at work throughout the book to develop a distinct "voice" and an original angle of vision. By using experimental forms, multiple narratives, and several versions of "language," and by his shifts between polemical-ideological and poetic styles of expression, he has tried to fuse the fragments of a wide-ranging and often engaging intelligence into a coherent, if not completely unified, construct.

In an attempt to deflect the glare of his sudden celebrity, the "Pretext" is deliberately mysterious at its inception, an oblique introduction that offers moments from the flow of a writer's consciousness. The first lines are a quatrain attributed to Sesson Yubai. In "End Notes," the reader learns that Yubai, a Japanese Zen monk of the thirteenth century, composed four poems by using each line of an older poem as a separate starting place. Almost incidentally, Breytenbach also notes that the poems were written in jail when Yubai was imprisoned by the Mongols and facing death. Several points of coordination are immediately established. First, history is cast into a multiple perspective as the reader is encouraged to move back and forth through the book, and accordingly, through the time span the book covers. Then, the factor of imprisonment is introduced, not obtrusively but as a constant that can never be completely escaped. The importance of poetry is claimed by its primacy, and the multinational nature of Breytenbach's literary education is also suggested. Finally, the reader is being prepared for an assault of compact, small units of communication, each so intense that the author has chosen to keep them compact to avoid overloading. Similarly, the subject changes abruptly and frequently to relieve the pressure on a writer who is often aware of the presence of death. The subject of South Africa seems to arrive in the fifth subsection without previous notice or conspicuous preparation, but within four pages, Breytenbach has stated with some clarity his reasons for condemning the policies of the South African government, his position that South Africa is a prison for all of its inhabitants, and his chilling explanation of what "exactly is it that happens to the prisoner during his stay behind the walls."

Partly because of his belief that the only real heroes of the South African nation are people such as Steve Biko, Nelson Mandela, and Bishop Desmond Tutu, and partly because he has the lag's knowledge that all forms of "heroic" behavior are a kind of empty posturing, Breytenbach has kept the intimate details of his own life in the background. Nevertheless, because he is also trying to show in *End Papers* how his instincts and attitudes as an artist have changed and progressed, his reactions to the contemporary world where he has achieved a measure of fame provide some of his most archly amusing pages. Breytenbach's devastating aphorisms on various forms of self-designated authority precisely skewer all sorts of pretense and pomposity, and his observations on the manner in which the media use the celebrity of the moment deftly expose the shallowness and parasitic behavior of various commentators and experts. "For so many of them," he writes, "journalism is a quick shuffle to find the shortest route to simplification and superficiality." Breytenbach is candid about his own uses of the media and about his gradual recognition of the personas he adopts—"Mr. Ex-Detainee," "Mr. Anti-Apartheid," "Mr. Odd(er) Afrikaner"—to survive "already out of prison but not yet arrived in paradise." Although his travel writing is not always very original ("Berlin the scarred . . . Rome eternally seductive"—

too often he settles for a melodramatic epithet), his observations of the way in which people live, particularly people down and out in the streets and slums of great cities, incline toward the bawdy, humanistic view of writers such as Geoffrey Chaucer and Miguel de Cervantes. His sense of historical parallels is acute, as when, for example, his observations of Europe and America lead him to the incisive conclusion that there has been a regression to "patterns of the Middle Ages: the unquestioned acceptance that misery and poverty are here to stay and should co-exist with blatantly reinforced opulence." His conviction that this mind-set is a part of the same global racism and economic imperialism that sustain Apartheid has not led him, however, to an acceptance of leftist dogma—much to the displeasure of some of his extremist acquaintances.

The two major divisions of the book are designated "Blind Bird" and "Burnt Bird" (playing on the root meaning of his name). The first of these includes essays and extracts from Breytenbach's diary written "during years of preparation for prison" (1967-1975). The second includes essays, addresses, and reflections written "since returning from No Man's Land." The early essays are clearly the work of a man with traditional academic inclinations and training. They are earnest, sincere in tone, and fairly optimistic. Their use of classical rhetorical devices assumes a rational audience; they try to persuade by force of logic and by dramatizing the justice of their argument. Almost nothing that Breytenbach says about the South African situation in the late 1960's and early 1970's has been discredited by subsequent events, and his skillful, scholarly use of historical material provides a solid background for anyone not familiar with the history of South African politics. His depiction of the Afrikaner as a transplanted European foisting a "Vulture culture" on Africa and his analysis of the manner in which Apartheid projects everyone, ruler and ruled, into an ethos of negativity, suppression, withdrawal, and confinement are strikingly clear; they offer a familiar message, but one rarely stated with greater eloquence. Still, these essays are not exceptional; merely rather impressive.

The years Breytenbach spent in jail inevitably altered the tone of his writing, and it is this man who is the most interesting voice in the book. Unlike such minimal figures as the media pet, the semibrilliant Jack Abbott, whose spasms of violence show that he emerged from "the belly of the beast" still infantile, Breytenbach was not diminished or brutalized by his experience. Perhaps because he risked jail to serve a series of principles upon which he had already committed his life, he found the strength to survive with his human inclinations deepened and amplified. The theoretical nature of his support for black activists such as Mandela and Biko was resolved and refined into an experiential understanding of their lives. The effect of his incarceration is most apparent in the change in his style of address to his audience in the essays of the 1980's. In "Burnt Bird," Breytenbach is sardonic, consciously strident, unabashed, and unsubdued regardless of the subject. Paradoxically, this makes him better company, less stiffly idealistic, more accessible, if a little more daunting as well. The authenticity of his observations lends a new gravity to his insights, and he does not seem to think that it is as necessary to be "serious" about everything. There is a marvelous piece of intellectual-artistic gossip wherein he meets Sophia Loren, Norman Mailer, Francis Coppola, and others at a cultural conference and chats about the events of the gathering in a parody of a "Society" column. There is a superb portrait of the great blind Argentinian writer Jorge Luis Borges receiving a medal at a reception in Paris, and for all that has been written about Borges, Breytenbach manages to see him clearly and afresh, the old man still intellectually honest and vibrant, alive to the things of the world, qualities Breytenbach admires immensely.

In a Dutch PEN Center address, Breytenbach makes a powerful case for a cultural boycott of South Africa, and at a poetry festival in Rotterdam, he explains that the "real" home for the artist (or exile) is his language. Throughout these essays, his enjoyment of the mundane is his way of expressing the value of life renewed after the limits of confinement. His definition of freedom includes a preoccupation with the pleasures of the commonplace. The essay "My Dear Unlikely Reader" is a wonderful excursion into the sensual joy of the mind and body responding to the world of the sun-struck Mediterranean in Sardinia. In all these essays, Breytenbach is never far from his sense of himself as a "Whitish" African whose homeland is one large prison camp. His thoughts on censorship ("the cold burning" of books), the task of the writer, the ethics of resistance, and the obligations of moral dissent are all a part of his essential philosophical position—that the South African government is not only an insult to human dignity but that it is actually aiding the spread of Communism as well by the creation of a justifiable rage which might be manipulated by unscrupulous forces.

Perhaps the most stirring expression of his convictions is his tribute to Desmond Tutu. Simple, deeply emotional, and very powerful, he describes Tutu as:

> . . . above all a passionate warrior for peace, where peace *must* come to mean: no more blatant racism, an end to institutionalized state terror, the abolition of the pass laws, stopping the forcible removal of millions, the dismantling of Bantu Education and its replacement by one educational system for all, the right of residence and the right to property for all. . . . Modest, minimal, realizable demands. What would pass anywhere else for basic human rights . . .

Like Tutu, like Mahatma Gandhi, like Martin Luther King, Jr., Breytenbach is one of those, in the words he uses to describe Tutu, who is "keeping the flame alive, giving a renewed sense and adding a depth to the liberation process." By the example of his life and his work, Breytenbach is a "courage teacher" (Allen Ginsberg's term for Walt Whitman), reminding us how precious democracy is, how hideous all forms of totalitarianism. His writing is a demonstration of his faith in the human spirit to bring about the changes he considers inevitable. His confidence in the ultimate success of a democratic evolution offers some comfort for those who might despair of any improvement in a centuries-long record of cruelty and repression. His book is unfinished, open-ended . . . much like the man and the politics of the world which he writes about with such integrity.

Leon Lewis

Sources for Further Study

Booklist. LXXXII, July, 1986, p. 1576.
The Guardian Weekly. CXXXV, July 6, 1986, p. 20.
Kirkus Reviews. LIV, July 1, 1986, p. 983.
Library Journal. CXI, August, 1986, p. 150.
Listener. CXVI, July 16, 1986, p. 26.
Los Angeles Times Book Review. August 17, 1986, p. 1.
The New York Times Book Review. XCI, November 30, 1986, p. 21.
Publishers Weekly. CCXXIX, June 13, 1986, p. 64.
Times Literary Supplement. September 19, 1986, p. 1028.
The Wall Street Journal. CCVIII, October 10, 1986, p. 26.

EROS THE BITTERSWEET

Author: Anne Carson (1950-   )
Publisher: Princeton University Press (Princeton, New Jersey). 189 pp. $20.00
Type of work: Literary criticism

The author explores the paradoxical nature of desire as expressed in the works of Sappho and other Greek lyric poets of the dawning age of literacy and contrasts their views with the interpretation of love in Plato's Phaedrus

Eros the Bittersweet is an odd, neat, duplicitous little book, written with double purposes for a double audience. One vein, much stronger in the early pages of the essay, is its generalizing bent: All lovers feel as Sappho felt. Leo Tolstoy's Anna Karenina joins with Jean-Paul Sartre, Jacques Lacan, and Emily Dickinson to present erotic love in its most paradoxical context. This epic sweep of generality is coupled with meticulous analysis of individual texts as they survive in the original Greek. The essay is both scholarly and personal in tone, at times holding the reader at a proper academic distance, at others dropping an arm about his shoulders and whispering cozily in his ear. The author's joy in paradox is so great and so apparent that the reader can sense its growth with each increment of paradox within the text; the more paradox, the merrier.

Eros the Bittersweet, significantly, has no numbered chapters, only coyly titled subdivisions, thirty-four in all, many accompanied by quotations from sources as diverse as Queen Victoria and Roland Barthes. In the preface, a character from Franz Kafka chases spinning tops for the sheer delight of the chase. The scholar, Carson assures us, is also engaged in a chase after spinning tops, and delights in the play of metaphor, while attempting to fix that movement in formal study.

The first movement of Carson's essay, generalizing, yet closely linked to specific analysis of a single term, is an inspection of Sappho's term *glukupikron*, or "bittersweet," and the interplay of its meanings in poetic context and in its English renderings. In succeeding pages, Anna Karenina and Simone Weil, as well as a host of ancient and modern authors, are cited as pondering the paradoxical nature of desire. Eros is seen as "limb loosener," tormentor of lovers and poets, qualified in terms of opposites polarized by the universal emotion of love-hate. Desire requires a three-part structure: lover, beloved, and obstruction. Examples of this "triangulation" (based in part on René Girard's concept of "mimetic desire") are drawn from meticulous analysis of Sappho's verse and also from ancient cultural practices. Carson cites the example of *harpagnos*, stylized Cretan homosexual-rape courtships, where the seeming opposition by a family to a boy's abduction was necessary for his desirability. Edges and boundaries of the self are felt only in desire, the outreach of self to other. The sweetness of desire is doubled by the bitterness of loss. The lover inevitably discovers that complete union of two individual selves is never possible, that two lovers can never dissolve into one. Permitting herself a pun, Carson suggests that, seeing his "hole" (lack, loss, wound), the lover sees his "whole." The lover's self-consciousness, born of Eros, is both aware of the superbeing which union with the beloved would produce and wounded by the impossibility of this union. Puns, like desire, increase awareness of edges. While erotic desire insists on the similarity and difference of two lovers, puns affirm the same for two words.

Carson's essay proceeds from a consideration of erotic love and puns to the development of Greek literacy and its effect on the ancient lyric poets. While Sappho and Archilochus inherited the oral tradition of Greek epic poetry, the lyric poets were estranged from that past by the development of the Greek alphabet and written words. The traditional language, formulas, and rhythms of oral epic were used by the lyric poets, but with the self-consciousness of lovers suffering from desire. Concentration on the hard-edged written word divided the poet from the immediacy of the living world. The impact of this consciousness of division was particularly acute for the generation of Greek poets who first sustained its assault. Alphabetization, Carson says, is erotic, and it is no coincidence that capricious Eros was first sung by these Greek poets. Wind, wings, and breath bind the complex of Eros and language. Vowels are moving air; consonants give edges to words. The development of the Greek alphabet, with its consonants as well as vowels, is thus significantly different from earlier syllabaries or pictographic writing systems. Students of words, like lovers, are seekers, wooers, stretching out in desire for the other. Union results in annihilation. The triangulation of desire, the tactics of imagination, are directed at preventing union while keeping desire alive in a search for "something more" than perfect union; metaphor, for example, brings two objects close in comparison yet lets the edges, the incongruence of the two, show.

As Carson builds up her dynamic of triangulation, she introduces the concept of a "blind point" of desire, with two examples as illustration: One is the Velázquez painting commonly known as *Las Meninas* (*The Maids of Honor*). Carson's interpretation of this complex painting is based, to a large extent, on Michel Foucault's well-known study in *The Order of Things* (1973). Understanding of her argument would have been assisted greatly by a reproduction of the painting itself, for her point of interest is not the familiar, luminous foreground group of a flaxen-haired infanta surrounded by her attendants. Carson concentrates, rather, on a detail in the background, a mirror hanging on the far wall, in which the viewer may dimly perceive a portrait of the king and queen of Spain. This mirror, Carson argues, draws the eye of the viewer and should reflect, not the king and queen, but the viewer himself; it is the blind point toward which one's view turns and loses itself. While this concept of blind points does not particularly aid in the understanding of a complex canvas, a series of frames and mirror reflections before which the mind boggles, the painting in its turn does serve to illustrate Carson's concept of blind points.

A second example of the blind point is drawn closer to home. Carson cites Homer's version of the myth of the hero Bellerophon, who represents in human form the blind point of Eros. The hero is beautiful, his face the sign of desire. He carries unsuspectingly a letter from a secret enemy, ordering his death. Carson suggests that, as Homer uses these two important qualifications, they remain inactive. Bellerophon's beauty is irrelevant; it is his heroism that counts for Homer. The letter ordering the hero's death is delivered unopened and has no decisive effect on Homer's story. Carson's argument is that for Homer, an oral poet, oral literature was the potent force. The written texts of Bellerophon's face and sealed death warrant were essentially uninteresting in an oral context. Homer's Bellerophon is a counterexample, offered in opposition to the consideration of Eros found in the lyric poets, treating the same themes of desire and the folded word with sublime indifference.

Carson briefly considers the tradition of ancient novels as an example of the delaying tactics of Eros-language-literature which developed as Greek literacy spread. These novels, *erotika pathemata* (erotic sufferings) as the Greeks called them, put pairs of lovers through separations, protracted wanderings, and series of adventures, all designed to create suspense and to delay union as long as possible. Reader and novelist tacitly agree in a reach of desire to triangulate and thus prolong the process; the union of the lovers and the end of the novel are identical.

A fragment from *The Lovers of Achilles*, a lost play of Sophocles, provides Carson with a metaphor used throughout the latter third of the essay, that of children holding ice in their hands, delighting in the ice yet watching it melt away. Desire is a melter of limbs. The ruses of Eros and the melting of ice are played out in time, both leading to eventual loss. Literacy affects the individual's use of time by attempting to fix the transient spoken word in written form like a piece of ice that "melts forever there."

It is the seeming ability of writing to fix the living word that is at the core of the final movement of Carson's essay, a study of Plato's *Phaedrus* and an examination of the argument that it is better to choose someone who does not love as an erotic partner. After all, desire can damage its recipient; a man in love with a beautiful boy will try to keep him unchanged physically and mentally and, further, will deny him education and the company of others in order to preserve him in a temporal state of desirability. When the boy becomes an adult and wishes the adult prerogatives of home and family, he is no longer desirable. A nonlover who chooses such a boy with an eye to the objective end point of their partnership will provide for his education and eventual welfare as an adult. The Socrates of the *Phaedrus* takes exception to this argument, objecting to its rhetoric (it has no proper opening) and to its perversion of the natural living order (considering the end of the affair before it starts and omitting its proper beginning: desire).

Three main examples of harmful desire are cited by Plato: Midas with his golden touch, cicadas that sing away their adult life until death from starvation, and the gardens of Adonis, festive pots of rootless plants forced into bloom and discarded after the festival of Adonis. In all cases, Carson notes, the interplay of time and desire is highlighted: Midas' touch petrifies the beloved; cicadas live in a "now" of desire; Adonis' gardens are predestined to wither when their brief time passes. In Plato's dialogue, these examples and the text of the nonlover argument intersect with a consideration of wisdom and the written word. If a text fixes not the living outlines of thought but only the outward forms of knowledge, what is the status of the wisdom thus absorbed by the reader? Written words lack desire. They are like Adonis' rootless plants or like Socrates' unloving lover. They possess only the outward form of Eros, not the substance. Inhabiting ritual time, rather than real time, they all lack a proper beginning.

Carson's Socrates suggests that the proper beginning is madness, *mania*, a divine invasion which joins the outer and inner selves and which gives a glimpse into the ideal realm of eternal forms inhabited by the gods. In searching for a painless, timeless security which expels Eros from love affairs or the written word, fixing time in its flight, man loses the divine madness that can free him. The loss and pain of desire expressed by the lyric poets is an occasion for growth, for the lover-searcher to grow and to take wing himself. Leaning at a major point in his argument on a pun culled from two spurious quotes from Homer, Socrates says that the gods' name for Eros is *Pteros* (winged). For Carson, the change from *Eros* to *Pteros* is a flash of insight which both distorts the metrical scheme of the verse (by lengthening the syllable preceding the added letters) and unites the acts of lover and writer. Both the poetic Eros and the Homeric word are winged. Eros is meant to rearrange meters and forms.

The topic of the *Phaedrus* is love one moment, writing the next. This written text, itself an example of Eros at work, discredits writing, Carson insists, by disappearing into a "blind point" in the logic. The final erotic exercise is thought, reaching out to know and employing ruse and subterfuge to continue a process directed toward an ever-receding object. Thought, too, is winged.

This short summary of Carson's argument cannot convey the charm with which the text lures the reader on to delight in the spinning top of literature. It also cannot convey the aggravation readers may feel in the early movement of the essay, when generalities and enthusiasm carry the text too far. Examples, swept together from many periods, say that "no one who has ever been in love" can deny a certain point and allege universality for one point or another. A surviving fragment of a poem by Sappho is analyzed as if its fragmentary nature were a deliberate poetic ruse, not a chance occurrence of transmission. The academic name-dropping of *Eros the Bittersweet*, ranging on one page from Aristotle to Paul Ricoeur and Roman Jakobson, is both exhilarating (so many pieces of the puzzle seem to fit) and exasperating (so many pieces seem truncated and forced into place). While Carson's "hole"/"whole" pun is forced and artificial, the point she makes about puns with it lends valuable support to her later reading of Plato's *Eros/Pteros*. The element of play which the pun introduces is seductive. Ultimately, even the reader incapable of judging Carson's work with Greek originals is cajoled into playing along, enjoying the increasing elegance of the argument, and forgiving the occasional frustrations of the early text. In narrowing its scope from "everyone who has ever been in love" to the Socrates of the *Phaedrus*, Carson performs the curious trick of broadening the resonance of her essay. The reader may not believe her when she speaks about erotic alphabetization, yet, by the last page, he is thoroughly seduced.

Anne W. Sienkewicz
Thomas J. Sienkewicz

Sources for Further Study

Choice. XXIV, December, 1986, p. 637.
Library Journal. CXI, November 15, 1986, p. 97.

THE FALL INTO EDEN
Landscape and Imagination in California

Author: David Wyatt (1953-   )
Publisher: Cambridge University Press (New York). Illustrated. 280 pp. $24.95
Type of work: Literary criticism
Time: The early nineteenth century to the 1980's
Locale: California

The relation of literature to the California landscape is explored, with illustrations from such writers as John Steinbeck and John Muir

If landscape has molded the American imagination, it is equally true that American artists have interpreted and molded the language, giving a definition of and a way of seeing the objective natural landscape. In *The Fall into Eden: Landscape and Imagination in California*, David Wyatt explores what is for him the particular characteristic of the California landscape: its resemblance to the Garden of Eden and its inevitable disfigurement and destruction, resulting from and imaging the Fall of Man. Defining literature broadly to include nature and travel writing, Wyatt supports his thesis with illustrations from eleven writers: Richard Henry Dana, Zenas Leonard, John C. Frémont, John Muir, Clarence King, Mary Austin, Frank Norris, John Steinbeck, Raymond Chandler, Robinson Jeffers, and Gary Snyder. The imagination under discussion is the Romantic imagination. In interpreting landscape in terms of their own experience and emotions, writers using this approach can become the "apotheosis of the Pathetic Fallacy." Wyatt uses critical theories about William Wordsworth and John Milton, in particular the former, to illustrate and elucidate his interpretations, as well as some concepts drawn from William Carlos Williams, Ralph Waldo Emerson, and Henry David Thoreau. For the Western writer, "poetic selfhood is imaged as a lonely figure in an empty landscape," a definition that could apply with equal force to the quintessential Western hero.

Organized chronologically, Wyatt's study begins with an analysis of Dana and Frémont, familiar to most readers, and Leonard, whose journals were one of the early sources of information about the Far West. Dana's experience of California differed significantly from that of most others. He arrived by sea rather than by land, and his perspective of California was the coastline, most of it seen from shipboard. His first impression was that of bleakness, and it was not until he returned years later to find the area, especially around San Francisco, settled and changed, that he saw the land as a paradise. Lost, Leonard, who arrived via a difficult trek over the Sierra Nevada and the desert, saw California as Eden indeed. In contrast to Dana, who tended to stand apart from the landscape as an observer, Leonard identified with it and colored his account with his own vision. Before photography, explorers had to rely on artists for pictures to accompany the written descriptions of their discoveries. Although even photography can and does reflect the sensibilities of the photographer, the artist's rendition, like that of the writer, is more decisively colored by the perception of the beholder. Though Wyatt does not emphasize the visual artist in relation to his thesis, he does include in the illustrations some early renderings by artists. Frémont, a controversial figure whose journals were the most popular and accurate sources for Western emigrants, not only gave his own perspective but also, by entering politics—a process Wyatt defines as turning landscape into real estate—participated in the Fall rather than merely observing it.

Muir, Wyatt contends, unlike most observers, "looks at landscape as if it were there," perhaps, Wyatt speculates, because Muir was once blind for a month. Though he introduced narrative into his writings to vary the descriptive passages, Muir, unlike Wordsworth, ignored or avoided experiences of the sublime. Even in describing the most awesome scenery or adventure, his accounts avoid emotional involvement. Muir's Eden was Hetch Hetchy, a valley much like Yosemite; in comparing the two, however, Muir gave primacy to Yosemite. After the San Francisco earthquake and fire of 1906, the valley was dammed as a reservoir for the city. Muir was devastated, but in the long run the conservation movement in the United States was strengthened by this irreparable loss, and Muir is credited with saving the Yosemite Valley. For Muir, Wyatt maintains, the Sierra Nevada landscape became both his Eden and his home, an Eden he achieved late in life. Muir's early childhood was spent outside the garden, literally and figuratively. He was the son of a severe Scottish father in whose garden Muir played at the risk of thrashings. When the family emigrated to Wisconsin, Muir worked a sixteen-hour day with two holidays a year, and learning was discouraged. At twenty-five, Muir left the University of Wisconsin for, in his phrase, "the University of the wilderness," to spend the remainder of his life in botanical and geological exploration. In marked contrast to his friend Emerson, Muir wanted to make people aware of the landscape, in this way becoming politically involved rather than imposing on and deriving from nature an inner vision.

In contrast to Muir, King, the first director of the United States Geological Survey and author of *Mountaineering in the Sierra Nevada* (1872), became actively involved in his accounts of the landscape. King's metaphor for material success became the conquest of a mountain; his life was a series of successes and failures, as were his mountaineering adventures. He finally did achieve Mounts Tyndall, Shasta, and Whitney. With Richard Cotter, he formed one of the "classic" American comradeships, and their climbs together took on the proportions of an epic. King, with his friend Henry Brooks Adams, shared the catastrophic theory of Earth's origins, to which Muir was opposed. Wyatt suggests that King's geological views mirrored his own catastrophic life; he attempted mining in Mexico, failed, and died in Arizona of tuberculosis. Eden, success, and even catastrophe eluded him:

He saw the geology of the Sierra Nevada as a series of upheavals and new beginnings, but his life took on a fated cycle of repeated failures.

Austin's conflict was between motherhood and the land, between the demands on her as a woman and the demands of her creativity as an individual and writer. She early realized that there was something wrong with her only child, Ruth, who had to be institutionalized; later, Austin was to attempt, unsuccessfully, to establish a mother-daughter relationship with her niece, Mary Hunter. Austin's own mother had rejected her, but later she was to develop a muted mother-daughter relationship with her father's former fiancée. Austin, Wyatt argues, in her career "explores the connection between a woman's experience of maternity and her orientation toward place." Her character, the Walking Woman, for example, having lost both child and lover, seeks freedom of movement and definition in space. The landscape of the stories has "little in it to love," a land in need of human care. In a number of Austin's works, Wyatt sees the natural lack in the land (the unproductive maternity) compensated for by some form of human intervention or imagination (literary creativity). Austin was to lose both her literal and metaphorical Eden after the defeat of the small landholders in the struggle for water in the Owens Valley in 1903. She moved to New Mexico, where in 1928 she revised an early essay, "The Lost Garden," a garden to which she now retreated—not to be with those she had lost but to be at one with herself. For Austin, landscape and the garden had the power to overcome death.

Norris, most notably in *The Octopus* (1901), created a highly mythical California. Norris' redesigning of California geography for symbolic reasons was an abrupt shift from the approach of those writers treated earlier. Although they presented a landscape colored with their own perceptions, they did not move natural phenomena from one place to another in the way in which historical novelists often manipulate person and event. Wyatt singles out as Norris' dominant image, or "ur-image," an isolated vertical figure and a vast, empty, horizontal space," a description very close to that which Wyatt gives of the poetic imagination. The two final and most telling images from *McTeague* (1899) and *The Octopus*, however, are those of the protagonists defeated by both landscape and man, pulled down literally as well as figuratively from their original stature. McTeague, pursued by the law, kills his pursuer only to find himself handcuffed to the dead man in the middle of Death Valley. In *The Octopus*, the final images are of Annixter and his fellow ranchers cut down one by one by the guns of the railroad's henchmen. Norris' emphasis is on Eden lost; a muted Paradise achieved by Presley and Vanamee scarcely offsets the tragic loss of Annixter and the ranchers. Not only have their lives ended but also their way of life.

Steinbeck is the author of the group most explicit in his Eden imagery and most conscious of having lost Eden. Yet, of the group, he is the least explicit about place. His concern is with the human drama, and, in *Of Mice and Men* (1937), the longing for a specific garden, a place where George and Lennie can be at peace, becomes a universal and archetypal tale of Everygarden rather than a specific California tale. In this novel, as well as in *East of Eden* (1952), the dominant emphasis is on male relationships (father-son-brother) rather than on Eve introduced into Eden. In *The Grapes of Wrath* (1939), Eden and home are no longer the object of the search, but the journey itself has merged with the Paradise within and has become the ultimate goal. Wyatt sees Steinbeck's three marriages as emblematic and symptomatic of his lack of settled domesticity and love relationships, and the final solution of wandering as the Paradise within.

Although landscape and the human will are key elements in the development of Southern California, "the most powerful work about the region deals with the human incorporation of space." For Wyatt, Chandler is the most powerful writer about the man-made elements of Southern California, especially those of Los Angeles. W. H. Auden observed that Chandler's books are not escape fiction but serious literature, studies not merely of crime and detection but of the "Great Wrong Place." Chandler's sense of loss came perhaps from his English upbringing; he lived in England from the ages of seven to twenty-three, settling in Los Angeles in 1912. Chandler's chronicles of the city focus almost exclusively on the man-made elements. The panoramic natural background is used, in Romantic fashion, to underscore the atmosphere of doom. The detective story becomes, in Chandler's words, "man's adventure in search of a hidden truth." It becomes a search for the serpent in Eden. The hidden truth in Chandler's life was his wife's concealment of her true age—she was seventeen years older than he—until well after their marriage had taken place. Chandler became reconciled with his wife and successful as an author. His character, Philip Marlowe, also finds the Romantic solution, the Paradise within, in relationship rather than in place.

From Wyatt's specific analyses, several general concepts emerge. One is the common element in the otherwise huge and diverse California landscape: the presence of the ocean. Bordering on the Pacific, California is seen both as the culmination of Manifest Destiny and as a dead end, the symbol of the failure of the Westward dream. The refrain of hope of the Joad family of *The Grapes of Wrath* becomes disillusionment: Ma looks with dismay on the Mojave and again reassures herself that when they get to California, it will be beautiful, only to be told that this *is* California. For Joan Didion and other writers of the Los Angeles scene, whose works often end in the classic car crash, many times on the coastal road, the end of the land becomes more oppressive, the ocean more deadly. Wyatt's discussion of Jeffers and Snyder compares their versions of life at the continent's end. Jeffers sees the ocean as the passage to the Pacific, the beginning of an endless cycle of repetition, with immigration coming full circle around the globe. Snyder, however, sees the ocean not only as an end but also as a possible beginning. "Westering," in Steinbeck the dream of an old man's youth, becomes transferred to the Pacific rim, with the influx of immigrants being the next generation of pioneers. Other common elements are the large landholders and the dependence of all the population on water rights, especially important in the work of Austin, Steinbeck, and Norris. The small landholder and the pastoral ideal are in constant jeopardy. Man-made structures dominating the landscape in diversity and monstrosity is another common element; they often contrast or clash with the landscape rather than obliterate it. Dana, Steinbeck, and Austin see these structures as encroaching on Eden. Dana's experience is both prototype and classic, with a fatally contemporary tone in his dismay at the discovery of a city of a hundred thousand (San Francisco) where he had last seen an almost deserted coastline. Chandler and Norris are ambivalent; Chandler has a love-hate relationship with the city he anatomizes in such telling detail. For Norris, the railroad is evil, but he is not against the idea of settlement and cultivation, and his ranchers are small landholders only in comparison to the giant tentacles of the railroad. Jeffers and Snyder manage to construct homes—Tor House and Kitkitdizze—which are external symbols of the Paradise within, set in areas that retain more than a little of Eden.

A brief survey does not do justice to the full scope of Wyatt's study. Complementing and supporting his theoretical analyses, some with actual charts and diagrams of the concepts, are concise and well-written biographical accounts stressing what for him are the writers' key experiences and, especially in the sections dealing with journals and poetry, ample and well-selected quotations. In addition, he occasionally gives another critic's viewpoint, contrasting it with or applying it to his own. The bibliography is excellent, organized by topic and succinctly annotated. The illustrations complement the text quite well, but the captions give rise to an admittedly minor criticism. The illustration for the frontispiece and dust jacket is, on the frontispiece, given almost full identification, but the others do not follow the style established, leaving the reader to search for the missing information on the reverse of the title page. The caption for *The Big Sleep* (1946) on page 167 should read either Philip Marlowe and Colonel Sternwood or Humphrey Bogart and Charles Waldron, but not Humphrey Bogart and Colonel Sternwood. These, however, are minor flaws in an otherwise handsome job of design and editing.

Wyatt's study is an important contribution to the growing body of literature on California, a region that traditionally has been a center for emerging new trends and influences in American culture. As Wyatt observes, for Americans, landscape fills much of the place that history and culture do in older civilizations. Source of both new ways of seeing and of a continuing innocence, it gives visual evidence of the Fall when it is defaced or destroyed. From the reality of the outer world, American writers have tended to turn to the inner world. Ultimately, landscape, even if preserved, is an illusion. One must deal with oneself and with others even if, perhaps especially if, one lives, like Jeffers and Snyder, at the end of the world. In just under three hundred pages, Wyatt has compressed an impressive range of information and interpretation. Though *The Fall into Eden: Landscape and Imagination in California* is addressed primarily to the reader with considerable literary background and a knowledge of critical theories and terms, Wyatt's style, especially in the biographical and introductory material, is readable as well as scholarly. As Wyatt himself is the first to admit, there are many authors who could have been included, and one would hope that he will pursue further his concepts of the relation of literature to the landscape and to the impact of human beings upon that landscape.

Katharine M. Morsberger

Sources for Further Study

Kenyon Review. New Series. IX, Winter, 1987, p. 129.
Los Angeles Times Book Review. August 24, 1986, p. 4.

FAMILY AND NATION

Author: Daniel Patrick Moynihan (1927-   )
Publisher: Harcourt Brace Jovanovich (San Diego, California). 207 pp. $12.95
Type of work: Current history and public policy analysis

A prominent liberal politician and scholar critically reviews the history of family policy in the United States, arguing for dramatic but consistent federal initiatives to strengthen family structures, especially among the nation's poor

If the United States is a nation of families—as both conservatives and liberals seem wont to say—then one has a right to inquire into the health of these families. Statistics are a vital way of beginning the examination, and the relevant statistics are truly alarming. Half of today's marriages are likely to end in divorce; currently, there are 1.2 million divorces per year. When the divorcing wife keeps the children, she becomes a good candidate for poverty. Eighty-five percent of divorced women are not awarded any alimony. When alimony is awarded, the average amount is around three hundred dollars a month for an average of two years. When child support is ordered by the court, it averages about one hundred dollars per month per child. Fifty percent of divorced fathers do not pay the full amount they owe and 24 percent pay nothing. Not surprisingly then, after a divorce, the typical former wife is placed at great economic risk. Currently, more than three million divorced and separated women, along with nearly 4.5 million of their children, live in poverty.

In 1979, the United States Bureau of the Census made a number of ominous projections about American households in the next decades. It forecast that by the end of the century, some three-quarters of American families will be of the traditional mother-father-children sort. This appears comforting until one recalls that in 1960 roughly 90 percent were of this description. Further, Moynihan states that, according to the census, it appears that for the period from 1980 to 2000, "the number of female-headed families will increase at more than five times the rate of husband-wife families. Family households headed by males with no wife present will increase at some six times of rate of the traditional sort."

While much has been made of the special crisis in the black family, it is clear that majority families have also been under tremendous stress. In 1960, only 9 percent of all white families were headed by a female. By 1984, census data showed that for white families with children the proportion had risen to almost 20 percent. By 1985, the issue of missing children had risen to public consciousness. Missing children are principally an expression of intense warfare within broken families, most of them "majority" families. Most missing children (more than one hundred thousand) have been abducted by a parent.

It is against this disturbing sociological background that Daniel Patrick Moynihan offers *Family and Nation*, a version of the talks he gave at Harvard University in the 1984-1985 academic year under the auspices of The Godkin Lectureship. (For the serious reader, the fact that the addresses are apparently printed verbatim becomes a source of much consternation.) That Moynihan is hugely qualified for this task goes without saying. For more than a quarter of a century, he has been a principal shaper of both public policy and intellectual debate in the related areas of family life, ethnic politics, and race relations. He served in all the administrations from John F. Kennedy through Gerald R. Ford, and in 1976 he was elected senator from New York. Among the former Harvard professor's numerous books are the provocative *Maximum Feasible Misunderstanding* (1969)—a rousing critique of the "community action" strategies against the War on Poverty—and *The Politics of a Guaranteed Income* (1973).

Moynihan's most famous work, a White House report, does not always appear in his bibliographies. It is *The Negro Family: The Case for National Action* (1967). Also known as the Moynihan report, this brief document argued that the ongoing civil rights revolution was certain to fail if the growth of single-parent black families living on welfare were not halted. Moynihan hypothesized that when a deprived group rears a large portion of its children "in the generalized disorder of welfare dependency," it will eventually discover itself falling ever further behind, unable to seize new economic and social opportunities.

Family and Nation is in many ways a return to the problem addressed in Moynihan's notorious report. The focus of the author's present concern is not so much the black family, however, but rather the impoverished family in America. His general thesis is that, at long last, the nation is receptive to the notion of "family policy" and ready to learn from its historic neglect of a crucial dimension of political economy. He is also at pains to put the War on Poverty in perspective, defending it from the assaults of Reagan intellectuals such as Charles Murray. Finally, Moynihan seeks to identify a convergence of concern and viewpoint between neoconservatives and liberals regarding possible legislative initiatives in the area of family policy.

Of the three lectures comprising the book, the first—"The Moment Lost"—provides the most useful historical data. (The author engages in a considerable amount of unsystematic reminiscing throughout the work.) Moynihan reminds readers that until the mid-1960's, social policy in America focused exclusively on individuals. Employment statistics, for example, did not distinguish those who were unemployed fathers of large families. In the eyes of the government, these men were no different from teenagers seeking part-time work or women returning to the labor force after a period of child rearing. This individualistic emphasis, Moynihan notes, was not to be found in other industrial democracies. There, family allowances, maternity leave, and vocational rehabilitation programs had the expressed intention of nurturing family units. Aside from instinctive individualism—Americans are repelled by the idea of a person being awarded a job partly on the basis of his or her status as a parent—a major cause of the American obliviousness toward "organicist" policy perspectives is the failure of Roman Catholic social thought to register deeply on the intellectual community. (It seems possible that the notoriety which has greeted the Roman Catholic Bishops' Pastoral Letter on justice in the American economy may eventually change this.)

What finally brought family policy to center stage was a developing awareness that a certain group of black people was simply not going to be able to take advantage of the opportunities gained through the Civil Rights movement. In preparing his report, Moynihan had noted that especially for poor urban blacks, a lowering of the nation's rate of unemployment brought no perceptible decline in the level of welfare dependency or family stability. This fact led Moynihan to W. E. B. Du Bois, E. Franklin Frazier, and Kenneth Clark, black scholars who had long warned of the "self-perpetuating pathology" in America's "dark ghettos."

At first, the Moynihan report galvanized action and was persuasive. As the long hot summers, assassinations, and furious war protest swept the nation, however, Moynihan and "family policy" were attacked as racist, irrelevant, and paternalistic. When in 1970 Moynihan counseled Richard Nixon to commence an era of "benign neglect" in race relations, Moynihan's image as a hopeless racist was confirmed. (Moynihan emphasizes that this phrase was immediately followed by these words: "We may need a period when Negro progress continues and racial rhetoric fades.")

In looking back at the era, Moynihan finds himself in agreement with Glenn Loury's view that if blacks were to have made authentic progress, a civil rights strategy (emphasizing the iniquities of racial discrimination and redressing these iniquities through the courts) needed to give way to an economic and cultural strategy. This, Moynihan avers, was not something he clearly understood at the time. Meanwhile, the moment for well-constructed policy initiatives to benefit poor families passed. Not surprisingly, the condition of these families steadily deteriorated. By 1981, reports Moynihan, half of all babies born in that year were destined to live in a female-headed household at some point prior to their eighteenth birthday. This would be true for 40 percent of majority children and 75 percent of minority. More distressing was the fact that by 1980, 56 percent of poor families were headed by a female. Reflecting on the 1980 data for New York City, Moynihan states: "It would appear that half of the children then being born in America's largest and most important and 'wealthiest' city can expect to be on public assistance before they graduate from high school."

The burden of Moynihan's middle lecture, "In the War on Poverty, Poverty Won," is to put President Lyndon Johnson's Great Society in perspective. Moynihan tries to show that the social legislation of the period (apart from Medicare and Medicaid) was neither excessive nor revolutionary—and it certainly produced budgets far smaller than perhaps one might remember them to have been. "For if you would look for a *true* increase in the size of government—to 24 percent of gross national product—you must await the advent of the Reagan administration," he notes. He also argues that the period bequeathed notable achievements in the effort to eliminate poverty. For example, longitudinal studies of federal preschool programs have demonstrated lasting and important impacts.

Nevertheless, Moynihan is at pains to illuminate a shameful paradox about the Great Society's successes. Because of steadily improving benefits from Social Security (which received a major boost in the 1960's), there has been a virtual elimination of poverty among the nation's elderly. This is, to Moynihan's mind, "the most extraordinary achievement in the history of American social policy." Yet this success now serves to cast a sinister light over a particular segment of the population still living in poverty—for it now turns out that "the rate of poverty among the very young in the United States has become nearly seven times as great as among the old." The pattern seems to be that the nation's elderly, who vote in very large numbers, are exacting income transfers from poor and working-class families through the tax system. What is one to say about a "generous" welfare system in which expenditures for children amount to about a sixth of the total spent on the elderly?

"Common Ground," Moynihan's final address, ranges over the broad terrain of welfare policy. He is concerned to show that a healthy point of convergence has been reached among liberals and conservatives. Both groups, he suggests, agree on the urgency of the issue. When James Coleman writes that "it would appear that the process of making human beings human is breaking down in American society," assent is forthcoming from all points on the ideological spectrum. There is agreement, first, on the need for social scientific expertise in these matters; second, on the limitations of this very science ("but the main lesson of enquiry is that behavior is hard to explain and harder yet to modify"); and, third, on the thesis that no strategy of pure neglect is even thinkable. A sign of the gathering convergence of thought is the Reagan Administration's second-term tax reform proposals, which advocate reducing dramatically the tax burden on poor and middle-income Americans. All tax systems contain an implicit family policy, and the reigning system has viciously antifamily features (such as personal and dependent exemptions which are drastically disproportionate to the real costs of child rearing).

Moynihan also offers some policy imperatives which can, he believes, be widely subscribed to. The federal government should assume the full costs of the Aid to Families with Dependent Children (AFDC) program, establish a national benefit standard, and regularly adjust benefit levels in accordance with the cost-of-living index. Job-training programs for AFDC females must be enhanced, their value having been abundantly documented. Low-income families which adopt poor children should be given both direct subsidies and tax advantages. The principle that children are, in effect, *entitled* to full-time fathers is, insists Moynihan, commanding increasing assent. Thus, the rise in teenage pregnancy is a phenomenon that *must* be reversed. The principle of "male responsibility" must be enshrined at all levels of policy and "pressed to the point of punitiveness." Moynihan's voice rises here: "Hunt, hound, harass: the absent father is rarely really absent, especially the teenage father, but merely unwilling or not required to acknowledge his children's presence."

The moral outrage evident here is worrisome. Apart from the question of whether "get-tough" policies toward these citizens will be effective, there is the larger issue of how they arise in society. Massive long-term unemployment levels for job-seeking teenagers are obviously a causal factor. Moreover, the foreseeable work opportunities for low-achieving schoolchildren will do little to inspire educational discipline. If insecure, low-paying food-service or assembly-line labor is the certain outcome of effort (or non-effort), many will opt for economic strategies that promise glamour, high returns, and excitement. When sports does not provide the proper avenue, crime may, and it is questionable whether the criminal father is doing his offspring any favors by assenting to "the principle of legitimacy."

Moynihan is aware that male responsibility must be sustained by far-reaching changes in the political economy. The question is whether his awareness leads him to reach for bold enough solutions. "For the too-much-pitied unemployed teenage male," he writes, "there would be nothing wrong with a federal work program—compulsory when a court has previously ordered him to support his children—with the wages shared between father and mother." Noting the link between drug abuse and family breakdown, he outlines a control program which dramatically enhances the role of federal authorities.

As for employment, Moynihan regards it as a fundamental starting point, but he offers no vision of an employment strategy and, very curiously, ignores completely the innovative weaving of welfare payment, job training, and vocational counseling in California's new "workfare" program. Indeed, at the very point in the book when he could have evaluated such efforts, he shifts the discussion to doomsayers such as William J. Goode. This is an abrupt and frustrating way to end a presentation which delights in announcing an emerging liberal-conservative consensus on the need for a national family policy. Surely at such a rare moment, the community of the powerful (Moynihan is very near its center) ought to be afforded something more than the assurance that since everyone is talking about a problem, solutions cannot be far behind.

Readers would do better to skim *Family and Nation* for its very useful statistics (which can rarely be checked, since Moynihan provides few citations) and then move on to Michael Harrington's *The New American Poverty* (1984). Here the intellectuals' despair over poverty and family policy is reflected and partially overcome by a well-developed plan for transformation—a plan not so radical that it is irrelevant in Ronald Reagan's America. Harrington's book preceded Moynihan's, but the latter apparently did not read it. If he had, he might have given a far better set of Godkin lectures.

Leslie E. Gerber

Sources for Further Study

America. CLIV, March 22, 1986, p. 230.
Booklist. LXXXII, February 15, 1986, p. 838.
Fortune. CXIII, April 14, 1986, p. 131.
Kirkus Reviews. LIV, January 15, 1986, p. 117.
Los Angeles Times Book Review. March 23, 1986, p. 7.
National Review. XXXVIII, March 14, 1986, p. 49.
The New Republic. CXCIV, March 17, 1986, p. 30.
The New York Times Book Review. XCI, March 2, 1986, p. 9.
Publishers Weekly. CCXXIX, January 3, 1986, p. 45.
Washington Post Book World. XVI, February 2, 1986, p. 3.

A FAMILY MADNESS

Author: Thomas Keneally (1935-   )
Publisher: Simon and Schuster (New York). 336 pp. $17.95
Type of work: Novel
Time: 1984; 1941-1945
Locale: Sydney, Australia, and Eastern Europe

An elaborate dramatization of the collision between old and new histories, cultures, and ideals

> Principal characters:
> TERRY DELANEY, the protagonist, who is a semiprofessional footballer and part-time security guard
> DANIELLE KAPPEL, his mistress
> RADISLAW (RUDI) KAPPELSKI/KAPPEL, his employer and Danielle's father
> BRIAN STANTON, Terry's best friend and a part-time security guard
> GINA TERRACETTI DELANEY, Terry's wife

While it is not yet possible to provide a general assessment of the impact made in the United States by contemporary works of Australian art, there is no doubt that an impact of some magnitude has been felt among critics and tastemakers. Contemporary Australian writers, musicians, and filmmakers currently receive, for the most part deservedly, the quality of attention previously reserved for their British counterparts. Indeed, it may be that the relative decline of Great Britain as a source of artistic innovation has facilitated the emergence of one of its juridical dependencies, an emergence marked by a distinctive accent, resonant voice, and commendable ambition. Cultural historians will probably date this development from the formation of the Oz group in London in the late 1960's. From the standpoint of literary history, however, the coming into fashion of Australian fiction dates, perhaps accidentally, from the awarding of the Nobel Prize for Literature in 1973 to the novelist Patrick White, until then the only Australian novelist with an international reputation of any magnitude.

Among the Australian novelists who have come to the fore since 1973, pride of place goes to Thomas Keneally. Not only has he been his generation's most prolific novelist, but he has also been the most varied and inventive in his choice of material and been less confined than some of his contemporaries to his native land. Basically known as a historical novelist, he has written well-received novels on, among other areas, the American Civil War, Joan of Arc, and both world wars. The particular fascination of *A Family Madness* (his fifteenth novel) is that it confronts his native Australia with historical phenomena not of its making, resulting in a work that is both a continuation of the author's meditation on history and its human costs as well as a critique of the historical phenomena typical of the twentieth century.

Australia as a fresh, new, naïve, shallow society is very much to the fore

in *A Family Madness*. Not all those attributes are embodied in the protagonist, Terry Delaney. In his ordinariness, however, or, rather, in the authenticity of his unadulterated Australian persona, he provides access to them.
The principal means by which the author characterizes Terry's definitively
antipodean personality is that he plays Rugby League.

Unlike Rugby Union, the game played in the United States, the United
Kingdom, and in former British colonies, Rugby League is played profes-
sionally. In fact, part of its distinctive character is that it was originally conceived and organized in the industrial areas of Northern England with pro-
fessionalism in mind. As a result, it is virtually impossible to think about
Rugby League without thinking about social class—in particular, about the
creation and survival of indigenous working-class leisure activity. Although
Terry Delaney only plays in the equivalent of the minor leagues, the fact
that Rugby League is the game he plays (rather, the game to which he is
devoted) gives him an air of refractory independence, a sense of physical
staunchness, and a socially significant undercurrent of solidarity with his
neighborhood and his class. The author is doing something more subtle than
exploiting the fact that his fellow countrymen are sports lovers, for the sport
which Terry loves carries with it a large amount of social and cultural
freight.

The possibility of becoming indifferent to a sport which he not only loves
but which is also a medium of expression for him is allied to other challenges that beset Terry's Australian identity in the course of the novel.
Though not a member of the family whose madness the book recounts, he
is vulnerable to it, implicated in it, and ultimately changed by his encounter
with it. As a result of his involvement with the Kappels, his marriage enters
a rapid decline, his traditional Catholicism is of no avail, and he finds that
there is nothing in his own cultural heritage (originally Irish, like that of a
large number of Australians) which might help him to confront and outwit
what the Kappels represent. Finally, Terry has to confront the fact that he
has only his own capacity to suffer and endure to see himself through the
devastating events that form the novel's climax.

From a larger perspective than that which the novel's characters offer, *A
Family Madness* provides a painful, serious challenge to the republican-
tinged, virile, limited brand of citizenship that Terry—almost uniquely (the
exception being his father, Greg)—embodies. This challenge is all the more
formidable in view of the jaundiced view of modern Sydney that the novel in
passing provides. Confining itself largely to suburbia, the novel presents an
unattractive picture of an all too recognizable modern community, characterized by opportunism, corruption, crime, and the craven and transparent inadequacy of most forms of community culture (Penrith, Terry's Rugby
League club, survives largely from the proceeds of its clubhouse bar and slot
machines). In addition, many of the old neighborhoods are now inhabited

by emigrants from Southern and Eastern Europe, who, while they adapt to the social codes of a material civilization, bring with them moral and emotional codes which ostensibly have no place in a society such as that of contemporary Australia. In a sense, the tensions which Terry Delaney is forced to experience as a result of the novel's plot already exist, though less dramatically, in the society from which the plot derives.

Yet, *A Family Madness* is rather more than a sociological treatise on the social ills of contemporary Australia. Its domestic dimension is at once defined and augmented by the role in the novel of the Kappel family, whose madness shapes Terry's destiny and the book's action. The Kappels are anything but Australian, an observation which obviously derives from their national origins, but which is also supported by the quirky, private, asocial form into which their national and family heritages deteriorate. At the same time, however, the Kappels profoundly bear the burden and penalties of history, a category of existence which has no real parallel to the experiences which their new world domicile can provide. History belongs to the old world: Terry Delaney belongs admirably but vulnerably to the here and now. Though while the removal of the Kappels to Australia is to be understood as their survival of the cauldron of World War II, it turns out that they cannot forsake the scars of being so close to history's fires. These scars are the sterile origins of their madness.

In the new world, the Kappels have assumed a new name and a new way of life. Their name originally was Kappelski, and in the old world they were among the elite. Along with the change of name, there is a change of status. Rudi Kappel, son of a police chief, runs a security business. Rudi Kappel, heir to an at least dubious political heritage, now has succumbed to the futuristic meanderings of a superstitious old man. It is as a result of these changes, and of the fact that Rudi forms a bridge between the two worlds of his experience, that he and his family fall victim to madness. In the immediate sense, Rudi's despairing, apocalyptic dementia is responsible for his family's destruction. Ultimately, however, Rudi is himself a victim of the hysteria and horror which was such a prominent feature of all forms of social reality on the Eastern Front in the 1940's. It is part of this novel's richness that it remains faithful to a complex sense of Rudi's destiny and the experiences that shaped it, thereby delivering itself and the reader from a facile moralism to which the material might well have lent itself in less capable hands.

The Kappelskis are White Russian (Belorussian) in origin. Rudi's father, Stanislaw, had been chief of police in the town of Staroviche during a large part of World War II and had left that position to take up a ministerial post in the short-lived Belorussian national government that had been formed in 1944. In order for these events to take place, it was necessary for Belorussian national aspirations to ally themselves with Nazi Germany, and the strain of doing so is vividly embodied in the characterization of

Stanislaw, who, for the sake of a dream, is obliged to turn a blind eye to extermination squads and other more intimate atrocities. Yet, for him, anger over the manner in which Belorussia has been abused by the Soviet government makes the moral compromises of the alliance with the Nazis, if, not justified, then, acceptable. Nevertheless, at the collapse of the Eastern Front and the evacuation of the Kappelskis and other members of the Belorussian elite—in other words, at the most critical juncture of his public life—Stanislaw places his family before his nation. This choice, in turn, however, leads to a further and more profoundly tormenting irony, when he discovers his wife's totally unsuspected role in events, a discovery for which Mrs. Kappelski eventually pays with her life. It is worth noting that Danielle, Rudi's daughter, is named for his mother and that the daughter repeats by the nature of her exclusively personal experiences the victimization which the mother underwent directly as a result of historical circumstances. In both cases, the emotional generosity of the female, her regenerative capacity to place life above ideology, is shattered by the degenerative power of the male.

The origins of Rudi's madness are in his childhood, which was spent following the trajectory of his father's political fortunes. To begin with, the child led a life of privilege, pointedly exemplified by the fact that while mass execution of the town's Jewish population was being carried out, young Rudi was attending a picnic. His genial host on that occasion was a Nazi officer whom he had come to name Oncle Willy, a fey pederast and close friend of Rudi's mother. In that perhaps somewhat facile sense, Rudi has been shaped by a hideously unreal experience as a result of his father's historical and political status, but the novel does not delineate Rudi's formative experiences in a facile sense. He is party to both a Nazi idyll, in which his guide is the inimitable Willy, and to the Nazi nightmare, and in the latter case it is Willy who unwittingly provides access. Rudi is an inadvertent witness to Willy's assassination, an event which marks the fragile tenability of Nazi security in Staroviche and the paucity of popular support for their Belorussian puppets.

With the collapse of the Eastern Front, and the Kappelski family's flight into exile, Rudi is exposed to yet further horror by being a pawn in the power struggle within the rapidly splintering Belorussian ranks. The child's impotence and abject vulnerability powerfully reenact the principal human effect of history's operation during the years in question. The survival of such an impact in the form of nightmare is all too credible in Rudi's case.

What gives Rudi his unnerving presence, however, is not his embodiment of history's deleterious effects but his compulsion to act on the destructive energies to which he is heir. In order to relieve the tension generated by such energies, he espouses survivalism, determined that when the nuclear holocaust (which he calls The Wave—perhaps the novel's most subtle employment of a term with a peculiarly Australian, beachlife connotation) occurs, the Kappels will finally inherit their posthistorical kingdom. When Rudi despairs of this eventuality, he exterminates the family.

This drastic event takes place precisely when the family has been enlarged by the arrival of its first unmixed Australian—Alexandra, daughter of Terry and Danielle. The new life which the baby symbolizes, however, cannot be allowed to develop. The perhaps morally childish, or at least underdeveloped, new world remains susceptible to the dark forces of the old. As Rudi tells Terry: "Sometimes, Mr. Delaney, history *does* make its claim on people." Rudi's tragedy is that he had no choice about the nature or quality of those claims. Terry, on the contrary, by virtue of his affair with Danielle, desires to create a history for himself and to choose the means of doing so. This is what Rudi can never permit; he will take all he holds dear to his grave rather than permit it.

The great strength of *A Family Madness* is its artful twinning of themes, destinies, and worlds. Belorussia, a history without a country, is the inverted double of Australia, a country without a history (that is, a history on the European model). Danielle, whose evening literature classes suggest her desire to imagine her way free of her heritage, is partnered with Terry, who finds himself helplessly attracted to the idea of outgrowing the obligations and expectations of his Sydney background. Stanislaw Kappelski's collaboration with evil in the name of political expediency is re-created by his son's identification with the forces of superstition and catastrophe. The irruption into the frail civic structure of everyday Sydney life of age-old unresolved hostilities and ineradicable nightmares violates the promise of ahistoric newness which Australia, a country originally conceived of in terms of expiation, may be perceived to offer.

Yet, in spite of the novel's rich material and the author's deft deployment of it, *A Family Madness* finally fails to cohere effectively. This failure is largely the result of Keneally's formal choices. The Kappel family history is communicated by means of two main documents. One is Stanislaw's wartime diary, miraculously preserved and fortuitously restored to Rudi's sister. The other—its latter-day counterpart—is Rudi's informal family history. While both these texts succeed in bringing to life the plot's larger personal and historical dimensions, neither succeeds in convincingly portraying Belorussia. The reasons for Stanislaw's collaboration are clearly stated, but the practical implications of the dream of Belorussian autonomy are never explored. Such an omission may be intended as a mute indictment of the collaborator's ardent but impossible romanticism. Yet, as the presumably intentional closeness of Kabbel to "cabal" suggests, it is difficult to view Belorussian political aspirations as more than a mixture of sentimentality and opportunism. By attempting to create their own history, the Belorussian nationalists become history's most problematical victims. As Terry Delaney testifies, the sins of the father are visited upon the children.

George O'Brien

Sources for Further Study

Contemporary Review. CCXLVIII, January, 1986, p. 45.
Kirkus Reviews. LIV, January 1, 1986, p. 9.
The London Review of Books. VII, November 7, 1985, p. 24.
New Statesman. CX, October 4, 1985, p. 28.
The New York Times Book Review. XCI, March 16, 1986, p. 9.
The New Yorker. LXII, May 19, 1986, p. 118.
Newsweek. CVII, March 31, 1986, p. 70.
Publishers Weekly. CCXXIX, January 17, 1986, p. 62.
Time. CXXVII, March 31, 1986, p. 70.
Times Literary Supplement. October 18, 1985, p. 1169.

A FATHER'S WORDS

Author: Richard Stern (1928-   )
Publisher: Arbor House (New York). 189 pp. $14.95
Type of work: Novel
Time: The 1980's
Locale: Chicago

A comic, sensitive novel about a father struggling to understand why his older son did not grow up as he had expected

> *Principal characters:*
> CY RIEMER, the protagonist, fifty-five years old, the editor of a science newsletter
> MOM and
> DAD, his parents
> JACK, his oldest son, a seeming ne'er-do-well
> JENNY,
> LIVY, and
> BEN, his other children, who are more successful and stable than Jack
> AGNES, Cy's former wife
> EMMA, Cy's lover, who is much younger than he
> BILLY JUGIELLO, an investment broker
> MARIA ROBUSTO, Jack's wife

A Father's Words, Richard Stern's seventh novel, has the same qualities that made his previous six critical successes: believable and humane characters, literate prose, and a fresh interpretation of a conventional story. In this novel, the refreshed convention is the tale of a son living out, up to, or short of his father's expectations. Usually the son is the dynamic figure in such a novel; his character is in flux and formation while the father is fixed. As the son decides whether to imitate, surpass, or rebel against the model of the parent, the father remains unchanging in his social and psychological identity. The father may be an admirable hero, a relentless tyrant, or a lovable eccentric, but he is fixed.

Stern's distinctive touch is to make the father as much a character in the process of development as his children. Cy Riemer may be fifty-five years old, may have worked at the same editing job for thirty years, and may have spent his entire adult life in Chicago, but he is still maturing intellectually, emotionally, and psychologically. The key to Cy's character is his realization that fatherhood is not a plateau but an upward slope. His four children are in their twenties or thirties, but Cy is not finished fathering them. At this age, other men may be content with being the lighthouse that signals a haven to the storm-tossed boats of their children's lives, but Cy is more like a buoy, in the same heaving sea as the boats.

The novel is Cy's first-person account of his eventful fifty-fifth year. It is a year of loss, separation, challenge, and reconciliation. The important losses are the deaths of his parents and his former wife's departure from Chicago.

The first causes Cy to meditate upon the legacies (emotional and psychological rather than financial) his parents have left and upon his own record of filial devotion. The second marks the end of a family tradition, because Agnes' home was the place, even after the divorce, where the Riemers gathered as one family for the holidays. The separations are also two: the open estrangement from his older son, Jack, whose knockabout life has always worried Cy, and the subtle estrangement from Emma, his lover, whose quiet hints about marriage and settling down Cy politely but firmly ignores. How Cy responds to the challenges posed by loss and separation composes the plot.

What pulls Cy through is the old-fashioned, rare virtue of love. He is able to live up to his qualified boast in the opening chapter, "I've always thought I was a loved father as I am—on the whole—a loving one." There is little sentimentality or posturing in Cy's love; it is not the maudlin, easy affection of the greeting card. It is rather an active caring, proving itself by constant involvement. Cy is frequently in touch with his children by letter, telephone, or visit. A steady stream of words keeps Cy informed about Ben, Livy, Jenny, and Jack: their work, their worries, the state of their hearts. These conversations can be rough-and-tumble; they consist of "accusation, analysis, and critical gossip" ("the family sport," Cy calls it). Father and children communicate by analyzing themselves and one another, just as Cy's mother taught him. She was the one who, as Dad put it, "knew the score" about an untrustworthy world and about the need for family members to guard one another from self-deception.

If Mom's legacy to Cy is the craving to analyze, Dad's gift is unflagging optimism and good cheer. Without them, the family sport could not endure. Cy has always supported his children with cheerful talk as well as timely checks. He has striven to "tell them about books and truths," so inculcating them with the spoken and written word that two have published books, and all four are relentless conversationalists and avid readers. Though not all of Cy's conversations or visits end peaceably, they never disrupt the family harmony: The stream of calls and letters continues, the children come home for the holidays.

Underlying Cy's active parenting is the realization that knowing his children does not mean automatically understanding them. Parenting is, after all, an art rather than a science. It possesses its own misconceptions and obstacles. As influential as a father is upon his children's lives, he cannot control them; at best he is a "semicompanion, semiprotector, and . . . semiconductor." The best moments for a father to accompany, protect, and conduct are not always apparent, but Cy has learned from experience that he cannot avoid intervening out of fear of making mistakes. Because he loves, he acts correctly most of the time; because he is loved, his mistakes are forgiven.

In his eventful fifty-fifth year, Cy finds that his children need different degrees of companionship and conducting. Ben hardly needs any. He is much like Cy: A successful writer, he has a relationship with a loving woman and is ready for the responsibilities of fatherhood. Jenny is almost as complete: A contented spouse and a successful writer like Ben, Jenny travels and researches with her husband. Only her reluctance to start a family worries Cy: Clearly, she needs some talking to. Livy, the younger girl, needs emotional support as well as practical advice. Lonely for a steady man in her life, Livy has thrown herself into a career in law enforcement; now with her third agency, Livy has yet to find her niche. Yet Livy is strong: After a hug and a homily from Cy, she is ready to go on. Jack is the child who really needs companionship and conducting, but he is the one who resists Cy the most.

Jack begins this year no better off than he was in any of the previous ten. Still unable to settle into a career, he moves from dead-end job to unemployment back to dead-end job. His personal life still consists of one-night stands and temporary liaisons. His personal habits remain slovenly: He is always content with one pair of jeans and a flannel shirt for a wardrobe and with popcorn and candy bars for sustenance. Jack's condition worries and frustrates Cy: He worries that Jack is in danger, and he is frustrated that Jack seems to care so little for the decent middle-class life toward which he was pointed.

During his fifty-fifth year, Cy finally seems able to conduct Jack positively. One of Cy's friends gets Jack a job with the Chicago stock exchange and introduces him to the beautiful, irrepressible Maria Robusto. Work and romance produce results quickly: Jack soon has a high income and a fiancée. Cy tries to be pleased, stifling his worry that Jack is making money too easily and laying aside any prejudices about Maria's father being a maker of pornographic films. When Maria marries Jack and takes him to New York, where both can make their fortunes, Cy believes that Jack has finally graduated from adolescence.

Cy's feelings are not all altruistic or parental. He and Jack have a special reciprocity that is both pleasurable and painful: "I'm both his model and his despair," Cy notes, "he's the dye which shows up my inadequacy." If Jack is now settled, then Cy must be as well, which is what Emma keeps hinting at.

Unexpectedly, the marriage and Jack soon fall apart. Cy visits him to hear the gory details but hears much more than merely a lover's lament. Jack repudiates everything his father taught him to want or value: self-pride, the good life, loving connections with others. Whether grandiose gesture or honest despair, Jack's outburst estranges him from Cy.

A lesser lover of family than Cy might have been dismayed. Jack's desertion could seem like the final blow in an already difficult year. Yet there is one more turn to the screw of Cy's emotional upheaval: Returning from the unhappy interview with Jack, Cy learns from Emma that she is pregnant and intends to keep the baby. For a moment Cy is tempted to think only of "the drudgery of a child's demands" that starting a new family—at his age, no less—will bring. He realizes, however, that this temptation results from his own fear of commitment. It is the same fear that Cy has always thought prevented Jack from choosing work and a mate and now makes him reject everything after the break with Maria. At this moment, Jack is indeed the dye revealing Cy's own potential inadequacy. To reject Emma is to choose Jack's way; to embrace her and the baby is to take a risk—but the one risk that can again bestow upon Cy the "bizarre, unearned excitement of family life."

A second surprise follows quickly upon the first. Unpredictably, Jack takes work as a television situation-comedy writer and scripts the season's most successful show. The most popular of the program's characters is the loud-mouthed father of a screwball family: Brash, funny, obnoxious, the father steals the show. Cy is stung by the characterization, convinced that Jack is simply venting hostility toward his father through the depiction of the fictional parent. Just as he makes the charge, Cy realizes that he may have done the same to Jack: "I've had this version of you, have thought about you in a certain way, have spoken to others about you that way, maybe even persuaded you that that's the way you are." In that realization that a father's words may inadequately define the son lies Jack and Cy's reconciliation. There is more to Cy than his words, though they seem so often to predominate. His visits, his nettled reaction to Jack's television show, and his embracing of Emma all prove that there is more to Cy than words.

Not surprisingly, in a novel where words are so important in revealing character, one of *A Father's Words'* strengths is its language. Stern's prose is crisp, allusive, and clever. The witty, epigrammatic style is signaled by the opening sentence: "I was raised by decent hypocrites to respect truth." The style befits a narrator who is intelligent, undergoes a rapid ebb and flow of emotion, and loves to communicate surprising truths to his children. When Cy narrates, the story is as sprightly as his thoughts. When the narration stops to record dialogue, the pace does not flag, because all Riemers are "athletes of the mouth," nimble verbal players in the game of words. Yet ultimately Cy is the authoritative voice, a wise philosopher about the paradoxical pains and pleasures of parenthood.

Stern's literary cleverness is also evident in the details of character and action that reverberate with meaning. Cy's newsletter, for example, is a marvelous measure of the man; it is an outward sign of his inward graces. He has been the sole editor for thirty loyal years, through lean subscription years and fat, as nurturing and attentive to its issues as to his children's growth. The newsletter's varied content (from the latest news in astrophysics to discoveries about animal mating habits) reflects the curious, restless intelligence of its editor, who cannot let go his mother's need to analyze the world and his father's strength to love it. The strange contortions the newsletter experiences in Cy's fifty-fifth year (first he opens its pages to kinky personal advertisements, then he anthologizes its best pieces with the pornographer's daughter's money) mirror this father's efforts to remain open to his children even when they explore unfamiliar territories.

Just as rich for its metaphorical implications is Cy's relationship with his stockbroker, Billy Jugiello. The way Cy invests is a subtle, yet precise metaphor for his involved, unpredictable, honest approach to fatherhood. Cy consults with Billy only by telephone, never in person, trusting as much in the man's voice and words as in his professional credentials. When stock prices rise and fall without forewarning or explanation, Cy's profits advance and ebb. Buoyed by Billy's reassuring tone and heartfelt sympathy, Cy learns to roll with the market's punches. After several years of envisioning a young, dark-haired, Italian-looking Billy on the other end of the line, Cy finally sees his picture on a Christmas card photograph—and discovers that he is a middle-aged, balding black man. Cy is no better at estimating how Jack will turn out than he is at guessing Billy's appearance. Yet being right about the externals matters little in comparison to knowing and understanding the internal qualities of a person. Parenting is like playing the market: a risky business attempted most safely when one trusts the person at the other end of the fragile communication cord.

Robert M. Otten

Sources for Further Study

Best Sellers. XLVI, July, 1986, p. 130.
Booklist. LXXXII, April 1, 1986, p. 1099.
Chicago. XXXV, August, 1986, p. 80B.
Kirkus Reviews. LIV, February 15, 1986, p. 246.
Library Journal. CXI, April 15, 1986, p. 97.
Los Angeles Times Book Review. May 4, 1986, p. 1.
The New York Times Book Review. XCI, June 15, 1986, p. 15.
Newsweek. CVII, March 24, 1986, p. 74.
Publishers Weekly. CCXXIX, February 21, 1986, p. 156.
Washington Post. May 9, 1986, p. D6.

FDR
The New Deal Years, 1933-1937, a History

Author: Kenneth S. Davis (1912-   )
Publisher: Random House (New York). 756 pp. $29.95
Type of work: Biography
Time: 1933-1937
Locale: The United States

A study of Franklin D. Roosevelt's first administration

Principal personages:
FRANKLIN D. ROOSEVELT, thirty-second President of the United States, 1933-1945
ELEANOR ROOSEVELT, his wife
LOUIS HOWE, Roosevelt's aide and political adviser
HARRY HOPKINS, a Works Progress Administration director
HAROLD ICKES, a National Recovery Administration director
RAYMOND MOLEY, a New Deal brain truster
HUEY LONG, a Louisiana senator and critic of FDR

In the grand tradition of richly textured biographies, this masterly account of Franklin D. Roosevelt's first presidential term in office is a worthy sequel to Davis' *FDR: The Beckoning of Destiny, 1882-1928, a History* (1972) and *FDR: The New York Years, 1928-1933* (1985). Tackling the most overworked and (arguably) least dramatic facet of FDR's life and times, the author recounts the New Deal years in a manner both subtle and provocative.

In a prologue aptly titled "The State of the World, March 2, 1933," Davis declares that out-of-control forces of barbarism and technology were threatening Western Civilization and that America seemed to be the world's last hope. Attention focused upon a "physically crippled man who had been chosen to lead a crippled nation out of sick depression." It was a moment of supreme crisis—and opportunity—for a leader whose physical affliction had bred courage, patience, and resilience.

Dividing his topic into four parts, Davis judges the New Deal to have been a political triumph but a disappointment in terms of its economic moderation. Part 1 describes the flurry of activity during the onset of the New Deal, the press conferences, fireside chats, and legislative accomplishments of the "First Hundred Days," when FDR gave the country a transfusion of hope, even though he had only a vague blueprint for recovery. Part 2 deals with the bogging down of the programs of the so-called First Hundred Days, as Roosevelt's policies failed to end the Depression or to satisfy critics on the Left and Right. Part 3 documents the high tide of reform during the so-called "Second New Deal" of 1935, as Roosevelt finally threw his weight behind meaningful labor, welfare, tax, and regulatory legislation. Part 4, entitled "The Man Becomes the Issue," shows how the 1936 election became a popularity contest rather than a mandate for specific policy issues.

Liberal historians, such as Arthur M. Schlesinger, William E. Leuchtenburg, and James MacGregor Burns, have richly mined this same topic, sympathetically portraying Roosevelt as a Progressive pragmatist. During the 1960's, new-left historians criticized the New Deal as a promise unfulfilled, which failed to help (in a meaningful way) those very groups—such as migrant workers and blacks—that were the least organized and the most dispossessed. The most compelling revisionist interpretation, Paul Conkin's *The New Deal* (1967), insisted that FDR's programs were neither pragmatically implemented nor logically consistent and failed to bring about either recovery or a social revolution. As Conkin glibly concluded: "The New Deal solved a few problems, ameliorated a few more, obscured many, and created new ones." For the most part, Davis accepts and amplifies upon Conkin's thesis to produce fresh and surprising conclusions cogently argued and buttressed with solid research.

The essence of the New Deal was improvisation: This was its genius and its flaw, for improvisation was no substitute for rational planning. Book 1 commences with lines from Walt Whitman's "Song of Myself":

> Do I contradict myself?
> Very well then I contradict myself.
> (I am large, I contain multitudes.)

Roosevelt compared his leadership role to that of a football quarterback who has a general game plan but who wisely calls but one play at a time. The key was flexibility: "If the darn thing doesn't work, we can say so quite frankly, but at least try it." As he knew, the times demanded immediate action. Coming on the heels of Herbert Hoover's cautious, orthodox, failed presidency, Roosevelt and his aura of confidence generated optimism. Justice Oliver Wendell Holmes keenly assessed the thirty-second President: "A second-class intellect, but a first-class temperament."

Roosevelt's values were basically those of an aristocratic country squire imbued with a sense of *noblesse oblige* and a love for the political process. The campaign trail invigorated him almost as much as sailing. Yet, Davis claims, he did not lust for power like, say, a Huey Long or an Adolf Hitler. "The fun and excitement of politics as game would have been lost to him in a grant of despotic authority." In economic matters, FDR's instincts were conservative. He believed in the efficacy of balanced budgets, save in times of dire emergency, and set out to save—albeit reform—the free enterprise system. Davis argues convincingly that public sentiment and the congressional mood were to the left of Roosevelt in 1933 and that he acted as a brake against more radical change. His National Recovery Administration (NRA) was more conservative than the congressional alternative, a thirty-hour work week. The Agricultural Adjustment Administration was less sweeping than proposals for a cost-of-production guarantee. Roosevelt's initial inclination was to oppose federal insurance of bank deposits, and he opposed veterans' bonus payments, even though he astutely arranged for the Bonus Marchers to be given food, shelter, medical care, rail passage home, and an exemption allowing them to join the Civilian Conservation Corps (CCC). Davis sums up the achievements of the First Hundred Days as a series of halfway measures, with the only real revolution being in the manner of FDR's political style.

Davis writes in a readable manner, although he frequently resorts to the old-fashioned device of introducing episodes with weather reports and has a tendency to piggyback adjectives in the manner of *Time* magazine during Henry Luce's heyday ("big, bald, immensely likeable James A. Farley," for example). There are also many nagging references to his two previous *FDR* volumes. Even so, the cumulative effect of the narrative is absorbing. One becomes convinced that the author is in command of his topic and is presenting just the right amount of detail. Richly anecdoted and gossipy— in fact, some might find excessive the details about the First Lady's lesbian friends and the sexual peccadilloes of Hugh Johnson and Harold Ickes— Davis' tome is enlivened with moments of comic relief as well as high drama. The flirtations, affairs, and petty rivalries which FDR seems to have encouraged reveal a human side too often left out of political biographies.

Most biographers have portrayed Roosevelt as somewhat of an enigma, who easily became a confidant to others but who maintained an inner reserve behind an exterior of unruffled affability. Davis shows how FDR needed the homey environment of Hyde Park, Warm Springs, and Campobello Island as well as the utter devotion of aides such as Louis Howe and Gus Gennerich. Their deaths grieved FDR deeply and increased his isolation. Gennerich suffered a cerebral hemorrhage shortly after hitting his head during a "pollywog" initiation ritual as the presidential party crossed the equator on board the *USS Indianapolis* en route to Buenos Aires. Howe had been a stabilizing influence who tempered FDR's tendency to "yield too much to his enemies, or as was equally likely, he might overreact and 'fly off the handle.'" His demise robbed FDR of a valuable adviser and, more important, someone who could "supply the toe-holds." While Roosevelt was more a manager than an inaugurator of policy, he took special interest in such conservation measures as the Tennessee Valley Authority, the CCC, and the shelterbelt program. Likewise, Eleanor's pet project was Arthurdale, a model program of the Subsistence Homestead Division of the Public Works Administration. The First Lady's paternalism was a mixed blessing, however, and in fact, Eleanor is portrayed during these years as rather pathetic—often crabby and carping when not dreaming of Lorena Hickok, who was often off on assignment for the Works Progress Administration.

Whereas Davis praises FDR's temperament as magnificent in so many ways, he also does not obscure his deviousness or his (in Davis' words) sadistic need to dominate others. This could come out in relatively harmless form in a conversation or in the way he teased sensitive subordinates. On the other hand, it could at times be cruel and vindictive. Liberal biographers have justified FDR's refusal to cooperate with lame-duck President Herbert Hoover during the Depression winter of 1932-1933, but Davis implies that FDR enjoyed his predecessor's discomfort, and by eschewing opportunities for cooperation he was negligent in a time of dire emergency. Likewise, by staffing agencies with men whose differences seemed irreconcilable, and then telling them to work out those differences, he virtually negated the chance of efficient bureaucratic direction.

One of the fascinating sidelights of the New Deal years is the irrational hatred of FDR among many of the wealthy class. The policies of the First New Deal were not antibusiness. Why then did the President come to be regarded as a traitor to his class? Why were there sick jokes, innuendoes, rumors, and malicious lies? This ingratitude stung, it was, in Davis' words, "more bitter than winter's wind, sharper than the serpent's tooth." Much of the anti-Roosevelt sentiment was partisan and at times pathological, but there was also the feeling that the President was devious and disdainful, that he could not be trusted. It was not so much what he had done as what he might do in the future. The very rhetoric that won for him such a large public following stuck in the craw of those whose status was threatened and who were accustomed to more deferential treatment.

Davis is a master of rendering three-dimensional character sketches—whether it be the sensitive curmudgeon Harold Ickes or the vain brain truster Raymond Moley, both of whom suffered frequent losses of face from the President. Before being undercut, Moley held forth at the London Economic Conference, where "the fawning attentions now paid him by the highest foreign dignitaries went to his head like wine." Congress of Industrial Organizations leader John L. Lewis is described as being "every bit as theatrically colorful as [NRA administrator] Hugh Johnson and far tougher, far braver, far more certain." The appointment of Joseph P. Kennedy as chairman of the Securities and Exchange Commission proved the old adage "Set a thief to catch a thief." Georgia governor Eugene Talmadge is dismissed as a "gallus-snapping racial bigot and total reactionary." On the other hand, Huey Long is presented as a shrewd politician and—for all his blarney—a perceptive critic of the "fundamental New Deal indecisiveness" over policies affecting agriculture, business, and relief. In fact, Long was on target in summing up the results of the First New Deal with this sarcastic epitaph: "It's all right to say it, but be damn sure you don't intend to do it." Most liberal historians stress what a threat the Louisiana "kingfish" was to democratic institutions while ignoring or justifying Roosevelt's unleashing of federal agencies in an effort to derail his political rival.

The summer of 1934 was a critical turning point in FDR's first administration. The economy was sluggish. Labor radicalism and farm militancy were on the rise. Surfacing was a host of critics espousing unworkable nostrums. It looked as though the New Deal had come to a grinding halt. Then came the Democratic mandate in the 1934 congressional elections and the move away from the politics of consensus during the Second New Deal with the passing of Social Security, the National Labor Relations Act, the Public Utilities Holding Company Act, and the Wealth Tax Act.

Not only had business hostility and the Supreme Court's intransigence forced FDR's hand, but the popularity of Francis Townsend, Huey Long, and Father Charles Coughlin had their effect as well. As Harold Ickes had recommended, a move to the Left was necessary "to hold" the country. A little reform was needed to stave off more radical change. Little noticed during the 1935 legislative session was the establishment, by executive order, of the Rural Electrification Administration, one of the most successful and far-reaching New Deal government agencies.

Then came the climactic 1936 presidential election. In his acceptance speech in Philadelphia, the President had thrown the gauntlet to the forces of "selfishness," as he labeled his opponents. "Better the occasional faults of a Government that lives in a spirit of charity," he intoned, "than the consistent omissions of a Government frozen in the ice of its own indifference." FDR's favorite campaign parable was about a gentleman in a silk hat saved four years before from drowning. Profusely thankful then, the old man later complained bitterly that his savior hadn't pulled out his hat, too. Campaigning in Emporia, Kansas, FDR spotted Republican editor William Allen White in the crowd, invited him onto the dais, and mischievously called him a "very good friend of mine for three and a half years out of every four."

Perhaps it would have been unrealistic to have expected Roosevelt to unveil a court-packing scheme or any specific legislative proposals at a time when businessmen were disseminating misinformation about Social Security payroll deductions and the constitutionality of the Wagner Act. Even so, the election was prelude to what Davis calls a series of "disastrous errors of judgment, psychologically motivated, which . . . followed hard upon the election's outcome." More on that will no doubt follow in volume 4.

Davis finds much to criticize in Roosevelt's first term: the failure to nationalize the banking system, the paucity of help for tenant farmers, the unwillingness to make national health insurance part of Social Security, granting to commercial airlines lucrative postal contracts rather than letting the Air Corps handle the mail, and, in foreign affairs, allowing trade with Italy despite its aggression in Ethiopia while forbidding arms sales to the Spanish Loyalists besieged by well-supplied Fascist forces. Summing up, Davis praises FDR as a marvelously inspirational leader who kept the worst from happening in an era where liberal democracies were faring poorly. Still, his caution and conservatism torpedoed any chance for a genuine social revolution.

Candid in revealing his own political biases, Davis achieves his purpose in conveying a sense of how worse the country could have been without a leader of Roosevelt's talents as well as a tragic sense of possibilities lost. Stimulating and liberating, the book leaves this reader looking forward with great anticipation to its sequel.

James B. Lane

Sources for Further Study

Booklist. LXXXIII, September 1, 1986, p. 25.
Kirkus Reviews. LIV, July 15, 1986, p. 1087.
Library Journal. CXI, September 15, 1986, p. 85.
The New York Times Book Review. XCI, September 28, 1986, p. 3.
The New Yorker. LXII, October 27, 1986, p. 144.
Publishers Weekly. CCXXX, July 4, 1986, p. 53.
Washington Post Book World. XVI, October 26, 1986, p. 5.

FIDEL
A Critical Portrait

Author: Tad Szulc (1926-   )
Publisher: William Morrow and Company (New York). 703 pp. $19.95
Type of work: Biography
Time: 1927 to the mid-1980's
Locale: Cuba

A life and times of Fidel Castro and the Cuban revolution

> *Principal personages:*
> FIDEL CASTRO, leader of Cuba since 1959
> RAÚL CASTRO, his brother and heir apparent
> FULGENCIO BATISTA, Cuban chief of state ousted during the revolution
> ERNESTO (CHE) GUEVARA, a revolutionary Cuban leader
> NIKITA KHRUSHCHEV, Premier of the Soviet Union, 1958-1964

In 1985, Fidel Castro put this question to journalist Tad Szulc: "Will your political and ideological viewpoint allow you to tell objectively my story and the revolution's story when the Cuban government and I make the necessary material available to you?" An impossible task, perhaps, but nevertheless, Szulc has succeeded admirably in fashioning a critical, yet admiring portrait of Cuba's "Maximum Leader" while disclaiming any intention of attempting a definitive history of the achievements and problems of the regime over which Castro has presided for more than a quarter century.

Szulc first met Castro in 1959 while a correspondent for *The New York Times*. Since then, some right-wing cold warriors have accused *The New York Times* of abetting Castro's rise to power by portraying him in flattering terms. Szulc's initial conversations, however, did not take place until shortly after the triumph of the Cuban revolution. The two men next met in 1961 when Castro took the reporter on a tour of the Bay of Pigs battlefield. After a twenty-three-year hiatus Szulc returned to interview Castro for *Parade* magazine. The idea for a book-length biography germinated from discussions held during a long January weekend in 1984. During subsequent discussions Szulc visited the site of Castro's imprisonment on the Isle of Pines, climbed the Sierra Maestra to survey Castro's rebel headquarters, inspected the site where Castro landed on board the *Granma* upon his return from exile in Mexico, and attended diplomatic receptions at the Palace of the Revolution. Szulc interviewed literally scores of old associates and comrades-in-arms, many of whom occupy high posts in the present regime.

Both the author and his subject believe that personality can be a crucial ingredient in social change. A student of history, Castro built his revolutionary movement on themes espoused by his nineteenth century role model, José Julián Martí: namely, nationalism, radicalism, racial equality, social justice, suspicion of the United States, and agrarian reform. "Dizzyingly imaginative" yet "ruthless and cunning," Castro, Szulc claims, is both "the hero of humble mankind and, at the same time, the repressive Communist dictator." Castro's life, the author concludes, proves the sad theorem that "without power, ideals cannot be realized; with power they seldom survive."

Castro is a man of paradoxes: both shy and boisterous; an intellectual yet a man of action; a moralist but also a Machiavellian; impulsive and manipulative. Fascinated with political theory as well as religious doctrine, Fidel sees in the "theology of liberation" a synthesis between Christianity and revolutionary socialism.

Szulc found that Castro at times "clearly desired to swathe his past, especially his early youth, in a cocoon of oblivion." Based largely on oral histories, *Fidel: A Critical Portrait* is sketchy on Castro's family life, detailed on the political activities of his law-school years, and absolutely riveting on his seemingly hopeless guerrilla activities during the period between Fulgencio Batista's 1952 coup d'état and the triumphant march from the Sierra Maestra. Most valuable is the section entitled "The Revolution (1959-1963)," which shows how Castro solidified his power despite the machinations of old-time Communists and the deep-seated American hostility that led to assassination plots, the Bay of Pigs invasion, and the Missile Crisis. The final section, entitled "The Maturity (1964-1986)," is the weakest; still it contains arresting anecdotes about Cuba's peripatetic ruler—"frustrated one day, triumphant the next"—who is certain of his own righteousness.

With style and sophistication, Szulc juxtaposes Castro's political coming of age as a law student in Havana with a synthesis of how Batista thwarted democracy and consolidated his political grip during the late 1940's and early 1950's. In many ways, university politics mirrored and influenced national developments. Castro emerged as a headstrong but cagey pragmatist whose frenetic activities during a time of gangsterism and factionalism seemed almost suicidal. An admirer of Karl Marx and Vladimir Ilyich Lenin, he nevertheless was wary of Cuban Communists. Instead, he belonged to the *Ortodoxo* Party, founded by the charismatic senator Eduardo Chibás. An anti-imperialist, he supported Puerto Rican independence, an end to American control of the Panama Canal, and the overthrow of Dominican dictator Rafael Trujillo. In fact, in 1949 he participated in an aborted invasion of the Dominican Republic, tried to orchestrate a popular revolt against the government of Colombia, and protested the desecration by American sailors of a statue of José Martí in Havana's Central Park.

Was Castro a Communist prior to taking power, or did American animosity force him into the arms of the Russians? Szulc believes that this frequently debated question oversimplifies the issue and that the Cuban leader was, above all, a nationalist radicalized by events. In fact, given the degree to which the island was a satellite of the United States, Szulc believes that social revolution was necessary in order for Cuba to achieve "its full national independence." The suspension of democratic elections by Batista in 1952 was a crucial turning point for Castro, who had been planning to run for a seat in the Chamber of Deputies. Shortly after Senator Chibás shot himself during a radio broadcast as an act of protest, Castro and other *Ortodoxo* Party members formed the 26th of July Movement. Castro proved especially adept at leading street actions—such as infiltrating a parade with protest marchers on the hundredth anniversary of José Martí's birth and holding a funeral procession for martyrs of police brutality. It was but a short step from such revolutionary gestures to the 1953 attack on the Moncada barracks.

The Moncada barracks incident was a fiasco from a military standpoint and resulted in a twenty-two-month prison sentence for Castro, yet it solidified his credentials as the most outspoken foe of the government. Defending himself at his trial adorned in a black robe, Castro concluded a two-hour summation by declaring: "Condemn me, it does not matter. *History will absolve me!*" Walking away in handcuffs, he asked a young reporter whether he had gotten it all down. Despite being immobilized in solitary confinement, he remained Cuba's most famous insurgent. Then followed his exile in Mexico, the nightmarish crossing aboard the *Granma*, twenty-five months of guerrilla activity from his base atop the Sierra Maestra, and finally his triumphant march to power in the wake of Batista's collapse.

Thirty years old at the time he took to the hills of Oriente province in December of 1956, the Jesuit-educated young lawyer seemed like "just another Caribbean troublemaker of whose existence the Eisenhower administration was not even aware." In fact, America was pretty much in ignorance about social conditions in Cuba, in contrast to Castro's awareness of the historical role played by the United States in making his nation a virtual colony. America's ignorance of Cuba and Castro's fascination with the United States are two themes running throughout Szulc's book.

Szulc suggests that Castro's love-hate relationship with the United States is not unlike that of a rebellious child who secretly yearns for approval from his spurned parents. His anti-Americanism dates to his student days, although he spent his honeymoon in New York and considered enrolling at Columbia University. While he foresaw his destiny as waging war against American imperialism, Castro has avidly courted American journalists, clerics, congressmen, and celebrities. His curiosity on these occasions is seemingly boundless. For example, he grilled an oilman on offshore drilling techniques, a pilot on jet aircraft, and a rice broker on planting techniques. He is fascinated by the Kennedy brothers and among his greatest regrets is that he never had the opportunity to converse at length with Ernest Hemingway (the two met only once at the Barlovento Yacht Club, where Castro caught the biggest blue marlin at the novelist's annual fishing tournament).

For America, the late 1950's was a time of missed opportunities. Szulc reports that the Central Intelligence Agency (CIA) actually gave the rebels some surreptitious support for a brief time. More indicative of American attitudes and future policy was the statement by Eisenhower's ambassador that Castro was a rabble-rouser.

Before long, the CIA was plotting Castro's overthrow and then his assassination. In fact, Szulc claims, as early as March of 1959—even before American property was seized—the National Security Council decided to get rid of him. Szulc believes that the collision course was inevitable, given the Cold War climate of the time:

> In a nutshell, Fidel Castro obsessively feared that his revolution would be stolen from the Cubans by the United States, as independence was stolen at the end of the Spanish-American War in 1898, while Americans . . . saw ominous threats to their national and economic interest, and were not always capable of distinguishing among real and imagined threats.

Just as the memory of José Martí inspired Castro during the 1950's, so does Simón Bolívar's vision of a united Latin America haunt him in the 1980's. Castro devotes an inordinate amount of time to hemispheric ambitions and perceives himself as the leader of the Third World. As Szulc writes: "He thinks other peoples in the Third World deserve the kind of dignity as nations and individuals that the revolution has granted the Cubans."

Aside from its validity and readability, one measure of any book is how much it alters one's perceptions about a subject. Szulc's book does not disappoint on this score. Because the Batista government collapsed so rapidly during the late 1950's, it is not sometimes recognized how difficult Castro's road to power was, how dangerous, and, indeed, how hopeless it must have seemed to all but himself. "There was a moment," Castro admitted later, "when I was Commander in Chief of myself and two others." Castro's faith in himself as a man of destiny has been almost mystical. He recognized Cuba's need for a national hero and at times performed acts of personal courage which, in the author's words, bordered "on the insane." He ordered his *guerrilleros* to pay cash for all goods they took from peasants and even had them helping with the harvest and starting primitive health clinics and schools.

While Castro has proved himself master of gaining and holding power—thanks in part to his oratorical talents ("crowds have never said no to Castro") and charismatic personality ("chants of 'Fidel, Fidel!' punctuate the mass rallies")—he seems to suffer from what Szulc describes as a "psychological inability" to delegate power, resulting in a state of affairs "that paralyzes all initiative on lower levels." Even so, he knows how to engender hope and faith during times of extreme hardship. When devastating Hurricane Flora struck the island, for example, Castro, according to Szulc, "was everywhere, on the front lines as usual, directing rescue operations, taking chances, leading and inspiring."

Going along with his actions and oratory, Castro's rebel image has been one secret of his political longevity. Indeed, the bogey of American imperialism serves this purpose. In 1962, Szulc notes, things could not have appeared worse for his fortunes: "There were guerrillas in the mountains, 'old' Communists were trying to undermine him, the farm economy was collapsing, and the Americans were after him." Turning to the Soviet Union, he concurred in the deployment of missiles, supposedly as a deterrent to an American invasion. The so-called Missile Crisis was ultimately resolved without significant input from Castro, an irritation which damaged relations between Cuba and the Soviet Union. On the other hand, the Missile Crisis probably solidified his popularity among his countrymen and facilitated his consolidation of Cuba "ideologically under a banner of a ruling Communist party that he would head." Szulc concludes: "After five years of the revolution, Fidel Castro had established himself as the undisputed, powerful, ruthless, imaginative, and unpredictable leader of Cuba as the country now edged toward a Communist system of life and governance."

Some of the issues Szulc addresses in *Fidel* are left unresolved. Why did revolutionary leader Che Guevara leave for the jungles of Bolivia? What is the relationship between Castro and his brother Raúl, his designated heir? Is Castro's insistence on absolute authority responsible for the failure of Cuba's economy? Finally, is an American-Cuban rapprochement possible? Perhaps at this juncture these questions are unanswerable. While *Fidel* produces no startling conclusions, this evenhanded biography provides valuable insights into a complex and towering personality. Certainly nobody's pawn, Castro has cast a long shadow over not only his own island's history but also that of the United States, Latin America, and, for that matter, the world.

James B. Lane

Sources for Further Study

Booklist. LXXXIII, October 15, 1986, p. 299.
Foreign Affairs. LXV, Winter, 1986, p. 400.
Kirkus Reviews. LIV, October 15, 1986, p. 1568.
National Review. XXXVIII, November 21, 1986, p. 56.
The New Republic. CXCVI, January 19, 1987, p. 28.
Newsweek. CVIII, November 24, 1986, p. 91.
The New York Times Book Review. XCI, November 30, 1986, p. 11.
Publishers Weekly. CCXXX, October 17, 1986, p. 46.
The Wall Street Journal. CCVIII, November 25, 1986, p. 26.
Washington Post Book World. XVI, November 2, 1986, p. 1.

THE FISHER KING

Author: Anthony Powell (1905-   )
Publisher: W. W. Norton and Company (New York). 256 pp. $15.95
Type of work: Seriocomic fantasy
Time: Summer, sometime in the 1980's
Locale: A cruise ship, circling Great Britain

Figures from various myths are identified with the characters embarked on a summer cruise, whose relationships with one another change during the course of the cruise

Principal characters:
> SAUL HENCHMAN, a highly successful photographer crippled in World War II
> BARBERINA ROOKWOOD, Henchman's assistant and companion, once a promising ballerina
> GARY LAMONT, a journalistic entrepreneur, in love with Barberina, suffering from heart trouble
> ROBIN JILSON, a young man afflicted with a degenerative disease, loved by Barberina
> MRS. JILSON, Robin's domineering mother
> SIR DIXON TIPTOFT, a retired civil servant
> DR. LORNA TIPTOFT, a domineering physician, daughter of Sir Dixon
> VALENTINE BEALS, a writer of popular historical novels, narrator of much of the action
> LOUISE BEALS, Valentine's wife
> PIERS MIDDLECOTE, an advertising executive and Beals's friend
> FAY MIDDLECOTE, Piers' wife
> WILLARD AND ELAINE KOPF, an American academic couple
> MR. JACK, an aged alcoholic, once a fervent womanizer

The Fisher King is the second novel published by Anthony Powell since the completion, in 1975, of *A Dance to the Music of Time.* That series of twelve novels presented a satiric social history of England from the mid-1930's to the 1970's and established Powell as one of the preeminent British writers of the postwar era. *The Fisher King* is more playful than the earlier series, more nearly a game in which the author challenges his readers to recognize and try to follow the mythological associations of the characters. Social commentary is present; Powell makes clear his views about advertising, popular novelists, the press, the civil service, and American scholars. He is less concerned with such matters, however, than with the shifting connections between the characters on his "ship of fools" and their mythic counterparts.

Powell sends his characters on a cruise around England, Wales, and Scotland aboard a ship called the *Alecto*, a name which suggests that this will be no peaceful voyage in the sun; Alecto was one of the Eumenides of Greek mythology, known as the "unresting," a source of grief who reveled in war, violence, and quarrels. No war breaks out on this voyage, nor is there much overt violence, but unrest and quarrels are omnipresent. Much of the unrest centers on Saul Henchman, "the Fisher King," a famous photographer who was crippled and disfigured in World War II, and his companion and assistant, the superbly beautiful Barberina Rookwood, who abandoned a highly promising career as a ballerina to devote her life to Henchman.

The action of the novel evolves from these two. It is Barberina's fate to attract the attention and admiration of men and women. Gary Lamont has loved her for a long time but has remained faithful to his wife. Now that the wife is dead, he joins the cruise at the last minute to try to win Barberina away from Henchman. Barberina, however, has never regarded Lamont as more than a friend, and bypassing Lamont, she gives her affection to Robin Jilson, a tentative young man in bad health. When Jilson proves incapable of meeting the challenge Barberina presents, falling instead into the clutches of the domineering female physician Dr. Lorna Tiptoft, Barberina announces through an impromptu performance that she is ready to resume her career in the ballet.

Saul Henchman demonstrates throughout the novel that he is a thoroughly unpleasant person. He uses his position to dominate others, he manipulates people through his physical condition, although when he wishes he can abandon his crutches and scale a difficult wall unaided, and he seems to compensate for his sexual impotence through sadistic treatment of others. At the same time, paradoxically, Henchman genuinely loves Barberina, whose departure is painful to him, and he is capable of kindness; when Jilson helps him and reveals that he has ambitions to be a photographer, Henchman offers to assist the younger man with his career. Even when it becomes clear that Barberina intends to leave him for Jilson, Henchman does not withdraw the offer of assistance, only modifying it with a promise to apprentice Jilson to another photographer. In the end, Henchman leaves the cruise to fish on the shore of one of the Orkney islands, in imitation of the Fisher King of Celtic mythology.

The tone throughout *The Fisher King* is that of comedy combined with and to some extent undercutting high drama. At the climax of the novel Barberina takes Jilson on deck after dinner to declare her love; apparently rejected, she returns to the salon where the ship's orchestra is playing a corrupt version of music from *Swan Lake*, dances beautifully as a way of announcing her return to ballet, and leaves to the applause of all who have seen her. It is the moment at which the major relationships among the characters are changed irrevocably.

This scene is followed by one of low comedy. Unable to sleep, Valentine Beals leaves his stateroom to go on deck to watch the sunrise. In the passageway he sees Jilson, evidently going to the lavatory; Lamont, Jilson's rival and cabin mate, emerges from Barberina's room and encounters Jilson.

From his hiding place, Beals then sees Henchman emerge from his cabin opposite Barberina's to confront the other two; Henchman sardonically compares the activity to a French bedroom farce. After it is made clear that Lamont's visit to Barberina has resulted in her final rejection of him, Jilson suffers an attack of weakness. Since Henchman cannot help Jilson and Lamont will not, Beals is forced to leave his hiding place to pick Jilson up. Beals offers a lame excuse for his presence and pretends that he has not been spying on them. Beals and Lamont, carrying Jilson to his stateroom, are stopped by a call from Henchman, who takes a snapshot of this disheveled trio and disappears. It is a farcical conclusion to a tension-laden evening.

The action of *The Fisher King*, however, is of less interest than its parallels in legend. Most of these are first pointed out by Valentine Beals, a writer of popular historical novels which are supposedly carefully researched and are filled with plenty of erotic detail. Beals is presented as the narrator of much of the action; he tells the story at a social gathering attended also by the Middlecotes, sometime after the end of the voyage. Some of the action is also reported by an omniscient third-person narrator, whose presence casts doubt on many of Beals's notions.

It is Beals, very early in the novel, who identifies Henchman with the Fisher King of legend, the figure whose wounds and impotence have condemned his lands to desolation and his people to poverty. This figure was central to T. S. Eliot's famous poem *The Waste Land* (1922) as a symbol of the barren state of modern life. The story of the Fisher King, despite its origins in pagan myth, had in medieval times become associated with the Christian myth of the Holy Grail and with the knights of King Arthur's Round Table. These associations permit Beals to play with a variety of ideas. Jilson, for example, can be associated with Sir Gawain, who was given a chance to recover the Holy Grail but who was distracted by the charms of the fair Elaine and failed in the quest. One problem with this particular identification is that while Barberina is the natural candidate for the role of Elaine, she does not become Jilson's lover; a further problem is that there is another Elaine present on the voyage in the person of Professor Kopf's wife, who is far more interested in Henchman than in Jilson.

Such problems abound, casting doubt on all of Beals's imaginative identifications. Even the central idea that Henchman is the Fisher King, despite some apparent validity, is in one way impossible because of the name Powell has given him; Saul, it is true, was an Israelite king, but the name "henchman" implies a very different role, and Henchman did begin his professional life as another's aide. Further, there is no evidence that Henchman's disabilities cause any wider desolation, as those of a king would. Finally, Henchman is too readily identifiable with figures from mythologies other than the Celtic or the Christian. In his relationship with Barberina, he is clearly the

Beast, of "Beauty and the Beast," a resemblance noted by several of the characters; the irony here is that the Beauty's love cannot turn him into a handsome prince. In turning the comically tedious old lecher Mr. Jack into his assistant in the final scenes, Henchman even echoes Don Quixote with his Sancho Panza. Mr. Jack himself suggests also Don Juan and, in his propensity for boring his fellow passengers, the Ancient Mariner.

The validity of Beals's speculative identifications is made even more doubtful by his own character. Although he pretends in certain situations that he is a scholar, he obviously is not, as his conversations with Professor Kopf make clear. He knows only as much about specific historical matters as he must know to incorporate them in his fictions. His real interest is in gossip. He tries by every means available to ingratiate himself with Saul Henchman, not through any knowledge or admiration of Henchman's art but through his desire to know the details of the lives of "the rich and famous." In a fine comic scene, Beals is frustrated in his efforts to overhear a potentially revealing conversation at the dinner table by Jilson's mother. A devoted fan of his fiction, she persists in questioning Beals about details in novels he had written years earlier and forgotten, preventing him from listening to more interesting diners.

The reliability of Beals's understanding is brought into question in other ways. His association with Fay and Piers Middlecote, before, during, and after the voyage of the *Alecto*, raises some questions. Middlecote is a windbag who contends with Beals for any available audience; as an advertising executive who seeks to inflate the significance of what he does, he is the object of considerable ridicule. Fay Middlecote, like Louise Beals and Beals himself, is primarily interested in gossip. Since his wife and the Middlecotes are the only audience for Beals's speculations, there is nothing to suggest that they are to be taken seriously.

On the other hand, since nothing in *The Fisher King* seems intended to be simple, there are kernels of truth even in Beals's speculations. Through the omniscient narrator as well as through Beals, Powell advances the idea that the old myths are still alive in modern dress, though substantially changed. In this, he is following in the footsteps of many authors who, in the first half of the twentieth century, examined similar parallels. Not only Eliot but also other writers, including James Joyce, who in *Ulysses* (1922) compared a Dublin advertising salesman to the Greek hero Odysseus, and Eugene O'Neill, who presented a modern version of the Greek Oresteia in *Mourning Becomes Electra* (1931), were fascinated by the ways in which the patterns defined in various myths could be portrayed in modern art.

When Powell allows Beals to become totally confused in his speculations, he is suggesting that any simplistic attempts to understand life, or the relationships among art, myth, and life, are doomed to failure. The fact that all three of the men most important in Barberina's life are physically ailing (besides Henchman's obvious disabilities, Jilson is the victim of a degenerative nerve and muscle disease and Lamont has been told that he has a bad heart) seems to point to the Greek myth (also found in many other cultures) of the wounded hero rather than to Celtic mythology. Barberina herself does not fit into the Fisher King pattern because, as a virgin goddess, she is associated with Artemis and, as one of the characters points out, with the dancer in the modern tale *The Red Shoes*. In her ill-fated relationship with the three men, she chooses the one who really does not want her, itself an archetypal situation. Beals lacks the understanding and the intellectual sophistication to see the implications of mythological patterns and is therefore an object of satire, but the patterns nevertheless exist.

The Fisher King makes the serious point that myths, old or new, are potential guides to recurring patterns in human behavior and in human relationships, but that those who look for simple patterns in myths or in life are doomed to befuddlement. It cannot be expected that people will follow expected patterns, even though at times they may seem to do so. In this novel, however, Powell is less interested in making serious points than in providing an enjoyment that is both intellectual and comic. *The Fisher King* provides a challenge to the reader's knowledge of various mythologies. At the same time, the novel's comic play ranges from the high comedy of the conversations between Fay Middlecote and Louise Beals, or Mrs. Jilson's questioning of Beals, to the low comedy of the meeting in the middle of the night of Lamont, Jilson, Henchman, and Beals in the corridor outside Barberina's stateroom. Anthony Powell, at the age of eighty, still seems to find great enjoyment in the ludicrous aspects of human behavior; his unerring eye for the comic situation, the sharpness of his wit, and his polished style make *The Fisher King* a highly enjoyable diversion.

John M. Muste

Sources for Further Study

Booklist. LXXXIII, September 15, 1986, p. 102.
Contemporary Review. CCXLIX, July, 1986, p. 45.
Kirkus Reviews. LIV, July 15, 1986, p. 1056.
Library Journal. CXI, September 15, 1986, p. 101.
The London Review of Books. VIII, April 17, 1986, p. 16.
New Statesman. CXI, April 18, 1986, p. 28.
The New York Times Book Review. XCI, October 19, 1986, p. 30.
Publishers Weekly. CCXXX, August 1, 1986, p. 66.
Punch. CCXC, April 2, 1986, p. 53.
Times Literary Supplement. April 4, 1986, p. 356.

FLASHMAN AND THE DRAGON

Author: George MacDonald Fraser (1925-   )
Publisher: Alfred A. Knopf (New York). 320 pp. $16.95
Type of work: Novel
Time: 1860
Locale: China, in the neighborhoods successively of Hong Kong, Shanghai, and
Peking

Harry Flashman, a British soldier, marches with Lord Elgin to Peking, there to be
captured and ravished by the emperor's concubine and to see the end of the Opium
Wars

> *Principal characters:*
> COLONEL SIR HARRY FLASHMAN, a coward, bully, and lecher
> JAMES BRUCE, eighth earl of Elgin, Queen Victoria's humane and
> kindly envoy to China
> SZU-ZHAN, a gigantic female bandit
> YEHONALA, THE ORCHID LADY, Imperial concubine, later Empress
> Tzu-hsi
> SANG-KOL-IN-SEN, a barbaric imperial warlord
> PHOEBE CARPENTER, a vicar's wife and gun-runner

George MacDonald Fraser took the central character of his sequence
"The Flashman Papers" (of which this is the eighth volume) from the classic
Victorian novel *Tom Brown's Schooldays* (1857) by Thomas Hughes. In that
earlier work Hughes set up an elementary contrast between hero and villain.
On the one hand there was the plucky, mischievous, cricket-playing, chapel-
attending Tom Brown (in several ways rather a close parallel to Tom Sawyer); on the other the cowardly, bullying Flashman, eventually dismissed in
disgrace from Rugby School for drunkenness. The years, however, have left
Hughes's ideas of virtue unfashionable and even mildly ridiculous; Tom
Brown's piety goes oddly with his aggressiveness, while his totally asexual
behavior has become unbelievable. It was then perhaps an obvious notion—
though like all such notions, brilliantly successful once conceived—for Fraser to seize Hughes's opposition and invert it, taking Flashman beyond his
expulsion from Rugby and making him, still as cowardly and cynical as ever,
a great Victorian hero: at the time of this story, Colonel Sir Harry Flashman, no less, knighted totally undeservedly for service to the Empire and
awarded the Victoria Cross even less deservedly for personal courage.
Where Hughes suggested that the British Empire ran on "muscular Christianity," Fraser suggested that its real constituents (at any rate in his hero)
were unscrupulousness, superior force, and an undeviating attention to the
main chance.

This appears on the surface to be especially true of the historical event
with which *Flashman and the Dragon* is primarily concerned; namely, the
conclusion of the Second Anglo-Chinese War of 1856-1860 with the combined Anglo-French march on Peking, and the burning of the Chinese em-

peror's summer palace. What had happened, in brief summary, was that the British had found themselves with nothing to trade for the Chinese tea and silk which they imported in great quantities. They, and other European powers, had accordingly fostered the Chinese taste for opium, which the British could produce in their Indian possessions. When the Chinese government attempted to stop this trade, and indeed to keep its country closed to Europeans, the British provoked successive wars, each ending with the imposition of commercial treaties. Finally, at the end of a march on Peking, designed to force the emperor Yüan-ming Yüan to sign one such treaty, the British envoy Lord James Elgin ordered the burning and looting of the summer palace, with all of its irreplaceable art treasures, as a punishment for Chinese breach of faith.

The aforementioned seems to be an example of the most colossal greed and barbarity. The British appear successively as commercial failures, drug pushers, and vandals; their superior Christian civilization (of which Hughes was so confident) has nothing to offer and indeed adds a vicious note of self-righteousness to the whole affair. Certainly this is Flashman's opinion. At the start of the novel, he is taken aback when an innocent-seeming vicar's wife, Mrs. Carpenter, whom he is trying to seduce, offers him a large bribe to run a cargo of illegal opium to Canton, claiming as excuses, first, that the new treaty will soon make the trade legal, second, that opium is only a sedative anyway, and third, that the profits will go to building a new church. Flashman's admiration for Mrs. Carpenter is only increased when he finds out that the cargo he is running is not even opium. It consists of Sharps carbines for the Taiping rebels, an insurrection against the Chinese government from 1850 to 1864. *This* trade would not even be accepted by the British government, which typically was trying to shore up the Chinese Empire against the Taipings while at the same time endeavoring to bully it into signing treaties. Mrs. Carpenter's resolute pursuit of profit characterizes not only her, however, but also Flashman, the British authorities, and almost every European Flashman meets.

Is this novel, then, a sustained attack on Victorian England and its official image? It turns out not. For there is another side to the colonialist experience, which Flashman also records carefully. He notes very early that the rulers of China are not Chinese, but Manchus, a race of invaders who have reduced their subjects to worse than slavery. He gives continual details of the appalling cruelties of the Chinese Empire, many of them verified by factual references from Fraser (posing as the"editor" of Flashman's memoirs). On Flashman's first opium-running trip, an Imperial galley orders his boat to heave to, threatening to drown twenty Chinese prisoners if he refuses. He refuses, and the prisoners are drowned. The point here is that the Manchus would only use this kind of moral blackmail against a European. One of their own kind would take no interest in the fate of Chinese petty criminals whatever. Having saved his credit after being caught later on with the guns, Flashman is then dispatched on a second trip to the Chinese interior, to act as envoy to the Taiping rebels, and there he finds what he calls the bloodiest war in history going on, a war in which, in all sober reality, more than thirty million lives were lost, more even than in World War I— many of them by deliberate execution and all of them without the slightest European instigation. Finally, on his third Chinese expedition to Peking and the summer palace, Flashman comes into horrifying contact with even grosser Manchu customs: specifically the "kow-tow" and the "wire jacket" (otherwise known as the Death of a Thousand Cuts). One may say in brief that unscrupulous as Flashman and his compatriots are, it is impossible to sympathize with their Manchu enemies or to see these as anything but an even crueler and far less efficient set of exploiters.

Morality in fact cannot be reduced to a matter of "sides" in *Flashman and the Dragon*. A further question which the book uncomfortably raises is the one of cultural superiority. There is no doubt that nineteenth century Europeans (and Americans) thought themselves superior to the Asiatic peoples they encountered, on grounds which were as much racial as technical or religious. This belief is now strongly and officially discouraged. The ironic fact, however, is that the Chinese Empire felt exactly the same way about Europeans. The Chinese word for ambassador is tribute-bearer, Flashman notes; the existence of powers outside China was simply denied. Queen Victoria was regarded as a barbarian vassal, and even educated Chinese officials were convinced that the prohibition of the export of tea to Europe would soon cause all Europeans to die of constipation. Lord Elgin's march on Peking, then, was intended above all to force the imperial ruling classes to admit that he existed and had a right to negotiate. Only force could achieve this goal.

Chinese and British perspectives clashed most dramatically over the ceremony of the kow-tow, the ritual prostration and banging of the head against the ground before a superior. Chinese officials demanded this of everyone. The British performed it to no one. Their motives may have been bad (racial pride) or good (refusal to accept that human beings had any right to demand such humiliation of one another). In any case, any Briton known to have kow-towed to a Chinese would have been forever disgraced. The whole complex of feeling was enshrined in another classic Victorian work, the poem "A Private of the Buffs," by Sir Francis Doyle, which recounts a genuine incident when a private soldier of the East Kent Regiment ("the Buffs") was captured and ordered to kow-tow by a Chinese mandarin. He refused and was instantly killed. Doyle made of this a hymn to racial pride, suggesting strongly that Private Moyes's action was both noble and instinctive and, furthermore, in classic Victorian style, that even the lowest Englishman was better than any foreigner. Flashman, however, as is his habit, is actually present at the incident and turns on it his cynical, penetrating intelligence. In the first place, he thinks the mandarin is an even crueler and more ignorant character than Doyle could imagine. Yet Moyes's refusal to submit is caused partly by drink, partly by sheer incomprehension, but mostly by fierce contempt for his captors. As side issues, one might note that Flashman himself kow-towed instantly and that Moyes turns out to be not an Englishman but a thoroughly truculent Scot.

Yet it remains hard not to have some admiration for Private Moyes, Victorian mythicizing apart. The custom of the wire jacket sharpens this feeling. One particularly atrocious form of Chinese punishment was to wrap a naked criminal in wire mesh, so tightly that the flesh poked through in small, separate lumps. Each of these lumps was then shaved off with a razor, so that the victim endured "ten thousand cuts" and was eventually flayed alive. One of the now-forgotten horrors of Elgin's march was that a British envoy, Harry Parkes, together with some twenty escorting soldiers and others including a reporter for *The Times*, was captured by the Chinese and, in defiance of all diplomatic convention, handed over to the Board of Punishments, under threat of the wire jacket or worse. Parkes in the end was rescued, but at least fourteen British and Indian soldiers and civilians, the *Times* reporter included, were tortured to death. It was this which provoked the burning of the summer palace, and irreplaceable as its art treasures were, they were arguably not as precious as life.

The historical parallel one can hardly avoid remembering is the Iranian hostage crisis of 1978-1980. On that occasion the American government was unable to act, though the hostages were returned. If they had not been, if they had been killed by their captors, one wonders what response would have seemed appropriate. It would naturally be anachronistic for Flashman in 1860 to draw any parallel of this nature, but Fraser, posing as a twentieth century editor, is able to drop hints in this direction, while he also uses the device of having Flashman write these memoirs many years later, already conscious therefore of declining European power and the likelihood—which he much regrets—of insults and injuries of this nature going unavenged. One may see this as simply part of Flashman's bullying character, established for him from the time of Thomas Hughes. One could also, however, see it as the opinion of a character certainly flawed and unreliable but with two major advantages denied to twentieth century historians: one being first-hand experience (and Fraser has certainly soaked himself in little-known period memoirs), the other being freedom from liberal illusion. Historical facts often tend to support Flashman. He is right in his estimate of the Taiping rebellion. There is an inevitable irony, also, for the modern reader in reading any account of the founder of that movement, Hung Hsiu-ch'üan, with his crazy millenarianism and his habit of having his "thoughts" read out to and memorized by all of his followers.

Flashman and the Dragon, in short, functions on at least three levels. At the most elementary, it is an exciting story of adventure, peopled by river pirates, imperial concubines, and soldiers of fortune. At the same time, it acts as a satire on official pretension and British Imperial hypocrisy; many "eminent Victorians" are accordingly given walk-on parts, mostly to their discredit. On a deeper level, however, it presents a challenge even to current illusions. Have matters improved since the nineteenth century? Wrong as the Victorians were, were they not at least small-scale in their depredations and capable of unexpected restraint? Does their descendants' higher morality not also look like reluctance to take responsibility? Flashman himself cannot say these things, for he has forfeited all moral authority by his selfishness, lust, greed, and sloth. Still, as he declares himself, "I know right from wrong"; his observation is accurate, even if his choices are bad. His cold and mordant eye gives one a view of the modern world evolving, a view at once comic, disturbing, and provocative.

T. A. Shippey

Sources for Further Study

Booklist. LXXXII, March 1, 1986, p. 913.
Kirkus Reviews. LIV, February 1, 1986, p. 146.
Library Journal. CXI, April 15, 1986, p. 94.
The New Republic. CXCV, August 11, 1986, p. 38.
New Statesman. CX, October 25, 1985, p. 31.
The New York Times Book Review. XCI, March 4, 1986, p. 19.
Newsweek. CVII, May 5, 1986, p. 76.
Publishers Weekly. CCXXIX, March 7, 1986, p. 86.
Time. CXXVII, June 2, 1986, p. 76.
Times Literary Supplement. October 11, 1985, p. 1125.
Washington Post Book World. XVI, May 4, 1986, p. 1.

FORD
The Men and the Machine

Author: Robert Lacey (1944-   )
Publisher: Little, Brown and Company (Boston). Illustrated. 778 pp. $24.95
Type of work: Historical biography/business history
Time: The 1860's to the 1980's
Locale: Primarily Dearborn and Detroit, Michigan

A vivid account of the major and minor personalities involved in the creation and growth of Ford Motor Company and of the automobile that transformed the United States socially, economically, and culturally

> *Principal personages:*
> HENRY FORD, founder of Ford Motor Company and one of the most influential personalities of the twentieth century
> EDSEL FORD, his son, a gifted man who was often humiliated and undermined by his father
> HENRY FORD II, Edsel's son, who saved Ford Motor Company from near collapse after World War II and built it into the fourth largest international industrial corporation

The year 1986 has witnessed a surge of interest in the American automobile industry in general and in the Ford Motor Company in particular. Pulitzer Prize-winning journalist David Halberstam has produced *The Reckoning* (1986; reviewed in this volume), which, while dealing in general with the Japanese challenge to the American automobile industry, focuses on Ford and Nissan, primarily in the post-World War II period. At the same time, Robert Lacey's massive study of Ford has appeared, and the autobiography of flamboyant Chrysler head and former Ford president Lee Iacocca has been issued in paperback. All three books have enjoyed considerable popularity, as is evidenced by their high standing on best-seller lists. This popularity can be explained by numerous factors. Each book is well written, and each author concentrates on colorful personalities in telling his tale. Each also deals with the automobile industry in general and Ford in particular, the only one of the Big Three whose family leadership has remained prominent until very recently. Ford, currently, is also the most successful of the Big Three in meeting the Asian (Japanese and Korean) challenge. By continuing to concentrate on its profitable international operations and by successfully responding to perceived Japanese-European superiority in quality and innovation with its introduction of the Taurus and Sable models for the Ford and Mercury divisions, Ford has sparked a positive response from car buyers and investors that accounts in part for current popular interest in it and its history.

British writer Robert Lacey, on the basis of his previous interests, would appear an unlikely chronicler of this distinctly American business, which had its roots in the rural America of the late nineteenth century. Lacey has devoted his talents in the past primarily to British aristocracy and royalty. In addition to biographies of Robert, Earl of Essex, Sir Walter Raleigh, and Henry VIII, Lacey authored the popular *Majesty: Elizabeth II and the House of Windsor* (1977). Perhaps he was attracted to the Ford family because it became America's closest approximation to an aristocracy, albeit one of wealth rather than birth. Indeed, the author consistently focuses on the family throughout the book, although he does not neglect others who have played significant roles in the company's history.

Once Lacey had decided on the Ford project, he made a firm commitment to research seldom exercised by even the most serious scholar. He relocated himself and his family from their home in England to Detroit for two years. There he had access to extensive collections of Ford documents as well as to members of the Ford family and present and former employees of the company. Lacey was admittedly aided in his research by members of the Ford family, including Henry Ford II (although he consented to only one interview by Lacey), and by the fact that Ford Motor Company has traditionally been unusually cooperative in making its records, which it has carefully preserved and organized, available to historians and researchers in the Ford Archives of the Edison Institute (the collective name for Greenfield Village, the Henry Ford Museum, and related research and educational facilities in Dearborn, Michigan) and in the Ford Industrial Archives. Not only did Lacey utilize the traditional sources of information about Ford, but also he conducted approximately two hundred interviews and consulted several collections of documents secured by application under the Freedom of Information Act. Most important of the latter are those which concern the activities of the shadowy Harry Bennett, the malevolent figure who monopolized access to Henry Ford in the latter's last years and thus exercised a high degree of unofficial control over the company—to its detriment and to that of Ford's son, Edsel. Finally, Lacey worked on an assembly line for several days in May, 1985. Lacey's major regret was the unavailablity of the personal papers of Edsel Ford. Although they were filed in the Ford archives when that invaluable collection was established in the early 1950's, they were removed from their boxes and taken away on the instructions of the company when the archives were transferred from the company to the Edison Institute in 1964. As a result, knowledge of the most compassionate and artistically sensitive member of the Ford dynasty is severely limited and must be pieced out primarily from company papers, interviews with family members, friends, and business associates, and from the FBI documents dealing with Harry Bennett, who successfully alienated the father from his son. As a result, the greatest disappointment of Lacey's book is its comparatively, but unavoidably, brief treatment of Edsel.

Not surprisingly, the dominant and most fascinating figure in Lacey's account is Henry Ford, the Michigan farm boy who founded Ford Motor Company, who became one of America's most admired and wealthiest citizens, who put the world on wheels and, in so doing, transformed it socially, economically, and culturally. Henry Ford was an authentic American folk hero who attempted to preserve the rural American values of the nineteenth century in an urbanized twentieth century, a new world which he had done more than anyone, with the possible exception of his idol Thomas Edison, to create. Unlike Edison and other creative geniuses of the late nineteenth and early twentieth centuries, Ford was not an inventor. Automobiles were built and sold long before Ford entered the field, and a century earlier, Eli Whitney had introduced the use of standardized, interchangeable parts. Ford's genius was as a manufacturer and marketer. His application of Whitney's ideas to his knowledge of automobile construction fostered his development of the moving assembly line of mass production, which enabled Ford to produce a rapidly increasing number of cars at an accelerated speed and at a steadily declining price. Ford expressed his vision in remarks made in 1903 and 1907. To attorney John W. Anderson, Ford had first stated: "The way to make automobiles is to make one automobile like another automobile, to make them all alike... just as one pin is like another pin when it comes from a pin factory." In 1907, Ford remarked to a company mechanic: "We're going to expand this company, and you will see that it will grow by leaps and bounds. The proper system, as I have it in mind, is to get the car to the multitude." In so doing, he wrought a revolution. Within a decade of the production of the fabulous Model T in October, 1908, this model, noted for its simplicity and durability, had come to dominate the world market, accounting for more than half the automobiles in the world. No longer was the automobile the toy of the rich. The common man could now own the world's most coveted consumer product. Any man making a good salary could "own one," Ford rhapsodized, "and enjoy with his family the blessing of hours of pleasure in God's great open spaces."

The heroic stature that Ford acquired with the average American is not difficult to explain, for he held fast to the prejudices and values of late nineteenth century America. Growing to manhood in rural Michigan, Ford identified with the Greenbackers and later the Populists, who raged against those whom they believed had destroyed the pastoral golden age of their forefathers. Their demons became his: railroad tycoons, easterners, hard money supporters, bankers, Wall Street speculators, intellectuals, and Jews. Ford's later wealth enabled him to vent his rage in print against his supposed enemies, especially the Jews, in the Ford-owned weekly, the *Dearborn Independent*. Indeed, Adolf Hitler later credited Ford as a source of inspiration in the development of his demonology. At the same time Ford held fast to the agrarian virtues of hard work, thrift, and a simple life-style, even after his acquisition of great wealth enabled him to live in a manner grander than that of any of his peers had he wished. Throughout his life Ford remained more interested in the mechanical features of his product than in ways to enhance and spend the wealth which his product brought him. Indeed Ford devoted expenditure to the creation of Greenfield Village and the Henry Ford Museum, an enterprise undertaken to re-create America's past, primarily though not exclusively its agrarian and technological past, a project to which he devoted not only money but much personal time as well. Ultimately, Ford's attachment to the rural ideal of simplicity and his distaste for modern business practices almost destroyed the company he had created. Unable to tolerate dissent from his employees and unwilling to adopt modern management skills and practices necessary to keep Ford Motor Company viable financially, the elder Ford was forced aside in 1945 by his grandson, Henry Ford II, who put together a management team that saved the company in the years following World War II.

Perhaps what is most interesting in the elder Ford are the contradictions in his personality. Outwardly a religious traditionalist, Ford was in actuality a spiritualist, whose vision of his own heroic goals was strongly based on his belief in reincarnation. Progressive in his hiring and advancement of blacks, he was also a violent anti-Semite. A model employer who introduced the revolution of the five-dollar day, he did not hesitate to employ thugs to intimidate and beat up union organizers. An avowed pacifist who funded and traveled on the Peace Ship in an attempt to bring World War I to a speedy conclusion, Ford soon after became a major war profiteer. (Parenthetically, Ford later claimed that his anti-Semitic views first took form as a result of his dealings with the Jewess Rosika Schwimmer, who convinced Ford to fund this ill-starred enterprise.) A loving and doting father, Ford openly supported a mistress, Evangeline Dahlinger, her husband, and her son, John, who was probably sired by Ford. Indeed, the Dahlingers became the closest personal friends of Henry and his wife, Clara Bryant Ford. A man who prided himself on his independence and good judgment, Ford allowed himself to come increasingly and almost totally under the influence of Harry Bennett, who, given free rein, allied himself with organized crime to intimidate union organizers in Ford's factories and worked successfully to alienate Ford from his only son, Edsel.

The most sympathetic of the three leading Fords was the son. Edsel Ford had most of the virtues, and others of his own, and few of the vices of his father and son. The only child of the union of Henry and Clara Ford, Edsel developed a strong sense of public service and filial obedience. He was without question the most artistically talented of all the Fords. Edsel was a leading patron of the arts in Detroit, whose most enduring and personal contribution was his commissioning and supervision of the Detroit industry frescoes by the Mexican muralist Diego Rivera for the courtyard of the Detroit Institute of Art. Gifted as a car designer, Edsel found his attempts at design changes continually frustrated by his father. Ironically, the automobile that proved to be Ford's greatest marketing fiasco, not in small measure because of its design, was named for Edsel, although it was designed and built long after his death. Indeed, the father took a perverse pleasure in undermining his dutiful son and in humiliating him publicly, even after Edsel had become president of the company. The treatment of Edsel Ford by his father reveals the dark side of Henry's personality and provides the saddest chapter in the family's history. Although Edsel died of cancer at the age of fifty, many, including his son Henry Ford II, were convinced that he really died of a broken heart, the victim of his father's cruelty.

Henry Ford II is more like his grandfather than father in temperament, although his skills were in management rather than engineering. He is, like his grandfather, a man of contrasts. Taking the company over when it was on the verge of collapse in 1945, he reversed its declining fortunes by hiring the so-called "Whiz Kids," who successfully introduced badly needed management skills and practices. Through his development of Ford of Europe, he made Ford into one of the world's largest and most successful companies. He acted forthrightly to improve race relations in the turbulent 1960's by inaugurating innovative hiring and training programs for Detroit's unemployed and undereducated blacks, and he tried with only marginal success to restore the vitality of Detroit's inner city by launching the Renaissance Center, a complex of shops, restaurants, and a hotel, built along the Detroit River and designed to lure people into the city. Unfortunately, Henry Ford II suffers from a vindictive and often boorish temperament, which contributed to two failed marriages and estrangement from some members of his family and associates. This trait inhibited the smooth functioning of the company toward the end of his tenure as chairman.

Also offered in Lacey's book are accounts of numerous personalities who have played important roles in Ford's history and in the company's triumphs and failures. Of considerable contemporary interest is the author's treatment of Lee Iacocca, who rode to the presidency of Ford in the 1970's on the basis of his creation and introduction in the 1960's of one of Ford's most popular models, the Mustang. Lacey's portrait of Iacocca is extremely unflattering and, as such, is an antidote to Iacocca's highly popular autobiography.

There is no shortage of histories of the Fords and their company. Indeed noted historians Allan Nevins and Frank Ernest Hill coauthored a highly respected three-volume account that has heretofore been regarded as the company's official history: *Ford: The Times, the Man, the Company* (1954); *Ford: Expansion and Challenge, 1915-1933* (1957); and *Ford: Decline and Rebirth, 1933-1962* (1963). The Nevins and Hill study ends, however, in the early 1960's. Other histories are also chronologically incomplete or narrowly focused on aspects of Ford's history. Lacey has made two major contributions to Ford historiography: bringing Ford's history in its totality up to date and shedding new light on the activities of the enigmatic Harry Bennett.

In addition to his unavoidably incomplete treatment of Edsel Ford, however, Lacey's account is disappointing in several other areas. A more complete discussion of Henry Ford's participation in the creation of Greenfield Village and the Henry Ford Museum and of the "Golden Jubilee of Light," the opening ceremony in October, 1929, which commemorated the fiftieth anniversary of Edison's invention of the incandescent bulb, would have been welcome. Also, nothing is mentioned of Henry Ford's role in funding educational facilities for the rural poor, notably the Berry School and Berry College in Rome, Georgia. This is significant because it modifies traditionally held assumptions about Ford's anti-intellectualism, which he himself helped foster. Finally, Lacey says little about how Ford Motor Company has successfully responded most recently to the Japanese challenge. Nevertheless, this is a fascinating account of a family and an institution that have had a profound impact on America and the world in the twentieth century. It can be read by scholar and general reader alike for enlightenment and pleasure.

J. Stewart Alverson

Sources for Further Study

Barrons. LXVI, August 4, 1986, p. 53.
Booklist. LXXXII, July, 1986, p. 1563.
Business Week. August 4, 1986, p. 10.
Kirkus Reviews. LIV, June 15, 1986, p. 910.
Library Journal. CXI, September 1, 1986, p. 197.
The New York Review of Books. XXXIII, August 14, 1986, p. 17.
The New York Times Book Review. XCI, July 13, 1986, p. 1.
The New Yorker. LXII, September 8, 1986, p. 137.
The Wall Street Journal. CCVIII, July 24, 1986, p. 20.
Washington Post Book World. XVI, July 13, 1986, p. 4.

FRANKLIN OF PHILADELPHIA

Author: Esmond Wright (1915-   )
Publisher: The Belknap Press of Harvard University Press (Cambridge, Massachusetts). Illustrated. 404 pp. $25.00
Type of work: Historical biography
Time: 1706-1790
Locale: The United States, England, and France

A biography of Benjamin Franklin, scientist and statesman

Principal personages:
BENJAMIN FRANKLIN, an American statesman, scientist, inventor, and writer
WILLIAM TEMPLE FRANKLIN, his son, governor of New Jersey
CHARLES GRAVIER DE VERGENNES, a French foreign minister
SILAS DEANE and
ARTHUR LEE, American commissioners to France
JOHN ADAMS and
JOHN JAY, members of the commission to negotiate peace with Great Britain

No eighteenth century American embraced many-sidedness more completely than Benjamin Franklin—journalist, essayist, scientist, inventor, statesman, and diplomat. His life spanned most of the century and his imprint is visible in its history. Of his contemporaries, only Thomas Jefferson was his equal in learning, inventiveness, and breadth of interests; no one was his equal in reputation. He was the most famous American of his time, an eminence at home, a celebrity abroad.

Despite his celebrated status, or perhaps because of it, Franklin attracted a sizable body of critics. The young man of the *Autobiography* (1771-1788), who claimed to embrace hard work, frugality, and virtue, was also the father of an illegitimate son and much at ease in the salons of Paris. He was known to enjoy a good table, a ribald story, and the company of flirtatious young women. John Adams, perhaps a little jealous, penned some acerbic criticisms of Franklin's abilities as a statesman and diplomat. William Cobbett denounced him as "a crafty and lecherous old hypocrite," and Thomas Carlyle found in him too much of the rationalist and too little of the heroic—he dubbed Franklin "the father of all the Yankees."

Esmond Wright's goal in this fluidly written biography is to examine the various public personae that Franklin assumed during his lifetime. He explores Franklin's complex and contradictory personality and assesses his contributions to the government for which he was both domestic architect and foreign advocate. Drawing skillfully on the Yale University Press edition of the Franklin papers, Franklin's own published writings, and the papers of his contemporaries, Wright traces Franklin's life from his birth in Boston in 1706 to his death in 1790 at the age of eighty-four.

Although Wright emphasizes that Franklin was a man of the Enlightenment—questioning, confident in the power of reason, and strongly optimistic about the future of humanity—he also views him as indelibly marked by the Puritan spirit of New England, where he spent the first seventeen years of his life. He knew Cotton Mather's *Essays to Do Good* (1710) and John Bunyan's *The Pilgrim's Progress* (1678) as thoroughly as he did Plutarch and John Locke, and he read (and counted the time lost) the books of polemical theology that his father, a candlemaker, owned. From the Puritanism of his youth Franklin derived his view of life as a serious endeavor, and like Mather he stressed works more than faith. Although he came ultimately to Deism, Franklin retained an abiding faith in virtue, the robust, active kind that brought material as well as spiritual reward. His first public voice was that of a moralist exhorting to good conduct, and he recognized that worldly success required some curbing of natural impulses. (Chastity was not his natural inclination, and he cheerfully admitted that he abandoned frugality as soon as financial success permitted.) In his writings Franklin claimed that virtue was an art to be practiced and perfected; he recommended it to others and drew up a list for himself of thirteen virtues that he worked to assimilate, concentrating on a different one each week.

The sixth virtue that Franklin set down was industry, and if he sometimes failed to live up to the others on the list, he practiced industry with conspicuous success. He educated himself by his own efforts (he had less than two years of formal schooling), reading voraciously and perfecting his prose style by imitating the *Spectator*. His first published writings, the famous "Silence Dogood" essays, appeared anonymously in his brother's *New England Courant* in 1722, when he was only sixteen, a year before he ran away to Philadelphia to escape his apprenticeship. In 1728, at the age of twenty-two, he opened his own printing office, and in the next two years he became publisher and sole owner of *The Pennsylvania Gazette* and official printer to the Pennsylvania Assembly. He launched *Poor Richard's* almanacs in 1731 and watched its circulation grow until its popularity with Colonial readers was second only to the Bible.

At the same time that he was becoming so successful in business that he would be able to retire at the age of forty-two, Franklin was busy with civic affairs and scientific observations. He brought together a group of inquiring friends and fellow tradesmen to form the Junto, a study and social club whose members were devoted to improving both themselves and their city. Under Franklin's guidance, the Junto organized the first circulating library in America, formed a city fire company and a police force, and set up the first Colonial fire insurance company (with Franklin as president). It was behind the founding of the city hospital, the academy that evolved into the University of Pennsylvania, and the American Philosophical Society. The Junto even drew up plans for improved street cleaning, paving, and lighting, using a four-sided ventilated lamp that had been invented by Franklin.

The lamp, which was easier to clean than the old closed globes, was only one of the many inventions that contributed to Franklin's fame. Always a devotee of "useful knowledge" and endlessly curious and inventive, Franklin was as fascinated by the challenge of curing smoky chimneys as by experiments in pure science. He was the first to prove the identity of lightning with electricity, and it was as a scientist that his name first became known in Europe. As a tinkerer he produced inventions that ranged from the supremely practical—the stove that bears his name, the improved fireplace damper, and the lightning rod—to a delicate musical instrument, the glass harmonica. Wherever he was, Franklin's ingenuity and his scientific curiosity were always at work. He made use of his Atlantic crossings on diplomatic missions to study the Gulf Stream; he installed a damper in the fireplace chimney of his lodgings in London and a lightning rod on his house outside Paris, where he observed the first experiments with hot-air balloons. Honors followed in the wake of scientific discoveries. Harvard, Yale, Oxford, and Saint Andrew's University pressed honorary degrees on him, and he was elected to the French Academy of Sciences and a Fellowship in the Royal Society. By the end of his life (when the American Philosophical Society had moved its meetings to his home because he was too infirm to go out) he was a member of twenty-eight learned societies and academies.

Wright devotes the majority of his text to a perceptive analysis of Franklin's activities as a statesman and diplomat, and with much insight he explores the complexities and contradictions of Franklin's political life. He portrays an instinctive cooperator who, despite his dislike of contention and his natural inclination for compromise, came finally and firmly to cast his lot with insurgents. Originally a moderate and an imperialist, Franklin evolved gradually and irrevocably into an "independence man" and a liberal.

His public career began in the Pennsylvania Assembly, to which he was elected in 1751. It carried him later to London, where he served as Colonial agent for Pennsylvania (and eventually for Massachusetts, New Jersey, and Georgia as well), and concluded in France, where he headed the American diplomatic mission. Between assignments in Europe he assisted at the birth of the new American nation: He was a delegate to the Second Continental Congress, serving on the committee that drafted the Declaration of Independence and, at nearly eighty, the most senior delegate to the Constitutional Convention of 1785. His last speech, which was read for him because he was too infirm to stand, was the famous plea to the delegates to set aside their private interests and reservations and, for the public good, adopt the Constitution unanimously.

Reasonableness and moderation were the essence of Franklin's political style. He preferred Socratic questioning to argument and confrontation; his motto was "Never contradict anybody." He lacked Patrick Henry's gift for oratory and eschewed Thomas Jefferson's impassioned prose. The language of natural rights was foreign to his straightforward style; it was through him that the truths held to be "sacred and undeniable" in Jefferson's original draft of the Declaration of Independence were modified to "self-evident" and that the foreign mercenaries sent "to deluge us in blood" became "to destroy us." Thoroughly urban and middle-class, Franklin was interested in the public good and his journalist's pen ever ready to promote it. He proposed a voluntary union of the Colonies for the purpose of defense and Indian policy as early as 1751, and Wright endorses the view of almost all historians except Lawrence Gipson that Franklin was the author of the Albany Plan of Union proposed in 1754.

Although a democrat by nature, Franklin was strongly drawn to the Old World. In the Pennsylvania Assembly he was known as a "popular man": He opposed the claims of the proprietary owners, the Penns, to tax exemption for their lands, and he clashed with the pacifist Quaker majority over defense of the state's Indian-ravaged Western frontier. Yet until the mid-1760's he was also an imperialist who looked forward to the infinite expansion of the British Empire and of the North American colonies within it. (He himself had hopes for a large grant in the upper Ohio Valley, where he proposed to start a new colony called Vandalia.) He held an imperial office—Postmaster General of North America—and his son, William Temple Franklin, was the royal governor of New Jersey. As tensions between England and her North American Colonies increased during the 1760's, Franklin's moderate views led some at home to regard the London agent suspiciously as an "Old England Man." He opposed the Stamp Act, preferring the traditional reliance on requisitions from Colonial assemblies to meet the expenses of imperial administration. Having lost the argument, however, he counseled making the best of it, relying on England not to endanger its own long-term interest by overtaxing the Colonies. He entirely failed to anticipate the angry reaction at home to the Stamp Act or the accusations that he himself had had a hand in drafting it. His skillful work on behalf of repeal salvaged his reputation in the Colonies, and over the ensuing nine years he emerged as a spokesman for all of Colonial America.

In his role as a middleman, Franklin acquired detractors on both sides—in America he was regarded by some as too much of an Englishman, in England as too much of an American. Gradually, as his attempts to smooth the troubled waters were rebuffed, he became less conciliatory. Parliament's increasing tone of belligerence offended him. In 1765 he questioned only the expediency of the Stamp Act, not Parliament's right to pass it. By 1770 he had moved much closer toward separation, accepting the sovereignty of the King but not that of Parliament. In 1774, when the Massachusetts petition to have Thomas Hutchinson removed as governor came up before the Privy Council, he was summoned and denounced as an organizer of rebellion. That moment was decisive, Wright stresses; after that time, Franklin no longer held out any hope for continuing union, and even his faith in the King was gone. When he reached Philadelphia in 1775, in time to take a seat in the Second Continental Congress, he was ready for the irrevocable split, and one that led to a permanent break with his son, who remained a Loyalist.

Franklin spent most of the Revolutionary War years in France, charged first with securing a treaty of alliance and later with negotiating peace. He was by this time past seventy, lionized by the French as the great scientist from the woods of republican America. His portrait appeared on medallions, snuff boxes, and rings, and he was as much at home in court society as he had been in his early years in England. As always, his amiable style and ability to get along with nearly everyone gave rise to criticism from some of his countrymen. His easy intercourse with the crafty foreign minister, Charles Gravier de Vergennes, who had no confidence in Franklin's fellow commissioners, Silas Deane and Arthur Lee, caused Lee to regard him with suspicion. When Lee succeeded in getting Deane recalled for financial misconduct, he tried to implicate Franklin as well. John Adams, who replaced Deane, disapproved of the gracious living that Franklin enjoyed at Passy and his flirtatiousness with the ladies. Adams and John Jay, appointed commissioners with Franklin to negotiate the final peace with Great Britain, distrusted him almost as much as they did Vergennes.

Wright's assessment of Franklin's role in the French mission is on balance favorable. He acknowledges that Franklin is vulnerable to criticism on several points, especially his casualness in supervising financial transactions and overseeing his staff—thus the Silas Deane affair. Yet Wright credits Franklin as the primary architect of the French alliance, and he contends that it was Franklin who secured the invaluable subsidies from the French government that financed so much of the American war effort. Cast in the role of a beggar asking for money that both he and the French knew Congress might not be able to repay, he managed not only to get much of what he asked for but also to convince Vergennes that France as well as the Colonies stood to gain if the struggle for independence were successful. Only Franklin, Wright concludes, was both adroit and respected enough to play the part with such success.

Franklin's other major service as a statesman, Wright argues, was his early and persistent advocacy of a Colonial union. Wright goes so far as to suggest, quoting Franklin himself, that if he had been listened to, the crises of the 1760's would have been averted: The united Colonies would have been strong enough to defend themselves against the French and the Indians, and there would have been no need for troops from England and taxes to support them. Franklin foresaw the option of dominion status for the colonies of the British Empire almost a hundred years before it occurred to the English, and Wright speculates that if they had been reasonable enough to listen to him, the break with America might have been averted.

Wright reasons that the quintessential Yankeeness that others have deplored in Franklin was more a virtue than a failing. Franklin recognized no limits to freedom: political, intellectual, religious, or economic. He had confidence in those whom he termed "the middling people" and in himself as one of them. If his soul had no poetry, as his critics have rightly observed, he compensated for this lack with abundant self-reliance, industriousness, and shrewdness. He has a stronger claim than any other man of his time, Wright concludes, to be called "the first specimen Yankee."

Judith N. McArthur

Sources for Further Study

American Heritage. XXXVII, August, 1986, p. 82.
The Atlantic. CCLVII, April, 1986, p. 122.
Booklist. LXXXII, March 1, 1986, p. 942.
Choice. XXIII, July, 1986, p. 1730.
Christian Science Monitor. LXXVIII, April 23, 1986, p. 21.
Commentary. LXXXI, June, 1986, p. 74.
Kirkus Reviews. LIV, March 1, 1986, p. 383.
Library Journal. CXI, March 15, 1986, p. 64.
The New York Times Book Review. XCI, May 18, 1986, p. 39.
Publishers Weekly. CCXXIX, March 14, 1986, p. 90.

FRIENDSHIP AND LITERATURE
Spirit and Form

Author: Ronald A. Sharp (1945-   )
Publisher: Duke University Press (Durham, North Carolina). 183 pp. $19.95
Type of work: Literary criticism and cultural analysis

A study of how friendship is practiced in society and presented in literature, with emphasis upon the parts played by form and the exchange of gifts

Friendship has metaphysical and ethical dimensions, according to Ronald A. Sharp, "for the friend not only validates and concretizes one's sense of identity and reality; he also in one way or another evaluates it." Sharp is not interested in the ways friends manipulate or betray one another but in the positive values inherent in close relationships; he is concerned with what makes a friendship successful: "How does it work when it does work?" Recognizing the potential scope of the subject, Sharp has chosen to concentrate on its more personal—though not sentimental—qualities.

The title of Sharp's study is somewhat misleading, since he invokes anthropology, sociology, and personal experiences almost as much as he does literature, drawing heavily upon Lewis Hyde's *The Gift: Imagination and the Erotic Life of Property* (1983) and Robert Brain's *Friends and Lovers* (1976). Sharp, chairman of the English department at Kenyon College and former editor of the *Kenyon Review*, considers his references to literary works "as examples, as points of departure, or as ways of illuminating particular points in my general argument about friendship."

His analysis of friendship is presented in three sections. The first, which makes up nearly half the book, examines the parts form and ritual play in friendship, how they promote rather than obstruct intimacy. The second looks at the effects of the gift on the spiritual dimensions of friendship. The last applies all of this to William Shakespeare's play *The Merchant of Venice* (1596-1597).

Sharp argues that those who consider forms suspect in matters of intimacy fail to realize that "friendship cannot flourish at all outside of forms." The way in which friendship is presented is as important as the friendship itself. He illustrates this point with the way three friends part at the end of a fiesta in Ernest Hemingway's *The Sun Also Rises* (1926). Their shaking hands, waving, and using affectionate terms such as "chaps," "fella," and "old kid" are formal and conventional means of "expressing affection in a culture that denies men more physical expressions." Modern American women in similar circumstances would have unself-consciously hugged one another. (The differences in male, female, and male-female friendships are of particular interest to Sharp.) Examples from the works of Ezra Pound and Friedrich Nietzsche suggest to Sharp that formality, ritual, artifice, and conventional hospitality do not impede intimacy but enhance it.

Those who promote a false or sentimental version of friendship are targets of Sharp's disdain. Yet the phony familiarity of encounter groups, insurance salesmen, and television weathermen calls attention to the necessity of formal conventions in preserving the authenticity of true friendship. The same is true in literature, since contemporary confessional poetry is less likely to express depth of feeling than the forms of the past, such as the sonnet. Sharp observes that confessional poems about friendship by such writers as Robert Lowell and Adrienne Rich "issue from an isolation that seems more profound than any intimacy that is achieved, or even yearned for." Good humor is more important in a friendship than an unburdening of emotions, as Sharp illustrates with Shakespeare's Prince Hal and Falstaff.

Friendship is more formalized than the worlds of business and popular culture would have one believe: "A friendship has its own history, its own founding, its own civil and foreign wars, its own mythic events, its own status quo, its own vision of the future, its own ethos, ideals, and legal system." For all its rituals, however, friendship is less a formal gesture presented in public than "a kind of private shelter from the demands of the public."

Sharp underscores these points with *Cranford* (1853) by Elizabeth Gaskell, in which the novelist seems to be ridiculing the public formality of the conventional friendships between the women in a community, only to reverse the reader's expectations when an old woman loses all of her money and is aided by the others. Beneath the forms of seemingly superficial intimacy, Sharp argues, lie forms capable of producing sincerity and compassion. Similarly, he uses Jane Austen to show how friendship thrives when forms are used creatively.

Sharp discusses how fear of being thought homosexual inhibits friendships, especially among Americans. In *The Sun Also Rises*, Bill Gorton tells Jake Barnes, "I'm fonder of you than anybody on earth," only to add, "I couldn't tell you that in New York. It'd mean I was a faggot." Gorton continues with a joke about Abraham Lincoln, Ulysses S. Grant, and Jefferson Davis being homosexuals to deflate the seriousness of his earlier remark. Sharp wants men to realize "that at some level there is no adequate substitute for self-disclosure, openness, and sincerity, and that in this respect the still dominant male inhibitions are indeed an obstacle to intimacy in friendship." Sharp, perhaps too easily, dismisses the presence of "an erotic element" as virtually irrelevant to the true nature of friendship. According to Sharp, many critics are quick to discover the homosexual content in Walt Whitman's poetry while ignoring the profound significance of friendship as theme and metaphor in his work.

The giving of gifts is crucial to Sharp's view of friendship because he regards it as "the quintessential friendly act; indeed, one way of defining the act of friendship may be to say that it is whatever is undertaken in the spirit of gift exchange." Inspired by Hyde's study of the role of the gift in human relations, he perceives all such relations as a form of exchange. For Sharp, friendship itself is a gift. "In gift exchange," he writes, "where the gift redounds to the giver, we have a perfect model for friendship at its best."

Among Sharp's literary examples of his theory of the gift is the "Julia" section of Lillian Hellman's *Pentimento* (1973), in which Hellman, at the request of her friend Julia, smuggles money into 1937 Germany to buy the freedom of political prisoners. That the money is disguised as a birthday present from Julia is appropriate since each is giving a gift to the other: Hellman's gift is assisting Julia's cause, and Julia's is giving Hellman the opportunity to help save people's lives, to be unselfish. Sharp considers this episode a perfect illustration of how gift exchange strengthens a friendship.

One of Sharp's best uses of literary sources occurs when he juxtaposes quotations from Aristotle, Cicero, Montaigne, and Samuel Johnson to compare their views of friendship and the role generosity should play in it. His skillful weaving of their views creates a compelling debate.

Sharp selects *The Merchant of Venice* to bring all of his ideas together because he regards Shakespeare as the "literary master of friendship" and this play his most thorough exploration of the subject. *The Merchant of Venice* is especially appropriate because its plot is built around a series of gift exchanges—a matter to which Sharp says other critics have devoted little analysis—and since so many legal, financial, and social forms are displayed.

Sharp counts eleven major exchanges of gifts involving nine characters in the play, the most important being the ring Bassanio gives to the judge, whom he does not know is Portia, for saving his friend's life. This act unifies all the elements in the play, because Portia's acceptance of the ring signifies her awareness and approval of her beloved's feelings for Antonio. The latter's presence in the marriage ceremony binds the three together more firmly.

Sharp interprets Shakespeare as saying that friendship is more vulnerable than marriage since it is not legally sanctioned and since it does not involve a sexual bond, but for the same reasons, it may be seen as nobler than married love. Shakespeare also shows how gift exchange offers the kind of sacrifice, risk, and creativity, as in the Lillian Hellman example, that helps give friendship its spiritual nature.

While one of the strengths of *Friendship and Literature* is the economy with which Sharp makes his points, some readers may justifiably see this apparent virture as superficiality. Sharp clearly does not offer as many literary examples in as much detail as he might, leaving the impression that he has failed to prove his case fully enough. Another problem is that he has buried many of his best observations and most interesting examples in eleven pages of notes where some readers may never find them. Henry Miller's account of how he, as a boy, gave all of his toys to his friends, only to be dragged to their homes by his mother to get the gifts back, is too good not to work into the text proper. The same is true for a striking quotation from Toni Morrison's *Sula* (1973).

For the most part, however, Sharp's study is a stimulating look at an aspect of life and literature which has had insufficient intellectual analysis. The book is also noteworthy for providing the kind of memorable writing too little seen in recent criticism: "When the gift is kept in motion, the universe becomes a familiar place, an answering place, a more intimate home; it feels like a living tissue of coincidence, a seamless web of purposeful accident. It becomes, that is to say, a friendly place."

Michael Adams

Sources for Further Study

Los Angeles Times Book Review. September 7, 1986, p. 4.
Playboy. XXXIII, September, 1986, p. 20.

THE GARDEN OF EDEN

Author: Ernest Hemingway (1899-1961)
Publisher: Charles Scribner's Sons (New York). 247 pp. $18.95
Type of work: Novel
Time: Approximately 1927
Locale: The Mediterranean coast of France and Spain and Madrid

A posthumously published novel which traces David Bourne's attempts to write as he confronts the growing demands of his new bride and the memories of his boyhood in Africa

> *Principal characters:*
> DAVID BOURNE, the protagonist, a young writer
> CATHERINE BOURNE, his rich, new bride
> MARITA, the bisexual lover of the Bournes

In a letter to Charles A. Fenton, Ernest Hemingway declared, "Writing that I do not wish to publish, you have no right to publish. I would no more do a thing like that to you than I would cheat a man at cards or rifle his desk or wastebasket or read his personal letters." Despite this objection, and despite his reservations about making certain manuscripts public, a number of these have been published since Hemingway's death. *A Moveable Feast* (1964) he had held back not for aesthetic reasons but because of its sometimes harsh assessments of colleagues still living. *Islands in the Stream* (1970), though, he never finished, nor was he ever able to shape *The Garden of Eden* to his own satisfaction. Hemingway, however, was not easily contented: He told the *Paris Review* that he had rewritten the last page of *A Farewell to Arms* (1929) thirty-nine times before he got the words right.

The Garden of Eden proved even more daunting. Begun in 1946, it grew quickly, though without any plan, as Hemingway wrote against what he suspected was imminent death. By the next year he had some thousand pages of manuscript. He then put the novel aside for a decade, though he did use some of its material for *Across the River and into the Trees* (1950). In 1958 he again tackled the story, incorporating material from his second African safari and his life with Mary Welsh, his fourth wife. Somewhat later he began a third revision, which he never completed.

Faced with these various manuscripts, Tom Jenks, an editor for Scribner's, has produced a remarkably coherent and nearly excellent novel of some sixty thousand words, about one-third the length of the original. In this version, he has removed the story of the painter Nick Sheldon and his wife, Barbara—apparently intended to parallel the lives of David and Catherine Bourne—and has made other editorial alterations. The book which has resulted is far better than *Across the River and into the Trees* or *Islands in the Stream* and hints at the greatness of Hemingway's earliest, and best, fiction.

The Garden of Eden is a semiautobiographical account based on Hemingway's honeymoon with his second wife, Pauline Pfeiffer, in May, 1927, at Le Grau-du-Roi, a fishing village in the Carmargue, on the Mediterranean coast of France. Like Hemingway, David Bourne, the novel's hero, has recently written a successful novel (*The Sun Also Rises*, 1926, in Hemingway's case) and has even more recently married.

Life for David and his bride, Catherine, is at first Edenic. They spend their days eating, drinking, and enjoying the beach; their nights they pass in lovemaking and peaceful sleep. As David reflects, "He had many problems when he married but he had thought of none of them here nor of writing nor of anything but being with this girl whom he loved and was married to. . . . It was a very simple world and he had never been truly happy in any other."

Like the first Eden, though, this paradise is short-lived. Hemingway described the theme of the book as "the happiness of the Garden that a man must lose," the same message he had developed in *A Farewell to Arms* and *For Whom the Bell Tolls* (1940). As early as the third page of the novel Catherine warns David, "I'm the destructive type, . . . and I'm going to destroy you." In the tradition of Frances Clyne (*The Sun Also Rises*) and Mrs. Macomber ("The Short Happy Life of Francis Macomber"), she becomes an emasculating heroine.

Unlike the ideal Hemingway heroine, Catherine has wants. At first these seem innocent—a tan and a haircut—but she wants to cut and dye her hair so that she can appear more masculine. Although Hemingway provides no details of what occurs in the Bournes's bedroom, the reader does eavesdrop on their intimate conversations, which again reveal Catherine's desire to be a man. She tells David, "I'm Peter. You're my wonderful Catherine. You're my beautiful lovely Catherine." Later, in La Napoule, near Cannes, they find Marita, a beautiful bisexual young woman whom Catherine sleeps with and then encourages David to bed as well. Again Hemingway draws on autobiography here, for in 1926 Pauline Pfeiffer joined the Hemingway household first as the friend of Hemingway's first wife, Hadley, then as Hemingway's lover and second wife. Pauline was smaller and darker than Hadley, as Marita is smaller and darker than Catherine. As in life, too, Marita finally supplants Catherine, for even though Catherine has proposed the ménage à trois, she becomes increasingly jealous of David's relationship with Marita. Her jealousy extends to David's work as well; she wants him to write about nothing except their life together.

He, however, is trying to confront the hard story of his boyhood in Africa. One night he and his dog, Kibo, spot an old elephant long sought for his huge ivory tusks. There had once been a pair of these elephants, but David's father had killed one years before. At first David is delighted at his discovery, which he quickly relays to his father. Together he, Kibo, his father, and their guide set off to find the elephant. As they get closer to their goal, though, David regrets having betrayed the animal, and he finally rejects the expedition and elephant hunting in general as barbaric.

Hemingway interweaves David's story of this youthful elephant hunt with his current life. Each morning David writes, then drinks, eats, and loafs with Catherine and Marita. Although the writing is physically isolated from the rest of the day's activities and its events are separated from the present by many years, the hunt parallels David's changing relationship with Catherine. Both the boy David and the man lose their innocence through an ordeal for which they bear much responsibility. Further, both losses of innocence lead to wisdom; both, then, like Adam's Fall, are fortunate. From the death of the elephant David learns respect for life, and his sorrow drives him to produce a powerful story. Although Catherine's increasingly bizarre behavior and jealousy cause her to burn David's manuscript and then desert him, he finds a more suitable mate in Marita. Catherine had wanted things for herself; Marita wants things for David. She is less demanding, more supportive. She will not destroy him or his work, and with her he is able to create an even better account of his boyhood adventure.

Hemingway's sentiments are with David and Marita, the writer and the docile mate. Still, the novel shows a movement toward new attitudes. An obvious shift emerges from David's story about the hunt, where the writing sympathizes with the hunted rather than the hunter. Similarly, Hemingway does not dismiss Catherine as merely a bitch. In Madrid, an acquaintance of the Bournes observes that Catherine reminds him of a "young chief of a warrior tribe who had gotten loose from his councillors." Her role-playing, both sexual and nonsexual, stems from her desire to escape the restrictions that society has imposed on women. Like Hemingway's new perspective on hunting, his understanding of Catherine marks a major shift in sensibility.

Toward the end of the book David reflects,

> There is nothing you can do except try to write it the way that it was. So you must write each day better than you possibly can and use the sorrow that you have now to make you know how the early sorrow came. And you must always remember the things you believed because if you know them they will be there in the writing and you won't betray them.

This observation illuminates the creation of *The Garden of Eden*. Hemingway uses the elements of his life—marital difficulties, African safaris, a lost manuscript—to create a powerful novel. Clearly, the work is unfinished. The style at times seems more a parody of Hemingway than his own lean phrasing: One sentence has no fewer than eleven and's. Further, the daily repetition of eating and drinking, complete with menus, grows tiresome.

Despite its weaknesses, though, this novel will not harm Hemingway's reputation as the other posthumously published works have. Rather, it suggests that in his last decade and a half he was struggling to fuse old material and themes with new attitudes and insights. One must regret that he never overcame the obstacles to completing and polishing *The Garden of Eden*. Yet one must be glad that Scribner's has chosen to publish even this truncated version. For one sees here a different Hemingway, one compassionately concerned with people's daily, inner lives. From this sympathy comes a sense of hope, uncommon in Hemingway's work, that while men and women must lose their Eden, they may yet find contentment in this flawed world.

Joseph Rosenblum

Sources for Further Study

America. CLIV, May 17, 1986, p. 413.
Choice. XXIV, September, 1986, p. 122.
Kirkus Reviews. LIV, March 15, 1986, p. 414.
Los Angeles Times. May 22, 1986, V, p. 1.
National Review. XXXVIII, May 23, 1986, p. 44.
The New York Review of Books. XXXIII, June 12, 1986, p. 5.
The New York Times Book Review. XCI, May 18, 1986, p. 1.
The New Yorker. LXII, June 30, 1986, p. 85.
Newsweek. CVII, May 19, 1986, p. 7.
Publishers Weekly. CCXXIX, April 4, 1986, p. 51.
Time. CXXVII, May 26, 1986, p. 77.
Washington Post Book World. XVI, June 6, 1986, p. 1.

GATHERING EVIDENCE
A Memoir

Author: Thomas Bernhard (1931-   )
Translated from the German by David McLintock
Publisher: Alfred A. Knopf (New York). 340 pp. $19.95
Type of work: Autobiography
Time: 1931-1950
Locale: Austria, Bavaria

An engrossing five-part memoir of the author's childhood and adolescence, during which he had to overcome a broken family, narrow-minded schooling, the aftereffects of war and deprivation, prolonged illness, and near death

> *Principal personages:*
> THOMAS BERNHARD, an Austrian novelist and dramatist
> JOHANNES FREUMBICHLER (unnamed), his grandfather, a philosopher, anarchist, and unsuccessful writer
> HERTA FABJAN, his mother

Although Thomas Bernhard's reputation as a major writer has become increasingly well established in the United States, the thematic and stylistic difficulties of his prose are still not likely to gain for him a wide readership. This translation of his five autobiographical sketches, which were published separately in German between 1975 and 1982, should make his novels and plays more accessible by providing a personal and historical context for the persistent Bernhardian themes of suffering, disease, death, despair, isolation, and suicide. Bernhard's recollections of the first nineteen years of his life are by no means an unrelentingly grim account of childhood suffering. Rather, he tells his story with remarkable detachment, even humor, most notably in *A Child*, the last of the five autobiographical books to appear in German (following chronology, it is placed first in the translation). The fascination which emanates from these works stems from the enormous contrasts and paradoxes of Bernhard's record of his life. It is the story of a continual overcoming of pain, of the struggle to transform suffering into meaningful endeavor and, eventually, into literature. Written in a gripping style and with considerable polemic energy, *Gathering Evidence* is a work of piercing honesty and integrity.

Each of the five books begins by focusing on a decisive moment in Bernhard's life. This initial focus, already suggested by the title of the books (*A Child, An Indication of the Cause, The Cellar: An Escape, Breath: A Decision, In the Cold*—David McLintock, it should be noted, takes some liberty in translating the titles as well as the body of the text), is then varied at length. *A Child* opens with the story of an illicit bike ride from Traunstein in Upper Bavaria, where the young Bernhard lived with his mother and guardian, to his Aunt Fanny's house, twenty-two miles east in Salzburg. He was eight years old at the time, it was his first time on a bicycle, which belonged to his guardian, and he never made it to Salzburg, ending up in a ditch instead. Nevertheless, it was the occasion of a major discovery, the elation brought about by the freedom of movement on wheels and the stretching of the limits of his previously confined existence. He felt a oneness with his dearly beloved grandfather, who would surely approve of such a daring, ambitious, and unheard-of undertaking. At the same time, however, the trip was in total disobedience to and rebellion against his mother, for whom he was an unwanted and intractable son. His return home was divided between feelings of "sublime pride" at his breaking away and dread of the "supreme penalty" that awaited him at home. After leaning the ruined bike against the wall of his mother's house, he immediately headed for his grandfather's house several miles away. As he climbed the foothills of the Bavarian Alps, he left behind the revolting petty bourgeois world of the flatlands and his own sense of worthlessness, feeling instead that he had become "a real person," someone who followed his own laws rather than the senseless and arbitrary laws of his parents, teachers, and institutions.

This love of anarchy Bernhard had learned from his grandfather, a restless and energetic man who had found little success as a writer and lived off his adoring wife and daughter. The tensions of Bernhard's upbringing resulted largely from the clash between his mother's desire for normalcy and middle-class security and his grandfather's penchant for conflict, "anything unusual and extraordinary, anything contradictory or revolutionary." His grandfather was "his great enlightener," his one true teacher, friend, adviser, and confidant. Bernhard's relationship with his mother, on the other hand, remained problematic for years, because he reminded her constantly of his father, the lover who abandoned her before Bernhard's secret, illegitimate birth in Holland in 1931. His mother returned to Vienna in 1932 and married Bernhard's stepfather in 1934, after which Bernhard moved with his grandparents to a town north of Salzburg, then to Traunstein in 1938. An outsider from his birth, Bernhard had the additional stigma of being an Austrian in a strongly Nazified Bavaria. He did poorly in school, detested the Nazi youth organization into which he was forced, and distinguished himself only in running.

At his grandfather's insistence, Bernhard was sent to a boarding school in Salzburg in 1943. It is significant that the first volume of Bernhard's autobiography to appear (*An Indication of the Cause*) describes his experiences under the blindly authoritarian rule, first of the school's National Socialist, then of its Catholic administration, in a city that he came to hate under the worst conditions of the war. While "the Cause" of the title is ambiguous, Bernhard makes it clear in his vituperative attacks that he associates it with Salzburg and all that the city came to represent for him: "renowned the world over for beauty and edification, as well as for the celebration of what is known as Great Art at its annual festival," Salzburg "is in truth nothing but a chill museum of death, open to every kind of disease and depravity."

Scene of the remaining four books, the city provides a uniformly bleak backdrop to Bernhard's narrative theater of human suffering. Salzburg, as the book's epigraph relates, holds the Austrian record for suicide, which, according to Bernhard, is the most fitting response to the city's deadly charms, yet a response for which he was too much of a coward. At the end of the war, the city traded one mindless ideology for another, just as smoothly as the sadistic Nazi school warden Grünkranz was replaced by an equally malicious young prefect, Nazi songs by hymns, and Adolf Hitler's picture by a cross. The death and destruction of the Allied bombing raids in autumn 1944, the terror and hopelessness of the air-raid shelters in tunnels burrowed into the city's hills, the stench of decomposition were all forgotten as quickly as the rubble was cleared and the city's architectural and cultural treasures rebuilt. The school itself remained for Bernhard an educational ruin and prison, "an institution for the destruction of the mind."

One morning at age fifteen Bernhard headed for the labor office instead of the classroom, and after protracted searching through the job file he found a position as an apprentice in the basement grocery store of Karl Podlaha in the Scherzhauserfeld Project, a notoriously poor district on the outskirts of Salzburg. *The Cellar* is the story of the two happy and productive years there among "the other people," Salzburg's victims and outcasts. Only his grandfather had understanding for the rash step of "going in the opposite direction," of rebelling against normality in order to search for a more authentic existence. Bernhard got along extremely well with Podlaha, a Viennese bachelor, who, like Bernhard, was an outsider seeking refuge in the slums as well as a musician at heart (after a disastrous start on the violin in the boarding school, Bernhard began during these years to take singing lessons and to dream of an operatic career). Bernhard delighted in his work, for not only was he free of the deadening institutional constraints, but also for the first time in his life he felt useful—Podlaha gave him an eminently practical education in dealing with people, in contrast to the philosophical and solitary teachings of his grandfather. Despite an impossible situation at home (he was living with his parents, siblings, and grandparents, all of whom had in the meantime moved into his aunt and uncle's three-room Salzburg apartment), Bernhard's work and musical studies combined to produce near euphoria.

This happy state of affairs was not to last long. In the fall of 1948, perhaps not coincidentally right after his grandfather was admitted to the hospital for possible minor surgery, a simple influenza deteriorated into a life-threatening case of pleurisy. When Bernhard was admitted to the same hospital, he was placed in what he calls the death ward. *Breath* and *In the Cold* follow the course of his illness over the next two years. Both books take as their point of departure two further turning points in Bernhard's narrative—namely, those moments when he decided to fight the death sentence imposed upon him by the disease and his inhumane and incompetent doctors. In *Breath*, this conscious decision not to stop breathing and "to *live*, to live *my life, the way I chose and for as long as I chose*" came in the washroom where terminal patients were moved just before their anticipated death. Back in the death ward that evening, Bernhard recognized his grandfather. It was the first of many visits over the next few months. In February, right before Bernhard's eighteenth birthday, the grandfather stopped coming. Twelve days later, Bernhard read in the newspaper of his grandfather's death, caused by a misdiagnosis of his illness by the hospital's chief physician. The shock of the death was accompanied by a sense of liberation from his grandfather's intellectual domination; for the first time in his life, Bernhard was completely on his own. Following years of estrangement, he became reconciled with his mother, and his recovery proceeded rapidly enough for him to be transferred to a convalescent hospital on the German border, where he began to read seriously for the first time in his life.

These positive developments, though, were again offset by catastrophe. Bernhard's mother was diagnosed with terminal cancer, and the convalescent hospital turned out to be a tuberculosis sanatorium; inevitably Bernhard contracted the disease and after a brief visit home was sent to another institutional prison, the Grafenhof sanatorium south of Salzburg. *In the Cold* opens with his initial acquiescence to the fatal hopelessness of his lung infection and to the cruel authority of the Nazi chief physician and his assistants. It was not long, however, before rebellion set in with the insight that he alone, and not the doctors or the disease, was responsible for his life and recovery. Isolating himself from the despair of his fellow patients, he observed the brutal workings of the sanatorium with new clarity and objectivity. He struck up a friendship with an ambitious young conductor, whose passion for music, optimism, and "absolute affirmation of existence" were exemplary. He began to write, "gathering evidence" about his past and his family on numerous small slips of paper. After nine months in Grafenhof, Bernhard was released and returned to Salzburg. Botched routine pneumothorax therapy sent him back to the hospital and eventually again to Grafenhof. Even more recalcitrant on his second visit, Bernhard surreptitiously undertook trips to the nearby village, where he began singing lessons with a woman organist. Fyodor Dostoevski's *The Demons* confirmed for him that he was on the right path, *"the one that led out."* Released again, Bernhard fell ill once more in Salzburg. This time, however, he refused to return to the detested sanatorium.

Gathering Evidence breaks off with this final refusal. At one point Bernhard admits that his autobiographical writings offer only "a collection of fragments which may readily be put together to form a whole, if the reader chooses to do so." Yet the five books resist integration, for their structure is dialectical, contrastive, and contradictory rather than linear and chronological. To borrow the quotation from Michel de Montaigne that stands as epigraph for *The Cellar*, Bernhard's writing can be said to be "an irregular, uncertain motion, perpetual, patternless and without aim." Indeed, Montaigne's moral skepticism and rigorous self-analysis are writ large across these pages, as Bernhard readily admits (Bernhard's admiration for the French philosopher, like so much else in his intellectual makeup, was owing to his grandfather). With such programmatic statements as "Truth is always wrong, . . every error is pure truth" and "Language can only falsify and distort whatever is authentic," Bernhard keeps open his search for authenticity and truth in the writing out of his recollections, a process that knows no beginning or end. The powerful desire for movement of thought and expression, which engenders the poses of ironist, anarchist, troublemaker, clown, and gadfly, lends these works their formal energy, a kinesis underscored by the percussive rhythm of Bernhard's complex, hypotactic sentences (which McLintock unfortunately fails to capture in his rather homogenized translation), his preference for hyperbole and extreme formulations, the hypnotic effect of the repetitions, the economy of the methodic, contrapuntal composition. Vitality resides within the images of movement and change—the bicycle ride, the walks with the grandfather, running, breathing, "going in the opposite direction," the forbidden sled rides from Grafenhof down into the Schwarzach Valley, death within the image of stasis and enclosure—the institutions, the air-raid tunnels, the endless lying in bed. Bernhard's conclusion that "absurdity is the only way forward" might be the most fitting epigraph for this memoir, for absurdity best describes Bernhard's tragicomic vision of the world as "pure farce." Yet Bernhard is not Albert Camus or Samuel Beckett, and these sketches, like Montaigne's *Essais*, ultimately function to provoke, instruct, and enlighten.

Peter West Nutting

Sources for Further Study

Booklist. LXXXII, February 15, 1986, p. 845.
Choice. XXIII, May, 1986, p. 1396.
Kirkus Reviews. LIII, November 15, 1985, p. 1232.
Library Journal. CXI, January, 1986, p. 78.
Los Angeles Times Book Review. February 16, 1986, p. 3.
The New York Times Book Review. XCI, February 16, 1986, p. 12.
The New Yorker. LXVII, July 21, 1986, p. 92.
Publishers Weekly. CCXXIX, January 10, 1986, p. 81.

GENTLEMEN IN ENGLAND
A Vision

Author: A. N. Wilson (1950-   )
Publisher: The Viking Press (New York). 311 pp. $17.95
Type of work: Novel
Time: 1880
Locale: England, primarily London

A look at Victorian life through the Nettleship family

> *Principal characters:*
> HORACE NETTLESHIP, a professor of geology; a beleaguered husband and father
> CHARLOTTE NETTLESHIP, his wife, considerably younger; bored and disillusioned
> MAUDIE, their sixteen-year-old daughter, very pretty and innocent
> LIONEL NETTLESHIP, a student at Oxford, who wants to become a clergyman
> WALDO CHATTERWAY, a social butterfly and incurable gossip
> SEVERUS EGG, Charlotte's father, seventy-six years old; a holdover from the eighteenth century
> TIMOTHY LUPTON, a mediocre society portrait painter

Although British author A. N. Wilson is still well under forty, *Gentlemen in England* is his eighth novel and twelfth book, his third novel to be released in the United States. Clearly, the man is a literary prodigy, and if he can mature as rapidly as he composes, he will take his place as England's greatest living novelist in a very short time. He is not there yet, but this novel shows considerable powers of invention and a flexible, witty style that marks so much of the best British writing of this century.

Set in 1880, the year in which Charles Bradlaugh refused to swear his oath in Parliament on the Bible and in which George Eliot married John Cross, this is more a modern novel set a hundred years ago than a historical novel. The difference is crucial, for Wilson is not so much attempting to recreate the late Victorian era (though he does so brilliantly) as to cast a critical eye upon it and dissect its social, sexual, and religious struggles. His vehicle is the intensely respectable and middle-class Nettleship family, ostensibly headed by Horace Nettleship, a professor of geology whose loss of faith while chipping fossils from a volcano remains the central event of his intellectual life. The most important happening of his personal life was his marriage to Charlotte, many years his junior. Long since emotionally estranged, they are kept together only by the social taboo against divorce and the Victorian passion for maintaining appearances. Charlotte has simply lost interest in Horace, realizing too late that she never loved him and was in effect coerced into the union by relatives determined to see her "well settled." Indifference turns to passion, however, when she meets Timothy

Lupton, the mediocre but socially successful portrait painter who, like every other man in the novel, falls in love with Maudie.

The novel's title, in fact, is somewhat misleading, since sixteen-year-old Maudie is its central figure. As Wilson observes in the first chapter, "All the world loved Maudie; it was her calling in life to be worshipped and adored." She accepts the world's homage as her natural right, though without pride or bad manners. Maudie is a young woman believable only in a Victorian context: childishly innocent about all worldly things and devoted to her brother Lionel. Unlike sixteen-year-olds of contemporary novels, she has no interest in men and no understanding of sex. She finds the hair that grows from men's faces repulsive, which is one reason why Lionel remains dear to her, without the slightest trace of incestuous feeling. The other man in her life, besides her adoring father, is the frivolous Chatterway, to whom she increasingly turns for advice and consolation. The great turning point in Maudie's life occurs over one of the family's painful meals when for the first time she lies to her father, thus becoming "a daughter of Eve." This defection to her mother's side is one more blow to her father's peace of mind.

The thematic concerns of the novel are explored through the conflicts among the characters. Lionel's embracing of the church and in particular the reform-minded Oxford Movement opens a rift between him and his father by which the claims of science and faith can be explored. One can see in Horace Nettleship's painful rejection of his once-firm faith the struggles of Victorians throughout the period, but one also sees its personal side, the toll it takes on the professor's spirit and the bitterness it causes in his relations with his wife. How, he asks himself, can Charlotte continue to observe the outward forms of Christian worship without showing any concern for his soul? Is she utterly indifferent toward him? Although father and son move toward respect for each other's position, the marriage deteriorates.

On her side, Charlotte has reached a state where she is angry at life and the people who betrayed her at an early age into a loveless marriage. On the surface, she seems calm and resigned, but when she falls violently in love with Lupton, the passionate side of her nature is finally revealed, erupting in a violent quarrel with Maudie, "shameless" behavior at a ball, and finally, after fifteen years of strained silence, an open quarrel with Horace that leads to his brutally raping her. There is an element of high comedy in Charlotte's passion for Lupton and the misunderstandings that result from her love for him and his for Maudie, but beneath the humor and the ridiculousness of a phony marriage lie the tragedies of Victorian sexual repression and hypocrisy.

Charlotte's father, Severus Egg, and his longtime friend Waldo Chatterway represent a departed way of life—the lighter, more frivolous attitudes of Lord Byron's time. In contrast to excessive Victorian earnestness, Egg and Chatterway idle away their lives in country-house parties, afternoon teas, and leisurely rubbers of whist at the club. Once a promising poet, Egg (whose black butler is named Bacon) dissipated his talents for literature by devoting them to the art of living, but in the process he allowed Charlotte to be reared by puritanical relatives who steered her in Nettleship's direction. Thus, while he can smile at the straitlaced lives and solemn attitudes of younger generations, he bears some responsibility for Charlotte's unhappy fate. Chatterway, who was close to Charlotte as a child and has now turned his attentions to Maudie, is both the most shallow and elusive character of the book. Utterly frivolous in his pursuit of titled, fashionable friends and up to the minute gossip, he is nevertheless a shrewd judge of character and on occasion a helpful counselor.

Timothy Lupton embodies both the sexual and artistic strains of the era. He is hopelessly in love with Maudie; his dreams and then his neoclassical canvases are invaded by erotic visions of her face and figure—he sees himself playing Odysseus to her Nausicaä. Frustrated in his wooing, he succumbs to debauches in London's bordellos and to grubby back-alley encounters with prostitutes. Having chosen a career in art, he has largely wasted his small talent in routine book illustration and society portraiture, but the Impressionists have awakened in him a dim recognition of his own truest bent, though he lacks the conviction and talent to pursue it. His is the struggle between art and commerce that became acute in the nineteenth century.

These are the ideas and struggles that preoccupy the characters of Wilson's novel. In many ways, the book can be read as an extended gloss on Matthew Arnold's "Dover Beach," that quintessentially Victorian poem on the loss of faith and the necessity of love. Paradoxically, however, the ideas and struggles of the characters in the book do not constitute the theme of the novel. In spite of Wilson's great skill at evoking the texture of Victorian life and his ability to dramatize the tensions that racked the period, the book remains strangely on the surface of these ideas. This can be traced in part to Wilson's urbane and witty style, which encourages distancing rather than involvement. In addition, his irresolute and anticlimactic ending leaves all the book's conflicts unresolved, further contributing to this feeling. Thus, *Gentlemen in England* seems to be "about" the Victorian period and its problems rather than "of" it. If a common thread runs through the various elements, it is the failure of communication. This is handled wittily in the case of Charlotte and Lupton, who talk at comic cross-purposes throughout much of the book, tragically in the fifteen-year silence between husband and wife, and wittily in Chatterway's ability to use gossip—the froth on the ocean of speech—to his own advantage. This theme, however, is at odds with the book's other major concerns and thus does not unify it successfully.

Make no mistake, however: *Gentleman in England* is an entertaining and provocative novel, technically accomplished and skillfully written. Much of its appeal lies in the fact that the difficulties its characters face have not changed much in the last hundred years or so. To say that this is not the best novel Wilson will write is not so much to criticize his current performance as to look optimistically toward his future accomplishments.

Dean Baldwin

Sources for Further Study

Booklist. LXXXII, March 1, 1986, p. 946.
Christian Science Monitor. LXXVIII, March 19, 1986, p. 26.
Kirkus Reviews. LIII, December 1, 1985, p. 1291.
Library Journal. CXI, February 1, 1986, p. 95.
The London Review of Books. VII, November 21, 1985, p. 20.
Los Angeles Times Book Review. March 16, 1986, p. 3.
The New York Times Book Review. XCI, March 9, 1986, p. 7.
Publishers Weekly. CCXXVIII, December 13, 1985, p. 46.
Time. CXXVII, March 17, 1986, p. 81.
The Wall Street Journal. CCVII, April 8, 1986, p. 28.

GHOST DANCE

Author: Carole Maso

Publisher: North Point Press (San Francisco, California). 275 pp. $16.95

Type of work: Novel

Time: The 1950's to 1986

Locale: New York City and environs

The daughter of a famous poet reckons with her mother's death by writing a fanciful, not-always-trustworthy family history

> *Principal characters:*
> CHRISTINE WING, a beautiful, doomed poetess
> VANESSA TURIN, her daughter, narrator of the book
> FLETCHER TURIN, Vanessa's brother
> SABINE, Christine's French lover
> MARTA, Vanessa's friend at Vassar College
> JACK, Vanessa's anonymous lover

The mid-1970's witnessed the birth in the United States of a new genre of nonfiction literature: the disgruntled memoirs of a celebrity's offspring. From Brooke Hayward's *Haywire* (1977) to Christina Crawford's *Mommie Dearest* (1978) to Angelica Garnett's *Deceived with Kindness* (1984), daughters of distinguished mothers have tried to dismantle, or at least analyze, the public and private personae of their famous relatives and in the process to squeeze themselves into the spotlight. Inspired perhaps by this dubious if fascinating phenomenon, Carole Maso has written a highly literary first novel about a fictional poet, written in the first person by the woman's daughter. Unlike her counterparts in real life, however, this daughter is inspired to write not by resentment or frustration but by a love so obsessive that it threatens to undermine the girl's very existence. *Ghost Dance* is a novel about a young woman living in the shadow of her mother's greatness, trying to accept her mother's death by spinning out a fanciful, not-always-factual family history.

The reader is introduced to Christine Wing, the poet, and Vanessa Turin, her daughter, in a scene at New York's Grand Central Station in the midst of the Christmas holidays. Christine has just returned from a month's vacation in Maine; Vanessa is on her way back to Vassar College for the winter semester. Christine seems distracted, oblivious to the time of day and the snowy weather outside. Vanessa is rapt, almost worshipful in her mother's presence. Nothing particularly eventful happens during the course of the scene, yet it becomes compellingly surreal as Vanessa, disturbed by her mother's gaudy appearance, strips her of her jewelry and as Christine, urging Vanessa to leave, whispers that she loved her even before she was born. It is clear that Vanessa, in describing the scene, is distorting it, imbuing it with a charged, desperate, romantic emotion, the reasons for which at this point remain unspecified.

During the course of the novel, Vanessa haltingly, circuitously explains the significance of that scene for her. Little in this book is told directly; everything is built up through allusion and repetition, until the facts spill out almost in spite of Vanessa. Initially, the reader learns only that Christine has apparently disappeared; that Vanessa's father has also vanished, leaving brochures in his car describing icy fjords; that her brother has taken to traveling around the country and mailing angry postcards alluding to various social injustices. During the course of the novel, however, the process of telling proves therapeutic for Vanessa. By the book's conclusion, she is able to confront (and communicate) the real reason for Christine's "disappearance": her death in a car accident a few days after that scene in Grand Central Station.

In segments which vary in length, Vanessa jumps back and forth from the distant past to the present day, touching on varied times and topics that all somehow tie back to her immediate family. Repeating scenes and motifs, building in intensity as Vanessa approaches nearer and nearer to the truth, the novel is structured musically rather than narratively. One of its central symbols is the Topaz Bird, a family metaphor for divine inspiration described by Christine to her young daughter. According to Christine, certain members of her mother's family were visited by this bird and thereafter showed glimmerings of genius bordering at times on insanity. Christine claims to have been privileged to see this bird at birth, and her daughter yearns for a glimpse of it, well aware that such a vision would be a mixed blessing.

While learning the Wing family mythology, the reader is provided a more concrete idea of Christine's past. The poet grew up in Paterson, New Jersey, the daughter of an Armenian factory worker and a sickly German-American mother who died while she was still a child. She and her sister, Lucy, led a deprived childhood, enjoying nothing so much as the travel brochures their father would read to them. Nevertheless, Christine managed to attend Vassar, where signs of her literary genius appeared early. She began publishing her renowned volumes of verse while just out of college.

It was at Vassar that Christine met Vanessa's father, the son of Italian immigrants, a mathematician from Princeton University attending a Vassar dance. As Vanessa describes it, her father fell in love with her mother at first sight. In her glorifying eyes, their marriage becomes an analogue for the marriage of Grace Kelly to Prince Rainier of Monaco. In this poetically conceived novel, it is not surprising that Christine Wing will eventually succumb to the same fate as Princess Grace, dying in an automobile accident.

The Turins' marriage turns out to be a most unconventional one. While Christine publishes several brilliant volumes of verse, her husband pursues a colorless career as a stockbroker, devoting himself utterly to nurturing his wife. Christine seems to return his love, but her distinguished poetry does not come without a price. Occasionally, the Topaz Bird pays a visit, and Christine's otherworldly calm gives way to what appears, in Vanessa's anxious descriptions, to be schizophrenia. The poet seems to have been institutionalized several times.

Throughout her marriage, Christine carries on a passionate affair with a Frenchwoman, Sabine, a friend from her Vassar days. Christine regularly flies to France or Maine to meet Sabine for month-long vacations. It is from a rendezvous with Sabine that Christine has returned the time Vanessa meets her in Grand Central Station. In writing about Sabine, Vanessa seems to suggest that, if Christine were never wholly satisfied with heterosexual love, neither did her love for Sabine threaten to disrupt her marriage. Vanessa's father apparently dotes sufficiently on her mother to accept whatever arrangement Christine desires.

Vanessa and her brother, Fletcher, grow up doting on their mother just as much, building their lives around her. Nevertheless, Fletcher does manage to develop a sure sense of his own identity—something Vanessa seems to lack. Inspired by a strong sense of morality and justice, Fletcher becomes an impassioned activist, crusading for environmental causes and minority rights. Vanessa, meanwhile, matures in her mother's image, attending Vassar and trying to re-create her own version of her mother's experience.

Soon after orientation, Vanessa meets a student named Marta, who is as haunted by another woman as Vanessa is by Christine, or, for that matter, as Christine is by Sabine. Marta's wealthy former girlfriend Natalie loved Marta, left her, went to France, and committed suicide. Taking Vanessa as a lover, Marta initiates the girl into a world of depression, drugs, and doom. Vanessa follows in Marta's footsteps, but only to a point. When Marta attempts to kill herself, Vanessa withdraws, though as a writer she cannot help entering into Marta's experience and describing her brush with death and narrowly missed reunion with Natalie.

Two other love affairs figure in Vanessa's autobiography, as she attempts to exorcise her mother's spirit. One is with Jack, a huge male stranger who accosts her at Grand Central Station, which she regularly visits as she relives her last meeting with her mother. Vanessa and Jack quickly become lovers, agreeing to keep their relationship anonymous and strictly erotic. As the affair develops, however, it becomes more personal, with Vanessa first playing the student to Jack's teacher and eventually submitting to bondage and sadomasochism. Nevertheless, Jack remains an almost faceless, helpful guide for Vanessa, leading her through an entire range of cathartic sexual experience.

Even more important is Vanessa's relationship with Sabine, her mother's lover, who appears at Vanessa's door after Christine's death. Sabine seduces Vanessa, then leaves her forever the next day. While the two women make love, it is Christine who is foremost on their minds. Indeed, Sabine is attracted to Vanessa simply because she looks so much like her mother. Their lovemaking becomes a kind of mourning ritual for the dead poet. It is a healing act for Vanessa, which finally enables her to accept her mother's death.

To accept Vanessa's love affairs as fact, however, is to ignore the dream-like tone of the book and to accept Vanessa herself as a reliable narrator— something she herself warns the reader against as the book's outset when she says that her mother always encouraged her to be highly imaginative. There is something too neat about Marta's resemblance to Christine to convince the reader of her reality, just as there is something blatantly contrived about Vanessa's entering into Marta's consciousness after her suicide attempt. Jack is anonymous in every sense of the word, appearing to be little more than a blank erotic presence Vanessa has failed to delineate, and Sabine's rendezvous with Vanessa is, transparently, a confused young woman's desperate wish fulfillment.

What then is one to make of the narrative of *Ghost Dance*? There are no clues to inform the reader of what actually happened to Vanessa; Maso is not interested in a Nabokovian game of detective, in which the astute reader can spot the reality beyond the narrator's distorted lens. Rather, what is important in *Ghost Dance* is Vanessa's telling. What matters is that she imaginatively enters into a particular incident, not whether it actually happened. Her summoning up her various lovers is writing as therapy, enabling her at last to confront her mother's death in a car accident that resulted from a 1973 Pinto's faulty gas tank. It is only after imagining sleeping with Sabine that she is able to take part, with her brother, in an Indian ghost dance, at last laying to rest the spirit of her mother.

Ghost Dance is, to be sure, a most elusive novel. What might have been a straightforward account of mother love becomes, in Carole Maso's hands, an ambitious tour de force combining influences as diverse as Gabriel García Márquez, Virginia Woolf, and Walt Whitman. That Maso manages to synthesize these various sources and to control her difficult technique marks the novel as one of the most interesting debuts in 1986.

Yet *Ghost Dance* is not a wholly successful novel. Though its various elements cohere formally, there is an overextended quality to the book that leaves one dissatisfied. There are too many parallel characters, too many hastily sketched relationships. Moreover, Maso is too anxious to make the Turin family stand for something larger than themselves. Throughout the novel, there is a vein of political concern running from Grandpa Turin's involvement in a 1964 Civil Rights march to Fletcher's own impassioned activism, which nevertheless cannot prevent Christine's death. Part of Vanessa's maturing, at the end of the book, seems to be her putting aside her resentment of America's political and social corruption. Yet when, at the end of the novel, Vanessa essays a Whitmanesque rhapsody embracing all forms of American life, one does not feel the sense of triumph intended; one is only aware of the novelist standing behind Vanessa, attempting to inflate her book beyond all bounds.

This, fundamentally, is the problem at the heart of *Ghost Dance*: that Maso never manages to establish authorial distance between herself and her narrator. Nowhere is this problem more crucial than in Vanessa's rendering of her mother. For the novel to work, one must believe either in the genius of Christine Wing or in some alternative version of her visible beyond Vanessa's portrait. Yet Christine remains only a breathlessly Romantic vision of The Poet, whose very schizophrenia becomes a glamorizing touch. Were one ever given samples of Christine's work, one might believe more readily in her powers, but Maso leaves the entire character of her writing to one's imagination.

One tries to picture Christine as an Americanized Virginia Woolf, but her past lacks the complexity of that novelist's, just as her madness lacks the pain. The heavy sense of doom surrounding Christine leads one, throughout the novel, to suspect her disappearance to be the result of her own self-destructive impulses, but when one discovers that the Ford Motor Company is responsible, one feels no shock of truth but only a vague sense of the arbitrary. The entire character of Christine Wing has become so dreamlike that virtually anything could be offered up as the cause of her disappearance. The novel's sense of aesthetic logic is finally that flimsy.

If *Ghost Dance* seems underrealized then, it nevertheless stands out as one of those rare novels that extend the realm of fiction. If Carole Maso shows a sometimes faulty grasp of her material, her stylistic control is that of a master, and it is not surprising that *Ghost Dance* garnered a respectful set of reviews and won the favorable attention of such novelists as Edmund White and John Hawkes. This first novel marks Carole Maso as a writer of real potential.

Richard Glatzer

Sources for Further Study

Best Sellers. XLVI, September, 1986, p. 204.
Booklist. LXXXII, May 1, 1986, p. 1283.
Christian Science Monitor. LXXVIII, July 18, 1986, p. 22.
Kirkus Reviews. LIV, April 15, 1986, p. 572.
Library Journal. CXI, July 16, 1986, p. 110.
Los Angeles Times Book Review. July 27, 1986, p. 3.
The New York Times Book Review. XCI, July 20, 1986, p. 18.
The New Yorker. LXII, September 15, 1986, p. 120.
Publishers Weekly. CCXXIX, April 25, 1986, p. 66.

GOING TO THE TERRITORY

Author: Ralph Ellison (1914-   )
Publisher: Random House (New York). 338 pp. $19.95
Type of work: Essays/literary criticism

A collection of sixteen thought-provoking essays on the black experience in America, on the concept of American democracy, on the poetics of the novel, and on various other aspects of American culture

One of the most venerated of American writers, Ralph Ellison was honored by a National Book Award in 1953 for his novel *Invisible Man* (1952), by his appointment in 1964 to the American Academy of Arts and Letters, by the Medal of Freedom in 1969, by the Chevalier de l'Ordre des Arts et Lettres in 1970, and in 1985 by the National Medal of Arts. These official honors are but one indication of Ellison's literary stature; he occupies almost a unique position among American writers because of the critical reputation of his powerful novel, *Invisible Man*. It is the kind of novel which only comes along once in a generation—a *Book World* poll of two hundred American writers and critics named it as the most significant work of fiction written between 1945 and 1965. The novel is the odyssey of a black man in contemporary America; it is characterized by the symbolic significance of the protagonist's experience, and it is narrated within an original intellectual context. This same formidable intellectual context is found in Ellison's nonfiction.

Although Ellison's essays, articles, criticism, and reviews have appeared in national publications since 1939, his first collection, *Shadow and Act*, did not appear until 1964. This present collection, *Going to the Territory*, is in many ways a companion volume to that first collection. Ellison's major concerns have not changed: He remains committed to exploring the nature of individual experience—particularly black experience—within the context of the social reality of the United States. He also remains committed to art—especially narrative art in the form of the novel—as an essential instrument in that exploration. All these essays, except for the longest in the collection, "An Extravagance of Laughter," which was written especially for this volume, have appeared previously in magazines, literary journals, or anthologies, most of them since the publication of *Shadow and Act*.

One of Ellison's foremost concerns is to define the nature of democracy for the individual in the United States. In several of these essays, he explores that concept of democracy in terms of a pluralistic society with one essential segment composed of the black experience. Ellison's position is that the experience of the black American has been the ultimate test of the democratic concept from the very founding of the nation to the present. With a critical eye on American history, he discusses the basic conflict between the ideal of equality for all people and the institution of slavery within the context of the framing of the Constitution. He points out that the most significant event in the nation's history—the Civil War—was a continuing development of that basic conflict. Ellison views the Reconstruction effort after the Civil War as a great failure of the democratic ideal. Instead of bringing the ideal of equality for all people closer to reality, the Jim Crow laws which were formulated during that period perpetuated a discrepancy between the ideals of the nation and the actual social reality of the country, particularly the social reality of the Deep South.

This discrepancy between the expressed ideals of the nation and its social reality is at the heart of much of Ellison's thought. He believes that it accounts for the way in which history has been written in the United States; those events which correspond to the ideals of the nation have been recorded formally, and they have been taught and consciously held dear by the people. Many of the events in the history of the nation, however, have not been recorded formally. This "unwritten history," or "underground" history, characterizes much of the black experience, and it is vitally important to the attempt to determine the nature of the country's moral identity. Folklore is one element of this unwritten history, and the very language in which black folklore is formed—black English—contains symbolic phrases and terms that indicate its subject. "Going to the Terr'tor' "—a line from a song of the great jazz singer Bessie Smith—is one such phrase, a phrase which Ellison identifies as indicating symbolic freedom for the black American.

Thus, Ellison believes that the experience of the black American is a factor which has not been adequately defined within the context of the national life. His point is made with the sure, confident reasoning that characterizes these essays in general. Ellison is very aware of himself within the historical context of the nation, and he can be passionate about the circumstances of that historical context, with its racism and its limited opportunities, as well as with its accomplishments and its potential. Always, his is a passion tempered with intelligence, a passion which is made to serve the point under consideration. It is the force of his logic that brings the reader around to Ellison's point of view.

Certainly, one of Ellison's strengths as a thinker is that he is aware that his concept of the black experience is generated from his own particular background. Indeed, it is often this awareness that gives his essays the insight of a significant writer. He declares that "geography is fate," and his personal geography is that of being reared in Oklahoma, which occupies a unique position in the unwritten history of the nation, a position which he explores in the essay "Going to the Territory." Ellison went on to college in the Deep South, at Tuskegee Institute in Alabama, and then he lived his young manhood in New York City. It is a combination of these experiences, dictated in part by geography, that has formed his vision. As a Southerner, Ellison declares that while growing up he learned that "one must listen beneath the surface of what a man has to say." One was forced always to listen for a threat on the accent of a white Texan, and one must continually be aware of the discrepancy between a man's statements and his conduct. The black provincial, Ellison points out, could not afford the luxury of not being aware of that difference, for the black man who was not so aware always faced the possibility of physical violence. In the essay "An Extravagance of Laughter," Ellison brilliantly explores the psychology of lynching, the ultimate physical violence perpetuated against the black man.

This discrepancy between what a man believes—as indicated by his public statements—and what he actually does—his conduct—parallels Ellison's idea of the discrepancy between the nation's ideals and its social reality. There is an interconnection: The individual's moral identity finds its correspondence in the nation's moral identity. On the deepest level, as with all significant thinkers, there is that consistent interconnection among Ellison's major ideas: His ideas on the black experience are integral to his concept of democracy, and, in turn, his concept of democracy is integral to his ideas on American art—in particular, his ideas on the American novel. His essays "The Novel as a Function of American Democracy" and "Society, Morality, and the Novel" explore the integral nature of that relationship.

Ellison's view of the novel is traditional in that it revolves around the concept of the art form as moral expression. He believes that the American novelist has upon his "shoulders the burden of conscientiousness." That burden is the American novelist's sense of duty, his sense of responsibility, for the health of society. In examining the changes in the American literary tradition, from Herman Melville to Mark Twain to Henry James, Ellison stresses the moral continuity of the novel form; he points out that Melville's *Moby Dick* (1851), Twain's *The Adventures of Huckleberry Finn* (1884), and James's *The Bostonians* (1886) are all concerned with the moral predicament of the nation. The serious American novelist, Ellison states, has a "moral cutting edge" in his work—a comment which certainly can be applied to *Invisible Man*. This comment also provides insight into how Ellison evaluates William Faulkner, a novelist for whom he has great respect. In part, Faulkner's achievement was to come "passionately to grips with the moral implications of slavery." As a "moral instrument," the novel is capable of "deadly serious psychological and philosophical explorations of the human predicament." Ellison views it as a "way of confronting reality, confronting the nature of the soul and the nature of society." These are high, serious claims for the novel, claims with which contemporary critics and writers disagree. The critical reception of John Gardner's *On Moral Fiction* (1978), in which Gardner's views on the novel are essentially the same as those of Ellison, indicates the controversial nature of these poetics.

If Ellison's poetics are debatable, his overall view of the artist is undeniably positive. Although the novelist must carry a great burden of responsibility, he is a privileged man in that his work allows him to come into possession of a certain part of reality that has been previously denied man. His art allows him to "realize and complete himself." Thus, the work itself is a vital, life-giving force.

The essay "An Extravagance of Laughter" is one of the most ambitious in Ellison's career. The essay is typical of Ellison in that he explores individual experience—in this instance, his own—within a broad intellectual context. The specific experience under consideration is the response Ellison had as a young man to a Broadway production of Erskine Caldwell's *Tobacco Road* (1932). Having recently arrived as a young college student from Alabama, Ellison was sorting through the different life-styles of New York City, with its radically different decorum for the behavior of black people. In so doing, he was becoming very sensitive to his own background as a black Southerner. The portrayal of Caldwell's characters caused him to go into an uncontrollable fit of laughter which he found extremely embarrassing, for his behavior distracted the audience from the performance. Ellison explores this uncontrollable laughter within the larger framework of the traditional function of comedy, which, in its broadest sense, is a "disguised form of philosophical instruction." He values comedy in that it provides an otherwise "unavailable clarification of vision." Ellison's vision of the South, its restrictions on the freedom of blacks, and the concept of the "mystery of black laughter" were clarified during this performance.

In "An Extravagance of Laughter," as in all of his major work, Ellison challenges the American reader to live up to his ideals. In so doing, he forces the reader to consider the discrepancy between stated ideals and actual conduct and, correspondingly, the discrepancy between America's beliefs and its social reality. Although seeing these discrepancies might be painful, Ellison believes that ultimately this awareness is essential to the moral life of the country.

Ronald L. Johnson

Sources for Further Study

Chicago Tribune. August 10, 1986, XIV, p. 44.
Christian Science Monitor. LXXXIV, August 18, 1986, p. 22.
Kirkus Reviews. LIV, June 1, 1986, p. 836.
Library Journal. CXI, July 16, 1986, p. 84.
Los Angeles Times. August 8, 1986, V, p. 1.
The New Republic. CXCV, August 4, 1986, p. 37.
The New York Times Book Review. XCI, August 3, 1986, p. 15.
Publishers Weekly. CCXXIX, June 6, 1986, p. 62.
Washington Post. July 23, 1986, p. C2.

GOLDEN DAYS

Author: Carolyn See (1934-   )
Publisher: McGraw-Hill Book Company (New York). 196 pp. $15.95
Type of work: Novel
Time: The 1950's to the 1990's
Locale: Primarily Los Angeles

A startling satiric novel about a brash Los Angeles woman whose quirky California optimism enables her to survive two bad marriages, a corrupt male-dominated society, and even a nuclear holocaust

> *Principal characters:*
> EDITH LANGLEY, a middle-aged divorcée and mother who becomes a tribal storyteller endowed with magical powers
> LORNA VILLANELLE, her friend, a psychic healer and television evangelist
> SKIP CHANDLER, an older financier who becomes her companion and lover
> LION BOYCE, a charismatic New Age guru
> AURORA and
> DENISE LANGLEY, Edith's daughters
> FRANZ DEGELD, a successful, handsome Hollywood producer who becomes Edith's lover
> AN UNNAMED MAN, the central character in a chapter on a day in the life of a typical brutish male

Edith Langley, the sharp-tongued first-person narrator of *Golden Days*, declares in its opening pages that this account of her friend Lorna Villanelle and herself "is the most important story in the Western World!" This brash assertion may provoke a skeptical smile, but by the end of this novel— Carolyn See's fourth—the author's potent combination of social satire and apocalyptic mythmaking compels the reader to feel the power of Edith's claim.

Like a number of other contemporary novels and films, *Golden Days* dares to imagine the aftermath of worldwide nuclear war in considerable graphic detail. Whereas such works as *On the Beach* (novel, 1957; film, 1959), *Testament* (1983), and *The Day After* (1983) place the outbreak of such a war early in the narrative and concentrate grimly on the emotional and physical torment accompanying the event, See introduces the theme of the holocaust much more gradually and—here is the major surprise of the novel—optimistically. Ultimately, she leads the reader into a vision of a new golden age of human renewal in the scorched world of the 1990's.

In the opening scene, Edith Langley remembers her experiences of 1980 as being part of "an entirely different world," and as her memories move back and forth in time and a number of such bittersweet asides accumulate, it becomes increasingly clear that Edith has in fact lived through the holocaust. See keeps these reminders of Edith's vantage point from a postholocaust future largely in the background throughout much of the narrative, for the novelist is ultimately less concerned with details of the holocaust experience itself (powerful and disturbing as those details are) than with the ways in which her characters' lives can illuminate two other purposes: a satiric, feminist critique of the forces in post-World War II society that are leading to nuclear war, and a comic but heartening look at the resources for psychological and spiritual survival that can be salvaged from that destructive society. To accomplish these purposes, See allows Edith Langley to tell her own story—a story in which she moves from rags to riches to ashes to transcendence—and the reader becomes so entertained, so moved, and eventually so attached to Edith's bizarre yet archetypal life that both her feminist critique and her triumphant survival ring emotionally true.

A first reading of *Golden Days* gives the impression that See wrote the novel in a rush, impelled by the urgency of her themes and by a determination to let her narrator's experiences and speculations range with a feminine freedom, somewhat in the manner of Virginia Woolf, rather than to confine them in a more classically "masculine" plot. A closer look at See's division of the book into three parts, however, reveals that the novel does have a highly effective structure that reinforces the concerns of each part and of the novel as a whole.

Part 1, the first five chapters, includes slightly more than half the book and covers the years from the spring of 1980, when Edith first returns to Los Angeles with her two daughters, Aurora and Denise, through the fall of 1986, when the city begins to respond to the certainty that a nuclear war which has started in Central America will soon spread to California. From the first page, Edith's vernacular, sardonic candor sets a highly contemporary tone, for her marital and career setbacks have made her a cynical survivor who is now determined to be one of the powerful rather than the powerless. In the first chapter, See also makes a concentrated and cleverly double-edged use of highly traditional plot conventions. Like many a hero and heroine of nineteenth century British fiction, Edith begins the novel as an outsider, a member of the lower classes, but whereas it would take such a character in the works of Charles Dickens or William Makepeace Thackeray many years and hundreds of pages to realize his or her great expectations of rising in society, Edith gains considerable wealth and power within the first eight months and twenty pages. On the one hand, this success is highly satisfying both for Edith and for the reader, who enjoys identifying with her gutsy ingenuity. On the other, the speed and facility of Edith's rise leads to a sense of underlying uneasiness, both in Edith and in the reader, that is central to See's satiric purposes. According to Edith, Los Angeles in the early 1980's was a place of widespread "personal chaos"—of great difficulty in trying to decide who to be and how to relate to others—that was exacerbated by the apparent lack of real businesses and careers. Los Angeles dealt in "intangibles"; driving around, Edith finds mainly "television stations or movie studios . . . or death factories where they made missiles, or think tanks where they thought them up." In such a society, Edith discovers that the path to success lies in acts of willful self-creation. She encapsulates the way in which she became a financial adviser and newspaper columnist by saying, "I made myself up," and throughout the novel she enjoys noting how other successful characters have done the same. For example, Edith discovers that the entrepreneurial guru Lion Boyce began with the name Hugh Boyce in "the Irish lower class—that's where he came from, just like me," while the phenomenally successful film producer Franz DeGeld (who is named with the German word for money, *geld*) began "twenty years ago at L.A. High as plain Len Bast."

With her history of unstable finances and relationships, Edith claims to put her primary faith in precious gems, believing in their constancy and indestructibility. With the benefit of hindsight, however, she also realizes later that there were other, more important values at work in her life in the early 1980's—values of home and family that the reader might well think are unexpectedly traditional. From the time that she first moves into a ramshackle house in the poorer section of Topanga Canyon, Edith finds that, for all the dangers from brushfires, mudslides, and rattlesnakes, she derives an inexplicable feeling of security from her home and daughters. This feeling is intensified when she meets Skip Chandler, an older financier who had moved with his family to Buenos Aires during the Cuban Missile Crisis because of his wife's fears of nuclear war but who has returned to Los Angeles to have medical tests performed on a lung problem that he thinks is fatal. Skip and Edith do not become lovers at first, but he nevertheless settles into her house, makes her the figurehead president of the Third Women's Bank of Santa Monica, and becomes a kindly father in a strangely reconstituted nuclear family. This arrangement suits Edith perfectly, for it adds to her feeling of "coming down in one piece, in one place" and does not disrupt the condition of rock-hard, secure "stasis" that she yearns to maintain.

Conventionally successful as Edith's life has become, however, it is only when she and Skip take a trip to San Francisco that her life begins to soar. When Edith is sent by her newspaper to write an exposé of a supposedly fraudulent self-realization seminar, she and Skip are converted to the ecstatic positive-thinking doctrines of madcap guru Lion Boyce and Edith encounters her old friend Lorna working as one of Lion's assistants. Flashbacks to the late 1950's and early 1960's reveal how Edith and the wildly energetic, perpetually angry Lorna supported each other through years of bad marriages and dull courses at Los Angeles City College. Through the renewal of their friendship and the teachings of Lion, Edith feels that she has entered paradise: Her finances flourish, Skip becomes her lover and recovers his health, the two enjoy wild weekends of risk-taking fun with Lion and his followers, her daughters become successful in school and in Skip's business, and she enters the highest circles of Los Angeles society.

Yet when the threat of nuclear war begins to darken this ideal existence, Edith becomes uneasy with changes in her friends and with her growing intimations that wealth, power, and even a stable home will not be enough to provide security in a society that has been deliberately oblivious to the approach of its own annihilation. At board meetings of the Third Women's Bank, where she is the token woman, Edith tries to take "some comfort" from the "magnificent impersonal[ity]" of "the iron rules of masculine commerce," but it becomes increasingly clear to her that such masculine impersonality, such greed and ambition cut off from moral scruples and understanding of the human heart, is ultimately destructive. Lion Boyce also displays this moral obliviousness when he turns from his failing seminar work to drug smuggling, and though he magically transports his body out of jail twice after being arrested, he finally disappears from the world of the novel. Partly in revenge against Lion—yet another man in her life who has jilted her—Lorna plagiarizes his doctrines and becomes a television evangelist under the name of Lorna Villanelle. Yet despite Lorna's success and enormous psychic power, Edith comes to believe that her old friend is, finally, "not very *good*" and does not deserve her supernatural gifts.

See takes her greatest stylistic risks in part 2 of the book: She allows her narrative to unravel into several strands as nuclear war comes closer to California and Edith explores her fears beyond the constraints of a single plot. At times, the writing in this section seems the weakest in the novel. The reader wonders, for example, why See bothers to provide Edith with another lover, for the character of Hal is unsatisfyingly sketchy and Edith's corrupt involvement in the destructive tendencies of Los Angeles has already been clearly established. At other times, though the writing reaches a blatant didacticism that See seems to have carefully avoided earlier, Edith's speculations and experiences rise to a new level of rhetorical and dramatic power. Edith urges on the reader a diagnosis of humanity's nuclear ills that is already overfamiliar and perhaps clichéd—that the obsession of male national leaders with nuclear missiles can be traced to the obsession of males in general with penis size and performance—but the idea takes on new substantiality and force as Edith's authentically profane voice recalls her own experiences with a variety of anxious men. Another memorable chapter involves Edith's portrait of a day in the life of an average brutish male—a portrait which captures his irresponsible treatment of his wife, family, mistresses, and job, but most of all his underlying despair and fear that his life and the world are out of control. A concise rationale for this widely ranging section of the novel occurs at a fashionable party where Edith discusses her numerous fears with a complacent psychologist. "Isn't it true," the psychologist suggests, "that your fear of nuclear war is a metaphor for all the *other* fears that plague us today?" "No," Edith replies resoundingly, "it's *my* view that the other fears, all those of which we have spoken, are a metaphor for my fear of nuclear war!"

In part 3, which takes up only about a fifth of the novel, Edith ultimately survives (along with a small number of those close to her), not through accumulated wealth or power, but through a gutsy fidelity to the Los Angeles milieu, her Topanga Canyon home, and her small tribal group. After five hard years in her canyon, which had been scorched but not destroyed by the war, Edith and her group make an arduous odyssey twelve miles down to Malibu Beach. Physically ravaged but undaunted, Edith emerges as a powerful storyteller who commands some of the psychic magic she had earlier witnessed in Lorna. She confidently prophesies that the surviving "race of hardy laughers, mystics, crazies" will now enter into new "Light ages" free of the fears and obsessions of the past.

Some readers may find that the optimism of *Golden Days* is ultimately a bit superficial, especially if they are familiar with the scientific arguments of Carl Sagan and others that such a war could create a "nuclear winter" that might well make organic life on Earth impossible. Nevertheless, as an indictment of the kind of aggressive value system that may destroy the world, as an exploration of the kind of expansive spirituality that might save it, and as an achievement in creating an appealing narrative voice and taking that voice into a powerful realm of social myth, *Golden Days* is a disturbing, an entertaining, and a cathartic reading experience.

Terry L. Andrews

Sources for Further Study

Booklist. LXXXIII, October 1, 1986, p. 190.
Chicago Tribune. November 9, 1986, XIV, p. 6.
Kirkus Reviews. LIV, August 15, 1986, p. 1241.
Library Journal. CXI, September 15, 1986, p. 102.
Los Angeles Times Book Review. October 12, 1986, p. 2.
The New York Times Book Review. XCI, November 30, 1986, p. 9.
Publishers Weekly. CCXXX, August 15, 1986, p. 69.
Time. CXXVIII, November 24, 1986, p. 94.

THE GOLDEN GATE

Author: Vikram Seth (1952-   )
Publisher: Random House (New York). 307 pp. $17.95
Type of work: Novel in verse
Time: The early 1980's
Locale: San Francisco and environs

A sonnet sequence about life among the young professionals of California, The Golden Gate *is a delightfully original work and an affectionate, witty, and thoroughly enjoyable achievement*

> *Principal characters:*
> JOHN BROWN, a successful but lonely computer specialist
> JANET HAYAKAWA, a sculptor and rock-band drummer
> PHIL WEISS, a bisexual single parent and activist
> ELIZABETH "LIZ" DORATI, John's lover, then Phil's wife
> ED DORATI, Liz's homosexual brother attracted to Phil

During the English Renaissance, the heyday of the sonnet, one popular long form was the sonnet sequence. William Shakespeare, Edmund Spenser, Michael Drayton, and Samuel Daniel are only a few of the poets in the age of Elizabeth I who left intriguing works in this form. Since that period, few successful long poems in sonnet stanzas have appeared, the nearest approximation being George Meredith's *Modern Love* (1862), a sustained sequence of sixteen-line units. Indeed, Meredith's title could stand as an effective subtitle for Vikram Seth's work; *The Golden Gate* is, among other things, a survey of contemporary love relationships. Love and survival are the author's central themes, and worthy themes they are for the dignity of the sonnet.

Seth's sonnets, however, are not so very dignified. Committed to a comic treatment of his material, this astonishingly assured poet bends the usually sober-sided effects of the sonnet to his will. One way in which he does this is by keeping his diction, for the most part, contemporary. It would be misleading, however, to give the impression that his vocabulary is narrow or commonplace: This is an eclectic, precise, and striking diction that harmoniously blends everything from glib hipness to scholarly erudition. Indeed, the voice of the engaging speaker who tells this tale is one of Seth's great achievements. He is a true humorist who has a lot of affection for those he chides. An opaque rather than transparent narrator, Seth's persona shows an affection for the reader, too. Time and time again he sets aside the narrative for a moment to engage the reader directly. Having sonnets written to the reader is a most pleasant form of flattery.

Another source of humor, though intimately connected to diction and voice, is the special sonnet shape that Seth has invented for this work. Typically, his rhyme scheme is *ababccddeffegg*. The poet borrows his opening quatrain from the English tradition, follows it with a quatrain made of two couplets, then a third quatrain in the Italian style, and finally the closing couplet—once again a feature of the English sonnet type. The formal device, then, is an eccentric version of a familiar shape that provides Seth with special opportunities that he is ready and eager to exploit.

The most obvious opportunity (and challenge) is adding more couplets to the sonnet than are usually found. The four couplets in each of Seth's sonnets are the traditional containers for poetic wit, the proximity of the rhyming words allowing them to call special attention to themselves. Seth often complicates his sound-play by adding another comic device—polysyllabic rhyming—both on the couplets and elsewhere. Add to this Seth's preference for the iambic tetrameter line, rather than the customary pentameter, and one has a complicated vehicle for whimsical and broad effects. (The tetrameter line simply shortens the intervals between rhyme words.) Here is an example from the first chapter. John Brown, one of the main characters, is describing himself:

> "I'm young, employed, healthy, ambitious,
> Sound, solvent, self-made, self-possessed.
> But all my symptoms are pernicious.
> The Dow-Jones of my heart's depressed.
> The sunflower of my youth is wilting.
> The tower of my dreams is tilting.
> The zoom lens of my zest is blurred.
> The drama of my life's absurd.
> What is the root of my neurosis?
> I jog, eat brewer's yeast each day,
> And yet I feel life slip away.
> I wait your sapient diagnosis.
> I die! I faint! I fail! I sink!"
> "You need a lover, John, I think."

The second speaker is John's former girlfriend, now his confidante, Janet Hayakawa. Her response continues in the next sonnet, exemplifying another feature of Seth's technique—the enjambing of materials from one section to the next so that the longer poem gains continuity at the expense of the independence of its hundreds of units.

For every obstacle one could name to the accomplishment of his goal, Seth has found a solution. By merging the two genres into a unique literary work, he has freshened both the tradition of the sonnet and the technique of the novel. If he had attempted a more conventional handling of either genre, his success might have been seriously limited—the plot and characters of *The Golden Gate* are not that exceptional or original.

John Brown is a man whose life lacks love. Although it goes against his inclination, he allows his friend Janet to suggest using a personals column in order to bring new relationships into his life. In fact, Janet takes over the writing of the ad and the screening of responses to it. John is at first dismayed, then entertained, and finally intrigued. One woman, Elizabeth Dorati, pens the response that fires his imagination. Liz, too, is finding the more conventional means of meeting people ineffective. Their relationship takes off, a relationship explored convincingly only because of the compression and illusion of texture and authority that Seth's handling of the sonnet affords.

From here, the novel begins its exploration of various types of relationships among San Francisco's young professionals. The affair between John and Liz, based first on their mutual loneliness and then on strong passion, flourishes for awhile, but then it begins to disintegrate. John lacks a flexibility necessary to maintain this match; Liz, willing to take risks in her profession and anxious to take strong liberal stands, finds John suspicious and then jealous of her causes and other relationships. John, a hireling of the military-industrial complex, refuses to question his complicity in the nuclear disaster that Liz and others see looming. Symptomatic of the problems in their relationship is the difficult time that John has with Liz's scheming cat, Charlemagne.

Seth's portrayal of this troublesome old cat is one of the great joys in this novel. Charlemagne senses John as an intruder into the comfortable life he has had as Liz's sole companion. The cat constantly finds ways to make John's life miserable, or so it seems to John. After several comic assaults on John's dignity, this self-important and humorless lover asks Liz to make a choice: either the cat or him. In effect, John's pettiness makes him no better than the cat—and far less attractive.

Meanwhile, other characters have been introduced, complicating the lives of this first couple and thickening the novel's social texture. Phil Weiss, John's old college chum, is nursing wounds from his failed marriage. While he goes about the loving business of rearing his son, Paul, he drops out of his profession and becomes an organizer for liberal activist causes. His idealism brings him together with Liz, who becomes his lawyer after a demonstration in which Phil is arrested. Prior to this, however, he becomes involved with Liz's brother, Ed.

Ed, a self-tormenting homosexual, is briefly Phil's lover, but he quickly becomes ashamed of his sexual needs and uneasy with Phil's bisexual identity. Some of the novel's most sensitive dialogue involves the arguments and attempts at understanding between these two men. Throughout his book, Seth manages to bring sufficient complexity and seriousness to touchy and modish subjects such as these. He avoids cheap jokes; his humor is gentle and redemptive, not cutting or abusive.

The relationship between Phil and Ed, though it shows a rich potential, is finally doomed in much the same way as that between John and Liz. There is not enough to it besides passion, and there is not enough self-confidence and generosity in the behavior of at least one member of each pair to permit the other sufficient peace of mind. Still, the struggle in each situation to find a basis for growth in the relationship is presented with delicacy and sophistication. These people are not quitters until it becomes only too clear that there is bound to be more pain than joy in trying to stay together.

As the problems between John and Liz mount, so does the possibility of a healthy arrangement between Phil and Ed dwindle. Liz and Phil are thrown more and more together, and in their misery-loves-company friendship they find a basis for much more than they expected. Before long, Liz decides to give up on John, and a rather hasty marriage to Phil shocks their friends and relations. By the time the author brings these two attractive people together, the basis for their relationship seems sound: Good humor, flexibility, mutual respect, and a lively interest in some of the same issues and in each other's talents takes the place of the grand passion that, by itself, was not sufficient to support their earlier relationships. Their haste is motivated in part by the pressure that Liz has felt to satisfy the longings of her mother, who desperately wants to see Liz married and starting a family. Liz, knowing that her mother is terminally ill, acts with less forethought than is characteristic of her.

John's anger is deep and, for a long while, inconsolable. Eventually, he finds himself turning to Janet, and, though he tries to keep the tone of their relationship light in the hope of avoiding future disappointment and pain, his attachment to her grows stronger and stronger. Ed, meanwhile, has begun to search for answers to his predicament in religious teachings.

The novel is about to move toward an easy happy ending when Janet dies from injuries in a car accident. John's period of mourning and Liz's term of pregnancy coincide. With a rather pleasant touch, Seth has Phil and Liz name their son after John, asking John to be the godfather. This gesture, coupled with the lessons learned from John's meditations on the meaning of Janet's life, allows the novel to end on a positive note of reconciliation.

The Golden Gate lives less in the bones of its plot than in the flesh of its vividly textured scenes. Seth conjures a sense of place that is enthralling. There are a number of party scenes in the novel that are spellbinding in their presentation of detail and evocation of mood—among them a housewarming party for John and Liz when they begin living together. A Thanksgiving gathering at the home of the Dorati family radiates with the love of the senior members of that clan while giving Seth an opportunity to draw a bit of the working life of a California vineyard. At one time or another, almost every important part of the San Francisco area is brought into view. Much of the charm of the novel depends on Seth's fine evocation of place.

In fact, given the experimental nature of this work, there is little with which to find fault. There are no established rules for Seth to break, no expectations for him to foil except the basic ones that he entertain and enlighten his readers. This he has done extremely well, mixing his boundless wit with compassion and tenderness. Though he is still a young man, Vikram Seth has written a very wise book. Moreover, he has found a way of bringing the languishing art of poetry back to a large audience—the audience of the novel.

Philip K. Jason

Sources for Further Study

The Atlantic. CCLVII, May, 1986, p. 99.
Best Sellers. XLVI, July, 1986, p. 154.
Commentary. LXXXII, September, 1986, p. 54.
Kirkus Reviews. LIV, February 15, 1986, p. 245.
Library Journal. CXI, July 16, 1986, p. 111.
Los Angeles Times Book Review. April 6, 1986, p. 1.
The New Republic. CXCIV, April 21, 1986, p. 32.
The New York Times. April 14, 1986, p. 18.
The New York Times Book Review. XCI, May 11, 1986, p. 11.
The New Yorker. LXII, July 14, 1986, p. 82.
Newsweek. CVII, April 14, 1986, p. 74A.
The Observer. June 22, 1986, p. 23.
Publishers Weekly. CCXXIX, February 21, 1986, p. 157.
The Spectator. June 28, 1986, p. 31.
USA Today. May 2, 1986, p. 4D.
The Wall Street Journal. April 29, 1986, p. 28.
Washington Post Book World. XVI, March 23, 1986, p. 1.

THE GOOD APPRENTICE

Author: Iris Murdoch (1919-   )
Publisher: The Viking Press (New York). 522 pp. $18.95
Type of work: Novel
Time: The 1980's
Locale: England

A prodigal son, his aunt, his half brother, his stepfather, and other characters struggle with the psychological and moral consequences of their actions

Principal characters:
> EDWARD BALTRAM, a college student, the illegitimate son of Jesse Baltram but reared by Harry Cuno
> MARGARET "MIDGE" McCASKERVILLE, a former model now married and Edward's aunt
> STUART CUNO, a college student, Harry's son and Edward's stepbrother
> HARRY CUNO, Stuart's dilettante father
> JESSE BALTRAM, Edward's father, a once-famous painter
> MAY BALTRAM, Jesse's wife
> THOMAS McCASKERVILLE, Edward's psychiatrist and Midge's husband
> MEREDITH McCASKERVILLE, Thomas and Midge's son
> BRENDA "BROWNIE" WILSDEN, Edward's love interest and the sister of his college roommate
> ILONA BALTRAM, May and Jesse's younger daughter
> BETTINA BALTRAM, May and Jesse's older daughter
> SARAH PLOWMAIN, Edward's lover for one night
> ELSPETH MACRAIN, Sarah's mother, a feminist journalist and novelist
> URSULA BRIGHTWALTON, Edward's doctor
> WILLY BRIGHTWALTON, Edward's tutor in French and Ursula's husband

In the opening pages of *The Good Apprentice*, Iris Murdoch seems to be writing a comedy of manners, lightly satirizing both the selfish indulgences of sexually liberated swingers and the philosophical pretensions of drug-consuming students; when the scene, however, ends abruptly in death, she begins to explore, in a detailed narrative that is alternately realistic and farcical, the unforeseen moral and psychological consequences of one's careless or self-satisfying actions. Her fictional parable grows to be as long as a nineteenth century Russian novel and as fantastically plotted as an opera. Within the narrative are realistically detailed descriptions of clothing, faces, and locales, as well as philosophical dialogues among characters arguing various concepts of the good life. Murdoch's technical brilliance in her twenty-second novel enables her to manage not only her initial shift from comic satire to tragicomic fiction but also wins the reader's acquiescence to her subsequent mixture of modes. Neither consistently solemn nor consistently silly, *The Good Apprentice* portrays individuals' search for the good, their responses to the accidental, and their moral responsibility for their actions in the world.

In the novel's opening scene, Edward Baltram, a college student of French literature, has just introduced his roommate, Mark Wilsden, to a mind-altering recreational drug, without Mark's knowledge or consent. Like an evil magician chuckling over his own power, Edward watches the drug take effect: Mark babbles happily about the true meaning of existence and then falls asleep. Edward is lured away from Mark by an unexpected telephone solicitation from a luscious college girl, Sarah Plowmain, who quickly seduces the willing boy. After intercourse, Sarah questions Edward about his very intriguing stepbrother, Stuart, who, in search of the good life, has given up sex. Sarah is also curious about Edward's mother, Chloe Warriston, who, pregnant by an artist, Jesse Baltram, had married Harry Cuno, then had died shortly after bearing Edward, who had been reared by Harry, who earlier had married another young woman, who had died shortly after giving birth to Stuart. Sarah herself reveals some details about her feminist mother, who had known Chloe at school, and her mathematician father, a suicide, who had been Stuart's teacher. Murdoch plants too many expository clues in this conversation, parodying the murder-mystery narrative which warns the reader that something of significance is about to happen. When Edward finally remembers that he has abandoned his friend Mark in a helpless state, the reader's suspicions are lulled by the context, which suggests that, actually, Edward is fleeing from the intrusive intimacy of Sarah's questions. Edward returns from his brief encounter to find the room empty. Mark's mind has flown out the window, but his body has landed on the ground below. Edward, plunged into a self-centered depression, struggles to recover in the remaining 516 pages of Murdoch's novel.

Despite being annoyed by Edward's unheroic pettiness, the reader is engaged by the moral dilemma that Murdoch unfolds. Edward was merely careless, not malevolent—and yet his deliberate actions made possible Mark's death. Edward is, to his credit, unable to shake off his feelings of guilt; his misery is genuine. His older brother, Stuart, whose behavior has been proper and careful, nevertheless suffers from feelings of nothingness and seeks, blindly, a sort of discipline that will allow him to enjoy life by helping others. Edward hopes to redeem himself by seeking forgiveness from his father; Stuart waits for some sign to direct his life. If Edward is a prodigal son, then Stuart is the prodigal's older brother, bewildered by the morality of his culture. Stuart and Edward both become apprentices to the idea of the good, but Edward, having lost conviction in his own identity, and lacking any system of belief, flounders in the shallows of his own mind.

Individual characters in this novel may strike some readers as silly, but their questions command serious reflection. Edward and Stuart, who are in their twenties, and an older generation of characters ask variations on these questions: How can one manage to live a good life, when neither avoiding pain nor seeking pleasure can prevent one from causing others to suffer? How can one choose the moderation of a good, productive life in a relativistic world in which there are many more than two extremes?

One definition of the good life which Edward rejects is high culture, associated with Bloomsbury and universities. Ignoring the clever conversation of the artists, doctors, and other upper-class intellectuals who form his social circle, Edward mopes throughout the dinner party planned by his aunt, Midge McCaskerville, to distract him from his troubles. Midge's husband, Thomas McCaskerville, a philosophical psychiatrist who combines a Jewish and Scots cultural heritage, treats his nephew Edward for his depression by listening and asking some questions, but he refuses to play the role of a priest granting absolution. Another guest, Ursula Brightwater, Edward's family doctor, treats him by prescribing tranquilizers. Her husband, Willy Brightwater, Edward's French tutor, has a mild crush on Midge, whose fashionable appearance still wins admiration, even though she has become plump. In the evening's conversation, two apparently stable young men are compared favorably with Stuart and Edward, who are regarded as mentally unbalanced. The conversation also compares Isaac Newton's faith favorably with the madness of quantum physicists and political terrorists. The dinner party conversation begins to resemble a philosophical dialogue. In response to the suggestion that computer logic could successfully imitate the human mind, Stuart, a brilliant mathematics student who seems familiar with the field of artificial intelligence, passionately asserts that only human intelligence can judge between good and evil. Stuart distinguishes justice from truth, and his vow of abstinence is related to his attempt either to embody good or to act justly—he is not yet certain which. At this dinner party, the philosophical seeker does not triumph; the others respond to Stuart with laughter, with a diverting complaint about pornography, and with a reversion to an old proof of reality: Midge knocks her wedding ring against the table top. Harry insists that good and evil are both relative and illusory concepts. There are buried ironies in Midge's and Harry's comments, for, as the reader learns later, these two have been carrying on an adulterous affair. In Murdoch's fiction, the good life cannot be located in a sophisticated, urban culture.

To find the way out of his labyrinthine depression, Edward, like any modernist hero, searches for his father. Although he resembles Harry more than he realizes—both are sons of famous artists, neither has settled on a career, and both cause suffering by selfish but pleasurable actions—Edward, nevertheless, leaves the stepfather who reared him to visit his biological father, who abandoned him.

After slogging through the contingent mud, this prodigal son reaches his father's house, only to find his father absent. In the odd castlelike house, named Seegard, May Baltram presides. She is attended by her daughters, Bettina and Ilona. These three self-sufficient, nearly vegetarian, herbal-brew-drinking women represent a caricature of the back-to-nature movement, and their life at Seegard is Murdoch's satirical version of the old utopian fiction. May makes wine; Bettina repairs tractors and machinery; Ilona dances and manufactures ugly jewelry. All share in the considerable labor of maintaining their existence; Edward even helps with the cleaning. In the literary tradition of utopias, Seegard appears to be the good place the traveler was seeking, but then its sinister aspect emerges.

Although Edward is no prisoner in this gothic castle, after several weeks he does begin to wonder whether his father is still alive and why he remains in this dank place. Are the women drugging him? Are they malevolent? Or are they simply odd? Because the narrative here remains within the mind and perceptions of Edward, who suffers not only from his depression but also from acid-trip flashbacks, these questions cannot be answered unambiguously, but the utopia at Seegard fails to satisfy his quest for the good life.

The absent patriarch, Jesse, who has designed the life as well as the house at Seegard, has left signs of his productivity: the architectural design of Seegard, the erotic paintings, the sketches and sculptures, and—apparently—the woven fabric of Mother May's, Ilona's, and Bettina's dresses. Is Jesse Baltram a godlike genius? May is certain that he is, but Murdoch convinces her readers only that Baltram's work will bring higher prices after his death. Jesse himself, a charming and successful philanderer, has impressed many people as either "evil" or "good." It seems that neither the artist's life nor his works can be judged consistently from all perspectives, for all time.

Finally, after many bumps and screams in the night, Edward explores a locked tower, and there, at the top, he discovers his father. The father the prodigal has been seeking cannot enact his role and forgive his son. Jesse has aged, and his behavior has grown unpredictable: Sometimes calm and sometimes destructive, sometimes recognizing his family and sometimes resenting them as strangers who are his jailers, Jesse appears to be suffering from the symptoms of Alzheimer's disease. His lucid moments and his violent paranoia are equally persuasive to the observing son, who can expect no guidance from Jesse in re-creating his own identity.

By the author's design, Edward's quest reenacts his Aunt Midge's visit years earlier. Then, Midge interpreted a remark Jesse had made as recognition that she might be beautiful. She re-created her own identity from that of Chloe's younger sister to that of a fashion model. Now, some years older and several pounds heavier, Midge listens to Harry, who has been incapable of guiding either Stuart or Edward, as he attempts to remake her identity according to his own vision: He wants her to make public their secret love. Midge, vulnerable because she enjoys escaping into the romantic fantasy of her improper affair with Harry, has delayed making an open declaration.

Midge is a more interesting character than Edward, in part because a character of her age (she is approaching menopause) is so rarely given serious psychological and moral problems in fiction. Much more familiar is the fictional exploration of a young man, such as Edward, in his early twenties. Midge seeks pleasure, but, unlike Edward, she can imagine the pain her pleasure will cause others—she thinks of her husband, Thomas. As it turns out, the first person in her family to discover her illicit affair is her thirteen-year-old son, Meredith, and that discovery corrupts his trusting nature. The addition of Meredith's perspective changes the reader's judgment of Midge's action, just as Murdoch's introduction of Mark's mother and sister changes the reader's judgment of Edward's action. Like Edward, Midge, though she was more experienced, could not foresee all the consequences of her actions, as they involved the repsonses of other people.

Murdoch makes her readers care about Midge, who is much less egotistical than Edward, so that, in a scene that is hilariously farcical, Midge's feelings, realistically detailed, are not only credible but also claim sympathy. When Midge is seduced into spending a long weekend in the country with her lover, she and Harry endure the long-expected exposure of their affair. On a dark and stormy night, their car gets stuck in the mud, and the house to which they are directed for aid turns out to be Seegard. Their partnership is witnessed not only by Edward, May, Ilona, and Bettina, but also by Stuart, who is visiting Edward, and by Jesse, who mistakes Midge for her sister Chloe and kisses her passionately. Her secret love, made public to Stuart and Edward and the Baltram women, becomes an ugly truth. Midge's suffering is prolonged on the drive back to London, because Stuart, fleeing Seegard, rides with them.

After their disastrous visit to Seegard, Midge refuses to continue her sexual liaison with Harry, but she also refuses to tell her husband, Thomas. Like Edward, she seeks some safe person to whom she can confess the details of her guilt and receive absolution; she chooses Stuart, who sensibly informs her that she is using him to avoid telling Thomas. Perhaps because Stuart is unreachable, Midge then declares her love for him—transferring her attachment from his father, Harry. Midge's temporary madness exactly parallels Edward's; both evade taking responsibility for the redefinition of their lives.

The morning after his encounter with Midge, Jesse disappears, and his son returns to London, seeking his father in his former haunts. Despite the damning testimony from Jesse's former companions, Edward, slow to learn that his father is no prophet, continues his quest. When he returns to the marshland around Seegard, Edward discovers Jesse's bloated body in a stream, apparently a suicide. Surely, now, Edward can abandon his false image of his father as prophet, whose authority can define his son's identity. By killing off the father, and by having the son discover his body, Murdoch seems to be demonstrating that physical reality is all—just the concept Midge had illustrated by tapping her wedding ring on the table. The success of the demonstration, however, always depends on the observer's perspective. Edward had repressed or denied an earlier proof.

Shortly after Jesse's disappearance, Edward had had a prophetic vision of his father's dead body, or perhaps he had actually discovered it in the stream, but he had then persuaded himself that he was having an acid-trip flashback. He refused to believe that he had actually touched his father's ring on his hand under water. At that time, Edward did not dally with a dead father, because he was rushing to a rendezvous with Brownie Wilsden, Mark's sister, through whom Edward thought he might find redemption for Mark's death. He had tried to transfer his dependency to a new figure, since his father seemed incapable of aiding him.

Edward ends his quest for his father's blessing only after he finds Jesse's will—Jesse has left his son all of his property. After considering various responses, Edward decides to burn the tangible evidence. As his heritage, he retains only the conviction that his father loved him. Secure in his belief, which can now never be proved, Edward begins to take responsibility for his life.

Edward, though he remains unaware of the philosophical implications of his choice, does make Midge aware of the necessity for her existential leap of faith. She returns to Thomas and Meredith, rejecting a false romantic fantasy and choosing the more commonplace identity she had living with her husband and son. Stuart's conscientious attempt to do good does actually bear fruit: Mark's mother gives up her hatred of Edward, but she does so freely, not because Stuart's persuasions forced her to do so. Midge's return to Thomas and Meredith has also been freely chosen.

The relatively happy ending is both engineered by the creative artist and created by Edward's and Midge's individual characters. Murdoch's characters remain responsible to other people, but they cannot command or control others' responses. *The Good Apprentice*, like her earlier novels, demonstrates Murdoch's concern with moral and psychological dilemmas. Despite her evident pleasure in outrageous artifice, this novel is not frivolous. Murdoch's intricately complicated plot does not imply the existence of a benevolent providence or of a malevolent fate. Seeking the good life, Edward and Midge slog through the existential mud; as Harry suggests, living is a muddle. Justice, neither an abstraction nor a relative concept, is one way of naming human responsibility.

Judith L. Johnston

Sources for Further Study

Booklist. LXXXII, October 15, 1985, p. 290.
Kirkus Reviews. LIII, November 1, 1985, p. 1156.
Library Journal. CX, December, 1985, p. 128.
The New Republic. CXCIV, March 31, 1986, p. 36.
New Statesman. CX, September 27, 1985, p. 30.
The New York Times Book Review. XCI, January 12, 1986, p. 1.
The New Yorker. LXII, May 12, 1986, p. 123.
Publishers Weekly. CCXXVIII, October 25, 1985, p. 58.
Time. CXXVII, January 6, 1986, p. 89.
Times Literary Supplement. September 27, 1985, p. 1047.

THE GOOD MOTHER

Author: Sue Miller (1943-   )
Publisher: Harper & Row, Publishers (New York). 310 pp. $17.95
Type of work: Novel
Time: The mid-1980's
Locale: Cambridge, Massachusetts

A beautifully written, deeply disturbing novel about a divorced mother's effort to retain custody of her child

> Principal characters:
> ANNA DUNLAP, a divorced mother in her late twenties
> MOLLY DUNLAP, her daughter
> LEO CUTTER, her lover

Even the most attentive and conscientious parents make mistakes. A mother leaves her three-year-old child safely asleep in the backseat of a parked car and goes inside a house to do an errand which takes a little longer than she anticipates. When she returns, she finds her child awake, weeping, distraught at the mother's absence. The mother is forever haunted by guilt, the child by fear of abandonment. Anna Dunlap makes this particular error in the opening pages of Sue Miller's stunning first novel, *The Good Mother*. Anna is devoted to her daughter, Molly, but circumstances, societal pressures, and Anna's own character contribute to a breaking of the vital connection between mother and daughter, leaving both irreparably damaged. Miller's characters are drawn with compassion, her writing is brilliant, and the questions her novel raises are timely and painful. Because of these strengths, *The Good Mother* is a deeply disturbing book.

At the time of the story's telling, Anna, the narrator and protagonist, works in the admissions office at Wellesley College. Her daughter, Molly, is seven years old. Anticipating without revealing the events of the plot, Anna recounts her own and Molly's recent past, beginning at the time of Anna's divorce, when Molly is three. The style of Anna's narration mirrors the style of her mothering—careful, intelligent, responsive to apparently insignificant details. She sees clearly that she is "the medium [Molly] lived in, as familiar to her, as taken for granted, as air and food." Later she compares her commitment to her child to an artist's commitment to art. In her own view and in that of the reader, Anna is a good mother, continually "monitoring and correcting...Molly's confusion" about her parents' amicable divorce, about the arrangements for Anna to have custody and for Molly's father to have regular visitation rights. Mother and daughter will share an apartment in Cambridge; Anna will give piano lessons and work part-time in a laboratory, and Molly will be in full-time day care.

After the opening chapter, which establishes the essentials of Anna's character and relationship to Molly, the narrative moves backward chronologically to an account of Anna's own childhood. Occupying several chapters, this account explores the development of her personality through her relationships with her mother and her mother's family, especially Aunt Babe. Anna's mother, known to her parents and siblings as Bunny, enjoys a "self-satisfied certitude in her correct mothering." In keeping with her father's dominant values of achievement and success, Bunny is ambitious for her daughter. She decides that Anna will become a musician and starts her with piano lessons at age five. Lessons, music camp, and the discipline of practicing become the means through which Anna's mother expresses love, the daughter's success as a musician the condition of the mother's and grandfather's approval. When it becomes clear that Anna's technical proficiency cannot compensate for her lack of genuine talent and that she will never be more than competent at the piano—she will be a piano teacher rather than a pianist—Bunny regards herself and her daughter as failures. She withdraws from Anna, now in early adolescence, leaving her in passive confusion about her sexuality—the passivity fostered by the mother's dominance, the confusion by the family's disapproving silence concerning Aunt Babe.

Bunny's striking youngest sister, Babe, was born late in their parents' marriage and is only five years older than her niece Anna. Separated by their ages both from the adults and from the children in the extended family, which gathers each summer at the grandparents' camp in Maine, Anna and Babe grow into comrades. At nineteen Babe becomes pregnant out of wedlock and is sent to Europe to have and give up her baby. Although Babe tells Anna what is happening to her, the adults never openly discuss these events, so Anna remains confused about their significance until she reaches adulthood. Even as a child, Anna senses that Babe thumbs her nose at the family values of success and achievement, and she envies her aunt's wildness. Too passive and approval-seeking to emulate what she so much admires, Anna realizes years later that Babe's lack of restraint, her openness, her contempt for convention are exactly the qualities to which Anna is attracted in Leo Cutter.

Leo enters Anna's life when she has been divorced for a year or so. He is an artist, gifted as a painter in a way Anna is not gifted as a pianist. The two meet in a Cambridge laundromat, and, several months after their tentative first encounter, they become lovers. Drawn to Anna's "withholding cool quality"—just as her father was drawn to her mother—Leo offers Anna the transforming power of "passionate intensity." The phrase from W. B. Yeats's "The Second Coming" resonates with meanings that include but are not limited to sexual desire: "I felt I'd been traveling all my life to meet him, to be released by him," Anna says. "It was what Babe had promised me,...what music had promised me: another version of myself, another model for being.... I became with him, finally, a passionate person." Leo and Anna spend time at Leo"s studio and at the apartment Anna and Molly share. At first the lovers are careful to keep from Molly the fact that they are sleeping together, but as she becomes aware that they are, she seems undisturbed by the slight differences in her life. Guided by Anna, Leo and Molly achieve first an easy friendship and then a strong attachment to each other, Molly enjoying Leo's uninhibited playfulness as much as her mother does. For a time the three of them live so comfortably and happily together that Anna imagines they are in some "boundaryless Eden" where she is the medium for their fusion. As Anna later explains it, Leo "had opened up [a whole world] where... I was beautiful, and our sex together was beautiful, and Molly was part of our love, our life." It is at this point, halfway through the novel, that Molly's father telephones Anna to say that he is keeping Molly, who has gone for a visit. He explains that he will sue for permanent custody on the grounds of Leo's having been involved in "sexual irregularities" with his daughter, and he tells Anna that he holds her responsible.

In the last half of the novel Anna recounts in detail the pretrial maneuvering, the custody trial itself, and the trial's outcome and aftermath. Because Miller has generated so much compassion and affection for her characters, the difficult situation in which Anna and Molly and Leo are now involved impels even the most reluctant reader forward. As the events of the novel's first half are recycled through the legal process, the reader becomes increasingly aware of Miller's virtuosity with language. Incidents that Anna has already described with a colloquial eroticism both arresting and fresh she must now repeat in clinical detail for lawyers, social workers, psychiatrists, and judges. Molly's favorite toys, her sleeping patterns, and her delightfully imaginative play must all be retrospectively analyzed for their darker significance. Leo, with a short haircut that makes him look frightened, and wearing a borrowed tie and jacket, must share blame for what Anna's lawyer, Muth, insists on calling a misunderstanding of the rules. Muth is one of Miller's best minor characters. She sketches his syntax and gestures with fine economy, clearly distinguishing him from his courtroom opponent and rendering him both likable and memorable. More memorable still is Anna's friend and piano student Ursula, who is writing a book on female infanticide. Ursula's bawdy wit and outrageous clothes make Anna and the reader smile even in the novel's most emotionally desperate moments.

Miller's characters, major and minor, are successful in part because of her skill at economical phrasing and her perceptive ear for dialogue. She is exceptionally good at shaping the startling phrase that captures a personality or brings a detail to life. To cite two of numerous examples, Anna's grandfather's children and grandchildren are "victims of his largesse"; a broken beer bottle shatters into "glittering curls of glass." As for dialogue, although Anna's interior voice dominates the narrative, she often quotes her own speech and that of other characters. Miller's differentiation of these various voices is masterful, with Molly's language especially impressive. Her speech is naïve but never cloying; it conveys a view of the world both childlike and distinctive to Molly herself. Her syntax and intonation patterns mature as she does, the reader's sympathy for her increasing as her language reflects her intensifying distress.

Miller also employs this technique of intensification in her use of reiterated references and symbols. Details, incidents, and objects appear casually, accumulate meaning as the narrative progresses, and reverberate with emotional significance by the end of the novel. The distant relationship between Anna and her mother, Aunt Babe's loss of her child, and Ursula's book on female infanticide make a pattern of this sort. The novel's numerous references to dancing and music work in a similar way. Anna's mother disapproves of her daughter's dancing, Leo teaches Anna to dance, and Anna plays for Molly's dancing. The country-and-western numbers Anna hears in the first chapter, with their trite themes of love and betrayal; the erotic lyrics of a Donna Summer song blasting from a box on a Cambridge street; the piano music Anna teaches and makes—or, in the depths of grief, does not make—these intensifying references form an ironic, emphatic counterpoint to Anna's emotions. Perhaps the most unusual symbol is the pacifier which appears in the first chapter and again in the last. In the first chapter, totally secure in the medium of her mother's physical presence, Molly falls asleep "sucking her pacifier rhythmically and twisting a strand of thin hair around her finger again and again. Her eyes were steady and blank.... She lisped through the thick nipple between her teeth. Her breath smelled sweet and rubbery." Playing a game with her mother, Molly tries to hold on to the pacifier as Anna pulls its ring, but eventually the child must let the rubber nipple go. In the last chapter mother and daughter see pacifiers in a drugstore, and Molly, now almost six, wishes for one, her words implying the unspeakable nature of her loss: "I can't *talk* about it, Mom. I just want to suck on a pacifier."

The sweet physical intimacy of the first pacifier scene is an effect Miller achieves over and over in *The Good Mother*. Her novel stresses the beauty and value of ordinary domestic life, dominated as it typically is by women's relationships and activities. Anna remembers her mother and aunts knitting and talking in the yellow lamplight during their long summer evenings in Maine: "Their conversations seemed to be about things that mattered— love, death, mutilation. This was the stuff that seemed important to me, although later I was to learn that it wasn't. It didn't count. And the preoccupation with it was what kept women from doing anything of consequence in the world." Making potato salad with her grandmother, Anna watches as "my thumb pressed a sliver of purple skin against my knife and pulled it away from the white flesh of the potato." The sensuous beauty of their silent work binds the two to a time "years before when I, the oldest granddaughter, was expected to help, and to learn from helping about the responsibility of being wife, mother, of serving others."

Disturbing questions about responsibility, especially maternal responsibility, pervade *The Good Mother*. Anna's mother fails to love her daughter unconditionally; as a result, Anna develops a conforming, self-mortifying passivity that becomes her fatal flaw. With Leo and Molly, Anna envisions a fulfilling freedom, a fusion without boundaries, a love that will "let go," but such freedom and fulfillment prove to be ephemeral ideals she cannot sustain. Instead, like the laboratory rats she trains, she has been conditioned to passivity, to the belief that certain events are beyond her control. Anna does not actively make wrong choices. She does, however, accept responsibility for the consequences her passivity sets in motion. In fact, she embraces, even helps to fashion, the punishment she must endure, so deeply does she believe that suffering is the price of pleasure. The emotional power of Miller's extraordinary writing forces the most idealistic reader to consider the possibility that, even from the best of good mothers, there can be no love without damage.

Carolyn Wilkerson Bell

Sources for Further Study

Booklist. LXXXII, March 1, 1986, p. 915.
Christian Science Monitor. LXXVIII, April 30, 1986, p. 21.
Kirkus Reviews. LIV, March 1, 1986, p. 331.
Library Journal. CXI, May 15, 1986, p. 79.
Los Angeles Times. April 14, 1986, V, p. 4.
Ms. XIV, June, 1986, p. 34.
The Nation. CCXLII, May 10, 1986, p. 648.
The New York Times Book Review. XCI, April 27, 1986, p. 1.
Publishers Weekly. CCXXIX, March 14, 1986, p. 101.
Time. CXXVIII, July 21, 1986, p. 72.
Washington Post Book World. XVI, May, 1986, p. 47.

GREAT AND DESPERATE CURES
The Rise and Decline of Psychosurgery and Other Radical Treatments for Mental Illness

Author: Elliot S. Valenstein (1923-   )
Publisher: Basic Books (New York). Illustrated. 338 pp. $19.95
Type of work: Medical history
Time: The 1930's to the 1950's

A case study of prefrontal lobotomy and other brain surgery shows that economics, ambition, professional rivalry, and mass publicity, fed by the desperation of patients and their families, led to the acceptance of radical therapies that did great harm

Principal personages:
> EGAS MONIZ, a Portuguese neurologist and the pioneer of psychosurgery, awarded the Nobel Prize for Medicine in 1949
> WALTER FREEMAN, the chief promoter of lobotomy in the United States

Priests and healers in ancient times are said to have drilled holes into the skulls of people who exhibited bizarre or destructive behavior to let the evil spirits out. Eminent surgeons as recently as in the 1950's did the same—but used the holes to insert picks and probes into the brain itself, thereby destroying some of the patient's personality, volition, and intellectual function. Tens of thousands of prefrontal lobotomies and similar surgical procedures were performed during the 1940's and 1950's, even though medical science failed to provide an adequate theory which drew on knowledge of the brain's anatomy and function to explain why the procedure should work. Practitioners recognized that even in the best "cures," patients lost initiative, ambition, creativeness, and reasoning ability; the lobotomized patient, when discharged from a mental hospital, was likely to be passive, childlike, and in need of constant supervision. As chemical therapies became available—and as more accurate neurological mapping suggested that lobotomy's tranquillizing function was merely an accidental by-product of the brain damage it caused—the procedure was gradually discontinued.

How could an operation which had no convincing theoretical support and never showed consistent evidence of success be performed on thousands of private patients as well as on the inmates of state institutions and, furthermore, be recognized with the award of a Nobel Prize? As Elliot S. Valenstein demonstrates in a book that serves as a cautionary tale about medicine in general, the circumstances were not unique to this one story. Science is still ignorant about the biochemical and physiological and neurological mechanisms of a great many diseases, both mental and physical. Patients and their families are desperate. Doctors feel compelled to do something— anything—so as to feel less helpless. The media uncritically publicize therapies that seem to offer hope. Physicians are often driven by ambition; medical specialties compete with one another; the market and related economic factors influence therapeutic decisions.

Described by Lewis Thomas as *The Youngest Science* (1983), medicine in the 1920's had very little support from the careful experiments and controlled research needed to understand the physical mechanisms of health and disease. In the mid-1930's, students at Harvard Medical School were told that 90 percent of the practice of medicine lay in keeping the patient comfortable while nature took its course. They were taught diagnosis and prognosis; they learned by observation to make predictions about the outcome of disease; they knew which drugs would alleviate certain symptoms or affect the action of some bodily processes. Except for surgery to remove or repair damaged organs and limbs, however, few of their interventions could actually change the course of a disease.

The treatment of mental illness had even less grounding in the kind of knowledge that could be verified through scientific method. Neurologists and psychiatrists disputed both turf and theory: Neurology studied physical mechanisms in the brain and nervous system, while psychiatry worked from the premise that mental illness was the consequence of life experience. Even among psychiatrists, however, most were convinced that psychoses had biological causes; psychotherapy was used primarily with neurotics and was, in any event, totally impractical for treating the large numbers of patients confined to asylums and state hospitals. In the 1930's, as in the 1980's, a variety of other specialists also competed to treat many of the same patients— neurosurgeons, psychologists, social workers, and trained or self-proclaimed therapists of various persuasions. In the face of the competition, psychiatrists as well as neurologists had a vested interest in promoting treatments unavailable to those competitors who were not actually licensed to practice medicine.

Since no treatment offered a proven cure for any variety of mental illness, almost anything was worth a try: the removal of one gland or another, ovariotomy, castration, sedated sleep (the patient was kept in a light coma for up to a month), drugs to stimulate respiration or metabolism, surgery which removed sources of infection, such as teeth, tonsils, uterus, and colon. During the 1930's, three radical shock therapies were introduced. The theories which explained how electroshock and the others worked were so vague as to defy credibility (and all were ultimately proved erroneous). Nevertheless, shock treatment was immediately hailed as a breakthrough and enthusiastically adopted by both private and state institutions. One can only suspect a desperate will to believe on the part of doctors, patients, and their families. If nothing previously available had offered any real hope, the violent convulsions induced by shock treatments may have appeared sufficiently dramatic to do battle with aberrations that had plunged patients and their families into years of disruption and despair.

Against this background, psychosurgery was shaped by men who saw themselves as heroes and could inspire others to follow them. Egas Moniz, a Portuguese neurologist, pressured colleagues to nominate him for a Nobel Prize in both 1928 and 1933 for his work in cerebral angiography. In 1935, a celebrated man in his field but still searching for the conclusive recognition he craved, Moniz attended a London symposium on the brain, heard a report about a chimpanzee whose frontal lobes were destroyed as part of a study on learning capacity and who had coincidentally failed to develop the neuroses that often struck laboratory animals, wondered if it might not therefore be possible to relieve anxiety states in humans surgically—and went straight home to begin operating, not even stopping for preliminary trials with animal subjects. Moniz theorized (without any evidence of experiments to back him up) that the abnormal thought processes of mental illness arose in the nerve-fiber pathways between the brain's cells. He rushed to announce his success less than four months after performing the first operation, and by the end of the year he published a monograph summarizing his first twenty cases, claiming that seven had been cured and seven significantly improved, with only six remaining unchanged.

The evidence in Moniz's monograph was extraordinarily slim. Observations of the patient's state before and after surgery—the primary data on which claims for a cure could rest—were made by different psychiatrists and were largely subjective. Moniz ignored the possibility that some patients were worse after the operation, and he apparently failed to appreciate the significance of the intellectual impairment that was reported in studies of brain injuries during World War I. For four of the seven "cured" patients, the last observation recorded in the monograph had been made less than eleven days after the operation. Moniz rushed into print because he wanted to be first, and he knew that other doctors were also considering the surgical treatment of insanity. His work gained credence because of his eminence in the field of neurology—and because both the medical profession and the general public so desperately hoped for something that could promise a quick and dramatic cure for mental illness.

Walter Freeman, one of the first brain surgeons in the United States, was also hungry for recognition. When he and his assistant James Watt saw Moniz's first article, they almost immediately began to perform similar operations. (Freeman and Watt supplied the name lobotomy.) More cautious than Moniz, Freeman admitted that patients lost some of their "sparkle," that there were relapses, that some patients deteriorated, and that a few died from hemorrhage during the operation. Furthermore, Freeman suggested that lobotomy was most effective in cases of depression. Since depression is often relieved spontaneously—regardless of what (if any) treatment is used—it seems likely that some of Freeman's cures had little to do with his operation.

Lobotomy did not immediately become widespread in the United States.

A number of physicians tried the operation (partly because they were willing to experiment on the mentally ill), but some of their studies reported a success rate as small as the 15 percent that Freeman claimed was his rate for failures. Freeman, meanwhile, cultivated attention from the popular press; one newspaper headline gives a flavor of the hopes that prefrontal lobotomy aroused: "WIZARDRY OF SURGERY RESTORES SANITY TO FIFTY RAVING MANIACS." Articles appeared in *Life*, *Coronet*, the *Saturday Evening Post*, and the *Reader's Digest*. In 1942, Freeman and Watts published a text, *Psychosurgery*, which gave precise details of their technique and provided suggestions on other aspects of patient care.

A surge of concern for the mentally ill in the postwar years exposed the barbaric conditions in underfunded state institutions which, lacking any therapies that could be used on large numbers of patients, provided only custodial care. (Even electroshock required more attendance than many asylums could afford.) More than half of all the hospital beds in the United States in 1949 were occupied by the mentally ill. Lobotomies were seen as a way to get people back into the world after years of psychiatric incapacity. Valenstein finds, in fact, no verified case of a patient who returned to a job that made any intellectual demands—but nevertheless, patients dulled by brain damage did often become passive enough to be cared for at home or on the open wards of an institution where they had previously been confined in restraints.

Freeman subsequently developed an even more extraordinary technique— the transorbital lobotomy—which was essentially an ice pick slanted up through the space between the eyeball and the skull. Freeman sometimes performed transorbital lobotomy as an office procedure, and he traveled around to state hospitals where—with a lecture, a demonstration, and a morning's supervision—he taught psychiatrists with no previous experience in surgery to perform the operation. Although a self-promoter, Freeman was not in it for the money; he paid his own expenses while traveling around the country to give demonstrations, and he visited hundreds of former patients to keep up with their progress. The second edition of *Psychosurgery*, in 1950, frankly admitted that patients who had undergone the lobotomy procedure inevitably lost mental acuteness and generally needed care and supervision to live outside an institution.

Although the introduction of chlorpromazine (Thorazine) in 1954 was the beginning of the end for lobotomy, the debate between organic and experiential causes—and therapies—for mental illness is far from settled. Freeman himself described the effect of the new drugs of the 1950's as "chemical lobotomy"; they, like brain surgery, have produced their share of unpleasant side effects and degenerative symptoms. Economically, however, psychoactive drugs have finally enabled states to empty their mammoth warehouse asylums—if all too often into urban streets, where patients who have escaped the old system of physical restraints are still victimized by degrading conditions and the lack of therapies that cure.

Sally Mitchell

Sources for Further Study

The Atlantic. CCLVII, May, 1986, p. 100.
Choice. XXIII, July, 1986, p. 1738.
Library Journal. CXI, April 15, 1986, p. 87.
Los Angeles Times Book Review. April 13, 1986, p. 2.
Nature. CCCXX, April 17, 1986, p. 568.
The New York Review of Books. XXXIII, April 24, 1986, p. 7.
The New York Times. April 1, 1986, p. 25.
The New York Times Book Review. XCI, April 6, 1986, p. 30.
Psychology Today. XX, September, 1986, p. 74.
Publishers Weekly. CCXXIX, March 21, 1986, p. 78.

GREAT DIRECTORS AT WORK
Stanislavsky, Brecht, Kazan, Brook

Author: David Richard Jones (1942-   )
Publisher: University of California Press (Berkeley). Illustrated. 289 pp. $25.00
Type of work: Dramatic theory and criticism

By exploring the work of four seminal theatrical directors, focusing on a major production of each, the author provides insight into the functions of the director, examples of various directorial models, and an understanding of the plays examined in this context

In the extensive critical literature devoted to the theater, there has been a marked shortage of works which take the director as their focus. Critics disagree concerning the extent to which directing is an art, and among the general public there is a lack of understanding about the role played by the director. Indeed, the concept of the "director" is less than a hundred years old, having evolved from the office of "actor-manager"; in time, direction became part of a complex collaborative effort, taking many forms.

Fundamentally, the director's role is to bring the script of a play to the stage and to establish its "style," the components of which include the aural and visual pace of the play, the mood, atmosphere, "sharpness of meaning," and the tone of the production. These choices are often made in collaboration with the playwright, set and lighting designers, and actors—all while observing the financial constraints of a commercial theater and the needs and expectations of the audience. Ideally, the director is what Gordon Craig called "an artist of the theatre," with jurisdiction over meaning, form, and style.

Great Directors at Work: Stanislavsky, Brecht, Kazan, Brook examines the craft of four directors, each representing a different model of this modern concept, with each chapter centered on the production of a significant example of its subject's work. The Russian director Konstantin Stanislavsky, founder of the famous "method" or "system," is represented by the 1898 Moscow Art Theatre production of Anton Chekhov's *The Seagull* (1896). The German playwright and director Bertolt Brecht is represented by his play *Mother Courage and Her Children* (1940), whose evolution is traced from 1948 to 1951. The American director Elia Kazan, a disciple of Stanislavsky by way of the Group Theatre, is represented by his famous 1947 production of Tennessee Williams' *A Streetcar Named Desire* (1947), which starred Marlon Brando, Jessica Tandy, Karl Malden, and Kim Hunter. The British director Peter Brook, representing the modernist trends in experimental theater, is discussed via his 1964-1965 production of Peter Weiss's play *The Persecution and Assassination of Jean-Paul Marat as Performed by the Inmates of the Asylum of Charenton Under the Director of the Marquis de Sade*, or, as it is better known, *Marat/Sade* (1964).

Although each chapter is organized somewhat differently, there is a set of underlying assumptions governing the choice of these four directors. All are identified as "intellectual figures" whose ideas about craft, art, and culture have been influential and historically important. Stanislavsky is identified as "the theatre's Freud, its Mendel." While Kazan is acknowledged to be the least intellectual of the four, his inclusion is justified because of his influence through the Actors Studio (of which he is a founder) as an American interpreter of Stanislavsky's theories, nurturing some of the most important actors America has produced.

Brecht represents a "theatre of point of view," composed of thinking actors, interpretive directors, and politically and intellectually aware and involved audiences. Brook, as noted above, represents avant-garde theater, characterized by radical views that challenge the centrality of the text in dramatic productions, mystical and incantatory theatrical language, and a growing trend toward deriving a production out of a highly collaborative "workshop" experience.

Jones employs different kinds of source material in each chapter. For the production of *The Seagull*, Stanislavsky's elaborate preproduction analysis of the play's *mise en scène* forms the core of the discussion. Brecht's similar *Couragemodell 1949* (1958) provides the core of the chapter on his productions of *Mother Courage and Her Children*. Kazan's *A Streetcar Named Desire: Acting Edition* (1953) is the central source for the third chapter. No central edition forms the basis of the chapter on Brook; rather, many sources are utilized, as they are used supplementally in all four chapters.

The use of these materials presents a problem of audience. The book presupposes a lack of knowledge about what directors do—thus its *raison d'être*. On the other hand, Jones's exhaustive analysis of the directorial choices and techniques employed in each case, and the intellectual and theoretical background which gave rise to them, assumes an intimate knowledge of the four plays discussed.

The discussion of Stanislavsky as director addresses the aspects of what he called "truth in directing," whose elements are "correspondence," or the relationship of a production to the world as the audience knows it; "coherence," or the internal harmony of design within a production, down to the smallest of theatrical detail; and the "spiritual meaning of life," a less technical truth, involving the study of both the stage representation of the naturalistic externals of the lives portrayed and the imagined and derived psychology and inner reality of the characters. Finally, Stanislavsky analyzed the relationship of the methods used to achieve a finished production and the effect of that production.

Brecht's *Couragemodell 1949* includes the script, production photographs, and notes. Jones discusses each aspect in considerable detail—a somewhat futile exercise in the case of the photographs, since they are not reproduced in the book and thus must be imagined. Brecht analyzed the content of the play, its scenic arrangements and blocking, and the treatment of details, providing advice about execution, tempos and running times, and divisions of the plot. Jones illustrates the evolution from Brecht's earlier position on theater for instruction to his mature emphasis on entertainment as the higher value, through which instruction might be effected. Brecht's theories, including *Verfremdungseffekt* (alienation effect), are explored with specific reference to both *Couragemodell 1949* and several productions of *Mother Courage and Her Children*. The discussion also provides a superb illustration of the essentially dialectic nature of Brecht's philosophy as exhibited through both his plays and his direction of them.

The chapter on Kazan, perhaps the least successful of the four, focuses on that director's relationship with the actors who played the leading roles in *A Streetcar Named Desire* and the collaboration among the director, the actors, the playwright, and the set designer, Joe Mielziner. Jones admits the impossibility of sorting out who provided which elements. Kazan served as "ringmaster," and it is hard to define his particular contributions with the precision evident in the other chapters. In addition, Jones's discussion of the actors' performances and the critical reception of the production is only tangentially related to the book's unifying subject.

The chapter on Brook, on the other hand, is excellent. Jones explores Brook's role in bringing to the stage the abstract theories of Antonin Artaud and the concomitant influence of such avant-garde theorists as Jerzy Grotowski. To understand the chapter, the reader must have both a thorough knowledge of *Marat/Sade* and of the historical events on which it is based. So equipped, one will profit from a superb explication of Brook's use of theater as ritual and as Brechtian political statement. Jones also provides an illuminating discussion of the acting and production techniques which Brook developed to render his visions on the stage.

As noted above, the four chapters do not follow a consistent pattern of organization. While this approach was no doubt deliberately chosen to reflect differences among the directors studied and the source materials used, some readers may find it confusing, especially since the design of each chapter is revealed only in the reading and is not outlined. Nevertheless, the book is not only a valuable exploration of the theories and practices of four seminal directors but also a unique and useful way of studying four significant plays. While there is no bibliography, there is an index, and the notes to each chapter document the large number of sources used in addition to the central texts, providing the reader with many avenues for further study.

David Sadkin

Sources for Further Study

Choice. XXIV, November, 1986, p. 491.
Kirkus Reviews. LIV, May 1, 1986, p. 698.
Library Journal. CXI, June 1, 1986, p. 138.
The New York Times Book Review. XCI, July 27, 1986, p. 11.

HANDLING SIN

Author: Michael Malone (1942-   )
Publisher: Little, Brown and Company (Boston). 544 pp. $17.95
Type of work: Novel
Time: Two weeks in March in the mid-1980's
Locale: Thermopylae, North Carolina; New Orleans; places in between

Handling Sin *is a comic quest, the story of a respectable insurance agent who leaves home to fulfill a set of tasks given him by his eccentric father and who thereby falls into many adventures*

> *Principal characters:*
> RALEIGH HAYES, an insurance agent and the hero
> AURA HAYES, his wife
> CAROLINE AND HOLLY HAYES, his sixteen-year-old twin daughters
> EARLEY HAYES, his father
> VICTORIA HAYES, his father's sister
> MINGO SHEFFIELD, his neighbor and companion
> JUBAL ROGERS, a black jazz musician
> BILLIE ROGERS, the granddaughter of Victoria Hayes and Jubal Rogers
> GATES HAYES, Raleigh's half brother and companion
> SIMON "WEEPER" BERG, a criminal and Raleigh's companion
> TOUTANT KINGSTREE, a black jazz musician

Michael Malone, right at the outset, takes great care to present this large comic novel as an old-fashioned entertainment. At the head of the epigraph from which the title is taken (a 1303 poem by Robert of Brunne), he writes, "This book is cald Handlying Synne. It contains Tales and Marvels." The descriptive chapter headings are reminiscent of Henry Fielding—"In Which the Hero Is Introduced and Receives a Blow," for example—and Fielding, along with Miguel Cervantes and Charles Dickens, is invoked in the acknowledgments.

These touches, in addition to an unabashedly farfetched plot, a great array of highly colored characters and settings, and the sheer number of pages in the book, suggest that Michael Malone set out deliberately to appeal to a mass audience. At the same time he is fundamentally serious. His novel is in some ways comparable to the fiction of John Irving, from *The World According to Garp* (1978) onward: Both writers seem to have ambitions to become the Dickens of contemporary American literature. Whereas Irving is often solemn and portentous, even embarrassingly sentimental, Malone, writing with tongue in cheek at least half the time, maintains with only a few lapses a deft seriocomic tone throughout. He depends for his appeal not on sex, of which the book contains very little, or violence, of which there is somewhat more, but on vividly detailed comic action in a variety of colorful landscapes. Though *Handling Sin* is by no means a profound psychological novel, Malone does pay due attention to his hero's inner life; while the focus is on the physical quest, the hero's inner struggle and eventual triumph ring true. This is a satisfying work of fiction, then. Much more than Irving, Malone gives value for money.

The device which Malone uses to set his story in motion is a good instance of the kind of compromise involved in writing a serious commercial novel. The hero, Raleigh Hayes, is a prosperous life-insurance agent, with a bright and attractive wife and troublesome sixteen-year-old twin daughters, living in Thermopylae, North Carolina. He owns, as Malone says in the prologue, "his own house, his own business, two oceanfront rental properties"; he is a member of "the Civitans, the Chamber of Commerce, the Baptist Church"; he is known to all his acquaintances as "respectable, smart, steady, honest, punctual, decent Raleigh Hayes." He is also ripe for a fall: "The day [comes] when the members of the court of Heaven [take] their places in the presence of the Lord." Specifically, Raleigh receives a mysterious tape-recorded message from his father, Earley, who is seventy years old and ill. Earley, by the time Raleigh receives the message, has discharged himself from the hospital against medical advice and set off for New Orleans in a yellow Cadillac convertible with a black teenage girl. He presents his son with a series of preposterous tasks: to locate a black musician named Jubal Rogers as well as Raleigh's black sheep half brother, Gates Hayes, and bring them, along with Grandma Tiny's trunk, a family Bible, and a bust which Raleigh will have to steal out of the public library, to Earley in New Orleans. Raleigh must also buy a tract of land from a man who, hating the Hayeses as he does, will surely be unwilling to sell it. If he succeeds, he inherits his father's fortune, which, Earley hints, is larger than Raleigh had ever guessed; if he fails, or worse yet declines to try, he gets nothing.

Raleigh thinks that his father is crazy, but he is not: Rather he is out to right an ancient wrong and at the same time to teach his son a lesson. Billie Rogers, the black girl in the Cadillac with Earley, is the granddaughter of Jubal Rogers and Victoria Hayes, Earley's sister; long ago, Earley had deliberately failed to deliver a message between the lovers and had advised his sister to give the baby up for adoption and put the whole affair behind her. This is to say that Malone has plotted his novel carefully. Still it is hard to escape the conclusion that whereas Tom Jones travels to London to seek his fortune, and Don Quixote rides in the service of his cracked vision, Raleigh Hayes sets off on his roundabout journey because his author wants to get him out of Thermopylae so that he can have picturesque adventures. (He does not, after all, have the least need of his father's fortune.) That the quest hero is a highly respectable and unadventurous man is part of the joke—and the joke is a good one—but it does require lively footwork from the author and willing suspension of disbelief from the reader.

Malone works his quest motifs hard, with tongue in cheek. If Quixote has his Sancho Panza, Raleigh has Mingo Sheffield, his fat, simultaneously obnoxious and endearing neighbor. These two become involved through an intricate sequence of events (Mingo is falsely accused of a murder which, as it turns out, was never actually committed). After a series of adventures in Thermopylae, in the course of which Raleigh succeeds in stealing the bust and buying the land, there two set off for the coast of South Carolina to look for Raleigh's half brother, Gates.

In his invention of adventures for his hero to fall into, Malone is at his best. In its structure, from Raleigh's departure until near the end, the novel is picaresque. The typical picaresque hero is a rogue, and Raleigh is anything but that. Nevertheless the events that make up the bulk of the novel are there primarily to entertain the reader, not because they serve any essential plot function. By sending Raleigh to New Orleans by so circuitous a route, Malone has given himself ample scope. What he puts his hero through is limited only by his own imagination and generosity, and this author has plenty of both.

Raleigh and Mingo run out of gas on an isolated stretch of highway, and then Mingo accidentally locks them out of the car. A van comes along with "'*Sympathy With The Devil*' in huge red script along [its] side, a skull-and-crossbones flying from its antenna, and a ring of spikes protruding from its hubcaps." They are mugged by the occupants, who if not actually Hell's Angels resemble them, then succored by nuns, one of whom happens to be a former thief and thus able to open a locked car. They drive into a swamp in Camp LeJeune and are rescued by a group of Marine recruits on a training exercise, whom they initially take to be spooks: "Out of the black stagnant woods, [the] rhythmic shouts grew louder and sharper, punctuated by clanking rattles, until Raleigh—frozen as a squirrel—distinctly heard the words of a grunted choral song." When they track down Gates, things begin to get difficult: Gates, being involved in drug traffic, is a natural target for assorted mobsters who think that he has double-crossed them. They fall in with Simon "Weeper" Berg, an escaped convict. They rescue a troupe of ballet dancers from the Ku Klux Klan and deliver a baby in Gates's truck. So it goes, all the way to New Orleans, by way of Charleston and Atlanta.

When at last they find Earley in New Orleans, he is clearly very ill; in fact, given that the Hayeses all seem to die young, mortality is a significant undercurrent throughout. The characters—including Jubal Rogers and his granddaughter Billie, both jazz musicians, and a third musician named Toutant Kingstree—assemble in a jazz club. Raleigh has not played his trumpet in years, but here he is caught up in the spirit of things, and to the strains of the music which brings the generations and races together in harmony at last, Earley dies: "Earley Hayes reached his hand up to put it around Raleigh's over the trumpet. The hand was cold. The blue eyes closed, and, smiling, he said, 'Play me on out, son.'"

Earley has left his son a code which leads him to a treasure in Civil War gold, buried by an ancestor on the land he ordered Raleigh to buy. The penultimate joke is that a Civil War sergeant with a hatred for the Hayeses stole the gold long ago; the ultimate one, however, is that it does not matter. In what he has learned about himself and the values which give life its true meaning, in his reconciliation with his father and the revitalization of his marriage, Raleigh has found treasure enough. The last chapter is entitled "Why Raleigh Married Aura": "because he loved her. Almost as much as he loves her now. And of all the sacraments and of all the sins, the greatest of these is love."

There is much more to *Handling Sin* than this summary suggests. In the first section, set in Thermopylae—and to a degree throughout—it is a family comedy; Raleigh comes across initially as very similar to the stereotypical fathers of any number of television shows: "On his rolled, seeded, fertilized, edged lawn where in precious leisure time he had crawled on hands and knees to tear out clumps of crabgrass, he saw leaping—her blond ponytail in the air like a deer's tail, her legs spread perpendicular, so that he could see her panties beneath a skirt as short and ruffled as a tutu—his sixteen-year-old daughter Caroline." When he confronts her she screams, "*Ew,* Daddy, you toedully terrified me, rilly!" His other daughter, Holly, is devoted to auto racing but at least speaks more or less normal English.

The comedy extends also to the manners and morals of the businessmen who make up Raleigh's circle, and Malone, along the way, has a lot of fun with the pretensions and foibles of all strata of Southern society. The novel is a romantic comedy as well. Raleigh's wife is attractive, loving, intelligent, and politically involved: While her husband chases Earley, she engages herself in libertarian causes, to the distress of Raleigh's friends, and ultimately runs for mayor. Raleigh, previously, had been too devoted to his work and his civic responsibilities to pay enough attention to her. Only when he has really grown up, as a result of his travails, does he become worthy of Aura.

Handling Sin would probably be a better book if it were shorter; to his desire for richness and the stature of comic epic, Malone sacrifices selectivity. In particular, long sections about Raleigh's past, designed to reveal the roots of the relationships and conflicts which move the quest along, are intrusive. At times, moreover, the author becomes preachy. When the Ku Klux Klan is about to attack the dance troupe, he pauses for almost a full page to explain why the Klan is at once evil and moribund: "Their Klavern chieftain gave the same speech month after month, and while this man possessed all the qualities (zenophobia, paranoia, a vile mind, and a frightened soul) that a demagogue needs to inflame other bigots, he lacked the oratory."

How large an achievement is *Handling Sin*? It is excellent entertainment, to start with, well worth the time of sophisticated and intelligent readers.

For just this reason, in an era when the critical establishment favors frail, self-consciously sensitive fiction, Malone's book is likely to be undervalued. It is worth rereading simply for the delight of rediscovering the author's power of comic invention.

It is nonsensical to accuse a book such as this one of being merely entertaining, then. It is moreover a right-thinking book, with whose humane values few readers are likely to quarrel. If it does not quite measure up to the highest achievements of Cervantes and Fielding, that is probably because those values are not fully tested in action. Malone wants his readers to close the book with a newly clarified vision of what it can mean to be human, certainly, but also, and perhaps primarily, he wants them to feel good. Yet in the most serious and ultimately rewarding comedy, the characters suffer real pain and so, vicariously, does the reader. Thus the triumphant resolution is all the more moving. Here Raleigh gets into serious trouble, yet there is always a hint of slapstick in it, the pie in the face which, onstage, neither hurts nor humiliates. The price Malone pays for his refusal to put his hero in true danger of his very soul is apparent in the climactic scene—the death of Earley—which is sentimental, reminiscent of Dickens at less than his best.

But then Raleigh Hayes is not Dante in the dark woods, nor is he meant to be. If *Handling Sin* does not quite offer the comic catharsis of a *Tom Jones* or a *Don Quixote de la Mancha*, what it does offer is more than ample compensation: a generous helping of high-spirited and high-minded fun.

Edwin Moses

Sources for Further Study

Booklist. LXXXII, April 1, 1986, p. 1098.
Christian Science Monitor. LXXVIII, March 26, 1986, p. 21.
Kirkus Reviews. LIV, February 1, 1986, p. 159.
Library Journal. CXI, April 15, 1986, p. 96.
Los Angeles Times Book Review. April 6, 1986, p. 3.
The Nation. CCXLII, June 21, 1986, p. 860.
The New York Times Book Review. XCI, April 13, 1986, p. 11.
The New Yorker. LXII, May 5, 1986, p. 132.
Newsweek. CVII, June 2, 1986, p. 74.
Publishers Weekly. CCXXIX, March 7, 1986, p. 84.
Washington Post Book World. XVI, April 13, 1986, p. 3.

THE HANDMAID'S TALE

Author: Margaret Atwood (1939-   )
Publisher: Houghton Mifflin Company (Boston). 311 pp. $16.95
Type of work: Novel
Time: The late twentieth century
Locale: The Republic of Gilead, formerly the United States

A fictional memoir narrated by a woman who contrasts her new role of Handmaid (a politically approved childbearer) to her previous roles as wife, mother, and wage earner

> *Principal characters:*
> OFFRED, the main character and narrator, a thirty-three-year-old woman
> THE COMMANDER, Offred's master, a high-ranking government official
> SERENA JOY, the Commander's wife, a former television evangelist
> MOIRA, Offred's best friend at one time
> NICK, another of the Commander's servants

Political climates have played major roles in several of Margaret Atwood's novels, particularly in *Life Before Man* (1979) and *Bodily Harm* (1982). In these novels, the sense of social upheaval provides not merely a social context for her protagonists, but it also mirrors their emotional conflict. What does society, so restless and discontent, need to become harmonious? Are revolutions or separatist movements genuine solutions to social problems? Individuals seem to have a greater range of possibilities for happiness: money, clothes, jobs, travel, sex. As any reader of Atwood's novels knows, these "remedies" are as shallow as those who promote them. Indeed, the twentieth century way of life, awash in banal hucksterism reducing people to products and solving complicated problems during thirty-minute television talk shows, seems perilously close to extinction. Just keeping afloat in a swill of pollution, exploitation, waste, racism, and sexism is problematical. Proposed "solutions" to these problems abound, a return to fundamentalist religion being one. *The Handmaid's Tale* gives its readers just such a political climate, and the results are both fascinating and chilling.

Late twentieth century America, saturated with pollution, pornography, sexual license, and a virulent strain of venereal disease, has erupted. Emerging from the fray is the Republic of Gilead, a theocracy even more conservative than that of the Puritans, where women are denied independence, education, even their own names—at least in the case of the Handmaids, who assume the names of their Commanders prefixed by the possessive preposition "of" (Offred is "of" added to "Fred," her Commander). In Gilead, women are reduced to mere functions—Wives, Daughters, Marthas (housemaids), Econowives, and Handmaids—and used as rewards for loyal service by men to the Republic. Dissident women are declared Unwomen and either shipped off to forced labor camps or publicly executed. Offred, the narrator of *The Handmaid's Tale*, is among the first group of Handmaids, fertile women assigned to high-ranking childless government officials and their wives to bear them a child. Haunted by memories of her former freedom, tortured because she does not know what has happened to her husband and daughter, and scornful of her moral cowardice, Offred struggles with her version of the truth.

The action of this novel is rather restricted, for Offred's movements are limited to grocery shopping and attending Prayvaganzas, Salvagings, and the rare Birthing. Her time is running out. At thirty-three, Offred has one more chance either to produce a child for her Commander or be killed. Thus, when Fred invites her to play an illicit game of Scrabble (books are forbidden in Gilead, and women are not allowed to read), Offred recognizes more than simply a change in her dull routine; she sees the beginning of an opportunity. Soon she finds herself caught among the desires of her Commander; those of his wife, Serena Joy, who wants a child; and her own need for human affection. She agrees to Serena Joy's arranged meeting with Nick, a fellow servant who is Offred's surest chance of becoming pregnant. Nick, however, arranges for an unexpected rescue.

Offred uses flat, almost emotionless prose to define and describe her existence. Weaving between past and an apparent present (which is later learned to be another past), Offred gives a picture of a terrifyingly real possibility. Her restrained prose seems at first to be extremely accurate and detached, as if she acts merely as an observer, one who declines to participate in her life at all. The fact is that Offred remains numb from all that has happened to her. Besides, she has learned not to trust anyone, least of all herself, a self she believes to be shallow and weak. Still, she is a grim survivor, planning to keep herself alive whatever the cost. As she goes forward with her narrative, however, Offred indicates gradual changes in her attitude, the need to take risks. Able to judge and in possession of an acerbic wit, Offred seizes opportunities when she can.

Not that she has many. Gilead is an almost perfect patriarchy, in which a few elderly men design rules for everyone else to follow. Ostensibly using the Bible as a guide and justification, the Commanders have structured a "safe" and orderly society, a society where they enjoy privileges denied to everyone else, where status is achieved by ideological rightness, where movements are constantly checked, and where anyone might be a spy. There is no longer any abortion or pollution, practically no rape, no apparent social discord, no lawyers, and no freedom of expression, movement, or religion.

This novel is not merely about a repressive patriarchy; it also explores the conflicts within women, their uncertainty between traditional values and liberation, their attitudes about behavior, their distrust of one another, and, most of all, their distrust of themselves. Offred is a prime example. Accepting the circumstances of her time, she thinks her mother's militant feminism archaic and her friend Moira's boldness merely entertaining. Because Offred thinks that her rights do not need defending, she thinks others' struggles are insignificant. Deprived of the very rights her mother and Moira defended, Offred recognizes their true value.

Offred's relation with the Aunts explores yet another relationship among women, for the Aunts in Gilead are one of the patriarchy's primary means of controlling women. As enforcers, they are granted some prominence and authority (but not guns) to become apostles of a woman's true purpose: bearing children. Needless to say, the Aunts ignore the contradiction between their relative freedom and the bondage they enforce when they preach submission and piety, assuring women that the protection they have is worth the cost of freedom.

Certainly, women are protected, not only by Angels and Guardians but also by apparel. Costumes identify role, with Wives in blue, Aunts in brown, Daughters in virginal white, Marthas in green, and Handmaids in red (still scarlet even in a new society that claims to revere their function). Color identifies rank and role; even as it separates women, it paradoxically makes them uniform. Offred frequently comments on her shapeless garment, comparing her protective red sack to the freedom of jeans and sundresses. She often alludes to her "wings," a wimple depriving her of peripheral vision, thus preventing her from seeing what goes on around her. The wimple further obscures her physical identity.

Identity is something to which Offred gave little thought in the past. She has been a stranger to herself and society, accepting the usual as if it has always existed. Deprivation, however, creates new hungers in her: curiosity about what goes on in the world, a subversive need for power, a longing for feeling, a willingness to dare. In many ways, *The Handmaid's Tale* is a novel about loss and what it creates. Gilead, in fact, has been created partially in response to loss. Offred's Commander explains that for men "there was nothing to work for, nothing to fight for. . . . You know what they were complaining about the most? Inability to feel." Offred finds little comfort in his assurance that feeling has returned.

Feeling, as Offred knows, can be mercurial, often unstable. Perhaps this is why her characterization of other figures in the novel seems distant. While Offred observes gestures, facial responses, and voice tone, she can only guess at intent. Messages seem to be implicit in simple language, and she attempts to decode all kinds of linguistic communication, beginning with the Latin inscription that she discovers scratched in her wardrobe: "*Nolite te bastardes carborundorum.*" When she is given a translation of this message, however, which becomes her motto, she discovers that it is corrupt. Language is subject to all sorts of twists. Even though Offred is desperate for communication, she intentionally obscures her own messages. All this struggle to understand reflects a familiar theme in Atwood's work, the inability to understand truly another person, another situation. Atwood further supports this through the very nature of Offred's narrative.

An extremely self-conscious narrative, *The Handmaid's Tale* constantly calls attention to itself. One plausible reason, readers later learn, is that Offred has recorded her experiences. Atwood, though, wants to emphasize the shifting face of reality by having Offred acknowledge the impossibility of telling the truth, by contradicting what she has said, by mixing hope with experience, by distrusting herself, by stating repeatedly, "This is a reconstruction." She goes on to confirm, "It's impossible to say a thing exactly the way it was, because what you say can never be exact, you always have to leave something out, there are too many parts, sides, crosscurrents, nuances; too many gestures, which could mean this or that, too many shapes which can never be fully described." While Offred's struggle to be honest makes her a reliable narrator, she constantly reminds readers of her limits.

Another interesting facet of this narrative is its place in time. Offred tells her story in the present, except when she refers to her life before becoming a Handmaid. Whatever experience she endures—from the Ceremony to a Salvaging—she gives her audience an intense sense of the present. Ironically, readers learn that not only is she telling her story after the events but also that her narrative has been reconstructed and presented to an audience at a still greater temporal remove. This latter audience, participants at the Twelfth Symposium on Gileadean Studies held in 2195, is concerned with authenticating Offred's story, in finding a truth that her message resists. Thorough research, however, fails to provide firm answers, and the entire narrative remains equivocal.

All of this is, needless to say, intentional. Atwood's fiction is rich precisely because of its ambiguity. The author does provide direction in prefatory quotations. The first, a passage from the Book of Genesis, recounts Rachel's reasons for giving her maid Bilhah to bear Jacob's child. More revealing, perhaps, is Atwood's quotation from Jonathan Swift's "A Modest Proposal." Like Swift's satire, Atwood's skates on the surface of reality, often snagging on familiar actions (such as bombing family-planning clinics), and only slightly exaggerating some attitudes, particularly those commonly held about women. Old issues concerning a woman's place, the value of her work, her real role in society are the heart of this novel. Atwood's sustained irony skewers not only attitudes but also the costumes they often assume. Her description of a dilapidated Playboy bunny costume, for example, is hilarious. This may lead to the novel's only weakness, if it is in fact a weakness.

Atwood has satirized popular culture so often in the past that readers familiar with her work will have no trouble recognizing her ironic references. Some novice readers of Atwood, however, will doubtless miss the author's understated digs at passing social trends. Still, this novel is so rich that even a morsel yields a pungent taste.

The Handmaid's Tale, in the guise of speculative fiction, is a deadly serious novel. Again, Atwood challenges her readers to look carefully at the world around them, to weigh the messages that besiege them, to interpret carefully the implications of action, and not to yield individuality. Offred certainly discovers that while submission may create the temporary illusion of safety, no one is safe. Ultimately human beings must risk life or lose what is most valuable to their experience.

Karen Carmean

Sources for Further Study

Commonweal. CXIII, April 25, 1986, p. 251.
Library Journal. CXI, February 1, 1986, p. 91.
Ms. XIV, February, 1986, p. 24.
The Nation. CCXLII, May 31, 1986, p. 764.
The New Republic. CXCIV, March 17, 1986, p. 33.
The New York Times Book Review. XCI, February 9, 1986, p. 1.
The New Yorker. LXII, May 12, 1986, p. 118.
Newsweek. CVII, February 17, 1986, p. 70.
Publishers Weekly. CCXXVIII, December 13, 1985, p. 45.
Time. CXXVII, February 10, 1986, p. 84.

THE HARVEST OF SORROW
Soviet Collectivization and the Terror-Famine

Author: Robert Conquest (1917-   )
Publisher: Oxford University Press (New York). Illustrated. 412 pp. $19.95
Type of work: History
Time: 1918-1933
Locale: The Soviet Union

A history of the collectivization of Soviet agriculture and the great famine of 1932-1933

Two twentieth century events have embedded themselves deeply in modern memory: the trench warfare of World War I and the massacre of the Jews during World War II. Robert Conquest wants to add a third: the staggering loss of life in the Soviet Union during the 1930's caused by the collectivization of agriculture and the purge of the Russian Communist Party. Already well-known for his history of the purges, *The Great Terror* (1968), Conquest has now written *The Harvest of Sorrow: Soviet Collectivization and the Terror-Famine*, an account of the collectivization of agriculture and the terrible famine that it caused. What Elie Wiesel is to Nazi Germany, Robert Conquest is to Soviet Russia.

Conquest would not find the comparison with Wiesel inappropriate. In the first sentence of his book, he compares the area of the Russian famine in the early 1930's to a Nazi concentration camp. He makes such a comparison because he is convinced that the famine was not a natural disaster, nor even the result of human miscalculation; rather he believes that it was a "terror-famine," a famine deliberately inflicted upon the Russian peasants to break their potential resistance to the Communist regime in Soviet Russia. Conquest calculates the total number of dead from the collectivization of agriculture and the famine at fourteen and a half million people, more than the combined death toll of all belligerents in World War I and more than double the number of Jews killed in the Holocaust. He bases this estimate on census figures, especially the census of 1937 which the Soviet government suppressed because of its appalling implications but whose total figure is referred to in scattered Soviet demographic studies during the Khrushchev era. Conquest emphasizes that his estimates are conservative and that the figures could very likely be much higher.

Despite the staggering scale of this enormous suffering, Conquest's book has the tone of an exposé of a little-known crime. Here one confronts the crux of his problem: Although it would be an exaggeration to say that the catastrophe of collectivization and famine was little known, it certainly has not commanded the attention which has produced the mountain of literature on trench warfare or on the Holocaust. This is the case for a number of reasons. First, the Soviet Union denied that there was a famine. Conquest calls this denial a use of Adolf Hitler's "big lie" technique. Despite an abundance of contemporary evidence and reports of famine, the official denial confused the issue and provided an opportunity for those who, consciously or subconsciously, did not want to know the truth to dismiss the reports as anti-Soviet propaganda. Although there can be little dispute that a great catastrophe occurred, the fear of anti-Soviet hysteria is still very real. There is a reluctance to emphasize the horrors of Soviet history because to do so might reinforce simplistic views of an "evil empire" and unloose a new wave of McCarthyism. Conquest's insistence that the failure of the current Soviet regime to conduct a thorough investigation of famine makes it heir and accomplice to the crime will not assuage such fears.

Finally—and this is the point Conquest emphasizes the most in explaining Western resistance to facing up to the implications of Soviet policy in the 1930's—the victims of this policy have not gained much sympathy. They were peasants, backward, ignorant, and superstitious. Many Westerners, fervent believers in progress, have consoled themselves with the thought that if the demise of the peasants in the Soviet Union took a form more rapid and terrible than would have been desirable, that demise was no less inevitable and necessary for the modernization of the Soviet Union.

Moreover, a large number of these peasant victims were Ukrainian. The Ukrainian claim to nationhood has never gained much support in the West. The culture and history of the Ukraine have not found a place in Western consciousness. The view of Ukrainians has generally been one of potential Nazi collaborators in World War II or fanatic anti-Communist émigrés in the United States. What will make Conquest's book controversial is not so much his statistics on the death toll as his insistence that the deaths were not the unfortunate by-product of necessary economic change but, rather, the result of a deliberate, genocidal war against a class and a nation. The fact that Conquest is associated with the conservative Hoover Institute at Stanford University and that he draws heavily on sources with such titles as *Communism: The Enemy of Mankind* (1955) and *The Black Deeds of the Kremlin* (1953) will cause some to adopt the comfortable position that his book is merely a Cold-War polemic which need not disturb them.

This, however, would be a mistake because Conquest has carefully researched his subject and utilized a variety of sources. Surprisingly, he was able to use a large number of Soviet sources. During the thaw of the Khrushchev era, especially in the early 1960's, a number of Soviet studies revealed new evidence about collectivization and famine, confirming that an enormous catastrophe had occurred. In addition, Conquest has found remarkably frank contemporary accounts in regional newspapers in the Soviet Union. Besides these more or less official Soviet sources, Conquest has also drawn on evidence provided by Soviet dissidents, both within the Soviet Union and without. Another important source from which Conquest draws is eyewitness accounts by émigrés from the Soviet Union. Especially important here are accounts collected and published by Ukrainian scholars and accounts deposited in the Harvard Research Interview Project. Finally, he has discovered vivid accounts of the suffering brought by collectivization in Soviet novels, which he utilizes with great effect.

These sources enable Conquest to go far beyond the abstractions of demographic statistics and generalizations. He describes collectivization and famine in vivid and horrible detail. There is an especially distressing chapter on how the famine affected children. Conquest notes in his preface that writing about the horrors which he describes was so painful that there were times when he could hardly proceed; indeed, his readers will be similarly moved.

Conquest interprets Soviet agricultural policy as a war against the peasants. This war began when Vladimir Ilyich Lenin launched the first campaign against the kulaks, or peasant proprietors, in the summer of 1918. Soviet propaganda depicted them as rich, selfish, greedy exploiters. Conquest demolishes this stereotype. The kulaks were mostly poor and were not hated by their fellow villagers. Indeed, they were often the most respected members of the village. The Communist effort to divide village society into classes of "kulaks," "middle peasants," and "poor peasants" was artificial and false and did not work. The idea that collectivization was a grass-roots movement of poor peasants against the kulaks was a fantasy. Conquest terms collectivization a revolution from above imposed on a peasantry which almost universally viewed it as a return to serfdom. Conquest believes that this was an accurate-enough understanding of the situation, describing collectivization as a sort of neo-feudalism and drawing several parallels between the collectivized farm and the aristocratic landed estate.

Lenin's war against the kulaks continued until 1921. At the same time that the Bolshevik regime was confiscating kulak land, it also requisitioned grain, the so-called "war communism" policy. There was massive resistance to land confiscation and grain requisitioning, at times reaching the scale of armed insurrection. Rather than give up their grain and their livestock, peasants quit producing or destroyed what they had. The result was a disastrous disruption of Russian agriculture that culminated in a major famine in 1921. Conquest uses Soviet census figures to estimate that six million people died in what he terms the Peasant War and in the famine of 1921-1922. Such a horrifying debacle forced an end to war communism in 1921 and the introduction of the New Economic Policy (NEP), which allowed the "rekulakization" of land in the countryside. Soviet leaders, however, viewed the NEP as a temporary retreat, and the conviction that peasant proprietors were a hostile threat to the regime remained strong. An especially unfortunate legacy of war communism was the belief that agricultural shortages could be solved by requisitioning.

From an economic point of view, the NEP was a success. By 1926, agricultural production had recovered to pre-World War I levels. The continuation of a class of peasant proprietors was a political defeat, however, for the Bolshevik regime. Hostile to the peasants and urban-oriented, the Soviet government followed a policy that discriminated against agricultural goods. Such a price policy inevitably led to market dislocations which produced a grain crisis in 1927. Conquest argues that the grain shortage of 1927 was by no means a crisis. It was simply the normal reaction of peasant producers to artificially low grain prices. An upward adjustment of prices would have easily brought an increase in production. The ways of a market economy were alien to the Soviet government, however, and it reacted to what it perceived as a crisis brought about by the hoarding of grain by resorting to emergency measures, the old policy of requisition.

This decision, taken in January, 1928, had fateful consequences. Requisitioning destroyed the peasants' confidence in the marketplace. They responded by evading confiscation and cutting production. These reactions convinced Joseph Stalin and the Soviet leadership that the peasants were incorrigible enemies. By November, 1928, open war was declared on the kulaks, and a massive drive to reorganize agriculture into collectivized farms began. The results were the same as during the era of war communism: massive resistance, massive dislocation of agricultural production, and terrible famine. Only this time it would all be on a much larger scale. Conquest believes that this war against the peasantry "may be seen as one of the most significant, as well as one of the most dreadful, periods of modern times."

Peasants who resisted collectivization, and many who did not, were either executed or deported to work camps in Siberia. About a third of the deportees died. Conquest estimates that about six and a half million people were killed or died in work camps. Many were women and children.

Although the horrors of collectivization and the consequent famine caused many lower-ranking Party members to balk, Stalin was able to carry through his policy without losing his grip on the Party because of critical moral weaknesses in Marxist-Leninist ideology. The language of class warfare depersonalized and dehumanized the victims. As the Soviet novelist Ilya Ehrenburg put it in his 1934 novel *The Second Day*: "Not one of them was guilty of anything; but they belong to a class that was guilty of everything." Party activists were capable of terrible deeds because they believed that they were agents of history. Indeed, hardness became a test of loyalty and commitment. Conquest has no difficulty finding Bolshevik rhetoric calling for the extermination or annihilation of class enemies. The comparison with the Nazi SS mentality is too obvious to require comment. Moreover, the principles of "democratic centralism"—that one kept one's mouth shut and obeyed orders—helped stifle thoughts of protest among those who had to endure the sight of starving women and children. Conquest does not fail to point out that the Nuremburg trials established the principle that obedience to orders did not exculpate criminal acts.

The catastrophic consequences of the rigid application of doctrine were most tragically shown in Kazakhstan. The Kazakhs were an Islamic people of seminomads. The effort to collectivize the agriculture of this partly pastoral people was a disastrous economic miscalculation rooted in a profound misunderstanding of human cultures. The Kazakhs were denied their pastures, but no fodder was provided for their herds. Rather than surrender their livestock to the collectivized farms, they slaughtered them. The result was a famine in 1932 in which at least one million people died, a higher proportion of the population than died even in the Ukraine. For Conquest, the tragedy of the Kazakhs is a paradigm for the moral blindness of rigid ideology to the rich variety of human culture.

Conquest focuses his book on the Ukraine where the collectivization was most aggressive and where the famine claimed the most victims. It is a significant triumph for Ukrainian nationalists that they have gained the support of a non-Ukrainian scholar of his prestige and influence. Conquest argues that it is no accident that the famine was worst in the Ukraine. (He is so sensitive to Ukrainian national feelings that he apologizes for using the term "the Ukraine," which implies a mere geographical area, instead of Ukraine, which implies a nation.) The famine was part of a policy to crush the Ukraine and to impose Russian rule securely once and for all. Particularly significant for Conquest is that the Soviet regime launched a vigorous purge of Ukrainian intellectuals and cultural leaders at the same time it was inflicting the terror-famine on the Ukrainian peasants. He tellingly quotes Stalin's statement that the "nationality problem is, in its very essence, a problem of the peasantry."

Conquest is convinced that the famine was not caused by grain shortages but by requisitioning on a scale deliberately calculated to cause famine. Bolshevik requisitioning of grain during the civil war had resulted in famine, so the Soviet government knew the consequences of its policy. Furthermore, the leadership of the Ukrainian Communist Party had pointed out clearly to the central government the implications of its grain-requisitioning policy, but to no avail. In contrast to previous famines in czarist times, or even during the civil war famine, the Soviet government continually denied that there was famine in the Ukraine and did not allow any relief efforts, either from within Russia or abroad. Even individuals traveling into the Ukraine were searched, and any food found was confiscated. The cities were closed to the countryside to prevent the starving from seeking food there. All of this leads Conquest to one of his central conclusions: The famine in the Ukraine was not an accident but a deliberate policy with a definite aim—to crush the Ukrainian nation. Indeed, he quotes the United Nations' definition of genocide and applies it to Soviet policy in the Ukraine. Conquest believes that the question of Ukrainian liberty should be "a key moral and political issue for the world as a whole."

The implications of Conquest's book are deeply troubling. It is a testimony to the almost unlimited human capacity to inflict suffering. When one considers that more than two million Russian soldiers died in Word War I, that this war was followed by a civil war and famine that claimed nine million lives, that fourteen and a half million died in the collectivization and famine between 1929 and 1934, that this was followed by Stalin's purges in which some three million were killed and that perhaps as many as twelve million died in labor camps, and that World War II brought perhaps as many as twenty million deaths in the Soviet Union, one is confronted with a twentieth century time of troubles almost beyond imagining. Most troubling, perhaps, is the thought that much of this horror was the result of men powerfully motivated by dreams of a better society. For Conquest, this millenarianism was the root of the irrational forces which produced the horrors of the terror-famine.

Paul B. Kern

Sources for Further Study

Booklist. LXXXIII, September 15, 1986, p. 98.
Kirkus Reviews. LIV, June 15, 1986, p. 903.
Library Journal. CXI, August, 1986, p. 145.
National Review. XXXVIII, September 12, 1986, p. 50.
The New Republic. CXCV, November 3, 1986, p. 34.
The New York Times Book Review. XCI, October 26, 1986, p. 11.
Newsweek. CVIII, November 17, 1986, p. 95.
Publishers Weekly. CCXXX, August 1, 1986, p. 65.
The Observer. September 14, 1986, p. 26.
Time. CXXVIII, December 8, 1986, p. 91.

HAWKSMOOR

Author: Peter Ackroyd (1949-   )
Publisher: Harper & Row, Publishers (New York). 217 pp. $16.95
Type of work: Detective novel and novel of ideas
Time: The 1980's and the early eighteenth century, with flashbacks to the middle of the seventeenth century
Locale: London, England

A richly evocative novel of ideas, disguised as a crime thriller, which simultaneously explores two centuries and the minds of two protagonists

> *Principal characters:*
> SIR CHRISTOPHER WREN, a famous English church architect
> NICHOLAS DYER, a master architect employed by Wren
> NICHOLAS HAWKSMOOR, a twentieth century London police officer
> WALTER PYNE, Dyer's apprentice
> WALTER PAYNE, a young detective, Hawksmoor's assistant

Has any period so embodied contradiction as the 1980's? From a distance, past eras can appear seamless, devoid of moral controversy or philosophical challenge. This impression regarding England's early eighteenth century, in particular, is reinforced by labels such as the Age of Enlightenment and the Augustan Age.

Yet Nicholas Dyer, one of two protagonists in *Hawksmoor*, is an uneasy representative of that period. An orphan of an earlier London—that of the Plague and the Great Fire—he has been reared by a cult whose philosophy is "Christ was the Serpent who deceiv'd Eve. . . . Sathan is the God of this World and fit to be worshipp'd." Paradoxically, Dyer becomes a builder of churches, employed by Sir Christopher Wren, that paragon of an age obsessed with scientific progress and the primacy of reason over what was called "enthusiasm." Dyer holds, contrary to Wren's beliefs, that "the miseries of the present Life. . . lead the True Architect not to Harmony or to Rationall Beauty but to quite another Game." Accordingly, he carries out the human sacrifice required for the "consecration" of every church he builds: "The Eucharist must be mingled with Blood."

In the twentieth century, Nicholas Hawksmoor, the second protagonist, is also an antirational holdout. A veteran police investigator, he relies heavily on intuition, rather than on scientific procedure and modern principles of criminology, to help him solve a series of murders on the sites of London churches built by Dyer.

Dyer and Hawksmoor have much more in common than renegadism: Each is also wracked by doubt and a feeling of mental disintegration. Events in their lives as well as in their minds seem to echo each other across the centuries. As the novel progresses by telling their respective stories in alternate chapters—and alternately in eighteenth century and contemporary prose—the two protagonists become virtual mirror images and eventually seem to merge in identity.

Although Dyer is a fictive character, the Hawksmoor of Peter Ackroyd's title actually lived (from 1661 to 1736; Dyer's dates are 1654 to *circa* 1715) and worked for Sir Christopher. Dyer's twentieth century fictive counterpart appears not to realize that he bears the same name as this historical Nicholas Hawksmoor, the brilliant and unconventional architect of "huge lushious Style" who actually built the seven churches where the murders in the novel occur. This is only one of many circumstances seemingly calculated to bewilder the novel's readers as well as its characters. As the irrationalist Dyer remarks, "There is a Mist in Humane affairs, a small thin Rain which cannot be perceeved in single Drops of this Man or that Man but which rises around them and obscures them one from another." The twentieth century murders suggest a pattern that Hawksmoor the detective never can quite grasp. He has a growing intuition regarding the murderer ("He's at my fingertips . . . I can reach him. I feel it"), but simultaneously his confusion grows, until "he considered the possibility that he had gone mad."

At the heart of this novel of ideas cum mystery thriller is an intense debate between deliberate cultivation of madness—Dyer's "Principles of Terrour and Magnificence"—and Wren's empiricist assault on superstition. Dyer's philosophy, in that it offers no consolation, proves the more realistic of the two. Or does it? The conflict receives definition in a pivotal scene between Dyer and Wren. Wren maintains that Dyer's superstition constitutes what in the 1980's would be called a self-fulfilling prophecy: "It is one of the greatest Curses visited upon Mankind . . . that they shall fear where no Fear is. . . . They fancy that such ill Accidents must come to pass, and so they render themselves fit Subjects to be wrought upon. . . . Nature yields to the Froward and the Bold." Dyer rebuts: "It does not yield, it devours: You cannot master or manage Nature."

In any case, one cannot master the action of this novel, so replete is it with overlapping frames of reference. How, for example, is one to interpret the apparent echoes of one century's events in the other century, as when Dyer expresses the fear "I have said too much" after his argument with Wren, and Hawksmoor hears the same words spoken behind his back? The novel itself offers contradictory hints: that its characters are reincarnated; that the same person can exist simultaneously in different periods; that the collective human spirit, like artifacts of civilization, is made up of accumulated archaeological layers; and that events simply recur eternally. Ackroyd never permits his reader to choose finally among these explanations.

Despite the story's intractability, then, the novelist cannot be said to side with the irrational; it is simply one among many frames of reference. Instead, Wren's observation on self-fulfilling prophecy suggests that one simply builds a world around one's chosen philosophy and lives or dies with the consequences. Hawksmoor, briefing his fellow investigators, speculates,

"Some people say that the crime which cannot be solved has yet to be invented. But who knows? Perhaps this will be the first"—an attitude that eventually gets him taken off the case.

Yet in the life of the novel in both centuries, there is a substratum undercutting all events and all philosophies. This substratum is revealed through the archaeological explorations in both centuries: Dyer, a true religious eclectic, is also a passionate amateur archaeologist, able to name the gods of ancient Syrian, Ammonite, Phoenician, Druidic, and Hebrew civilizations—and to him they are all the same god. He remarks that the temples of pagan gods have been uncovered at his church sites. "We live off the Past," he declares, striking a blow for his side in the eighteenth century battle of Ancients versus Moderns: "We can scarce walk across the Stones without being reminded of those who walked there before us. . . . It is the dark of Time from which we come and to which we will return."

Hawksmoor's archaeologist friend says, "As far as I'm concerned we could keep on digging for ever," and Hawksmoor himself echoes this thought while trying to fix a starting point for his investigations: "Perhaps there is no beginning. . . . I never know where anything comes from." It is like admitting that one cannot unearth the origin of evil.

The substratum of life also is manifested in the sad existence of both centuries' derelicts, who huddle perennially around sputtering campfires. They are presented as fully rounded human beings, although it is from among them that most of the sacrificial murder victims are drawn. Indeed, there is a suggestion that the murderers, even while fulfilling their own religious obligations, believe that they perform a kindness by delivering their victims from such squalor—another case of multiple frames of reference.

Dyer extends this "merciful" way of thinking to all human existence. Like a medieval Albigensian heretic, he believes that life is a curse and time "the Deliverance of Man." "No Wish more frequent among Men than the Wish for Death," says Dyer, and he imagines a murderer telling his intended victim, "You will be sure to get what you Want." Dyer's own first victim is a would-be suicide, a derelict who could not summon enough courage to kill himself. Hawksmoor the detective carries Dyer's reasoning to its logical conclusion: "There was always so strong a sense of fatality that it seemed to Hawksmoor that both murderer and victim were inclined towards their own destruction; it was his job only to hurry the murderer along."

In this respect, *Hawksmoor* echoes a moral issue of vital importance in the 1980's, when it is sometimes argued that crime victims invite their own fate; that they are subconsciously in collusion with the perpetrators. Much modern psychotherapy consists of retraining clients not to think or act like victims. While reflecting this current issue, *Hawksmoor* characteristically does not take a stand. Instead, in recounting the story of Little Saint Hugh, for whom one of Dyer's churches is named, the novel suggests that whoever becomes a sacrificial victim under one system of belief may be seen simultaneously under another system as a martyr, hero, or saint:

> He was "a child of ten years, the son of a widow. One Koppin, a heathen, enticed him to a ritual house under ground where he was tortured and scourged and finally strangled. Then his body was left there unknown for seven days and seven nights. Immediately Hugh's body was recovered from the pit a blind woman was restored to sight by touching it and invoking the martyr; other miracles followed."

Legends such as this—along with the archaeological finds—become the archives of the novel's world, indications of why rationality is no cure for its ills. There is sad irony in a remark of Hawksmoor's assistant regarding a police computer: "You know, you could put the whole of London in the charge of one computer and the crime would go right down.... A memory bank ... makes the world a safer place." Yet the murders continue unsolved; Hawksmoor, seeing a figure on the computer screen, mutters sarcastically, "Ah, ... the green man did it." Dyer mocks the "Philosophy of Experiment and Demonstration ... poor Particles of Dust which will not burie the Serpents."

Hawksmoor's archaeologist friend tells him that she has dug down to the sixth century, well before any of the action in the novel. Although she had hoped to dig out a key to human motivation, she now ventures the idea that perhaps human behavior has no fundamental explanation—neither in rational theory nor in superstition. Again, given the worldviews that can lead to sacrificial murder, there is irony in Hawksmoor's reply: "It's a theory, and a theory can do no harm."

Neither, however, is there any safety in theories for the novel's protagonists. Overwhelmed by life's incurable dilemmas, both become weary unto death. The narrative is full of phrases such as "the full weariness of the evening" and "the full weight of the world." Dyer lives oppressed by terror of having his murders found out, belying his own credo that "the highest Passion is Terrour." Eventually both he and Hawksmoor seem to dissolve and to become virtually invisible, their personal identities rendered meaningless: "I saw a man who is not, nor ever could he be,/ Hold up your hand and look, for you are he."

Yet, while conveying the protagonists' own sense of their unreality, *Hawksmoor* gives the reader a strong sense of both character and place, evoking vividly the worlds of eighteenth and twentieth century London. With his usual air of disgust, Dyer describes a tavern he enters with a man he is about to murder: "There was a handful of Fire in a rusty Grate and a large earthern Chamber Pot in the chimney-corner; the Mixture of Scents that met us when we first entred were those of Tobacco, Piss, dirty Shirts and uncleanly Carcasses."

Aside from its characteristically vivid style, *Hawksmoor* would seem to have few points of similarity with Peter Ackroyd's other writings, which include *The Last Testament of Oscar Wilde* (1983) and *T.S. Eliot: A Life* (1984). Yet they share the ability to enter another time and place as well as another consciousness in a wholly convincing manner. Ackroyd has given some evidence that this is one of his main objectives as a writer. He spoke of "re-creating Eliot's presence" in the biography, and *The Last Testament of Oscar Wilde* ends with the dying Wilde imagining that he might enter another man's heart as a way of salvation: "In that moment of transition, when I was myself and someone else, of my own time and in another's, the secrets of the universe would stand revealed." With the richly suggestive *Hawksmoor*, Ackroyd has taken a major step in that direction, though the path has hardly led to his characters' salvation.

Thomas Rankin

Sources for Further Study

Kirkus Reviews. LIII, November 15, 1985, p. 1200.
Library Journal. CXI, January, 1986, p. 98.
The London Review of Books. VII, October 3, 1985, p. 18.
New Statesman. CX, September 27, 1985, p. 34.
The New York Times Book Review. XCI, January 19, 1986, p. 3.
The New Yorker. LXII, March 3, 1986, p. 104.
Newsweek. CVII, February 24, 1986, p. 78.
Publishers Weekly. CCXXVIII, November 22, 1985, p. 47.
Time. CXXVII, February 24, 1986, p. 76.
Times Literary Supplement. September 27, 1985, p. 1049.

HENRY THOREAU
A Life of the Mind

Author: Robert D. Richardson, Jr. (1934-   )
Publisher: University of California Press (Berkeley). Illustrated. 455 pp. $25.00
Type of work: Literary biography
Time: 1837-1862
Locale: Concord, Massachusetts

The growth of Henry David Thoreau's intellectual life is traced through a careful examination of his formal schooling and his diffuse reading, as well as the political and social movements of his time

Principal personages:
HENRY DAVID THOREAU, an American author, philosopher, and
naturalist
RALPH WALDO EMERSON, Thoreau's mentor and lifetime friend

Henry David Thoreau has always been, at least for the general reader, an author one preferred to read rather than to read about. Indeed, his *Walden* (1854) is essentially a selective and controlled autobiographical memoir of his almost two years of self-sufficiency in the cabin and bean field beside Walden Pond near his native Concord, Massachusetts. What one learned about Thoreau that was not contained in *Walden* was essentially apocryphal, such as the fabled jail visit of his mentor Ralph Waldo Emerson after Thoreau had been arrested for not having paid the poll tax. Thoreau had always enjoyed seeing human life as well as nature in mythic terms and avoided detailed considerations of personal affairs, even in his private letters and journals.

Logically then, the first biographies of Thoreau by his friend Ellery Channing and by his acquaintance Frank B. Sanborn are anecdotal family histories, informal and readable to be sure, but without real attempts to discern what formed Thoreau's mind, original even among his distinctive Transcendentalist contemporaries. Perhaps Channing and Sanborn were too close to Thoreau, either by friendship or in time, to make such judgments. Paradoxically, Emerson's own Thoreau references are least helpful of all for objective study, and in the first quarter of the twentieth century interest in Thoreau had generally waned. *Walden* was suddenly rediscovered during the Depression, however, and with its renascence came the biography written by Henry Seidel Canby. Canby's treatment was more scholarly than any that had come before it, but it essentially depended on Sanborn's book for family history and material on nineteenth century Concord.

Clearly, a hundred years after Sanborn's book and a hundred twenty-five after Thoreau's death is the right time for a documented intellectual biography of Thoreau. Robert D. Richardson, Jr., provides this needed treatment in his *Henry Thoreau: A Life of the Mind*. This is not to imply that Richardson writes only for scholars, though Thoreau and Emerson scholars will no doubt read this book with profit and enjoyment. Richardson's study is as much a social history of America between the Revolutionary and Civil wars as it is literary biography.

This period, in every sense, shaped Thoreau as it did his country. It produced a man for whom independent action was privileged and prized. The young Thoreau glorifies the soldier as a descendant of the Homeric heroes. Even so, great-souled independence could be won less easily as the United States adopted the mechanization which was primarily responsible for its collective greatness by the mid-nineteenth century. One solution was the withdrawal of the individual, but Richardson rightly rejects the all-too-often assumed notion that Thoreau would, had he been able, have remained beside the pond forever.

As Thoreau grew older, his soldier's courage was increasingly channeled toward support of unpopular and controversial political causes. His essay "Civil Disobedience" is one indication of this involvement; another is his enthusiastic support of Emerson's public position as an abolitionist. Richardson recounts Thoreau's racing to announce Emerson's famous address on the injustice of slavery and his ringing of the Concord church bell when the verger who normally performed that task refused to do so because he was not in sympathy with Emerson's position.

One related motif thus clearly emerges in Thoreau's life: his personal idealism. This led him to take courageous unpopular stands even as it militated against his joining organizations and movements which were clearly in harmony with his own views. Thoreau, for example, had no immediate family responsibilities (unlike Emerson) and so could easily have joined Margaret Fuller's experiment in communal living at Brook Farm. As things turned out, he was wise not to have done so, for that community of philosophers quickly dissipated its energies through small-mindedness and ultimately disbanded when fire destroyed its main building. Thoreau saw Brook Farm as institutionalized reform, and he believed from its beginning that it could not succeed.

Fuller was always cold to Thoreau's notions of independence. Richardson rightly implies that her resentment probably cost Thoreau an important ally in the publication of his work, for Emerson had made Fuller editor of *The Dial*, the famous Transcendentalist journal. Most of Thoreau's essays did eventually appear in *The Dial*, though not without Emerson's prodding. Even so, Thoreau remained throughout his life a man of generous feelings. When Fuller died tragically with her husband and son in a shipwreck off the Long Island coast, famous stay-at-home Thoreau raced to the scene in a futile attempt to rescue one of her manuscripts.

Richardson argues compellingly that although Thoreau's travels were geographically confined to southern Canada and a brief period of residence on Staten Island, New York, and though he rejected several opportunities to travel in Europe, Thoreau was actually a far-ranging traveler. His furthest journeys were made intellectually through his broadly based readings. He chain read, and one important work would inevitably lead to several others related to it. Then, too, the time in which he lived, one of scientific as well as philosophical ferment, allowed him to see a typically Transcendentalist oneness in all that he read. The works of Charles Darwin, so controversially popular in the mid-nineteenth century, became for Thoreau at once notes of scientific observation, travel writing, and fortuitous nature discovery.

Indeed, perhaps the most engrossing feature of Richardson's book is his careful examination of Thoreau's intellectual growth. This is most apparent in Thoreau's reading, which changed markedly from his student years at Harvard College. Richardson notes Harvard's smallness and provincialism in the years before and during Thoreau's attendance. (The biography itself begins with Thoreau's graduation in 1837.) Thoreau read the Greek and Latin classics, as did all the Harvard men of his day. He was excited by the bold strength of Homer's heroes, but he was equally taken by Vergil's poetry. Significantly, he appreciated both the adventuresome boldness of Odysseus and the orderly cycle of the farmer's year as delineated in the four books of Vergil's *Georgics*. Thoreau increasingly became convinced that the circularity of nature produced heroes in every age, though these necessarily had to suit the requirements of the times in which they lived. He recognized, in a way that has become popular only since Sigmund Freud and Carl Jung, the essentially mythic nature of life. Thoreau's Odyssean adventures were confined to his raft journey on the Concord and Merrimack rivers, to his ascent of a New Hampshire mountain, or merely to a winter walk around Walden Pond, but for a man who could see the world in a leaf these adventures were no less epical than those of Homer's poems.

Thoreau came to the English poets late, only after his Harvard years and only because of Emerson's urging to read them. He always found them sterile by comparison with the classics of his college years. He certainly admired Geoffrey Chaucer, William Shakespeare, and John Milton, but he enjoyed much more the nature poetry of William Wordsworth and Samuel Taylor Coleridge.

One might assume as much. Emerson's substantial correspondence with Thomas Carlyle led Thoreau to that author's prose and to praise it, extravagantly by contemporary tastes. In a sense, Thoreau's greatest intellectual task became having to balance the childlike wonder of his philosophical reading against an increasing need for empiricism fed by his reading in the biological sciences. He would, consequently, never have wanted to be considered a scientist but, rather, a careful observer of science's workings. He felt close to Darwin's works, primarily because they managed to balance a philosophical and scientific inquiry into nature.

Certainly, Thoreau was closer to no contemporary than he was to Em-

erson. Emerson was only ten years older than Thoreau, a fact often overlooked, and a fellow Harvard graduate. He was an established author when
Thoreau left Harvard; he had also acquired by this time his interest in
American Idealism, an outlook adapted from Immanuel Kant and Eastern
sources and more popularly called Transcendentalism. Richardson's study
reveals more profoundly, even than Thoreau's letters and journals, the deep
intimacy of the connection. On the one hand, it was personal. Thoreau lived
in the Emerson house for several years, supervised the running of the
household during Emerson's long European and American lecture tours,
and even tutored the child of William Emerson and lived for a year in his
Staten Island home. He was possibly even more deeply affected by the death
of Emerson's son Waldo than he was by that of his own brother John.

Just as important, Thoreau found an intellectual guide in Emerson. This
is not to imply that Thoreau allowed Emerson to choose the subjects of his
scholarly inquiries or even that their writings were similar. Emerson, in fact,
was never enthusiastic about Thoreau's poetry or even the bulk of his travel
writings. What Thoreau most valued in Emerson was his friend's candid
advice, criticism, and tireless efforts in propagating the younger man's work.
The Dial, which Emerson founded, was a primary outlet for Thoreau's earliest writings, and Emerson sponsored Thoreau's foray to New York City in
what turned out to be an unsuccessful attempt to find the young man a
permanent publisher.

Success, or the lack of it, remained a delicate subject for Thoreau
throughout his lifetime. After leaving Harvard, he became a supervising
instructor in the Concord public schools. He had important administrative
as well as teaching responsibilities, and by contemporary standards he was
well compensated. Nevertheless, teaching in these schools was difficult, and
Thoreau found it impossible to employ corporal punishment, the traditional
method of maintaining class control. The result was that he left his post
barely two weeks after the start of his first term of teaching. For a time, he
maintained his own private academy, founded with the help of his brother
John, but this was never a profitable venture. Thoreau's father was a merchant turned pencil maker, and from time to time Thoreau would return to
this trade, even perfecting a process for the manufacture of purer and more
efficient leads. Thoreau also pursued surveying, charting the portion of
Walden Pond shorefront (owned by Emerson) on which he would eventually
build his cabin. Emerson wrote several letters of recommendation on
Thoreau's behalf in this regard, and for a time it seems as though Thoreau
actually considered joining the teams of surveyors then sweeping the newly
annexed Western territories.

Though his never having acquired wealth seemed not to bother Thoreau,
he became defensive whenever he described his attainments in the question-
naires sent regularly to Harvard graduates. Richardson notes that Thoreau

once offered in one of these to show any of his classmates who cared to ask him the way of acquiring true wealth. Indeed, Thoreau's outlook did not require wealth as a concomitant of success, but his America, the country of Benjamin Franklin and Adam Smith, equated wealth with industry. It was accusations of laziness that Thoreau most feared.

Thoreau insisted throughout his life that he was content; nevertheless, his life certainly held unhappiness and frustration. The early deaths of his brother John and Emerson's young son Waldo affected him deeply. Much as he tried to compare the loss of those he loved with the passing of the seasons, it is hard to believe that he entirely managed to translate philosophy to practice in this area. Then, too, winning widespread acceptance for his writings during his lifetime was a goal he never accomplished. Richardson wisely refrains from such sentimental reflections; nevertheless, it is worth noting that at his death Thoreau asked that his sister read to him the section of his *A Week on the Concord and Merrimack Rivers* (1849) which narrates his swift journey home quickened by a favorable wind. His pleased response to the cyclical nature of his journey was a simple smile.

Robert J. Forman

Sources for Further Study

American History Illustrated. XXI, December, 1986, p. 6.
Booklist. LXXXIII, September 1, 1986, p. 20.
Chicago Tribune. September 4, 1986, V, p. 3.
Choice. XXIV, December, 1986, p. 628.
Library Journal. CXI, August, 1986, p. 151.
Los Angeles Times Book Review. November 30, 1986, p. 11.
Publishers Weekly. CCXXX, July 18, 1986, p. 72.

HIGH JINX

Author: William F. Buckley, Jr. (1925-   )
Publisher: Doubleday & Company (New York). 261 pp. $16.95
Type of work: Novel
Time: 1954
Locale: England, Washington, D.C., Moscow, and Stockholm

The seventh in Buckley's series of sophisticated espionage entertainments featuring CIA agent Blackford Oakes begins with an abortive plot to overthrow the Communist regime in Albania and dramatizes the Kremlin struggle for succession to Stalin

> *Principal characters:*
> BLACKFORD OAKES, a Yale-educated CIA agent
> RUFUS, his CIA control
> ANTHONY TRUST, the CIA London bureau chief, his classmate and
>   recruiter
> SIR ALISTAIR FLEETWOOD, a Cambridge professor and Nobel laure-
>   ate, inventor of the Zirca
> ALICE GOODYEAR CORBETT, Fleetwood's lover and a KGB recruiter
> BERTRAM OLIVER HEATH (aka HENRY), a KGB mole recruited at
>   Cambridge by Fleetwood
> BORIS ANDREYEVICH BOLGIN, the KGB London bureau chief
> GEORGI MAXIMILIANOVICH MALENKOV, Soviet premier
> LAVRENTI PAVLOVICH BERIA, head of the KGB

Probably best known as the best-known conservative author in the United States, William F. Buckley, Jr., continues to be both versatile and prolific. *High Jinx* is the seventh Blackford Oakes novel he has produced in ten years, in addition to his activities as editor, columnist, television host, and yachtsman. Buckley has even published *Overdrive* (1983), a journal of his febrile activities during the course of a week that testifies to just how busy he has been being busy. His best-selling novels have enlarged his intellectual influence into popularity.

Like its predecessors in the Blackford Oakes series, *Saving the Queen* (1976), *Stained Glass* (1978), *Who's on First* (1980), *Marco Polo, If You Can* (1982), *The Story of Henri Tod* (1984), and *See You Later Alligator* (1985), *High Jinx* belongs as much to the genre of political-historical fiction as to that of the spy novel. Indeed, much of the pleasure in reading the Blackford Oakes novels comes from their dramatic exploration of the possibilities in recent history.

In *High Jinx*, the interplay between fact and fiction is particularly pro-vocative—and timely, because the novel's donnée is based on one of the best-kept secrets of the Cold War: a joint British-American operation in Al-bania, conducted between 1949 and 1953, designed to overthrow the Com-munist regime of Enver Hoxha and destabilize the entire Soviet Bloc. This ill-fated plan, sabotaged by Soviet mole Kim Philby and by sheer incom-petence, was fully revealed for the first time in Nicholas Bethell's book *Be-*

trayed (1985; first published in Great Britain as *The Great Betrayal*).

In *High Jinx*, too, Buckley again offers deft and amusing portraits of public figures—Dwight David Eisenhower, John Foster Dulles, Allen Dulles, Lavrenti Pavlovich Beria, and Georgi Maximilianovich Malenkov are given plausible dialogue and tantalizing roles in the plot—and, as in the other Oakes books and as with Alfred Hitchcock's brief cameo appearances within his own films, reference is even made to the name William F. Buckley, Jr., when Eisenhower's national security adviser happens to mention the author's early work *McCarthy and His Enemies* (1954).

Early in his career, Buckley himself worked for the Central Intelligence Agency (CIA), and he has had the confidence of important government officials. Hence much of *High Jinx* seems to bear the authority of an insider's version of major international developments. Yet Buckley slyly reminds his reader that, while *High Jinx* is no idle fabrication, it is a work of fiction. The queen of England in his rendition of 1954 is named Caroline, not Elizabeth, and her prime minister is Anthony Brogan, not Winston Churchill or even his successor, Anthony Eden. In a statement that he appends to the completed narrative, Buckley also confesses to a deliberate inaccuracy in his chronology.

Buckley also chides two critics of *See You Later Alligator* for complaining that Blackford Oakes was not interesting enough. "I find him fascinating" is Buckley's final comment. Given the fact that he has commissioned him for espionage duty seven times, the author's attraction to his own protagonist is not surprising. Oakes is about the same age as Buckley was in 1954, and he shares his political views and his background at an English public school, Yale University, and the CIA. Oakes is irresistibly handsome, while Buckley is certainly witty.

High Jinx begins on a military base somewhere in England where Oakes, just back from Germany, is assigned to help train a special commando group composed of British, American, and Albanian volunteers. They are preparing for Operation Tirana, a top-secret mission to depose the Marxist regime in Albania and replace it with one more sympathetic to the Western alliance. The book invites the reader to speculate on turning points in history: What if, at an early stage in the Cold War, one nation in the Soviet Bloc had chosen to defect? The novel suggests that the loss of Albania as a fiefdom would have constituted a serious, consequential blow to Kremlin prestige and that the world of 1986 would be a better place for it. It is hard, however, to conceive of installing democracy in the xenophobic rural state that for more than thirty years has not only been a scourge of the West but a pain in the Warsaw Pact's Balkan flank as well. Even without the intrusion of the CIA and MI5, Albania has been almost as hostile to Moscow as it has to Washington.

Like its real-life prototype (from which, however, it differs considerably in detail), Operation Tirana is an utter failure: All forty-one of the commandos are reportedly intercepted immediately on arrival in Albania and are presumably executed. A reasonable assumption is that the local authorities were waiting for them, that they had been tipped off with exact details of the secret mission. Much of the novel traces the efforts to discover the source of this deadly leak in Western intelligence. Someone must have had access to the most confidential military and diplomatic information, and until the mole is exposed the governments of the United States and the United Kingdom face paralysis.

Although it is a capital offense for book reviewers to divulge too many of the intricacies of an espionage novel's plot in which the gathering of information is a chief source of the reader's pleasure, *High Jinx* is not quite a whodunit, and suspense is not the engine that gets its pages turned. Though the book is much more pallid on a second reading than the first, it is not so much to learn who or what but how that one reads on.

The fact that Sir Alistair Fleetwood, a brilliant and vainglorious young English physicist, is somehow implicated in the breach of security is suggested rather early in the narrative. Fleetwood has been a committed Marxist ever since his precocious student days. For twenty years, he has been the lover and the operative of KGB officer Alice Goodyear Corbett, an American who lives in the Soviet Union. At the age of thirty-eight, Fleetwood wins a Nobel Prize for his invention of the Zirca, an extremely powerful telescope that he surreptitiously makes available for service to Soviet intelligence. It also turns out that one of the Operation Tirana commandos, Bertram Oliver Heath, is a protégé of Fleetwood. Heath does not share the gruesome fate of his forty comrades, inasmuch as it is he who betrays them to the KGB.

Blackford Oakes directs the investigation into Fleetwood and Heath, which is of urgent interest to the highest circles of both the British and American governments. Though fascinating as Buckley finds his fictional alter ego, Oakes is much less interesting than the characters he pursues. He is a useful agent, of the CIA and of the plot, but Oakes is too bland to be the focus of the novel's narrative energies. In Buckley's Manichaean universe of good combating evil, the villains are ultimately, if temporarily, foiled. Oakes, however, is merely a foil to more complex figures.

The Tirana intrigue is set against the contemporary jockeying for power among the Politburo heirs of the recently deceased Joseph Stalin. Malenkov is in tenuous command of the Kremlin, but Nikolai Aleksandrovich Bulganin, Nikita Khrushchev, and, most ominously, Beria are formidable rivals eager for him to stumble. *High Jinx* is most engaging when it takes the reader into the midnight fastness of Lubyanka to observe Beria's diabolical machinations to eliminate his associates and wrest absolute control for himself. Beria enlists the services of the KGB and of Fleetwood's Zirca in his personal factional struggle, while his opponents even go so far as to collude with American and British intelligence services to obstruct him. The novel, in fact, derives its title from the astonishment of Allen Dulles, director of the CIA, at learning of the intricacies of the internecine battles among the Soviet leaders. "He had been many years in the intelligence system. He had never before come across high jinx at such a level."

It is a matter of historical fact that during the fierce conflict to determine who would succeed Stalin on his death in 1953, Beria was executed in 1953 (not 1954, as Buckley admits to misplacing it), Malenkov was forced out of the premiership by Bulganin in 1955, and Bulganin was forced out by Khrushchev in 1958. Though no Western, or probably Eastern, scholar can be certain about the exact circumstances under which these developments occurred, Buckley's vivid scenario of crude personalities and brute force is probably as plausible as any other speculation. More than most others, it makes for a compelling story.

Buckley's imagination is animated more by political themes than by psychological ones, and *High Jinx* is more effective when set in government offices than in bedrooms. Yet the novel is a variation on the motifs of trust and betrayal: personal and geopolitical. Couples exploit the confidences of each other, just as moles within the Soviet and Western commands do. CIA officer Anthony Trust is cannily named. Through it all, the reader welcomes the offer of a perspective based on a stable system of values.

The hindsight of thirty years enables Buckley to provide the illusion of certitude more difficult to construct for the profusion of contemporary events. As a conservative essayist, Buckley has railed against liberal agnosticism toward the vision that sees this planet as a battleground between the forces of leftist totalitarianism and those of capitalist democracy. In his novel, he is able to re-create a world in which the Cold War is the dominant, and indubitable, reality. Buckley has been an outspoken supporter of Ronald Reagan, and he sets *High Jinx* during a period when another genial old Republican, Dwight Eisenhower, sits in the White House. The implication seems to be that in the 1980's as in the 1950's a popular president recognizes what is the inescapable truth: that Soviet imperialism is the principal menace to free societies throughout the world.

Upon publication, *High Jinx* shared the best-seller list with such espionage thrillers as John le Carré's *A Perfect Spy*, Robert Ludlum's *The Bourne Supremacy*, and Ken Follett's *Lie Down with Lions*. Each was very popular at the time the United States retaliated for terrorist incidents by bombing Libya. These novels were launched into an anxious world beset not so much by the nuclear confrontation of superpowers as by pandemic fears of random personal violence. Nuclear annihilation is grotesque, but at least it follows a grotesque logic; terrorist incidents, industrial accidents, and natural disasters do not. The headline stories which share the same historical moment with *High Jinx*—Bhopal, TWA flight 847, the *Achille Lauro*, the Mexico City earthquake, Chernobyl—document a world in which at any moment, for no coherent reason, anyone can be singled out for knee-capping, machine-gunning, or radiation poisoning.

Spy fictions reflect this sense of an untidy universe in which bad things happen to good people, by chance and by grenade. They do so obliquely, in books that imagine an alternative world in which human beings still make war, but they also make sense. Though the espionage story deals in danger and destruction, its characters recognize that there are rules to the game, as its author accepts the conventions of his traditional literary form. *High Jinx* offers the added balm of retrospection. Its fictional spies inhabit a world of stable values; if there are betrayals—and there are many—they occur as deviations from a code that all acknowledge. Yet when a child is maimed by a suitcase that happens to explode nearby, where is the code? Buckley's seductively lucid vision offers an escape from the gratuitous. His Blackford Oakes is Rambo with a Yale degree, and what makes him so enticing to readers is that Buckley creates for him another world, one in which intelligence matters.

This is not true for the fundamentally ambiguous ideological intrigues created by Fyodor Dostoevski and Joseph Conrad. *High Jinx*, however, is educated entertainment organized by an author who knows how to parse an English sentence and to please a sophisticated reader. Part of the pleasure is in imagining a world very much like the reader's own except that it not only has a design on his sympathies but also that it has one for him; there is never any doubt over who is a villain and who a hero, and how to react to either. Central intelligence, and its agency, governs all.

Steven G. Kellman

Sources for Further Study

Booklist. LXXXII, February 15, 1986, p. 834.
Kirkus Reviews. LIV, January 15, 1986, p. 69.
Library Journal. CXI, March 15, 1986, p. 77.
Los Angeles Times Book Review. March 23, 1986, p. 11.
National Review. XXXVIII, May 23, 1986, p. 43.
The New York Times Book Review. XCI, April 6, 1986, p. 15.
Publishers Weekly. CCXXIX, January 31, 1986, p. 365.
Time. CXXVII, March 31, 1986, p. 72.
The Wall Street Journal. CCVII, May 1, 1986, p. 30.
Washington Post Book World. XVI, March 9, 1986, p. 4.

THE HISTORY OF STATISTICS
The Measurement of Uncertainty Before 1900

Author: Stephen M. Stigler (1941-   )
Publisher: The Belknap Press of Harvard University Press (Cambridge, Massachusetts). Illustrated. 410 pp. $25.00
Type of work: History of science
Time: 1700-1900
Locale: Western Europe and England

A scholarly and technical history of statistical science, focused on the concept of uncertainty

Principal personages:
ADRIEN LEGENDRE, a French mathematician
PIERRE-SIMON LAPLACE, a French astronomer, physicist, and mathematician
ABRAHAM DE MOIVRE, an expatriate French mathematician
ADOLPHE QUETELET, a Belgian astronomer and sociologist
GUSTAV FECHNER, a German experimental psychologist
FRANCIS GALTON, a English statistical biologist
FRANCIS EDGEWORTH, an English mathematician and philosopher
KARL PEARSON, an English statistician and philosopher
GEORGE YULE, an English statistician

Statistics is one of those disciplines, relatively rare, which leads an unconfined existence. Unlike zoology or geometry, statistics ministers to an immense variety of needs, both academic and practical. The techniques and skills of statistical science serve the quantum physicist, the economist, the sociologist, the psychologist; they are to be found at work in virtually all government departments, bureaucracies, and corporations which shape and control the modern world. How many people poring in puzzlement over complex numerical tabulations have paused to wonder where and when the characteristic ideas and methods of this powerful and pervasive discipline originated and grew to maturity?

Stephen Stigler has the answers to such questions in this lengthy, technical, and learned history of statistics. The story he tells is a European one, with a specifically English finale. It covers the two centuries between 1700 and 1900, that period in which the discipline of statistics was formed out of the concepts and requirements of several diverse fields. His guiding theme is the notion of uncertainty, which is the main preoccupation of modern statistical thinking. All scientific activities which engage with and depend upon measurement have to be concerned with uncertainty, the degree to which measured quantities and the propositions based upon them are accurate. Uncertainty, technically speaking, is the name of the concepts and techniques which estimate quantitative accuracy, and is at the heart of the statistical enterprise.

Stigler partly discerns the origins of this science of uncertainty within the

problems encountered by astronomers in the eighteenth century. The elimination of potential errors was of vital importance for astronomy, because
crucial theoretical issues, notably those of planetary and lunar motion,
depended on the degrees of accuracy which could be brought to bear com-
putationally upon observations of complex dynamical systems. This line of
origin traced by Stigler therefore runs through a tradition of mathematician-
astronomers, such as Pierre-Simon Laplace, culminating with Adrien Legendre's formulation of the method of least squares of 1805. The other
route he follows is the sequence of efforts made by mathematicians to
produce an effective probability calculus; first, by showing how the chances
of error decrease as the number of observations increase and, second, by
performing calculations based upon the mean value of results produced by
observation. With the following of such methods, it was claimed, large
errors would almost certainly be eliminated, and the likelihood of small
errors persisting would be considerably diminished.

The motivations for such work, and the store of empirical materials upon
which it drew, indicate a largeness and complexity to the question of the origins of statistical science that is not immediately apparent in Stigler's opening chapters. By the eighteenth century, astronomy was a long-established
and thoroughly mathematicized discipline, and it is therefore unremarkable
that astronomers in their pursuit of theoretical accuracy should contribute
significantly to the design of mathematical techniques for the elimination of
error. Nevertheless, equally striking in the eighteenth century was the drive,
both general and profound, to submit the whole observable world to number and measure where at all possible. This drive was apparent not merely
where one might have expected it, in experimental physical sciences such as
electricity and chemistry. It was equally present in attempts to formulate a
viable social science which might prove as successful for the understanding,
prediction, and control of the social world as physics and astronomy had
proved for the natural world. The eighteenth century was in this sense a sci-
entistic age, and mathematicians such as Laplace, who pursed the possibility
of a genuine social science, were by no means untypical in their pursuit.

Stigler, in his close and necessary focus on technical mathematical
advances, is by no means unaware of these larger features of eighteenth
century development, but in his account, for the eighteenth century at least,
the quest for social science remains in the background, and statistics moves
into the nineteenth century armed with its technical achievements in probability theory and error distribution.

With the advent of Adolphe Quetelet's work in the 1820's, the issue of the
historical relationship of statistics to social science became more pressing,
and Stigler presents Quetelet's project as a definitive step toward incorporating probability theory within practical social science. The first half of
the nineteenth century was a period of great expansion for practical statis-

tics, with work going forward especially in the study of population and of public health. Quetelet's early statistical work on regional variations in birth, death, and marriage rates raised acute questions of sampling and of the often imponderable nature of the factors that produced the data under examination. In terms of data, what the social field evidenced was variation, and Quetelet was understandably reluctant to treat his data on the assumption of statistical homogeneity across large geographical and social areas, where the potential range of factors behind observed statistical fluctuation was both large and diverse. Quetelet continued to expand and refine his data base to include topics such as crime and insanity. His eventual aim was to produce a social physics, a thoroughly qualified discipline which would contain scientific laws describing major functional features of society. The device he memorably originated for this purpose was the concept of the "average man."

Stigler's account of Quetelet's notion aptly captures its several meanings. The average man was at once a social symbol, an important sociological concept, and a fiction. He was a fiction insofar as he was a purely statistical construct, an abstraction whose existence was literally a calculation drawn from numerical data on the physical and moral qualities of a given population. Stigler's treatment of this focal point of Quetelet's science is among the best things in the book. He reveals both the moral and ideological resonances which the idea of the average man possessed for Quetelet and his readers, as well as providing a lucid analysis of its significance for the development of statistics. This significance centered on the measurable norms for a given sector of the social field, say criminal convictions, the constant causal factors producing such norms, their standard deviations, and the variable causes which underlay small changes in standard deviations from year to year. This realm of social causation did, however, produce undeniable difficulties: If Quetelet intended to produce statistically embodied social laws, his intention was frustrated by his failure to designate and discriminate the relevant causal parameters and their relation to one another. Thus, one is left with a curious impression of Quetelet's enterprise. Here was a genuine attempt at a practical social science which dealt with concrete social realities, a world composed of death rates, marriage rates, insanity, criminal convictions, and the like, but Quetelet's endeavor to demonstrate and explain observable social regularities on the model of physics seemed to lead him into notably metaphysical areas. How to define a social cause, and its mode and force of operation in combination with other potential causes, proved to be deeply problematic for Quetelet. His program lacked crucial intellectual foundations, despite the aura of sophistication and precision provided by the techniques of statistical abstraction.

Before 1860, the other science whose practitioners contributed to the growth of statistics was psychology. Experimental psychologists, notably

Gustav Fechner in Germany, focused their efforts on the experimental quantification of sensory response to physical stimulus, aiming to produce a general quantified statement of the relationships between sensation and stimulus. This raised problems comparable to Quetelet's, for the range of possible variables affecting sensory responses was considerable, even under tightly controlled experimental conditions. Prompted by this realization, Fechner further developed probability calculus and error theory, through methods which distributed doubtful responses and averaged out error. He did not, however, provide uncertainty estimates for the constants that his experimentation had uncovered. This latter step was taken, in the 1880's, by Hermann Ebbinghaus.

Why did astronomy, social science, and experimental psychology play such a decisive role in the advance of statistical methodology? After all, there were many other fields, notably those within the physical sciences, where comparable problems of accuracy could occur. Reading between the lines of Stigler's account, one concludes that the answer has to do with the quantity and complexity of the observable data in question, the difficulties of experimental observation, and the problematic discrimination of the causal realm posited as relevant to the production of constancy and variancy of results. Whenever these factors were strongly in play, uncertainty would accompany them and hence require techniques for an estimation.

These considerations might help explain the culminating location of nineteenth century statistical progress, which lay predominantly in the field of biological inheritance. This was simultaneously relocation and revolution so far as statistics was concerned. The combined work of Francis Galton, Francis Edgeworth, Karl Pearson, and George Yule developed the most powerful new concepts and techniques statistical science had yet seen. By 1900, the key ideas of regression and correlation were well established at the core of the discipline. Both ideas emerged in the work of Galton on the heredity of a wide variety of factors with given biological populations and were given much more generalized application, abstracted from the biological data base, by Galton's successors. Statistics now had precise ways not only to estimate uncertainty in relation to generalized quantitative propositions but also to focus on the differences, as opposed to the norms, which any statistical array evinced. It could do better than average.

Stigler, a professor of statistics, is interested primarily in the mathematical elements which came together by 1900 to provide a coherent paradigm for statistical scientists. His treatment is therefore necessarily technical, and his history is a model account of the conceptual development within a series of scientific environments. Statistics appears to have developed in response to the requirements of astronomers, sociologists, psychologists, and biologists. It is an applied science therefore, but its applications are within science itself and are geared to the quintessentially scientific pursuits of accuracy.

Yet, it is possible to ask, what of the purposes of those sciences served by statistical methodology? Further, what of the purposes of the whole burgeoning statistical movement itself in the nineteenth century?

To ask such questions is to envisage a history of statistics rather different from Stigler's. It would have to investigate the origins, growth, and institutionalization of statistics in the statistical societies that appeared between 1800 and 1850. It would need to take account of the attempts during the French Revolution to institute a totally rational polity. Above all, it would take notice of the relocation of statistics not only in biology, broadly conceived, but also within that late nineteenth century integration of social engineering and the science of heredity, the eugenics movement.

With these sorts of considerations in mind, it is possible to gain a deepened sense of the contexts and motivations for the work undertaken by many of Stigler's most important figures. Quantitative accuracy appears as its own reward for the statistician conceived as mathematical expert. Why, however, is quantitative accuracy necessary for a social scientist of the French Revolution or a mathematical biologist with socialist inclinations in late nineteenth century England? Karl Pearson's science expressed, among other things, his preoccupation with the possibilities of degeneration and progress for his society, as well as the desire not only to understand and estimate such tendencies but also to control them. For Pearson, Quetelet, and others, science, even such an abstract and mathematical science as statistics, was less a disinterested conceptual inquiry than a socially interested practice. It is not finally accidental then, as sweeping economic and political changes made the direction and nature of Western society increasingly uncertain to its inhabitants, that a science of uncertainty, focused on the human subject within psychology, biology, and sociology, should grow apace. These other historical meanings need to be set alongside the elegant, formal mathematics which Stigler so expertly describes, for the meaning of a science resides as much in its uses as its content.

John Christie

Sources for Further Study

Choice. XXIV, December, 1986, p. 646.
Nature. CCCXXIV, December 17, 1986, p. 519.
The New York Times Book Review. XCI, October 5, 1986, p. 47.
Times Higher Educational Supplement. December 19, 1986. p. 15.

HOME
A Short History of an Idea

Author: Witold Rybczynski (1943-   )
Publisher: The Viking Press (New York). Illustrated. 257 pp. $16.95
Type of work: Cultural analysis and social history
Time: The 1400's to the mid-1980's
Locale: The Western nations

An interdisciplinary exploration of the historical forces which helped to create the relatively modern idea of a comfortable, Western, bourgeois home

Anyone who has ever looked with admiring disbelief at the pristine modern interiors which grace the pages of periodicals such as *Architectural Digest,* and has searched in vain for a clue to the kind of person who lives in those neatly organized, highly polished, entirely uncluttered spaces, will no doubt appreciate Witold Rybczynski's exploration of this, as well as many other conundrums, in his book *Home: A Short History of an Idea.*

Home is an eclectic book; one does not have to read very far before realizing that Rybczynski, a professor of architecture at McGill University in Montreal, is not so much interested in the idea of "home" as he is in the idea of domestic "comfort." This focus on the idea of comfort is a result of several realizations: first, that during his own otherwise rigorous architectural training, he only heard the word comfort mentioned once, and then only in the most mechanical way; second, that his clients, for whom he designed homes in the approved modern style, were decidedly uncomfortable with the results; and third, that when he designed his own home, he was constantly struck by the incompatibility of personal comfort with the modern architectural idiom. What begins as an interdisciplinary, and admittedly sketchy, history of a neglected idea eventually becomes a rather impassioned criticism of modern architecture. It is as if Rybczynski must first create and define the notion of comfort before he can forcefully decry its loss.

Rybczynski begins his book with an engagingly written analysis of the work of fashion designer Ralph Lauren, whom he believes has a profound understanding of popular, as opposed to elite, tastes. Lauren's richly textured furnishings, with names such as "Thoroughbred" and "New England," become a kind of touchstone against which the reader can measure the comfort quotient of a succession of historical styles from Louis XIV to Walter Gropius' Bauhaus. Lauren is important, Rybczynski argues, because his popularity shows that people are longing for a recent past and seeking not a true historical revival in domestic interiors but a renewed sense of ease in their lives.

Rybczynski's main thesis is that domestic comfort, as it is now understood, is a relatively modern idea. It was, he says, unknown in the Middle Ages. Castles were less lived in than camped in, and the hordes of people who gathered in the great halls to eat, sleep, and entertain themselves were accustomed to an appalling lack of privacy and sanitation. Indeed, in the Middle Ages, the idea of comfort could not even be conceived, as one could not afford it. Domestic comfort would have to emerge slowly, and incrementally, and it would get its start at a much later date, in bourgeois seventeenth century Holland.

One of the most provocative ideas in *Home* is that comfort is the natural result of a bourgeois life-style, in which women dominate the domestic sphere. Rybczynski believes that the Dutch house of the seventeenth century differed considerably from its medieval predecessor, primarily as a result of the removal of men's work from the house, which put a new emphasis on the home as a private dwelling, and women's consequently enlarged role in the management of the home, which was partly the result of a Dutch prejudice against the use of servants. As the household chores fell to the woman of the house, she soon devised new and more convenient arrangements for cooking, cleaning, and other domestic chores; she also began to demand more rigorous standards of cleanliness from the other members of her family. The Dutch house was light, airy, and meticulously clean; it was the perfect place for a nascent sense of domesticity to develop. In Rybczynski's view, the understanding of privacy and domesticity which flourished in the neat row houses of the Netherlands, and subsequently spread to all of Europe, set the stage for the next advancement in the idea of comfort.

In the eighteenth century, historical interest in the home shifts from the Netherlands to France, where French women "demanded, and got, furnishings which were more informal and more convenient." This century also brought some welcome technological changes to the home. Builders improved fireplaces and chimneys so that they would create a draft, making houses less smoky and much cleaner. Porcelain stoves became fashionable, and bathrooms were becoming more common. The idea of comfort had clearly made its entrance.

At this point the narrative moves to the homes of nineteenth century England, of which Rybczynski says, "The continued attractiveness of the Georgian interior is no accident of fashion. It typified a period that combined domesticity, elegance, and comfort more successfully than ever before." Just as for the sense of seventeenth century Dutch life Rybczynski relied heavily on the evidence of the minutely detailed images of the Dutch school of interior painting, so for the Georgian period he took as his model the writings of Jane Austen. It is this comparatively recent period of *Sense and Sensibility* (1811), calling cards, and Chippendale chairs that Rybczynski eulogizes as the high point in the history of comfort. It is this period that he sees echoed in the bourgeois fashions and furnishings of Ralph Lauren. It is this period that he apparently learned to admire so intensely at the feet of the historian Mario Praz, whose own book *An Illustrated History of Interior Decoration* (1964) is a lavishly illustrated, and extremely eccentric, paean to this particular aesthetic.

Not that Rybczynski does not give the later Victorians their due. After all, it was the Victorians who enthusiastically incorporated the wonders of modern technology into their homes. They pioneered ventilation and the use of the gaslight. They welcomed electricity with its fans, its incandescent lights, and its resistance heaters. They embraced the small electric motor. Furthermore, according to Rybczynski, women once again showed the way, by expecting comfort "not only in domestic leisure, but also in domestic work." The age of the domestic engineer had dawned, bringing with it smaller, more intimate houses, with rooms clearly set aside for particular functions, as well as reachable counters, efficient storage, and an almost unimaginable array of labor-saving devices. The Victorian paterfamilias, both English and American, governed by the dictates of domestic engineers such as Ellen H. Richards and Mary Pattison, incorporated these modernizations into his comfortable little home until, at least to some tastes, the multitude of things started to displace the home dweller.

Comfort had arrived and was perhaps beginning to suffocate itself when Art Deco came jazzily along and played out a few ephemeral variations on the theme before the beginning of the Great Depression. It is at this point that Rybczynski introduces the book's dark villain: the new spirit of modern architecture, with its plain white walls, its minimalist attitude toward furniture, and its complete disdain for interior design. Any reader who has read Tom Wolfe's biting satire of modern architecture, *From Bauhaus to Our House* (1981), will find much familiar territory in Rybczynski's castigation of Le Corbusier, the god of immaculate white walls and antibourgeois architecture, and in his criticism of Le Corbusier's coterie of largely academic sycophants.

It is no coincidence that Wolfe satirizes, with considerable relish, Mies van der Rohe's highly modern, leather and stainless steel, Barcelona chair, which is in many ways the epitome of the reductionism of the Bauhaus style, and that Rybczynski singles out Marcel Breuer's Wassily chair to exemplify everything that is wrong or, more to the point, uncomfortable about the austerity of modern architecture, and its continued influence on furniture, as well as exterior and interior design. "A well-designed easy chair," contends Rybczynski, "must accommodate not only relaxed sitting, but also having a drink, reading, conversation, bouncing babies on the knee, dozing, and so on." The Wassily chair, he contends, "is an easy chair in which one cannot relax for more than thirty minutes at a time." The Wassily chair, like the Barcelona chair, may well be appreciated intellectually, or aesthetically, but it is not likely to be enjoyed by that hypothetical bourgeois man who has come home from a hard day at work and simply wants to relax. Both chairs, and all the remaining artifacts of the new spirit of modern architecture, dismally fail the ultimate, and relatively simple criteria, defended by *Home*: the criteria of domestic comfort.

Having dismissed modern solutions to the age-old problems of comfort, Rybczynski does not simply suggest a naïve return to the historical styles of prior times, not even to his cherished nineteenth century Georgian interiors. What he does suggest is a realization that homes which are visually exciting are frequently impossible to live in; that the open plans of many new houses not only create an intriguing flow of space but also make personal privacy as unlikely as in the great halls of the Middle Ages; that domestic efficiency relies as much on having pots and pans out in the open where they are accessible as it does on having a counter full of unused Cuisinarts and pasta makers; that architects, schooled in the modern style, should perhaps be the last people to consult when building a home. To put it in Rybczynski's own concluding words: "Domestic well-being is too important to be left to experts; it is, as it has always been, the business of the family and the individual. We must rediscover for ourselves the mystery of comfort, for without it, our dwellings will indeed be machines instead of homes."

Cynthia Lee Katona

Sources for Further Study

Christian Science Monitor. LXXVIII, July 10, 1986, p. 28.
Kirkus Reviews. LIV, May 15, 1986, p. 773.
Los Angeles Times Book Review. July 13, 1986, p. 3.
The New York Times Book Review. XCI, August 3, 1986, p. 1.
The New Yorker. LXII, September 1, 1986, p. 96.
Newsweek. CVIII, August 18, 1986, p. 57.
Publishers Weekly. CCXXIX, June 13, 1986, p. 63.
Time. CXXVIII, August 4, 1986, p. 64.
Vogue. CLXXVI, July, 1986, p. 92.
The Wall Street Journal. CCVIII, July 2, 1986, p. 24.
Washington Post Book World. XVI, July 6, 1986, p. 3.
Wilson Library Bulletin. LXI, September, 1986, p. 84.

HOPKINS, THE SELF, AND GOD

Author: Walter J. Ong (1912-   )
Publisher: University of Toronto Press (Toronto). 180 pp. $20.00
Type of work: Literary criticism and intellectual history

An exploration of previously unexamined reasons for Hopkins' uniqueness in his distinctive attention to the self

Gerard Manley Hopkins, Jesuit priest and poet, lived from 1844 to 1889 and thus would seem to be situated in the middle of the Victorian period. Unfortunately, at least for those who like their literary and historical chronicles neat and orderly, Hopkins refuses to fit neatly anywhere. He certainly lived in the heart of the Victorian period, but his poems were almost all published after World War I. In anthologies, he is sometimes found among the Victorians and sometimes with the modern poets, with whom he is seen to have more in common. There is also a continuing debate about whether Hopkins is to be considered a major or a minor poet; on the grounds of influence and of studies about him, he would seem to qualify as major, but (say others) he must surely be minor, simply on the grounds of the relatively small number of poems that he produced. The easiest way to duck such questions is perhaps to state simply that whether major or minor, whether Victorian or modern, Hopkins is certainly an important poet.

Hopkins, the Self, and God, however, admits of no havering about these questions: Hopkins is definitely modern (though perhaps not for specifically literary reasons, as will be seen below) and just as definitely Victorian—and certainly major. In this work, Father Walter Ong, the noted Jesuit scholar, continues his concern for the evolution of consciousness and the understanding of human identity. Ong's most recent work in this area is *Orality and Literacy: The Technologizing of the Word* (1982). The present volume actually dates from 1980 to 1981, when the material was first presented at the University of Toronto in the prestigious Alexander Lectures, but it was not published in its present form until 1986. Other works by Ong that bear upon the same themes are *Ramus, Method, and the Decay of Dialogue: From the Art of Discourse to the Art of Reasoning* (1958), *The Presence of the Word: Some Prolegomena for Cultural and Religious History* (1967), *Rhetoric, Romance, and Technology: Studies in the Interaction of Expression and Culture* (1971), and *Interfaces of the Word: Studies in the Evolution of Consciousness and Culture* (1977). In all these works, as well as in the present work, the overriding theme, under one guise or another, is the history of consciousness and the development of the modern awareness of consciousness.

Ong is insistent that in his awareness of the self, the "I," the nameless which is immediately before each of us and is absolutely other than anything in the physical world or even God, Hopkins is very modern, not only ahead of his own time but also well ahead of the present time, and that in this Hopkins is unique. Ong then discusses in detail this one single characteristic and theme of Hopkins (preferring the term "awareness of self" to the more modern jargon of "self-awareness"), presenting in three chapters the backgrounds of and influences on Hopkins that led him to this awareness of self and, in a final chapter, estimating the effect of all of this on Hopkins and emphasizing the modernity of it. In each of the first three chapters, Ong pursues the related themes of Hopkins' sensitivity to particularity in the external world (a quality immediately noticeable to even a cursory reading of Hopkins' poetry and one of the first things that strikes a reader) and of Hopkins' equal sensitivity to the particularity of the individual self. As Ong clearly demonstrates, the two go hand in hand, two sides of the same coin. If, upon occasion, the writing is pockmarked with abstractions and the technical jargon of the social sciences, the reader must remember that essentially Ong is trying to talk about something for which ultimately he has no words (as Hopkins also did not).

Chapter 1 demonstrates how the Victorian Age in which Hopkins was inevitably immersed was an age of growing awareness of self and an age of growing particularity in much literature, art, and, especially, science and technology. His detailed example of how Hopkins used the details of the shipwreck of the German steamer *Deutschland* from the London *Times* (obtained by telegraphy) in his major poem "The Wreck of the *Deutschland*" demonstrates in one small way how the age itself influenced the poet. In chapter 2, Ong presents the Catholic ascetic tradition, especially as found in the *Spiritual Exercises* (1548) of Ignatius Loyola, the founder of the Society of Jesus, and its influence upon Hopkins. He ranges widely over this tradition, which was present to Hopkins as an element of his membership of the Jesuit order, of his seminary training, and of his priestly life. There is here a lengthy discussion, interesting in its own right, of the nature of Ignatian discipline and life, and Ong makes clear how the *Spiritual Exercises*, though presented in manual and outline form, are more than simply a list of topics about which to think and practices to perform. Chapter 3 follows the same basic pattern, tracing the influence on Hopkins of the Thomistic academic theology which he studied in the seminary, especially moral and systematic theology. Perhaps of equal importance to Hopkins' background, however, was his interest in and knowledge of the work of John Duns Scotus, whose philosophy tended to emphasize the individual rather than the universal; Duns Scotus was perhaps not quite in the main line of official Catholic theology and philosophy, but his particularism undoubtedly reinforced other strains of thought in Hopkins and his background.

It is in the final chapter that Ong brings together his three key concepts; to summarize them is not simple, for Ong's argument and demonstration are not simple and straightforward. The concepts are awareness of the self, decision making, and freedom; Ong argues that awareness of the self and of particularity leads to the ability to make decisions, and that it is in decision

making that man is in fact most free and most human. It is impossible to reproduce here the subtlety of the argument.

Ong is a true scholar who has at his fingertips many strands of modern
intellectual life—science, psychology, literature, art, theology, philosophy,
history, and more. What is most impressive about this book is not what is
specifically said about Hopkins but the demonstration it gives of the unity
and interrelatedness of knowledge. In the space of a few brief pages in the
course of chapter 1, for example, Ong connects Samuel Taylor Coleridge,
depth psychology and phenomenology, Plotinus and Saint Augustine, the insights of Jacques Derrida, the "self concept" of current literary criticism,
semiotic structuralism, and proto-Indo-European linguistics to illuminate his
discussion of Hopkins and his Victorian milieu. Such connections are certainly not made to show off learning, but because they illuminate the specific figure he has under examination. Ong does not criticize or evaluate in a
vacuum; he can take knowledge of the distant past or of the present and use
it in a fresh way to say something new about Hopkins.

At the same time, it must be said that this wide-ranging play of intellect
can create problems for the reader. A general reader may well not be aware
of or sufficiently up on the various sorts of knowledge and disciplines that
Ong brings to bear. Frequently his references are too compact, too brief,
too elliptical for full understanding except by a specialist. This aspect of the
book is probably a result of the original presentation of the work as a series
of lectures, when time and space did not permit the full development of
material which perhaps requires a more discursive treatment. Thus it is that
the book is probably most appealing to Hopkins scholars and to those familiar with modern psychological currents of thought; the work has its insights
about Hopkins, but it is definitely not the first book on Hopkins that the
student or general reader should attempt. While the overall pattern and thesis of the book is clear, it is, though brief, formidable.

In specific terms of Hopkins criticism, this work may be said to be more a
commentary than an analysis. It takes its rather narrow topic and asserts
and presents it from several angles. It deals not at all with much else about
Hopkins than awareness of the self and its implications. It proves its point
with much evidence and intricate argument. The book will not at all change
the basic or standard view of Hopkins as a poet, though it will certainly emphasize the importance of self as a major theme and concern, as well as the
importance to the poetry of Hopkins' Jesuit background and his priesthood,
an importance occasionally denied and even lamented.

At times the book seems to treat Hopkins as an example of the movement of mind in modern thought rather than as the subject under discussion. At times, the reader even receives the impression that Ong would like
to claim for Hopkins a stature as a modern thinker or philosopher, but Ong
manages to resist the temptation. What Ong has done is demonstrate that

Hopkins is not a freak, that he is the product of his background, upbringing, training, and education. Yet, there is more than this that accounts for an individual and a poet—and that is the "self" which Hopkins and Ong, each in his own way, wish to father forth. It is a noble concept and one that penetrates to the most secret sources of what it is to be truly human.

Two items might have been given a bit more treatment. Walter Pater and the Pre-Raphaelites are mentioned only in passing, yet one would have thought that such notable particularist artists would have had more connection with Hopkins' Victorian milieu, especially since Pater was one of his tutors at Oxford. At the end of the book, Ong raises the subject of Hopkins' "suffering." This is an aspect, especially of Hopkins' later years, that has attracted the attention of a number of commentators. Ong argues that the suffering, the agonizing that can be found in many of Hopkins' poems and in his notebooks and papers, was well within the mainstream of Christian teaching, according to which "any suffering, accepted with love, has positive value." Some critics have explained Hopkins' intense suffering as the result of ill health and overwork, some as reflecting a sense of frustration, and a few as a sign that Hopkins was chafing at the bit of his Catholicism or his priesthood. Whatever the reasons (and Ong persuasively contends that Hopkins was not wavering in his commitment to the Church), Ong either cannot or does not supply reasons for this specific man at this time and place to feel as he did. Perhaps again the reasons are too interior for anyone to know at this remove. Perhaps we shall never know, as much as we would like to know.

Hopkins, the Self, and God is, then, a brief but packed work. It is well organized and aided by the brief subheadings under each chapter. There is a brief index and a lengthy and useful, if rather specialized, bibliography. The book also includes a complete list of all the Alexander lecturers since 1928, with their respective topics. It is sad to relate, but, for a book produced by a university press, there are a distressing number of typographical errors.

Gordon N. Bergquist

Source for Further Study

Choice. XXIV, January, 1987, p. 764.

THE HORNES
An American Family

Author: Gail Lumet Buckley (1937-   )
Publisher: Alfred A. Knopf (New York). Illustrated. 262 pp. $18.95
Type of work: Biography, autobiography, and social history
Time: 1865-1986
Locale: Primarily the United States

Beginning after the Civil War, the author traces the history of her family, the Hornes, as illustrative of the heretofore unrecorded story of the black bourgeoisie in America

Principal personages:
GAIL LUMET BUCKLEY, the author
SINAI (SINIA or SINY) and
HENRY REYNOLDS, her great-great-great-great-grandparents
NELLY REYNOLDS, her great-great-great-grandmother
MOSES CALHOUN, her great-great-grandfather
CORA CALHOUN, her great-grandmother
EDWIN HORN, her great-grandfather
TEDDY HORNE, her grandfather, Cora and Edwin's son
EDNA LOUISE SCOTTRON, her grandmother, the first wife of Teddy and mother of Lena Horne
LENA HORNE, her mother and the most famous of the Horne family

With the Emancipation Proclamation and the end of the Civil War, a new group, the black bourgeoisie, began to evolve in America. After flourishing for a century, however, that social class became obsolete, as a consequence of the Civil Rights struggles of the 1960's and early 1970's. Gail Lumet Buckley chronicles this century of black life, viewing her own family history as the embodiment of the black-middle-class experience during the period. While Buckley's mother, singer and actress Lena Horne, is certainly by far the most famous member of the family, she is not the only Horne to have made significant contributions to American life or to have lived an essentially middle-class life.

Because Buckley was brought up a child of Hollywood, New York, and Europe, with a white stepfather and all the privileges of money and fame, and because she grew up to marry a rich and famous white man, director Sidney Lumet, she herself was not aware of her family's unique position in American social history until she discovered years of family history in the photographs and memorabilia in her grandfather Teddy Horne's trunk. By discovering what her family had been, Buckley came to a great understanding of herself and of the segment of black America that her family typifies.

In her concise and insightful introduction, Buckley traces the origin of the black bourgeoisie to three groups: "free Northern blacks, free Southern blacks, and 'favored' slaves." The class that grew out of these groups took great pride in being separate from ordinary black life. Buckley writes of black Brooklyn children who responded to requests to perform menial chores by chanting, "We're not field niggers! We're house niggers!" In this world, the Hornes were considered among the elite of the elite: *"old* (as in not *'nouveau'*), *comfortable* (not super-rich, but property owners), *intellectual* (with teaching degrees and a certain appreciation for 'the arts'), *political* (from suffragettes to civil rights) and famously *good-looking."*

The Horne ancestors who were slaves were fortunate in two ways. They were among the favored house slaves, and their masters tended to treat them well. Sinai Reynolds' master allowed her and her husband, Henry, to live together without white supervision, something that eventually brought him before the court because such living arrangements were illegal. Cora Calhoun's master was also a member of the white aristocracy, and his prestige and power carried over to his slaves when they were freed and began to participate in black society.

In addition, from the earliest recorded family history—the story of Sinai and her family—a recurring theme is the enormous value placed on literacy and education. Thus, when freedom came, Buckley's ancestors were better prepared to assume the leadership role of the bourgeoisie than were many of their less educated counterparts. Edwin Horn first made a reputation for himself by publishing poems, essays, and editorials in the black press, and one of Teddy Horne's brothers, Frank, was a poet associated with the Harlem Renaissance, a teacher and college administrator, and finally a member of Franklin D. Roosevelt's unofficial group of black advisers known as the Black Cabinet.

Buckley's purpose, however, is not merely to document the accomplishments of her family. She is equally candid when she discusses the career of her grandfather Teddy and the oddly disturbing behavior of his first wife and Lena's mother, Edna. Although Teddy was the product of Edwin and Cora's firmly traditional life, he was not a traditional man, even for the black bourgeoisie. He did not find sedate, middle-class life fulfilling and left Brooklyn, his wife, and his baby daughter to pursue the life of a dashing and slightly shady sportsman, sustaining himself and often being generous with his daughter by means that were never exactly clear even to his family.

Edna, too, eventually left her young daughter to the care of her grandmother Cora and traveled in pursuit of success on the stage. At irregular intervals, seized by guilt or a sense of her power as the mother of Lena or some other irrational impulse, she would appear to spirit away the frightened child from the familiar world of Brooklyn and her grandparents' home. Lena would then spend time living in a variety of unconventional situations, often left with strangers while her mother pursued the theater or men, or both.

Because Lena was the product both of her parents' unconventional lifestyles and her grandparents' much more traditional middle-class world, she entered adulthood and her show-business career with conflicting values and aspirations. Part of her was dominated by the "correct" world of her schooling and social life, especially by the female friends and debutante social clubs that pervaded black Brooklyn. Part of her wanted to please the grandparents who provided the only security she knew as a child, and to please them she should make an acceptable marriage and rear well-bred bourgeois children. Another part of this complex woman contained the charm and the talents of her less conventional parents, and she was perhaps the most beautiful of a family famous for its stunning good looks. The adulation and attention of audiences and critics also may have helped to satisfy the need for approval that her absentee parents left unfilled for most of her life.

The most interesting part of Buckley's discussion of her mother's show-business career is not so much what Lena Horne has accomplished—the most familiar information in a book filled with surprising facts and conclusions—but rather what Lena felt about her position in the business, in black society, and in the larger, more comprehensive society to which her career gave her access. By becoming successful, as she did at a young age and with relative ease, Lena suddenly found herself being used, manipulated by the white power structure of the film industry, at the same time that demands began to be placed on her to do something for the vast portion of black America that was still excluded from the securities and privileges she had known all of her life as a member of the black bourgeoisie. Her role as the first true black movie star (Buckley's description) placed enormous pressures on her that involved social, political, and cultural consequences far beyond the immediate career path she sometimes reluctantly took.

In addition, Lena had not completely given up on the more traditional family life that she had learned from her grandparents. She married early, before her first real breaks in show business, and had two children, Gail and her brother, Teddy, with her first husband, Louis Jones. Realizing early that her career and the marriage to Louis would not mix, Lena sought a divorce that left her separated from her son for much of his childhood, a cruelly ironic echo of her own separation from her mother.

Buckley is quite skillful in her rendering of this pain, as well as in her portrayal of her mother's disillusionment with the film industry and indeed with much of American life. When Lena decided to marry Lennie Hayton, a classically trained white pianist, in 1947, they had to go to Europe to be joined as man and wife. As a result of this marriage and her mother's enormous success, Gail Horne Jones grew up even more removed from the world of the black bourgeoisie than her mother had come to be.

While Lena was involved in many political issues, her daughter was receiving a boarding-school education where she was so absorbed in the white world that she need not consider her own blackness. Despite occasional forays into the world of black society, to take part in the dances and socials that her mother had relished as a girl in Brooklyn, Gail was more at home in the white world. A Radcliffe graduate, she drifted into and out of jobs in the theater and journalism, and without very substantial credentials, she relied on networking to get positions.

A beautiful, well-educated woman who had been spared almost every difficulty associated with growing up black in America, Gail Horne eventually married a famous white artist and gave birth to children and hosted beautiful parties attended by equally famous people. In a sense, she was living a continuation of the dream begun a century before in Sinai Reynolds' determination to be free and educated and to provide a better life for her children than she had known—the classic American middle-class goals. As Gail Lumet, however, child of a star and wife of a celebrated film director, she was cut off from her family's heritage in the black bourgeoisie; she was, she came to believe, without real identity.

Thus began Buckley's search, which led eventually to her grandfather's trunk and the century-long history that ultimately became this book. Buckley underwent a religious conversion during this odyssey, but she presents that facet of her experience with remarkable restraint. Her main point—and she never loses sight of it—is the history of this little-discussed class, what she calls "America's historic family secret."

When one writes about the life of one's ancestors and one's own life, the question of objectivity is not really appropriate. What Buckley achieves here is an admirable perspective that carries her far beyond personal reminiscence and indulgence. Because she is willing to show the broad range within the Horne family—she calls her great-grandfather Edwin Horn a boulevardier in addition to extolling his virtues as a leader and a moral force, and she readily portrays the failures as well as the triumphs in this history—they do become the symbol that she wants them to be.

The Hornes: An American Family is a respectful and loving account, but it is also thorough and professional. The author's judgment is sound, her conclusions logical. The photographs and other memorabilia reproduced within the volume enhance the text and serve as a fascinating synopsis of the whole. At the end of her book, Buckley turns briefly to her daughters and their attitudes toward racism. As they are still another generation removed from the genesis of their family history as recorded by their mother, she understands their irreverent attitude toward race: "My daughters refuse on principle to take race seriously in America. They have no illusions about it, but they refuse not to laugh. . . . Like most of their generation, my daughters seem to ponder the past more in terms of how people dressed than how they thought."

What Buckley provides in this thoughtful, highly readable book is a record of her own journey toward understanding how an important segment of the American people thought, how they lived. Thus, when her daughters, who are, in her words, "variations of the family theme," do decide to consider more seriously their heritage, they will have an admirable guide. So will other readers of *The Hornes*.

Jane Bowers Hill

Sources for Further Study

Black Enterprise. XVII, October, 1986, p. 18.
Library Journal. CXI, July 16, 1986, p. 76.
Los Angeles Times Book Review. July 6, 1986, p. 3.
Ms. XV, August, 1986, p. 77.
The New York Times Book Review. XCI, July 6, 1986, p. 5.
Publishers Weekly. CCXXIX, May 23, 1986, p. 94.
Smithsonian. XVII, August, 1986, p. 126.
Time. CXXVII, June 23, 1986, p. 81.
Vogue. CLXXVI, June, 1986, p. 120.
Washington Post Book World. XVI, June 22, 1986, p. 3.

HURRICANE LAMP

Author: Turner Cassity (1929-   )
Publisher: University of Chicago Press (Chicago). 68 pp. $15.00; paperback $6.95
Type of work: Poetry

A description of the paradoxes that define human life and behavior

In *Hurricane Lamp*, Turner Cassity visits the geography and history and art of mankind, and in each he finds examples of paradox. On one side of the paradoxes he considers are life, desire, and immortality, and on the other are death, corruption, and mortality. Each side presupposes the other, and time is the lens through which he often looks at both. Time for him is the past where man's lust for power and immortality lies in the arms of ruin; it is also the present, where man looks back and finds the mirror image of himself, and the future, where he sees the failure of desire as well as the fact that desiring names him. In some of Cassity's poems, time is youth, where desire focuses on its goals, and maturity, where desire focuses on itself. In youth, excess predominates; in age, moderation does.

In searching for lost treasure in "News for Loch Ness," divers encounter an image of doom in the figure of a trumpeting angel and actual doom in the figure of Leviathan. Man searches, the poem says, for what will make him powerful, even immortal, and finds what his ancestors found: mortality. Moreover, the monuments to idealism in the past become, in surviving ruin, debased in the present to commercial ventures, as "Berolina Demodée" points out. The formulations of man's idealism never seem to last; what does seemingly survive the process of time from the past to the present is human striving itself. As the Nile in "The Aswan Rowing Club" was once the scene of galley slaves rowing the ships of their masters, it is now the scene of a crew club striving as energetically as its predecessors. One of the major forces behind this striving or desire is egotism, which at one time may be images of the divine, such as Diana, through which man worships himself, and at another may be the gold in those images by which man feeds his avarice. In one's personal time span, desire is again the common element, though in different ways: In youth (as "U-24 Anchors Off New Orleans" shows), desire and pain depend on each other to produce pleasure, and in maturity, they occur as a paradox that produces understanding. Youth and maturity, in fact, define a temporal process which desire as imagination begins and desire as responsibility ends.

No matter the time or the place, desire or striving is accompanied by failure and ruin because man, the creature who experiences desire, is mutable. One type of ruin generated by desire is sin. In "The Chinaberry Tree," for example, desire as temptation leads to ruin, but this ruin leads not to wisdom but more temptation. The paradox is this: If sin is ruin, man longs for more ruin. In pursuing self-gratification, man ends up, like the demon-ridden swine in "I the Swineherd," paradoxically pursuing self-destruction, even when he sees what is happening and tries to restrain himself. For man's greatest sin is pride, and it is stronger than the humility that restraint requires. Like the diver in "After the Fall," who discovers a huge statue of Apollo underwater, man exults in the discovery itself of images of his own godliness, forgetting that these images are subject to corrosion and point to the fact that man is anything but immortal.

Cassity underscores the paradox of a mortal creature with pretensions to immortality in a trope in "Pausing in the Climb." The thistle in the poem flourishes on a mountain, which puts it between earth and sky. Man derives his energy from what he cannot escape (mortality) and expends it on what he cannot have (immortality). Man hangs between the limited and the limitless, the former making him harsh, the latter beautiful.

Other natural phenomena provide Cassity with images for the paradox of which man is an extension. In "Dispensations of the Date Fairy," day and night in the desert show the cold in heat and the heat in cold; the life symbolized by dates in the death symbolized by the desert, and the idea that life and sustenance are the result of death, belong in this paradoxical framework. "Phaëthon" presents the sun as an extended trope for an ontological paradox: Energy ordered is life, and energy disordered is death. The paradox of energy in a specifically human context is explored in "The Space Between the Andirons": The ashes on the hearth (failure) depend on the fire which produced them (desire), just as the fire itself would not exist without the ashes.

Cassity notes that maturity, though it may not escape desire, inclines one to moderation. One gets tired, after all, and has accumulated the experience to know what desire is all about. As an artist, and aware in his maturity of the paradoxes of a cultivated temperament, Cassity uses the title poem of the book to support the idea of caution when dealing with desire and the idea of containing desire in a work of art. Beyond this, he shows the inclination of an artistic personality such as his to satire; that is, inclined to moderation, he notices excess, and perceiving paradox, he is inclined to irony.

There are many satires in the book, and each has a message. "The Consultant" shows a modern professional type being consulted about building the Tower of Babel. The reach of man in this poem turns out to make more sense in the concept than in practice. "Imputations" describes man's mania (excess) in attributing values and symbols to everything—in this case, finance. Man the émigré is the target in "A Dialogue with the Bride of Godzilla," in which the Anglo heroine, in making a life for herself in Japan, ironically becomes the dubbed human (English) voice of the "ingenues" in films about inhuman monsters. The satire in "Anastasia" is not so much leveled at the irony of the heroine being and not being at the same time the murdered czar's daughter as at the illusory aspect of royalty itself, in that the woman who claims to be Anastasia is turned into a kind of middle-class toy in America. "Eniwetok Mon Amour" focuses on the irony of those minds which showed their genius in creating the atom bomb and their stupidity in reckoning its consequences, while "At the Mercy of the Queen-Empress" considers the irony of the draft dodger who, having escaped to the safety and comfort of Canada, longs to return to the United States—that is, to the place and laws to which he originally said no. "Page from a Bar Guide" satirizes nostalgia, and "Wine from the Cape" pleasure by highlighting the insubstantiality of life itself. As for dreams, they are either sparked by extravagant clichés (and thereby silly), as in "Scheherazade in South Dakota," or they conceal conflicts which their achievement reveals, as in "Cendrillon," or they are a prison, as in "Maeterlinck in Ontario."

A straightforward summary of Cassity's view of human life and of his advice to the reader who must live that life occurs in the last poem in the book, "A Song for Clines Corners." No matter what direction the "Hitchhiker" in the poem takes, he ends at the shore of death where the "boatman" (Charon, it seems) awaits him. The common element is movement or process itself, in which light and energy gradually fail. The random element is the "silent driver" in the poem, who seems to be the unpredictable means by which a given journey is conducted. The common and random elements contribute to the paradox which lies at the heart of the journey, and the poet himself is the traveler-reader's "host" in that he presents the features of the journey. The poet also presents himself as a paradox when he calls himself the "endless coast" that terminates the journey, for he is death in that he will die, but his words about the journey (the poem, especially the end of it where the trope of the "endless coast" is situated, and especially the poem's position as the last one in the book) will live on, thus extending his life. Moreover, his "last" words come in the form of advice. "Lift up your tongue and put the cost," he says, by which he seems to mean that one must accept death as the price of the journey and praise or do justice to the journey in art.

Though Cassity's range of occasions and subjects is broad, and the metrical formats he uses are various, his work is consistently reflective and, as such, multilayered. His taste for moderation recalls the Latin poet Horace, and his taste for antithesis and satire the English poet Alexander Pope. There is much in his work to bring one back to it, much to savor and weigh. If there is a flaw, it is the syntax, which is often so involuted and elliptical that one is forced to go back to the poems to puzzle over what they are saying. "News for Loch Ness" provides an example of this kind of syntax:

> Outside the orbit of the diving helmets, name
> Without a genealogy and life for salt,
> Leviathan engenders: "Bonnie," of the Lake
> Its legend guardian, a symbiont of gulls. . . .

There is a kind of intellectual pride in such usage that does a disservice to themes whose truth and importance should be more available than Cassity's poems allow them to be.

Mark McCloskey

Sources for Further Study

Booklist. LXXXII, April 1, 1986, p. 1112.
Library Journal. CXI, February 15, 1986, p. 183.
The London Review of Books. VIII, December 18, 1986, p. 22.
The New York Times Book Review. XCI, April 20, 1986, p. 19.
Poetry. CIL, no. 3, December, 1986, p. 173.

I THE SUPREME

Author: Augusto Roa Bastos (1917-   )
Translated from the Spanish by Helen Lane
Publisher: Alfred A. Knopf (New York). 438 pp. $18.95
Type of work: Novel
Time: The late 1830's
Locale: Paraguay

The fictionalized memoirs, musings, and pronouncements of José Gaspar Rodríguez de Francia, Supreme Dictator of Paraguay between 1814 and 1840, here also the dictator of the text

> Principal characters:
> JOSÉ GASPAR RODRÍGUEZ DE FRANCIA, Supreme Dictator of Paraguay, 1814-1840
> POLICARPO PATIÑO, his secretary
> SULTAN, his dog
> COMPILER, the assembler and annotator of the text

Augusto Roa Bastos' *I the Supreme* (published in Argentina in 1947 as *Yo el Supremo*) has been acclaimed as one of the most important novels of twentieth century Latin America. It may be seen as the culmination of a distinguished series of novels by major Latin American writers (including Miguel Ángel Asturias and Gabriel García Márquez, both of whom won the Nobel Prize) which consider the phenomenon of dictatorship and the nature of power. It is also the most ambitious and complex of many recent novels which undertake the scrutiny and reevaluation of the nineteenth century, particularly the euphoric period just after independence from Spain when it seemed possible to implement idealistic visions of how countries and governments should be.

José Gaspar Rodríguez de Francia, the central subject and primary narrative voice of *I the Supreme*, was the absolute dictator of Paraguay between 1814 and 1840. His emphasis upon personal rule and national self-sufficiency cut Paraguay off from neighboring countries in ways which still affect the isolated, dictator-ruled Paraguay of 1986. Augusto Roa Bastos, who has lived most of his life in exile from his native land (not only exiled but forbidden to return), weaves an awareness of subsequent events into his evocation of the past.

Paraguay was the first Spanish American country to repudiate Spanish rule. It declared its independence in 1811 and was then governed for two years by a national executive committee whose principal member was Francia. After a year as consul, Francia assumed the title of supreme dictator in 1814 and ruled the country possessively until his death in 1840. A lawyer and serious student of theology, Francia was honest, frugal, and abstemious, and he himself lived with the austerity and isolation he imposed upon the country. Steeped in the ideas of the French Enlightenment (his passion for Voltaire and Jean-Jacques Rousseau is frequently evident as he tells his story in *I the Supreme*), Francia severely limited the power of the Catholic Church and of the aristocracy or upper class in Paraguay. He forbade immigration and emigration, and, insofar as possible, sealed Paraguay off from the rest of the world. He introduced modern methods of agriculture, built roads, bridges, and forts, and maintained a large army. Constantly suspicious of conspiracies against him, Francia maintained his absolute power over the some three hundred thousand Paraguayans by means of spies, state police, and the incarceration of large numbers of political prisoners. He burned all of his private papers right before his death, just as he does at the end of *I the Supreme*.

The genre of *I the Supreme* eludes definition: It is neither historical fiction nor fictional history, neither free of historicity nor limited by historical fact. Roa Bastos has called it "another kind of history," a fiction which makes more sense of history than an array of documented facts. Gerald Brenan, the distinguished historian of modern Spain, when asked to contribute to the *Oxford History of Modern Europe*, said: "I've given up history, you cannot get at the truth by writing history, that only a novelist can discover." It is this complex truth of history that Roa Bastos seeks, and in his pursuit of this ever-changing, elusive truth, he presents his readers with a kaleidoscopic, multilayered, hilarious account. The book is a patchwork of texts. Francia writes official pronouncements, private diary entries, and talks to his secretary or his dog. The Compiler of these hundreds of varied texts, although he says that he is merely assembling the book, is more than a fictional editor. He splices in sections of documents (both real and spurious), footnotes, and long quotations which comment upon and often contradict what the Dictator has just said. In addition, some of the supposed texts have already been annotated, sometimes by the Supreme Dictator himself, sometimes by other writers, sometimes by an unknown saboteur who may be an unacknowledged aspect of the personality of the Dictator.

Readers of *I the Supreme* are made constantly aware of the work of the Compiler and of their own role as readers of a text (who are trying to make sense of it) by the annotations about the fragmentary nature of the documents. In many places, the manuscript (says the Compiler) has been burned or worms have chewed great holes in it. Often, just those sections where the Dictator seems about to reveal something particularly personal and interesting about himself are the ones that are missing. Readers are never allowed to forget the precarious and temporary nature of a written document and hence of truth itself. The text of the novel constantly threatens to fall apart into fragments which undermine and contradict one another, shift and change meanings, conceal and obscure just what they seem to want to illuminate.

Even the words of which the novel is made assume new dimensions and meanings as the reader forges onward through a forest of puns and verbal jokes that mock and double back on themselves. Most of the jokes relate to the problematic relationship of words to physical objects and the creation of literature as opposed to the practical use of words in everyday contexts. Francia speculates that "writing within language makes every object, present, absent, or future, impossible," for "what meaning can writing have . . . when by definition it does not have the same sense as the everyday speech of ordinary people?" Francia laments the writing mania which has afflicted his age (or the present?), insisting that "there is no more deadly merchandise than the books of these convulsionaries. There is no worse plague than the scribonic. Menders of lies and benders of truths." Language as a representation of reality is suspect, but it creates its own reality, its own system of signs and references. Verbal fireworks ("Yet the genes of gens engender tenacious traitorous taints"; "the filigreed fleuron in the vergered-perjured paper, the flagellated letters") serve to emphasize Francia's isolation and increasing paranoia about conspirators; his writing is his refuge as well as his way of trying to understand himself, yet it also distances him from the Paraguay he loves and controls so obsessively.

I the Supreme has no plot in the usual sense of chronological action and the dramatization of cause and effect. Many different events and encounters are recounted, but most of the cumulative interest of the novel lies in the revelation of the obsessions and perceptions of Francia himself. The main action is that of producing the story, but along the way, the reader is entertained by interwoven anecdotes, elements of suspense, and fierce arguments between the Supreme Dictator and his various antagonists. The novel begins as a mystery: The Dictator rages about a villifying poster that has just been found nailed to the cathedral door and demands to know who would have put it there. Throughout the novel, the Dictator returns periodically to this outrage of the pasquinade, and the mystery becomes a basis for a variety of diatribes and reminiscences only to be resolved at the end of the book when it is apparent that the Dictator dictates or imagines many different texts, some of them critical and even condemning of his own actions.

At first, the novel seems to be a series of statements made by a dying (or already dead) Francia to his secretary Policarpo Patiño. This dictation is interspersed with the conversations of Patiño and Francia as they discuss the text being dictated. Francia corrects himself, adds more commentary, contradicts his earlier observations, and often reacts abusively to Patiño's comments, which seem finally to be part of his own self-mockery. These conversational monologues tell anecdotes of the past, recount interviews and meetings, and discuss his readings.

The Dictator also dictates the statements of a Perpetual Circular to instruct the nation, directed particularly to "Commissioners, Commanders of Garrisons and of Urban Militia, Appointed Magistrates, Administrators,

Overseers, Revenue Agents, Tax Collectors and other authorities." Here he interprets historical events, explains national principles, and defends himself publicly against calumnious accusations.

Francia also writes in his private notebook. According to a footnote by the Compiler, it is an ordinary accounting ledger, one of many in which the Dictator set forth "in a disjointed, incoherent fashion, events, ideas, reflections, minutely detailed and well-nigh maniacal observations on any number of entirely different subjects and themes: those which in his opinion were positive in the Credit column; negative, in the Debit column. In this way words, sentences, paragraphs, fragments are divided, continued, repeated, or inverted in the two columns, in an effort to strike an imaginary balance."

Passages labeled as the tutorial voice tell the story of the Dictator's father. Sequences of imaginary dialogues with Patiño and many others and the lively documents appended by the Compiler provide an illusion of a large cast of active characters. In the logbook, the Dictator dialogues with the Compiler, dividing himself into "I" and "HE," an I who is mortal, subject to time, and a HE who is the mythic Dictator, the image that endures. Extensive historical commentaries by the Dictator are included, and these, in combination with the Compiler's lengthy footnotes, quotations from other writers (some real, some invented), and documents, provide a sense of the context of the Dictator's life. This strange and marvelous collection of texts and fragments, of multiple points of view about a vast number of subjects, is interwoven into a coherent whole.

The Dictator seeks to elucidate the meaning of history in *I the Supreme* and simultaneously seeks an understanding of what it is to write about history, to describe experience in words. Myth, legend, multiple accounts, statistics, contradictory points of view, blurred memory, and fiction itself are all part of history. The complex man, José Gaspar Rodríguez de Francia, is presented from a vertiginous number of perspectives, and through this composite—through a personal interpretation of the words that represent this reality—readers can glimpse their connection to the past, their participation in the past. The novel never ceases to examine itself, refute itself, transpose itself into new forms and perspectives. As Francia reflects, "To write does not mean to convert the real into words but to make the power of the word real." Roa Bastos has written elsewhere that

we all know that a genuine literary work has merit not for its good intentions or for the ideas and opinions proclaimed by its author, but rather for the truth or *force* of truth that emanates from the collective social energy unconsciously projected through the sensitive filter of subjectivity: that of the particular author.

It is this force of truth that makes *I the Supreme* so remarkable and fascinating.

Mary G. Berg

Sources for Further Study

Booklist. LXXXII, April 15, 1986, p. 1183.
Choice. XXIV, September, 1986, p. 130.
Commonweal. CXIII, May 23, 1986, p. 314.
Kirkus Reviews. LIV, February 15, 1986, p. 243.
Library Journal. CXI, April 1, 1986, p. 163.
Los Angeles Times Book Review. July 13, 1986, p. 1.
The New York Times Book Review. XCI, April 6, 1986, p. 1.
The New Yorker. LII, September 22, 1986, p. 106.
Publishers Weekly. CCXXIX, March 7, 1986, p. 82.
Washington Post Book World. XVI, May 11, 1986, p. 1.

IN THE PENNY ARCADE

Author: Steven Millhauser (1943-   )
Publisher: Alfred A. Knopf (New York). 164 pp. $14.95
Type of work: Short stories
Time: The distant past, the late nineteenth century, and the mid-1980's
Locale: Germany, the northeastern United States, and China

> *A truly distinctive writer achieves some wonderful effects in his latest fiction and offers some stimulating insights into the nature of art*

Steven Millhauser established himself as a writer to watch with the publication in 1972 of *Edwin Mullhouse: The Life and Death of an American Writer, 1943-1954, by Jeffrey Cartwright*. The originality of the wit and of the intense attention to the minutiae of everyday life in middle-class America makes this parody of literary biography immensely appealing. Millhauser has yet, however, to live up to the promise of his delightful first novel. *Portrait of a Romantic* (1977), his second novel, while original and moving, is clearly a lesser work but leaves the reader still looking forward to more Millhauser fiction. After a nine-year wait, a collection of seven short stories may at first seem disappointing, but *In the Penny Arcade* shows Millhauser attempting to refine his art further, to move beyond the concern with childhood, melancholy, and death in his novels to become a truly distinctive writer. While the result may fall short of his obvious potential, he achieves some wonderful effects in this new fiction and offers some stimulating insights into the nature of art.

The three most conventional stories in *In the Penny Arcade* depict the emotional confusions of women. In "A Protest Against the Sun," Elizabeth Halstrom is making the transition from adolescence to adulthood. Spending an afternoon on a beach on Long Island Sound with her mother and her adored professor father, whose shifts from playfulness to irritation hurt her, Elizabeth contrasts the world of the present with memories of her happy childhood. When a teenage boy dressed in black stalks angrily past the sun worshipers, only Elizabeth perceives that he is mocking them. She understands his revulsion for their complacent normality but recognizes that she has passed this stage of adolescent revolt.

Catherine, in "The Sledding Party," is a younger version of Elizabeth. Catherine has been enjoying the party with her high school classmates when Peter Schiller, whom she has considered only a friend, suddenly tells her that he loves her, then abruptly leaves. Outraged at his spoiling the festiveness of the occasion, Catherine is nevertheless forced to reflect on the mysterious nature of love. Struggling against the complexity of such emotions, she feels "an immense pity for Peter Schiller, and for herself, as if someone had done something to them and gone away." This realization leads to an epiphany which allows her to return to the party and deal with whatever may lurk beneath the simplistic surface of adolescence.

A more mature woman appears in "A Day in the Country," though Judith, a thirty-six-year-old editor, is no less uncertain about her relationship to her world. She goes to a mountain resort to escape New York and the pain of a failed romance and to work on a manuscript, but she is annoyed by the presence of the only other unaccompanied woman there. Everywhere she turns she encounters this dark, younger woman who seems to pose some type of threat that Judith does not understand or want to confront. She is shocked when the dark woman suddenly dares to say that Judith is unhappy. Judith runs to her room in tears, weeping even more as she becomes outraged at "the banality of tears." She does not want to be understood because she does not understand herself. She is bored by her suffering yet realizes that she cannot run from it.

The remaining four stories are more concerned with artifice than with the banalities of everyday existence. "Cathay" is a series of vignettes describing the exotic splendors of the ancient Orient. The emperor's miniaturists create elaborate paintings on the eyelids and breasts of the ladies of the court to aid them in enticing and exciting their lovers. Other miniaturists reproduce the innumerable chambers, corridors, courtyards, and parks of the Imperial Palace in jade. Inside this miniature palace the size of a small table is, barely perceptible to the naked eye, a miniature of the miniature itself. Millhauser clearly intends the people and objects of "Cathay" to be a miniature of the entire book. The last vignette in the story, the last in the collection, presents a competition among magicians. One of the two finalists turns a jade statue into a living woman. The other magician wins by transforming a similar statue into a moving jade woman. *In the Penny Arcade* becomes an examination and celebration of artifice, of the power of the imagination. Even in the three more conventional stories, the protagonists find some peace through resorting to their imaginations.

"Snowmen" dramatizes the relation between art, reality, and the imagination. A group of boys is thrilled by the opportunities offered by a heavy snowfall. After they create elaborate snowmen, other, even more detailed ones appear throughout their town. It is as if the entire community is competing to see who can create the most realistic snow jugglers, birds, and fountains. When the snow sculptures begin to melt, creating unrealistic figures, the narrator recognizes the aesthetic superiority of these accidental gargoyles:

> They were nothing less than a protest against the solemnity, the rigidity, of our snowmen. What had seemed a blossoming forth of hidden powers . . . suddenly seemed a form of intricate construction. It was as if those bird-filled maples, those lions, those leaping ballerinas and prancing clowns had been nothing but a failure of imagination.

Failures of imagination are at the center of the title story. The protagonist of "In the Penny Arcade" spends his twelfth birthday revisiting the tacky, run-down arcade he remembers vividly from when he was younger. He is disappointed that nothing—the mechanical gunfighter, the stripper in the peep show—is as dramatic and romantic as he remembers it. "It seemed as though a blight had overtaken the creatures of this hall: they were sickly, wasted versions of themselves." Gradually, he begins to understand why the arcade is no longer magical: The creatures "had lost their freedom under the constricting gaze of all those who no longer believed in them. Their majesty and mystery had been crushed down by the shrewd, oppressive eyes of countless visitors who looked at them without seeing their fertile inner nature." The boy understands that he has betrayed the creatures of the arcade: "I saw that I was in danger of becoming ordinary, and I understood that from now on I would have to be vigilant." Millhauser seems to be asking for a similar vigilance from his reader, for the imaginative effort necessary to see beneath the surface of his stories.

What these stories say about art, imagination, reality, loneliness, the loss of innocence, and the need for love is presented on a larger scale in "August Eschenburg," the first and longest story in the collection. August, the son of a watchmaker in Mühlenberg, Germany, becomes fascinated at an early age by moving toys. After seeing a clockwork magician whose face seems to express emotion, young August begins creating automatons. One of his creations is displayed in his father's shop window and is seen by the owner of Berlin's Preisendanz Emporium. Two years later, eighteen-year-old August goes to Berlin to make automatons for Preisendanz's windows.

August loves his work so much that he begins living in his workshop, and all Berlin soon becomes entranced by his lifelike creations. Preisendanz's competitors begin displaying their own automatons, many of them sexually suggestive women with realistic breasts and hips. August wants to create beauty with his clockwork art; his employer wants whatever the public wants. August is fired and returns to Mühlenberg.

Two years later, Hausenstein, the maker of the sensual automatons, asks August to return to Berlin and create his art for a clockwork theater because he wants to see what August is capable of when given the opportunity to do as he pleases. August is suspicious, wondering if Hausenstein needs "to bathe himself in the fluid of another's creativity, in the hope that he would be washed clean of all that was common in him." Nevertheless, he accepts the challenge.

The Zaubertheater is initially a huge success, but soon imitators flood the market again. A pornographic automaton theater, started by Hausenstein behind August's back, drives the true artist out of business and out of Berlin. August has failed, ironically, by being too good an artist, by using his clockwork creations "to express spiritual states, and such lofty experiments were bound to seem rather confusing to all but the most stubborn adherents of the Zaubertheater."

Millhauser's purpose becomes even clearer in the final pages of "August Eschenburg." He uses this story not only to establish the themes to be explored in the other stories, and to do so in a way which underscores how they are all interrelated, but also to present a philosophical argument about the uses and abuses of art. August recognizes that there is "no law requiring the world to pay the slightest attention to him or his work, but by the same token he saw no reason to bend himself out of spiritual shape in the hope of pleasing a corrupt public. He would do what he had to do, in obedience to the only law he knew." The true artist creates only what pleases him, and it is the role of his audience to attempt honestly to understand what he is trying to do before dismissing his work. Both artist and public must ignore what is merely fashionable. Hausenstein explains that while his fellow late nineteenth century Germans "chatter about the soul, I give them what they really want, and in the process I satisfy a sense of world-irony and a love of truth. Yes, I drag them down, the swine—I drag them down." Such cynicism is destructive not only to the artist but also to his potential audience; it corrupts the sensibility necessary for art to flourish.

At the end of the story, August rationalizes his lowly status as a man creating an anachronistic art only a handful can appreciate and decides to abandon it. The irrational side of his nature perseveres, however, and he decides to remain what the fates have damned him to be: an artist. This is the only ending possible for Millhauser, a romantic despite his awareness of the dominance of the Hausensteins of the world.

Although admirers of Millhauser's novels may miss their humor and playfulness in these stories, such elements appear in a more subtle form: the intricate detailing of August's automatons, the ephemeral snow sculptures in "Snowmen," and the exotic artifice of "Cathay." Millhauser's stories will remind readers of works by James Joyce, Herman Hesse, Vladimir Nabokov, Jorge Luis Borges, J. D. Salinger, Italo Calvino, and many others, but in his ability to delineate the strangeness of reality, to see the potential magic in the commonplace, Millhauser continues to be an original artist.

Michael Adams

Sources for Further Study

Booklist. LXXXII, January 1, 1986, p. 658.
Choice. XXIII, July, 1986, p. 1677.
Esquire. CV, February, 1986, p. 117.
Kirkus Reviews. LIII, November 1, 1985, p. 1155.
Library Journal. CXI, January, 1986, p. 103.

The New York Times Book Review. XCI, January 19, 1986, p. 9.
Newsweek. CVII, March 17, 1986, p. 74.
Publishers Weekly. CCXXVIII, November 1, 1985, p. 55.

THE INNER REACHES OF OUTER SPACE
Metaphor as Myth and as Religion

Author: Joseph Campbell (1904-   )
Publisher: Alfred van Der Marck Editions (New York). Illustrated. 155 pp. $16.95
Type of work: Philosophy and religious theory

A proposal of a new metaphysical theory of unification based on an analysis of metaphors and myths common to all religious traditions

Joseph Campbell, long known for his ability to deal with nonlinear subjects such as dreams and myths, has once again tackled the intuitive level of man's understanding and attempted to present it in a logical, linear fashion. The result is a book that challenges the reader to bring to bear everything he has ever read about metaphysics, art, mythology, and religion and to connect these ideas into an intricate pattern that does indeed lead from outer to inner space. Arranged in a logical way, this book leads the reader from the overview of the prologue through three dense and articulate chapters: "Cosmology and the Mythic Imagination," "Metaphor as Myth and as Religion," and "The Way of Art." These are not, however, separate entities but parts of a universal structure, a harmonious symbiosis, which Campbell believes, optimistically, to be the message of the future. In his search for meaning in metaphor, Campbell moves from the universal to the particular, from religious traditions to the human imagination, and thus from inner to outer space. For most readers, this journey through outer and inner space will require both attention to detail and faith that all the disparate parts will come together in the end.

After Campbell introduces certain concepts in the prologue that are common to all religious traditions, including the dread triad of god-given urgencies—feeding, procreating, and overcoming—he turns to the relevance and meaning of mythology and the modern world. Beginning with a reference to Immanuel Kant and the idea that the laws of space are known because they are of the mind, Campbell challenges our ideas about the universe. A major thesis states that outer space is within us, for outer and inner space are the same. With this metaphor, Campbell encompasses both art and religion. The reader must also travel through outer space (the realm of religious and philosophic theory) and inner space (his own dreams, visions, and intuitive connections) in order to follow Campbell's connections between universal and local ideas. For example, he is intrigued by the importance of the number 432,000 and its significance in Indian Kali Yoga, Icelandic Eddas, Germanic and Babylonian legends, the Old Testament, and the writings of the ancient Greeks. Of more interest, perhaps, to the Western reader is his discussion of the split in Western religions: the ethical protest against an uncritical submission to the will of nature, the distinction between good and evil, rather than a belief in oneness. This division has been widened by the separation between science and religion and the failure of mythology to encompass the advances of science. Mankind is forced to choose one or the other. Campbell notes parallels between Western and Eastern mythologies. The fact that man has chosen not to go along with nature but to align himself with the good in nature to fight the bad is the beginning of divisions and distinctions where there, in reality, are none. All groups assert that "God is with us"; according to Campbell's hypothesis, all are right. The path of chapter 1 leads to some sort of metaphysical transcendentalism. The point seems to be that man has outgrown this old concept of good and evil; man's new knowledge of space and the universe requires that he create and learn a new mythology that fits the world as it is known today. Science and religion must be brought together as one, not as opposites. To begin with, Campbell suggests that man give up defined good for the experience of the transcendence. "The Holy Land is everywhere," mythologized as home. Campbell's use of Hindu parables for analogies may leave the Western reader stumbling along behind because the analogy is thick and complicated and the story is unfamiliar. At the end of one such story, the old man who tells the tale simply vanishes, as does the young boy listening to it; the king, Indra, sits "alone, bewildered and unstrung." The reader may indeed understand how he feels; yet the logic and wholeness of Campbell's argument are convincing.

Fortunately, the second section of this book begins to answer some of the questions raised in the reader's mind. Campbell's mind (best described by a metaphor from the future—a magnetic sponge) collects and assimilates information from diverse sources, fitting them together so that there is an unexpected coherence. Beginning with the accepted idea that what one people call myth another may call religion, Campbell suggests that much, if not all, of the misunderstanding in religion derives from a confusion between mythic metaphors and hard facts. Most religious events and concepts are, in reality, metaphors. Myths, productions of the human imagination, are psychologically symbolic; the rituals that sustain these myths are metaphors or direct expositions of life-sustaining patterns. Mythic figurations are both psychological and metaphysical. Thus, the concept of God is a metaphor in an unknowing mind, connotative beyond itself and beyond thought—the realm of metaphysics. "Our Father" is a metaphor; its import is psychological, but its meaning is transcendent or metaphysical. Contemporary allusions to the religious conflict in Beirut help pin down this point. Campbell believes that tribal literalism can contribute only agony to an intercultural world. He believes that all this division and conflict comes from misreading metaphors, mistaking denotation for connotation, confusing the message with the messenger, from sentimentality and banality, all of which throws life and thought off balance. Tribalism or ethnocentrism causes and perpetrates the old mythologies. His argument is both loaded and convincing.

Moving through an intricate discussion of the moon and sun as metaphor, Campbell takes on some of the basic concepts of Christianity: the Virgin Birth, Salvation, and the Fall. The metaphor of the Virgin Birth, for example, is that of a life lived not for economic or biological ends such as survival, progeny, prosperity, or pleasure, but for the metaphysical end. Thus, "folk heroes" who die for causes or who give of themselves totally often have virgin births attributed to them in folk legend and memory. This is metaphor confused as fact. As metaphors, rather than facts, these become only parts of universal mythology.

Yet this is no attack on religious beliefs but, rather, an exploration of metaphysical meaning. Connectedness is of central importance throughout this work; each time Campbell introduces something new, there is an attempt to link it with the concepts previously discussed. Thus, when he considers in depth the Indian Yogic schools and the spinal centers of consciousness, he connects this to his earlier discussion of the basic urgencies of life, and he attempts to integrate the psychological impact of man's gods with cultural expectations. He synthesizes, seeing similarities and relationships between images and concepts that appear on the surface to have little in common. This book creates a whole greater than the sum of all of its parts. In order to make these connections, Campbell recognizes the necessity of threshold figures that stand at the interface of time and eternity. Readers of this book will find that Campbell himself becomes a "threshold" figure, helping them pass from one field of thought to another. One interesting example of this is his interpretation of the myth of the Garden of Eden. Campbell proposes that the serpent is a "threshold figure," attempting to release mankind from the bondage of an unknowing god who had identified himself with the absolute and had blocked the way to the tree of eternal life. The frequent juxtaposition of concepts and images from different cultures and time periods is part of what holds his theory together. If the kingdom is within us, then immortality is already available to us if we detach our minds from mere mortal aims: Eden is here; there was no exile. This assumption finds validity in Sir James G. Frazer's concept of "homeopathic magic," Adolf Bastian's "elementary ideas," and Carl Jung's "archetypes of the unconscious." One becomes convinced that Campbell has surveyed the ancient writings and the artistic renderings of the world. The similarities in structure and the correlations create for Campbell macrocosm, microcosm, and mesocosm, all equal, all important. Similarities noted in images from Indian gurus, Tibetan rimpoches, and Japanese Zen masters from the late Neolithic and the early Bronze Ages are not surprising perhaps, but some of the same image patterns can be found in Navaho sand paintings. Here Campbell poses another possible connection, that of the hallucinogen experience, which he claims was common to the entire Mayan-Aztec culture field as well as to the Greek mysteries of Eleusis and the mysterious Vedic sacraments;

he further suggests that some of these same experiences are produced through intense Yoga practice. If this hypothesis is true, it validates the idea that the source for metaphor, myth, and symbol is the individual psyche. This accounts for the appearance of the same symbols, independent and parallel, in many places at or near the same time—in other words, what folklorists and anthropologists call polygenesis.

Campbell's study of American Indian culture, in particular that of the Navaho, seems to have provided much impetus for this section of his book. He is especially interested in parallels between the vision quest of the Ushumna, a tribe of ancient India, and that of the Navaho; both, Campbell suggests, may be interpreted as "a single mythological epic of the human imagination." His detailed comparisons lead him to assert that Bastian's "elementary ideas" are of the human psyche, regardless of culture, while differences in mores and ethical precepts reflect the geography, history, and societal expectations of local groups.

The question each reader of this work must answer is whether Campbell proves his case. Certainly there is no lack of evidence, but a certain leap of faith is required, for few readers will have read as widely as Campbell himself. When he asserts that what distinguishes all mythological thought and communication is an implicit connotation of a strong sense of identity of some kind which transcends appearances and unites behind the scenes the oppositions of the world, it is easy to believe that he has, indeed, studied all "mythological thought and communication" before making such a statement. With this theory, Campbell can encompass individual biographies and dreams as interlocking parts of the Indian image of the "Net of Gems," the Buddhist doctrine of "mutual arising," the Mahāyāna "Flower-Wreath sūtra," the Japanese *Avatamsaka*-sūtra, the Hindu Cosmic Serpent dreaming the dream of the universe, and finally James Joyce's vision in *Finnegans Wake*. Intuitively and logically, the universe becomes, at least for Campbell, one concise, coherent, metaphysical, and transcendent whole.

In the concluding section of this book, Campbell turns to the question of art. Beginning with the distinction between the mystic and the artist (the mystic has no craft to hold him to this world), Campbell connects the Indian god Vishnu the Preserver with the Greek god Apollo and Shiva the Destroyer with Dionysus. He continues to connect the roles of artist and priest: They are seen in the same light, for both must learn to master metaphorical language. Nevertheless, they do differ—the priest uses an established vocabulary while the artist must be creative and innovative to be effective. Thus, art is seen as the way of innovative insights, the mystic way, beyond mere religion. Campbell sees the microcosm of the artist's nature and the macrocosm of the nature of the universe as two aspects of one reality. Having set the perimeters of theory, Campbell turns again to the concrete. Mixing art, symbol, and metaphor, he gives a detailed analysis of the

Great Seal of the United States which is engraved on the back of all one-dollar bills. One is forced to confront the mystical in the mundane, to see mystery in this common symbol, for the idea of money itself is also symbolic. It is curious to contemplate the spiritual inspiration behind economic values. It seems that not only the message but also the vocabulary in which it is written has been lost. Moving back to focus on the artist and his work, Campbell turns to Joyce's *A Portrait of the Artist as a Young Man*, in which Stephen Dedalus translates the values of art according to Aristotle. These ideas (beauty, harmony, and radiance) are relevant to myth and metaphor as well. Campbell presents these ideas as touchstones, noting their presence in the teachings of Buddha and in the life and death of Martin Luther King, Jr. Such prodigious leaps of thought seem simple under Campbell's guidance.

Somehow it all begins to come together with a quotation from T. S. Eliot's poem "Burnt Norton." Here is the transcendent vision, the classic goal of Yoga, Nirvana. Campbell has drawn convincing connections between Shiva, Dionysus, Joyce, Aristotle, Richard Wagner, Kant, Friedrich Nietzsche, Cervantes, Nathaniel Hawthorne, Thomas Mann, Sigmund Freud, Jung, and even the "antihero" created by Charles Chaplin. The "whatness" of Joyce is fused with the Indian term "Brahman." Campbell poses a final question, however, not about individual psychology, alienation, or resentment, but about the irreducible conflict of metaphysics vis-à-vis morals within the jurisdiction of art, myth, religion, and social action. What can be done about the schism between materialism and industrialization and the world of the artist? Campbell seeks to unify coldness and passion; perhaps this is the fusion of inner and outer space. The book concludes with another quotation, from Robinson Jeffers' poem "Natural Music," which calls together the archetypal images that Campbell has been tracing: old voices, birds, rivers and oceans, divisions and one language, desire and terror, and the dreams of lovers, both personal and of the world. Poetry may be the answer to Campbell's question, not in the language of the scholar or the priest but in the metaphors and symbols of the artist. Perhaps only in poetry, art, or music can one see the whole that Campbell proclaims and understand the unification of all and the one in metaphor, myth, and symbol.

Few books of such short length contain so much information. Campbell has combed the world's mythologies and metaphors, bringing order to what on the surface seems scattered and disconnected. Because of the breadth and depth of this work, many readers will want to reread it. In addition, Campbell's notes at the end of the book provide a reading list of sources. Although light in weight, this is not a book to be taken lightly. For those in search of a new mythology for a new world, *The Inner Reaches of Outer Space* is a good starting point.

Linda T. Humphrey

Sources for Further Study

Choice. XXIV, March, 1987, p. 1084.
Parabola. XI, Winter, 1986, p. 101.

JANE AUSTEN

Author: Tony Tanner (1935-   )
Publisher: Harvard University Press (Cambridge, Massachusetts). 291 pp. $20.00;
paperback $8.95
Type of work: Literary criticism

A reading of Jane Austen's novels that demonstrates her concern with society, education, and language

Tony Tanner, Fellow of King's College and Reader in the Faculty of English at Cambridge University, is an authority on the English and American novel. He has edited Charlotte Brontë's *Villette* and has published books about such writers as various as Thomas Pynchon and Henry James; his other works include *City of Words: American Fiction, 1950-1970* (1971) and *Adultery in the Novel: Contract and Transgression* (1979). Tanner's experience and expertise pervade his most recent book, *Jane Austen*. According to his acknowledgments, Tanner sees his book not as an addition to the already extensive scholarship on Austen but rather as a reading of her work, addressed to a general audience, and demonstrating Austen's concern with society, education, and language. Tanner has written introductions to Penguin editions of three of Austen's novels—*Sense and Sensibility* (1811), *Pride and Prejudice* (1813), and *Mansfield Park* (1814)—and he has spoken to the Jane Austen society about *Persuasion* (1818). Versions of the talk and introductions have been incorporated into this book, and Tanner has added an introductory section as well as chapters on *Emma* (1815), *Northanger Abbey* (1818), and *Sanditon* (1975), the fragment written in the months before Austen's death in 1817. *Jane Austen* thus represents twenty years of Tanner's thinking and writing about this important and enduringly popular English novelist. Although familiar with Austen scholarship and with recent developments in literary theory, Tanner presents his reading of her work in a manner so informal as to be described as casual. As a whole, the book is best approached as a series of insightful lecture-commentaries, replete with parentheses and digressions, presented by a delightfully erudite don. The reader who comes to *Jane Austen* in this way will be impressed by the book's many strengths and may manage to avoid being disturbed by its weaknesses.

Tanner's chapters take up seven of Austen's novels—*Northanger Abbey*, *Sense and Sensibility*, *Pride and Prejudice*, *Mansfield Park*, *Emma*, *Persuasion*, and *Sanditon*—in order to delineate changes in her appraisal of English society. Preceding these seven chapters is an introductory essay divided into four sections which lay groundwork for matters to which Tanner returns in his discussions of specific works. Beginning with a section called "Jane Austen and the Novel," Tanner presents and then dismisses the conventional view of Austen as a remarkable but restricted novelist. He quotes her famous comments about "the little bit (two inches wide) of ivory on which I work with so fine a brush" and her interest in "three or four families in a country village," and he cites the opinions of James and Ralph Waldo Emerson concerning Austen's "narrowness," only to assert what other readers have also discovered: that the "two-inch" view of Austen that she herself helped to perpetuate does not adequately account for her obvious awareness of the political, economic, and social conflicts from which her works arise. Even her heroines' absorption in making good marriages, Tanner points out, reflects Austen's broader concern with marriage and the family as basic social units.

In the second section of the introduction, "Jane Austen and Society," Tanner offers an analysis of money and property as forces in Austen's world. Austen, like many of her contemporaries, believed that the concept of the rule of property rested on the propriety—that is, the proper behavior—of the landed class. According to Tanner, Austen saw her society as threatened from within by the failure, on the part of landowners responsible for supporting and reinvigorating the social order, to provide a strong moral example. "Thus the ideal marriage at the end of a Jane Austen novel," according to Tanner, "offers itself as an emblem of the ideal union of property and propriety—a model to be emulated, a paradigm for a more general combination of the two on which the future of her society depends." In the introduction's third section, "Jane Austen and Education," Tanner briefly considers works by Lord Chesterfield, Edmund Burke, Thomas Gisborne, John Locke, and Thomas More to illuminate Austen's emphasis on education, not as knowledge of facts and skills, but as the cultivation of wise conduct and prudent manners. The fourth section, on language, describes Austen's diction and syntax, her use of dialogue and scene, and her sense of her audience to show that, taken as a whole, her novels move from acceptance, to skepticism, to rejection of the values implicit in the changing social milieu of early nineteenth century England. Although this material on language formally concludes the introduction, the next chapter, ostensibly on *Northanger Abbey*, also has an introductory quality, since it offers numerous useful generalizations about Austen's work. There is no concluding chapter.

By far, the most impressive part of Tanner's book is his commentary on *Sense and Sensibility*, a novel often faulted for its too-geometric assignment of sense to Elinor Dashwood and sensibility to her sister Marianne. Rejecting this rigidly dualistic view and drawing on Michel Foucault's *Madness and Civilization* (1967), Tanner sees *Sense and Sensibility* as an examination of "the tensions between the potential instability of the individual and the required stabilities of society." He asserts that the illness which overtakes Marianne when Willoughby jilts her is madness, a bona fide neurosis brought on by the necessary repression of powerful feelings. Maintenance of the society to which the Dashwood sisters belong requires adhering to forms, putting up screens, and even telling polite lies—all activities at which

Elinor excels and which Marianne believes to be hypocritical. Through the contrasts between the two sisters, says Tanner, Austen brings

> into focus a problem right at the heart of that, or indeed any other, society: namely, how much of the individual's inner world should be allowed to break out in the interests of personal vitality and psychic health; and how much should the external world be allowed to coerce and control that inner reality in the interests of maintaining a social structure which does provide meaningful spaces and definitions for the lives of its members?

Tanner suggests that the novel's numerous references to eyes and vision show Austen's exploration of the boundary between the inner and outer worlds, between consciousness and externality, while Marianne's marriage to Colonel Brandon represents a sacrifice of her emotional energy to the "overriding geometry" of the novel and of the social forces that it depicts. Observing that the nonconforming Marianne is the ancestor of Cathy in *Wuthering Heights* (1847) and Maggie Tulliver in *The Mill on the Floss* (1860), Tanner persuasively argues that the conclusion of *Sense and Sensibility* is far more complex than it seems. His own conclusion, drawing on ideas he has subtly laid down in the course of the chapter, is a breathtaking example of his skill as a prose stylist.

Other particularly strong chapters are those on *Mansfield Park*, *Persuasion*, and *Sanditon*. In all three cases, Tanner illuminates works that have not been as widely read or as enthusiastically appreciated as *Pride and Prejudice* and *Emma* have been. What is often a problem for readers of *Mansfield Park*—the extreme passivity and goodness of its Cinderella heroine, Fanny Price—becomes, in Tanner's hands, a virtue absolutely essential to the larger purposes of a book which he considers "one of the most profound novels of the nineteenth century." He demonstrates that modest, steady, humble Fanny is actually the moral center of Mansfield; the Bertrams, who should be assuming responsibility for moral leadership, abdicate in various ways, leaving their house vulnerable to the temptations represented by those attractive Londoners, Henry and Mary Crawford. With sensitive close readings of two key passages, the trip to Sotherton and the theatricals, Tanner explains that the book Austen said was about "ordination" is not only about a young clergymen's entry into his profession but also depicts the reinstatement of order and authority in a family nearly destroyed by corruption from within as well as from without. *Mansfield Park*, says Tanner near the end of this beautifully constructed chapter, "is a book about the difficulty of preserving true moral consciousness amid the selfish manoeuvring and jostling of society."

As for *Persuasion* and *Sanditon*, Tanner uses these novels to show that by the last years of her life, Austen had begun to question and even to reject values implicit in her earlier novels. The "rare autumnal magic" of Anne

Elliot's story is—Tanner's wordplay here is characteristically witty and effective—"deeply shadowed by the passing of things, and the remembrance of things past." Anne must learn romance, just as earlier heroines have had to learn prudence; she is emotionally constant, as Fanny Price is, while everything around her is changing or threatening to change. In *Persuasion* the locus of hospitality and familial affection has shifted from the landed gentry to the navy, from land to sea. As Tanner explains, "Society in the form of Sir Walter Elliot has become all empty self-regarding form and display; he has no sense of responsibility to his position, to the land, and it is significant that he rents his house to go and participate in the meaningless frivolities in Bath." In his remarks on communication as a theme of *Persuasion*, Tanner again makes good use of close reading as he examines chapters 22 and 23, the expanded conclusion which replaced Austen's original ending. The subject of this expansion—constancy in love—is particularly relevant to Tanner's thesis. Anne's constancy represents what is best in the old order, while the resort town of Sanditon, or "sandy-town," which gives its name to Austen's final fragmentary work, shows "the infiltration, if not invasion and colonisation, of the signs of a new consumer culture and fashion and leisure industry, into an older rural economy." In Sanditon, activity and conversation are almost meaningless; health, sickness, and the sea itself have become commodities to be exploited for profit. In this final work, Tanner claims, Austen herself abdicates, and there is no authority, not even authorial authority. While it seems risky to base the conclusion of a book's entire argument on an unrevised fragment, Tanner's treatment of *Sanditon* is plausible in the context of his discussion as a whole.

The rewards of Tanner's chapters on *Sense and Sensibility*, *Mansfield Park*, *Persuasion*, and *Sanditon* must be balanced against relatively weak treatments of *Pride and Prejudice* and *Emma* and against distracting mannerisms in Tanner's often admirable style. The chapter on *Emma* is especially disappointing, opening as it does with lengthy quotations from Otto Weininger's misogynistic *Sex and Character* (1906), quotations which Tanner uses only to establish what even the most naïve reader can surely discern for himself: that Emma is a matchmaker. The stylistic weaknesses are in some ways more irritating than the substantive ones because they could so easily have been eliminated by careful editing. Tanner is fond of parentheses and of parentheses within parentheses; a single paragraph in the chapter on *Emma* boasts six pairs. The otherwise splendid chapter on *Persuasion* features five postponements of the "But-I-shall-return-to-that-subject-later" variety, three of them occurring in two pages. There are occasional lapses from syntactic clarity and even a who/whom mistake. Further, one sentence actually begins this way: "As far as my memory and my notes go, I think I am right in saying that. . . ." Although this sort of thing may be perfectly acceptable in a lecture, many readers will consider it unacceptable in print.

These stylistic irritations are related to the more distressing matter of documentation. Readers who may wish to explore some of the many sources Tanner mentions will be hard pressed to locate specific passages, since Tanner provides no page numbers and in some cases no specific editions. While it is true that British and American conventions differ in certain respects and that Tanner has said that he is writing for the general reader, still, the absence of precise documentation is likely to frustrate the more scholarly members of his audience—and scholars there undoubtedly will be among his readers; no academician who refers with such ease to thinkers as diverse as David Hume, John Locke, Sigmund Freud, Karl Marx, Roland Barthes, and Gaston Bachelard can expect to keep scholars away. These problems with style and documentation should have been solved before publication. Tanner's and his editors' failure to establish and maintain a clear, consistent relationship with the audience of *Jane Austen* seriously undermines a book which offers fascinating and occasionally brilliant readings of some of the finest novels in English.

Carolyn Wilkerson Bell

Sources for Further Study

Library Journal. CXI, October 15, 1986, p. 97.
The Library Review of Books. IX, February 5, 1987, p. 15.

JEWISH SELF-HATRED

Author: Sander L. Gilman (1944-   )
Publisher: The Johns Hopkins University Press (Baltimore, Maryland). 461 pp.
$28.50
Type of work: Cultural and social history

This study deals with problems of Jewish acceptance and identity as reflected in the lives and writings of Jews in German-speaking countries and the United States, with particular emphasis on the "language" and discourse that marked Jews as different in the eyes of non-Jews as well as in their own eyes

A disturbing phenomenon of social history is the unholy fascination exerted by victimizers on their victims and the tendency of the latter to "identify with the aggressor" (Anna Freud)—what Guy Stern has described as "the willingness of pariah groups to embrace the calumnies of their oppressors and to affix them to subgroups within their own ranks." In the light of the Holocaust, this phenomenon has acquired particular poignance in the case of the Jews. Sander L. Gilman has now produced the most searching analysis of Jewish self-hatred since Theodor Lessing's paradigmatic study *Der jüdische Selbsthass* (1930), providing an entire typology of Jewish modes of alienation, insecurity, compensation, self-laceration, and other outward projections of inner anxieties. He defines self-hating Jews as individuals who accept and internalize the premises underlying anti-Jewish rhetoric and behavior. "This present study," the author writes, "examines how a group defined as different by society as well as by itself responds to one very specific stereotype, the image of its language and discourse." Gilman then goes on to elucidate what he terms the "classic double bind situation":

> Society has stated, through its literary institutions: Become like me—speak my language, think within my constraints, express yourself within my forms, undertake the same search for origins as I do—and you will become one with me. The state says: If you speak like a Jew, you are treated like an object; I can see beyond your superficial attempts to disguise yourself as a member of the intelligentsia and identify you.

Full acceptance by the reference group seems to beckon if the marginal group agrees to abandon its otherness and play by the majority's rules, as it were. That is the liberal promise, but there is also a conservative curse: "The more you are like me, the more I know the true value of my power, which you wish to share, and the more I am aware that you are but a shoddy counterfeit, an outsider." In this way acceptance becomes a mirage, a double-bind situation. Gilman is careful to point out that

> "self-hatred" among Jews is not the special prerogative of any specific group of Jews; it is the result of the internalized contrast between any society in which the possibility of acceptance is extended to any marginal group and the projection of the negative image of this group onto a fiction of itself that leads to "self-hatred" or self-abnegation.

What distinguishes Gilman's wide-ranging, impressively researched study from other books on anti-Semitism or problems of Jewish acculturation and identity is its in-depth treatment of the perception of the Jew as a marginal member of society, as "Other." This otherness has been expressed in a certain language or discourse. The Other can never possess "true" language; the hidden language, the true articulation of Jewishness, is the language of otherness: "The Other's language is hidden, dark, magical, dangerous, private." What is meant by "hidden language" or "damaged discourse" is whatever is perceived as being at the core of the Jews' otherness, and at various times and in different places this has been Hebrew, Yiddish (or Yiddishized German), language and rhetoric generally, journalism, trading, materialism, wit, sexuality, and (after the Holocaust) even the silence of the survivors. The author points out that on one level or another everybody is an Other to some group. Certain ethnic, racial, or religious entities—Jews, blacks, homosexuals—have always been labeled as different. The trouble starts when culturally determined, more or less arbitrary and "unfair" patterns of Otherness are applied whoesale to groups rather than individuals, and "self-hatred arises when the mirages of stereotypes are confused with realities . . . when the desire for acceptance forces the acknowledgment of one's difference."

The author sets out to "use the written words of Jews about the Jews in a number of historical and cultural contexts to examine the articulation and implication of self-hatred for Jewish indentity." Gilman's breadth and interdisciplinary orientation are evidenced by the fact that as a professor of humane studies he is a member of the departments of German and of Near Eastern studies at Cornell University in addition to serving as a professor of psychiatry at Cornell Medical College. The present book was suggested to the author, who has also written on blackness, insanity, and psychiatric photography, by his seminar on stereotypes of women in nineteenth century thought. (Paradoxically, he excludes Jewish women from consideration—because of "the double-double bind of being Jewish and being female" and the "discontinuity of texts by women and . . . their essentially private nature.") Since Gilman is primarily a Germanist, his study gives pride of place to German Jewry.

In tracing Jewish anti-Semitism (or anti-Judaism) as a "label for a specific mode of self-abnegation that has existed among Jews throughout their history," Gilman points out that in the sixteenth century Haim ben Bezalel described one of the first examples of Jewish self-hatred: baptized Jews railing against the Talmud. In the Christian medieval world, Hebrew was the "hidden language"; its status as an arcane, magical language explains the importance of Jewish physicians in the Middle Ages: They were thought to have access to occult knowledge. Johannes Pfefferkorn, a Jew baptized in 1504, became a willing tool of the hidebound Cologne Dominicans. The polemics between him and the "wise Christian" Johannes Reuchlin became a *cause célèbre* of European intellectuals in the struggle between the old order and the new humanism. The model of self-hatred supplied by Pfefferkorn and other Jewish converts—the "good" Jew who accepts Christ and gains true insight, and the "bad" Jew whose blindness and obduracy lead him to evil and destructive acts—decisively shaped Martin Luther's vulgar Jew-baiting and became part of a tradition that continued to generate negative self-images within German Jewry. Luther dehumanized the Jews by denying their claim to control of the magical Hebrew language and disseminated the notion that thieves' argot derived from Yiddish, which Johann Christoph Wagenseil and Johann Andreas Eisenmenger later presented as the new magical, conspirative language. In the early eighteenth century, the writings of Jewish converts to Christianity reinforced the popular image of Yiddish as the language of corruption and crime. It was so viewed by the Maskilim, the adherents of the Jewish Enlightenment ("The Maskil uses Yiddish to exorcise the image of himself as a speaker of Yiddish"), and a hundred years later Theodor Herzl, the father of political Zionism, described it as "the stealthy tongue of prisoners."

Gotthold Ephraim Lessing's play *The Jews* (1749), the first German attempt to present a Jew in a favorable light, was followed by the same author's *Nathan the Wise* (1779); in both plays the Jewish character speaks a flawless German. Lessing's friend Moses Mendelssohn helped German Jewry take the giant step from the ghetto into Europe by translating the Hebrew Bible into German. Henceforth this was to be the language of German Jewry, but there were many impediments on that path. With or without anti-Semitic intent, German playwrights used stock Jewish characters in their works, including the schlemiel, that "quintessential Jewish literary persona," a hapless fool with a damaged language that entraps him at every turn. The author supplies poignant pen portraits of a number of Jews— Moses Ephraim Kuh, Solomon Maimon, Isashar Falkensohn Behr—who failed in their attempts to "craft an integrated identity out of fragments of the German-Jewish self." The convert Ludwig Börne, born in the Frankfurt ghetto as Löw Baruch, criticized the Rothschilds, and Moritz Gottlieb Saphir, another convert, attacked the "rootless and languageless" Jews as separate from himself. In his memoirs, Saphir sanitized his family background, as it were, by having his mother and grandfather speak a perfect literary German. The ambivalent Heinrich Heine, who fought Börne as his "double," converted in 1825 in the hopes of receiving an "admission ticket to European culture," only to be relegated to a cultural sphere viewed by German society as the dominion of the outsider, the Jew, spending half of his life in a sort of intellectual limbo as a Jewish journalist living in Paris but writing in German and striving to fashion for himself a poetic discourse not contaminated by an "alien" rhetoric. Karl Marx, also a convert, tried to distance himself from the Jewish discourse of "haggling" by adopting the language of a prophet and revolutionary, but society still regarded him and his polemics as quintessentially Jewish. Attacking another self-hating Jew, the socialist Ferdinand Lassalle, in terms of vulgar racism, Marx labeled him a "black" hybrid.

Gilman writes that "within a generation of the granting of civil emancipation to the Jew, German society had created a new language that it attributed to the Jew. . . . It was called *mauscheln.*" The author defines this term, which derives from the name Moshe, as "the use of altered syntax and bits of Hebrew vocabulary and a specific pattern of gestures to represent the spoken language of the Jews." *Mauscheln*, that polluted language, was perceived as an impediment to the complete acculturation of German Jewry.

The special language of the Jews became one of the salient features of the new "science" of race. Whether it was Richard Wagner writing on Jews in music, Theodor Billroth on Jews in medicine, or Heinrich von Treitschke on "German-speaking orientals," Jews were deemed incapable of any acceptable form of discourse, and consequently they created a subgroup of Jews whose discourse stamped them as inferior. Fritz Mauthner developed an entire philosophy and psychology of language in which to embed his projection of the language of the Jew, and Eduard Engel set himself up as a "language-purifier" and arbiter of linguistic "Germanness." In 1912, Moritz Goldstein sounded a warning: "We Jews administer the cultural possessions of a people who deny us the right and the ability to do so." Until the late nineteenth century, the Eastern Jew had provided the touchstone for the exorcism of feelings of insecurity for the Western Jew; later the assimilated Jew became the "bad" Jew. Martin Buber was a notable proponent of a positive view of Eastern Jewry; his sense of self was shaped by Zionism and his presentation of Hasidism to a German readership as well as his translation of the Old Testament into a sort of Hebraized German. Arnold Zweig discerned self-hatred as a specific disease of the Austrian Jew because of the blandishments of Austria's culture and life-style. In analyzing Eastern Jewish humor, Sigmund Freud, the writer of "scientific" German, distanced himself from the *Mauscheln* of other Jews—"laughter as a means of expiating Jewish self-hatred"—yet, in writing about Jews, Freud's language is itself tainted; since the new hidden language was that of the Jew as anti-Semite, Freud invented a new one, the language of the unconscious. In his influential book *Sex and Character* (1903), Otto Weininger, a precocious self-hater and a suicide at age twenty-three, linked anti-Semitism and misogyny. Later the paranoid Arthur Trebitsch discerned a hidden language in the Jews' gestures, wit, and sexuality. Franz Kafka was both attracted to and repelled by the world of the Eastern Jew. In his story "A Report to the Academy," an ape acquires speech and thus escapes from brutish obscurity, but his discourse (like that of the Jews) is still damaged, and he is not accepted as a full member of human society. Gilman characterizes the Viennese satirist Karl Kraus as "one of the most complex examples of the creation of the Jewish Other as a substitute for the hatred of the self" and a fighter for a language free from *Mauscheln*, but the Berlin satirist Kurt Tucholsky, the author of the revealing "Herr Wendriner" monologues, is mentioned only in passing.

Under the rubric "The Survivor as Author," Gilman discusses the work of Elias Canetti, who grew up multilingual and continued to write in German during his decades of residence in England; Arthur Koestler, who thought that the paradox of the Jew required either emigration to Israel or gradual assimilation to a host nation; Polish-born Jerzy Kosinski, who writes in English; and Jurek Becker, a native of Lodz, who writes in German and in his novel *Jacob the Liar* (1969) reverses the image of the lying Jew by having a Jew's lie serve a higher truth and sanity in a world gone mad. "The Language of the Mad" is illuminated by the novels of Israel Joshua Singer, Saul Bellow, and Mordecai Richler. Among contemporary American Jewish writers, Cynthia Ozick has tried to re-create a "Jewish" discourse in the tradition of Henry Roth's *Call It Sleep* (1934), while Anne Roiphe has cut herself off from any "Jewish" language. "In Germany," the author writes, "the myth of the damaged discourse of the Jew absolutely defined the Jews' difference in society. In the United States, it appeared that such a distinction also existed, except that it was paralleled by a number of like images of other groups." His discussion of the work of three (unrelated) Roths— Henry, Samuel (a self-hating pornographer-publisher), and Philip (the creator of such self-hating personas as Portnoy and Zuckerman)—might have included a fourth, the Austrian storyteller Joseph Roth, who once signed a letter as "Moishe Christus." The author concludes that increased articulation of the problem has defused self-hatred as a motivation for writing and that Jews need no longer project their own insecurities onto other groups of Jews.

At the burning of the books in Nazi Germany (May, 1933) there was a reference to "the Jew who can only think Jewish but writes German lies" as well as the preposterous demand that "Jewish works appear in Hebrew; if they appear in German, they are to be labeled as translations." George Steiner, himself a survivor, believes that the Germans now speak the corrupted and corrupting language they once ascribed to the Jews. Gilman discerns as the double bind of post-Holocaust Jewish identity the muteness, inarticulateness, or silence of the (direct or indirect) survivors and places the poetry of Paul Celan in this context. He also discusses Meyer Levin's dramatization of the diary of Anne Frank, which the producers rejected as "too Jewish." The founding of the State of Israel, the rebirth of Hebrew as a national language, and the novel image of the militant Jew (the "Jews with muscles" called for by Herzl's associate Max Nordau) have created a new sense of national identity and a more favorable climate. Nevertheless, a recent form of Jewish self-hatred is Jewish opposition to the existence of the State of Israel (the Austrians Bruno Kreisky and Hans Weigel are cases in point). In the cultural pluralism of the United States, with its many different Others, self-hatred still persists as part of the human condition.

Gilman displays an admirable command of both primary and secondary sources, and his book is replete with incisive analysis, cogent argumentation, and highlights and sidelights not readily found elsewhere. It is not easy reading, however, and not merely because of the author's difficult locutions ("succuba," "apotropaic," "mephitic," "mythopoesis") and cryptic references ("Turnvater Jahn," "water-pollack Jews"). His practice of giving titles of books or periodicals in English where no translation exists is misleading (*Flying Pages* for *Fliegende Blätter*, *The Artguard* for *Der Kunstwart*, *Jewish Panorama* for *Jüdische Rundschau*, *The Attacker* for *Der Stürmer*, *Menzel, the Eater of the French—Franzosenfresser* is a colloquial term for "Francophobe"). At the risk of ending on a low note: Adolf Hitler's *Mein Kampf* is an exception.

Harry Zohn

Sources for Further Study

Choice. XXIV, September, 1986, p. 192.
Chronicle of Higher Education. April 2, 1986, p. 6.
Congress Monthly. LIII, November-December, 1986, p. 16.
Kirkus Reviews. LIII, December 15, 1985, p. 1374.
Jewish Quarterly. XXXIII, No. 4, 1986, p. 28.
Judaica Book News. XVII, No. 1, Fall-Winter, 1986, p. 40.
London Review of Books. May 8, 1986, p. 7.

JOURNALS, 1939-1983

Author: Stephen Spender (1909-   )
Edited by John Goldsmith
Publisher: Random House (New York). Illustrated. 511 pp. $19.95
Type of work: Diaries
Time: 1939-1983
Locale: England, Germany, the United States, the Soviet Union, and other locales

Stephen Spender, a respected figure in British letters, presents a selection from the journals he has kept throughout his varied career as poet, editor, critic and essayist, playwright, and author of fiction

By his own admission, Stephen Spender is a collector. Indeed, one of the final entries of his journals records his rummaging through his London attic. He sifts with a certain melancholy through mementos and outlines, and drafts of uncompleted and unpublished works, private memorials to a career in literature. When he receives the word that he has been proposed for a knighthood, he accepts gratefully despite his brief, early fling with Communism, recalling that the seventeen-year-old Spender had said that a poet with a title could never be trusted. Even as he accepts, he believes that it would have been a greater honor to have refused the honor. Like it or not, the always politically involved Spender has suddenly found himself in the inner circle of the British establishment and is somewhat disconcerted that he rather enjoys being there.

Still, what haunts Spender even more, so much so that it ironically emerges as a theme throughout these journal entries, is the fear that he has wasted his career in what he calls "journalism." By this, he means everything except poetry. He wishes that he could revise even the poems he has already published, and he regularly slips into moods of depression and frustration at what he perceives to be his inability to find words which measure up to his ideas. Even in his lighter moods, he analyzes how it feels to be "a minor poet" and reviews with agreement as well as amused masochism Virginia Woolf's mordant observations of himself as a young poet.

To some extent, it is understandable that Spender has these concerns. It was his curse as well as his good fortune to have been the contemporary and close friend of poets such as T. S. Eliot and W. H. Auden, to have been the disciple of intellects such as Ernst Robert Curtius and Isaiah Berlin; more tellingly, Spender witnessed the decline of promising individuals such as Christopher Isherwood and Robert Lowell. Then too, he realizes that he lacks the zeal of a missionary (like Eliot) or the personality of a hierophant (like Auden). One wonders if he realizes that it is precisely this sense of inadequacy which makes several of his poems, such as "What I Expected," "The Funeral," "Rough," or even "Icarus" (his answer to Auden's "Musée des Beaux Arts"), immortal. Fortunately, a new edition of Spender's *Collected Poems, 1928-1985* (1986) has been issued side by side with these journals, and readers will now have the opportunity to judge Spender's poetry on its own, revised and apart from the shadows of others.

The hundreds of names resoundingly dropped in these diaries and the anecdotes which fill their pages are often of more than passing interest. The entries written in Germany just before and just after World War II, for example, contrast impressions of a young man ten years down from Oxford and enjoying his first success as a poet with those of a still young but now seasoned member of the Civilian Military Forces doing a survey of German intellectuals in occupied Germany for the British Foreign Office. While the 1939 journal reads like passages from Thomas Mann's *Doctor Faustus* insofar as it analyzes German patriotism, racial theories, and conceptions of *Freundschaft*, the 1945 journal contains vivid pictures of a dispirited, conquered people. Cynical librarians calmly remove and store Nazi approved materials, replacing them with the Jewish literature they had saved ten years earlier from Nazi book burnings. There are anti-Nazi intellectuals such as Ernst Robert Curtius, who invites Spender to a lunch of cabbage and boiled potatoes, the only foods available, yet worries about appearing to be a collaborator by fraternizing with a member of the occupying forces. Curiously, but logically, there is not a word about the often recorded war years in England. This is but one example of the extent to which Spender has controlled the content of the published volume.

The postwar years are also the period of Spender's greatest involvement as an editor of the literary and political magazines *Horizon* and *Encounter*, the latter discredited when it was revealed that its funding came through the American Central Intelligence Agency. Spender was unaware of this, and he resigned his position when the facts came to light, though he felt that he had been used and betrayed. The third section of *Journals* deals with his feelings during this politically charged early period of the Cold War. Again, Spender avoids obvious references he might have made to the Army-McCarthy hearings or the House Un-American Activities Committee. Much more revealing are the fears of the dean and the English department chairman of the University of Cincinnati, where former Communist Spender, having been awarded a guest lectureship, gives an interview to the student newspaper. It is only toward the end of the journals that one learns Spender's American visa had, during the 1950's and 1960's, been coded to indicate that he was a Socialist. It is amusing and reassuring that the 1980's customs officer has to ask his superior the meaning of the code.

Spender travels increasingly in the mid-1950's; these trips are varied and somewhat bold considering the prevailing political climate. For example, he attends the European Cultural Association conference of Soviet and Western intellectuals in Venice during March, 1956. The conflicts between Soviet Bloc representatives and Western writers disillusioned with Communism in the wake of Stalinism are particularly profound. Italian writer and Socialist

Ignazio Silone attacks one of the Russians as a Soviet agent. Jean-Paul Sartre publicly states that dialogue with Communist intellectuals is impossible given the irreconcilable nature of Western and Soviet ideologies. All the while the Russians sit by, occasionally murmuring how glad they are to be in Venice. Spender is quick to note in his journal the absurdity of the situation; his satiric novella *Engaged in Writing* (1958) was based on this failed attempt at rapprochement.

Following a brief tour of India and trips to Japan for the International PEN Conference (1957) and the Congress for Cultural Freedom (sponsor of *Encounter* magazine), Spender increasingly involves himself in a series of teaching engagements, the first of these a six-month stay at the University of California, Berkeley, which he begins in 1959. His teaching activities are one of the most curious elements of his career. He fills guest lectureships at numerous American universities, some major institutions like Berkeley, but many more at schools that are mediocre, isolated, and undistinguished. Having arrived at one of the latter, Spender inevitably bemoans the poor preparation of his students, his accommodations, his loneliness. In a way, his teaching, editorial, and conference activities are at the heart of his often repeated feelings of self-dissatisfaction, for though pursued for financial reasons, they limit the time available for writing verse, Spender's first love.

Spender consistently resists sensationalism in these journals, though he had countless opportunities to introduce it. He treds very lightly when discussing reasons for the failure of his first marriage, though he establishes a neat synthesis between this personal crisis and the chaotic events in Europe preceding the onset of World War II. He similarly avoids extended discussion of his homosexuality or that of many of his friends, though he inevitably notes it (even when not particularly relevant) and makes observations and speculations, particularly about Auden and Isherwood. He is less chary about his own sexuality as the journals enter the 1970's, often referring to a young man whom he calls "B." Even here, however, Spender's frankness mirrors changed times rather than indicating a turn to gossip or sensationalism.

The Moscow entries, which focus on Spender's meeting with the Communist spy Guy Burgess after the latter's defection, are among the most poignant sections of the journals. The year is 1960, and Spender is traveling with his friend Muriel Buttinger Gardiner, the Elizabeth of his celebrated autobiography *World Within World* (1951) and the woman to whom he dedicated the present volume. Burgess lives comfortably by Soviet standards. His apartment, though in an ugly building, is furnished with a Chagall reproduction and a pair of tasteful paintings by gifted amateurs. Bach and Mozart sonatas stand open on an upright piano, and the room is filled with books, including an inscribed edition of Winston Churchill's memoirs. Burgess appears content, though he suffers from homesickness and would like to see his aging mother. Even more, he is hurt by former friends who have written unkindly about his defection. One in particular had himself been a paid Communist agent in Vienna. Upon returning to London, Spender takes it upon himself to explore the possibility of Burgess' coming home. It is curious to see the noncommittal and equivocating statements made by those in power in regard to this.

Spender's meetings with major contemporary artists fill the pages of his journals. English sculptor Henry Moore, interviewed for *Encounter*, discusses six varieties of drawing, arranged in hierarchic order from exploratory and descriptive to "metamorphic" (in which the realistic becomes the abstract) and imaginative (which verges on fantasy and dream). Francis Bacon notes with distress the loveless style of his painting since the death of a friend, while David Hockney enthusiastically describes how he superimposes film images to create what Spender calls neo-Cubist, or Expressionist, photographic portraits. Spender enjoys these photos immensely; he himself paints in a style that resembles that of Paul Cézanne, and Spender's son Matthew has pursued a career in painting.

Entries increasingly turn to preoccupations with death. Spender had been both witness and participant in the new style of the Oxford poets. Eliot and Auden overshadowed Spender, but Spender has outlived them both, and many of the entries from the 1970's deal with the numerous lectures and symposia on this movement in which Spender participates. More significantly, these years provide the long-sought opportunity for Spender to return to his verse, to revise old works, and to compose new poems. It is both encouraging and hopeful that Spender, by the latter 1970's, resists the temptation to write new critical works. His preoccupation, indeed near obsession, is to complete his elegy "Auden's Funeral." Implied in this work is his burial of the past as well as his determination to face the future. The former literary and political radical appears content in his London and Provence homes. He enjoys the recognition he has received and finally has the leisure a poet's life demands.

Robert J. Forman

Sources for Further Study

Choice. XXIII, June, 1986, p. 1543.
Library Journal. CXI, February 15, 1986, p. 184.
The London Review of Books. VII, December 5, 1985, p. 6.
Los Angeles Times Book Review. January 19, 1986, p. 3.
New Statesman. CX, December 6, 1985, p. 28.
The New York Review of Books. XXXIII, April 24, 1986, p. 15.

The New York Times Book Review. XCI, January 26, 1986, p. 1.
Publishers Weekly. CCXXVIII, December 13, 1985, p. 49.
Time. CXXVII, January 20, 1986, p. 68.
Washington Post Book World. XVI, January 12, 1986, p. 1.

KATE VAIDEN

Author: Reynolds Price (1933-   )
Publisher: Atheneum Publishers (New York). 306 pp. $16.95
Type of work: Novel
Time: 1937-1984
Locale: North Carolina and Virginia

A powerful first-person narrative of a young woman's struggle against death and despair

Principal characters:
  KATE VAIDEN, the narrator
  DAN VAIDEN, her father
  FRANCES VAIDEN, her mother
  CAROLINE PORTER, her aunt
  SWIFT PORTER and
  WALTER PORTER, Caroline's sons
  NOONY, the Porters' black maid
  GASTON STEGALL, Kate's first love
  DOUGLAS LEE, Walter's companion, the father of Kate's child
  LEE VAIDEN, Kate and Douglas' child

With the first page of this stunning novel the reader enters the mind and life of the title character, who becomes as real as one's closest friend. Reynolds Price's achievement in creating a believable female narrator should not be too surprising for readers of his earlier work, who will remember, among other characters, the appealing Rosacoke Mustian of *A Long and Happy Life* (1962). His accomplishment here is even greater, for Kate is a richer, more mature, more introspective creation, a character who commands sympathy and respect.

Kate freely admits in her opening words that "the best thing about my life up to here is, nobody believes it." Price's plot is, indeed, melodramatic in the extreme. Before Kate reaches her eighteenth birthday, she has endured her father's fatal shooting of her mother and himself, the suicides of both the men with whom she has been intimate, and the birth of an illegitimate child. The measure of Price's skill is that he is able to use these sensational plot elements to bring his reader's attentions to his real concerns—how human beings deal with their choices, what control they have over their own destinies, and how the ties of compassion and caring bind them together.

The novel begins in 1984, when Kate is fifty-seven. As the reader discovers late in the book, she is recovering from cancer surgery, and she has, after forty years, decided to try to find the son she had abandoned when he was only four months old. The story she tells in her unforgettable voice is for him, for Lee. It is her explanation and her justification of her life and the choices she has made; as she tells the story, she explores again its meaning and her responsibility for what has happened to her.

The setting of Kate's account is territory familiar to readers of Price's earlier work: rural North Carolina and the nearby Piedmont cities of Greensboro and Raleigh, with journeys as far as Norfolk, Virginia. The scenes of Price's childhood in Macon, North Carolina, are Kate's—"scraggly spirea bushes" in the yard of her home, rocky creek banks, overgrown country graveyards. She rarely ventures farther than two hundred miles from her family, but for forty years they manage to be as remote from one another as if they lived on different continents.

The narrative begins with a death and a trip to a funeral—events that recur with appalling frequency in Kate's early life. It is the death of her mother's first cousin Taswell Porter in a motorcycle accident that sets off the first and most catastrophic of the incidents that determine her future. Eleven-year-old Kate and her mother, Frances, leave her father fuming at home in Greensboro while they go to Frances' childhood home in Macon for the burial. Although Kate does not discover the real reason for Dan's anger until many years later, she senses the tension between her parents and particularly Dan's resentment of Frances' attachment to her family: Caroline Porter, the sister who has been a mother to her; Caroline's husband, Holt; and their son Swift, only a few years younger than his aunt.

On the day after the funeral, Swift whisks Frances off, ostensibly to check the flowers on his brother's grave. Dan arrives unexpectedly and follows them into the countryside. Hours later, Kate is summoned from the dark garden where she has been sitting alone beside the tiny "penny garden" her mother made for her under the roots of a tree. Caroline forces Swift to tell the child what her instincts have already revealed. Dan and Frances are dead.

In their end is the shape of Kate's whole future. She first feels guilt, believing that her parents' quarrel was somehow her fault. If she had accepted her father's invitation to go with him to find Swift and Frances, she thinks, she might have saved them. Then she feels a deep sense of abandonment, an emotion that is to condition many of her later actions.

Price characterizes Kate as an inherently lovable person. She is, throughout most of the novel, surrounded by people who want to care for her. Caroline and Holt take her in as their daughter after the death of her parents, and their black servant, Noony, soon appoints herself Kate's adviser on sexual matters. Fob Foster, a middle-aged cousin, teaches her to ride, buys her a horse, and later gives her five hundred dollars with the instruction, "*Make* something of yourself." Kate returns their affection, yet she always withholds something. Angry with Caroline over an apparently trivial matter, she tells her on the fateful afternoon when Dan and Frances die, "I'll never trust anybody else." Indeed, she never seems absolutely secure again.

The nearest Kate comes to real happiness is in her inarticulate relationship with Gaston Stegall. They become lovers when she is almost thirteen and he only three years older. They meet as often as they can in a secluded mossy spot not far from the creek where her parents died, and there is in their uncomplicated loving more security and contentment than she is to find again. Yet latent in that happiness, as in her happy childhood with Dan and Frances, is death. When Gaston is graduated from high school, he joins the marines and writes Kate of his plans to come home. Then, inexplicably, near the end of a training exercise that requires him to crawl under machine-gun fire, he stands up and is killed instantly. His death increases Kate's sense that she is a kind of Jonah, a bringer of disaster on those she loves.

Once again Kate must face the lesson she had first learned on the afternoon when Caroline had left her alone with her "penny show" garden: *"People would leave you."* The only way to avoid being abandoned is to be the first to leave. This knowledge sets the pattern of Kate's life.

Kate's first flight is to Norfolk, to Caroline and Holt's son Walter. She knows of his estrangement from his family and community, connecting it with his leaving town some years earlier with a young orphan boy, Douglas Lee, but she is too young to understand the full implications of their relationship. She only recognizes Walter's kindness and senses that the same impulse which led him to take Douglas from the orphanage where he was stifling for lack of love will provide her with warmth and acceptance as well.

Nevertheless, Kate's quest for stability leads inexorably to further pain. She and Douglas Lee become lovers—Kate, chiefly because her body is hungry for the comfort she found in being with Gaston; Douglas, as a gesture of defiance against Walter, whose help and devotion have aroused in him more resentment than gratitude. Kate soon becomes pregnant. She quickly realizes the inadvisability of following Walter's plan to have Douglas marry her and incorporate the baby into their strange household. She knows that Douglas does not love her in the way she wants to be loved, and she runs again.

This time Kate takes refuge for two weeks with Tim, the widower taxi driver who had taken her under his wing on her first day in Norfolk, before she had found Walter. He, too, begins to care for her, and she takes another escape route—the train to Raleigh with Douglas, who offers her a new, independent life. It takes only a few hours to convince her that this is the wrong course, and when the train stops in Macon, she slips off and returns to Caroline and Holt. Remarkably patient, they accept her without question and nurse her through her pregnancy and her son's early months.

In her child, Lee, Kate sees yet another individual demanding commitment from her. She tries to meet his needs and reestablishes contact with Douglas Lee; he has settled in Raleigh as chauffeur to a blind piano tuner, Whitfield Eller. She delays her move to Raleigh, however, until she sees in the city newspaper a report of the wounding of Eller by an unknown intruder. Remembering that Douglas had stabbed Walter in the hand before she left Norfolk, she guesses what has happened. She leaves Lee with Caroline and goes to Raleigh. Douglas has disappeared; she takes his job of driving his attractive young employer, who joins the list of those who want to share their life with Kate.

Douglas puts an end to that hope with a final act of resentment and defiance. He kills himself in Whitfield Eller's bathtub, knowing that he will hurt all three of the people who have cared most for him—Eller, Walter, and Kate. Once again Kate sees herself as the bringer of death. When she leaves Eller with his aunt in the mountains shortly after Douglas' death, the reader senses that she does it as much for his protection as for her own. She has left despair and death in her wake, and she is determined to do it no more. She goes to Norfolk to join Walter for Douglas' burial, then walks out of the lives of everyone in her family for the next forty years; her life, for all intents and purposes, ends when she is seventeen. Memories of Lee haunt her, but she knows that she has left him in the hands of a saint—Caroline, who now takes on a third generation of motherless relatives.

The long next chapter in Kate's life is quickly told. She returns to Greensboro, where she had lived with her parents, and seeks help from the woman who had been her much-admired fifth-grade teacher. With Miss Limer's help, she finishes high school through a correspondence course and works for a time in a college library. She sets for herself a path of deliberate restraint and limitation, reaching out for love only once more, with a returning World War II veteran. They are almost ready to marry when she is impelled to tell him her story. He cannot accept it. As she ruefully admits, "An outlaw mother is the black last nightmare any man can face." Thus she is abandoned once again.

Miss Limer retires, and Kate moves to Raleigh, where she becomes a legal secretary. She lives quietly, makes friends, male and female, but never lets them get too close. What her experience has taught her, she says, is to recognize the truth when she hears it—a skill that makes her a valuable employee. In the back of her mind is always guilt about her son, but nothing forces her to take action until she takes a trip to Rome. There she is thrust unexpectedly into the crypt at Saint Peter's and shown the bones of the apostle, whom she calls "the biggest quitter in human history." The experience seems a message to her. It is time to go home, find those *she* has abandoned, and ask forgiveness. She suddenly realizes that Caroline and Holt would be by now more than a hundred and Lee nearing forty. "That I hadn't laid eyes on any of them, or sent the simplest message, seemed a brand of denial past understanding."

Before she can seek reconciliation, Kate must go through her illness, then make her peace with Swift Porter, whose unwelcome attentions had precipitated her first flight to Walter and Douglas and, ultimately, Lee's birth.

From Swift, now tied to a bed in a nursing home, she learns at last the truth about his love for Frances, which helped to destroy her parents' marriage. He gives her a letter her father had left for her many years earlier, just before he set off on his ill-fated visit to Macon. Dan had written of his hope that he would be able to "watch [her] grow up and have [her] own children, maybe one boy at least." Instantly Kate's perspective on her life shifts, and the apparently calamitous choices she has made now appear to be part of a divine design leading to Lee's birth. "Beyond that," she adds, "I was still blind as Whitfield to all the rest—whether I'd moved to anybody's will except my own rank notions, needs and fears." She is now ready to find her son, who is not very far away; he has joined the navy and lives in the Norfolk house he inherited from Walter. All that remains is to tell Lee her story, the story that makes up the novel. She begins, as the reader ends.

What is it that makes this book so moving? First and foremost, there is Kate's voice, honest and real, rooted in Price's native country and in the experience of people he has known. There can be few male writers who have entered more convincingly into the mind of a female protagonist. Second, there is the fully developed cast of characters, each one depicted compassionately. Almost all of them have their own private anguish, from the tormented Douglas Lee to the selfless Caroline, who can rise beyond loss and betrayal again and again to nurture others. Finally there is Price's world as a whole, a place where people care deeply for one another, establish bonds, and provide loving support. It is this world which gives Kate the courage to persevere and triumph against what appear to be insuperable odds and which makes the reader respond so positively to her story.

Elizabeth Johnston Lipscomb

Sources for Further Study

Booklist. LXXXII, May 15, 1986, p. 1358.
Christian Science Monitor. LXXVIII, June 25, 1986, p. 21.
Kirkus Reviews. LIV, April 15, 1986, p. 575.
Library Journal. CXI, June 1, 1986, p. 142.
The New Republic. CXCV, September 29, 1986, p. 40.
The New York Review of Books. XXXIII, September 25, 1986, p. 55.
The New York Times Book Review. XCI, June 29, 1986, p. 1.
Newsweek. CVII, June 23, 1986, p. 78.
Publishers Weekly. CCXXIX, April 25, 1986, p. 67.
USA Today. IV, June 27, 1986, p. 4D.
Washington Post Book World. XVI, July 6, 1986, p. 1.

KRIPPENDORF'S TRIBE

Author: Frank Parkin (1940-   )
Publisher: Atheneum Publishers (New York). 192 pp. $13.95
Type of work: Novel
Time: The 1980's
Locale: Great Britain

A savagely comic vision of contemporary family life in a decaying British society, the corrosive satire and black humor of which intensify as the novel progresses

> *Principal characters:*
> JAMES KRIPPENDORF, an unemployed anthropologist
> VERONICA YARDLEY, his wife, a television journalist
> SHELLEY, their thirteen-year-old daughter
> MICKEY, their twelve-year-old son
> EDMUND, their seven-year-old son

Krippendorf's Tribe, Frank Parkin's first venture into fiction, is an irreverent black comedy about the decay of family life in a British society ravaged by riots, strikes, bomb scares, racism, unemployment, and vandalism, to list but a few of the evidences of decline and unrest that Parkin cites in the course of his novel. Although Parkin's previous works—*Middle Class Realism* (1968), *Class Inequality and Political Order* (1971), *Marxism and Class Theory: A Bourgeois Critique* (1979), and *Max Weber* (1982)—are academic treatises in the field of political science, he betrays none of the tentativeness and unevenness of performance that often characterize inexperienced novelists. On the contrary, *Krippendorf's Tribe*—a sustained assault on propriety buttressed by brilliant intellectual wit and mordant social commentary—places him in the company of such fine contemporary British satirists as Kingsley Amis, Tom Sharpe, David Lodge, and Malcolm Bradbury.

James Krippendorf, who is an unemployed anthropologist, finds himself in charge of a chaotic and unruly family. His wife, Veronica Yardley, is perpetually out of town, her career in television journalism involving her with lepers in Calcutta, the misappropriation of earthquake funds, political riots, guerrilla warfare, and so forth. As the sole force against domestic entropy, Krippendorf inherits an unenviable situation. His twelve-year-old son, Mickey, is passing through an incendiary and sadistic phase, napalming the neighbor's cat and trying to flush his brother down the toilet in order to extort a confession from his "political prisoner." His seven-year-old son, Edmund, is seemingly incapable of mastering the rudiments of alimentary ingestion. As Krippendorf conjectures, "One reason why Edmund was so thin . . . was that although a great quantity of food got as far as his mouth it proved merely to be in transit to various other external destinations." His thirteen-year-old daughter, Shelley, who resents Mickey's stealing the batteries from her vibrator, sports green and magenta hair, wears dresses fashioned out of aluminum foil, and passes through various ideological phases, ranging from Hare Krishna to the Young Conservatives. Resigned to endless defeats for the cause of rationality, Krippendorf regards his own children with scientific detachment and scholarly reserve. The ironic disparity between his professorial attitude and the bizarre, if not brutal, behavior of his children, not to mention his fellow citizens, is the source of much of the novel's outrageous humor.

The plot revolves around Krippendorf's accepting a lucrative research grant to do anthropological fieldwork in the Amazon Basin. Unfortunately, he has already spent the £14,800 bestowed upon him by the Malinowski Research Institute; the allure of a new Volvo, a three-month vacation, and other amenities of civilized life proves stronger than the desire to study primitive savages in South America. As a result, he is compelled to adopt an inventive strategy: that of concocting an imaginary tribe—the Shelmikedmu—whose culture and customs are based upon the systematic observation of his children's behavior and the role reversal implicit in his own domestic situation. Krippendorf reflects that although his children's behavior

> did not appear to conform to any recognizable norms of social behaviour . . . they were too consistent and predictable to be classified as random. There must be some hidden pattern underlying the apparent chaos, some implicit logic which could render their behaviour perfectly intelligible. He took a pencil and notebook from his pocket and recorded the order and frequency with which they punched, bit and gouged one another, and the approximate ratio of physical to verbal assaults.

The particular observations recorded in this notebook are eventually transformed into "Savagery and Socialization in Amazonia," the fourth chapter of his manuscript.

The role reversal in Shelmikedmu society that Krippendorf posits may reflect wish fulfillment on his part, for in this imaginary society the women are the breadwinners while the men are responsible for household chores. Hunting is contemptuously referred to as women's work, whereas sweeping, scrubbing, and cooking are honorific activities that confer superior status upon the men. His research project—"The Hegemony of Myth: Social and Symbolic Reproduction Among the Shelmikedmu of the Upper Amazon Basin"—is predicated upon this fertile premise. As Krippendorf suggests, rationalizing his unusual strategy,

> the more he thought about it the more certain he felt that he could give value for money by producing as good a piece of fieldwork as he might have done if he had actually gone there to do it. In some respects he might even be able to create a work of greater originality and insight than would be possible for somebody on the spot. Familiarity gave rise to its own peculiar blindness. In any case, anthropology was an unusual science. It was a well-known fact that if two anthropologists of different schools were to study the same tribe they would come up with two entirely different and contradictory accounts. If actually being in the place and witnessing things at first hand led to such confusion there was a sound case to be made for keeping one's social distance.

The objects of the satire in this novel are thus threefold: First, the decaying British welfare state—Krippendorf receives both research funding and unemployment insurance, his self-designated field of applied hermeneutics guaranteeing the unlikelihood of his procuring a regular job; second, academia in general—"I am no longer in the employ of the university," Krippendorf affirms, "but that hardly qualifies as an impediment these days, now that they teach nothing but commercial arithmetic and fisheries science"; third, anthropology in particular—empirical research, objective data, and painstaking fieldwork are not only dispensable, but they also have no bearing upon academic acceptability. Scholarly discourse itself seems also dispensable, for an enterprising, innovative, and demographically conscious young editor successfully has waged war against the scientific jargon and theoretical obscurantism of the *British Journal of Structural Anthropology*, converting that stodgy journal into *Exotica*, an anthropological *Playboy* of sorts which combines popular journalism and pornographic titillation. *Exotica* offers Krippendorf munificent sums per illustrated article and provides the novel with rich opportunities for comedy. The heavily edited version of Krippendorf's "Cognitive Dissonance and Symbolic Mediations: A Neo-Structuralist Account of Circumcision Rites Among the Shelmikedmu" becomes "Fantasies and Foreskins"; his "Witchcraft and Wittgenstein: Utterances as a Mode of Social Control" becomes "Amazonian Knockers"; and his treatise on uxoricide becomes "Bumper Boobs and Bums."

Moreover, the machinations he must practise in order to fabricate the photographs that accompany his articles make for hilarious comedy. Krippendorf covers his sons with grease paint and induces them to act out a ritual circumcision. He seduces the Filipino mother of one of Edmund's friends and photographs her mammoth breasts, for Shelmikedmus believe that the bigger a woman's breasts the greater her power of black magic, and the men, as a consequence, live in terror of being victimized by malevolent nipple pointing. Indeed, this mammary preoccupation is even reflected in their language: There are seventeen terms for different types of nipples and twenty-two for different types of cleavage. Fondling the Filipino woman's breasts in the midst of his conquest, Krippendorf is led to ponder the impoverishment of "our own classificatory vocabulary":

> Given the tremendous interest in that part of the body, in western culture at least, one might have supposed that an adequate descriptive nomenclature would by now have evolved. . . . Does it not strike you as anomalous that anatomical objects which are so palpably venerated, and so proudly displayed, should nevertheless fail to yield a set of classificatory terms designed to capture their multiple forms and varieties? . . . After all, the Eskimos have a dozen or more names for different types of snow.

Further, Krippendorf must also gull an Ethiopian baby-sitter and a Thai nurse into posing for him. The result of his lust for full-frontal centerfolds is gonorrhea, and even this inspires an article—"Notes on Shelmikedmu Conceptions of Disease"—an interpretation of disease as punishment for bad behavior. As Krippendorf muses, his kind of anthropology continually throws up new challenges not generally encountered by the more orthodox schools.

Suffice it to say that Parkin's parody of anthropological language, which many believe is inadvertent self-parody in and of itself, is delightfully wicked. Moreover, the satiric effect is compounded by the fact that all of these laughably improbable events take place against the pervasive backdrop of a British society in real decay.

The hyperbolic absurdities escalate as the life-style of Krippendorf's imaginary tribe and that of his real family intertwine and interfuse to the point that they become virtually indistinguishable. After an elaborate kinship ceremony celebrating Shelley's first menstrual period, Mickey inadvertently electrocutes the Welsh housekeeper, a recent and unwelcome addition to the household. The storage of the corpse poses some logistical problems since freezing has caused it to bloat and expand. Some dexterous work with a Black and Decker saw, however, divides the problem into manageable parts, and protracted cannibalism causes it to disappear altogether. At the atavistic climax of the book, the children have regressed to the point of utter savagery: They live in a tree house, Mickey and Edmund kill neighborhood domestic pets for food, they cook their meals over a fire in the barbecue, Mickey and Shelley cohabit incestuously, and Krippendorf's only regret is that the boys engage in hunting, which, after all, is women's work. At the end of the book, Krippendorf and his tribe are headed for the jungle, leaders of Exotica Tours's first Shelmikedmu expedition.

A novel whose master tropes are irony and hyperbole in some sense resists criticism; either it is funny or it is not, and *Krippendorf's Tribe* is funny. Even though this novel is radically unlike its serious counterparts, works such as *Lord of the Flies* (1954) and *Heart of Darkness* (1902), which also thematize the possibilities of savage regression when the external restraints of society are removed, it is nevertheless discomfiting to be reminded, in however humorous a fashion, that civilization is based upon the renunciation of instinctual desire and that the gap between savagery and propriety can be bridged in an instant.

Greig E. Henderson

Sources for Further Study

Kirkus Reviews. LIII, December 1, 1986, p. 1286.
Library Journal. CXI, February 1, 1986, p. 94.

Los Angeles Times Book Review. February 9, 1986, p. 3.
New Statesman. CIX, March 22, 1986, p. 30.
The New York Times Book Review. XCI, March 2, 1986, p. 13.
Newsweek. CVII, January 27, 1986, p. 62.
Publishers Weekly. CCXXVIII, November 29, 1986, p. 36.
Time. CXXVII, February 17, 1986, p. 78.
Times Literary Supplement. April 12, 1986, p. 406.
Wilson Library Bulletin. LX, May, 1986, p. 72.

LAND OF SUPERIOR MIRAGES
New and Selected Poems

Author: Adrien Stoutenburg (1916-1982)
Edited by David R. Slavitt
Foreword by James Dickey
Publisher: The Johns Hopkins University Press (Baltimore, Maryland). 122 pp.
  $16.50; paperback $7.95
Type of work: Poetry

A complex, vivid, and personalized drama of nature, history, and time is Adrien Stoutenburg's poetic legacy

This posthumous collection of Adrien Stoutenburg's best work establishes that relatively obscure poet as a major voice of conscience. The new poems, as well as those selected from her three earlier volumes, show her to be a vivid, passionate writer whose concerns touch the most fundamental issues in human experience. There are poems here of pain and outrage, as well as poems of more gentle emotions—but there is never merely an unfelt thought. While ideas are plentiful in her work, they are always ideas cloaked in sensation. Moreover, though her works reveal her great skills and her attentiveness to finding the most effective word or image, one never gets the impression that her style is showy. Every poem, every trope, is in the service of something else.

In his foreword, James Dickey calls attention to Stoutenburg's blend of delicacy and power. This quality is nowhere more apparent than in the selection of new poems that David R. Slavitt has decided to place first in this collection. These pieces are mostly short sketches, hoarse lyrics of stubborn frailty and a tough courage that does battle with despair. The section is framed by "Next Door to the Rest Home Laundry" and "Intensive Care Unit," two poems that seem most directly autobiographical as responses to the poet's battle with esophageal cancer. The poems surrounded by this pair reflect a time of summing-up, something Stoutenburg does not only for herself but for everyone as well. A characteristic passage is the following one from "Before We Drown":

> We are here to measure waves
> and the length of the marlin's gill
> and to gather up into castles
> the wandering, witless sand
> before the tide turns
> and we see our dead selves
> mirrored, open-mouthed,
> in its glass shoulders.

Mankind's civilized pursuits and the question of how these test the claims of time and nature are Stoutenburg's subjects over and over again. Here, they are quietly joined in the poem's closing images. "Storm's Eye" is another kind of farewell, a poem of lashing sounds and images in which the valiant but doomed flight of Icarus feeds the speaker's imagination: "But when I arrive there/ at the fire-ringed hub,/ I shall not blaze any more fiercely/ than I do here and now."

As a poet, Adrien Stoutenburg burned fiercely through her whole career. Her first book, *Heroes, Advise Us* (1964), announced her intense ambition with the long poem "This Journey," an imaginative re-creation of Captain Robert F. Scott's arduous effort to reach and return from the South Pole. This powerful work is really a sequence poem in various voices and mixed styles. Generally, though, the lines are rough-hewn into a kind of verbal echo of the nerve- and muscle-shattering experience. "This Journey" illustrates Stoutenburg's fascination with history and her startling ability to throw herself into the past so as to extract and project its constant human meaning. Though sometimes individual units in this long sequence go flat, they are more than redeemed by the majority of strong passages and the cumulative effect—Stoutenburg creates here an impression of epic energy and magnitude.

While "This Journey" risks being downright prosaic for the sake of certain kinds of verisimilitude, many of Stoutenburg's poems from *Heroes, Advise Us* gain their power from the poet's sure and appropriate handling of traditional devices. A stanza from "The Allergic" can serve to demonstrate that formal ease:

> Gazelles must keep in bounds, and orioles
> transport their gold combines to darker trees;
> the world of pelt and plume and naked rose
> is battered by the dust's duplicities.

The world of pelt, plume, and rose is man's world, too, but in a great many of Stoutenburg's most majestic poems, she reminds her readers that the world is not only man's and that man's exploitation of it is a crime of such proportion that it calls into question the very notion that humankind constitutes a higher order of life.

The title poem of her next volume, *Short History of the Fur Trade* (1968), will always stand as Stoutenburg's major achievement. In this magnificent poem, her passion for history and for the animal world has found its perfect subject. "Short History of the Fur Trade" is also a sequence poem, though much shorter than "This Journey." Each of its parts is densely textured with imagery, and almost every line blazes with the fierceness one has learned to expect from this powerful poet. The first sequence reviews how the monarchs of the ancient world began the unnecessary exploitation of those creatures who ruled the animal kingdom. From the opening lines, Stoutenburg's tone is unmistakable:

Lions were always high style,
the tail, a bearded rope,
glowing from angular pharaohs' belts;
the paws, chrysanthemums with thorns,
flung over priestly torsos
in a dead embrace.

This combination of precision and imagination runs through the entire poem, which is surely one of the most important long poems written in the United States in recent decades. In whole or in part, it is deserving of being included in any anthology of contemporary poetry.

The ravaging of the North American wilderness by traders and trappers is the main subject of this poem, though Stoutenburg does not forget that Jacques Chartier, Samuel de Champlain, Henry Hudson, and John Astor were performing as agents of investors or governments. These heroic men are viewed, finally, as savages and predators; they are devalued to the status of the creatures they killed. Indeed, Stoutenburg's compassion is all on one side.

Stoutenburg's attitude toward the American Indian nations is mildly ambiguous. While she records the uses they made of the bison, the antelope, the bear, the beaver, and other animals, it is clear that she considers these activities less exploitative. Moreover, full use was made of each animal. Rarely was one killed merely for ornament or luxury. Stoutenburg's language, as always in this poem, is richly evocative:

Beaten hides of bison kept out the cold
and their swift horns, headgear for warriors,
blazed like new moons turned into bone,
or served as flagons for an antelope's blood. . . .

Still, she writes of the "cosmetic bear" and the "ornamental porcupine"—reminding one how man takes more from the rest of living nature than he will ever need. These Indians, the poem suggests, were at least conscious of their questionable intrusions upon the rights of other members of the animal domain. The poet imagines that the spirits of the animals were reconciled to what the Indians did because they heard, in the tribes' ceremonies, "the ritual grunt of brute apology."

Other parts of this amazing sequence poem, particularly the section called "John Jacob Astor," deserve far more attention than they have so far received. *Land of Superior Mirages* provides a new opportunity for readers to find Adrien Stoutenburg's best work—"Short History of the Fur Trade" being the best of the best. Other fine poems selected from her second volume include "Sky Diver," "Avalanche," "Hunter's Cabin," and "Who Loves to Lie with Me," the latter of which records, with a quiet intensity, the busy world of life to be discovered where the stems of plants enter the soil. This varied universe of insects moves Stoutenburg as much as the larger and more obvious scale of nature that one is accustomed to observing. Over and over again, it is her passionate attention that one learns to admire:

> There is such a buzz here;
> my ears whirl with it
> and the wind spinning it
> into legs, arms, squeaking trees,
> motes, mites, and the precise blue tick
> inside my wrist, my temple—
> the same inside you
> with your forehead and mouth beside me
> and your eyes watching me
> watch the rounded earth
> where the lizards run,
> their tongues flicking what seems sunlight
> and is love.

When a person beholds with the acuteness and intensity of an Adrien Stoutenburg, then what he sees, as the lines above suggest, becomes a part of him: Subject and object, outside and inside, merge and lift to a new plane of being. The person inside the poem—or outside it—who shares this penetrating vision is also lifted. Stoutenburg, sooner or later, brings to every careful reader his or her own moments of transcendence.

The concluding segment of the present volume offers selections from the final gathering compiled by the author, *Greenwich Mean Time* (1979). Although all of Stoutenburg's poetry is finally personal, however obliquely, the poems in this section seem most directly so, especially the shorter lyrics. Poems such as "The Sleep of Animals," "Cellar," and "Message" continue and deepen the poet's exploration of her nature-consciousness. The world out there is more and more inside her, and she is less and less bound by the man-made, conventional perceptions of time and space. In these poems, as in the final ones chosen by Slavitt for the initial section, Stoutenburg's talent for finding the daring image with which to register an emotional truth is undiminished. Her interest in nature, history, and the conserving role of art now is enfolded by a rich and wise fascination with time itself.

"Greenwich Mean Time" is the title of the third major poem of Stoutenburg's career. This, another sequence poem, is a complex meditation on the nature of time and on the history of man's attempts to manage his experience, his memory, and his future. Stoutenburg regards man's various time-telling schemes, calendars, and adjustments as part of his natural flight from his mortality. Solar time, star time, calendar time, lifetime, jet time—these are some of the subjects through which Stoutenburg builds a portrait of man's valiant, absurd, and inevitable struggle with the unstoppable passing moments.

With the final section of this sequence, "Beyond Greenwich," the book closes—though few readers will want it to end:

> I shall plunge through
> the green gut of the abyss,
> far below serpent or urchin
> down where blackness and silence
> make midnight seem a blaze of operas.
>
> I shall dive deep, deeper.
> I shall become a fish of sorts.
> I shall wear a skin of icicles.
> I shall avoid all hooks
> though my teeth be as sharp
> as the cutting edge of the wings of swans.

This closing simile may again remind the reader of Stoutenburg's special blend of delicacy and power that James Dickey applauds in his preface. Adrien Stoutenburg's poetry is a mature, impassioned, and innovative art and makes much of what is praised in contemporary poetry seem pallid and ephemeral by comparison. David R. Slavitt must be commended for his judicious selections that allow one to discover, or rediscover, the work of this most significant poet. *Land of Superior Mirages* offers a poetry of permanence. A complex, vivid, and personalized drama of nature, history, and time is Adrien Stoutenburg's poetic legacy.

Philip K. Jason

Source for Further Study

The New York Times Book Review. XCI, February 15, 1987, p. 42.

LAST POEMS

Author: Paul Celan (1920-1970)
Translated from the German by Katharine Washburn and Margret Guillemin
Introduction by Katharine Washburn
Publisher: North Point Press (San Francisco). 256 pp. $20.00
Type of work: Poetry and autobiographical fable

The most celebrated figure in contemporary German poetry reflects on the Nazi Holocaust and his own approaching death in this bilingual collection of surreal, minimalist poems

The catastrophic fact of the Nazi Holocaust has been considered so estructive to the human spirit that one critic, Theodore Adorno, has proclaimed, "After Auschwitz there can be no more poetry." Among the millions of lives devastated by the Nazi regime was that of Paul Ancel, a Romanian Jew who survived the forced labor camps but was lastingly haunted by that experience and by the Nazis' execution of his parents. After years of exile in Paris under the name of Paul Celan, he took his own life in 1970 by jumping into the Seine. Tormented as he was, however, and as strongly as part of him subscribed to the sort of absolute pessimism expressed in Adorno's dictum, Celan nevertheless completed nine volumes of poetry. In these brilliantly paradoxical books, he somehow draws creative force from the abiding sense of nothingness and despair that the Holocaust produced in him.

Last Poems constitutes an ideal introduction to Celan's work, for this collection of ninety-nine poems (most of which have not been previously translated into English) presents the writer in the final, most powerful stages of his development. Selected and ably translated by Katharine Washburn and Margret Guillemin, these poems from Celan's last three volumes—*Lichtzwang* (1970; *Force of Light*), *Schneepart* (1971; *Snow-Part*), and *Zeitgehöft* (1976; *The Farmstead of Time*)—show the poet reaching his minimalist limits of hard-edged compression while also continuing to achieve the effects of verbal wit and strangely hypnotic lyricism that always characterized his work. In addition to these poems from Celan's three posthumous volumes, the translators also include Celan's short autobiographical fable "Conversation in the Mountains" (1959), and Washburn provides an informative (though sometimes formidably academic) introduction to Celan's life and writings that suggests the impressive range of his learning and allusions.

Although "Conversation in the Mountains" is the earliest piece of writing in the book in its date of composition, the translators place it last in the volume—perhaps because, even though it is written in prose, its meanings are often more elusive and enigmatic than those of many of the poems. Nevertheless, the fable helps locate Celan's moorings in the tradition of Holocaust literature, and it also provides a sardonic dramatization of Celan's problematic relation to his poetic self, his audience, and the worlds within and around him. Significantly, Celan wrote the fable after a failed attempt at communication—according to Washburn he had "missed [a] meeting with an unnamed person on a mountain road"—and the stuttering, halting conversation that occurs in the fable fails to establish much more than that both the speaker and his interlocutor are Jewish "babblers" who are prevented by "veils" and "shadows" (images of their dark and cloudy past) from experiencing any direct communion with the beautiful Alpine countryside around them. In the manner of a Samuel Beckett play, their interactions with the external world are comically and pathetically reduced, yet in this dark world in which "the sun (and not only the sun) had gone down in the west," there are images of a limited achievement and hope. Though the two Jews are mostly blind, they do perceive and express images of the natural beauty around them, if only in a strangely twisted way: "an image barely enters [the eyes] before it gets caught in the web[;] . . . a thread from the veil . . . winds itself around the image and gets it with child, half-image, half-veil." Celan thus suggests a metaphor for his strangely internalized, surrealistic mode of poetry: Images from the natural world are covered over by the "veil" of his brooding, Holocaust-haunted imagination, and a new sort of poetry is born.

Though the Romanian Celan knew a number of languages, emigrated to Paris after the war, and was strongly influenced by the French surrealists, he chose—perversely and paradoxically—to write in German, to create in the language of the oppressor and the destroyer. The Washburn-Guillemin bilingual edition of the poems helps the reader (even the reader who is not expert in reading German) appreciate one of the reasons for Celan's strange choice: The use of German compound nouns greatly enhances his effects of minimalist density. Thus, many of his lines in German consist of only a single word that requires several English words to translate.

Another aspect of Celan's minimalism is that he severely narrows his range of imagery. In poem after poem, the reader enters a dark and usually silent world of snow and sand, stones and boats, blood and litter. Just as Celan chose to confine himself in the German language, he also characteristically fixed his poetic vision on the fundamental elements of his experiences in forced labor camps, where he worked hauling debris out of rivers and shoveling rocks onto roads. Yet even while asserting these poems as petrified Germanic reactions to his dehumanizing experiences, Celan also transforms these static and depressing elements into what he calls in one poem "the lark-shaped stone" of verse that moves and sings. Though Celan's surrealistic indefiniteness seems to discourage narrowly clarified interpretations of any of of the poems, many of them seem to be in one sense poems about the attempt to create poetry, with language of voyages, journeys, and walking conveying the speaker's movement toward his goal of poetic expression and spiritual fulfillment. Images of leaves and flowers,

have/ everything/ for this evening." On the other hand, a later series of poems seems surprisingly and joyfully to be referring to Celan's visit to Israel in 1960, where he apparently enjoyed an intimate, loving relationship with another person:

> There was
> the fig-splinter on your lip,
>
> there was
> Jerusalem around us
> . . . .
> there was I
> within you.

In the final twelve poems of the Washburn-Guillemin collection, Celan once again addresses himself to the approach of death; he seems once more to be addressing his parents in an imagined underworld and drawing himself ever more closely into their "circle" or "ring." Nevertheless, his jubilant experience of love in the Jewish homeland seems to have rejuvenated his wit and playfulness. At the end of one poem, Celan declares almost jauntily, "from the fate-engine falls/ our measure," with a pun on the "measure" of their lives and the studied "measures" of his verse. In another poem, he describes dying as "the game of the highest gravity/ of fallingsickness."

Thus the final verses in *Last Poems* show Celan moving toward his suicide, after more than two decades of struggling with that temptation. Yet, simultaneously, the book also shows him striving for, and often achieving, spiritual sustenance through his continuing quest for the authentic expression of his extraordinary states of mind. Throughout the book, this quest often seems almost literally to be keeping him alive, as he moves back and forth in his imagination between the lands of the living and the dead. In the end, it is his enduring quest for spiritual sustenance, and his achievement in eloquently expressing the human experience of that quest, that makes Paul Celan's work such a resounding refutation to Adorno's idea that poetry could ever be impossible.

Terry L. Andrews

Sources for Further Study

Booklist. LXXXIII, October 15, 1986, p. 321.
Library Journal. CXI, June 15, 1986, p. 70.
The New York Times Book Review. XCI, November 9, 1986, p. 21.
Publishers Weekly. CCXXIX, April 18, 1986, p. 57.
TriQuarterly. Fall, 1986, p. 172.

LESS THAN ONE
Selected Essays

Author: Joseph Brodsky (1940-   )
Publisher: Farrar, Strauss and Giroux (New York). 501 pp. $25.00
Type of work: Essays

Literary, political, and autobiographical essays by one of the most talented living Russian poets

Joseph Brodsky is considered by many contemporary critics to be not only the finest poet currently writing in Russian but also one of the preeminent living poets. A Soviet Jewish exile since 1972, Brodsky has been poet-in-residence at several American universities, notably the University of Michigan and Columbia University. *Less Than One* is a generous collection of his essays on such Russian poets as Anna Akhmatova, Marina Tsvetaeva, and Osip Mandelstam; the Russian prose writers Fyodor Dostoevski and Andrey Platonov; the Western poets W. H. Auden, Constantine Cavafy, Dante, Eugenio Montale, and Derek Walcott; the cities of Constantinople, Alexandria, and Saint Petersburg/Leningrad; and two largely autobiographical memoirs serving as opening and concluding chapters: "Less Than One" and "In a Room and a Half."

In "Less Than One," Brodsky introduces two themes that he will weave through most of his work: his conviction that poetry is man's supreme achievement (even a writer's "biography is in his twists of language"), and his personal sense of estrangement, isolation, solitude ("the rest of my life can be viewed as a nonstop avoidance of its most importunate aspects"). His tone is candidly intimate, self-confident, sometimes astringent, but never self-pitying. His prose is energetic, incisive, often eloquent, occasionally grandiose.

Brodsky's parents lived in a cramped apartment, termed "a room and a half," in Saint Petersburg (he abhors the city's Soviet name, Leningrad); the poverty, vigor, and cleanliness of his parents constitute his first memories. His father was a journalist and photographer who became a naval officer during World War II, then served as curator of the photography department in Saint Petersburg's Navy Museum, which the boy would visit admiringly. The son recalls frequent walks home with his father from what he regarded as the city's most magnificent edifice. He yearns for the splendor of Russia's naval history, poor in victories but rich in "nobility of spirit":

> To this day, I think that the country would do a hell of a lot better if it had for its national banner not that foul double-headed imperial fowl or the vaguely masonic hammer-and-sickle, but the flag of the Russian Navy: our glorious, incomparably beautiful flag of St. Andrew: the diagonal blue cross against a virgin-white background.

In 1950, the poet's father was demobilized because of a Stalinist decree that no Jew could rise higher than a commander's rank in the navy. At the age of forty-seven, he began a new, unstable career as an itinerant free-lance photographer, while the mother earned an equally meager living as a council clerk. Joseph left his schooling at fifteen to contribute to the family's income by working in a factory. After a year as a milling-machine operator, he became a hospital morgue attendant and began writing poems. When he applied for admission to a submarine academy, he was rejected because he was Jewish.

Brodsky's reminiscences are vague about his subsequent imprisonment. All that is known is that he had already made a reputation as a talented poet when Soviet authorities summoned him before a Leningrad court in 1964 to answer to the charge of "social parasitism"; he was sentenced to three years' servitude in a *kolkhoz* near the Arctic Circle. By 1972, the Soviets had decided that they had had enough of this rebellious individualist and exiled him to Vienna. From there, Carl Proffer, a professor of Russian literature at the University of Michigan, took Brodsky to W. H. Auden's summer house in the Austrian village of Kirchstetten. Auden gave him shelter and friendship.

In a glowing essay, "To Please a Shadow," Brodsky anoints Auden as "the greatest mind of the twentieth century" and states that in 1977, after only five years' residence in the United States, he undertook to write in English to please the shadow of the Anglo-American poet who had died in 1973. Brodsky had been reading Auden's work in "limp and listless" Russian translations since the early 1960's; while hauling manure in Siberia he was confronted by Auden's "In Memory of W. B. Yeats"; Auden's poetry, and photographs of his deeply lined face, kept him company during the difficult years before his ejection from his homeland. In the summer and fall of 1972, during what turned out to be Auden's last year, the older poet became Brodsky's mentor and sometime companion, even though Brodsky did not share Auden's homosexual proclivities. The Russian's last memory of Auden is of seeing him perched atop two volumes of the *Oxford English Dictionary* while dining at a high table: "I thought then that I was seeing the only man who had the right to use those volumes as his seat."

Brodsky is the only Russian poet who has successfully achieved bilingual status after having been uprooted. Vladimir Nabokov's is the only other remotely parallel history, but the latter spoke English since his childhood, and for him, as a writer of fiction, the challenge of adaptation was far easier. The first volume of Brodsky's poems to appear in English was *Elegy to John Donne and Other Poems* (1967), translated by Nicolas Bethell, followed by *Selected Poems* (1973), translated by George L. Kline, and *A Part of Speech* (1980), which combined Russian works translated by such distinguished peers as Richard Wilbur, Derek Walcott, and Howard Moss, with poems written by Brodsky in English during the late 1970's.

Brodsky's adroit mastery of the lyric and elegiac modes has been hailed by Auden, Stephen Spender, and other poet-critics. In his introduction to Brodsky's *Selected Poems*, Auden expressed his admiration for the Russian's command of diverse tones of voice and variety of rhymes and meters. He compared Brodsky to Vincent van Gogh and Virginia Woolf in his "capacity to envision material objects as sacramental signs, messengers from the unseen. . . . For Brodsky, as for Rilke and Eliot, poetic language has the same degree of 'reality' as the world; words regularly interact with things."

Two key images inform Brodsky's poetry: One is of his native land, *rodina*, which he writes about eschatologically, as the realm where an individual or community stands stripped before God; the other is separation, *razluka*—the apartness of one aspect of the self from other aspects, from other people, from life, from God. Pain, loss, pessimistic introspection, martyrology, and religiosity are the poems' overriding moods, with Brodsky rooting his perception of God in an earth-centered, Old Testament perspective from which he identifies with an Isaac or a Jacob. He is, however, also attracted to the Christian motifs of the Nativity and Crucifixion as signs of both the limits of mortality and triumph over death.

Brodsky's poetry is notable for its embrace of a worldwide culture. To be sure, he reaches deeply into Russian tradition, being particularly drawn to the lofty yet rugged idioms of Gavrila Derzhavin. Yet he draws more heavily on the English Metaphysicals—John Donne's dramatic spiritual discourses and intellectual complexity have influenced Brodsky since the early 1960's. From Donne he naturally moved to T. S. Eliot's poetry, particularly in the use of a persona or speaker, as in "Anno Domini." He has learned not only from the masterful modern Russian poets Mandelstam, Akhmatova, and Tsvetaeva, but also from Greek and Roman literature, Dante, Cesare Pavese, Montale, and Auden.

Joseph Brodsky is thus a unifier of East and West, tradition and modernity, whose work serves as a vital link between the silver age of early twentieth century Russian poetry and the Western achievement of Eliot, Auden, Cavafy, and others. In *Less Than One*, which won the 1986 National Book Critics Circle Award for literary criticism, he plays a number of variations on the primary theme of poetry's primacy. What, he asks, does it mean to be a poet? What role can poetry perform in the community at large?

The answer that Brodsky gives, again and again, is reminiscent of the views of both Rainer Maria Rilke and Percy Bysshe Shelley: Not only is the poet superior to the prose writer, but also metrical language is civilization's Himalayan glory, its highest altitude. Thus he salutes Akhmatova, whose poetry was refused publication from 1922 on: Her poems "will survive because language is older than state and because prosody always survives history. In fact, it hardly needs history; all it needs is a poet, and Akhmatova was just that." Of Mandelstam's persecution by the state, Brodsky writes:

A poet gets into trouble because of his linguistic, and, by implication, his psychological superiority, rather than because of his politics. A song is a form of linguistic disobedience, and its sound casts a doubt on a lot more than a concrete political system: it questions the entire existential order. And the number of its adversaries grows proportionally.

Reflecting on Nadezhda Mandelstam's splendid testimony to her husband's genius in her twin memoirs, *Hope Against Hope* (1970) and *Hope Abandoned* (1972), Brodsky builds this syllogistic pyramid: Reality is given its meaning only through perception; the most valuable perceptions are the most refined and sensitive; refinement and sensitivity are imparted by civilization; civilization's main instrument is language; the monarch of language is poetry; and Osip Mandelstam's wife and widow, in possession of "the best Russian poetry of the twentieth century," has therefore recorded a version of reality that is "unchallengeable.... Basically, talent doesn't need history." In an essay on Tsvetaeva, Brodsky raises his paeans to poetry to religious exaltation: "Ideally... it is language negating its own mass and the laws of gravity; it is language's striving upward—or sideways—to that beginning where the Word was."

It would be a disservice to the nature of these essays if the reader were left with the impression that Brodsky is content to limit his criticism to a lyrical celebration of poetry as the most valuable carrier of culture. In "Footnote to a Poem," he subjects Tsvetaeva's poem "Novogodnee" ("New Year's Greetings") to a stringent generic, linguistic, and biographical analysis: The poem is an elegy to the memory of a great poet who was also an intimate friend, Rainer Maria Rilke, and as such the lyrical monologue is also a self-portrait. Above all, it is an intensely moving confession, with the author using Rilke as her trusted confidant, whom she elevates from dead mortal to an idealized immortal, "who has ceased being a body in space and has become a soul—in eternity." The result is "a maximum tension of poetic diction." Brodsky then analyzes the poem's structure with minute care, noting Tsvetaeva's preference of trochees and dactyls over iambs, her skillful use of the caesura and truncated metrical foot, her fondness for dactyline endings, her surpassing precision of detail, her balance of ecstatic charges with grounding prosaisms.

The seventy-two-page analysis, "Footnote to a Poem," is rivaled by the fifty-two-page tribute to Auden's ninety-nine-line poem, "September 1, 1939," which was delivered as a lecture at Columbia, taped and transcribed by two students. Here Brodsky again uses a formidable arsenal of historical, biographical, and prosodic knowledge, including subtle distinctions between British and American idiomatic usage—Auden wrote the poem within weeks of leaving England for the United States. Brodsky's tone is chattily colloquial: "Words and the way they sound are more important for a poet than ideas and convictions." Yet his mind is in high metaphorical and metaphysical gear, though mellowed by the nostalgia of his attachment to the dead poet. He examines the poem's organization brick by brick, with acutely alert attention to theme, rhythm, metrics, imagery, symbolism, tone, voice, political context, stanzaic patterning, literary tradition, Auden's life—the works. The result is an inspired invitation, not only to visit this particular poem but also to befriend the muse of poetry.

In a stirring address to the 1984 graduating class of Williams College, Brodsky posits extreme individualism as the most effective antidote to evil. He cites an overtly autobiographical anecdote: In a Soviet prison camp, the inmates were challenged to a grueling "socialist competition" in lumber chopping, with the guards pitted against the prisoners. By noon all were tired, by late afternoon they were totally exhausted. One young man, however—guess who?—kept swinging his ax through the lunch break and into the night, before he finally stopped. The result was that "for the rest of his stay in that prison, no call for socialist competition between guards and inmates was issued again, although the wood kept piling up." Brodsky draws a lesson from this episode analogous to the message of Jaroslav Hašek's *The Good Soldier Schweik* (1921-1923): "Evil can be made absurd through excess. . . . The victory that is possible here is not a moral but an existential one."

In an overriding sense, Brodsky's essays are also Schweikian: He knows that he can defeat neither the totalitarian politics of the twentieth century nor a technologically oriented culture's indifference to poetry. Any frontal assault would be futile. He therefore uses his talent to expose, to a minority of discerning readers, the meaninglessness of contemporary history and the void of a mechanized age. All Brodsky has at his disposal are his gifts as a major poet and challenging critic; he makes the most of them, working into the spiritual night.

Gerhard Brand

Sources for Further Study

Christian Science Monitor. LXXVIII, May 21, 1986, p. 21.
Kirkus Reviews. LIV, March 1, 1986, p. 353.
Library Journal. CXI, April 15, 1986, p. 82.
Los Angeles Times Book Review. April 27, 1986, p. 11.
The New Republic. CXCIV, May 12, 1986, p. 26.
The New York Review of Books. XXXIII, June 12, 1986, p. 3.
The New York Times Book Review. XCI, July 13, 1986, p. 3.
Publishers Weekly. CCXXIX, March 28, 1986, p. 46.
Time. CXXVII, April 7, 1986, p. 70.

The Wall Street Journal. CCVII, June 4, 1986, p. 28.
Washington Post Book World. XVI, May 25, 1986, p. 7.

LETTERS FROM PRISON AND OTHER ESSAYS

Author: Adam Michnik (1946-   )
Translated from the Polish by Maya Latynski
Foreword by Czesław Miłosz.
Introduction by Jonathan Schell
Publisher: University of California Press (Berkeley). 354 pp. $25.00
Type of work: Essays

Incisive essays by a historian who was a founder of the important organization known as KOR (Workers' Defense Committee) and of Solidarity, the independent workers' union

Although the writings of Adam Michnik are usually in the form of the essay or letter, it is not appropriate to call him an essayist any more than it is to call, for example, Martin Luther King, Jr., an essayist. Michnik has been one of the most active organizers of the KOR and Solidarity movements—this activism has taken priority over his writing, although the two activities, as with King, overlap and reinforce each other. Michnik has spent many years in a variety of prisons, where he has found that he is able to write effectively. He admits that he has been more productive as a writer inside prison than outside. The routine of prison life has not favored lengthy projects requiring research in libraries, but Michnik has adapted his genre to his circumstances, favoring the short essay. Some of the essays are in the form of letters, either to his friends and colleagues or to his jailers. One of the latter, "A Letter to General Kiszczak," which was excerpted in *The New Yorker*'s "Talk of the Town" section of February 6, 1984, is a masterpiece, and it can be set beside Martin Luther King's "Letter from Birmingham Jail" or Henry David Thoreau's "Essay on Civil Disobedience."

The essays vary in length from six to sixty pages. Some are brief communications giving practical advice; others are lengthy discussions of a problem presenting a full historical perspective and a variety of considerations. Occasionally they lack polish or development, revealing the constraints of prison life: the lack of information available to those in the outside world, absence of library facilities, or leisure to refine the expression of the essay. On the other hand, the essays often gain in concrete immediacy and dramatic relevance. Michnik has already written a second collection of essays in prison, (*Z Dziejów Honoru w Polsce*, 1985), not yet translated into English, that focuses on different aspects of the theme of honor; the length of these essays is slightly longer, the range broader, including literature and poetry in the material he considers, but the form is similar.

Paradoxically, Michnik was, to a large extent, a willing prisoner. He looked forward to a trial so that he could prove his innocence in a public forum. As he makes clear, he was jailed for obeying, not disobeying, the law. The government admitted that he had not prepared to overthrow it by force, that his sentence had been prepared long before his trial, and that the purpose of the legal proceedings was to get rid of an embarrassing political adversary. The government promised Michnik his freedom if he would emigrate. He declined. The authorities decided to grant amnesty to Michnik; with a fair trial, the regime's lawlessness—not Michnik's—would have been in full view.

The essays which are collected here present objective and provocative analyses of the events in Poland that led to the formation of autonomous (nongovernmental) social structures in the 1970's, the growth of Solidarity, the struggle within the Polish Communist Party in 1980-1981, and General Wojciech Jaruzelski's declaration of martial law on December 13, 1981. The significance of these events, however, goes far beyond the borders of Poland. Michnik describes them not only as an apologist for Solidarity but also as a historian with an extremely broad perspective. Average Americans probably sympathized with the Polish attempt to create Solidarity; when it was finally crushed by the military, many people thought, "This is unfortunate, but such are the realities of naked force—the Polish people will have to give in." Very likely this was the impression formed by the average observer at a great distance from the actual events. Adam Michnik presents a strikingly different picture and interpretation.

In Michnik's version, the declaration of the state of war was a political disaster for the regime. The period between August, 1980, and December, 1981, was only one phase in a longer struggle that Michnik describes as "a dramatic wrestling match between the totalitarian power and a society searching for a way to attain autonomy. . . . It ended with a setback for the independent society and a disaster for the totalitarian state. For disaster is an appropriate name for a situation in which workers are confronted by tanks instead of debates." Michnik's analysis of the evolution of Polish society after World War II—and especially after the revolt of 1956—is revealing. Throughout the forty-year postwar period, constant pressure was exerted by society to reform the Communist regime, resulting in different attitudes and approaches. Michnik calls the two major concepts of reform "revisionist" and "neopositivist." The revisionists wanted to act within the framework of the Communist Party and Marxist doctrine. They wanted to transform from within both the Party and doctrine in the direction of democratic reform and common sense. Party members and adherents to Marxism, he says, were not completely people of ill will; many had democratic, progressive instincts. In this group were thinkers and writers such as Leszek Kołakowski, Edward Lipiński, Kazimierz Brandys, Adam Ważyk, and Wiktor Woroszylski. The neopositivists looked for structures outside the Party to provide reform or evolution, such as the Catholic Church; they took for granted Poland's loyalty to the Soviet Union while at the same time rejecting Marxist doctrine and Socialist ideology. These two groups shared, however, the conviction that change would come from above. Both revisionists and neopositivists counted on positive evolution in the Party that would derive from the rational policies of wise leaders, not from incessant public pressure. According to Michnik, most of the oppositionist initiatives during the period from 1956 to 1968 came from these two groups—especially the revisionists—and not from the consistent anti-Communists.

Nineteen sixty-eight was the year, Michnik writes, that revisionism died. It was the year of the Soviet invasion of Czechoslovakia and the enforced end of the Czech attempt to create a broadly based Communist government with significant civil rights and freedoms. With the demise of both revisionists and neopositivists in Poland after 1968, the society was forced to create groups and institutions outside the government and outside Marxist doctrine. Groups such as KOR and eventually Solidarity did not try to overthrow the Communist regime (as some Westerners mistakenly imagined) but simply to create autonomous structures alongside it. Among these were discussion groups, the so-called "Flying University," and groups dedicated to helping families of those who were imprisoned.

Michnik calls Jaruzelski's declaration of war in 1981 a disaster, but this disaster was already prefigured in the evolution of Polish society during the decade 1968-1978. Both the Party and Marxist doctrine became increasingly irrelevant as society was forced to solve its own problems and minister to its own needs. It was less a confrontation than a filling of a vacuum. To a large degree, the government had abdicated its functions, relying on what were (and still are) euphemistically called "administrative measures" (jailings, beatings, loss of jobs, threats) to control society. The autonomous, or "self-governing," organizations were improvised to fill this vacuum. Once they were created, the government felt threatened and tried to destroy them, but it did not really try to duplicate them or replace them once they had been destroyed. The government's role was purely negative.

Throughout this evolution of institutions, it was the civil society and ordinary people who suffered the most, while Party members were enjoying positions of privilege—but if it is possible to speak of an "agony" of the Party, this occurred in 1979 and 1980, when there was great pressure inside the Party to reform itself. It had to deal with society's demands, and to honor (or not honor) the Gdańsk accords concluded with the Solidarity movement. The Party leadership rejected the attempts at reform from within, and as a result there were mass resignations from the Party. At this time, and after Jaruzelski's declaration of war, people spoke of bucketfuls of Party membership cards being turned in as the result of protest. Loss of membership and turnover inside the Party approached 50 percent.

It is against this background that Michnik's description of the declaration of war as a disaster for the regime must be interpreted. It was the culmination of a forty-year period of evolution within Polish society, with the Party itself turning its back even on most of those cooperative and conciliatory elements which had never really challenged it. During 1980, want ads appeared in leading Warsaw daily newspapers offering high starting salaries—the equivalent of the salaries of doctors and full professors—for police recruits, to be paid even during their first six months of training. The security forces and Party members came increasingly from outside normal society. Criminal elements were employed to perform tasks such as beatings, kidnapings, and murder. Michnik writes that the murder of the priest Jerzy Popiełuszko was only one of many. Popiełuszko was abducted by policemen, tied and imprisoned in the trunk of a police car, strangled, and thrown in a reservoir. A police thug once threatened Michnik, "There's room in the trunk of our car for you, too!"

As a result, Marxist doctrine has suffered an almost total defeat in Poland. Other Eastern European countries have had similar experiences. Louis Aragon, a believing Communist if there ever was one, has described contemporary Czechoslovakia as "the Biafra of Europe." Serious thinkers, such as Czesław Miłosz, the 1980 Nobel Prize-winner in literature, now often refer to "Post-Marxist Eastern Europe."

Michnik analyzes this evolution meticulously and dispassionately. His study gains in depth by other essays that are historical case studies. One of the finest essays in the collection is about ethics and compromise. It is entitled "Maggots and Angels" (a literal translation would be "Nits and Angels"), and in it Michnik discusses the moral implications of collaboration, conciliation, and resistance. The essay is a reply to an essay by Piotr Wierzbicki, "A Treatise on Maggots." For Wierzbicki, maggots or "maggoty" people are collaborators with the regime, and he describes a broad spectrum of collaboration, ranging from the occasional opportunist to the informer to the full-fledged collaborator, with or without his full free consent, often ensnared by a bargain with the Party. All of them are maggots. Wierzbicki contrasts them with the "angels," who have held out and resisted all overtures to collaboration. Michnik takes issue with Wierzbicki—he is not in favor of the maggots, but his essay is a remarkable demonstration of practical tolerance, defining the myriad circumstances that force the average person to compromise or seek conciliation if he is not to live in total poverty. Job, publication, school for children, place of residence, vacation, trip abroad, medical care in an acceptable hospital or with an adequate doctor—all of these require minor negotiations with authorities, and Michnik accepts them as necessary. He is above all concerned to accept and understand the average citizen who makes compromises—"maggoty" ones, perhaps—because he is forced to, but who would prefer another way of acting if he had a choice. It was to provide just such a choice, and to help ordinary people find help in areas abandoned by the regime, that Michnik and others founded KOR in 1976, and then Solidarity, which was actually not a single union but an umbrella of hundreds of various autonomous or self-governing groups. Ethical or "angelic" purity is fine, according to Michnik, but he realizes that it is found most often among those who are far from the concrete pressures of constraint. The irredentists, those who are morally steadfast, are often in emigration and live in democracies.

In many of his essays Michnik follows a procedure that in the United States would be called a "Rogerian" argument (named after psychological theorist Carl Rogers). This approach requires sympathy for an adversary in an effort to understand his motivation, thought processes, and language. A similar technique was followed by King in his "Letter from Birmingham Jail," addressed to eight Southern clergymen; King's argument was as much an act of compassion as of intense disagreement. In a similar spirit, Michnik tries to understand the ordinary person who is forced into collaboration but would prefer other, better routes if given a choice.

Michnik's approach is usually objective. It could be argued, however, that he identifies too closely with the revisionists who were at home with Marxist ideology and believed in reform from above. After 1946, a large number of Polish intellectuals deliberately chose fields outside politics, becoming doctors or scientists, writing excellent works in fields such as art criticism, music, and philosophy. They were neither revisionists (such as Michnik himself) nor neopositivists, neither angels nor maggots. They were outside these categories.

Michnik's case studies on Polish and Russian history are excellent. Readers who know little about Polish history will find analyses of movements, parties, and personalities with which they are perhaps unfamiliar, but these are well argued, always original, and bear upon the present. Michnik follows the same procedure of trying to understand those whom others often reject out of hand. His discussion of the "organic work" school of the 1860's and 1870's is cogent, as is his description of the "shock" following the failure of the January, 1863, uprising and similar "shocks" after 1956 and 1981. His essay on Józef Piłsudski ("Shadows of Forgotten Ancestors") is one of the best in the book. The rehabilitation of Roman Dmowski and the National Democrats is unexpected, as they are often rejected by contemporary writers. Michnik's argument is subtle, and he carefully distinguishes between the positive, creative elements in their thinking and that which is negative or sterile. His analysis of the components of nationalism has great breadth; his essay on nineteenth century Russian Slavophile and liberal thinkers is particularly well balanced, and his discussion of the racial and "pretotalitarian" elements of the Slavophiles bears strongly on the present.

Finally, Michnik's discussions of the Socialist Party, of the Catholic Church, and of anti-Semitism are models of fairness and objectivity. In areas where people often become violently emotional, seeing issues in terms of black and white, he consistently avoids oversimplification. No doubt this has not been easy, requiring extreme discipline. Jewish and Socialist in his own upbringing, he is nevertheless sharply critical of the prewar Socialist Party, and he finds much that is both positive and useful for the present in the programs of its adversary, the National Democrats. He analyzes anti-Semitism—a "frightening illness"—in its complicated nineteenth and twentieth century contexts with a historian's surgical precision, noting that the Jewish Socialist Bund, with its philo-Russian orientation, had a negative attitude toward Polish aspirations for independence and that "one should remember that common sense is not the same as philo-Semitism."

Letters from Prison and Other Essays is a superb collection which makes a major contribution to an understanding not only of contemporary Poland but also of that large part of the world which calls itself "Marxist" and has decisively entered a new, post-Marxist stage. Many admirable insights that come from a close study of both the present and the past are brought to bear on this crucial juncture.

John Carpenter

Sources for Further Study

Library Journal. CXI, October 1, 1986, p. 100.
Los Angeles Times Book Review. November 9, 1986, p. 3.
Macleans. XCIX, November 10, 1986, p. 68.
National Review. XXXVIII, October 10, 1986, p. 50.
The New Republic. CXCV, October 6, 1986, p. 29.
The New York Review of Books. XXXIII, October 9, 1986, p. 45.
The New York Times Book Review. XCI, October 5, 1986, p. 11.
The New Yorker. LXII, November 10, 1986, p. 146.
Publishers Weekly. CCXXX, August 15, 1986, p. 63.

LIFE AND FATE

Author: Vasily Grossman (1905-1964)
Translated from the Russian by Robert Chandler
Publisher: Harper & Row, Publishers (New York). 880 pp. $22.50
Type of work: Novel
Time: 1941-1945
Locale: The Soviet Union and Germany

A sprawling novel that reflects the aspirations of two brief periods in contemporary Soviet history when there were widespread hopes for greater freedom: during World War II (1942-1945) and during Khrushchev's "thaw" (1956-1962)

Principal characters:
  VIKTOR SHTRUM, a physicist and member of the Academy of Sciences
  LYUDMILA SHAPOSHNIKOVA SHTRUM, his wife
  NADYA, their daughter
  ALEXANDRA SHAPOSHNIKOVA, Lyudmila's mother
  YEVGENIA SHAPOSHNIKOVA and
  MARUSYA SPIRIDONOVA, Lyudmila's sisters
  KRYMOV, Yevgenia's former husband, a commissar in the Red Army
  STEPAN SPIRIDONOV, Marusya's husband, director of the Stalingrad power station
  PYOTR SOKOLOV, a mathematician in Shtrum's laboratory
  MARYA SOKOLOVA, his wife
  MADYAROV, a historian, Sokolov's brother-in-law
  CHEPYZHIN, director of the institute where Shtrum and Sokolov work
  MOSTOVSKOY, an old Bolshevik
  LISS, an SS representative in a German concentration camp
  GETMANOV, a Red Army commissar
  GREKOV, the captain who commands the unit holding out in House 6/1 in Stalingrad

Vasily Grossman died of cancer in the Soviet Union in 1964. His novel *Life and Fate* was composed over a period of ten years, from 1950 to 1960, and is his most ambitious work, but was never published during his lifetime. At the height of the "thaw"—the period of partial de-Stalinization under Nikita Khrushchev—Grossman took his thick manuscript to Vadim Kozhevnikov, editor in chief of the review *Znamia* (banner), which in the past had published much of his work. For some time nothing was heard from the editorial board; indeed, the board had taken it upon itself to send the manuscript directly to the Lubyanka Prison. (Ironically, the Lubyanka is the setting for some of the events in the second half of the novel.) Grossman's apartment was visited by the police; it was thoroughly searched for every carbon copy, handwritten script, notes, even old typewriter ribbons. Everything was confiscated. Grossman sought an explanation from the Central Committee, still hoping that the manuscript would be returned. He finally met with one of the committee's members, the ideologist and theoretician

Mikhail Suslov, who told him: "We are not about to discuss with you whether the October Revolution was a good thing. As to your book, it could not be published for three hundred years." Until his death, Grossman continued to revise sections of the book in his mind, even though he no longer possessed a single page. Indeed, at the time of his death he thought the manuscript was lost forever.

Two microfilms of the text, however, were smuggled from the Lubyanka archives. How this was done is not known—photographing the manuscript would have been a very lengthy process. While Grossman was alive, the KGB certainly wanted to keep evidence that could incriminate or justify the arrest of a famous living author. With Grossman dead, however, the events become less clear. When the dissident writer Vladimir Voinovich was expelled from the Soviet Union in 1974, he managed to bring the microfilm of the manuscript with him. The Russian text was first published in Lausanne, Switzerland, in 1980.

Life and Fate describes in a panoramic manner many of the layers of Soviet society and directly confronts some of its major problems: the prison camps, the lack of individual freedoms and civil rights, the important role of race in that society, the crucial political changes after World War II ended, the evolving ideological role of the 1917 Revolution, and the outlook for the future. The destructive nature of the Soviet past is touched upon, especially the death of millions of peasants during the period of collectivization (this was called the "liquidation of the kulaks," but kulak was a euphemism for peasant) and the purges that reached their climax in 1937. The totalitarian nature of Soviet society is explored, although not at length; also the key analogy between Germany under National Socialism and the Soviet Union under Joseph Stalin is debated. Russians and Germans are presented as "two poles of one magnet"; a character even mentions the historical fact that Stalin's purges of the 1930's were carried out in imitation of the earlier Nazi purges, organized by Ernst Röhm, the Sturmabteilung, or SA, leader.

These themes would be enough to make the novel one of the more interesting Soviet products of the postwar period, even though they are not treated in depth and the author's position often remains ambiguous. All the themes are developed more forcefully by writers properly called dissidents, such as Vladimir Bukovski, Andrei Amalrik, Alexander Solzhenitsyn, or A. V. Antonov-Ovseyenko, or by writers in other Eastern European countries who would use Grossman's conclusions only as a starting point, for example Leszek Kołakowski. There are, however, two other themes, treated in real depth, which represent the greatest strength of Grossman's novel. First, there is a convincing, highly interesting exploration of the character traits of those who conform and manage to rise to positions of power within the Party hierarchy. Grossman is especially good at describing the numerous political commissars in the book who fought alongside (or behind) the officers of the Red Army and ensured morale as well as correct political thinking among the troops. The portrait of the commissar Getmanov is a minor masterpiece, a three-dimensional incarnation of hypocrisy that ranks with Molière's Tartuffe.

Second, the novel explores the real meaning—as opposed to the myth—of Stalingrad, and of the Soviet victory as a whole. Grossman had already written a rather conventional novel about the victory at Stalingrad, *Za pravoye delo* (1952); it was a best-seller, and *Life and Fate* was to be the second part of a dyptich. It was hoped that it would also be a success, profiting from the new opportunities for publication opened by the twenty-second Party Congress in 1961 and by the example of Solzhenitsyn's *One Day in the Life of Ivan Denisovich*, published in 1962 with Khrushchev's personal blessing. Grossman knew the battle of Stalingrad well. He had been a war correspondent and had filed many dispatches from near the city during the crucial weeks of the fighting. According to the myth—partly created by Grossman himself with his propagandistic dispatches—Stalingrad represented the turning point of the war, won by the Soviet army virtually alone before a second front was opened by the Western Allies in Europe. The victory supposedly proved the superiority of the Soviet political and social system over Germany; by implication, this decisive victory (according to the myth) proved also the Soviet superiority over the Allied armies and capitalism in general.

Life and Fate presents a very different, far more sober version of Stalingrad and its importance. The reader might be surprised to learn that during the dreadful wartime years in the Soviet Union, there was what might be called a controlled revolution. In the period from 1941 to 1944, the greatest freedom in the Soviet Union was to be found, of all places, at the front. The soldiers and officers were given a relatively large amount of personal initiative and independence—far more than the officers of the *Wehrmacht*. Before the battle of Stalingrad, Adolf Hitler had assumed personal control of German strategy on the Eastern front, effectively crippling the initiative and flexibility of the German armies. *Life and Fate* contains a superb scene, set in the shell of a building during the house-to-house fighting in Stalingrad, in which a rather unlikable Red Army commissar is sent to regain political control over a small unit that has been cut off (abandoned?) from the regimental command for an extended period of time and is known to be openly flouting the less important forms of army discipline. The commissar tries, and fails, to take control. The scene is beautifully described. Finally the commissar is shot by a "stray bullet" that unquestionably came from the gun of one of the rebellious, highly patriotic Russian soldiers defending the house.

The broader significance of Stalingrad is shown in several different ways in the novel. It is, actually, a family novel, and Grossman follows the fortunes of the members of the extended Shaposhnikov family as the war proceeds. They have been evacuated to the east, and the novel ends with the mother's return to her ruined apartment in Stalingrad. More important, by what Grossman meaningfully calls a "coincidence," the turning point in the lives of many of the members of the family occurs exactly at the moment of the Russian victory at Stalingrad. Often it is a turn for the worse. In the case of Viktor Shtrum, the theoretical physicist who is married to Lyudmila Shaposhnikova, his most productive work was done during the period when he was evacuated to Kazan; when he is permitted to return to Moscow and better working conditions, his career takes an abrupt downturn, and he is almost removed from the Academy of Science. Other family members are killed or arrested during this time of victory.

After the initial defeats of 1941, a nationalist revival occurred in the Soviet Union, bringing about a reversion to pre-Revolutionary ideology. It was the composer Dmitri Shostakovich who wrote in his memoirs, "Spiritual life, which had been almost completely squelched before the war, became saturated and tense, everything took on acuity, took on meaning.... You could finally talk to people. It was still hard, but you could breathe. That's why I consider the war years productive for the arts." Grossman captures this atmosphere—in the conversations that took place in a city such as Kazan and in the fighting around House 6/1 in Stalingrad, also in his probing of the directions taken by individual lives after the victory was won and the war's relative freedoms were lost. Grossman constantly returns to the question: Stalingrad was a victory for what?

It should be stressed that *Life and Fate* was written for publication, intended for a broad audience, presumably a Soviet audience. Grossman's more conventional novel *Za pravoye delo* was scathingly attacked for political reasons, but that was in 1953, just before the death of Stalin. Grossman was a member of the presidium of the Soviet Writers' Union for the ten years before his death, and he was never what is now called a "dissident." Grossman hoped that, like Solzhenitsyn's *One Day in the Life of Ivan Denisovich*, *Life and Fate* would be officially acceptable, which, thus, explains the form of the book, a peculiar combination of socialist realism and the nineteenth century bourgeois novel. Like the Rostovs in Leo Tolstoy's *War and Peace* (1865-1869), the Shaposhnikovs are presented as a typical family with which the reader can easily identify. The sisters Lyudmila and Yevgenia Shaposhnikova are distinguished primarily by their beauty and a certain dissatisfaction with their personal lives—they are in no way intellectual, and it would be hard to find more "bourgeois" characters in Western European literature. Their sentimental life is of primary importance. Although an average reader might find the family congenial, those who have read extensively in dissident Eastern European literature may well be irritated by many features of the book that seem to be compromises. For example, Stalin makes an appearance as a *deus ex machina*, as he does in so many novels of the late 1940's and early 1950's. No doubt this episode is inserted for both dramatic and ritual value, but it does not ensure a happy ending. Although in structural terms it momentarily rescues the career of the physicist Viktor Shtrum and avoids tragedy, the same problems shortly resurface and nothing is resolved.

In addition, there are many superficial clichés in the novel—political, social, and historical. Very likely they are deliberate, symptoms of Grossman's intention of appealing to a broad audience. Also, some of the characters in the book are real historical personages: Not only does Stalin appear but also Friedrich Paulus, Adolf Eichmann, Basil Chuikov, Nikita Khrushchev, and others; the character Chepyzhin, who is director of a scientific institute, is only a faintly disguised portrait of Pyotr Kapitsa, the famous physicist and pupil of Ernest Rutherford. In this way, *Life and Fate* resembles Herman Wouk's *The Winds of War* (1971) and some of the popular potboilers of the late 1940's and 1950's, where historical personages have a tendency to appear in just those places where the action is most crucial and intense. The sections in which Grossman attempts to animate these historical personages are among the weakest in the book. There are others which indicate that old habits die hard, recalling that Grossman was for many years of his life a propagandist, not so very different from the commissars whom he describes so well. Slogans and political formulas still come readily to the tip of his pen, even though the Grossman of the years from 1950 to 1960 was a very different person from the successful careerist before the war. The reader is constantly reminded that *Life and Fate* was intended for "official" publication and is not in the same genre as the books by Solzhenitsyn, Amalrik, or Bukovski.

Life and Fate has been highly praised by serious critics, compared to Tolstoy's *War and Peace*, Boris Pasternak's *Doctor Zhivago*, Solzhenitsyn's *The First Circle*, and called "*the* great Russian novel of the twentieth century." These claims are no doubt well-intentioned but are only partly borne out. In reality, the novel is a desperate attempt to reconcile truth with false claims and propaganda. It is an effort to create a genre that does not exist, which combines sincere, truth-seeking exploration and the hollow, ritualistic conventions of socialist realism. The novel is constantly falling between two or more chairs. Everything about it is mixed, from what Ronald Hingley calls its "puddingy and conformist technique" to its lack of resolution at the conclusion, the evocation of a blind, unpredictable fate. In scope it is massive. In artistic achievement it remains mixed.

John Carpenter

Sources for Further Study

Commentary. LXXXI, April, 1986, p. 39.
Library Journal. CXI, March 1, 1986, p. 108.
Listener. CXIV, September 26, 1985, p. 31.
The London Review of Books. VII, September 19, 1985, p. 3.
National Review. XXXVIII, June 6, 1986, p. 53.
The New Republic. CXCIV, May 5, 1986, p. 34.
New Statesman. CX, November 15, 1985, p. 30.
The New York Times Book Review. XCI, March 9, 1986, p. 1.
The Observer. September 29, 1985, p. 23.
Publishers Weekly. CCXXIX, January 24, 1986, p. 63.
Times Literary Supplement. November 22, 1985, p. 1315.
World Literature Today. LIX, Winter, 1985, p. 46.

THE LIFE OF LANGSTON HUGHES
Volume I: 1902-1941
I, Too, Sing America

Author: Arnold Rampersad (1941-   )
Publisher: Oxford University Press (New York). Illustrated. 468 pp. $22.95
Type of work: Literary biography
Time: 1902-1941

The first volume of a projected two-volume biography, a thorough, scholarly chronicle of Langston Hughes's early development and establishment as the most prominent voice of the emerging black literary movement in twentieth century America

> *Principal personages:*
> LANGSTON HUGHES, a poet, playwright, short-story writer, and author
> MARY LANGSTON, his maternal grandmother
> CARRIE HUGHES CLARK, his mother
> JAMES NATHANIEL HUGHES, his father
> GWYN "KIT" CLARK, his "brother" by his mother's remarriage
> COUNTEE CULLEN, his friend and a rival fellow poet
> ARNA BONTEMPS, his lifelong friend and an occasional coauthor
> CARL VAN VECHTEN, his friend and a prominent New York music critic
> CHARLOTTE MASON, his patron and adviser for a time
> JESSIE REDMON FAUSET, his friend and an editor of *Crisis* magazine

It is true almost invariably that some kind of childhood or adolescent trauma shaped the careers of the literary masters. Yet, as biographer Arnold Rampersad illustrates, few writers have taken conscious hold of those traumas and used them so relentlessly yet generously to broaden their artistic vision as did Langston Hughes. Naturally sensitive, young Hughes was both scarred by the hurts of his parents' abandoning him at separate times during his childhood and impressed by his grandmother's tales of abolitionism and the plight of runaway slaves. To his credit (and to readers' good fortune), the "genius child" was sufficiently bright and bold enough to realize that his recoil and anger could best serve him and others by being used to expose the many broader hurts of his race. That selfless vision cost him dearly, both financially and in terms of intimacy, but, as with many artists, the cost seemed not to compare to the satisfaction he enjoyed from the purity of purpose he found in writing.

Hughes's selflessness, notes Rampersad, was magnified in his life and work more so than in any other writer of the celebrated Harlem Renaissance and, as succeeding decades proved, other black writers. By choosing (somewhat against his nature) as his lifelong subject matter race over love or family (but with always a brooding over the absence of the latter two), Hughes, whose work truly became his life, charted a course that would provide both a life of observation that took him across four continents and gave him insight into all humanity, but one also of constant restraint from romantic and familial inclinations. The choice cast him as a wanderer, a political leftist, a loner (though his gregarious nature and ingratiating effects on friends and acquaintances indicated otherwise), and as the sole guardian of his literary gifts, although the form of his output was occasionally influenced by his patrons. Hughes himself was fully aware of the consequences of his decision, and the realization surfaced often in his poetry, as in the poem "Today":

> This is earthquake
> Weather:
> Honor and Hunger
> Walk lean together.

Hughes's self-imposed yet well-disguised alienation attracted the attention of Carl Van Vechten, one of his literary advisers, who remarked on one volume of his poetry that "the whole book sings with that kind of wistful loneliness you have made peculiarly your own." Even Hughes's peers, such as fellow Harlem writer Countee Cullen, simultaneously marveled and gaped aghast at the poet's scorning of what he saw as an emerging black bourgeoisie in favor of the unrelenting pursuit of his vision. Dorothy Parker wrote the following of Ernest Hemingway in regard to the uncompromising personal vision in his writing, but the same could be said of Hughes and his quest to speak for the black race: "He has never turned off on an easier path than the one he staked for himself. It takes courage."

In a comprehensive treatment of Hughes's life, Rampersad takes painstaking account of biographical and historical detail to reconstruct definitive scenarios within which the young writer's literary talent and instincts bloomed. To his credit as a scholar, Rampersad, like his subject, never veers from his own appointed course. In doing so, he remains consistently and judiciously removed from speculation in most instances. As a result, his work is exactly the kind of definitive biography needed to chronicle the life and work of his prolific subject. Rampersad's unswerving reconstruction from detail recalls Matthew J. Bruccoli's rigidly factual and excellent work on the relationship between Hemingway and F. Scott Fitzgerald, *Scott and Ernest: The Authority of Failure and the Authority of Success* (1980). Because Rampersad relies chiefly on this technique, however, certain events which warrant explanation but for which little factual evidence may be provided, such as Hughes's decision as a young seaman to throw his precious books overboard—save for one copy of Walt Whitman's *Leaves of Grass*—are cited with apparently no logical motivation for their occurrence (Rampersad does mention in passing, more than one hundred pages later, that the act was irrational). In addition, Rampersad's technique is so invariable throughout the 395 pages of text that his themes at times become muted by the weight of description and, occasionally, seemingly irrelevant facts. Even so, by building detail upon factual detail, when Rampersad does allow himself the room to explain his subject at certain points in the narrative, such as Hughes's conscious and precocious decision to become an adult after suffering years of a parentless, suspended identity, he does so with success. As he sets forth from the outset the causes and influences behind Hughes's vocation—parental neglect, spiritual alienation, and a family background that included several radical abolitionists—his portrait of Hughes becomes all the more convincing and revealing.

Though his own research was exhaustive, Rampersad relies as well on the outline that Hughes established in his own self-appraisal, the autobiography *The Big Sea: An Autobiography* (1940). This includes three important admissions on Hughes's part: his despair at not having genuinely "seen" Jesus at a church revival (and having lied to his favorite aunt that he had); his hatred for his father; and his anguish and deep depression over a break with his most influential patron, Charlotte Mason, an episode linked notably to the others as a result of his formative experiences. Rampersad, in fact, renders a great literary service in this first volume of biography by his painstaking establishment of Hughes's younger character; for when Hughes decided to become an adult, it was only after a thorough inventory of his life, and he never (seriously) looked back thereafter. His sexual identity already established (apparently he was reticent throughout his life, and Rampersad takes pains to discount suggestions from various corners that Hughes was homosexual), he remained suspicious of women's love for him throughout his adulthood and seldom indulged his passions (though one encounter, at one particularly low point in his career, resulted in his contracting gonorrhea). Rampersad reveals that although Hughes was pursued several times by both women and men, he was careful to keep his emotional distance, preferring as the years passed "the almost sensual gratification that his words in print gave him."

Even though he would pursue life with open arms and eyes, as a wanderer and explorer, Hughes knew that what he was after was an examination of people, especially the black people whom his black father loathed and about whom his grandmother had spun tales of slavery revolts and underground railways. (Rampersad skillfully shows, however, that Hughes, more so than other artists of the Harlem Renaissance, possessed an international vision of his race, and for this reason, he was elevated above his peers.) Hughes suffered relatively few and unmomentous personal affronts of racism, in some cases avoiding confrontation by virtue of his light skin by explaining that he was of Latin descent, and, in others, protesting dutifully and eagerly against racism in even its petty but nevertheless effective forms. Again, in this case, Rampersad's narrative method brings Hughes fully to life. At different points in his life, under the various influence of Carl Sandburg and, later, Latin poets such as Nicolás Guillén, Hughes's naturally passive reactions gave way to the passion of revolt, which seemed to give his quest a deeper meaning. (He scorned a potential lover in Elsie Roxborough, in part because he was put off by her racial shame.)

Because of Rampersad's chronological treatment, Hughes is portrayed in the context of history exactly as events affected him, and he them. In a few instances, Rampersad writes that Hughes was influenced by, among other events, a race riot in Chicago, a black coach's lynching in the South (for having parked in a white man's space), and the Scottsboro case in Alabama. Though his political convictions (which grew with each trip he took, through the Deep South, to Europe, Mexico, Africa, the Soviet Union, Japan, China, and the Caribbean) were revealed in a shift in the subject matter of his poems, the poet was praised by critics for what Rampersad suggests was perhaps Hughes's greatest gift: "He would have a child's charm and glittering sense of wonder and innocence, a child's fondness for the dream." It was just that quality, an innocent wisdom which transcended yet was sorely influenced by political realities, that led biographer-critic Richard Barksdale to laud Hughes as "the literary spokesman for a divided and insecure racial minority" during "his long years of authorship."

Indeed, between his most severe political forays, Hughes maintained a stream of works that explored terrains of torment, obviously prompted by his quest to discover the adult significance of his childhood hurts. Rampersad points out that Hughes's play *Mulatto* (1935), which had an extended run on Broadway, revealed these personal concerns, yet gave them a significance which transcended their occasion. Similarly, when readers interpreted Hughes's "Song for a Suicide" exclusively as a poem about race, Hughes protested vociferously. "The poems about race and politics," notes Rampersad, on a theme central to Hughes's life, "in fact, routed his innate tendencies toward melancholy; in a real sense, they kept him alive."

One theme with which Hughes dealt in his early writings, yet to which he did not return wholeheartedly, was death. Rampersad mentions this as one of Hughes's major themes yet does not return to it himself; it must be assumed that the subject, which appears to be integral to an understanding of Hughes and his work, will receive attention in the second volume of the biography. Rampersad ends the first volume in 1941, at what appears to be a turning point for Hughes. After having achieved literary acclaim for a career of almost twenty years, Hughes, who himself has no magnum opus to tout, dwells with fascination (and somewhat morosely) on the overwhelming success of the novel *Native Son* (1940) by his colleague Richard Wright. In addition, Hughes at this point received renewed criticism from religious groups for his poem "Good-bye Christ" and in general for his loud praise of the Soviet Union, a country in which his writing received recognition and acclaim, but which, in the early days of World War II, had signed a non-aggression pact with Nazi Germany.

In *The Life of Langston Hughes*, Rampersad excels at the singular task of the literary biographer: He provides an account of the writer and his environs that will significantly extend and deepen our understanding of his works. Hughes early made himself a citizen of the world, and his works are enriched by a humane insight that transcends racial differences. In that respect, Rampersad shares the noble vision of his subject.

Scott Sawyer

Sources for Further Study

Black Enterprise. XVII, December, 1986, p. 103.
Booklist. LXXXIII, November 1, 1986, p. 381.
Kirkus Reviews. LIV, July 1, 1986, p. 1005.
Library Journal. CXI, August, 1986, p. 151.
National Review. XXXVIII, October 10, 1986, p. 50.
The New York Times Book Review. XCI, October 12, 1986, p. 7.
Publishers Weekly. CCXXX, August 15, 1986, p. 60.

THE LOST LANGUAGE OF CRANES

Author: David Leavitt (1961-   )
Publisher: Alfred A. Knopf (New York). 319 pp. $17.95
Type of work: Novel
Time: The 1980's
Locale: Manhattan

Two homosexuals, father and son, must come to terms with their sexuality and the crises their "coming-out" causes in their family relationships

> *Principal characters:*
> PHILIP BENJAMIN, a young homosexual
> OWEN BENJAMIN, his father, also a homosexual
> ROSE BENJAMIN, Owen's wife and Philip's mother

In this, his first novel, David Leavitt treats several themes found in his widely praised collection of short stories, *Family Dancing* (1984). Among these themes are homosexuality, family relationships, and the sense of personal isolation characteristic of modern urban life.

Structurally, the book is divided into four sections. In the first section, "Voyage," the reader is introduced to the principal characters and their lives. The story centers on Owen and Rose Benjamin, a solid, middle-class couple, and their adult son, Philip. Owen Benjamin is the first character introduced, although he is not named at the time. He is seen as a nameless, shadowy figure on an anonymous, faintly sinister errand that takes him through the deserted streets of Manhattan. In contrast, Rose, his wife, is introduced clearly and is seen in the warmth and coziness of their apartment. Philip, their twenty-five-year-old son, is barely mentioned at first, although he is a catalyst for much of the action.

Ostensibly, the Benjamins are threatened by outside forces. The apartment in which they have lived for more than twenty years is going co-op, and they must either use most of their savings to purchase the apartment or move to another location. This problem, however, only serves to divert the reader's attention from the real threat to their security. All three of the Benjamins have been harboring secrets, but it is Owen's and Philip's homosexuality which will endanger their basic family relationships.

Even at twenty-five, Philip is portrayed as rather callow. He is openly gay and for the first time in his life has a lover, Eliot Abrams. Yet this affair is doomed by Philip's adolescent clinging and need for reassurance. His almost puppylike affection and enthusiasm make him seem much younger than he really is. Philip also seems to be somewhat superficial and thoughtless. In his self-centered view that his sexuality is the central thing in his life and therefore should be revealed to his parents, he gives little thought for their feelings or reactions.

In contrast to Philip's openness, Owen has hidden his homosexuality for twenty-seven years of marriage. His one guilty concession to his obsession has been regular, furtive trips to a pornographic-film theater each Sunday. Owen, representative of an earlier, closeted generation of homosexuals, believes that his shameful secret must be kept hidden, but he is balancing on a thinner and thinner edge as he realizes that his Sundays no longer satisfy him.

"Myths of Origin," the second section of the novel, further explores the natures and backgrounds of the characters. Throughout the section there is an emphasis on personal distance and alienation and the keeping of secrets. This is especially true in the descriptions of the father-son relationship of Owen and Philip. Owen purposely has kept a distance between Philip and himself, fearful that his unnamed obsession will be transmitted to his son like a disease.

Leavitt again presents a contrast to the Benjamins' closed, secretive lifestyle as he introduces Philip into the open atmosphere of Eliot's "family." Orphaned as a child, Eliot was reared by a gay couple in an accepting, supportive atmosphere. It is shortly after meeting this family that Philip finally tells his parents of his own sexual orientation. The section closes with Owen's devastation at the news and Rose's immediate rejection of her first acknowledgment of Owen's potentially more damaging secret.

The novel's third section, "The Crane-Child," is the briefest, covering only three pages, but it presents an allegory of the central motif. The story is, in fact, a report of a psychoanalytic case study of a neglected child, who, in the absence of human models, began to imitate the sound and actions of construction cranes, which he could see from his window. When the boy was found by authorities, the screeching and whirring of the cranes was his only language. For Leavitt, the story shows how one does not necessarily choose whom or what to love and how one becomes like whatever is loved. A basic tragedy and alienating factor of life is the inability to find a common language to communicate these different kinds of love. The languages are lost to all but those who already understand them.

The final section, "Father and Son," is the longest of the four divisions of the book. Philip, Owen, and Rose all must deal with their personal crises. Their decisions and actions are made in isolation but continue to have great impact on the others.

Philip is floundering, set adrift when Eliot suddenly leaves him and goes to Europe. Having just begun to feel the security of being part of a couple and enjoying the freedom of having "come out," he is stunned and overwhelmed by Eliot's defection, although he has feared that just such a thing would happen. In a sense, being without Eliot forces Philip to grow up. He responds first with intense self-pity and turns to anonymous meetings in pornographic theaters. He even has the opportunity to play an Eliot-like role when he rejects a younger, overly eager man with whom he has had one brief encounter. Gradually, however, he drifts into a relationship with a former college acquaintance. One senses that this bond, based as it is on friendship, will be more solid than was Philip's bond with Eliot.

As Philip is rapidly maturing, Owen struggles to come to terms with himself and his nature. For him it is an agonizing process that takes almost more courage than he has. Like Philip, he progresses quickly through several stages. He moves from anonymous encounters, to being able to talk about his needs on the phone, to finding someone in a gay bar with whom he can share a more personal involvement. His final step in this evolution, however, reveals how far he is from really accepting his nature and what it means. Under the guise of reaching out to Philip, Owen invites for dinner with his family a young teacher with whom he works. He says that he wants to introduce the young man to Philip, but it becomes increasingly clear that Owen is himself interested in him. At the disastrous dinner, Rose is forced to sit apart and observe her husband and her son competing for the attentions of a man only she, of all the Benjamins, can recognize as being heterosexual. This bizarre situation forces Owen's secret life into the open and destroys Rose's last, illusory defenses against a truth she wanted to avoid. It is Rose who will ultimately pay the price of the secrets disclosed. She realizes that Owen and Philip have achieved a sort of liberation, however painful, but that freedom means that the basis for her marriage, her life, has been a lie.

Although the narrative of the novel flows easily and Leavitt displays a real talent in his use of language, there are problems with *The Lost Language of Cranes*. One is the basic plot. The narrow focus on the sexual orientation of two of the three major characters loses impact after a while. Coming out to one's family has become a frequent subject of books, films, and television programs, and Leavitt's treatment of this theme offers no strikingly new insights. Leavitt does present a certain twist by having both father and son struggle with the same problem, but even this seems somewhat commonplace since the focus is more on the generational acceptance of homosexuality rather than on any true familial link.

Leavitt also has included a subplot involving a black lesbian friend of Eliot which never quite seems to be integrated into the narrative flow. The character's in-progress dissertation becomes a device to present the idea of the tragedy of lost languages and failed communication and is used to explain the allegory of the crane child, but the character herself remains peripheral.

At times Leavitt becomes a bit heavy-handed in his use of symbols. One must wonder at the name given to the publishing house for which Rose works: T. S. Motherwell. Is it, intentionally or subconsciously, a comment on Rose's primary role of mother? In the flashback to Philip's youth which ends the first section of the book, Leavitt describes Philip's experience in a pornographic theater, showing it to be very similar to Owen's experiences. The description of the circumstances is powerful enough to convey Leavitt's idea, but he seems to want to be sure that the comparison is obvious. Therefore, he closes the section by describing a scene from the film in which a boy imitates the actions of an older man, who then says, "Come to Daddy, boy." Such obviousness tends to dilute the impact of what has just been conveyed more subtly.

Perhaps the greatest weakness of the novel, however, is found in the shallow definition of most of the characters. Both Owen and Philip are one-dimensional. Almost nothing is known about them beyond their preoccupation with themselves. Because they are so limited by their single-minded obsession, they become boring. Take away the central focus of their lives, their homosexuality, and there is little left to make them interesting human beings. In contrast, Rose is much more clearly portrayed. From the first, the reader knows of her passion for order, sees her working at home and in her office, learns of her outside interests. She is more real because she is presented as a more rounded character.

Additionally, Rose has the advantage of simply being more likable than either her husband or her son. Although it may be easy to sympathize with Owen's dilemma, his constant panic and hysteria are tiresome. Both Owen and Rose face enormous upheavals in their lives, yet their reactions are almost diametrically opposed. Rose's relative calmness is admirable under the circumstances.

Philip's immaturity also begins to grate. Although he seems to begin to control his overzealous affections, he maintains very childish attitudes and beliefs. He seems to live in a world where his points of reference are children's books and Saturday morning television shows. He has a child's self-centeredness, especially in relation to his parents. To Philip, Owen and Rose are not real individuals with personal lives and secrets—they are only his parents. At one point he even dismisses the idea that his father could be homosexual precisely because Owen is his father and is married to his mother. Given his personal experience, one would hope that Philip would be more broad-minded than that.

In spite of these criticisms, Leavitt has provided some worthwhile insights and expressions of the human condition. When he writes, "Little changed visibly in their immediate vicinity, but Rose knew it was the invisible changes that in the end would be the most damning," Leavitt is speaking of more than the changes in a Manhattan neighborhood. He expresses the common feeling that life really is beyond the control of an individual. Instead, forces of which one is unaware move behind the scenes, only to catch him off guard.

It is not surprising that it is again Rose, the best-defined and most sympathetic character, who speaks for the necessity of keeping some illusions and secrets in life. Although she might be accused of hiding from the truth, she realizes that total honesty can often be more damaging than long-held secrets, because once the truth is spoken, what was reality becomes a sham.

Leavitt uses his most powerful and complex images, however, to express his feelings about the private languages which allow a special level of communication among those graced with the ability to understand. Yet this secret communication can also isolate and alienate those who use it, so the language generally is destroyed by others for the good of all. Those isolated must be integrated with society. While this might be necessary, one senses that it is a cry from the heart when Leavitt writes, "It makes me sad. It seems to me the world has enough lost languages."

Leavitt demonstrates sensitivity, a literate style, and an ability to express universal concerns. *The Lost Language of Cranes* is not a great work, but it is an impressive and affecting first novel.

Barbara E. Kemp

Sources for Further Study

Booklist. LXXXIII, September 15, 1986, p. 102.
Commonweal. CXIII, October 24, 1986, p. 558.
Kirkus Reviews. LIV, July 15, 1986, p. 1051.
Library Journal. CXI, September 15, 1986, p. 100.
Los Angeles Times Book Review. September 14, 1986, p. 8.
The New Republic. CXCV, November 17, 1986, p. 43.
The New York Times. September 11, 1986, p. 23.
The New York Times Book Review. XCI, October 5, 1986, p. 3.
Newsweek. CVIII, October 27, 1986, p. 100.
People Weekly. XXVI, November 3, 1986, p. 19.
Publishers Weekly. CCXXX, August 8, 1986, p. 55.
Tribune Books. September 21, 1986, p. 7.
The Village Voice. XXXI, October 14, 1986, p. 51.
The Wall Street Journal. CCVIII, September 16, 1986, p. 26.

LOUIS SULLIVAN
His Life and Work

Author: Robert Twombly (1940-   )
Publisher: The Viking Press/Elisabeth Sifton Books (New York). Illustrated. 530 pp.
$29.95
Type of work: Biography
Time: 1856-1924
Locale: Primarily Chicago

A detailed interpretive biography which seeks to discover how Louis Sullivan's difficult and secretive character affected his architectural designs and the shape of his career

> *Principal personages:*
> LOUIS SULLIVAN, an architect
> PATRICK SULLIVAN, his father, a dancing master
> ALBERT SULLIVAN, his brother, vice president of a railroad
> DANKMAR ADLER, an architect and engineer, his business partner
> from 1881 to 1895
> MARGARET HATTABAUGH SULLIVAN, his wife

"Throughout his life," Robert Twombly writes, "Sullivan seemed intent upon revealing almost nothing personal about himself, either in print or in public." The biographer of Louis Sullivan is, therefore, forced to construct a collage of evidence in which the architect's character and genius can be discerned, to draw conclusions from what went unwritten, and to read between the lines of those documents Sullivan did commit to paper. Thus Twombly's account of the early years of Sullivan's life draws heavily on Sullivan's *The Autobiography of an Idea* (1924) yet judiciously questions the accuracy of much that is recorded there. The portrait of Sullivan's dancing-master father, for example, is "not to be trusted," Twombly says. Because Sullivan wrote the autobiography only two years before his death, when his own career was in eclipse and he had suffered both economic and physical decline, he may well have felt an urge to exaggerate his father's physical repulsiveness and poor immigrant origins. The tale Sullivan tells of his father's coming to America is "full of improbabilities," according to Twombly, who hypothesizes, "Had he written in 1893, from the height of glory, his feelings about his father might have been altogether different." In form, too, the autobiography is deceptive. Rather than refer to himself as "I," which would be customary in such a work, Sullivan wrote about himself in the third person, implying that his story should be read not as the life of one individual but as "a case study in human development." Twombly sensitively characterizes the effect of this formal decision, noting that although Sullivan's life story at first appears quite revealing, "his seemingly candid self-analysis was, in fact, a kind of scrim through which the real man was only vaguely perceived."

Perhaps because the challenge of writing a personal, informative, and revealing study of so guarded and private a person is great, Twombly's biography is the first major account of the architect's life to appear in fifty years. Yet a reassessment of Sullivan's work is long overdue. In 1935, when Hugh Morrison's *Louis Sullivan: Prophet of Modern Architecture* was published, a modernist aesthetic prevailed among architectural critics. Those aspects of Sullivan's work which foreshadowed the sleek office towers of the mid-twentieth century were celebrated. It was as "father of the skyscraper" that Sullivan was admired; his formula for the tripartite division of the tall office building into base, body, and capital, which allowed for undifferentiated and easily convertible office space throughout all the floors of such a building's shaft, and the strong vertical thrust of his designs were praised as progressive, while his opulent use of applied ornament was overlooked as an embarrassment. Twombly's study helps to rectify this injustice. In dealing with some of Sullivan's early works, such as the six-story building he designed for A. F. Troescher in 1884, Twombly sometimes seems to follow conventional modernist standards, arguing that the ornamental arches with which the building is capped "weaken the effect" of a structure which might have been "a clean, successful composition of geometrical relationships." Yet in dealing with the later buildings, Twombly properly appreciates the complex interplay of structural form and surface ornament that Sullivan achieved.

Twombly rightly praises the florid cast-iron decoration of the base of the Schlesinger and Mayer (now Carson Pirie Scott) store constructed in Chicago in 1902 and 1903. This ornamentation, according to Twombly, associated the large plate-glass windows along the street with a row of paintings enclosed in ornate frames, thus presenting commodities in an aesthetic form designed to attract the eye of a new type of middle-class woman with leisure time on her hands and money to spend. Many earlier historians of modern architecture focused attention on the pure structural design of the upper floors of the building, ignoring the dynamic contrast of their stark verticality with the profusion of intertwining decorative curves below.

Similarly, Twombly acknowledges the importance of ornament in discussing the Bayard Building, with its cornice of angel figures; the mammoth "Golden Doorway" composed of profusely ornamented concentric arches which was the design focus of Sullivan's Transportation Building at the World's Columbian Exposition of 1893; and Sullivan's masterpiece, the Guaranty Building. Constructed in Buffalo in 1894 and 1895, this structure is elegantly simple in structural design yet decorated on every square inch of nonglazed surface. In this building, Twombly observes, Sullivan's ornamentation complemented the underlying structure: "The ornamental particulars became a rich, textured skin, if anything emphasizing, certainly not contradicting, the steel frame."

Twombly's discussion of the tension between form and ornament in Sullivan's work is marred only in one later section of the biography where the hypothesis is advanced that Sullivan was homosexual, although perhaps "so repressed he may not have known it himself." Twombly's evidence for this assertion is largely conjectural, which is not surprising given his subject's extreme reticence about his private life. Yet Twombly's manner of making his case, suggesting his conclusion with pointed innuendo long before he makes an outright statement of it, is overly portentous. It implies that his reading of Sullivan's sexuality is an important revelation, a key to interpreting the works, rather than simply one possible conclusion that can be drawn from the facts of his late, unhappy, and childless marriage, his aesthetic attraction to the male form, his participation in men's athletic clubs, and his close working relationships with a succession of older men. Twombly does indeed proceed to argue that Sullivan's "sexuality informed and is visible in his work," leading to the bonding of male structural forms with female ornament. Twombly even suggests that the heavy ornamentation of some of the later buildings is a result of the feminine and emotional aspects of Sullivan's character coming to dominate his male and rational side. Twombly's discussion of the Gage Building shows the extremes to which he takes this questionable interpretive approach. The "columns can be read as part of the geometric male form, but when they exploded into huge decorative symbols of femininity... the imagery was almost ejaculatory: the male sexual organ emitting a female form." Twombly goes on to argue that this should be read not as the male giving birth to the female but, rather, the "male *becoming* female."

It is as a historical scholar, rather than as an interpreter of Sullivan's imagery, that Twombly excels. His discussion of Sullivan's fruitful partnership with the German-born structural engineer Dankmar Adler is richly detailed and informative. He devotes an entire chapter to painstaking description of the process of design and revision that led to the firm's landmark success in constructing the Auditorium Building in Chicago between 1886 and 1890. Illustrations chronicle the design's progress from preliminary sketches to final realization; photographs of the interior show Sullivan's elaborate decorative scheme, and floor plans give a sense of the structure's internal organization. The building was a monumental accomplishment; it took up an entire city block, contained a theater which was at once decoratively and acoustically superb to house the Chicago Opera Festival, and rose to seventeen stories in a massive tower. When the building was completed, Adler and Sullivan took up offices in its top two floors. Twombly even provides a floor plan of these offices, showing Adler's office adjacent to the reception area, while the irascible and secretive Sullivan's was in the most remote corner. Adjacent to it was "Mr. Wright's room," the office of Sullivan's personal assistant, the young Frank Lloyd Wright. Twombly, who is also the author of an excellent biography of Wright, is particularly interesting on the troubled relationship between these two famous fathers of American architecture.

Twombly's careful documentation and rich sense of historical milieu are also evident in his explication of the factors underlying Sullivan's decline from the peak of his success in the years following the World's Columbian Exposition. While Sullivan was committed to the creation of an indigenous American architecture, most of the buildings at the fair (which was also known as "the white city") were slavishly imitative of classical European models. It was not long after the fair that the depression in the national economy was felt in the decline of commissions that came to Adler and Sullivan. By 1895, Adler had withdrawn from the firm, and without him Sullivan had an increasingly difficult time securing and holding clients. Because his fame rested largely on his reputation for designing large commercial structures, Sullivan was dependent upon economic conditions in which companies were prepared to make substantial investments in buildings. Twombly's discussion of the last twenty years of Sullivan's life is poignant, revealing that even as his fame within the architectural community grew more secure, his clientele disappeared almost completely.

In his detailed description of this period in Sullivan's life. Twombly illustrates that success is dependent not simply on genius, but also on historical and personal circumstances, on luck and personality. Sullivan's passion, ire, and guardedness, his brilliance, opinionatedness, and unwillingness to compromise all contributed to the painful circumstances in which he lived out his last years. Twombly's book is excellent in documenting the works and professional ideas of this private man; he is also successful in stirring sympathy for Sullivan. Twombly is finally unable, however, to give a vivid and intimate picture of this man who refused to be fully revealed.

Patricia Sharpe

Sources for Further Study

Barron's. LXVI, May 19, 1986, p. 111.
Booklist. LXXXII, February 1, 1986, p. 789.
Choice. XXIV, September, 1986, p. 107.
Kirkus Reviews. LIII, December 1, 1985, p. 1322.
Library Journal. CXI, January, 1986, p. 76.
The Nation. CCXLII, June 28, 1986, p. 393.
The New York Times Book Review. XCI, April 6, 1986, p. 3.
The New Yorker. LXII, May 12, 1986, p. 127.
Publishers Weekly. CCXXIX, February 7, 1986, p. 64.
Washington Post Book World. XVI, March 16, 1986, p. 3.

cans have taken too much pride and proportionately too little interest in their frame of government." In support of this contention, he juxtaposes two illustrations of public interest in the Constitution. After establishing the Center for the Study of Democratic Institutions in Santa Barbara, California, Robert M. Hutchins invited Rexford G. Tugwell there to conduct a reassessment of the Constitution. Between 1966 and 1976, in a series of conferences, Tugwell discussed revision of the Constitution with scholars, jurists, and politicians. The publication of Tugwell's proposed revisions in 1974 and 1976 did not spark a public debate on constitutional revision.

In contrast to the negligible impact that this effort to revise the Constitution had on the public, Kammen describes the overwhelming attention devoted to a *Star Trek* episode entitled "The Omega Glory," which first aired in 1966. The starship *Enterprise* lands on a planet where the people (now known as "Yangs," presumably a corruption of "Yanks") are governed by a Prime Directive. The Yangs revere the Prime Directive, a worn parchment document, and can recite its opening lines. Captain Kirk and the crew realize that the Yangs worship "freedom" but do not understand what it is. A court scene presided over by a jury, however, demonstrates that the institutions of justice have survived.

In a moving final scene, Captain Kirk explains the meaning of the preamble of the Prime Directive to the Yangs. Summarizing the message of the episode, Kammen concludes that the "great question—is the Prime Directive still operative, and does it apply to this planet?—achieves a satisfactory resolution." Juxtaposing the popularity of *Star Trek*'s "constitutional homily with a happy ending" to the lack of public interest generated by Rexford Tugwell's revised constitution, Kammen comments that many younger Americans can still recite "The Omega Glory." He concludes the anecdote with a noncommittal statement: "How much of the homily got through, however, is another matter."

The homily of Kammen's *A Machine That Would Go of Itself* bears a striking resemblance to that of the "The Omega Glory" episode. Citing polls, surveys, excerpts from school and popular texts, as well as inadequate press coverage of constitutionalism and the Supreme Court, Kammen sets out to demonstrate that Americans, like the Yangs, venerate a document which they do not understand. Faced with the vast amount of evidence Kammen has amassed, that statesmen, jurists, and legal scholars have found in the Constitution whatever message they wished to find, it is difficult not to sympathize with the Yangs' lack of comprehension of the meaning behind the Prime Directive.

Kammen cites many statistics which indicate that Americans are ignorant of basic issues discussed in the Constitution and facts about the Bill of Rights. Kammen's interpretation of one study released in 1983, however, might be questioned. Four groups defined as the mass public, community leaders, legal elite, and police officials were asked: Suppose that the people want an important law passed and that Congress and the president would have to violate a constitutional principle to pass that law, would you support them? Three replies were possible: Yes, because the Constitution should not be allowed to stand in the way of what the people need and want; no, because protecting the Constitution is more important to the national welfare than any law could possibly be; and undecided. Kammen calls the results "depressing" because of the number of undecided people and the response of the mass public.

It could be argued that indecision is an appropriate response to such a general question. The nature of the specific issue—for example, the right to bear arms as opposed to the freedom of the press—could be important. If the specific issue were gun control and involved a limitation on the right to bear arms, the respective responses of the mass public and the legal elite might reflect credit upon the mass public. The responses were as follows: mass public: no (49%), yes (22%), and neither/undecided (29%); legal elite: no (81%), yes (7%), and neither/undecided (11%). It may be heartening that the mass public appears more objective about the inviolate nature of the Constitution than the legal elite.

It is to be hoped that Kammen's *A Machine That Would Go of Itself* will prompt thoughtful examination both of the knowledge that Americans have of the Constitution and of the instruments used to measure that knowledge. A particularly impressive facet of Kammen's study is his examination of the anniversary celebrations of the Constitution in 1837, 1887, and 1937. That record is indeed depressing. To ensure that materials for the study of the Constitution are available during the 1987 bicentennial for the use of teachers, librarians, and civic leaders, Kammen has also edited *The Origins of the American Constitution: A Documentary History* (1986). This anthology contains an introduction by Kammen, an excellent selection of original source readings, a chronology, bibliography, and suggestions for special projects. *A Machine That Would Go of Itself* draws upon unpublished manuscript sources, hitherto unexamined immigration records, the iconography of paintings, street names, legal commentary, and political speeches, to mention only a few of the kinds of materials the author has examined. If Kammen had done nothing more than identify these fresh sources for students of American cultural history, his book would be an important one, but in fact he has done more. Brilliantly researched and intelligently written, this study supplies a history for the Constitution's bicentennial and a challenge to future celebrations.

Jeanie R. Brink

Sources for Further Study

Booklist. LXXXIII, November 15, 1986, p. 454.
Christian Science Monitor. LXXVIII, September 22, 1986, p. 23.
Commonweal. CXIII, October 24, 1986, p. 567.
Kirkus Reviews. LIV, July 15, 1986, p. 1099.
Library Journal. CXI, October 1, 1986, p. 95.
Los Angeles Times Book Review. October 12, 1986, p. 11.
The New York Times Book Review. XCI, September 14, 1986, p. 11.
Publishers Weekly. CCXXX, August 1, 1986, p. 62.
Washington Post Book World. XVI, October 5, 1986, p. 9.

MAGDALENA AND BALTHASAR
An Intimate Portrait of Life in Sixteenth-Century Europe
Revealed in the Letters of a Nuremberg Husband and Wife

Author: Steven Ozment (1939-   )
Publisher: Simon and Schuster (New York). Illustrated. 190 pp. $16.95
Type of work: Social history through personal letters
Time: The late sixteenth century
Locale: Germany and Italy

The lives and daily cares of a sixteenth century married couple from the merchant city of Nuremberg, including their personal and family concerns, business dealings, health, and religion

Principal personages:
BALTHASAR PAUMGARTNER, a traveling merchant of Nuremberg
MAGDALENA BEHAIM PAUMGARTNER, his wife

Traditionally, history has been the study of past politics, of wars and treaties, of the lives and times of philosophers and kings. That continues to be true, but only partly. Historians and their readers are becoming increasingly interested in social history, particularly the lives of the "common people," however that term might be defined. This "new history," as it is sometimes called, is really not so new at all, as Steven Ozment shows in this well-crafted little volume devoted to a middle-class couple from sixteenth century Nuremberg, whose letters were uncovered in a local archive and published in 1895. Now these letters, translated, arranged, edited, and illuminated by a creative and well-informed scholar, provide the American reader with a window into everyday life four centuries ago.

Magdalena Behaim and Balthasar Paumgartner belonged to prominent merchant families in one of the most bustling European cities north of the Alps. In the twentieth century, the name Nuremberg calls to mind visions of endless columns of marching Nazis, of laws which institutionalized racist prejudices, and of post-World War II trials that sought justice. In the sixteenth century, however, Nuremberg meant guildsmen and merchants, the encompassing walls of an Imperial Free City, and the Renaissance culture of Hans Sachs and Albrecht Dürer. The city had some thirty-five thousand inhabitants at the time, and the rosters of its councils contained the family names Behaim and Paumgartner again and again. Yet when Magdalena and Balthasar were betrothed in 1582, neither was in a position of great wealth or power. Throughout their lives they remained solidly middle class, she a wife and mother, he a merchant traveling each year to market fairs in Italy and the German states, striking deal after deal to keep the family business going. Whenever he was away, the two corresponded regularly, leaving a fascinating though tantalizingly incomplete record of themselves and their world. The reader sees them first as a young couple in love, then as business partners, as parents of a child in declining health, and finally as aging adults seeking to avoid illness and to maintain a proper relationship with their

God in the Lutheran faith.

Steven Ozment, a professor of history at Harvard University, and a gentle partisan of the "new history," has organized the letters around these themes, ignoring strict chronology when it suits his purpose and occasionally repeating himself when it seems convenient to do so. He has numerous scholarly books and articles to his credit; this one seems to be intended more for leisure reading. (Indeed, it might make a very nice wedding gift.) Of the 169 letters in the German original, he publishes only fourteen in their entirety. From the others there are fragments where they are meaningful to the story he tells. There is no index. The scholarly apparatus is discretely understated in unnumbered back notes. Simon and Schuster has printed and bound the book in such a way as to give it a modest but special attractiveness. It is no glossy coffee-table book, but, with its occasional sixteenth century prints and manuscript facsimiles, it is a publication of genuine quality.

Ozment has written elsewhere that "new historians are particularly devoted to popular or vernacular culture—the study of the masses, the simple folk." He realizes that Herr and Frau Paumgartner were not from the lower ranks of their society. Nuremberg struck a commemorative medallion for Balthasar upon his death. Magdalena had unusual ability. "I do not know," Ozment writes, "of another example in the sixteenth century of a woman speaking her mind so freely and so fully on such a variety of issues." Yet, though literate and well connected, the couple wrote of daily cares rather than of high politics, and they speak to the modern reader in a way which shows how much (and how little) life has changed in the intervening centuries.

In the very first letter, dated 1582, Balthasar showered his fiancée with endearing compliments—"honest, good, true, friendly, dearest, closest bride"—and then pardoned himself for not having written sooner. Throughout their correspondence she chided him for not writing more often, and he, as a loving fiancé and then as a dutiful husband, responded with the best excuses he could think of. The view one gets of the Nuremberg business system is enlightening but inevitably incomplete. Balthasar is apparently a general merchant, dealing in wine, textiles, grain, cheeses, fruits, and in the several coinages of the time. One learns the costs of individual items (twenty-three gulden for a large measure of wine and fifteen gulden for a suit of men's clothes), but even Ozment cannot put together a balance sheet for the Paumgartners or offer much of an idea of how well-to-do they actually were. He does demonstrate that in spite of the legal superiority of the husband in that age, the two were in effect full business partners. Balthasar was often absent from Nuremberg for weeks at a time plying the mercantile trade in Lucca, in north central Italy, or in Frankfurt am Main, many days' travel from Nuremberg. At home Magdalena became his "distributor, bookkeeper, and collection agency." She was not merely his subordinate; he clearly valued her business judgment. The letters also show how important family relationships were to business. Magdalena cultivated her relationship with an influential aunt, for example, and Balthasar complimented her on her skill in "stroking the tail of the fox."

The most poignant exchanges, however, were in the letters picturing the couple as parents. "Little Balthasar" was born one year after their marriage and remained their only child. One sees the three of them as the boy grew, learned, and tried to please his parents. His health, however, was delicate from birth. Ozment points out that infant and child mortality was high in that age, with perhaps one third of all children dying before the age of twelve. Little Balthasar had the best medical help available, but that consisted of purgatives to drive worms from his digestive system, enemas, and "white Bohemian beer." He survived nearly eight years. As the little boy's health declined and he could no longer attend school, he dreamed of having his very own horse. During his final sickness his father was away again on business; Magdalena's long letters describe the illness, her constant worry, and finally her grief at the loss. "We have unfortunately known in him a short-lived joy," she wrote. "I must accept God's will and let him go in peace to God, for there is nothing left in this for me now except suffering, heartache, and tears."

Invocations of the divine were very common in both Balthasar's and Magdalena's letters. It was a very religious age. Nuremberg had become Protestant in 1525, very early in the Reformation, and the city remained officially and staunchly Lutheran thereafter. The Catholic Mass was banned in the city, yet individual Roman Catholics were permitted to live there unmolested, and Catholic services were accessible in neighboring communities where the old faith had been retained. Commerce with Italy was very important for the city, and some forms of religious tolerance had practical advantages. Italian Catholics continued to reside in Nuremberg, even while Lutheran Germans, such as Balthasar, continued to travel and trade regularly with Italy. Balthasar and Magdalena frequently wrote of God's will in their letters, reflecting a theology that recognized His sovereignty. Yet it is remarkable that there is virtually no commentary on religious issues in their letters. They lived the generation between the upheaval of the Lutheran break with Rome and the chaos of the Thirty Years War (1618-1648). They never agonized over questions of faith, or did they comment on the faith or the practices of others. Ozment shows the reader no evidence of religious, national, or ethnic prejudices. Did Balthasar ever complain about the ways of Catholics, of Italians, or of Jews whom he encountered on his trading ventures? Apparently not, though he often lamented other aspects of the hard life of a commercial traveler.

Historians are necessarily limited by their sources. An epistolary novelist can invent whatever letters are helpful to tie up loose ends and bring a story to its conclusion. The historian has no such option. The final extant letters, written in 1597 and 1598, indicate that the couple had acquired a small estate in the countryside near Nuremberg. They looked forward to the life of genteel landowners, but they found that the new situation brought its own set of legal and practical problems. A year and a half later, Balthasar died, forty-nine years old, but Ozment could learn none of the details. Magdalena amazingly lived on to the age of eighty-seven, but—alas—she left no more written records. The reader is left, therefore, with only a slice of life, but a richly varied one. Ozment has permitted his readers to meet and partially understand two unknown but admirable members of a merchant family who lived long ago and far away but who seem now very close indeed.

Gordon R. Mork

Sources for Further Study

Best Sellers. XLVI, January, 1987, p. 395.
Library Journal. CXI, October 15, 1986, p. 93.
The New Yorker. LXII, February 2, 1987, p. 100.
Publishers Weekly. CCXXX, August 29, 1986, p. 381.

A MAN OF LETTERS
Selected Essays

Author: V. S. Pritchett (1900-   )
Publisher: Random House (New York). 306 pp. $19.95
Type of work: Literary criticism

A selection of essays on English, American, and European novelists and artists from the eighteenth to the twentieth centuries by England's foremost man of letters

V. S. Pritchett began writing literary essays and reviews in the 1920's when, as a struggling young author, he needed money to put food on the table. Unlike many of his contemporaries, university wits with classical educations and systematic training, Pritchett had nothing to guide him but his own haphazard if voracious reading and his native wit. He has survived through the years on these same qualities, producing an astonishing volume of reviews and essays, in addition to novels, biographies, stories, and memoirs. He reigns as the presiding grand old man of English literature, still a voice to be heard and a presence to be reckoned with. This new selection of his critical essays, his first since *The Tale Bearers* in 1980, reminds one that the days of the dedicated, humane critic are not yet over, that it is still possible to write cogently and without jargon about literature simply because the written word really matters. In Pritchett's criticism, the classics are treated as if they were newly published, while the contemporary is given the same serious but unsolemn attention as the classical.

Pritchett's methods and approach have changed little since the war years when he was given the "Books in General" column for the *New Statesman* and asked to write a weekly literary essay of eighteen hundred words. With paper rationed and books in short supply, Pritchett, like his readers, was forced to take up again the works of the past, often finding in them an unsuspected contemporary relevance. He has continued to do so ever since, in essays on figures as diverse as Samuel Richardson, Edith Wharton, and Alessandro Manzoni, to name only three of the authors discussed in *A Man of Letters*, a collection of essays written between 1942 and 1985. At times the reader might think that Pritchett has read everything of significance ever written, but poetry and drama are outside his range. He writes almost exclusively about prose fiction and seems most at home in the nineteenth century novel, which he reads in English, French, and Spanish. He is drawn irresistibly to the Russians in translation, and like all modern short-story writers he owes a debt to Anton Chekhov and Ivan Turgenev. Pritchett's catholic tastes in fiction mirror his lack of methodology as a critic: He belongs to no school, uses no one's jargon, and happily ignores the battles in literary theory that have raged around him. What he brings to his task instead of method or ideology is a commitment to literature and a reader's desire to understand both the form and the substance of what he has read.

He confronts each work on its own terms, explaining and evaluating by its own internal aesthetic. If he uses any recognizable approach, it is the biographical, for many of these and other essays are in part reviews of authors' biographies.

At its best, Pritchett's criticism supplies what all good criticism should—a clear sense of what the work under consideration is like, a feeling for its successes and failures, and the motivation to read or reread the work itself. Pritchett always has his eye on the book and its author; he has no desire to parade his own learning or to ridicule the author. The result is criticism that takes the reader into, not away from, the work. These qualities are observable in nearly all of Pritchett's essays, but in the best they are raised to the level of art. The essay on Laurence Sterne, for example, says more about *Tristram Shandy* (1759-1767) in a few witty pages than do most academic critics in their ponderous tomes. (American criticism, Pritchett wryly observes, "must begin by stunning its victim with the obvious.") Pritchett's lively prose mirrors Sterne's "eccentric" writing, and his thumbnail descriptions of *Tristram Shandy*'s characters have the pith and wit of Joseph Addison's character sketches. In slightly more detailed analyses, he characterizes Mr. Shandy and Uncle Toby as bores made comic by Sterne's wit and imagination. He then turns to Sterne himself and remarks in a highly characteristic passage:

> The bother was that Sterne was a bore himself, as boring in his way as Mr Shandy is. That Irish loquacity which he got from his mother and his early years in Tipperary had deluded him. He has that terrible, professional, non-stop pedantry of the Irish. One feels, sometimes, that one has been cornered by some brilliant Irish drunk, one whose mind is incurably suggestible.

Such remarks may not ring equally true for all readers; nevertheless, they have the virtues of lively writing, astute observation, and wit. After reading Pritchett's essay, one wants to take *Tristram Shandy* from the shelf and read it.

The discipline of condensation, strengthened by Pritchett's lifelong commitment to the short story, produces tightly written and highly polished essays in which every word counts. On occasion, the demands of the form make Pritchett overly compact and allusive, as he tries to cram too much into a short space and hence leaves out material the reader needs to understand his point. The best essays for each reader, therefore, are likely to be those concerning authors or works already familiar. Following Pritchett's discussion of an unknown writer or unfamiliar work can sometimes be difficult. Nevertheless, such economy has its compensating virtues. It produces incisive remarks and pithy definitions, such as his observation in the essay on Henry Fielding that "satire is anger laughing at its own futility." Pritchett can be brilliant, as when describing Richardson's style, or positively Shakespearean in his usage of verbs: "Later she [Amelia Opie] was to harden into the vivacious snob and to fatten into the determined celebrity hunter who bosomed her way into the limelight with the infallible flair of the woman who knew her geniuses." He can even rival Falstaff: "Wine has the triple merit of enriching the vocabulary, cheering the heart, and narrowing the mind, and the sooner one cuts the cackle of the intellectuals with some good food and drink the sooner comes peace on earth." He can turn the same witty eye on modern psychology and economics with equally good effect.

Although Pritchett has never written a nasty review, another of his virtues as a critic is seeing the limitations or failings of a book as clearly as its strengths. His contention that Anthony Trollope's political novels, for example, are all about the machinery of politics but none of the issues points to one of the novelist's weaknesses and to a reason that his books seem to lack substantive ideas. Equally provocative is his observation that Joseph Conrad is better at conveying the horror in a specific instance of evil than at capturing evil in the abstract. Thus, Pritchett contends, Conrad's masterpiece *Heart of Darkness* (1902) suffers from a vagueness which is at least as frustrating as it is suggestive. The point is not so much whether such points are right or wrong but rather that, unlike most who write about the classics, Pritchett is prepared to challenge his readers with statements they can test against their own reading. In Pritchett's view, the function of the critic is to elucidate and evaluate, not merely to dissect, and he applies this approach to all works, classic and contemporary.

Having noted that Pritchett's critical essays are refreshing in their wit and charm and often valuable for their insights, one is left with the question of whether this book best represents its author. The forty-six essays included here derive from two early, out-of-print collections (not one, as the dust jacket asserts) and from previously uncollected pieces first printed in the *New Statesman*, *The New Yorker*, and *The New York Review of Books*. This is, then, neither a retrospective collection of Pritchett's best nor a gathering of essays written since *The Tale Bearers*. Thus there is a certain haphazard quality to the book, entitling the reader to wonder why these particular essays were chosen (especially the three on visual artists). Like *More Collected Stories* (1983), *A Man of Letters* is less good overall than its individual parts. Pritchett's criticism, like his short fiction, deserves a genuinely retrospective collection of the author's best work. If and when such a volume is assembled, Pritchett's achievements as an essayist and critic will be plain for all to see. Meanwhile, this book exists to refresh readers awaiting such a happy eventuality.

Dean Baldwin

Sources for Further Study

Christian Science Monitor. LXXVIII, July 9, 1986, p. 21.
Library Journal. CXI, July 16, 1986, p. 87.
Los Angeles Times Book Review. June 29, 1986, p. 8.
The Nation. CCXLIII, August 16, 1986, p. 121.
The New York Review of Books. XXXIII, June 26, 1986, p. 7.
The New York Times Book Review. XCI, May 4, 1986, p. 12.
The New Yorker. LXII, June 9, 1986, p. 108.
Smithsonian. XVII, July, 1986, p. 144.
Times Education Supplement. December 27, 1985, p. 16.
Times Education Supplement. January 31, 1986, p. 27.
Times Literary Supplement. November 22, 1985, p. 1309.
Washington Post Book World. XVI, June 22, 1986, p. 3.

THE MAN WHO MISTOOK HIS WIFE FOR A HAT
And Other Clinical Tales

Author: Oliver Sacks (1933-   )
Publisher: Summit Books (New York). Illustrated. 233 pp. $15.95
Type of work: Essays
Time: 1970-1985
Locale: London and New York

A collection of twenty-four unusual case histories from the neurological practice of Dr. Oliver Sacks

Principal personages:
> DR. P., the patient of the title, who has lost his ability to recognize concrete objects
> JIMMIE G., a man whose memory stopped in 1945
> CHRISTINA, a woman who has lost all muscle, tendon, and joint sense
> WITTY TICCY RAY, a man with involuntary tics
> MRS. O'C, a woman whose epileptic seizures have brought her music from her Irish past
> STEPHEN D., a man who experiences heightened powers of smell
> JOHN AND MICHAEL, twenty-six-year-old twins with IQ's of 60, who have astonishing numerical abilities

The Man Who Mistook His Wife for a Hat: And Other Clinical Tales could be, in the hands of a lesser writer, a mere compendium of neurological grotesqueries. As Dr. Oliver Sacks himself points out, in one of two important epigraphs (this one by William Osler): "To talk of diseases is a sort of *Arabian Nights* entertainment." What saves this book from charges of medical voyeurism is that Sacks has several significant underlying concerns, not the least of which is reconsidering the very fundamental issue of what constitutes a neurological disease.

The Man Who Mistook His Wife for a Hat is divided into four sections: "Losses," "Excesses," "Transports," and "The World of the Simple." In each section, Sacks tells a number of clinical tales, which particularize the behavioral consequences of various right hemisphere brain disorders and also pose questions of philosophical and ethical importance. Sacks is working in a rich tradition of narrative case histories, begun by Hippocrates in Greece and perfected in the nineteenth century, lost with "the advent of an impersonal neurological science," and revived in the twentieth century by the Soviet psychologist A. R. Luria. This tradition encourages physicians to listen, with professional interest, to their patients' accounts of their illnesses, and to focus not only on obvious "deficits" but also on patients as complete human beings. This attitude of affectionate attention is characteristic of *The Man Who Mistook His Wife for a Hat*.

In "Losses," the reader is introduced to Dr. P., or "The Man Who Mistook His Wife for a Hat." Dr. P. is a patient whose case negates one of the fundamental axioms of classical neurology: that any brain damage will reduce or remove the ability of an individual to think in abstract or categorical ways. Dr. P., contrary to the received wisdom, has lost instead all ability to recognize the individual and the concrete. Looking at a picture, he attends to color or shape but not to the picture as a whole. Given a red rose, he comments, "About six inches in length. A convoluted red form with a linear green attachment... I think this could be an inflorescence or flower." Dr. P. cannot be entirely sure until he smells it. He is unaware of anything unusual in his method of perception. As the title of this piece suggests, because of a similarity in size and shape, he is even capable of mistaking his wife's head for a hat.

In this opening essay, Sacks suggests that Dr. P.'s case holds a metaphorical warning for the science of neurology, which has moved inexorably toward abstraction, at the same time eschewing the particular and the personal. Sacks sees this branch of science developing an agnosia, or perceptual difficulty, not unlike Dr. P.'s—a difficulty of which it is unaware. It has pursued the abstract idea of disembodied diseases, has paid exclusive attention to the measurable, and has become sadly mechanistic and dehumanized. Such cases as Dr. P.'s not only call into question established ideas about brain damage but may also point the way toward a neurology which can reintegrate brain and mind, science and art, patient and disease.

"Excesses" allows the reader to contemplate some symptoms of brain damage in other than the traditional context of "deficits." Witty Ticcy Ray is a patient with Tourette's syndrome; he has an excess of energy which exhibits itself in involuntary and extravagant motions. On the one hand, his tics are a severe handicap, stigmatizing him since the age of four and making a normal life nearly impossible. On the other hand, his abnormally quick reflexes and abrupt movements add a manic energy to his career as a weekend jazz drummer, where he has made a name for himself with his wild improvisations. His story raises intriguing therapeutic questions. When he is treated with Haldol, his tics are controlled, but so are the rest of his reactions. He is less quick, less playful, less impulsive. He feels only half alive. When he is unmedicated, he loses all muscular control, but he gains a wit and vibrancy, which he can express brilliantly on the drums. Which is the "real" Witty Ticcy Ray? Which Witty Ticcy Ray is preferable? Who should answer these questions? His wife, his doctor, or the patient himself?

In the long run, Witty Ticcy Ray has made an interesting and courageous decision. He takes his Haldol regularly on weekdays, functioning as a solid citizen and taking care of his responsibilities, but on the weekend, he is medication free, taking full advantage of the creative bursts that his disease affords him. His case makes one ponder not only the "deficits" of Tourette's syndrome but also its possible compensations, as well as the very nature of sickness and health. Sacks finishes this clinical tale with a quote from

Friedrich Nietzsche: "As for sickness: are we not almost tempted to ask whether we could get along without it?" One suspects that Witty Ticcy Ray would probably answer: not entirely.

In "Transports," the reader is presented with symptomatologies that might be referred to as beyond deficit and excess. They are the stuff of dreams, hallucinations, and reminiscences. In this section, one meets Hildegard, a medieval nun and mystic, whose visions have survived from the twelfth century; a medical student, Stephen, who awoke one day with a dog's unbelievably rich sense of smell; Mrs. O'C., whose "incontinent nostalgia" has brought her Irish melodies from her childhood at such a volume that they have drowned out the sounds of the present; and Donald, who murdered his girlfriend while under the influence of PCP and has only slowly recovered the gruesome details of his crime. How is one to evaluate such bizarre phenomena? Are these transports gifts, like Fyodor Dostoevski's epileptic ecstasies? Are they in any way devalued because of being physiological in origin? Are science and magic and religion more closely allied than the modern neurologist would like to believe? Certainly, these right hemisphere disorders generate more questions than they, at present, answer.

In "The World of the Simple," the reader is introduced to John and Michael, twenty-six-year-old twins with IQ's of 60 and the unusual ability of picking six-figure prime numbers seemingly out of the air. These two, who cannot perform simple arithmetic operations, can repeat numbers of three hundred digits without hesitation. They do not calculate; they seem to imagine in numbers. They are numerical geniuses, and yet they are at a loss in the practical world. Eventually, they were separated "for their own good," and while they have gained some social independence, it has clearly been at the expense of their overwhelming gift.

John and Michael's story raises disturbing issues: Is there some painfully reciprocal relationship between excellence, ecstasy, and normalcy? Are such questions in the province of neurology or theology, or both? The raising of these and other provocative questions seems to be Sacks's real purpose in recording his searching clinical tales.

The Man Who Mistook His Wife for a Hat is an unusual blend of scholarly documentation, medical terminology, lively narration, philosophical allusion, and subdued humor. Sacks is a writer who is comfortable referring to Gottfried Wilhelm Leibniz (the philosopher), Ernst Toch (the composer), Jedediah Buxton (the "tenacious calculator"), and David Garrick (the actor) within the space of a single page. He mixes Pythagoras with Bertrand Russell and Bette Davis with Plato.

It is no wonder that his view of neurology is somewhat less than traditional. It is not surprising that he has written a book that can be profitably read by both layman and medical specialist alike.

Cynthia Lee Katona

Sources for Further Study

The Atlantic. CCLVII, March, 1986, p. 112.
Commonweal. CXIII, March 28, 1986, p. 182.
Library Journal. CXI, February 15, 1986, p. 189.
The Nation. CCXLII, February 22, 1986, p. 211.
New Statesman. CX, December 13, 1985, p. 28.
The New York Review of Books. XXXIII, March 13, 1986, p. 11.
The New York Times Book Review. XCI, March 2, 1986, p. 3.
Psychology Today. XX, February, 1986, p. 80.
Publishers Weekly. CCXXVIII, December 13, 1985, p. 49.
The Wall Street Journal. CCVII, May 6, 1986, p. 28.

MARINA TSVETAEVA
The Woman, Her World, and Her Poetry

Author: Simon Karlinsky (1924-   )
Publisher: Cambridge University Press (New York). 296 pp. $44.50; paperback
  $15.95
Type of work: Literary criticism and literary biography
Time: 1892-1941
Locale: Moscow, Czechoslovakia, and Paris

*A comprehensive study of Tsvetaeva, including a thoroughly researched biography,
contemporary historical and cultural background, and interpretation of individual
works—the best single volume on Tsvetaeva to date*

> *Principal personages:*
> MARINA TSVETAEVA, a Russian poet
> VLADIMIR and
> EKATERINA TSVETAEVA, her parents
> SERGEI EFRON, her husband
> ARIADNA EFRON, her eldest daughter
> IRINA TSVETAEVA, her second daughter
> GEORGY "MUR" EFRON, her son

The abiding impression produced by this admirable study of the Russian
poet Marina Tsvetaeva (1892-1941) is of an archaeological discovery performed under the reader's eyes. No matter that Tsvetaeva is almost a contemporary, twentieth century poet whose lifetime might overlap with that of
the reader. Her life was lost—she committed suicide in the Soviet Union in
1941—and her work was almost lost too. Many manuscripts were destroyed
during World War II or are still missing, probably permanently, both in the
Soviet Union as well as those she left behind in Paris, prior to her return to
the Soviet Union in 1938. Much of her work is still unpublished and unwelcome in the Soviet Union itself. In addition, she was at odds with many
in the Russian émigré community in Paris, where she lived for thirteen
years. More important, however, several of the major events which occurred
during Tsvetaeva's life were not understood as they were happening, nor are
they well understood to this day; this applies both to the Soviet Union and
to the West. As this study shows repeatedly, the present moment is far from
being privileged; people today are the heirs of misrepresentation and ignorance as well as of knowledge. This book highlights in a dramatic form
what creative scholarship can do. In 1966, Simon Karlinsky wrote his first
book about Tsvetaeva. So much new information has come to light in the
intervening period that he has written a second and very different book
about her. *Marina Tsvetaeva: The Woman, Her World, and Her Poetry* is not
a revised edition, as some critics have suggested; a completely different
work has been written, and the reader is able to see a new, fascinating poet,
vividly and accurately described against her contemporary background.

It is not for nothing that the concerted resources of the literary bureaucracy in the Soviet Union have hindered publication of information about Tsvetaeva. She was hostile to the revolution in February, 1917, and even more hostile to the second revolution in October. She was explicit about her attitudes in her poetry and openly expressed her allegiance to the cause of the White Army; she assumed the role of "chronicler of the White Army" and even wrote a narrative poem about the war entitled "Perekop," the name of the isthmus that connects the Crimea to the mainland. On the other hand, her views do not easily fit those of Western readers either. As Karlinsky writes in his foreword, "Some of the historical issues I felt compelled to emphasize... are extremely unpopular with some Western readers today." Tsvetaeva was a remarkably critical and unprogrammatic poet. For example, she could write (in 1921):

> Migrating
> To what kind of New York?
> With universal enmity
> Loaded on our backs,
> What bears we are!
> What Tatars we are!
> Devoured by lice,
> We bring conflagrations.
> ....
> 'In the name of the Lord!
> In the name of reason!'
> What a fester we are,
> What a leprosy we are!
> With a wolfish sparkle
> Through the snowstorms' fur,
> The Star of Russia
> Against the World!

The irony of the last four lines of this poem, "Sidestreets," and its critical nature probably did not endear Tsvetaeva to either side of the struggles of the period known as "War Communism." Her irony indeed alienated both sides as well as puzzled those readers of poetry who expected it to be consistently elevated, euphoric, or noncritical.

Tsvetaeva was writing in the sharp, mordant tradition that came to be associated with the later poems of Osip Mandelstam, who wrote: "I'm being conscripted still/ for new plagues, for seven-year massacres." Tsvetaeva's poem, however, was written sixteen years before that of Mandelstam. In some ways, Tsvetaeva was far ahead of Mandelstam in her poetic evolution. These poems give a glimpse of the tantalizing possibility of a critical or even adversary contemporary Russian poetry, and it is precisely this which has not been permitted. After a brief existence in the 1960's, the dissident movement in the Soviet Union has been totally eradicated, the writers in the movement either imprisoned or exiled. The poems by Tsvetaeva and Mandelstam represent one of the interesting might-have-beens of Russian literary history: a biting, extremely powerful kind of poetry, critical but ultimately patriotic and positive, which could have put Russian poetry at the forefront of twentieth century literature. It was not to be.

What kind of a woman was Tsvetaeva, and what was her personality like? Karlinsky's study is scholarly, and he takes the reader as close to the intimate workings of Tsvetaeva's mind as evidence permits. The reader sees a woman who had three children with a rather weak, ineffectual husband; she was estranged from this husband for long periods of time throughout her life but never broke with him. She had a large number of romantic affairs, both with men and with women. Although her involvements with women might be termed Sapphic or lesbian, she herself was the first to admit that these relationships were inevitably doomed and must lose to the greater force of the maternal instinct—a woman's more powerful need to have children. As Karlinsky shows, these involvements of Tsvetaeva's were above all "infatuations," and she needed the intense, passionate relationship without scrutinizing too closely the object of her affections. Her poetry seemed to require this too. The relationship was often short-lived, but the poems it inspired would be important, permanent additions to her oeuvre.

This gives rise to an important question about Tsvetaeva's poetry that Karlinsky only partly answers. Joseph Brodsky maintains, for example, that Tsvetaeva's was the most passionate voice in Russian poetry of this century. To what extent was this passion contrived? As Tsvetaeva herself wrote, with a certain irony, "It's not your fault, it's my sin./ I force feed my insatiability/ To everyone." In another poem Tsvetaeva writes, "I'm a rebel in my mind and my guts," and several critics have drawn attention to her supreme candor; yet this candor often lacked deliberateness and philosophical depth. Its freewheeling, centrifugal quality is captivating on the linguistic level, where Tsvetaeva can produce dense textures. Yet her poetry frequently strives for deliverance from everything transient and petty, even from reality itself. She detested Anton Chekhov. She does not explore *byt* (everyday life) but *bytie* (the subjective, elevated level of existence). It is a poetry of spirit and transcendence—a specialized conception of poetry which avoids many of the major issues poetry is capable of confronting. Only in a limited sense is it a poetry of revolt.

Karlinsky's book has many great strengths. It draws a broad canvas, paying close attention to Tsvetaeva's life from birth to death, her writings, and the political, cultural background. It is difficult to combine these in a single study, to keep them in correct proportion so that one theme informs the other, and at the same time to maintain narrative flow. The scholarship can easily be too cumbersome or too superficial. The proportions in this book are almost perfect; the reader becomes interested in Tsvetaeva as a person and also in her individual works and in the fate of the period as a whole. Although the study is primarily a contribution to literary scholarship—and all specialists in twentieth century Russian literature will want to read it—the general cultural commentary is particularly well done. Tsvetaeva's poems frequently refer to cultural and political currents of the age. Many studies of poets treat their subjects as if they lived above sea level (to appropriate a phrase of Wallace Stevens); Anglo-Saxon literary critics in particular tend to treat texts of poems as if they existed in a timeless, ideal domain outside the welter of history. Karlinsky, however, can combine both close attention to textural effects of rhythm and sound with a high level of generalization about a period. One example is the parallel he draws between the period in Russian history from 1905 to 1917 (a span of relatively great prosperity and liberalization after the czar's October Manifesto of 1905, important land reforms, and the establishment of the legislative duma), the Weimar Republic in Germany in the 1920's, and post-Vietnam America. All three periods, Karlinsky suggests, were epochs in which new rights and freedoms were granted but were perceived by contemporaries as times of decline and oppression. The comparison incites the reader to rethink much of twentieth century history.

Another example of excellent evocation of a cultural period and milieu is Karlinsky's treatment of the Russian émigré community in Paris between the two world wars. He shows, very effectively, that this group was far more diverse, even left-wing, than is generally believed. Many of the Russian liberals who took part in the February revolution of 1917 were driven out eight months later by the very different revolution in October and eventually made their way to Paris. Karlinsky's discussion of the intellectual movement known as Eurasianism is especially interesting. The Eurasians included some of the most important philosophers, historians, and theologians of the Russian emigration: D. S. Mirsky, George Vernadsky, Nikolay Berdyayev, and George Fedotov. They held that because of Russia's geopolitical position and past history (centuries of domination by Mongol nomads), its revolution could have taken no other form but the Bolshevik. The democratic institutions developed in Western Europe were by their nature unsuitable to Russia, since Russia was not only a European but also an Asian country. The ideas of the Eurasian group led thousands of exiled Russians to reexamine their views of the Soviet regime and to opt for repatriation. Tsvetaeva's husband, who had fought with the White Army in 1921-1922, became attracted to the Eurasian movement, and this involvement eventually provoked his decision—then that of Tsvetaeva herself—to return to the Soviet Union in 1939. Unfortunately, the Eurasian movement in Paris had become infiltrated by the Soviet G.P.U., or secret police. Tsvetaeva's husband became an agent for the G.P.U. without her knowledge. This did not prevent his being shot a year after his return. Two months after Tsvetaeva's return to the Soviet Union, her daughter was arrested and shortly afterward made pregnant by her police guardian. Tsvetaeva was under constant suspicion of working against the Soviet government. She gave up all hope. The last job for which she applied was as dishwasher in the writers' mess hall in Chistopol. She committed suicide by hanging herself on August 31, 1941.

A recurrent theme in Karlinsky's study is how little the Russian émigré community knew about events in the Soviet Union and also how little the West knew about what was happening there. It is interesting for the reader to observe important events both in the arts and in contemporary history through the eyes of these communities as they grasped at shreds of information. It is ironic that for several years Tsvetaeva did not know of her own husband's status as agent for the secret police and his involvement in the murder of Ignace Reiss (his real name was Poretsky) as well as the sensational abduction of the White general and émigré Yevgeny Miller. After her husband fled to the Soviet Union and the French police came to arrest Tsvetaeva, she persuaded them that she knew nothing of her husband's activities—and several of her friends from this period verify that this is true. Yet the split between the activities of husband and wife is perhaps not so astounding. In a somewhat less drastic form, a similar split in American and Western European attitudes toward the Soviet Union remains to this very day.

These same contradictions existed within Tsvetaeva but were united in her art. As she herself described one of her books, "Omens of the Earth":

> This is a book of living life and truth, which politically... is a failure in advance. In it, there are charming Communists and irreproachable White Guards. The first will see only the latter, the latter—only the first....
>
> The danger shoals of this book are: counter-revolution, hatred of the Jews, love of the Jews, glorification of the rich, vilification of the rich; despite an undoubted White Guard attitude, certain irreproachable living Communists are given their full due of admiration. Yes, and also a fierce love for Germany....
>
> In a word, the publisher, like my own ribcage, should be able to encompass EVERY-THING. Here, everyone is involved, everyone stands accused, everyone is acquitted. This is a book of TRUTH. There.

John Carpenter

Sources for Further Study

British Book News. May, 1986, p. 315.
Choice. XXIV, November, 1986, p. 485.
Christian Science Monitor. LXXIV, August 4, 1986, p. 21.
The London Review of Books. VIII, March 20, 1986, p. 9.
The New Republic. CXCV, October 27, 1986, p. 42.
Times Literary Supplement. July 11, 1986, p. 768.